'Within the sometimes bewildering world of Ol[...] its modern and postmodern presuppositions, Cr[...] way forward, one that takes fully seriously the[...] logical dimensions of the Old Testament, and [...] Old Testament fully seriously as one who acts and reveals. For anyone who finds the Old Testament irrepressibly fascinating, this will be an exciting as well as a learned and coherently argued book.'
**Richard Bauckham**, Emeritus Professor of New Testament Studies, University of St Andrews, Scotland

'In this far-reaching and ambitious work, Bartholomew compellingly contends for an audacious notion: the Old Testament needs God and, above all else, enacts deific truth. This claim stands in sharp contrast with modernity reinforced by its tacit atheism and sardonic rejection of the supernatural. Consequently, the most central aspect of the Scriptures is absent in most post-Enlightenment biblical criticism. *The Old Testament and God* models an alternative, post-critical approach that is both overtly theistic and particularly Christian.'
**H. H. Hardy II**, Associate Professor of Old Testament and Semitic Languages, Southeastern Baptist Theological Seminary

'In this introductory volume, Bartholomew makes an impressive start to a project that seeks to do for the Old Testament what N. T. Wright has done for the New Testament. A great strength of his approach is an in-depth philosophical and methodological awareness. This enables him to provide a sharp critical evaluation of a number of traditional scholarly views. His careful attention to the historical, literary and theological dimensions of the Old Testament sheds new light on many disputed issues, as well as illuminating the rich Old Testament portrayal of the living God.'
**Philip Jenson**, Teaching Associate in Old Testament, Ridley Hall, Cambridge

'Only Craig Bartholomew could have written this book! The range of interlocutors is vast; Old Testament scholars mingle with philosophers, literary theorists and historians of the Ancient Near East, and Bartholomew's immensely creative and constructive mind orchestrates a powerful symphony by means of a running commentary upon the scholarship. At the heart of the matter is the possibility – indeed the firm conviction – that the living God has revealed himself to Israel. A joy to read, this book should fund a new and multifaceted conversation grounded in the question of God.'
**Matthew Levering**, James N. Perry Jr and Mary D. Perry Chair of Theology, Mundelein Seminary

'Craig Bartholomew brings his wide knowledge and insight to the question of God in the Old Testament. His training and sensibilities as both an Old Testament scholar and a philosopher are on full display here. This book, the first of four, is a big book in the best sense of the term. He considers the most important questions and utilizes the best approaches to study of the Old Testament. In my opinion, Bartholomew sets the study of God in the Old Testament on its proper foundation, which makes this essential reading for all scholars and serious students alike.'
**Tremper Longman III**, Distinguished Scholar and Professor Emeritus of Biblical Studies, Westmont College

'Who but Craig Bartholomew could have imagined this book, much less actually written it? In *The Old Testament and God*, he takes the reader on an exhilarating quest to answer the biggest question not only in biblical studies, but in our lives: the question of God. Along the way, Craig introduces us to a vast array of voices, from philosophers and historians to narrative critics and specialists in the Ancient Near East. The end result is part manifesto, part invitation. *The Old Testament and God* is sure to guide and inspire students and scholars alike.'
**Michael J. Rhodes**, Lecturer in Old Testament, Carey Baptist College, Auckland, New Zealand

'This *opus* breathes intelligence, learning and creativity as it frames what it means – and could mean – to study the Old Testament. True to form, Bartholomew assesses the academy critically, with breadth of vision and philosophical rigour. He methodically advances a theological vision of the Old Testament that takes as fundamental its kerygmatic force. Faith and theology inform Bartholomew's work as resources rather than obstacles, while he rightly pleads for genuine pluralism in the academy. Although it will be possible to interrogate Bartholomew's argument, it will be impossible to ignore it. This volume exhibits the characteristics of a classic.'
**Heath A. Thomas**, President and Professor of Old Testament, Oklahoma Baptist University

'Many of us were apprenticed into the guild of Old Testament scholarship under the paradigm of alleged academic "objectivity" in which "God" could not be the subject of a sentence that presumed his living reality and power, other than as a fictive character in the narrative. Craig Bartholomew challenges that paradigm in a way that enables an encounter with the living scriptures to be an authentic encounter with the voice of the living God.'
**Chris Wright**, Global Ambassador and Ministry Director, Langham Partnership

**The Revd Dr Craig G. Bartholomew** is the Director of the Kirby Laing Centre for Public Theology in Cambridge.

Dedicated to Tom Wright for his magisterial work in New Testament studies. May new generations rise up to receive and develop your work in both New Testament and Old Testament studies.

# THE OLD TESTAMENT AND GOD

## Old Testament Origins and the Question of God 1

Craig G. Bartholomew

First published in Great Britain in 2022

Society for Promoting Christian Knowledge
36 Causton Street
London SW1P 4ST
www.spck.org.uk

The publisher and author acknowledge with thanks permission to reproduce extracts from
the following:

Craig G. Bartholomew, 'Old Testament Origins and the Question of God.' *Bulletin for
Biblical Research* 27/2 (2017): 169–184. Used with permission from Penn State University
Press.

Figure 4 is taken from N. T. Wright, *The New Testament and the People of God*,
Christian Origins and the Question of God 1 (London: SPCK, 1992), p. 124.

The maps were produced by Baker Academic.

Every effort has been made to acknowledge fully the sources of material reproduced in this
book. The publisher apologizes for any omissions that may remain and, if notified, will
ensure that full acknowledgements are made in a subsequent edition.

*British Library Cataloguing-in-Publication Data*
A catalogue record for this book is available from the British Library

ISBN 978–0–281–07393–1
eBook ISBN 978–0–281–07394–8

1 3 5 7 9 10 8 6 4 2

Typeset by Manila Typesetting Company
First printed in Great Britain by Clays

eBook by Manila Typesetting Company

Produced on paper from sustainable sources

# Contents

## Part 1
## WHAT SHOULD WE DO WITH THE OLD TESTAMENT?

# Contents

# Contents

# Contents

## Part 3
## THE WORLD VIEWS OF THE ANCIENT
## NEAR EAST

# Contents

# Contents

# Contents

# Contents

# Illustrations

**Figures**

**Maps**

# Preface

> Disciplines develop questions of their own and by doing so function as a mnemotechnique [method for memorizing] of forgetting with regard to concerns of a more general and fundamental character.[1]

These are the words of the distinguished Egyptologist Jan Assmann. In recent years he has produced a series of important books weighing in on the more general and fundamental questions in relation to the Hebrew Bible (HB) / Old Testament (OT) and the Ancient Near East (ANE), including a commentary on Exodus.[2] He has become well known for what he calls *the Mosaic distinction*, according to which Israel's revolutionary monotheism sets her apart in the ANE by resisting the 'translatability' of gods across cultures in the ANE, and insisting on truth and falsehood in religion. Assmann engages critically and controversially with the legacy of this distinction,[3] but it is greatly to his credit that he has put this general and fundamental topic on our agendas for discussion. This is the sort of issue that is central to this book and series.

As someone trained in OT wisdom and hermeneutics, I have found it exhilarating, hard work and wonderfully insightful to immerse myself in ANE studies. Nowadays, OT and ANE scholarship have become so specialized that just staying up to date with one's own small area is a challenge. However, the needs of the day cry out for us to look at questions of a more general nature and fundamental character, and to give them the sort of attention that Assmann calls for.

In New Testament (NT) studies no one has done this with greater panache and expertise than N. T. Wright. In my view his work is extraordinarily significant and calls for a new generation/s of scholars to receive, deepen and develop the new paradigm that he has opened up for NT studies. I have long felt

---

1   Assmann 1997, 6.

2   Assmann 2018.

3   In his *The Price of Monotheism*, Assmann (2010) responds to some of his critics and provides a more nuanced account of his position.

that some sort of equivalent project needs to be attempted in OT studies. But is it possible, let alone for one person? Eventually, I plucked up courage and spoke to Philip Law at SPCK, the originating publisher for N. T. Wright's project. Things moved quickly to a contract, and more recently Jim Kinney and Baker Academic have come on board as my US publisher, for which I am very grateful. I have no illusions that this work will be on a par with that of Wright, but I remain convinced that the attempt needs to be made. My hope is that other scholars will pick up the *direction* of this work and do it far, far better than I have done.

After more than a hundred years of rigorous historical criticism, and more recently postmodern interpretation, in my view OT studies cries out for a paradigm shift. Not, it must be noted, a move to a pre-critical paradigm, but a move to a post-critical one. Historical criticism has examined the data of the OT with unprecedented rigour and its gains are too many to abandon. The enormous developments in ANE studies are also vitally important. However, we have learned from philosophy of science, no less, that *theory is underdetermined by the facts*, and time and again I have been struck by how the data to which historical critics refer is patent of alternative interpretations and, in my opinion, more convincing ones. A great deal of excellent work has been done on the OT in the modern era, but 'after' historical criticism and postmodernism the field is severely fragmented and jaded, with signs of hard secular approaches emerging in the West, even while we live amid a global resurgence of religion and not least of Christianity. The danger I perceive is a lapse back into historical criticism where believing Christians simply try to do more conservative versions of such work. I am convinced that we need an alternative paradigm for Old Testament studies, akin to that provided by N. T. Wright for New Testament studies, that can catch all the many, many insights of modern interpretation into a coherent whole and open the way forward to exciting new developments.

As with N. T. Wright, at the heart of my proposal is *the question of God*. Modernity privatized religion with the result that we allow freedom for a personal, leisure-time faith, but we insist that it must be kept out of the great spheres of public life, out of the university and thus out of OT studies. Especially after the postmodern turn, it is fine in mainstream OT studies to be a naturalist, a Marxist, a new historicist, a Foucauldian, a Derridean, an exponent of queer and transgender theory, a postcolonialist and so on, but heaven forbid one should be a theist, let alone a full-blown Christian theist. As we witness each year at the Society of Biblical Literature (SBL), HB/OT studies has become more diverse as the academy has become more diverse. Gone are the

days when the field was dominated by white males. And yet the religious taboo often remains. In some of the best and richest work in HB/OT and ANE
scholarship the question of God never even enters the picture, as we will see.

At a deep level, every scholarly paradigm is rooted in philosophical presuppositions – ontological, epistemological and anthropological ones – as
scholars such as Charles Taylor and Jacques Derrida have pointed out. Alas,
much of modernity had a vested interest in obscuring these presuppositions,
claiming that with the modern triumph of human autonomy, objective, neutral scholarship was now the name of the game, and it alone would get us to
the truth, including the truth about the OT. In the first half of the twentieth
century, when positivism and classical foundationalism[4] dominated, it was,
perhaps, understandable that OT scholars were wary of bringing their religious beliefs with them into their scholarship. However, positivism has been
hoisted on its own petard, and once classical foundationalism was allowed
to come fully into view through the penetrating work of philosophers such
as Alvin Plantinga, Nicholas Wolterstorff, Bill Alston, C. S. Evans and many
others, it was found thoroughly wanting. Indeed, by the end of the twentieth century the hubris of the modern project had been shattered after what
many consider the most brutal century in history.

In this context it is notable that we have witnessed a truly remarkable renaissance of Christian philosophy in recent decades. In 1980, *Time* maga-
zine reported that God was making a comeback – in philosophy no less, and it
identified Alvin Plantinga as the foremost Protestant philosopher of religion.
Since then, Plantinga and many others have produced a vast corpus of rigorous work. In his inaugural address at the University of Notre Dame, 'Advice
to Christian Philosophers',[5] Plantinga noted that 'even if Christianity is on the
move, it has taken only a few brief steps; and it is marching through largely
alien territory'.[6] His advice to Christian philosophers is as follows:

> My counsel can be summed up on two connected suggestions, along with
> a codicil. First, Christian philosophers and Christian intellectuals gen-
> erally must display more autonomy – more independence of the rest of
> the philosophical world. Second, Christian philosophers must display
> more integrity – integrity in the sense of integral wholeness, or oneness,
> or unity, being all of one piece. Perhaps 'integrality' would be the better

---

4  On classical foundationalism see Bartholomew and Goheen 2013, 214–17.

5  Plantinga 1984.

6  Plantinga 1984, 253.

word here. And necessary to these two is a third: Christian courage, or boldness, or strength, or perhaps Christian self-confidence.[7]

Plantinga's call has been heeded in philosophy, but far less so in other disciplines and hardly at all in OT studies. At the Scripture and Hermeneutics Seminar on history and biblical interpretation, we hosted a fertile dialogue between Plantinga, Robert Gordon and myself.[8] This remains well worth reading. Plantinga, Wolterstorff, C. Stephen Evans, Alston and others have made courageous forays into biblical interpretation, recognizing its importance. But we have yet to see Plantinga's advice and call taken up with rigour in OT studies. This series is an attempt to do just that.

For some 14 years I occupied the H. Evan Runner chair in philosophy at Redeemer University in Ontario, Canada. It was my daily privilege there to teach philosophy across a range of courses, including philosophy of language, philosophy of history and the history of philosophy. Those years of immersion in philosophy have been indispensable for this project. As I began to immerse myself in ANE studies, I was wonderfully awarded a year-long Senior Fellowship by the Carl Henry Center at Trinity International University in Chicago. Although this time was interrupted by the onset of the coronavirus, engagement with colleagues there and the opportunity to do the immersive work has been a gift, for which I am very grateful.

It should also be noted that concurrent with beginning this project I was appointed a Senior Fellow at the Herzl Institute in Jerusalem for two years, funded by Templeton. This time provided me with a rich opportunity to excavate Jewish and Christian thought. The book that emerged from this period is my *God Who Acts in History: The significance of Sinai*.[9] In many ways it is a prequel to this series. I have come to see that in the OT *all paths lead to and away from Sinai*, and in this volume I appropriate, summarize and develop further the argument in that book.

As N. T. Wright notes of his own work, the proof of the pudding is in the eating. Thus, while ranging across OT studies, ANE studies, philosophy and theology, I have attempted always to keep my eye on actual OT interpretation. If a new paradigm/s is to emerge, it has to demonstrate a capacity to handle the OT better than other paradigms. I have tried to keep this in mind throughout.

---

7  Plantinga 1984, 254.

8  In Bartholomew et al., eds, 2003.

9  Bartholomew 2020.

I am immensely grateful to Michael Rhodes and Robby Holt for their close reading of the manuscript. My thanks too to Trey Nation, Chip Hardy, Jim Eisenbraun and Chris Wright for their input. As my SPCK editor, Mollie Barker has done truly excellent work in bringing order to a complex manuscript. I am beyond grateful for her work. This has helped to make the book much better than it would otherwise have been. The weaknesses, of course, remain my own. I am also grateful for permission to draw on my article, 'Old Testament Origins and the Question of God.' *Bulletin for Biblical Research* 27/2 (2017): 169–184. If this project is pointing in the right direction then it will require a community of scholars to move it forward, and I am grateful for the community of the Kirby Laing Centre here in Cambridge.

Craig Bartholomew

# Abbreviations

| | |
|---|---|
| AB | Anchor Bible |
| ABD | *Anchor Bible Dictionary.* Ed. D. N. Freedman. 6 vols (New York, NY: Doubleday, 1992) |
| ALASP | Abhandlungen zur Literatur Alt-Syrien-Palästinas und Meso-potamiens |
| AnBib | Analecta Biblica |
| ANE | Ancient Near East(ern) |
| ANET | *Ancient Near Eastern Texts Relating to the Old Testament.* Ed. J. B. Pritchard. 3rd edn (Princeton, NJ: Princeton University Press, 1969) |
| AO | Tablets in the collection of the Musée du Louvre |
| AOAT | Alter Orient und Altes Testament |
| BA | *Biblical Archaeologist* |
| BAR | *Biblical Archaeology Review* |
| BASOR | *Bulletin of the American Schools of Oriental Research* |
| BBRSup | Bulletin for Biblical Research, Supplements |
| BCOTWP | Baker Commentary on the Old Testament Wisdom and Psalms |
| BETL | Bibliotheca Ephemeridum Theologicarum Lovaniensium |
| BibInt | *Biblical Interpretation* |
| Bo | Field number of tablets excavated at Boghazköy |
| BR | *Biblical Research* |
| BRev | *Bible Review* |
| BTM | Biblical Theology Movement |
| BZAW | Beihefte zur Zeitschrift für die alttestamentliche Wissenschaft |
| CBQ | *Catholic Biblical Quarterly* |
| CBQMS | Catholic Biblical Quarterly Monograph Series |

| | |
|---|---|
| *CD* | K. Barth, *Church Dogmatics* (Edinburgh: T&T Clark, 1936–69) |
| ConBOT | Coniectanea Biblica: Old Testament Series |
| *COS* | *The Context of Scripture.* Ed. W. W. Hallo and K. Lawson Younger Jr. 3 vols (Leiden: Brill, 1997–2002) |
| *COS IV* | *The Context of Scripture, vol. 4: Supplements.* Ed. K. Lawson Younger Jr (Leiden: Brill, 2018) |
| *CTH* | *Catalogue des textes hittites.* Ed. E. Laroche (Paris: Klincksieck, 1971) |
| *CTJ* | *Calvin Theological Journal* |
| CUP | Cambridge University Press |
| DAP | Divine Action Project |
| *DDD* | *Dictionary of Deities and Demons in the Bible.* Ed. K. van der Toorn, B. Becking and P. W. van der Horst. 2nd edn (Leiden: Brill; Grand Rapids, MI: Eerdmans, 1999) |
| EDP | Early Dynastic proverb collection |
| *EE* | *Enuma Elish* |
| EG | Epic of Gilgamesh |
| EWO | Enki and the World Order |
| FzAT | Forschungen zum Alten Testament |
| HB | Hebrew Bible |
| *HUCA* | *Hebrew Union College Annual* |
| *IAAM* | H. Frankfort et al., *The Intellectual Adventure of Ancient Man* (Chicago, IL: University of Chicago Press, 1946) |
| *IAS* | R. D. Biggs, *Inscriptions from Tell Abu Salabikh* (= OIP 99, 1974) |
| ICC | International Critical Commentary |
| *IEJ* | *Israel Exploration Journal* |
| *ISBE* | *International Standard Bible Encyclopedia.* Ed. G. W. Bromiley. 4 vols (Grand Rapids, MI: Eerdmans 1979–88) |
| IVP | InterVarsity Press |
| *JAJ* | *Journal of Ancient Judaism* |
| *JAOS* | *Journal of the American Oriental Society* |
| *JBL* | *Journal of Biblical Literature* |

| | |
|---|---|
| JCS | *Journal of Cuneiform Studies* |
| JISMOR | *Journal of the Interdisciplinary Study of Monotheistic Religions* |
| JNES | *Journal of Near Eastern Studies* |
| JPS | Jewish Publication Society |
| JQR | *Jewish Quarterly Review* |
| JR | *Journal of Religion* |
| JSOTSup | Journal for the Study of the Old Testament: Supplement Series |
| KAI | *Kanaanäische und aramäische Inschriften.* Ed. H. Donner and W. Röllig. 2nd edn (Wiesbaden: Harrassowitz, 1966–9) |
| KAR | *Keilschrifttexte aus Assur religiösen Inhalts.* Ed. E. Ebeling (Leipzig: Hinrichs, 1919–23) |
| KBo | *Keilschrifttexte aus Boghazköi* (Leipzig, 1916– ) |
| KTU | *The Cuneiform Alphabetic Texts from Ugarit, Ras Ibn Hani, and Other Places.* Ed. M. Dietrich, O. Loretz and J. Sanmartin. ALASP 8 (Münster: Ugarit-Verlag, 1997) |
| KUB | *Keilschrifturkunden aus Boghazköi* (Berlin, 1921– ) |
| LHBOTS | Library of Hebrew Bible / Old Testament Studies |
| LXX | Septuagint |
| MAL | Middle Assyrian Laws |
| MT | Masoretic Text |
| NAC | New American Commentary |
| NBC | Tablets in the Babylonian Collection, Yale University Library |
| NC | New Criticism |
| NICOT | New International Commentary on the Old Testament |
| NRSV | New Revised Standard Version |
| NT | New Testament |
| OIP | Oriental Institute Publications (Chicago, 1924ff.) |
| OLA | Orientalia Lovaniensia Analecta |
| ORA | Oriental Religions in Antiquity |
| OT | Old Testament |
| OTL | Old Testament Library |
| OUP | Oxford University Press |

| | |
|---|---|
| *RAW* | *Religions of the Ancient World: A guide.* General ed. Sarah Iles Johnston (Cambridge, MA: Belknap, 2004) |
| RS | Field numbers of tablets excavated at Ras Shamra |
| SAHS | Scripture and Hermeneutics Series |
| SANER | Studies in Ancient Near Eastern Records |
| SAOC | Studies in Ancient Oriental Civilizations |
| SAT | Speech Act Theory |
| SBL | Society of Biblical Literature |
| SBT | Studies in Biblical Theology |
| SDA | special divine action |
| *SLT* | E. Chiera, *Sumerian Lexical Texts* (= OIP 11, 1929) |
| THOTC | Two Horizons Old Testament Commentary |
| TOTC | Tyndale Old Testament Commentaries |
| Ukg | Inscriptions of Urukagina, in E. Sollberger, *Corpus des inscriptions 'royales' présargoniques de Lagash* (Geneva, 1956) |
| Urk. | Urkunden des aegyptischen Altertums (series). Ed. K. Sethe, H. W. Helck, H. Schäfer, H. Grapow, O. Firchow. 8 vols (Leipzig/Berlin, 1903–57) |
| *VT* | *Vetus Testamentum* |
| VTSup | Supplements to Vetus Testamentum |
| WBC | Word Biblical Commentary |
| YBC | Yale Babylonian Collection |

# Introduction: A road map for *The Old Testament and God*

This book is volume 1 in a four-volume series entitled Old Testament Origins and the Question of God. As such, the book lays the foundation for the series, attending to the relevant introductory issues and to the question of God in the Old Testament. The series is intentionally designed as something of a companion to N. T. Wright's Christian Origins and the Question of God. Indeed, readers will note similarities between this volume and N. T. Wright's *The New Testament and the People of God.*

The overarching shape of this book is clear:

- **Part 1** seeks to answer the question 'What should we do with the Old Testament?'
- **Part 2** develops a range of tools for answering this question from a critical realist perspective.
- **Part 3** examines the major world views of the Ancient Near East against which background we read the Old Testament.
- **Part 4** brings all this to bear on the central character of the OT, YHWH, the God of Israel.

However, there is a lot of detail amid this fourfold division, and this road map is designed to alert readers to the journey and act as a guide that you can refer back to if you get lost in the details. I have tried to make the signposting throughout as clear as possible, but you should read this section at the beginning and then return to it whenever you need to.

**A puzzle**: in many ways this book is a response to a puzzle. The OT is unique in its communicative power when compared to other ANE literature and yet, so often, whether among liberals or conservatives, we seem to fail to hear it with its full acoustics. Why is this the case, and how can we change it?

It is surprising how many different things are done with the OT by scholars today and so we start by posing the question 'What *should* we do with the OT?' We begin our journey by attending to the small land of Israel situated among the nations and empires of the day. Within the OT there appear to be strikingly different descriptions of this land, and through close attention to these we *inductively* – from the descriptions themselves – foreground three dimensions of OT texts that must be recognized if we are to hear the message of the OT today, namely:

- the historical;
- the literary;
- the theological or what I prefer to call the 'kerygmatic'.

These three strands and their complex interrelationships are a central part of OT texts and must be attended to closely if we are to hear what the OT wishes to communicate.

*Readers should note my strategy here,* not least because it is one I use throughout the book, and if it is not understood it might be confusing. Through close consideration of an OT text, a theme or a topic, I allow the central issues to come to the fore and *then* attend to them. I do this deliberately in order to show that I am not imposing an agenda on the OT but rather allowing issues to emerge that are already and truly present. For example, the literary dimension, foregrounded by the different descriptions of the land in the OT, alerts us to the fact that when we read the OT we are dealing with words, books, texts. It follows that if we are to study the OT as such, we need to be sure that we have a (reliable) OT text to read, and thus I *then* attend to the hot-button issue of textual criticism and the OT.

The theological, kerygmatic or religious dimension of the OT also alerts us to the role of theology (or not) in the approach the reader brings to the OT. Historical criticism of the OT emerged in *modernity* and has often been attached to a refusal to allow religion or theology to be part of what the reader brings to the text. This marginalization or erasure of religion has been very damaging to OT study, bearing in mind that YHWH is at the very heart of the OT. Here and elsewhere, 'modernity' will be attended to as the matrix out of which modern OT scholarship has emerged, for better and for worse. We argue that this sort of historical criticism is deceived if it thinks that by bracketing out religion it is doing neutral, scientific scholarship. Instead, it is argued that we need a paradigm shift in OT studies with room made for *an* approach to the OT, among others, in which God is allowed to play his full role.

All of this, and more, is covered in **Part 1**.

Very different views of history, literature and theology are held by OT scholars, and so we need an approach to the underlying issue of *knowing* the

OT (i.e. the field of epistemology) that maximally allows these strands and their interrelationships to come to the fore. In **Part 2**, as with N. T. Wright and the NT, we argue that a *critical realist* approach to knowledge is best suited for this task. It does justice to the objectivity of the text of the OT as well as to the different perspectives that scholars bring to the OT and allows us to delineate the overtly theological or Christian perspective that we bring to the OT while recognizing the plurality of other approaches. Our tools for the task of hearing the OT in its full communicative power are developed in this second part of the book, namely narrative, literature, reading, world view, history and theology.

Once again, the reader should note our inductive strategy. Literature and narrative, for example, are close companions, and attention to *narrative* will back us into the storied nature of the *traditions* (MacIntyre) out of which we think and do our scholarly work. A common term for what MacIntyre gets at with his 'traditions' is *world view*. At base, world views are storied, and we will see how world view with its storied nature is wonderfully suited to analyse:

- the world views of the ANE with their myriad stories of the gods;
- the world view/s of the OT;
- the world views of the readers of the OT.

The OT comes to us embedded in history as a collection of ANE texts, and this historical dimension means that we need to know as much as we can about its historical and cultural context. In **Part 3** we attend to the main world views of the ANE in order to gain an understanding of the world in which the OT was forged. As we will see, this is a very useful way to enhance our hearing of the OT with its full acoustics. The ANE nations' stories about their many gods are commonly called 'myths', and we begin with an examination of 'myth' in the ANE and in the OT. We then explore nine major world views in the ANE. They reveal that the ANE was awash with gods, and that the various peoples of the region were thoroughly polytheistic. How does their view of the gods relate to the view of YHWH in the OT?

Jan Assmann has developed his notion of *the Mosaic distinction* in this respect, according to which the OT uniquely regards YHWH as the only true God and all other gods as false, so that 'translatability' is ruled out. By 'translatability' Assmann does not mean the use of ANE motifs to explain YHWH, which is obviously the case in the OT, but rather the ready equation of gods across the ANE, so that, for example, the solar god in one culture could be readily recognized as the solar god in another. Mark Smith has engaged with

Assmann's view in detail, and, since this is such an important issue, we discuss and critique Smith's view in detail at the end of Part 3.

The central character of the OT is YHWH, and it is the wager of this series that it is only as we take God with full seriousness that we will be able to hear the OT in its full communicative power. Thus, in **Part 4** we attend to YHWH as he is portrayed in the OT and bring this portrayal into dialogue with the issues raised thus far, so that our investigation of the origins of the OT can be fully informed by what we know about him. Readers should note that they will intentionally find exegetical sections juxtaposed with sections on the theology of divine action and of revelation, with such sections *informed by* what we learn of YHWH in the OT, and *providing lenses through which* to read the OT. Such a dialectic or circularity, it is argued, is unavoidable, indeed essential, if we are to take YHWH with full seriousness as we listen to the OT in order to hear it with its full acoustics.

Historical criticism has been woven into our discussions throughout and we conclude by asking 'What then should we do with historical criticism?' This issue, as with many others raised in this first volume, will be explored in detail in relation to specific areas of the OT in subsequent volumes.

The OT is an extraordinary book on which to focus one's scholarly attention. We urgently need to find a way to hear the OT in all its communicative power today. I have loved writing this book, but it has been a Herculean task and it calls for a community of scholars to attend to the issues raised. My hope is that some readers will be inspired to join me in refining and honing the agenda set forth, and in developing it in fruitful ways as we listen to the OT today.

# Part I

# WHAT SHOULD WE DO WITH THE OLD TESTAMENT?

The above question may strike the reader as an extraordinarily strange way to begin a series of books on the OT. Is it not obvious that we should simply get on with reading the OT? Oh, that it were so simple!

Enter the world of OT studies and you will soon discover that a great variety of things are done with the OT. A legacy of historical criticism is that some readers, accepting the argument that on the surface the OT is very fragmented, move quickly towards reconstructing the underlying sources of the historical books and the prophets, and then devote most of their energy to an analysis of these reconstructed sources and tracking them within the OT.

Postmodernism greatly increased the number of things that are done with the OT and it has become common nowadays to find ideological, feminist, deconstructionist, queer, postcolonial and other readings of the OT. Postmodernism generated a wild pluralism of readings of OT texts, and, although postmodernism seems to be in demise, we are left with a breathtaking sense of the immense variety of things that can be and have been done with this body of writing.

Many Evangelicals continue to read the OT along grammatical–historical lines with a strong sense of the unity of the OT, an approach with which I have many sympathies. However, it is rare in Evangelical literature, sophisticated as it has become, to find anything like the rich and comprehensive vistas opened up by Leon Kass in his exceptional work on Genesis and Exodus.[1] It is worth pondering why this is the case.

Thus, while the question in the heading might strike the reader as strange, in fact it cuts to the very heart of contemporary OT study. To cut to the chase, I will argue in Part 1 that we need to find a way *to listen* to the OT so that we hear its acoustics in all their rich, personal and public dimensions. However, we will need to travel a fair and complex distance in order to unpack this. The rewards make the journey well worthwhile!

---

1   See Kass 2003; 2021.

# 1
# Old Testament origins

## 1 Introduction

An inscription found in Amaseia in Pontus in western Asia Minor (modern-day northern Turkey) describes the ancient region it calls 'Palestine' as a 'God-trodden' land.[1] Such it is, but surprisingly this God-trodden land is small, with its fertile parts, including the semi-arid sections of the Negev to the south of Israel and the inhabitable land east of the River Jordan, amounting in total to only about 7,700 square miles (20,000 sq. km),[2] about the size of El Salvador or Slovenia.

In some form or another, the OT has been around as long as 'the land of Israel' since it is only as a result of the Israelites' occupation of the land that the 'land *of Israel*' comes into existence, and it is this small strip of land that forms the geographical and historical context in which, to a large extent, the drama of the OT plays out. Aharoni observes that:

> This was the stage for His [God's] dramatic and redemptive acts. Without an awareness of the stage, the action of the drama cannot be fully understood. Thus, the historical geography of the Holy Land is a reflection of the mutual relation between God and Israel as understood and interpreted by Israel's national faith.[3]

It is mainly in this context that the OT, three quarters of the Christian Bible, came into existence.

Speech Act Theory (SAT) is a theory of how language – speech and writing – operates, an important consideration for anyone working on a corpus of books such as the OT. Central to SAT is the insight that by means of language we not only make statements but also *perform* acts – acts such as warning, inviting, exhorting, praying, promising. In order to get at this, SAT distinguishes between

---

1 Wilken 1992, 192.
2 Mazar 1990, 1.
3 Aharoni 1962, 1967, xi.

three elements in a speech act: locution, illocution and perlocution. The locution is the basic meaning of a portion of speech or writing, the illocution is the force or act performed by that speech or writing, and the perlocution is the effect of it. The key and insightful distinction is that between locution and illocution. Take a statement such as 'There is a snake in the garden'. The basic meaning or locution is clear, but what is the force, the illocution, of the statement? It could be a warning; it could be an invitation to come and see; it could be simply providing information. The context is, of course, crucial in alerting us to the precise illocution at work. An important point is that understanding the locution alone does not get us to the full meaning of a speech act.

A speech act can perform multiple acts at once.[4] After Moses' encounter with God at the burning bush, YHWH instructs him to tell Pharaoh: 'Israel is my firstborn son . . . Let my son go that he might worship me' (Exod. 4.22–23).[5] The description of Israel as YHWH's *firstborn son* is evocative. The statement could function as an invitation: if YHWH has one son he could have another, and in this sense the statement is an invitation to Pharaoh, opening up the possibility that Egypt might also become a son of YHWH.

From another angle the statement is a shocking affront to Pharaoh, ruler over one of the most ancient civilizations. In the ANE, primogeniture (being the firstborn child) was the norm, with the oldest son the heir. As Pardes notes of Exodus 4.22–23:

> The priority given to Israel by the Father represents a translation into national terms of the reversal of the primogeniture law . . . The late-born nation that came 'to the stage after all its neighbors had assumed their historical roles' is elevated by God to the position of the chosen firstborn.[6]

In terms of the ANE, Israel was indeed a latecomer.[7] By the end of the fourth and start of the third millennium BC, the foundations of the great civilizations of the ANE had been laid in the lands of the great rivers: Egypt with the Nile, and Mesopotamia with the Tigris and the Euphrates, forming the bulk of what we know as the Fertile Crescent. Great expanses of land, and rivers for irrigation and transport, provided economic and geographical possibilities that allowed for the emergence of these powerful kingdoms. Depending on

---

4   In the language of Speech Act Theory, a speech act can have more than one illocutionary force.

5   Unless otherwise indicated, Scripture quotations are from the NRSV. Emphasis in Scripture quotes is mine throughout.

6   Pardes 2000, 6, quoting Greenberg 1969, 12.

7   See, e.g., Saggs 1989.

how one understands the conquest of Palestine by the Israelites and when one dates 'it',[8] Israel emerges on the stage of the ANE with her own land in the late second millennium BC at the earliest.

# 2 Israel among the nations

The situation of Ancient Palestine was entirely different from that of Egypt and Mesopotamia. Its geography divides the country into small parcels. 'Though in itself quite small, it is divided into many tiny regions, each possessing its own peculiar geographical features.'[9] Unlike Mesopotamia and Egypt, Palestine is a middle ground, a bridge between Egypt and Syria-Mesopotamia and thus a thoroughfare for the great kingdoms, nestled as it is along the Mediterranean coastline between the Great Sea (the Mediterranean) on the west and the desert to the east. Brague refers evocatively in this respect to Israel's 'tormented geography'.[10] Because of its crucial role as a thoroughfare for trade and travel, the superpowers of the day sought to impose their control over it.

> This made it very difficult for any kind of independent economic and political development, but it also gave access to all the accomplishments of ancient civilization. In this melting pot of cultural contact some of the greatest human cultural achievements came into being, e.g. alphabetic writing and monotheistic faith.[11]

Intriguingly, Israel possessed a unique awareness of its geopolitical position among the nations (see Map 1 overleaf). This is apparent in so many ways throughout the OT but particularly in the Table of the Nations in Genesis 10 (cf. 1 Chron. 1.1–23), in which the nations of the world are traced as descendants of Noah's three sons, Shem, Ham and Japheth. Wiseman notes that '[w]hatever date and interpretation is followed . . . the chapter remains unique in ancient

---

8   Moore and Kelle (2011, 81) note that '[m]ost histories of ancient Israel no longer consider information about the Egyptian sojourn, the exodus, and the wilderness wanderings recoverable or even relevant to Israel's emergence'. They (2011, 111) identify the three classic models of the emergence of Israel as conquest, peaceful infiltration and peasant revolt, but point out that different approaches continue to be proposed. Intriguingly, many scholars writing in this area still think that religion – Yahwism – played an important role in uniting Israel (Moore and Kelle, 2011, 126–9). The mention of 'Israel' on the Merneptah Stela dated *c.*1210 BC provides extrabiblical confirmation that by this time an entity called Israel existed in Palestine.

9   Aharoni 1962, 1967, 19.

10   Brague 2007, 30.

11   Aharoni 1962, 1967, 6.

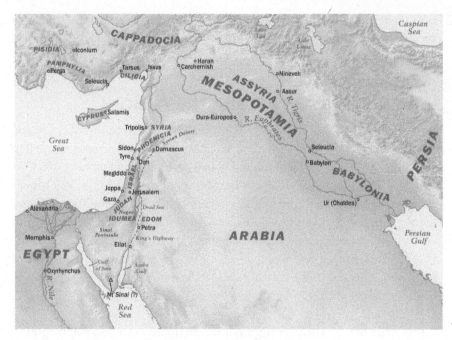

Map 1 **Israel among the nations of the Ancient Near East**
(© Baker Publishing Group)

literature'.[12] F. Delitzsch writes: 'Nowhere is there a survey of the relationship of peoples to each other comparable to the biblical table of the nations, so universal in its horizon and sweep, so utterly comprehensive in its intent.'[13] For von Rad, Genesis 10 is a document of 'amazing theoretical power', embodies the complex world in which Israel found herself, and embraces and affirms it as God's creation.[14] Many of the nations mentioned in the Table were great enemies of Israel and yet remarkably the Table insists that all humans and nations come from God. Von Rad makes much of the fact that Israel is not mentioned; nor is she the centre of the nations. She is represented in the Table by 'Arpachshad' in 10.22.[15] He argues that in contrast to the *polis* (city state) religions which drew a direct line between primeval times and themselves,

---

12  Wiseman 1973, xviii. Westermann (1984, 501) similarly observes that 'the table of the nations is unique and has no parallel either inside or outside the Old Testament'. The date assigned to Gen. 10 is contested, ranging from fourteenth-century Egypt (Wiseman) to tenth- or seventh-century Jerusalem (Westermann). Source critics find J and P material in it (Wenham 1987, 214–15). See also Aharoni (1962, 1967, 6–8) who argues that its composition fits best in the early monarchy.

13  Quoted in Westermann 1984, 528.

14  Von Rad 1972, 143–4.

15  But see Westermann 1984, 512; Wenham 1987, 228; Hess 2009, 77–8.

leaving no room for what lay outside them, in Genesis 10 the line from Noah to Abraham is interrupted by the Table of the Nations. Thus:

> Israel looked at herself in the midst of the international world without illusion and quite unmythically. What Israel learns and experiences of Yahweh occurs exclusively within the realm of history. For biblical theology the inclusion of the table of nations means a radical break with myth.[16]

## (a) The Table of the Nations

The Table of the Nations (Gen. 10) comes prior to the call of Abram in Genesis 12, and to the Tower of Babel narrative plus a genealogy of Shem in Genesis 11. Genesis 10 is framed by an inclusio[17] with the evocative, judgement-ridden words 'after the flood' (10.1, 32). Shem, Ham and Japheth are Noah's three sons, and the inhabitants and the nations that filled the earth following the Flood are said to be descended from these three. Genesis 10.1 refers to 'Noah's sons, Shem, Ham and Japheth', and then their lists of descendants are given in reverse order, starting with Japheth. The recurring refrain in this list is based on the pattern: 'These are the descendants of X in their lands, with their own language, by their families, in their nations' (cf. Gen 10.5, 20, 31). This refrain closes each section of Genesis 10, pulling the variety of names together into a unity and indicating 'that the origin of all the peoples of the earth lies in the creator's will and blessing'.[18] Amid the genealogy, peoples are seen as constituted of land, language, families (clans) and nations:

> As far as we know this is the first attempt in the history of humankind to conceive and define the basic elements of the entity 'people.' It arose from the theological impulse to express how the separation of humankind into people is grounded in the will and blessing of the creator.[19]

Wenham[20] notes that Genesis 10 differs from the genealogies in the primeval history (Gen. 5; 11) in that: no ages are mentioned; although many of the names are personal, some are place names or gentilics (names of tribes, nations, races);

---

16 Von Rad 1972, 145. Note that in Part 3 we will discuss myth in the ANE and in the OT.
17 An inclusio is a repetition at the beginning and end of a section indicating the range of the section and its main theme/s.
18 Westermann 1984, 509.
19 Westermann 1984, 509.
20 Wenham 1987, 215.

the terms used to express the relationship among those listed should not all be regarded as eponyms (persons from whom something takes its name); sonship and brotherhood not only referred to blood relation in ancient times but could also refer to a treaty relation. Thus, the Table is complex in terms of its historical background and the data it pulls together.[21] Genesis 10 is also literary in that it shows a fondness for 7-numbered lists and it is likely that the total number of nations listed is 70, the same number as constituted Jacob's family.[22]

Japheth's line deals with nations most remote from Israel; from Israel's perspective they are peoples of the far north. Ham's line deals with nations of most relevance to Israel, and Shem's genealogy is placed last because it is picked up again in 11.10–31, leading to Terah and his son Abram. Terah took his extended family to Haran, intending to go on to Canaan, but settled in Haran, and it is from there that Abram leaves in response to God's call.

Thus, prior to the *particularity* of God's call to Abram in response to the Tower of Babel episode, we have the Table of Nations with its *universal* concern for nations and territories. 'This is the known world from Israel's perspective in the Old Testament period.'[23] There are not many people mentioned in the OT who are not included in this list. Thus, the list is historically particular but also symbolically comprehensive – the number of nations listed is 70, suggesting completeness on a large scale,[24] so that they symbolize the nations of the earth. It is instructive in this respect to take note of the 'inner map' of the author; the nations are listed and expanded upon in terms of their relation to Israel.[25] Geographers have come to recognize that maps do not simply mirror realities on the ground, as is often popularly thought. Maps are human constructions through which we comprehend places and spaces. This is profoundly true of the Table of the Nations.

Wenham observes that just as Jacob's family numbered 70 (Gen. 46.27; Exod. 1.5; Deut. 10.22), so do the nations of the world: 'Israel is thus seen as a microcosm of the wider family of humanity described in this chapter.'[26] Nations furthest from and of least consequence to Israel are mentioned first and with no details about them (10.2–5). Genesis 10.6–13 includes the elaboration on the activities of Nimrod and his establishment *inter alia* of Assyria,

---

21  See also Sarna 1989, 68. Sarna (1989, 68) notes that '[t]he Table itself is riddled with difficulties, many of which remain insoluble in the present state of knowledge'.

22  Wenham 1987, 213–14.

23  Bauckham 2003, 56.

24  Sarna 1989, 69.

25  Thus, von Rad is incorrect to assert that Israel is not at the centre of the nations.

26  Wenham 1987, 214.

Nineveh and Egypt, places of great interest and relevance to Israel.[27] Similarly, the detail in 10.15–19 with respect to Canaan is explained by its relevance to Israel. '[A]ll the children of Eber' in verse 21 – 'Hebrew' is the gentilic of 'Eber'[28] – anticipates the emergence of the Hebrews from Shem's line. By implication, Israel is seen as residing at the centre of the inhabited world with the nations most distant from Israel at the edges of the world. The vision is not ethnocentric but one in which the particularity of Israel extends to the nations as part of God's universal purposes.[29]

Eichrodt observes that:

> As creatures of the one God the peoples are members of one great family, and the list of the nations in Gen. 10, which is unique in ancient Eastern literature, includes Israel, proudly conscious though it is of its preferential historical position, in the general context of humanity. No claim is made for Israel of any fundamentally different natural capacity or 'inherited nobility' which might set it apart from the rest of the nations. The Old Testament knows nothing of races which are 'naturally inferior' or un-worthy of designation as human, just as the dividing wall between Greeks and barbarians, or between master races and slave natures, which was never wholly overcome in the ancient world, is completely foreign to it.[30]

Vriezen makes a similar point. He discerns 'communion' between God and humankind as the main theme of the OT, and finds it implicit in the covenant with Israel as that which makes Israelites family. In connection with Genesis 10, he evocatively observes that communion applies 'over the borders of Israel . . . But this was only possible because the God of the Covenant, in whose nature it is to seek communion, was confessed as the God of Creation.'[31]

Gordon notes of Egypt that '[t]he Land, almost sealed off from the rest of the world, is ideally suited for nurturing a distinctive civilization'.[32] Bearing in mind the emphasis on holiness and distinctiveness in the OT, one might expect that Israel would occupy a similar land in which she would be left relatively free to nurture and develop her distinctive life. In his *Fear and Trembling*,

---

27  See Wenham 1987, 243.

28  Wenham 1987, 228.

29  cf. in this respect Zeph. 3.9, 10 and Isa. 66.18, 19, which envisage the reversal of the judgement on Babel.

30  Eichrodt 1951, 36.

31  Vriezen 1970, 171.

32  Gordon 1962, 1965, 98.

Kierkegaard begins with several meditations on Genesis 22, imagining various different tellings of the story of Abraham's journey to Mount Moriah to sacrifice Isaac. Similarly, one could examine a map of the ANE and consider different routes and destinations that Israel might have taken to different possible lands. However, as the narrative unfolds, it is to Palestine that Israel is led, and her situation in this land-between-lands is quite the reverse from that of Egypt. Geographically, she is compelled to be aware of the major empires of the day and in constant contact with them and the surrounding nations in one way or another.

As we begin to reflect on what to do with the OT, the Table of the Nations is already instructive. It highlights three aspects of the OT that are central to its acoustics if we are to listen to it fully. Clearly, first, there is a *historical* dimension to this text, as the detailed studies of the persons, nations and places referred to demonstrate. Second, the *literary* nature of Genesis 10 is clearly important with its inclusio, refrain and strong symbolism. Third, there is the remarkable ideological, *theological* or kerygmatic dimension[33] that surfaces once we ask how this unique account emerged in Israel, how Israel perceived herself in relation to the other nations of the world, and so on. If it is right that the Table represents the first attempt in history to think through the nature of a people, then we are in the presence of truly remarkable *political theology*, compelling us to ask how such questions and answers were able to emerge in Israel. No account of the Table of the Nations will be adequate that fails to consider all three of these dimensions and their interrelationships.

The reader should note how these three dimensions have appeared inductively, through close attention to Genesis 10, rather than being imposed on the text. The centrality of these three dimensions to any acoustics of the OT will become clearer as we move on to an examination of the land of Israel below. After we have introduced the geography of Israel, an essential component in OT study, we will look at descriptions of the land in the OT itself, and then we will see in greater clarity just how important it is to attend to the historical, literary and kerygmatic dimensions.

# 3 Palestine: the land

Place and time are the two great constituents of the context of human life, and that applies as much to Israel as it does to us today. Place is ubiquitous

---

33 Scholars commonly use 'ideological' or 'theological'. My preference is for 'kerygmatic' because it foregrounds the message the OT seeks to convey.

but always particular, and it shapes us even as we shape it.[34] Place and placial metaphors abound in the OT, so that we do well not to ignore the geography of the Holy Land in our reading of it. As Monson notes: 'The text of the Old Testament exhibits a geographical rootedness and cultural expression that is woven into the tapestry of the eastern Mediterranean and its ancient civilizations'[35] so that 'the land offers a kind of "hermeneutic" of its own'.[36]

Psalm 84, for example, is a marvellous psalm, celebrating Zion as the dwelling *place* of YHWH, the living God (v. 2). It is perhaps a pilgrim song,[37] written for Israelites as they engaged in the mandatory pilgrimages to Jerusalem each year. It contains three beatitudes ('Blessed are . . .'), and for our purposes the second one is the most interesting:

Happy are [Blessed are] those whose strength is in you,
  *in whose heart are the highways to Zion.*
  (v. 5)

Here the experience of place, of regular journeys to Jerusalem over the years, amid the often-challenging terrain of Palestine, is mapped on to the domain of 'the heart', the 'headquarters' of the human person,[38] in order to unpack what it means to ground one's strength in YHWH. Given the diverse geography of Palestine – its plains, hills, mountains and valleys, as well as the range in elevations from 3,500 feet (167 m) at the peak of Mount Hermon to 1,300 feet (396 m) below sea level at the Dead Sea[39] – no Israelite who had experienced pilgrimage to Jerusalem would imagine that, although 'blessed', it was an easy thing to put one's strength in YHWH if it meant having the highways to Jerusalem engraved on one's heart.

As the most cursory glance at a map of Palestine reveals, it lies between the Great Sea on the west and desert on the east. The result is that its *climate*, despite varying across the land, is subtropical with rainy winters and dry summers. Most rain falls on the coastal strip and the northern highlands. Unlike Egypt with the Nile, and most of Mesopotamia with the Tigris and

---

34  See Bartholomew 2011.

35  Monson 2018, 26.

36  Monson 2018, 28.

37  cf. the psalms of ascent, Pss. 120—134.

38  Chrétien (2019, 69) notes that '[t]he heart, which is the headquarters, biblically speaking, of both intellect and volition, becomes the receptacle of the divine presence when God's Word is understood and put into practice'.

39  Losch 2005, 1.

Euphrates, Israelite crops grew mainly without irrigation, dependent on the winter rains and the soil. Deuteronomy 11.10–12 captures this contrast with Egypt well:

> [10] For the land that you are about to enter to occupy is not like the land of Egypt, from which you have come, where you sow your seed and irrigate by foot like a vegetable garden. [11] But the land that you are crossing over to occupy is a land of hills and valleys, watered by rain from the sky, [12] a land that the LORD your God looks after. The eyes of the LORD your God are always on it, from the beginning of the year to the end of the year.

The shadow side of this was the perennial danger of drought:

> Years of drought and famine run like a scarlet thread through the ancient history of Palestine. In such times it often happened that part of the population was compelled to seek refuge in Egypt which is supported by a permanent water supply from the Nile. Only in parts of the Jordan Valley,[40] especially the eastern sectors, rich in wells and tributary streams, was there irrigation in ancient times.[41]

The river valleys were conducive to urban settlements, with Jericho being one of the most ancient such centres along the Jordan Valley (cf. Gen. 13.10).

Although the coastal strip is extensive, it has a dearth of natural harbours so that Israel was never a great seafaring nation, in contrast to Phoenicia to her north which did indeed have significant harbours, those of Tyre and Sidon being the most notable.[42] Equally extensive is the eastern desert, home to nomads and bedouin, who were always in search of pastures and thus presented a perennial threat to Israel.

Palestine is divided longitudinally into four strips encompassed by the Great Sea on the west and the desert on the east. There are small fissures that cut latitudinally across it, the Jezreel Valley being the only valley that extends right across the land, connecting the coastal strip with the Jordan Valley. The Jezreel Valley separates Galilee from Mount Ephraim. Palestine's division into distinct topographical areas was recognized by the Israelites, as is made clear

---

40   The major river in Israel is the Jordan. On the Jordan Rift see Aharoni 1962, 1967, 29–33.
41   Aharoni 1962, 1967, 13.
42   See Casson 1971.

in several verses (Deut. 1.7; Josh. 10.40; 11.16; Judg. 1.9).[43] Deuteronomy 1.7 contains an abundance of geographical terms:

> Turn and set out and enter into the mountain of the Amorites and into all the neighbouring regions in the Arabah, in the mountain, in the Shephelah, in the Negev, and in the seacoast – the land of the Canaanites and the Lebanon, up to the great river, the Euphrates.[44]

From this we can identify the following descriptors:

- 'the mountain of the Amorites' = the central mountainous region;
- 'the Arabah' = the Rift Valley;
- 'the Shephelah' = the range of low hills lying between the coastal plain and the central mountain range;
- 'the Negev' = the dry land in southern Palestine stretching from north of Beer-sheba to the mountains of Judea;
- 'the seacoast' = the coastal plain.

'The land of the Canaanites' refers to all of the above. 'The Lebanon' refers to the region to the north of Israel. The Euphrates is the great river north of Lebanon that defines the southern boundary of the Fertile Crescent.

Five major areas of Palestine are thus recognized in this verse (see Map 2 overleaf).

*(a) The coastal plain.* The coastal plain is very narrow in the north of Palestine but widens as one moves south and then becomes quite broad as the coastline sweeps round to the west in the south. Three major plains occur along the coastal plain from north to south: the Plain of Akko/Phoenicia, the Sharon Plain and the Philistine Plain. The Plain of Akko is enclosed by two mountain ridges jutting out from the Mediterranean: Ras en-Naqurah in the north and the forested Mount Carmel in the south. The city of Akko on the coastline was one of very few important harbour sites in Palestine. To the south of Akko lies the Jezreel Valley, best taken with the coastal zone.[45] The Jezreel Valley, constituted along the lines of an equilateral triangle with each side approximately 20 miles (32 km) long, was vital for its agricultural fertility and as part of the **Via Maris** (the Way of the Sea; cf. Isa. 8.23(9.1)), which divides in the Jezreel

---

43  Aharoni 1962, 1967, 37.

44  My translation.

45  Aharoni 1962, 1967, 21.

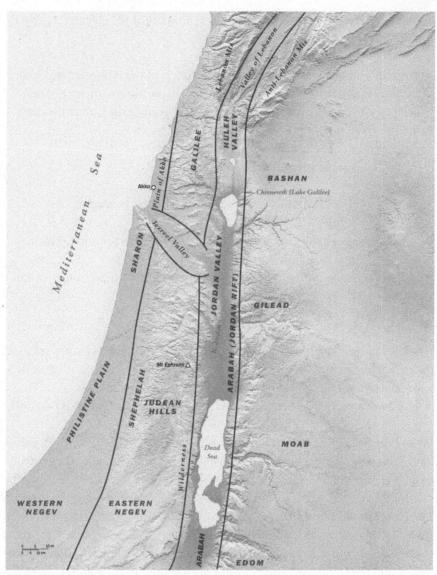

Map 2 **The major regions of the land**
(© Baker Publishing Group)

Valley, one route going north to Ugarit and then Anatolia, another going east and then north-east to Mesopotamia.

The Via Maris was one of three major trade routes in Ancient Israel. The other two were the Ridge Route and the King's Highway. The Via Maris follows the coastline from the border of Egypt to the Plain of Sharon. At this point it splits into several branches, and only the westernmost continues along the coast through Phoenicia. The eastern branches pass along the Valley of Jezreel and from there to Lebanese Beqa', to Damascus and then to Mesopotamia.[46]

*(b) The Shephelah.* This consists of the low hills between the coastal plain and the central mountain range.

*(c) The central mountainous region.* The major parts of this are Galilee (upper and lower), Mount Ephraim, the Judean hill country and the eastern Negev.

*(d) The Jordan Rift.* This long valley consists of the Huleh Valley, Chinnereth (Lake Galilee), the Jordan Valley, the Dead Sea and the Arabah.

*(e) The Transjordan area.* To the east of the Jordan Valley lies a region that is not specifically mentioned in this verse but may be included in the sweeping description 'up to the great river, the Euphrates'. It consists of Bashan, Gilead, Moab and Edom. To the east of the Transjordan lies the eastern desert.

We referred to the Via Maris above. There were other major routes in and through Israel (see Map 3 overleaf). **The Ridge Route** is also known as the Beer-sheba–Jerusalem–Jenin highway, the National Highway or the Way of the Patriarchs.[47] This north–south route connected prominent cities such as Beer-sheba, Hebron, Jerusalem, Gibeah, Ramah, Bethel, Shechem, Ibleam and Jezreel. It followed the watershed ridge line of the Samarian and Judean mountains, running from Megiddo and Hazor down south to Beer-sheba via Shechem, Bethel, Jerusalem, Ephrath and Hebron. Unlike the Via Maris and the King's Highway, which were international routes traversing multiple territories, the Ridge Route was situated wholly within Ancient Israel. A section of this 'highway', namely that from Bethel to Shechem, is mentioned in Judges 21.19: 'So they said, "Look, the yearly festival of the Lord is taking place at Shiloh, which is north of Bethel, on the east of the highway that goes up from Bethel to Shechem, and south of Lebonah."'

---

46   cf. Aharoni 1962, 1967, 41–9.
47   Dorsey 1991, 117.

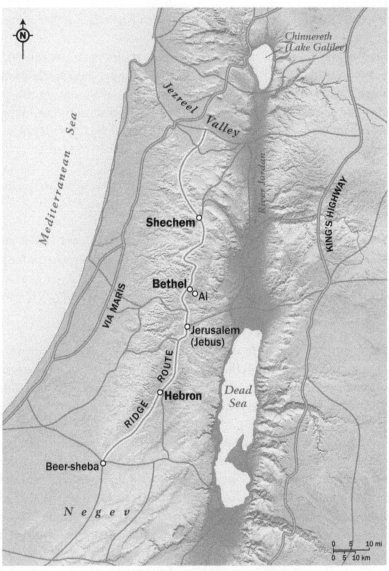

Map 3 **The highways of Ancient Israel**
(© Baker Publishing Group)

The Ridge Route is also referred to as the 'Watershed Route' because it follows the watershed of the highlands for much of its length. This is not quite accurate since, especially in Samaria, it departs from the watershed and follows alternative ridges or valleys.[48] Aharoni describes the route as follows:

---

48    Dorsey 1991, 117.

One longitudinal road of some importance is that through the hill country . . . which runs along the length of the north-south mountain ridge.
In this section between Hebron and Shechem it follows a single track
corresponding approximately to the watershed, and the deep wadis on
both sides prevent any deviation to the right or left. The main cities in
the hill country are situated near or on this route, e.g. Debir, Hebron,
Bethlehem, Jerusalem, Mizpah and Bethel . . . From Shechem the road
forks out into two branches: the western one passes through Samaria,
Dothan, Ibleam and Beth-haggan via Tirzah and Bezek . . . South of
Hebron the road also forks to form additional branches: the westernmost descends via Debir and Madmannah to Beer-sheba, whence it
continues southward past Nissana towards the 'Way of Shur' which
leads to Egypt. The eastern branch turns from Hebron towards Juttah
and Eshtemoa and descends towards Arad and Hormah. From here it
extends southward through the heart of the Negeb past Aroer, Oboda
and Bir-Hafir to Kadesh-barnea.[49]

**The King's Highway** starts in Heliopolis (Egypt), and from there goes east
to Clysma (modern-day Suez), through the Mitla Pass and the Egyptian forts
of Nekhl and Themed in the Sinai desert to Eilat and Aqaba. From there the
highway turns north through the Arabah, past Petra and Ma'an to Udhruh,
Sela and Shaubak. It passes through Kerek and the land of Moab to Madaba,
Rabbah Ammon / Philadelphia (modern Amman), Gerasa, Bosra, Damascus
and Tadmor, concluding at Resafa on the upper Euphrates.

These are the major regions and highways of the land, but, as ever, place
is particular and it is helpful to attend to particular places if we are to combine 'the intertextual "web" of canon with the contextual "web" of regions,
sites, cognate texts, and realia', as Monson proposes.[50] For example, the literary and geographical setting of the sermons of Moses in Deuteronomy
is the plains of Moab (Deut. 1.5). Intriguingly, Moses is commanded to
ascend Mount Nebo in 3.27 in order to see the extent of the land but only
does so in 34.1–4, an example of *resumptive repetition*. We will have occasion to refer to this literary technique again and so it is worthwhile quoting
Brichto's definition here:

---

49  Aharoni, 1962, 1967, 57–8.
50  Monson 2018, 32.

Essentially it is the treatment of one event two times. The first narration of the event . . . is usually briefer . . . than the second [and] is an independent, freestanding literary unit. The second treatment or episode, usually longer than the first, may or may not be able to stand by itself . . . The second treatment seems to go back to the opening point of the first episode and, resuming the theme of that treatment, provide a more detailed account . . . of how the bottom line of the first episode . . . was arrived at . . . The variety and richness of effects made possible by this technique are such that a full appreciation can only be achieved by examining each instance in situ.[51]

Mount Nebo is an elevated ridge some 2,330 feet (710 m) above sea level. On a clear day, the summit of Nebo ('Pisgah' (Deut. 3.27) may mean summit) provides the viewer with a panorama of the land. Craigie notes that:

The places are listed as they would appear to an observer facing north, following the horizon round to the west, and then down to the south; then the eye travels, as it were, back to the starting point by encompassing the great rift valley, containing the Dead Sea.[52]

Monson proposes that:

One way to appreciate the 'hyper-canonical' quality of Deuteronomy is to view its canonical centrality through the focused lens of the land hermeneutic introduced earlier. The reader not only shares Moses's perspective but can also see beyond him to the subsequent canonical and chronological layering of Deuteronomy's message being lived out and recited in the regions and locations that are visible from Nebo. *Locations of biblical episodes create associations between texts that might not otherwise be noticed.*[53]

He then goes on to explore some of the places visible from Nebo and their role in the OT.

Already in Genesis 10.19 in the Table of the Nations we find a description of the land. It may seem from this and the above that the boundaries of Ancient

---

51  Brichto 1992, 13–14. Fishbane 1985 refers to this trope, but it is surprising how many remain apparently unaware of the way in which it explains phenomena that historical critics lean on in texts such as Exod. 19—24 and 32—34. For resumptive repetition and Exod. 19—24 see Bartholomew 2020.

52  Craigie 1976, 404–5.

53  Monson 2018, 36. Emphasis original.

Palestine are clearly defined. To a large extent that is true of the west and the east, but, intriguingly, in the OT we find two rather different descriptions of the land. We get a sense of this in Deuteronomy 1.7 with the terms 'and the Lebanon, up to the great river, the Euphrates'. This extends Palestine greatly beyond what we typically think of as the northern boundary. What are we to make of this?

# 4 The land of Israel: different views in the Old Testament?

'The land' is one of the central themes throughout the OT. The Hexateuch (Genesis–Joshua) is held together by the axis God–people–land.[54] However, we appear to find divergent descriptions of the land in the OT.[55] In Genesis 15.18–21, part of one of the major passages in Genesis dealing with the covenant with Abram, a spatial merism follows 'this land', setting out the extent of the gift, namely from the river of Egypt to the River Euphrates:

> [18] On that day the LORD made a covenant with Abram, saying, 'To your descendants I give this land, *from the river of Egypt*[56] *to the great river, the river Euphrates*, [19] the land of the Kenites, the Kenizzites, the Kadmonites, [20] the Hittites, the Perizzites, the Rephaim, [21] the Amorites, the Canaanites, the Girgashites, and the Jebusites.

As scholars note, this depiction differs from the far more precise and restricted description of the land in Numbers 34 and Ezekiel 47.15–20. As is clear from Map 4 below, Numbers sets out the boundaries of Israel with precision. Similarly wide-ranging descriptions of the land to that in Genesis 15 are found in Exodus 23.31; Deuteronomy 11.24; Joshua 1.3–4; and 1 Chronicles 13.5.

How do we deal with such divergent data? Weinfeld discerns two different conceptions of the extent of the land in the OT: first, the 'unbiased' accounts fit with the common description of the land as stretching from Dan to Beer-sheba,[57] which describes the land by referring to the largest cities at its northernmost and southernmost extremes. Wherever a more precise

---

54  Wazana 2013, 1.

55  See Wazana 2013 for a comprehensive discussion of the major descriptions of the land in the OT.

56  Sarna (1989, 117) argues that the 'river of Egypt' here is not the Nile but its most easterly branch.

57  Judg. 20.1; 1 Sam. 3.20; 2 Sam. 3.10; 17.11; 24.2, 15; 1 Kings 5.5; Amos 8.14.

specification is required of this view of the land, we find a topographic one (cf. Josh. 11.17; 12.7). The so-called priestly description of the land in Numbers 34 (repeated in Ezek. 47—48) is an example of such a topographic description:

> **34** The LORD spoke to Moses, saying: [2] Command the Israelites, and say to them: When you enter the land of Canaan (this is the land that shall fall to you for an inheritance, the land of Canaan, defined by its boundaries), [3] your **south sector** shall extend from the wilderness of Zin along the side of Edom. Your southern boundary shall begin from the end of the Dead Sea on the east; [4] your boundary shall turn south of the ascent of Akrabbim, and cross to Zin, and its outer limit shall be south of Kadesh-barnea; then it shall go on to Hazar-addar, and cross to Azmon; [5] the boundary shall turn from Azmon to the Wadi of Egypt, and its termination shall be at the Sea.
>
> [6] For the **western boundary**, you shall have the Great Sea and its coast; this shall be your western boundary.
>
> [7] This shall be your **northern boundary**: from the Great Sea you shall mark out your line to Mount Hor; [8] from Mount Hor you shall mark it out to Lebo-hamath, and the outer limit of the boundary shall be at Zedad; [9] then the boundary shall extend to Ziphron, and its end shall be at Hazar-enan; this shall be your northern boundary.
>
> [10] You shall mark out your **eastern boundary** from Hazar-enan to Shepham; [11] and the boundary shall continue down from Shepham to Riblah on the east side of Ain; and the boundary shall go down, and reach the eastern slope of the sea of Chinnereth; [12] and the boundary shall go down to the Jordan, and its end shall be at the Dead Sea. This shall be your land with its boundaries all round.[58]
>
> (Num. 34.1–12)

Map 4 illustrates this depiction of the land.

Second, there is the broader description of the land in Genesis 15 and related texts.[59] Map 5 illustrates this broader description.

For Weinfeld, both are 'idealistic systems'.[60] However, the first does not include Transjordan south of Chinnereth, which is difficult to comprehend since the Israelites occupied Transjordan from the outset of their settlement in that

---

58   cf. 1 Kings 8.65.

59   Weinfeld 1993.

60   Weinfeld 1993, 55.

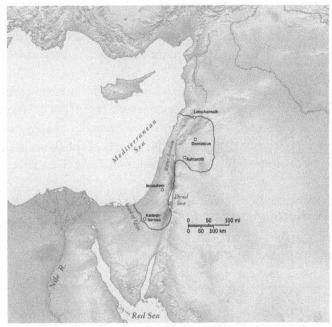

Map 4 **Borders of the promised land (Num. 34.3–12)**
(© Baker Publishing Group)

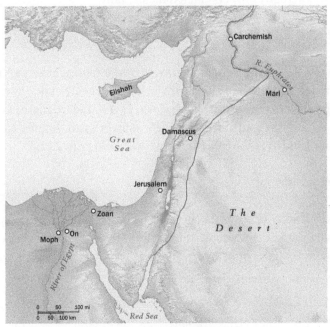

Map 5 **Borders of the promised land (Gen. 15.18–21)**
(© Baker Publishing Group)

area (Judg. 11.26). This issue was addressed by B. Mazar and R. de Vaux, who noted that this first border description corresponds to the boundaries of the Egyptian province of Canaan prior to the conquest. Aharoni notes that:

> In fact, the biblical description matches perfectly the boundaries of the Egyptian district of Canaan during the second half of the thirteenth century. This is one of those most instructive examples of ancient sources being preserved among the geographical texts of the Bible, because we have here a document that makes no sense whatever in later periods.[61]

Such a view, according to Weinfeld, fits with most biblical sources according to which the crossing of the River Jordan marks the beginning of the Israelites' conquest of the land (cf. Josh. 3—4). This is confirmed by data such as the fact that the manna of the wilderness ceased *after* their crossing of the Jordan (Josh. 5.12; Exod. 16.35; cf. Josh 5.2–11; Deut. 27.2–3; Josh 5.14).

> It is clear, then, that the realization of the promise of the Land of Canaan to the Israelites did not begin until Israel arrived at Gilgal. The territory of Transjordan was not included, at the outset, in the borders of the promise, and it was actually only conquered incidentally.[62]

Weinfeld notes further that:

> Settlement east of the Jordan, then, was considered secondary and therefore was not apportioned along with land on the western side by the casting of lots before the Lord at Shiloh (Josh. 14–19). Indeed, the eastern side of the Jordan is regarded in the ancient sources as an 'impure land' that was not included in the inheritance of the Lord (Josh. 22:19).[63]

Janzen comments:

> The second 'map' (Deut 11:24), in this schema, originated in the expansive era of the Davidic-Solomonic empire, was formulated in grand, utopian ancient Near Eastern royal terminology (river to river, sea to sea, etc.),

---

61   Aharoni 1962, 1967, 69.
62   Weinfeld 1993, 59.
63   Weinfeld 1993, 63.

and received its final crystallization by 'the so-called Deuteronomistic author or school' in the Josianic era.[64]

As one can see from Map 5, the broader description 'from the river of Egypt to the ... river Euphrates' sweeps up the Transjordan within its remit, and this is Weinfeld's focus. According to Weinfeld, it was only after the conquests of David in Transjordan and the priestly ascendancy of the house of Zadok that the view of Israel's borders changed, a perspective evident in Psalms 60.8–9 and 108.8–10:

### Psalm 60

[8] 'Moab is my washbasin;
   upon Edom I cast my shoe;
   over Philistia I shout in triumph.'
[9] Who will bring me to the fortified city?
   Who will lead me to Edom?

### Psalm 108

[8] 'Gilead is mine; Manasseh is mine;
   Ephraim is my helmet,
   Judah my sceptre.
[9] Moab is my washbasin;
   upon Edom I cast my shoe;
   over Philistia I shout in triumph.'
[10] Who will bring me to the fortified city?
   Who will lead me to Edom?

These psalms envisage no distinction between the eastern and western sides of the River Jordan, and it is this sensibility, according to Weinfeld, that stands at the foundation of the ideal model of borders in Genesis 15, whose ten peoples include the peoples of the Transjordan. According to Weinfeld, '[d]elineations of borders using seas and rivers as boundaries are typical of imperial descriptions',[65] and the imperial borders were adopted by the Deuteronomic circle as the borders of the land. 'Thus, what was in Numbers a settlement outside the borders of the Promised Land becomes in Deuteronomy a legitimate

---

64  Janzen 1992. Quoted in Wazana 2003, 55–6.
65  Weinfeld 1993, 68.

inheritance, which includes expansive territories.'[66] This change in perspective on the description of the promised land took place during the reigns of kings Hezekiah and Josiah.

> Until this period, the sources adhered to the ancient view, according to which the Transjordan is not part of the Promised Land, and only during the period of nationalist pride that characterized the time of Hezekiah and Josiah was a new view elaborated.[67]

Wazana attends to *exactly the same data*, but she interprets it in a significantly different way. She says of Weinfeld's analysis that 'the assumption that these are "boundary descriptions" is not valid. The Deuteronomistic corpus does not present a set of borders of the Promised Land that differs from the priestly source.'[68] Central to her analysis is close attention to the *literary* tropes at work in such texts. She states: 'The Bible, a literary document, communicates perceptions of mental pictures molded in words.'[69] Consequently, readers have to decipher their meaning. This, she argues, is felt strongly in relation to texts dealing with borders and territories. Whereas scholars tend to take all such descriptions as data for cartography, Wazana proposes

> that we regard images of the Promised Land in the Bible as literary descriptions; hence, the basis for examining them must begin with a literary analysis. Like all other biblical texts, they too are part of a charged ideological document, bearing religious notions and, sometimes, polemical undertones.[70]

Wazana points out that Israel's natural borders are hard to define, especially its northern and eastern ones:

> The Land of Israel is characterized by two main geographical features – the variety and diversity of its topography, climate, and plant and animal life in a relatively small area, and its configuration as a bridge

---

66  Weinfeld 1993, 73.
67  Weinfeld 1993, 74.
68  Wazana 2003, 56.
69  Wazana 2003, 45. Cf. Wazana 2013 for her comprehensive analysis of boundaries in the OT.
70  Wazana 2003, 45.

between three continents, part of the larger civilized continuum that was the ancient Near East. From a historical point of view, the events that shaped the history of the land were a manifestation of the interaction of those two factors, the meeting point of the forces from within and without.[71]

The land grant is at the core of the covenant with Abram, and according to Wazana it is remarkable that the first mention of the land in Genesis 12 does not specify its boundaries. Such covenant texts have, at least, a quasi-legal nature and yet 'Numbers 34 is . . . the only extensive description of the Promised Land in the traditions of the formative periods'.[72] Against the background of Hittite diplomatic texts, Wazana argues that this is not as unusual as it might seem. As with such diplomatic texts, the OT often relies for its concept of 'the land' on a territorial concept defined elsewhere.

However, Genesis 15 is far more specific, including a list of ten nations as opposed to the traditional six or seven in such texts, and, as such, is the foundational text of the greater Israel. Similar idioms are found in four other places: Exodus 23.31; Deuteronomy 1.7; Deuteronomy 11.24; and Joshua 1.3–4. Scholars deal with such texts as though they are descriptions of boundaries, but, for Wazana, this is a mistake.

Wazana attends closely to the literary nature of the spatial merism in Genesis 15 – 'from the river of Egypt to the . . . river Euphrates' – a phenomenon that most scholars do not take adequately into account.[73] Such merisms sometimes employ border sites, but sometimes the sites are within or without the totality being referred to. 'River' is common to all five texts; other elements include sea, wilderness and mountain. The 'great river' refers to the Euphrates, but, as with the other terms, this is a vast area and it is unclear which part of the Euphrates is being referred to. As Wazana notes, such concerns are not trivial. For Wazana:

> Problems and questions arise only when the spatial merisms are being forcefully transformed into exact border descriptions, contrary to the impression of indefinite vagueness inherent in them all . . . [T]hese texts are simply not what scholars have constantly tried to make of them.[74]

---

71  Wazana 2003, 46.

72  Wazana 2003, 51.

73  cf. Wazana 2013, ch. 2.

74  Wazana 2003, 62.

For example, Genesis 15.18 refers to 'from the river of Egypt'. Clearly, this is the Nile, but, as we know, it runs throughout the whole of Egypt. Because scholars treat texts such as Genesis 15.18–20 as boundary descriptions, they interpret the river of Egypt to refer to the eastern branch of the Nile. However, '[t]his exegetical act is not required by the text but derives from an attempt to read these passages as border descriptions on the basis of which cartological lines may be drawn'.[75]

As we will see in Part 3, the Nile was the heartbeat of Egypt and, as such, was awash – excuse the pun – with gods. This makes us reflect on whether or not the more expansive descriptions of the promised land are more ideologically or theologically charged than is often realized. In the context of the ANE – again see Part 3 – this is likely, and Wazana connects the spatial merism of the two rivers in Genesis 15.18 to the river flowing out of Eden and its four branches, including the Euphrates (Gen. 2.10–14). She notes of the Euphrates that it 'holds a special position, because it is considered equivalent to the cosmic ocean, perhaps by virtue of its extraordinary length and breadth'.[76]

Wazana asserts of the two different descriptions of the land in the OT that '[t]he differences in form and context reveal that these are two separate genres that convey two different *conceptions* of the Promised Land, but not two different *territorial units*'.[77] The literary form of the sort of spatial merism that we find in Genesis 15.18 has an instructive background in Neo-Assyrian imperial claims, in which they evoke world rule.[78] However, Assyrian imperial descriptions refer to past events, whereas '[b]iblical promise traditions are just that: a promise to be fulfilled in the future, that is, Israel's vocation'.[79] Thus, in the OT, '[t]he spatial merisms in promise terminology reflect a land that has no borders at all, only ever-expanding frontiers; they are referring to universal rule, using stock terminology typical of Neo-Assyrian royal inscriptions'.[80]

Most of the references to the land in the OT reflect a *multicentric* world view, according to which Israel is one nation among others,[81] as we have seen above with the Table of the Nations. Empires generally articulate a *monocentric* world view evoking world dominion. In the world-dominion texts of the OT we do indeed find a monocentric perspective: 'Contrary to the message

---

75  Wazana 2013, 108.

76  Wazana 2013, 111–12.

77  Wazana 2003, 63–4. Emphasis original.

78  Wazana 2003, 67–71. Cf. Deut. 11.25.

79  Wazana 2003, 70.

80  Wazana 2003, 71.

81  Wazana 2013, ch. 3.

that the Assyrian king is the vanquisher and ruler of the world, the Deuteronomistic promissory texts assert that the Israelites are destined for dominion over the whole earth.'[82]

# 5 Land and the different dimensions of the Old Testament

Wazana's approach to the different descriptions of the land in the HB/OT is fascinating. I think she is right, and we will return to this issue in subsequent volumes. For now, we need to note that what she does with these texts – examining their literary dimension closely – allows fresh new questions and perspectives to emerge, including the possibility that the different descriptions are not contradictory but complementary. Rather than representing different sources, together they enable us to gain a rich understanding of what is going on with YHWH's gift of the land to the Israelites, namely the beginning of a process that will extend to the whole of his creation.

Wazana's approach to the HB thus merits close attention, and in what follows we will use it as the springboard for a more wide-ranging discussion of key elements in what we should do with the OT. Indeed, in this way, our brief examination of these two very different approaches to the descriptions of 'the land' in the OT, with significantly different outcomes, enables us *inductively* to bring into the foreground central issues that determine what we do with the OT.

## (a) The Old Testament communicates[83]

Wazana draws our attention to the fact that the HB/OT '*communicates* perceptions of mental pictures molded in words'.[84] In this section we will use Wazana's statement as a springboard to explore the unprecedented communicative nature of the OT. In the following section we will use it to explore the lingual nature – 'mental pictures molded in words' – of the OT.

The first word that calls for our attention in Wazana's statement is *communicates*. Language and texts, including the OT, are best understood primarily as

---

82  Wazana 2013, 125.

83  I first developed a model of a communicative hermeneutic in Bartholomew 1998, 212–26. See that section for a detailed explanation of this approach.

84  Wazana 2003, 45. Emphasis added.

human communication or discourse. Such a communicative approach to texts positions a text in the hermeneutical framework:

sender – message – receiver

This may seem obvious, but in modernity scholars have too often attended to just about every aspect of the OT texts without ensuring that all the rigour of their work is directed towards listening to the message of the text/s as we have received them. We will see below why this has been the case.

## The Old Testament's unique communicative power

Communication is at the heart of the nature of the OT in a powerful and unique way. In the Preface to his very stimulating book *The Invention of Hebrew*, which will be the main focus of this section, Sanders states that:

> For over two thousand years, people have recognized the Bible as speaking directly to them, calling them to new forms of belonging that can threaten or transform the orders in which they find themselves. *But no other Near Eastern texts talk like the Bible does; virtually all other literature was by and for scribes, courts, and kings.*[85]

For those of us in churches where the OT is regularly preached, we hardly notice just how distinctive is this dimension of the text. But Sanders is clear that in its ANE context:

> *The Bible*[86] [HB/OT] *is the first text to address people as a public.* It is this call that the Bible's audiences have been answering for more than two thousand years. The way the Bible refuses to let go of us – and we of it – suggests a challenging question: What can biblical scholarship tell us about the Bible's power as political communication?[87]

## The problem with modern Old Testament interpretation

Sanders' question hints at a major problem with modern OT interpretation, a problem of which he provides an acute analysis. He discerns two major

---

85   Sanders 2009, xi. Emphasis added.

86   Note that when Sanders refers to the Bible he means the Old Testament / Hebrew Bible.

87   Sanders 2009, 1. Emphasis added.

reasons why we are in a situation in which the Bible's power as communication is not attended to. Figures such as Wilhelm de Wette and Julius Wellhausen are often seen as the great fathers of modern biblical criticism, but Sanders rightly points out that their work would not have been possible without more foundational conceptual shifts. As he asserts, HB/OT studies emerge out of modernity. Sanders identifies two major ways in which modernity shaped OT studies: seventeenth-century political philosophy and eighteenth-century folklore and philology.

Modernity involved the restructuring of European societies from the ground up,[88] and not least politically. At the onset of modernity the OT was linked with the rights of kings and queens, and to clear the space for modernity its authoritative political communication, however distorted, needed to be muted and marginalized. The key figures in this muting were Hobbes and Spinoza. Both rightly saw the connection between the OT and politics, and had to close it down as a political authority in order to make way for their own views of how politics should work.[89] Elsewhere, I have explored Spinoza's philosophy and biblical hermeneutics in detail.[90] In order to mute its authority, Hobbes and Spinoza had to reduce the OT to a text like any other text; it could convey ideas about its own time but could not speak powerfully and authoritatively to modern readers. Sanders notes that the HB/OT only became vulnerable to *source criticism*, a central method in the arsenal of historical criticism, because it could now be seen as just a text. Spinoza and his contemporaries shattered the link between language and power in the HB/OT, reducing it to 'just words'. According to Sanders, by the nineteenth century so devastating had this effect been on studies of the HB/OT that scholars were reduced to arranging its pieces in different strata. For example, it remains common to identify and concentrate attention on J, E, D and P as the major sources in the Pentateuch.[91] When I read theology at Oxford, a source of humour among students was identifying how many layers of Deuteronomistic editing our different lecturers identified in Deuteronomy. For Sanders, an effect of endless attention to such strata is that people lost sight of how the HB/OT speaks – and speaks so powerfully.

If Hobbes and Spinoza played a central role in muting the power of the OT's communication, Locke and then eighteenth-century folklore and philology muted the OT's capacity to convey knowledge. Under the influence of studies

---

88   See Goudzwaard and Bartholomew 2017; Israel 2001.

89   cf. Hahn and Wiker 2013; Hahn and Morrow 2020.

90   Bartholomew 2020.

91   J, E, D and P refer to the following sources: Jahwist, Elohist, Deuteronomist and Priestly.

in folklore and philology, the authentic core of the HB/OT and Ancient Israel was located in its earliest poetry. Thomas Blackwell had used orality to explain the aesthetic power of Greek poetry, and this approach, mediated by figures such as Herder, was applied to the OT and to Ugaritic poetry by Cassuto, Albright and Cross, utilizing, *inter alia*, the theories of orality and literacy of Havelock, Ong and Goody. The earliest authentic strata of the OT, it was argued, were poetry, which was good culture but bad history.[92] Sanders comments: 'Strikingly absent [from these debates] is theory developed through thinking about the Bible.'[93]

Indeed, Sanders' project develops through thinking hard about the Bible: 'this book asks if the originality of ancient West Semitic texts can be understood not in terms of their faded archaism but in terms of their innovation as political communication.'[94] For Sanders, recent epigraphic discoveries in Israel can help us sever the Gordian knot that has held HB/OT studies captive for too long.

## Iron Age Israel

Sanders recognizes that the uniqueness of the HB/OT requires a historical explanation. However, he seeks a naturalistic one which is anchored in hard evidence. For Sanders we need to avoid reconstructions that cannot be based on external evidence.[95] Sanders argues that recent epigraphic texts discovered in Israel shed new light on the historical change that facilitated the uniqueness of the HB/OT. He notes: 'For two thousand years, Near Eastern kingdoms and empires shared cuneiform, a script, not a language. Hebrew, as the first widely written vernacular, changed this.'[96] He maintains that:

> Israelite writers in the Iron Age did not have a national language handed to them: instead they created a form of political communication that could address a group called Israel, narrate its history, and let its audience see itself as part of that group and that history.[97]

---

92   Sanders sees this trajectory of thought manifesting itself recently in the debate between maximalists and minimalists about the historicity of the HB/OT. Maximalists see as historical as much of the OT as they can, whereas minimalists reduce the historicity of the OT to a minimum.

93   Sanders 2009, 34.

94   Sanders 2009, 33.

95   He notes of van der Toorn's 2007, and Carr's 2005, work on scribal culture that they rely on Mesopotamian and Egyptian evidence. The problem with this is that we do not know much about scribal culture in Israel. Furthermore, a focus on scribal culture attends to how texts were edited rather than why people cared so passionately about their message.

96   Sanders 2009, 2.

97   Sanders 2009, 38.

In the HB/OT we find a theological and political call to enter into and participate in a distinctive order; this pervades the HB/OT. The critical question is how the writers were able to do this.

Around 1200 BC, the dominant system of foreign empires collapsed, opening up a space in Palestine and elsewhere for the rise of kingdoms and peoples. Liverani writes:

> Thus, Palestine was – for the first time in 500 years – free from foreign occupation and from the menace of external intervention . . . 'Little' Palestinian kings, accustomed to submission to a foreign lord, were now beholden to no superior authority apart from their gods.[98]

It is in this context, and with the emerging shadow of Assyria as the new empire of the day, that Sanders locates the historical change he documents: 'By showing how writers began to speak in a deliberately local way and address a people, not a king or his subjects, this book documents a shift in communication and argues for seeing it as a major historical event.'[99]

For example, HB/OT ritual texts address the readers as 'you' and include the people in the rituals, an emphasis found elsewhere only in Ugarit. Sanders discusses the Ugaritic text *KTU* 1.40 and Leviticus 16 – the famous ritual of the Day of Atonement – in this respect, noting their similarities and important differences. Their similarities are not an accident. Both texts presuppose and speak to a new audience. However, the differences are equally important. First, through sending out the scapegoat beyond the camp and thus to the world's margins, the ritual of the Day of Atonement establishes Israel as the axis of the world, over against the margins. The Ugaritic ritual, while including its readers in the atonement ceremony, has, however, no sacred centre, nor does it cast anything out of its polity, as does Leviticus 16 with the sending of the second goat out into the wilderness to Azazel. Second, Leviticus 16 differs in terms of its narrative context, which has no parallel either in the ANE or at Ugarit. 'Its place in a founding narrative simultaneously decontextualizes it from any other history and encourages its readers to recontextualize it through reuse.'[100]

Sanders traces the emergence of vernacular writings across Palestine during this time. Assyrian imperial ideology – which we will come to in Part 3 – made use of the vernacular to assert its authority over local areas, but this very

---

98   Liverani 2005, 38. Quoted in Sanders 2009, 106.

99   Sanders 2009, 7.

100  Sanders 2009, 65–6.

use was also turned against Assyrian power. In this way a non-monarchic literature emerged, especially in Israel. In Israel, genres from Mesopotamia are now found: history, law, and new ones such as narrative about prophets. However, they have all been reconceived, addressing the public, namely Israel as a whole. 'No literature addressed such a "you" before the Bible.'[101]

## Distinctive Israelite literature

Sanders argues that it is in this period that Israel develops a distinctive voice in the vernacular – Hebrew – in the genres of law, history and prophecy.[102] History-telling began to address its audience in a non-monarchic voice. It is in and through this address that we witness the OT genres of history, law and prophecy being reconfigured. Israelite law has much in common with ANE law, but whereas in Mesopotamian law the identity of the citizen addressed is static, HB/OT law is grounded dynamically in an identity that develops through engaging with the text of the Torah. This is evidenced by its deictic markers, namely, general words that refer to specific times and places. It is no longer presented as 'I am the king' but rather 'This is the story . . .' and the readers are exhorted and invited to make this their story.[103]

Earlier, in the Deir 'Alla inscription[104] we find references to Balaam as a prophet; importantly, his prophecy is instigated by the gods and not the king. Balaam's renown is demonstrated by his occurrence in Numbers 22—24 but in a significantly different role.[105] For the first time, we find a narrative concerning a prophet who delivers divine messages irrespective of the desire of a king. The appearance of the prophetic books also marks an important shift in the message and medium of ANE prophecy, with its dynamic of reader participation. According to Sanders, 'in prophetic narratives from the late Iron Age, the decisive feature of a text was its communicative power, not its written nature'.[106]

With its origin in God and not the king, the triumph of prophecy in this way marked a major contribution of Israel, facilitating, for example, the profound political edge of the Torah. It enabled the universal emperor to be

---

101  Sanders 2009, 104.

102  There are multiple books on the history of Hebrew. Schniedewind (2013) is fascinating in his attention to the relationship between Hebrew and the life of the Israelites as well as his focus on written Hebrew. He engages with Sanders' work.

103  The Siloam Tunnel inscription (*KAI* 189) is a good example of this.

104  This inscription was discovered in 1967 in Deir 'Alla in Jordan. See <https://en.wikipedia.org/wiki/Deir_Alla_Inscription>.

105  Sanders 2009, 141.

106  Sanders 2009, 146.

recontextualized as God, the speaker of Torah, whose law could never be fully and truly mediated through a human king. Peter Machinist tracks in this respect how Judah and Urartu, a kingdom to the north of Assyria, reacted to Assyrian writing:[107]

> The genres of power from which history-writing in the Levant emerged are revisited and subverted, their voices taken over by a new double speaker: the prophet and the god he ventriloquizes. If the Urartean king claims to speak as the equal of Assyria and challenges its limitations, Judean prophecy claims to speak as Assyria's superior, challenging it by both echoing and inverting it.[108]

Sanders refers to this revolution as Israel's *negative political theology* which – especially in First Isaiah – discerns the foundation of political power in God and rejects the very ground rules of ANE sovereignty. For Sanders, the success of the Bible indicates that its claim to address 'my people' turned out to be true!'[109]

Sanders claims that this revolution in *prophecy* reframes both *law* and *history*. Prophecy frames the law and narrative: 'Biblical law is handed down by a prophet, and biblical history is framed as the working out of prophecy. It is as prophecy above all that biblical genres of discourse reflect on, and empower, their own mediation.'[110] Narrative prophecy in particular 'serves as a kind of meta-genre, framing biblical history and law'.[111] Sanders discerns this particularly in Deuteronomy: 'Deuteronomy's very notion that the covenant takes place between the people and God establishes this negative political theology at the ritual basis of the covenant.'[112] For Sanders, the Deuteronomistic movement enthrones a covenant and a text but not a king! He compares the discovery of a king – the youngster Joash – in the Temple in 2 Kings 11 with the discovery of a text in the Temple in 2 Kings 22—23.[113] The discovery of a king leads to the destruction of a Baal temple; the discovery of a text results in the destruction of all other cults in Judah. Text trumps king!

---

107  Machinist 2006. Referenced in Sanders 2009, 149.
108  Sanders 2009, 151.
109  Sanders 2009, 152.
110  Sanders 2009, 165.
111  Sanders 2009, 165.
112  Sanders 2009, 153.
113  cf. Grottanelli 1999.

Alongside the concept of the people as a protagonist of history, the vernacular revolution enabled the creation of a negative political theology. With the emergence of a divine narrator for history, an eternal political threat became possible: that no history could speak in the voice of the state and be true.[114]

Alongside this threat a new promise emerged, that of a people bound to God through a covenant embodied in a repeated ritual.

Sanders refers in this regard to a remarkable lecture by the postmodern philosopher Michel Foucault.[115] In it Foucault argues that for most of history, history-recording was a ritual that reinforced sovereignty and absolute power. Foucault identifies three axes of such history: the genealogical grounded the present in the heroes of the past; memorialization (annals, chronicles) demonstrated that what kings do is pregnant with significance; the exemplary function is to provide examples which are 'the law functioning in the luster of a name'.[116] Foucault writes:

History is the discourse of power, the discourse of the obligations power uses to subjugate; it is also the dazzling discourse that power uses to fascinate, terrorize, and immobilize. In a word, power both binds and immobilizes, and is both the founder and guarantor of order; and history is precisely the discourse that intensifies and makes more efficacious the twin functions that guarantee order. In general terms, we can therefore say that until a very late stage in our society, history was the history of sovereignty, or a history that was deployed in the dimension and function of sovereignty.[117]

Foucault thinks of Rome in particular as embodying this tradition, but his analysis applies equally well to the ANE nations that we will examine in Part 3. As we will see, in nation/empire after nation/empire, 'king–law–power' form a tight triad. However, this discourse of history has an alternative, a counter-testimony. For Foucault, this emerges in the sixteenth and seventeenth centuries AD, and disrupts the identification of people with king:

---

114 Sanders 2009, 154.
115 Foucault 2003, 65–85.
116 Foucault 2003, 67.
117 Foucault 2003, 68.

And the history or counterhistory . . . will of course speak from the side that is in darkness, from within the shadows. It will be the discourse of those who have no glory, or of those who have lost it and who now find themselves, perhaps for a time – but probably for a long time – in darkness and silence.[118]

This counter-testimony is disruptive and prophetic: it is

much closer to the mythico-religious discourse of the Jews than to the politico-legendary history of the Romans. We are much closer to the Bible than to Livy, in a Hebraic-biblical form much more than in the form of the annalist who records, day by day, the history and the uninterrupted glory of power.[119]

For Foucault, this is 'the counterhistory of prophecy and promise';[120] 'a history that sought to unmask Rome as a new Babylon, and which challenged Rome by demanding the lost rights of Jerusalem'.[121]

Foucault paints in very large brush-strokes, but his point is incisive. The so-called Roman discourse of history dominates the ANE, as we will see again and again. Rome, however, has a shadow, that of biblical history, which is exceptional in that it subverts this tradition. We have already noted above, in our discussion of the Table of the Nations, the potential political theology in the OT, and Foucault's discussion raises that notch several levels. Neither Foucault nor Sanders, however, takes God seriously in accounting for this radical shift.

For Sanders, our limiting factor in assessing the OT is that the manuscript evidence is so very late. In the OT, we are dealing with streams of traditions in which we find these radically new ways of conceiving of and writing about history, law and prophecy. 'The Bible's narrative prose represents a turning point in the history of literary forms, as Robert Kawashima (2004)[122] has brilliantly demonstrated.'[123] Law is reconfigured with performative, apodictic law

---

118  Foucault 2003, 70.
119  Foucault 2003, 71.
120  Foucault 2003, 73.
121  Foucault 2003, 74.
122  Note that we will come to Kawashima's work below.
123  Sanders 2009, 161.

at its heart,[124] and '[t]he genres of law and covenant had never before appeared within the genre of narrative'.[125] Sanders notes that we cannot identify the moment/s when a brilliant scribe or ruler inaugurated this shift. However, the epigraphic evidence that has come to light enables us to position this remarkable shift in the Iron Age. The public to whom this shift was directed needs to be imagined, and Sanders argues that he has found the context in which this remarkable change took place, as noted above.

There has been much discussion about the existence – or not – of schools in Israel. Sanders points out that no archaeological evidence for buildings to house large numbers of students has been found in Israel. The epigraphic evidence points to scribes operating outside the large institutions, much like metalworkers and potters.[126] The literary turn in OT studies has revealed just what a complex poetics existed in Israel.[127] For Sanders, this complexity does not mean that we need to assume an earlier written Hebrew literature. A highly developed culture of poesis must have existed in the Iron Age and earlier, long before there was any attempt to set it down in a standardized Hebrew. In a comparable way to Sanders, Schniedewind argues that:

> in particular, the rise of the Assyrian Empire would – for the first time – serve as a catalyst for the creation of the language of the Judean state – that is, Standard Biblical Hebrew (SBH), which would develop as the literary language of Judean scribes from the late eighth century until the disappearance of these scribes by the end of the sixth century B.C.E.[128]

Scholars typically think of the state as giving rise to writing, but '[w]hat we find is not an Israelite state establishing writing but writing being recruited by an Israelite state to establish itself'.[129] During the Iron Age, the Bible facilitated roles for its readers far beyond those of typical ANE readers – either mute subject or king. As Sanders concludes:

---

124  It is common to distinguish between casuistic ('If . . . then . . .') law and apodictic law ('You shall . . .') in the ANE.

125  Sanders 2009, 164.

126  Schniedewind 2019, 3.

127  cf. esp. Sternberg 1985.

128  Schniedewind (2013, 74) asserts that '[t]here is no evidence for formal "schools" in ancient Israel; rather, scribal education was done in an apprenticeship context'.

129  Sanders 2009, 124.

What emerges as remarkable about the Hebrew Bible is not only that it speaks in the voice of God, but how this voice at once directly addresses its audience and represents that audience's responses as both determinative and unpredictable. It speaks in the voice of a God who can inflict terrible punishment, but not coerce obedience. Instead it circulates through and by means of the people it addresses.[130]

## Evaluation

For our purposes, Sanders' work is vitally important for its rediscovery of the unique communicative dimension of the OT in the ANE world. As he notes: 'Ultimately, this book hopes to offer a way of understanding the Bible's *astonishing fertility as a communicative form*.'[131] As we ask the question 'What should we do with the Old Testament?' Sanders' work helps us answer it. First, all our labour needs to be directed towards hearing the OT's address. In a footnote of Sanders we get a sense of why this may be so very important:

> This question seems especially urgent since it is arguable that the last work within biblical studies to have had an enduring theoretical impact outside of the field was W. Robertson Smith's *Lectures on the Religion of the Semites* (1894). The source criticism of W. M. L. de Wette and Julius Wellhausen had already been deployed in classics.[132]

If we are to unleash the power of the message of the OT, then a great deal is at stake in what we do with it. Not only does this extraordinary literature call to us and invite us to become participants in the world it opens up, but it does so with the whole of life in view: politics, law, history, ritual, family, sexuality and so on. As Sanders' quote indicates, the OT has much to say to all areas of life and to the other disciplines in the academy, and if it has been muted in modernity then we need to read it in a way that unmutes it and allows it to speak with all its power and insight for today. Sanders draws our attention in particular to the political dynamite of the OT message. Thus, any OT hermeneutic will need to train itself first of all *to listen* afresh to the OT, before merely applying the analytical tools of historical criticism, as beneficial as these have been.[133]

---

130  Sanders 2009, 170.
131  Sanders 2009, 10. Emphasis added.
132  Sanders 2009, 174, n. 2.
133  See Bartholomew 2015 for my argument that biblical hermeneutics should be grounded in listening.

Second, Sanders' work is important for our project because it teaches us that we urgently need to *rethink the origins of modern biblical interpretation*. From Sanders' perspective, we are heirs to traditions of reading the OT that intentionally and unintentionally mute its powerful message and resist its transmission of knowledge so that it is at best good culture but bad history. If OT studies is as wedded to *modernity* as Sanders argues, then we need a handle on modernity, and on how modernity shapes OT studies, for better and for worse.

Third, for all the fecundity of Sanders' work, it too is quintessentially modern in its *naturalism*. We might say that Sanders attends to the OT historically and as literature, but the question of God never appears. Prophecy frames the redirection of the genres of the HB/OT, but the possibility that YHWH spoke is never investigated. In other words, his account is *theologically* deficient, as is that of Foucault. The originality of the OT is accounted for entirely in terms of naturalistic categories of historical change. At one point in his book, Sanders quotes Wittgenstein's famous saying from the Preface to his *Tractatus*: 'What can be said at all can be said clearly; and whereof one cannot speak thereof one must be silent.'[134] For Sanders, the latter is that for which we have no concrete evidence. For Wittgenstein, by contrast, it may well refer to the really important things in life which cannot be captured in propositions. Indeed, the later Wittgenstein radically changed his whole philosophical approach, and we will argue in this book that any approach to the OT which ignores its theological dimension is bound to be deficient.

## (b) The Old Testament communicates in language

Wazana draws our attention to the fact that the OT 'communicates *perceptions of mental pictures molded in words*'.[135] In this section we will use Wazana's statement as a springboard to examine the OT as language.

At its most basic the OT is made up of words, sentences, books, that is, texts, mostly in Ancient Hebrew[136] but with a small portion in Aramaic. In other words, the OT is a *lingual* artefact and needs to be attended to as such. Wazana's use of 'communicates–perceptions–mental–pictures–molded' alerts us to the complexity of issues involved at this point, a complexity which recent philosophy of language and postmodernism, in which language is central, have drawn to our attention.

---

134 Wittgenstein 1922, 18.

135 Emphasis added. Note that the relationship between thought and language remains contested in modern philosophy.

136 See Schniedewind 2013 for the classifications of the different types of Ancient Hebrew.

Of course, if we are investigating what to do with the OT, then there needs to be an OT to do something with. This brings us to the complex issue of textual criticism.

## Textual criticism

Textual criticism is commonly thought of as the discipline that works to determine the original text of the OT, what is often referred to as the autograph/s. We do not possess any of the original manuscripts of the OT but rather copies, and copies of copies, coming to us over hundreds of years. Through this process of *transmission*, errors and mistakes were introduced into manuscripts by scribes, and – so the idea goes – it is the role of the text critic to get us as close as possible to the original manuscripts of the OT.

On all accounts, the challenges of textual criticism are far more complex than this.[137] Tov defines textual criticism as dealing 'with the nature and origin of all the witnesses of a composition or text, in our case the biblical books'.[138] In recent decades this discipline has moved from being – at least from the outside – dry and dusty to hugely controversial, with some arguing that the fluidity of the text/s goes all the way down, as it were.[139] Clearly, there is a great deal at stake in this debate if we are to have confidence that there is a reliable OT text to be attended to. It would be a joy if I could claim to have solved the challenging issues of textual criticism of the OT! My goal in this section is the far more modest one of orienting the reader to the current issues, through the work of Tov and Ulrich in particular, and asking whether or not the question of God, our major concern in this book, impinges on this debate.

In a publication in 1863, Paul de Lagarde provided the first significant articulation of the theory of an original text of the OT underlying the witnesses to which we have access. This fits with the common understanding of textual criticism above. However, not all agree with Lagarde's assumption of an *Urtext* or *Urschrift* (original text or original writing). *The* issue that has come to the fore and that complicates matters is *the relationship between the composition of a book* and *its transmission*. Brotzman and Tully point out that this issue has still to be solved.[140] As they note, a book could have been produced, copied, subsequently revised and then the new 'version' copied again. 'This meant

---

137  For an accessible and up-to-date work on textual criticism and the OT see Brotzman and Tully 1994, 2016.
138  Tov 2012, 1.
139  See Bartholomew 2015.
140  Brotzman and Tully 1994, 2016, 22.

that there might be two versions of the same book which were being copied and circulated at the same time.'[141]

As if this were not complex enough, mainstream OT scholars assume nowadays that an OT book only reached its final form after a long process of oral tradition, editing, revision, updating and so on. From this perspective, the books of the OT came into existence over a long period of time, and many different scribes were involved in their production. This means that during this long process, parts of a book could have been copied, transmitted and revised, with new versions and parts thereof being copied, transmitted and revised, alongside the process whereby the final form of the book was achieved, leaving us with multiple possible streams of transmission and complex interactions. It is not hard to see just how messy is the picture that emerges.

Tov identifies two major models that have emerged in relation to these challenges: that of multiple original texts (Kahle, Barthélemy, Goshen-Gottstein, Talmon, Greenberg, Walters) and that of an original text or determinative (original) texts. Lemmelijn, an example of a scholar holding the former position, states: 'I would rather start from the observation that at a certain moment in history several texts have indeed been current . . . without positing anything about their origin and the phases of their prior textual history.'[142] Tov astutely points out that textual critics cannot *not* have a position on this issue: 'almost all scholars are involved with the evaluation of textual variants, but often they may not be aware that this procedure actually requires the acceptance of the idea of an original text in some form.'[143] According to Tov, there is no clear manuscript support for the theory of multiple original texts.

In Tov's view we need to define what we mean by the *Urtext* very carefully: 'we refer to the written text or edition (or a number of consecutive editions) that contained some form of the finished literary product.'[144] It is argued that such an approach to the *Urtext* is the simplest assumption, assuming that as literature the biblical books were completed at some point; the alternative theory of multiple original texts is improbable; a sense of linear development is central to textual criticism's analysis of the biblical text. For Tov, textual criticism of the OT attends to the original text, or a series of determinative or original texts. However:[145]

---

141  Brotzman and Tully 1994, 2016, 22.

142  Quoted in Tov 2012, 5, n. 12.

143  Tov 2012, 5. Cf. Childs 1979, 84–106.

144  Tov 2012, 9.

145  Tov 2012, 11.

- only some elements in one or more of these stages can be reconstructed;
- the original text existed in a written unvocalized form;
- if the original text were ever discovered it would most likely contain errors and inconsistencies.

Tov is keenly sensitive to the complexity of textual criticism and especially to the distinction between the following:

1  differences created during the transmission of a text;
2  variants created during the process of production or the literary growth of a text.

It is worth pausing to make sure we have understood this. The first point relates to what we stated above; namely, in the process of transmission of a text through copying and transmission errors and mistakes crept in, and the goal of the textual critic is to recover the original text.

Regarding the second point, Tov notes that the assumption that, before the completion of a book, textual transmission was already in operation is a major complicating factor for textual criticism.[146] He argues, furthermore, that during all stages of the development of books of the OT, parts of them were written up. An example is Baruch's writing of an early scroll of Jeremiah's prophecies, and then Jeremiah's dictation to Baruch of an additional scroll (Jer. 36). Intriguingly, for Tov these stages and any others are outside the concern of textual criticism. Rather, attention to them is the responsibility of other specialists within the study of the HB/OT.

The problem for Tov is that, try as we might, it is not always possible to distinguish between the transmission of the text of a book and the transmission of parts of the text of a book.

The recognition of literary variants symbolizes the progress made in modern textual criticism. However, at the next stage, we often recognize that lack of clarity requires us to take a step back when evaluating certain variants. I consider this a worrying aspect of post-modern textual criticism.[147]

---

146  In this regard, Tov identifies books or parts thereof in OT texts such as Joshua, Ezekiel, 1 Samuel, Proverbs and Jeremiah.

147  Tov 2012, 16. Waltke (quoted in Brotzman and Tully 1994, 2016, 22) comparably notes: 'As a result of [the literary achievements of scribes] the line between literary criticism and textual criticism has been attenuated.'

However, earlier in his article, Tov does note that most differences between textual witnesses can be explained as genetic ones emerging from linear developments: 'The acceptance of an original text model is based on the admittedly subjective understanding that the great majority of the variants are genetic.'[148]

It is intriguing to see how, as Tov explores the challenge of the fluidity of divergence all the way down, the *literary* nature of the OT texts plays an important role in the arguments he identifies for an *Urtext*. Tov notes that there is no 'absolute proof' for the model of an *Urtext* because our evidence is dated late. The simplest assumption, or so it is argued, is that the editing or composition of a biblical book was completed at some point; there was a time when each biblical book was extant as an *individual textual unit*. The OT books are literary creations, and one can appeal to data such as literary unity, and the mind, logic and style of individual authors which are often visible. These point to a composition that was completed and not to 'a multi-stage process of composition'.[149]

Ulrich takes a somewhat different approach. He is a major authority on the Qumran manuscripts and argues that they illuminate the history of the biblical texts. The Scrolls are a thousand years older than what fifteenth-century scholars referred to as the original text of the OT, and the books of the Samaritan Pentateuch are not bad translations or paraphrases, as scholars have proposed, but rather translations of alternative forms of biblical texts, now partially rediscovered at Qumran.

The books of the Hebrew Bible evolved organically 'until their final, perhaps abrupt, freezing point of the Masoretic tradition'.[150] In this process, authors or tradents worked creatively to produce new versions of books or passages:

It is well known that many parts of Scripture began as small, oral units and were told and retold, grouped into small collections of related material, and gradually written down. The oral and written forms were occasionally reformulated to meet the varied needs of the times and were handed down and repeated faithfully for generations.[151]

---

148  Tov 2012, 12.
149  Tov 2012, 10.
150  Ulrich 1999, 108.
151  Ulrich 1999, 108.

Ulrich argues that in this process the 'base text' remains stable:

> The base text functions with respect to subsequent variant editions in a manner analogous to an original or correct reading in relation to variant readings, whether expansions, revisions, or errors. That is, it is what one expects to find – the 'default reading' – and so its occurrence is unremarkable. In a sense, all witnesses of a given book exhibit the base text; the material that indicates a variant literary edition is the coordinated pattern of intentional variants intended by a creative author.[152]

The base text is what we should see as the standard, and not the Masoretic Text (MT). The latter is a 'nonunified collection of texts, the nature of which varies from book to book'.[153] Ulrich says of the MT that:

> We should not look to it as the standard by which to judge the text of the various books, but to the base text, or earliest available literary edition of each. The base text of each book, that is, the earliest edition of that book attested in our extant witnesses, must be individually assessed and determined. It already stands late in the succession of reworked editions of that book, but for the sake of general applicability we can call the first extant edition of each book the base text. For some books only one edition appears to be attested, and for those books one can skip to the level of individual textual variants to refine the interrelationship of preserved manuscripts. But for many books our witnesses document variant literary editions.[154]

In this regard Ulrich differs from Tov. Textual criticism must focus on *the base text*, which is:

- a developing text;
- diachronic;
- pluriform.

The result, for Ulrich, is that

---

152  Ulrich 1999, 113.
153  Ulrich 1999, 113.
154  Ulrich 1999, 114.

the target of 'textual criticism of the Hebrew Bible' is not a single text. The purpose or function of textual criticism is to reconstruct the history of the texts that eventually became the biblical collection . . . it is not just to judge individual variants in order to determine which were 'superior' or 'original.' 'The original text' is a distracting concept for the Hebrew Bible; in a very real sense, there was no 'original text,' at least none accessible, except for those relatively late parts contributed by redactors.[155]

Ulrich sums up his position as follows:

Thus I propose that the main lines in the picture of the history of the biblical text were formed by the deliberate activity of a series of creative scribes who produced the new or multiple literary editions of the books of the Bible. These multiple literary editions have been demonstrated for us over the past forty-five years in the biblical manuscripts from Qumran; they have been under our noses for centuries in the new literary editions preserved in [the Samaritan Pentateuch] and [the Old Greek] or attested in Josephus; and they have been described for us by literary and historical critics since the Enlightenment as the successive literary editions constituting the history of the very composition of the Scriptures from the beginning.[156]

Clearly, the Qumran evidence needs to be attended to closely. What all of this has done is to massively complicate our understanding of how we got the OT. Brotzman and Tully identify the different periods in the history of the development of the OT. We appear to know least about the period up until *c.*300 BC, during which time the OT texts were written, copied and updated, written on scrolls initially in an archaic script and then later in the square script.[157] We do have textual witnesses in the period from *c.*300 BC to AD 135 since this is the period of the production of the Septuagint, and that of the Dead Sea Scrolls, which came to light in the second half of the twentieth century. The Bar Kokhba revolt took place in AD 135, after which time the OT text was fixed among Jewish scribes and remained stable. The different text types evident at Qumran were standardized by AD 135 at the very latest. For Childs, it is this stabilization that is definitive: 'The term canonical text denotes that official Hebrew

---

155  Ulrich 1999, 114–15.
156  Ulrich 1999, 107.
157  For an illustration of the difference see Brotzman and Tully 2016, 22.

text of the Jewish community which had reached a point of stabilization in the first century AD, thus all but ending its long history of fluidity.'[158] The period of the Masoretes begins in the fifth century AD; these were Jewish scribes who transmitted the text carefully and established a system to retain the reading tradition they had received. The Leningrad Codex, the basis for the *Biblia Hebraica Stuttgartensia*, comes from early in this period. Childs qualifies affirmation of the MT by noting that it is the vehicle for recovering the canonical text.

Brotzman and Tully say of this history that:

> It is ... amazing that we have access to a generally faithful copy of the OT that is substantially the same as the autographs written so many years ago. There are places in the OT where the text may be in doubt, and in places the testimony of the ancient versions will be necessary to restore the text. But by and large, the Hebrew text that we have has been faithfully (though not perfectly) transmitted down through the years.[159]

I think this is correct, but it should be obvious from the above that OT textual criticism is in a state of diversity and potential crisis. Especially if one brings together the quintessentially modern historical criticism of the OT with postmodern views of language, one is in deep trouble. Are there ways in which our project orients us towards this situation?[160] In my view there are.

First, it needs to be noted how Ulrich's approach is woven throughout with what used to be called the 'assured results' of historical criticism. This is evident above in his reference to what is 'well known'; he states that 'intense and voluminous literary and historical-critical study of the biblical literature over several centuries has solidly grounded the assumption of a rich and continuous literary history of Israel spanning more than a millennium'.[161] He refers, as one would expect, to source criticism of the Pentateuch, the development of the Deuteronomistic history, the layered nature of prophetic texts, and the collections that underlie Psalms and Proverbs.

Ironically, Ulrich arrives at a position that Tov calls 'postmodern textual criticism', *inter alia* through a strong return to historical criticism, a product of

---

158  Childs 1979, 100.

159  Brotzman and Tully 1994, 2016, 35. See also Bazak 2020, 171–234.

160  For an example of how theology may bear on OT textual criticism see Childs 1979, 84–106, for his canonical approach to textual criticism. Childs (1979, 102) asserts that 'the failure . . . to take seriously the effect of the canon, lies at the heart of the methodological controversy over Old Testament text criticism'.

161  Ulrich 1999, 100.

modernity. One is reminded here of Alvin Plantinga's perceptive tracing of the creative anti-realism – we are the creators of the world and not God – of post-modernism back to the idealism of Kant, *the* proponent of human autonomy, alerting us to the way in which the DNA of modernity itself provides an impetus towards the relativism of postmodernism.[162] Recent decades, and especially the literary and postmodern turns in OT interpretation, have, however, rendered the assured results of historical criticism far from sure. Furthermore, the explosion of ANE evidence since Wellhausen does not always support the core views of historical criticism. As we will see below, for example, when we come to the Babylonian world view in Part 3, Van De Mieroop argues for the primacy of the written text from the outset in Mesopotamia. He rejects the view of a long oral tradition underlying the written texts. He does see scribes as playing a very creative role in the transmission of texts, but, nevertheless, his argument raises questions about Ulrich's acceptance of the view that OT texts began in small units of oral tradition.

Second, the way in which textual criticism has backed into literary analysis of the OT must be noted. The issue of an original text/s has now become one of the major issues in OT textual criticism. And clearly, it has major implications not only for textual criticism but also for OT interpretation in general since *the text* is what we aim to understand. What is intriguing and calls for attention is that this debate encroaches on issues such as the nature of the OT books *as literature*, the nature of textuality and ultimately the nature of language and linguistics. One can ask, for example: what view of a text is Ulrich working with when he refers to the 'base text' of an OT book? To me this sounds like one of Plato's forms or ideas which is thought to be out there and determinative but bears no precise relationship to actual texts on the ground, as it were.

Early on in their *Biblical Hebrew Reference Grammar*, van der Merwe, Naudé and Kroeze note under a heading, 'Textual Cohesion', that '[e]very language community has its own conventions that determine the form that their texts should take in order to be understood as coherent texts'.[163] They say this, of course, in relation to Ancient Hebrew, and, if it is true, then we should indeed be able to access such conventions and assess OT texts as coherent – or not – and this could/should support the notion of an *Urtext*. Similarly, Sanders notes that 'texts must draw on preexisting forms to communicate to their audiences'.[164] If there is one thing that the literary turn in OT studies has alerted

---

162  Plantinga 1995.

163  Van der Merwe, Naudé and Kroeze 2017, 64.

164  Sanders 2009, 14.

us to, it is that the poetics of OT texts – their nature as literature – is extremely well developed and complex. As we will see below, OT scholars struggle to account for this emergence of a fully fledged poetics in Israel, and Israel's view of God bears on it.

Third, insofar as this debate is informed by postmodernism, at the heart of which is a view of language as inherently violent and slippery, we need to note that the postmodern view of language is decidedly not the only option. Derrida, for example, views texts as inherently unstable, an approach which he embodies in his own works, making their meaning very difficult to discern and contain. It is easy to see how such a view resonates with some of the current approaches to OT textual criticism. In my view, we are emerging beyond postmodernism, bearing in mind that it was only ever one view among many in the academy.

Fortunately, there are major alternatives to the postmodern views of language, and the two we will mention specifically invoke theology. In his *Real Presences*, George Steiner notes astutely that it is to Derrida's credit that his work confronts us with either nihilism or 'In the beginning was the Word'![165] Steiner notes that for most of history we have worked with a notion of *a covenant between word and world* so that 'being is sayable'.[166] Steiner tracks the attack on this view which culminates in postmodernism, in which all language contains aporia – contradictions or disjunctions – and is inherently unstable.

Among the New Phenomenologists, Jean-Louis Chrétien's work on language, *The Ark of Speech*, similarly stands out as an exceptional work articulating a very different philosophy of language from that of the postmoderns.[167] When one hears the title of Chrétien's book one thinks that 'Ark' is 'Arc', that is, a trajectory. Remarkably, it is, however, an allusion to Noah's ark which contains Noah, his family and the animals and protects them. Far from viewing language as violent, for Chrétien it is a gift that enables humans to protect the otherness of the other. He argues that Adam's first great test came when the animals were brought to him to be named. Would he use language to dominate them, or would he use it to safeguard their otherness and integrity?

While we should not underestimate the challenge of OT textual criticism and its complexity, we are in real trouble if we bring a postmodern view of language to bear on the discipline in combination with the so-called assured results of historical criticism, and then, not surprisingly, find resonances of

---

165 Steiner 1989.

166 i.e. we can speak truly about the world.

167 Chrétien 2004.

such a view all over the place. When it comes to our view of language, as noted by Steiner above, there is a *theological* dimension that is unavoidable. Steiner argues that we need a *grammar of creation* to account for the real presences we encounter in literature and art and so that we can escape what he calls the 'secondary city' of criticism and commentary that has so taken on a life of its own that we are prevented from engaging with the major texts themselves. It is hard here not to find resonances in recent developments in textual criticism. Of course, if we are to engage with the major texts, then we must grant them the courtesy of assumed coherence unless the evidence is overwhelmingly in the other direction. Indeed, in his *Real Presences*, Steiner sets out in exquisite detail what I call his 'courteous' hermeneutic.

Fourth, of course, we also need to attend closely to the nature of textuality and language in Ancient Israel and in the ANE. Is it true that the Ancient Israelites had their own conventions that determined the form that their texts should take in order to be understood as coherent texts? And, as Joshua Berman[168] and others have rightly pointed out in recent years, the *criterion of similarity* also needs to be taken seriously; namely, how did literature and textuality work in the ANE and how can this illuminate scribal practice in Israel? As we will see below, in its formative stages historical criticism operated without the huge amount of ANE material we now possess, and scholars working in this field imposed on the OT, relatively uncritically, views of composition for which there is little evidence in the ANE.

In a conversation I held with Eric Tully, he made the insightful point that contemporary textual criticism operates *downstream of redaction criticism*. Schart, for example, identifies five phases in the redaction of Amos 9 from different time periods.[169] Such work and the assumption that we can with confidence reconstruct these stages lends credence to the view that fluidity of the OT text goes all the way down, but, of course, such reconstruction of multiple layers of redaction is itself highly speculative.

Fifth, we need to revisit the issue of the origin of the OT. Childs asserts: 'One of the least satisfactory elements in the text-critical manuals is the failure to relate the text-critical enterprise to the history of the Old Testament canon . . . Yet the two subjects are closely related.'[170] This strikes me as correct, but Childs proceeds to relate the history of the canon to the *terminus ad quem* of the production of the OT, whereas in my opinion we need to go back to the *terminus*

---

168 Berman 2017.
169 Schart 1998.
170 Childs 1979, 94.

*a quo*, to what Ulrich evocatively but unhelpfully describes as the 'shadowy beginnings' of the OT texts.[171]

Much mainstream OT scholarship works without the view that God revealed himself in history and to Israel.[172] Similarly, studies of the history of the formation of the OT canon tend to focus on the *terminus ad quem* rather than the *terminus a quo*. However, it is to the *terminus a quo* that the OT draws our attention, namely God's revelation of himself in history. Later in this book, we will develop a model of God's disclosure of himself that takes revelation fully into account as well as the Israelites in their reception of that revelation. Clearly, if God did disclose himself to the Israelites and remained deeply involved in their life, then this bears strongly on the origin of the OT texts and on their transmission, which we would expect to have been handled with great care.

The current complexity of OT textual criticism will be clear to the reader of this section. We have made no attempt to solve all the issues or to dive into actual examples which are readily available in the textbooks. Instead, we have sought to orient ourselves towards the debate with the assurance that we can proceed with the confidence that we do indeed have a text/s to 'decipher', and our very deciphering of it/them will confirm – or not – their integrity as texts. There is a circularity here that is simply unavoidable.

## Dimensions in deciphering the Old Testament

A synonym for 'decipher' – Wazana's language – is 'interpret', but 'decipher' helpfully alerts us to the fact that this is not always simple. We have witnessed this first-hand above in the discussion of descriptions of 'the land'. It is helpful to distinguish various levels and/or dimensions in interpretation, as follows.

*The semantic.* I have in mind here what Speech Act Theory (SAT) refers to as the locution. Words have meanings, and for a sentence to be meaningful we need to be able to obtain some sense of the meanings of the words in their context and how they fit together to make linguistic sense. In Genesis 15.18, for example, to interpret 'To your descendants I give this land, from the river of Egypt to the great river, the river Euphrates . . .', we need to know what a river is, to know that the river of Egypt is the Nile, and so on. We also need to know how this promise hangs together – that is, understand its syntax – with the two rivers expanding on 'this land', the object of 'I give', which YHWH promises to Abraham and his descendants.

---

171 Ulrich 1999, 108.
172 Childs is, of course, an exception to this.

*The literary.* A major mistake is to think that once we understand the locution, we have understood what the OT is saying. As we will see in this volume, this mistake is not uncommon among OT scholars. Meaning, as SAT recognizes, is far 'thicker' than mere locution. SAT identifies, as noted above, three dimensions to a speech act: locution, illocution and perlocution.[173] In my view, the identification of the illocutionary force/s of speech acts is a major insight. Genesis 15.18, for example, has the force of a promise to Abraham, and needs to be read as such. Paul Ricoeur and others have rightly pointed out that meaning cannot be located in the individual word but is spread across the sentence, the paragraph, the discourse.

Comparably, Wazana highlights the *literary dimension* of the HB/OT, noting of the twentieth-century scholars who did vital work on the geographical-historical boundaries of Israel that they 'largely eschewed literary analysis'.[174] A major contribution is her creative attention to spatial merism in the texts articulating the greater Israel, indicating how crucial it is to attend to this trope in such texts. Indeed, it is through close attention to this trope in the relevant texts that Wazana arrives at a significantly different interpretation from that of Weinfeld, whose reading is more typically historically critical.[175]

## The underdetermination of theory by facts

An important lesson emerges here. Historical criticism has been rigorous in its work and has played an invaluable role in alerting us to *the data of the OT.* However, what has not often been noticed is that, as philosophy of science has taught us, theory or interpretation is *underdetermined* by facts. Our discussion above illumines this well. Both Weinfeld and Wazana deal with the same textual data but arrive at different 'theories' or interpretations to account for that data. A deficiency in historical criticism and much conservative interpretation has been to fail to attend consciously and closely to the other elements in interpretation apart from identification of the data, such as illocutions, and this has major implications for any assessment of historical criticism. For example, as we saw above, for Weinfeld the P source has a different view of the land from the later D source, and even D has various layers of recension. Wazana's literary analysis enables us to see that their views of the land may not

---

173  Austin 1975.

174  Wazana 2013, 4.

175  This is not to argue that Wazana ignores historical criticism. Cf., for example, her 2013 treatment of Joshua. She (2013, 298–302) identifies four views of the promised land in Joshua. She (2013, 297) asserts that 'Joshua is a complex, layered composition that has undergone a greater degree of reworking and transmission than other biblical historiographical texts'.

in fact differ. Weinfeld, as a typical historical critic, has failed to attend closely to the literary nature of the texts that articulate a broader view of the land.

In the history of modern OT interpretation I identify four turns: the historical, the literary (from the 1970s onwards), the postmodern (from the mid 1980s onwards) and the recent renaissance of theological interpretation.[176] As is well known, and as we see in the above discussion, the literary turn raised the most acute questions about the historical-critical approach, but, before the implications could be fully explored, the postmodern turn was upon us with its wild pluralism. The result is that the historical-critical approach/es remains the default mode for most OT scholars.

Wazana's work points to the inadequacy of this. We need an approach to the OT that *integrates the historical with the literary and the literary with the historical*, if we are to find a healthy way forward in our post-postmodernist era.

The historical aspect of the OT remains vitally important, but our discussion above shows how it is bound up with the literary nature of the text. Note Wazana's conclusion above that the two types of texts relating to the land 'are two separate genres that convey two different *conceptions* of the Promised Land, but not two different *territorial units*'. In Ricoeur's language the historical relates to that which underlies the text or, as we might say, that to which the text refers. Wazana's literary analysis concludes that the historical and geographical *reference* of the two types of texts is the same, namely the land of Israel. And 'the land' was not imaginary but geographically and historically real.

This brings us to the central role of the ANE context in both Weinfeld's and Wazana's analysis. Israel herself was an ANE nation and, positioned where she was, it is simply impossible that Israel should avoid the influence of the powerful surrounding cultures. Wazana's and Weinfeld's analysis demonstrates the vital importance of reading the OT as literature against its ANE context, not least in relation to Assyrian ideology.

## The theological

Aharoni refers to Israel as the stage of God's dramatic acts. He relates the historical geography of Israel to the relationship between God and Israel as it was interpreted by Israel's 'national faith'. Wazana notes that the OT is an *ideological* document conveying religious and polemical notions. She also, appropriately, notes that, as a literary document, the OT 'communicates'.

We have referred above to the lingual, literary, geographical, cultural (ANE) and historical aspects of the OT. These dimensions of the OT alert

---

176 Bartholomew 2015.

us, potentially at least, also to its *religious* nature. In our discussion above of the borders of Israel, this comes to the fore in multiple ways but particularly in relation to the vision of a greater Israel, which in the OT amounts to the universal rule of Israel's God, YHWH. Within the OT, YHWH's election of Israel is always held in relation to his purposes for the whole of his creation, for all nations or what is called 'the kingdom of God'. Thus, the way in which greater Israel is depicted, if Wazana is right, which I think she is, relates to the dominant *religious* dimension of the OT which is communicated through such texts.

It is the religious dimension of the OT that tends to be ignored – as with Sanders – or seen as causing most problems. In a recent work on biblical criticism, for example, John Barton argues that the bracketing out of 'questions of theological truth' is 'methodologically essential' for biblical criticism.[177] In his useful book *The First Historians*, Bruce Halpern nevertheless insists that:

> For believers, the history in the Bible is constitutive of a religious community . . . Such a confessional history must be uncritical history: to question the canonized reports is to threaten the cohesion of the community. The straitjacket of doctrinal conservatism therefore prohibits critical historical analysis of the Bible.
>
> The confessional use of the Bible is fundamentally antihistorical . . . Worshippers do not read the Bible with an intrinsic interest in human events . . . Confessional reading levels historical differences . . . because its interests are life present . . . and eternal.[178]

There are, of course, two different issues here, but ones that are intimately related. The first is the role of religion *in the OT*; the second is the role of religion *in the interpreter of the OT*. These should be neither equated nor completely separated. Both will be attended to in this series, but for now we simply demonstrate ways in which serious attention to the religion in the OT is explanatorily fertile.

In his fascinating *Biblical Narrative and the Death of the Rhapsode*, Robert Kawashima provides us with an example of why taking the theological or religious dimension of the OT seriously is important and fecund in terms of its explanatory power.[179] Kawashima begins by comparing the rhapsode[180]

---

177  Barton 2007, 164.

178  Halpern 1988, 3–4.

179  See Kawashima's forthcoming *The Archaeology of Ancient Israel's Knowledge*.

180  A rhapsode is one who recites epic poems, especially as part of a group in Ancient Greece whose job it was to recite from memory the Homeric poems.

of Plato's *Ion* with Ezra, the scribe (Neh. 7.72b—8.8). For Kawashima, 'Ezra and Ion, whom one might take as emblematic figures of their respective narrative traditions, help bring into focus the contrast I would like to trace in the following study: the art of biblical narrative versus that of epic'.[181] He points out that, way before Herodotus, the supposed father of history, and Homer, Israelite scribes practised an innovative narrative art that anticipates the modern novel's craft.

There are important connections between OT narrative and Ugaritic narrative poems but also important differences. Something radically new emerges with OT historical narrative, and Kawashima surveys different approaches to this issue. Von Rad expresses wonder at the emergence of narrative history in relation to the succession narrative of King David, but argues that while we cannot trace the origins of this development – we cannot provide history with a history – we can trace predisposing factors:

> We cannot trace the origins of ancient Israelite historical writing. At a particular point in time it is there, and already we have it in its fully developed form. We can, however, trace the predisposing factors which made such an achievement possible to such people.[182]

Von Rad locates the predisposing factors in the era of Solomon:

> Only in Solomon's era did the new order, which began in the time of David, develop its cultural potential to touch every facet of human existence . . . In short, the time of Solomon was a period of 'enlightenment,' of a sharp break with the ancient patriarchal code of living.[183]

For von Rad, J is also 'redolent of the untrammeled days of Solomon',[184] but here certain cultic legends developed and were historicized into the history-like prose narratives of J.

Cassuto similarly comments that:

> When we consider the earliest stages of Biblical literature, we are confronted by an amazing phenomenon. They do not give the impression of having

---

181  Kawashima 2004, 4. 'Epics' are long, narrative poems, typically from the Greek tradition.
182  Von Rad 1966a, 167.
183  Von Rad 1966a, 203.
184  Von Rad 1966a, 69.

an embryonic character, or of being literary first fruits; nor are there any signs of experimentation or of searching for the right path discernible in them. On the contrary they present us with finished and perfected writings that bear witness to a well-established artistic tradition, as though they had been preceded by a centuries-old process of development. But Israel's history does not provide sufficient time for such development, since the beginning of Biblical literature coincides with the commencement of the life of the nation. How then can we explain this phenomenon?[185]

Cassuto finds formal parallels in Ugaritic literature, so that the biblical innovation is a formal continuation of the Canaanite tradition while unique in terms of content:

> This being the case, it is clear why Biblical literature is already at a stage of artistic completeness when it first originates. Its rules of literary expression and its path among the Canaanite dialects were already firmly established in the past. Therefore our ancestors, when they first came to express their thoughts in literary form, did not have to fashion techniques of expression; these were quite ready to hand, and it was easy to use them in order to create a new literature, a literature new in truth, in its content and spirit, but a continuation of the old in its forms – new wine, so to speak, in an old flagon.[186]

Kawashima also attends to the epochal work of Erich Auerbach. Auerbach's *Mimesis* is fascinating, not least because it is 'ideologically unintelligible without the Christian doctrine of Incarnation'.[187] In his Chapter 1, Auerbach compares Genesis 22 – the story of Abraham's journeying to sacrifice Isaac – with book 19 of Homer's *Odyssey*. From Genesis 22 Auerbach comments in general on the biblical stories. Intriguingly, he notes that:

> their religious intent involves an absolute claim to historical truth. The story of Abraham and Isaac is not better established than the story of Odysseus, Penelope, and Euryclea; both are legendary. But the Biblical

---

185  Cassuto 1975, 16.

186  Cassuto 1975, 18. Frank Moore Cross revisits in essence von Rad's approach, but now in the full light of the Ras Shamra and the Ugaritic discoveries. He sees J and E as different forms of an older, mainly poetic epic cycle; J transformed cultic poetry and tradition into prose and 'history' at a time when Israel's cultic traditions had fallen into disuse.

187  Said, 2003, xi.

narrator, the Elohist, had to believe in the objective truth of the story of Abraham's sacrifice – the existence of the sacred ordinances of life rested upon the truth of this and similar stories. He had to believe in it passionately; or else (as many rationalistic interpreters believed and perhaps still believe) he had to be a conscious liar . . . lying in the interest of a claim to absolute authority.[188]

The Elohist aimed not primarily at realism but at *truth*:

The Bible's claim to truth is not only far more urgent than Homer's, it is tyrannical – it excludes all other claims. The world of the Scripture stories is not satisfied with claiming to be a historically true reality – it insists that it is the only real world, it is destined for autocracy . . . Far from seeking, like Homer, merely to make us forget our own reality for a few hours, it seeks to overcome our reality: we are to fit our own life into its world, feel ourselves to be elements in its structure of universal history.[189]

Auerbach argues that the Old Testament presents *universal history*, beginning with creation, and concluding with the last days, the fulfilling of the covenant: 'As a composition, the Old Testament is incomparably less unified than the Homeric poems, it is more obviously pieced together – but the various components all belong to one concept of universal history and its interpretation.'[190]

A fascinating aspect of Auerbach's analysis of the Bible is that its literary nature develops a view of the world in which the sublime (divine) and the everyday are integrally woven together.[191] In Chapter 2 of *Mimesis*, Auerbach compares chapter 37 and part of 38 of Peronius's *Fortunata*, the ancient view of the instability of fortune, and part of Tacitus's *Annals*, book 1, with the narrative of Peter's denial of Jesus in Mark's Gospel. In contrast with the ancient literature, Peter 'is the image of man in the highest and deepest and most tragic sense',[192] and the scene of his denial 'fits into no antique genre'.[193] Auerbach explores why this narrative arouses in us strong sympathy:

---

188 Auerbach 1953, 2003, 14. This is not to suggest that Auerbach simply sees all OT narratives as historical. There is legendary material present, but (1953, 2003, 19) 'the material of the Old Testament comes closer and closer to history as the narrative proceeds'. C. S. Lewis held a similar view.

189 Auerbach 1953, 2003, 14–15. Lesslie Newbigin makes comparable points.

190 Auerbach 1953, 2003, 17.

191 cf. Auerbach 1953, 2003, 22–3.

192 Auerbach 1953, 2003, 41.

193 Auerbach 1953, 2003, 45.

Because it portrays something which neither the poets nor the historians of antiquity ever set out to portray: the birth of a spiritual movement in the depths of the common people, from within the everyday occurrences of contemporary life, which thus assumes an importance it could never have assumed in antique literature. What we witness is the awakening of 'a new heart and a new spirit.' All this applies not only to Peter's denial but also to every other occurrence which is related in the New Testament . . . Peter and the other characters in the New Testament are caught in a universal movement of the depths which at first remains almost entirely below the surface and only very gradually . . . emerges into the foreground of history . . . What we see here is a world which on the one hand is entirely real, average, identifiable as to place, time and circumstances, but which on the other hand is shaken in its very foundations, is transforming and renewing itself before our eyes. For the New Testament authors who are their contemporaries, these occurrences on the plane of everyday life assume the importance of world-revolutionary events, as later on they will for everyone.[194]

Auerbach's work alerts us, first, to the value of historical, *comparative study*, but of a certain sort.[195] Auerbach attends to the world represented by the text; such a focus makes his writing fresh and powerful, and pushes the issue of history to the fore. Second, Auerbach's work illustrates the need for a *literary sensibility* when it comes to the Bible. Indeed, the most creative work on the Bible as literature has largely emerged from Jewish scholars whose speciality is not primarily biblical studies but literature. Third, it is clear from Auerbach's work that the literary, the historical *and the theological* – note his emphasis on the Incarnation – are intertwined in the Bible. Kawashima notes that

the contrasts he [Auerbach] so brilliantly illuminates between Homer and the Bible, which we might take as the dual foundations of the Western literary tradition, help us to differentiate between two fundamental

---

194 Auerbach 1953, 2003, 43.

195 cf. Lewis 1971, 126, for his critique of seeing the Gospels as legends. He (1971, 126) notes that, as a literary historian, he is quite convinced that the Gospels are not legends. Apart from parts of Plato's dialogues, Lewis knows of no conversations comparable to those in John's Gospel in ancient literature. This is true even of modern literature until the emergence of the realistic novel some one hundred years ago.

narrative modes – not premised, one might add, on any direct historical relationship.[196]

Kawashima also attends to the work of Alter, Damrosch and Gresseth, the latter two of whom seek to lessen the distinction between the OT and the ANE in terms of the OT's distinctiveness. Nevertheless, even Damrosch observes that:

> In a small country, in a society younger and less prosperous than the great cultures of Egypt and Mesopotamia, literary composition reached a degree of power and beauty previously unknown in the Near East. Soon after the unification of the country, not one but two extraordinary bodies of material were created: the first historical accounts of the monarchy, and the first version of the materials that became the Pentateuch. How did the biblical writers come to produce the greatest historical writing ever seen in the ancient Near East?[197]

Damrosch speaks of 'the manifest superiority of biblical narrative over the historical prose of neighboring countries'.[198]

Kawashima concludes that 'the novelistic art of biblical narrative ... results from decline of the epic arts in ancient Israel'.[199] Biblical narrative marks the death of the rhapsode so that its novelty results from a shift from the spoken to the written word. For our purposes, what is particularly significant is not only Kawashima's documentation of the uniqueness of OT narrative but also *the way in which he finally accounts for it*. He locates the source in what Assmann has described as 'the Mosaic distinction'. Kawashima asks, 'Why did the biblical writers prefer past-oriented narrative – and, indeed, exert much effort in developing it as an art form – while virtually all their neighbors, past and present, and with strikingly few exceptions, preferred the drama of epic?'[200] Alter refers to Israel's reflex away from polytheism as a powerful influence on its literature, and Kawashima invokes Michel Foucault's concept of a change in 'episteme', an epistemic breakthrough, to account for Israel's achievement in the OT. In my view, Yehezkel Kaufmann's multivolume work *The Religion*

---

196 Kawashima 2004, 8.
197 Damrosch 1987, 1.
198 Damrosch 1987, 1.
199 Kawashima 2004, 10.
200 Kawashima 2004, 192.

*of Israel* remains vitally important as an alternative to the tradition of Well-hausen in OT studies, and it is to Kaufmann's definition of monotheism in the Hebrew Bible that Kawashima turns:

> The mark of monotheism is not the concept of a god who is creator, eternal, benign, or even all-powerful; these notions are found everywhere in the pagan world. It is, rather, the idea of a god who is the source of all being, not subject to a cosmic order, and not emergent from a pre-existent realm; a god free of the limitations of magic and mythology. The high gods of primitive tribes do not embody this idea.[201]

For Kawashima, the key element in this definition is the implied dualism of mind and matter:

> Apparently for the first time in the history of knowledge, a metaphysical distinction, however implicit, is made between mental and physical entities. For in conceiving of God as 'not subject to a cosmic order' and 'utterly distinct from, and other than, the world,' the biblical writers/thinkers abstracted or projected divinity outside of the physical universe, simultaneously constituting the realms of spirit and of matter as such.[202]

The effect of this move is that:

> By reducing the material world to a mere object henceforth submitted to his Will, Yahweh becomes (as has frequently been noted) the God of history. I would suggest that it is this gesture of thought, whose first appearance is typically attributed to the pre-Socratic philosophers in ancient Greece, that lies at the heart of what has generally been referred to as the distinctiveness of biblical religion.[203]

Kawashima refers to another earlier and important work in support of his thesis, namely *The Intellectual Adventure of Ancient Man*.[204] Israel uniquely stressed the transcendence of God, thereby enabling the world epistemically to be engaged as an 'It'. To explore the operation of this new episteme,

---

201  Kaufmann 1960, 29.

202  Kawashima 2004, 198.

203  Kawashima 2004, 198.

204  Frankfort et al., 1946. This older work is receiving a surprising amount of re-engagement.

Kawashima attends to Genesis 1—11, noting that while 1—11 function as myth insofar as they explain how the present world came to be as it is, 'they present an understanding of the world entirely at odds with "pagan" myth, which is based upon a monistic cosmos'.[205] Israel's thought, according to Kawashima, is distinctive in the ANE in being dualist. With Kaufmann, Kawashima sees P as early, and finds in the J and P accounts of the creation of humankind none of the divine–human continuity so common in the ANE. He thinks that Friedman is right to argue that the *imago Dei* amounts to nothing other than 'consciousness'.[206] The absence of theogony and battle-like cosmogony in the creation accounts is significant, and while it has some parallels in Ugarit, Ugarit knows nothing of the dualism of Israel. The aniconism – refusal to tolerate images of YHWH – of Israel's cultus further supports this view: 'Specifically, the aniconism of Israelite religion, even in its de facto stage, implies the nonmateriality of God, putting into perspective whatever anthropomorphisms of God we do find in the Bible.'[207]

Kawashima argues that there is both gain and loss in this epistemic revolution in Israel. The development marks a loss of a natural bond between humankind and nature, but the relationship becomes human rather than natural. The epistemic shift involves alienation but also possession: facts are alienated from the subjective, allowing a society to possess its past; facts are alienated from necessity, thus allowing humans to recognize their own contingency. By transcending human nature, YHWH can be seen to rule over it, thus providing a whole new significance to earthly events.

> As a result, biblical time emphasizes that which changes through time, the linear movement of history as one generally thinks of it. Correspondingly, one sees the tendency in Israel to historicize festivals, to make them commemorations of divinely appointed events in history.[208]

This new view of time is seen in the form that the relationship between Israel and YHWH takes on, namely that of a covenant, whereas, by comparison, Marduk's and Baal's reign over the citizens of Babylon and Ugarit is part of the eternal order.

---

205  Kawashima 2004, 200.
206  Kawashima 2004, 202.
207  Kawashima 2004, 206.
208  Kawashima 2004, 208.

This epistemic shift in Israel is *anthropologically and ethically weighted*. Humankind now possesses a unique sense of responsibility in relation to God's will. Apodictic law of the form 'You shall . . .' is known in the ANE but is rare in treaties, whereas it is at the heart of the Sinai covenant, which is modelled on ANE treaties. Biblical narrative furthermore signals the triumph of *écriture* (writing). 'In fact, as a symptom of this new technology, the world of biblical narrative exhibits a thoroughgoing and . . . mundane familiarity with writing without parallel, moreover, in Homeric, Ugaritic, and Mesopotamian narrative traditions.'[209] In line with von Rad, Kawashima relates this triumph to the loss of the comfort of ritual and myth, and their associated institutions. 'In ancient Israel *écriture*, the death of the rhapsode, announces the birth of the scribe, the advent of Scripture.'[210]

Kawashima sums up his argument as follows: 'We have already seen how biblical narrative communicates a new knowledge appropriate to the episteme of ancient Israel: knowledge of a transcendent God, of history, of the human subject.'[211] We noted above the distinction between attending to religion in / as part of the text and a religious orientation towards the text. If Kawashima embodies the former, we find both in the work of the Jewish scholar Will Herberg.

Herberg argues that '[t]he uniqueness – the "scandal" – of biblical faith is revealed in its radically historical character'.[212] He insists that we cannot eliminate the historicity of the Bible without destroying faith itself. Herberg identifies three major ways in which humans have sought to understand history. First, there is what I call the pagan approach, which equates reality – including human beings – with nature, a type of immanence philosophy. Second, there is the Greek approach, which focuses not on nature but on the timelessly eternal beyond nature. Third, there is the biblical view, which breaks with both of the first two – both nature and time are real but contingent, dependent on God. This, for Herberg, allows history to come into proper focus for the first time: 'it is in and through history that God calls to man; it is in and through history, human action in history, that man responds; and it is in and through history that God judges.'[213] The Bible presents us with a great drama of existence in a threefold pattern: our present woes result from falling away from the original good creation, and the fallen creation is destined

209  Kawashima 2004, 211.
210  Kawashima 2004, 214.
211  Kawashima 2004, 214.
212  Herberg 1976, 32.
213  Herberg 1976, 35.

for restoration in the kingdom of God. All human history is contained within this drama. Its range is universal, but its centre is particular: Exodus–Sinai for Judaism and the Christ event for Christians. Herberg discerns a double inwardness to the biblical view of history. First, it interprets events through the lens of faith, 'acts and events that, from another standpoint, might well be interpreted in an altogether different way'.[214] Second, it is inward in that the biblical view can only become redemptive for me, personally, if I indwell it as my history.

Herberg's work indicates that the Bible developed a unique view of history which allowed history for the first time to come properly into focus. In this respect it is comparable to Kawashima's work. It differs, however, in its insistence that the perspective of the OT needs to be inwardly appropriated. Where both Kawashima's and Herberg's work is extremely helpful is in foregrounding the theological dimension of the OT and demonstrating its explanatory power.

## A threefold cord

We have ranged far and wide from our base in Wazana's work as we have identified the significance of the historical, the literary and the theological as crucial dimensions in a threefold cord of OT interpretation. Indeed, Wazana is insightful and in line with the best recent work on hermeneutics in attending to these three aspects of the descriptions of borders in the OT, namely:

- the literary;
- the historical and factual;
- the ideological (religious and political)[215] or kerygmatic.

Identification of these three central dimensions constituting the text of the OT marks a major way forward for OT studies.[216] However, as is apparent in Wazana's work, it is as we tease out the interrelationship between them that vital differences emerge. Thus, Wazana identifies as *the starting point* for her examination of the border descriptions in the OT the idea that

despite their geographical nature, the numerous locations that they mention, and the lines delineated in them, the biblical texts do not constitute

---

214  Herberg 1976, 40.

215  Wazana 2013, 5.

216  Meir Sternberg, N. T. Wright, Anthony Thiselton and others have identified a similar triad as central to biblical interpretation.

genuinely geographical documents. They are more appropriately to be understood and examined as literary texts that were composed in the service of an ideological agenda.[217]

First of all, it is startling that this should be her starting point; one would think it might rather be her conclusion! Second, this illustrates well how crucial it is that we examine in detail, as we will below, what we understand by the literary, the historical and the theological and how we should conceive of their interrelationship. Certainly in English, 'ideological' tends to have negative connotations, and intriguingly the question of God never really surfaces in Wazana's otherwise rich analysis. However, as I have argued in my *God Who Acts in History*, bracketing out questions of theological truth only allows alternative world views to govern OT interpretation, generally unconsciously.

Likewise, Halpern's assertion that a confessional history of the OT must be uncritical is quintessentially modern and ironically betrays a lack of a sense of history. Are we to regard all the Christian and Jewish scholarship preceding the Enlightenment as by definition 'uncritical'? Or is Halpern working with a quintessentially modern view of what is allowed to count as 'critical'? And it is hard to be sure which worshippers Halpern has in mind or what body of evidence he is referring to when he asserts that believers do not read the Bible with an intrinsic interest in human events. As we have seen above, it can – and will – be argued that the OT produced the major breakthrough in philosophy of history which allowed history to become a focus of interest in its own right. Certainly, one can find examples of believers who do not manifest such an interest, but, in my view, it is precisely the religious vision of the Bible that pushes the OT *and* believers to take a deep, genuine interest in history. YHWH cannot be so easily displaced from the task of interpreting the OT, try as scholars might. The main reason the Bible is studied so intensively is precisely because of the religious communities it reflects and has given birth to, so that scholars like Halpern are in danger of sawing off the branch on which they sit.

If we think back to our discussion of the border texts above, in Genesis 15.18, for example, YHWH is portrayed as *speaking*. Much biblical scholarship either works with the assumption that there is no God or, as is recently the case, argues that God exists but he cannot speak.[218] Doubtless, there are many dimensions in any assessment of the historicity of Genesis 15, but one

---

217 Wazana 2013, 4.
218 Sommer 2015. Cf. Bartholomew 2020.

is hard-pressed to see how the question of whether or not God speaks does not bear on the historicity of such a text in a major way. Our view of God and of divine action will have a strong impact on how we engage with such a text, especially in terms of its (possible) historicity.

# 6 What then shall we do with the Old Testament? The case for a new paradigm

## (a) Polarization in Old Testament studies

Wright notes that NT studies is a *battleground* and that it will continue to be one.[219] If this is true of NT studies, it is even more the case in OT studies. For a long time now, OT studies has been polarized between what we might call liberal and conservative approaches. This has been significantly less the case in NT studies. Why? A major reason is that as biblical criticism was taking hold in the UK in the second half of the nineteenth century and following on from F. C. Baur's comprehensive work in Germany, a moderate, believing criticism emerged through the exceptional labours of three Cambridge friends: J. B. Lightfoot (1828–89), Brooke Foss Wescott (1825–1901) and Fenton J. A. Hort (1828–92).[220]

> For forty years, from 1860 to 1900, Lightfoot, Westcott, and Hort were names profoundly venerated throughout the whole world of scholarship, and especially in the English-speaking world. Hardly ever in the history of the Church have three men of such distinction worked together over so long a period on the accomplishment of what was essentially one great purpose.[221]

Lightfoot was above all else the historian, Westcott the NT exegete and Hort the philosopher.

F. C. Baur died in 1860, and his work on the NT plus the publication in England of *Essays and Reviews* ensured that the critical problems were brought to the attention of thinking Christians in the UK. Lightfoot, Westcott and Hort toyed with the idea of replying to *Essays and Reviews* but decided an entirely different approach was needed.

---

219  Wright 1992, 1.
220  I am indebted to Brevard Childs for this insight. Cf. Neill and Wright 1988, 35–64.
221  Neill and Wright 1988, 35.

The only way adequately to deal with this situation was to carry out an equally comprehensive survey [to that of Baur], on basically the same critical principles, but far more soberly, far more realistically, with far greater attention to accuracy, and with far fewer presuppositions than those which Baur had brought with him into the field.[222]

These three friends embarked on an extraordinarily ambitious plan: to produce a critical Greek NT, to do philological, historical, exegetical and doctrinal work, and thereby to present the entire vista of Christian truth against its historical background. Not surprisingly, the plan was never fully achieved, but what they did produce was remarkable.

In the history of biblical criticism this creative, rigorous and moderate tradition was established fairly early and provided a base for a tradition of comparable work in the UK and USA by NT scholars such as C. E. B. Cranfield, Ralph Martin, C. F. D. Moule, George Caird and F. F. Bruce, and on into the work of contemporary scholars, including James Dunn, Richard Bauckham, David Wenham and N. T. Wright. In OT studies, by contrast, it was really only in the second half of the twentieth century that a comparable moderately critical approach started to develop among Evangelical thinkers, led by scholars such as R. K. Harrison (1920–93), Derek Kidner, Gordon Wenham and Gordon McConville, by which time a liberal, critical approach to the OT was entrenched, developed and dominant. In recent years, even as we have witnessed an extraordinary revival of religion worldwide and especially in Africa and Asia, a hardened secularism has appeared in the West and become manifest in OT studies, enhancing the already existing polarization.

## (b) Mirror images? The standard account of modernity and Old Testament studies

By early in the twentieth century, historical criticism had come to dominate OT studies in the UK, Europe and North America. Inevitably, a reaction set in among Evangelical scholars, and understandably they focused on historical issues, feeling that this was where the battle was most intense. Sanders argues that HB/OT studies emerges out of modernity, and a danger of the Evangelical reaction to historical criticism is that *both* historical criticism *and* the 'Evangelical' reaction are expressions of the Enlightenment tradition, both accepting as basic what Toulmin refers to as the *standard account of*

---

222  Neill and Wright 1988, 37.

*modernity.*[223] It is thus imperative that we spend some time familiarizing our-selves with modernity.

Toulmin asserts that in the twentieth century a narrative of modernity came to be accepted, according to which the modern age had originated in the seventeenth century with the transition from the medieval era to mod-ernity achieved through applying rational methods to all areas of study: in science Galileo, in epistemology Descartes and in political theory Hobbes. The retrieval of autonomous rationality plus the rejection of superstition con-stitutes modernity, and this is a good thing. Toulmin calls this the standard account of modernity.

Toulmin argues that since the 1950s this account has been strongly chal-lenged,[224] and he proposes a dual origin for modernity: first in Renaissance humanism and later in the seventeenth-century Enlightenment. Renaissance humanism emerged in a predominantly Christian European context, sought to balance practical and theoretical concerns, and was aware of its limitations epistemologically. However, in the 1600s

> [t]here is a shift from a style of philosophy that keeps equally in view issues of local, timebound practice, and universal, timeless theory, to one that accepts matters of universal, timeless theory as being entitled to an exclusive place on the agenda of 'philosophy'.[225]

Toulmin discerns this shift in the move from Montaigne to Descartes. Descartes's philosophy is often presented acontextually, but it was in fact forged amid deep sociopolitical uncertainties. 'Descartes was convinced that we can build a secure body of human knowledge, if we scrap our inherited systems of concepts and start again from scratch – with a clean slate – using "rationally validated" methods.'[226] This view seeped through all disciplines. Toulmin shows how a world view developed out of this Cartesian soil which dominated the West for some 200 years:

> After 1660, there developed an overall framework of ideas about human-ity and nature, rational mind and causal matter, that gained the standing of 'common sense': for the next 100, 150 or 200 years, the main timbers of

---

223 Toulmin 1990.
224 Toulmin 1990, 17–21.
225 Toulmin 1990, 24.
226 Toulmin 1990, 81.

this framework of ideas and beliefs were rarely called in question. They were spoken of as 'allowed by men' or 'standing to reason', and they were seen as needing no further justification than that . . . Between them, they defined a system of ideas that we may refer to as the Modern world view, or the 'framework of modernity'.[227]

At the heart of this Cartesian world view is the dichotomy between humanity and nature. The main elements of the world view thus divide into two groups, reflecting this dichotomy.[228] On the nature side are the following principles:

- Nature is ruled by fixed laws established at creation.
- The structure of nature was determined a few thousand years ago.
- The material substance of nature is essentially inert.
- Physical objects and processes are unable to reason or think.
- At creation, God formed natural objects into stable systems.
- Lower and higher things are linked, with the result that motion in nature, and action in society, flow from 'higher' to 'lower' creatures.

On the humanity side are the following:

- The essence of humanity is the ability to think and act rationally.
- There can be no science of psychology.
- Human beings also have the power to establish social systems.
- Humans are mixed beings – partially rational, partially causal.
- Reason is mental; emotion is bodily.
- The emotions distort and frustrate reason.

Toulmin sees 1750–1914 as the time of dismantling this scaffolding of the modern world view.[229] 'By 1914, then, all the material was ready to hand to justify dismantling the last timbers of the intellectual scaffolding that had, since the late 17th century, established the parameters of acceptable thought.'[230] However, any renewal of the Renaissance tradition was deferred in 1920–60;

---

227  Toulmin 1990, 107–8.
228  Toulmin 1990, 109–17.
229  Toulmin 1990, 145.
230  Toulmin 1990, 150.

indeed, during this time things went into reverse, epitomized by logical positivism and the architectural theory of Mies.

> The ideas of strict 'rationality' modelled on formal logic, and of a universal 'method' for developing new ideas in any field of natural science, were adopted in the 1920s and 1930s with *even greater* enthusiasm, and in an *even more extreme* form, than had been the case in the mid-17th century.[231]

The Second World War symbolized, for Toulmin, the culmination of modernity.[232] It was the last time that the great ideals and goals of modernity could be put into practice unselfconsciously.

In Toulmin's view, the 1960s counterculture represents the delayed reaction to modernity. Within 20 years, postmodernism broke upon the West. Toulmin clearly regards modernity as in a crisis:

> If an historical era is ending, it is the era of Modernity itself . . . What looked in the 19th century like an irresistible river has disappeared in the sand, and we seem to have run aground . . . we are now stranded and uncertain of our location. The very project of Modernity thus seems to have lost momentum, and we need to fashion a successor program.[233]

In his view, it is too simplistic to label modernity as a success or failure. We need to humanize modernity.

The importance of this analysis by Toulmin lies in his argument that the received or standard account given of modernity is but one among several accounts, and it is not neutral; it has its particular prejudices. Toulmin maintains that '[b]oth the received view of Modernity, and the standard narrative of its origins, were thus rationalist constructions'.[234] Especially in the light of the plurality of accounts of modernity, the rationalist prejudices of the standard account can no longer be assumed; if they are to be presupposed, then a case has to be made for adopting them rather than alternatives. As we investigate

---

231  Toulmin 1990, 159. Emphasis original.

232  See Bauman 1989 for a penetrating study of the connection between the Holocaust and modernity. 'The truth is that every "ingredient" of the Holocaust . . . was normal . . . in the sense of being fully in keeping with everything we know about our civilization, its guiding spirit, its priorities, its immanent vision of the world' (1989, 8).

233  Toulmin 1990, 3.

234  Toulmin 1990, 81.

the emergence of historical criticism/s in modernity, we must recontextualize it and interrogate its prejudices.

In his *At the Origins of Modern Atheism*,[235] Michael Buckley argues that a mistake made by Christian thinkers was to imagine that one could concede the epistemic ground to Enlightenment thinkers as neutral and objective, and hope that one could nevertheless arrive at the right, orthodox conclusions. Indeed, this has been one of James Barr's criticisms of 'fundamentalism', namely that it claims to operate on the same epistemic foundations of OT studies but already knows the conclusions that it is going to come to.[236]

What needs to be added to Toulmin's and Buckley's analyses is Lilla's point that we now live – alluding to Nietzsche – amid the postponement of the twilight of the idols. Lilla notes of modernity that:

> By attacking Christian political theology and denying its legitimacy, the new philosophy simultaneously challenged the basic principles on which authority had been justified in most societies in history. That was the decisive break. The ambition of the new philosophy was to develop habits of thinking and talking about politics exclusively in human terms, without appeal to divine revelation or cosmological speculation. The hope was to wean Western societies from all political theology and cross to the other shore. What began as a thought-experiment became an experiment in living that we inherited. Now the long tradition of Christian political theology is forgotten, and with it memory of the age-old quest to bring the whole of human life under God's authority.[237]

Now, however, we are in the unexpected situation in which '[t]he twilight of the idols has been postponed'.[238] During the twentieth and twenty-first centuries, religion has returned in a major way, and the West is badly unprepared to cope with this. Lilla says of *The Stillborn God* that:

> The story reconstructed here should remind us that the actual choice contemporary societies face is not between past and present, or between the West and 'the rest.' It is between two grand traditions of thought, two ways of envisaging the human condition. We must be clear about those

---

235 Buckley 1990.
236 Barr 1981.
237 Lilla 2007, 2008, 5.
238 Lilla 2007, 2008, 3.

alternatives, choose between them, and live with the consequences of our choice. That *is* the human condition.[239]

Lilla notes that for most moderns:

> To think that the West could produce its own political theology, in a thoroughly modern vein, is surprising and unsettling. More unsettling still is the fact that these new political theologians produced original and challenging works not to be dismissed lightly.[240]

The crisis of the Enlightenment tradition is widely acknowledged. One response is to find ways, in Habermas's language, to get modernity back on track. Lilla's analysis, however, alerts us to another possibility, namely, to retrieve the Judeo-Christian tradition. It is, of course, this latter option that I am most interested in for OT studies, albeit in post-critical mode, taking account of all the vital insights of historical criticism.

That much historical criticism and its critics often operated on the same principles is evident in the words 'on basically the same critical principles' above in relation to Lightfoot, Westcott and Hort. Similarly, I am told that when asked what theology contributes to exegesis, F. F. Bruce answered 'Nothing!' Comparably, Kenneth Kitchen is clear in the Preface to his *On the Reliability of the Old Testament* that:

> Absolute truth in any deep philosophical sense is not the concern of this book, and thus will not be discussed. But individual absolute truths in the shape of objective fact, 'hard facts' that exist independently of what any human being may choose or wish to think – these abound around us in their hundreds of thousands in everyday life, and (quite simply) cannot be gainsaid or wished away . . . The facts are wholly independent of me, my prejudices, or my knowledge, and of everyone else's.[241]

To be clear, I have the greatest respect for Lightfoot, Westcott and Hort, and for F. F. Bruce and Kitchen. I am deeply indebted to all their work. Methodologically, however, the realist and empiricist epistemologies they embody have been seriously critiqued in the twentieth and twenty-first centuries. The

---

239 Lilla 2007, 2008, 13. Emphasis original.
240 Lilla 2007, 2008, 11.
241 Kitchen 2003, xiv.

danger is that historical criticism in its various forms *and* its critics in their various forms embody different aspects of a common Enlightenment tradition – the standard account – for better and for worse, but nevertheless a tradition that has been seriously critiqued in the latter part of the twentieth century. Intriguingly, it is in the history and philosophy of science that the problems with this sort of approach have become clear, and this shift is now manifesting itself in the re-evaluation of science in the ANE.[242]

In his *What Is This Thing Called Science?* Chalmers devotes the first four chapters to arguing that

> the idea that the distinctive feature of scientific knowledge is that it is derived from the facts of experience can only be sanctioned in a carefully and highly qualified form, if it is to be sanctioned at all. We will encounter reasons for doubting that facts acquired by observation and experiment are as straightforward and secure as has traditionally been assumed. We will also find that a strong case can be made for the claim that scientific knowledge can neither be conclusively proved nor conclusively disproved by reference to the facts, even if the availability of those facts is assumed.[243]

Chalmers points out that 'seeing' is more complex than we think, an approach to knowledge that is already, in my view, scrutinized and evaluated in Ecclesiastes.[244] To illustrate this, Chalmers uses a simple picture of stairs. At first blush it appears perfectly clear what one is seeing, until the realization dawns that one could be looking at the stairs from above or from underneath. The 'seeing' of analysis is more complex than it appears; what an observer sees is not just related to reflections on the retina of the eyes but also shaped by the experience, knowledge and expectations of the observer.[245] As a (critical) realist, Chalmers accepts that a single unique physical world exists apart from observers, but this does not mean that all the perceptions of observers are identical. Our perceptions are affected by the dispositions and background of observers so that what an individual discerns to be an observable fact may not be so for another.

---

242 cf. Rochberg 2016; Van De Mieroop 2016.

243 Chalmers 1999, xxi.

244 Bartholomew 2009.

245 Chalmers 1999, 7.

Furthermore, Chalmers argues that observable facts are to some degree fallible and subject to revision. Ironically, scientific facts can be both objective and fallible.[246] What is needed in science are *relevant* facts, but what is relevant is determined by the current state of that science. The world in which relevant facts are sought is complex and multidimensional so that the observer often needs to intervene in experiments to secure such facts. It is commonly thought that theories arise from facts in a sort of inductive move, but once again the relationship between facts and theory is complex. As Chalmers observes: 'Judgments about what is a significant question and about whether some specific set of experiments is an adequate way of answering it will depend heavily on how the practical and theoretical situation is understood.'[247] In fact, the acceptability of experimental results is theory-dependent.

Someone with a strong view of science who sees it as dealing in facts would argue that theories are derived from the facts. However, '[g]eneral scientific laws invariably go beyond the finite amount of observable evidence that is available to support them'.[248] The view that theories are arrived at *inductively* from the facts is belied by two issues:

- it is very difficult to explain just what is an adequate inductive argument;
- there is an unavoidable circularity in justifying induction.

Thus, according to Chalmers:

We have seen that facts adequate for science are by no means straightforwardly given but have to be practically constructed, are in some important senses dependent on the knowledge that they presuppose . . . and are subject to improvement and replacement.[249]

Intriguingly, perhaps astonishingly for many of us, Chalmers makes this comment early on:

One reaction to the realization that scientific theories cannot be conclusively proved or disproved and that the reconstructions of philosophers bear little resemblance to what actually goes on in a science is to give up

---

246  Chalmers 1999, 25.
247  Chalmers 1999, 34.
248  Chalmers 1999, 45.
249  Chalmers 1999, 58.

altogether the idea that science is a rational activity operating according to some special method.[250]

He refers in this respect to Feyerabend's (1975) *Against Method: Outline of an anarchistic theory of knowledge.*[251] On the strongest reading of Feyerabend's text there is nothing special about science that makes it superior to ancient myths or voodoo! Chalmers resists this account. In his Chapter 15 on anti-realism and realism he seeks to find an approach that captures the best of both. He proposes what he calls *unrepresentative realism*,[252] which is similar to John Worrall's (1989) *structural realism.* From this perspective, science is realist insofar as it attempts to articulate the structure of reality and has made steady progress in this respect, but its representations are often replaced. In *What Is This Thing Called Science?* Chalmers also attends to Popper and falsification, the Bayesian approach and the new experimentalism, and has two chapters on Thomas Kuhn. For our purposes, Thomas Kuhn's influential work on paradigms is particularly relevant. Chalmers concludes:

> The production of scientific knowledge always takes place in a social context in which that aim is interrelated with other practices with different aims, such as those involving the personal or professional aims of scientists, the economic aims of funding agencies, the ideological interests of religious or political groups of various kinds and so on.[253]

## (c) Changing paradigms?

Thomas Kuhn's *The Structure of Scientific Revolutions* was hugely influential and is of significant relevance to our work.[254] Kuhn was a physicist who came to devote his research to the history of science. What he discovered there shattered his preconceptions about how science developed. He begins his *Structure* as follows: 'History, if viewed as a repository for more than anecdote or chronology, could produce a decisive transformation in the image of science by which we are now possessed.'[255] Historically, science appears to operate within

---

250  Chalmers 1999, xxi.

251  Chalmers 1999, 149–60.

252  Chalmers 1999, 244.

253  Chalmers 1999, 249. On the social sciences and science see Chalmers 1990.

254  First published in 1962. I am using the 2012 50th-anniversary edition.

255  Kuhn 2012, 1.

theoretical structures, and observation appears to be theory-dependent so that concepts receive their meaning at least *in part* from their function within a theory. These insights are central to Kuhn's approach.

Kuhn attended to how science 'progresses' and argued that it does so through revolutions, which involve the abandonment of one structure or paradigm for another, *incompatible* one. Chalmers sets out Kuhn's view of how science progresses as follows:

pre-science – normal science – crisis – revolution – new normal science – new crisis

Pre-science becomes structured, and thus a science, when a scientific community embraces a paradigm. Kuhn's use of the word 'paradigm' has generated controversy,[256] but it is the nature of a particular paradigm to defy precise definition. 'A paradigm is made up of the general theoretical assumptions and laws and the techniques for their application that the members of a particular scientific community adopt.'[257] A paradigm in science includes elements such as fundamental laws, theoretical assumptions, standard ways of applying the laws, and general methodological prescriptions. Once a paradigm takes hold, *normal science* ensues.

'Normal scientists must be uncritical of the paradigm in which they work.'[258] Only thus can they channel their energies in developing the paradigm and execute the hard work to probe it in detail. 'It is the lack of disagreement over fundamentals that distinguishes mature, normal science from the relatively disorganised activity of immature *pre-science*.'[259] Because of how they are trained, normal scientists generally will be unable to explain in any detail the paradigm within which they work. Anomalies exist within all paradigms, resisting solution through the resources of the regnant paradigm. It is only when anomalies persist and begin to challenge the foundations of the paradigm that a *crisis* looms. Some scientists start to express concerns with and doubts about the regnant paradigm. The crisis becomes really serious when a rival paradigm emerges.

---

256 Masterman (1970) identified 21 ways in which Kuhn used the word 'paradigm'.
257 Chalmers 1999, 108.
258 Chalmers 1999, 110.
259 Chalmers 1999, 110. Emphasis original.

'The new paradigm will be very different from and incompatible with the old one.'[260] It will see the world as constituted of different things, regard different questions as right and/or meaningful and embrace different standards and metaphysical principles. A switch in paradigms is likened by Kuhn to a gestalt switch or a religious conversion. Intriguingly, '[t]here will be no purely logical argument that demonstrates the superiority of one paradigm over another and that thereby compels a rational scientist to make the change'.[261] One cannot appeal to generally accepted rational criteria to argue for one paradigm over another, since these are contained within a paradigm. A new paradigm is incommensurable with the old one.

> This is the idea that, in the course of a revolution and paradigm shift, the new ideas and assertions cannot be strictly compared to the old ones. Even if the same words are in use, their very meaning has changed. That in turn led to the idea that a new theory was not chosen to replace an old one because it was true but more because of a *change in world view*.[262]

Chalmers identifies a major problem with Kuhn's approach: the difficult question of which standards can be used to judge that one paradigm is better than another.

How might this help us with what to do with the OT today? In several ways.

(i) By the early twentieth century, the historical-critical *paradigm* had become entrenched in OT studies, dominating mainstream OT study in the UK, Europe, North America and beyond.

(ii) As such, normal OT 'science' assumed this paradigm and got on with developing it and solving the remaining puzzles within OT studies, using the resources of this paradigm. Naturally, from Kuhn's perspective, practitioners were inducted into its methodologies without particular attention to the paradigm. This is, for example, what I and my fellow students experienced at Oxford University. We were inducted into source, form, redaction and tradition criticism and were expected to be able to apply it to the OT without ever

---

260 Chalmers 1999, 114.

261 Chalmers 1999, 115.

262 Hacking, 2012, xi. Emphasis original.

learning where this method had come from. In other words, it was assumed we were doing normal OT science within the regnant paradigm.

(iii) Especially in Germany, but also in other centres, historical criticism was exceptionally rigorous in scrutinizing the data of the OT, but *within* the regnant paradigm. Looking back, it is astonishing to witness the extent to which this paradigm has been pursued within OT studies.

(iv) Emerging as it did within and as an embodiment of modernity, historical criticism assumed what Toulmin refers to as the standard narrative of modernity, whereby the paradigmatic aspect of historical criticism was obscured so that what historical criticism was doing was just neutral, objective, OT science. Thus, to use Kuhn's vocabulary, not only was the practice of normal science detracting from scrutiny of the paradigm within which most scholars were working, but also this tendency was reinforced by an emphasis on objective neutrality, thereby obscuring the existence of the paradigm.

(v) Kuhn's attention to the history of science alerts us to the vital importance of the *history of OT interpretation* if we wish to foreground the paradigm within which historical criticism/s operates. It was attention to the history of science that shattered Kuhn's preconceptions about how science progresses, and in my view, as I have argued elsewhere,[263] deep attention to the history of OT studies has the potential to shake up the discipline to its very foundations.[264] OT studies has not been nearly as well served as NT studies in terms of its history, and this needs to change. Kuhn may be right that within normal science practitioners need to get on with their science and assume the paradigm. However . . .

(vi) The paradigm of historical criticism has been challenged repeatedly in OT studies in recent decades. The literary turn from the 1970s onwards raised acute questions about many of the assured results of historical criticism, but before it could be fully appropriated, postmodernism was upon us, threatening with its wild pluralism to cast OT studies back into what Kuhn calls a pre-science.

Postmodernism introduced a veritable smorgasbord of new ways of reading the OT: deconstructionist, new historicist, queer, postcolonial and so on,

---

263 Bartholomew 2015.
264 cf. Bartholomew 2020 etc.

so that it has been the fashion to celebrate ever new readings of OT texts from a whole range of ideological positions. Where this wild pluralism has been attached to a view of texts as inherently unstable (Derrida), or to the 'strong reader response' approach found, for example, in *Is There a Text in This Class? The authority of interpretive communities* (Fish),[265] we soon end up with the view that there are as many legitimate readings of a text as there are readers, so that such readings become impossible to evaluate.

In many ways, postmodernism savaged historical criticism, but they also have important elements in common. Mary Hesse, the Cambridge philosopher of science, noted perceptively of postmodernism that its background in Western liberalism is so strong that it goes unnoticed.[266] In a dialogue held in Capri on the theme of 'Religion', involving Derrida, Vattimo, Gadamer and others,[267] Gadamer notably argued that we cannot, of course, go behind Kant and return to the doctrines of the Church. As I show in *God Who Acts in History*, Kant is a major influence on the emergence of historical criticism, and we do indeed need to go behind and beyond Kant. Gadamer's comment reveals the extent to which both historical criticism and postmodernism are deeply wedded to some version of the modern or post-Enlightenment world view with human autonomy at its heart. Where postmodern readings have been as, if not more, debilitating when it comes to what to do with the OT is in constantly directing attention and energy away from what the OT *says* – its communicative trajectory – towards ransacking it as a resource for ideological interpretations.

More than a decade ago, David Clines, who has probably done more in terms of postmodern readings of the OT than any other UK scholar, came to give a lecture in Cheltenham on this topic. He compared OT interpretation to a supermarket and encouraged us to choose the cans of interpretation that we enjoy and that will sell. In the lecture, he did a highly creative reading of the nursery rhyme 'Little Bo Peep' from a range of postmodern perspectives. The creativity was impressive, but what was glaringly absent was a reading which helped us to hear 'Little Bo Peep' as the exquisite nursery rhyme that it is.

Ironically, therefore, postmodernism has served to entrench historical criticism as the default mode or overarching paradigm for OT studies, especially since it failed to produce constructive work in terms of a new paradigm.

---

265  Fish 1980.

266  Hesse 1994.

267  Derrida and Vattimo, eds, 1998.

(vii) We are now in a situation where some are seeking to shore up historical criticism whereas others are adrift amid the remnants of postmodernism, while yet others attempt to do more conservative work in the current situation. Many of us would argue that the historical-critical paradigm has reached a crisis, but before a revolution can take place we need an alternative paradigm to gain traction. To refer back to Buckley, clearly this will not happen as long as those seeking an alternative paradigm concede the epistemic grounds to historical critics. For example, as long as both sides think they are simply fighting about the facts, we are unlikely to witness the emergence of a new paradigm.

(viii) In my opinion, in relation to OT studies, Kuhn may overstate the case when he argues for the incommensurability of two paradigms. In Part 2 we will come to MacIntyre's view of traditions as the matrix out of which scholars do their work, and his analysis is helpful in seeing how different traditions in OT scholarship can coexist and dialogue with one another. Nevertheless, different traditions or paradigms are incommensurate, and Kuhn argues that a new paradigm will see the world as constituted of different things, regard different questions as right and/or meaningful, and embrace different standards and metaphysical principles. However much this is overstated, it is related to what in my view is a crucial insight of recent science, namely the underdetermination of theory by facts. To put this in plain language, historical critics have probably been more rigorous than any preceding generation in attending to the data of the OT but within a very particular paradigm, and the very data they identify are capable of fitting within more than one paradigm. We would all agree with Philip Rieff, the American Jewish sociologist, when he says that with good theory the facts rise up to meet the theory,[268] but we cannot even try to compare the way the OT fits within different paradigms as long as only one major paradigm dominates the field.

(ix) Kuhn claims that there can only be one paradigm in a science at any one time, but I am not sure he is right about this. Postmodernism has foregrounded the pluralism in the academy, and it seems to me inherently possible that different paradigms can operate simultaneously, especially in a subject such as OT studies. In my view, we need to face up to the plurality of perspectives in OT studies, identify the contours of the different paradigms at work and allow different paradigms to come to fruition so that we can compare them from the ground up.

---

268  Rieff 1973, 5.

# (d) Contours of a new paradigm?

What are we to do with the OT today? Of course, we need to do many things, but even as the old paradigm/s is in crisis, at the outset we need to orient ourselves towards our destination amid the forest of activity in contemporary OT studies. Perhaps the Romans can help us here! Four years after invading Britain in AD 47, the Romans had constructed 1,000 miles (1,600 km) of roads, largely replacing the old tracks the Britons used. Large parts of these roads ran straight, and it is this that the Romans are remembered for. How did they achieve this? Their engineers used an instrument called a *groma*. A pair of boards were fastened together to form a cross shape, and then lines with weights were hung from each corner so that they could achieve a straight line by correlating the weights with a pole some 330 feet (100 m) away. In a forest this was, of course, more challenging, and so the Romans built fires in a straight line and the smoke functioned as markers for the *groma*.

As we seek to plough a straight line towards a re-engagement with the OT, what might a fire look like that can hold our attention as we traverse the many dimensions of the forest of OT study today? Tom Wright points out that many things can be done with a volume of Shakespeare's plays: such a large volume might function as a good doorstop; one could cut out words at random and assemble them in poems; one could do a smorgasbord of analyses of the contents much as is done in postmodern OT study today. However, it is not hard to see that making use of the plays for dramatic productions is by far the most appropriate use of the volume. 'There is a general appropriateness about using Shakespeare as a basis for staging plays which justifies itself without much more argument.'[269]

What, we might ask, would such an equivalent for the OT look like today? Our answer relates back to the communicative hermeneutic set out above and to Sanders' insightful analysis of the unique communicative dimension of the OT in its ANE context. In essence, our answer is the same as Wright's for the NT: the OT

> must be read so as to be understood, read within appropriate contexts, within an acoustic which will allow its full overtones to be heard. It must be read with as little distortion as possible, and with as much sensitivity as possible to its different levels of meaning. It must be read so that the stories, and the Story, which it tells can be heard as stories, not as rambling ways of declaring unstoried 'ideas'. It must be read without the

---

269  Wright 1992, 6.

assumption that we already know what it is going to say, and without the arrogance that 'we' – whichever group that might be – already have ancestral rights over this or that passage, book, or writer. And, for full appropriateness, it must be read in such a way as to set in motion the drama which it suggests.[270]

Nowadays, a great deal is done with the OT. Within mainstream biblical studies a veritable industry has arisen of doing diverse things with the OT. Historical critics have majored in detecting the cracks in the tablets, as it were, of the OT, with an enormous amount of detailed work devoted to source, form, redaction and tradition criticism since the late eighteenth century, originating in particular from Germany. It is still common to find monographs appearing that claim to discern multiple redactional layers in OT books or parts thereof. Zechariah and Amos are good examples in this respect. The gift of such work has been its microscopic attention to detail; its curse the constant picking apart of the OT so that we are never in a position to attend to what the OT and its parts are communicating. Postmoderns have luxuriated in doing a thousand things with OT texts, almost all involved with reading them against the grain in the service of a contemporary ideology. Conservatives have tended to allow the regnant paradigm to set the agenda for their work so that even amid the plethora of commentaries appearing, many overtly theological in name, the message that the OT communicates is rarely attended to, especially in its public dimensions, whereas what we are aiming at is an approach which leverages all the most rigorous work in the service of listening for the address of the OT. Meyer observes:

As Freudian suspicion generated psychoanalysis and Marxian suspicion the critique of ideology, so the suspicions of Reimarus generated the quest for the historical Jesus and those of Strauss and Baur, the inquiries into the nature of the gospel literature and into the drama of early Christian development. Still, all these adepts of suspicion – Freud and Marx, Reimarus, Strauss and Baur – were reductionists whose work had to be selectively salvaged by correction from outside their own suspicions. By contrast, the greatness of the great biblical interpreters of the past generation – to mention two, Gerhard von Rad and Joachim Jeremias – lay

---

270 Wright 1992, 6.

in the acuteness that informed their capacity to listen and to hear. It was greatness *ex auditu*.[271]

A related issue to the bifurcation between conservative and liberal approaches to the OT is that between academic and ecclesial reading of the OT. A great deal could be said about this, but suffice it to note that a recovery of a communicative hermeneutic with our threefold cord at its heart for the OT in the academy – and in the Church – would go a long way towards healing this unhealthy divide.

An issue which we will need to attend to in detail is what the 'appropriate contexts' are for understanding the OT. One would hope that the NT cannot be read without sustained attention to the OT, and that is certainly true of N. T. Wright's incredibly fertile work. But what of the OT? Can it be read with appropriate contexts apart from the NT? In my view, we need to read the OT from right to left and from left to right, as it were! Childs, and many others, are correct in my view, that we need to take the *discrete witness* of the OT seriously, seeking to listen to it as Ancient Israel would have heard it. At the same time, we are seeking to understand the Old Testament, which overlaps with but cannot and should not be equated with the Hebrew Bible.[272] To speak of the *Old* Testament is to speak of the *New* Testament and their relationship as part of Christian Scripture. We discredit the Old Testament – and the New – if we insist on only reading from left to right, as it were, only reading the OT through the lens of the NT. The NT cannot be understood without the OT, but at the same time the Christ event is an explosion of good news which casts its light in all directions, so that we would be foolish to think that our reading of the OT cannot and should not benefit from this illumination.

When I was a student in Oxford, I recall a panel discussion at Christ Church in which Oliver O'Donovan argued that we should read the OT as did the apostles. Maurice Wiles and others strongly opposed this. However, it is hard not to feel that we find adequate precedent for this in Acts 2.42 where the early believers devoted themselves to the apostles' teaching. *Paul's conversion*, not least as described in Galatians, is a rich node in this respect. As a devout and highly intelligent Jew, Paul was very familiar with the OT. However, in Galatians, for example, Paul alerts us to his 'conversion' – 'God . . . was pleased to reveal his Son to me' (Gal. 1.15–16) – and his subsequent time in Arabia and Damascus as the formative elements in his theology. N. T. Wright is cautious

---

271 Meyer 1989, 94.

272 cf. Levenson 1993; see my Bartholomew 1995 review.

about describing this as a 'conversion': 'But Saul – Paul the Apostle – saw it [the OT] as the same narrative, now demanding to be understood in a radical, but justifiable, new way. The narrative in question was the hope of Israel.'[273] According to Wright:

> This moment shattered Saul's wildest dreams and, at the same split second, fulfilled them. This was – he saw it in that instant – the fulfillment of Israel's ancient scriptures, but also the utter denial of the way he had been reading them up to that point.[274]

Paul mentions that he spent sustained time in Arabia, which Wright argues means in the vicinity of Sinai. Like Elijah, at this time of crisis Paul went back to the place where the Sinai event occurred:

> Saul was starting to come to terms with the possibility that, if the divine purposes had been completed in Jesus, it might mean that a whole new phase of the divine plan, hitherto barely suspected, had now been launched, a place in which the Torah itself would be seen in a whole new light.[275]

So, how then did Paul come to read the OT in the light of his encounter with Christ?

He thought his way backward from the 'new fact', as he saw it, of a crucified and risen Messiah, back into the world of Israel's scriptures and traditions, back into the long, dark, and often twisted narrative of Israel that had been groping its way forward to that point without glimpsing its true goal. He reread Genesis. He reread Exodus. He reread the whole torah, and the prophets, especially Isaiah, and he went on praying the Psalms. With hindsight (and, he would have insisted, with a fresh wisdom that came with the spirit), he saw Jesus all over the place – not arbitrarily . . . but as the infinite point where the parallel lines of Israel's long narrative would eventually meet.[276]

---

273  Wright 2018, 44–5.
274  Wright 2018, 52–3.
275  Wright 2018, 65.
276  Wright 2018, 71.

This, in my view, is right, and we need to follow the example of Paul and the apostles. Indeed, it seems to me that one of N. T. Wright's great achievements has been to show us how we might read the OT with the early Church, without in any way subverting its discrete witness.

Now that we have some sense of what to do with the OT – to listen to it by means of a communicative hermeneutic with our threefold cord at its heart – we turn to an examination of the tools we will need for this task.

Part 2

# TOOLS FOR THE TASK

# 2

# Knowledge: towards a critical realist paradigm

## 1 Introduction

You could sum up what I am trying to achieve in this series as *to know the OT truly*. We are after nothing less than true knowledge of the OT. A postmodernist will find this ridiculous, but, pursued consistently, the relativism of postmodernism ends in absurdity with no reasons for taking it seriously. If you are a 'normal' practitioner of OT study, you might say, 'Well, yes, isn't that what we all do?' To which I reply, 'Not so fast!' When it comes to the truthful acquisition of knowledge (epistemology) there are many different views nowadays, and we need to think through the issue of 'knowledge' in relation to the 'OT' carefully.

In Part 1, using the issue of boundary descriptions of the land in the OT, we identified three dimensions that must be taken seriously if we are to understand the OT today, namely the historical, the literary, and the theological or kerygmatic. Of course, we never encounter these as distinct elements but interwoven together as integral parts of the text of the OT. However, as is typical of what philosophers do, we can abstract them in order to take a close look at them and endeavour to see how they fit together within various texts, with a view to *knowing* far better how to listen to the OT.

As soon as we do this, we will quickly realize that when it comes to literature, history and theology there is not one view but a plurality of views, and these cash out in different ways in OT studies. Take the OT as literature, for example. We can ask two major questions in this respect:

1 How do the OT/Israel and the ANE nations conceive of literature?
2 How do *we* conceive of literature? In the wake of postmodernism we should all be aware that today there is no one accepted view of what literature is and how it works. Thus the OT scholar will need to reach a considered view on this topic.

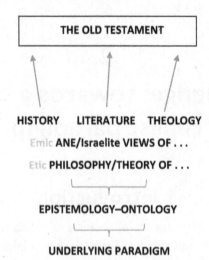

Figure 1 **The emic and etic approaches to the study of the Old Testament**

In other words, attention to these strands is complex. It will soon back us into the views of literature, history and theology in the OT and the ANE, *as well as* philosophy[1] of literature, philosophy of history, and the relationship between theology and philosophy. To use the language of social anthropology, an *emic* (from within) and an *etic* (from outside) approach will be required, while remaining aware of differences among etic and emic approaches to the OT. We can envisage this as shown in Figure 1. Scholarly work such as OT studies can also be imagined as an ice cream (see Fig. 2).

As we would expect, most scholars are in OT studies because they love studying the OT. In terms of our ice cream, it is the actual ice cream, not so much the wafer cone, that attracts them, and this is where almost all their energies are expended. In Kuhn's language we would expect that most OT scholars accept the paradigm into which they were inducted and then devote their time to exploring the OT using the resources of that paradigm, that is, practising normal science. As we are aware, it takes years of specialist study nowadays to become an OT scholar and there is enough to keep one busy for more than a lifetime.

However, as the Canadian philosopher Charles Taylor points out, in any discipline – including OT studies – you can ask deeper and deeper questions about the discipline until you reach the really foundational questions, and this

---

1  If the word 'philosophy' is off-putting for you, I suggest you think of the 'theory of literature, theory of history', etc. Alvin Plantinga defines philosophy as 'thinking hard about something' and that is what we have in mind here.

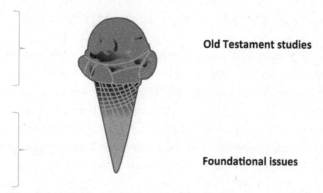

Old Testament studies

Foundational issues

Figure 2 **Old Testament studies imagined as an ice cream**

is philosophy. Once again, let's take the issue of the OT as literature as an example. Wrestle with this and you will find yourself asking questions such as:

- What is literature and how does it work?
- How is literature different from other types of writing?
- What is the relationship between speech and writing?
- How does language – underlying both speech and writing – work?
- How does language relate to my view of the human person and to the nature of the world?

As you can see, attending closely to the OT as literature backs one into deep philosophical questions about the nature of language, the nature of being human (called anthropology in philosophy) and the nature of the world (called ontology in philosophy). This is what the cone represents. Few of us would obsess about the cone – it is the ice cream we are after – but we know well that a cone is indispensable if we are to enjoy the ice cream to the full! Understandably, OT scholars are generally neither philosophers nor theologians, but there are times when we need to attend to the cone, and *this is such a time.*

Kuhn points out that most practitioners of a science are largely unaware of the paradigm within which they operate, but when a crisis starts to develop in relation to the regnant paradigm they become more conscious of it and begin to examine it critically. In my view, the historical-critical paradigm/s has been in crisis for a while now, and in this situation, as well as in relation to our quest for a new paradigm, we simply have to take time out to examine the cone, the foundations of OT studies, anew. In this and the following chapters that is precisely what we will do with a view to proposing a new, critical realist cone for OT studies.

As with the history of science, examination of the history of OT studies is very illuminating in bringing foundational issues to the fore, and elsewhere I have attended to this in some detail.[2] Much more work remains to be done. What the history of OT studies clearly reveals is that historical criticism/s is not simply objective, neutral and scientific, but works from the basis of a very specific, very modern cone/s.[3] Thus, if we are after true knowledge of the OT, then we need to reflect on just what we mean by 'knowledge'.

# 2 Knowledge

## (a) Outdated paradigms: the tale of two 'p's: from positivism to postmodernism

Looking back at the twentieth century, it is astonishing to track the move in theories of knowledge from positivism at the outset to postmodernism at the end. Both, I argue, are connected, have deeply influenced OT studies and are now outdated.

### Positivism

Anthony Thiselton notes perceptively that biblical scholars often work with philosophical approaches that have been discredited by philosophers [of religion].[4] Positivism is one such philosophy. Comte (1798–1857) coined the expression 'positive philosophy', and its abbreviation 'positivism' has remained with us.[5] Positivism came to refer to a philosophical movement that was very influential in the West in the latter part of the nineteenth century and the first half of the twentieth, the very time when historical criticism became the dominant mode of OT study. However, there is diversity within this movement. Kolakowski tracks positivism from Berkeley and Hume, through Comte, Bernard, Mill and Spencer, and then through conventionalism and pragmatism on to the logical positivism of the twentieth century.[6]

---

2  Bartholomew 2015.

3  cf. Bartholomew 2020; etc.

4  Thiselton 1999, 137.

5  According to Abbagnano (1967, 414), Comte appropriated it from Saint-Simon .

6  Kolakowski 1968, 1972.

Nevertheless, Kolakowski discerns the following major characteristics of positivism as an epistemology (theory of knowing) that clarifies rules and criteria for knowledge:[7]

1 phenomenalism, which rejects any distinction between substance and essence;
2 nominalism, according to which 'we may not assume that any insight formulated in general terms can have any real referents other than individual concrete objects';[8]
3 a resistance to seeing value judgements and normative statements as knowledge;
4 an affirmation of the unity of the scientific method across disciplines, with the result that positivism aimed at applying its epistemology across all disciplines.[9]

In this way, a science of literature comparable to that of the natural sciences developed.

## Positivism in literary studies

In the late nineteenth century, it was normal for literature to be analysed on the basis of:

the genesis of the art-work in terms of 'influences' and 'sources'; to search for similar or analogous motifs and themes in earlier literature; to probe the origins of the political, cultural and social background of the period or the biographical background of the author – all in order to give a causal explanation of how the work came into being.[10]

Causality was central to the scientific method and it was similarly used to explain literature. As Jefferson and Robey note:

In its pure form positivistic scholarship studied literature almost exclusively in relation to its factual causes or genesis: the author's life, his recorded intentions in writing, his immediate social and cultural envir-

---

7   Kolakowski 1968, 1972, 9–18.
8   Kolakowski 1968, 1972, 13.
9   On positivism and Protestant thought in the UK and USA see Cashdollar 1989. On the relationship between positivism and philosophy of history see Collingwood 1946, 126–33.
10   Weiss 1984, 2.

onment, his sources . . . It was not interested in the features of the literary text itself except from a philological and historical viewpoint . . . it disregarded questions concerning the value or the distinctive properties of literature, since these could not be dealt with in a factual and historical manner. Or more exactly, while it took for granted that literary texts possessed a special value, in practice it treated them as if they were indistinguishable from other sorts of historical document.[11]

During the course of the twentieth century, positivism was thoroughly discredited, but it is not hard to see resemblances with historical criticism; for example:

- historical criticism as the scientific approach to the OT;
- a major concern with sources and a causal explanation of how the text came into being; although this was called 'literary' criticism, historical criticism has generally not attended closely and in detail to the OT texts as *literary* entities, and moved quickly from apparent discrepancies in the texts to sources;
- a naturalistic, causal approach to the OT, which excludes value and normative statements as real knowledge, including, of course, religion.

Not only has positivism been discredited in philosophy as a kind of naive realism which fails to account for the social location of the knower, but within literary studies there was a major reaction to positivism, first with New Criticism, and then with a host of other approaches which sought to attend to the literary text in itself.

## Postmodernism as creative anti-realism

If positivism leaves us with a real but deeply reduced OT, the creative anti-realism of postmodernism leaves us wondering with Stanley Fish whether or not there is an OT text at all. If positivism focuses almost entirely on what underlies the text, the creative anti-realism[12] of postmodernism places all the power in the reader and sees the text as a construction of the reader so that we potentially end up with as many readings and texts as there are readers of

---

11  Jefferson and Robey 1986, 9.
12  This is Alvin Plantinga's (1995) expression.

the OT. Elsewhere, I have explored postmodernism and the OT in detail and readers are referred to my discussions there.[13]

We are, in my view, on the other side of postmodernism, bearing in mind that postmodern approaches to the OT were always only one approach, albeit manifesting in a wild pluralism of readings. If positivism left us with a real but reduced text, postmodernism left us without a text but with an important sense that what the reader brings to the text does indeed influence our reading/s of it. If positivism foregrounds the reality – albeit reduced – of the text, postmodernism foregrounds the social location of the reader/s.

We need an approach to knowledge and to knowing the OT which retains *both* the reality of the OT text *and* the social location of the reader. Clearly, if we are to find such an approach and to move beyond positivism and postmodernism, we need to attend to the foundations of OT studies. My hope is that the above diagrams are helpful in starting to identify key issues at play in such foundations. What we are after is *true* understanding and *true* knowledge of the OT, and thus we will enter our discussion through the door of knowledge, or what is more technically known as *epistemology*. As Ben Meyer asserts in his *Critical Realism and the New Testament*, we need to make sense of the ways we make sense of things,[14] and more particularly the way we make sense of the Old Testament.

Attention to philosophy inevitably involves a technical vocabulary. I would encourage readers not to be wary of such technical philosophical terms, and I will attempt to provide useful definitions of such terms throughout.

**Epistemology:** how we go about knowing something so that we can trust the results of the knowing process

If you think about this definition, then there is never a course we take or teach, never a research project we engage in, an article or book we write, without an epistemology at work. It would be extraordinary, even in the most postmodern context, to teach a course or engage in a research project without any aim of moving towards the truth of what we are studying.

Epistemology is, of course, a large subdiscipline of philosophy in itself. In recent decades, Christian philosophers have done extraordinary work in this

---

13   Bartholomew 2015.
14   Meyer 1989.

area: I think of scholars such as Alvin Plantinga, Nicholas Wolterstorff and William Alston, among others. In our foray into the epistemology of science in Part 1 we have already seen how the work of Thomas Kuhn is fertile for OT studies. Kuhn's work, however, raised the spectre of relativism, although he himself rejected this. A response to the insights and challenges of Kuhn's work is *critical realism*, stemming in particular from the work of Roy Bhaskar and developed by a number of Christian scholars.[15] As with N. T. Wright and the NT, I think that critical realism has the resources to resolve the conundrums thrown up by positivism and postmodernism, and can help us find an approach to knowledge that fits with the OT. My major work philosophically has been in hermeneutics, and once we have traversed critical realism and its rich insights for knowledge and OT studies, we will explore how this fits in relation to philosophical and biblical hermeneutics.

## (b) Critical realism

The Enlightenment project has unquestionably failed; it is not obvious what will succeed it.
(Alister McGrath, *Reality*, xxii)

The father of modern critical realism was Roy Bhaskar (1944–2014), although it has many antecedents.[16] Since the publication of his *A Realist Theory of Science* (1975), and many other works by Bhaskar and others, critical realism has become a major influence in many disciplines. Bhaskar's work developed through three major phases:

1  His transcendental naturalism, or what came to be known as *critical realism*, focused on the ontology (the nature of reality) and the epistemology of the natural and social sciences.
2  His *dialectical* critical realism – think of the background of this in Hegel and Marx – sought to develop critical realism to address issues of human liberation.
3  His philosophy of *meta-reality*, a result of his spiritual turn, attended to issues of ultimate reality and the purpose of life.

We saw with Kuhn the challenge of holding together epistemic shifts and revolutions in science with some sort of ontological realism and some way of

---

15  cf. A. Wright 2013; McGrath 2002, 202–9.
16  A. Wright 2013, 1.

assessing progress from one paradigm to another. If different paradigms are seen as strongly incommensurate then it is hard to see how progress can be assessed and how one paradigm can hold on to the genuine insights of preceding ones, leading us down the slippery slope towards Feyerabend – see above – and relativism. There is also the question of how we can avoid the modern problem of collapsing ontology into epistemology so that the world simply is as *we* perceive it to be, an approach which has led to debilitating reductionisms.

It is these sorts of problem that critical realism answers.

> The term 'critical realism' arose by elision of the phrases 'transcendental realism' and 'critical naturalism', but Bhaskar and others in this movement have accepted it since 'critical', like 'transcendental', suggested affinities with Kant's philosophy, while 'realism' indicated the differences from it.[17]

Readers may recall that in Kant's *idealism* we cannot know the world as it actually is but only as it appears to us, and its appearance is a result of experience filtered through the mental grid by means of which we appropriate that experience. Behind the *phenomenal* – the world as it appears to us – lies the *noumenal*, the world as it actually is, but *we* cannot know the noumenal. As with Kuhn, critical realists agree with Kant that the knower influences the results of the knowing process; the paradigm or epistemology within which one works shapes the outcomes of one's work in important ways, although it should be noted that they disagree that every rational human person will filter the data of experience in the same way, as Kant thought. However, where critical realists strongly disagree with Kant is in his view that we cannot know the world as it is. *Realism* argues that the world has a discernible shape and humans can know it as it is, and critical realists are concerned to hold fast to this view.

## An intransitive ontology and a transitive epistemology

It is this sense of there being a real world out there beyond and more encompassing than us and our knowing that critical realists want to preserve. There is a well-known question in modern philosophy: if a tree falls but there is no human to witness it fall, does it actually do so? For critical realists, the answer is an unequivocal 'yes'. Things exist and events happen independent of whether we know about them or not. Whereas pre-moderns began with ontology – the nature of reality – and then moved to epistemology, modern philosophers

---

17   Bhaskar 1998.

start with the knowing subject, and in the process ontology has moved to the margins or virtually disappeared. Critical realism seeks to retrieve the centrality and importance of ontology, and to maintain the inseparable relationship between ontology and epistemology but without collapsing the one into the other. Of ontology they note: 'Of course being contains, but it is irreducible [cannot be reduced] to, knowledge, experience or any other human attribute or product.'[18]

From language studies, we will be familiar with *transitive and intransitive verbs*. This contrast is used by critical realists to argue *inter alia* for an *intransitive ontology* (the world has a fixed, discernible shape apart from us as knowers) and a *transitive epistemology* (as with Kuhn, the frameworks or structures within which we seek to understand the real world vary).

> The process of scientific development can be explained in critical realist terms as the uncovering by experimentation of deeper layers of the causal forces which operate within nature. While these forces exist independently of any scientific investigation of their nature and domains, that scientific investigation itself must be considered to be a historically contingent and socially located process.[19]

Critical realists refer to this as *epistemological relativism*.

> A problem for all these [modern] trends was to sustain a clear concept of the continued independent *reality* of *being* – of the intransitive or ontological dimension – in the face of the *relativity* of our *knowledge* – in the transitive or epistemological dimension.[20]

Critical realism seeks to account for meaning variance: different frameworks read the world in a different way, while holding on to ontological objectivity: it is the same world that holds for all knowers.

## A stratified world

As part of their retrieval of ontology, critical realists have developed a rich account of the *stratified* nature of the world:

---

18  Bhaskar 1998, xii.
19  McGrath 2002, 211.
20  Bhaskar 1998, x.

A transcendental argument from the conditions of the possibility of experimentation in science thus establishes at once the irreducibility of ontology, of the theory of being, to epistemology and a novel ... *stratified and differentiated ontology*, that is characterized by the prevalence of structures as well as events (stratification) and open systems as well as closed (differentiation).[21]

Since academics can develop multiple accounts of the same things or events, it would appear that reality is pluriform and stratified.[22] Take a fire in our neighbourhood, for example. A house near where we live catches fire and burns down. This event has multiple dimensions to it, and these can be analysed in complementary ways by diverse scholars or practitioners from different disciplines. A physicist will be able to explain the physical aspects of the event. A local historian may be able to tell us how common or unusual such an event is in our neighbourhood. A builder may be able to alert us to why certain materials made such an event more or less likely. A detective will investigate whether we are dealing with arson – was the house deliberately set on fire or not? An ecologist would be able to assess the damage done to the environment. An artist or poet might enable us to enter the aesthetic and tragic dimensions of the fire. The family who lived there can tell us about all that the house meant to them as a home. And so on and so forth. Critical realism is not alone in developing a rich stratified view of reality. We find similar emphases in Arthur Lovejoy, Michael Polanyi, Schumacher's *A Guide for the Perplexed* and the work of the Dutch philosopher Herman Dooyeweerd.

For Bhaskar, stratification is found in nature and thus also in science, both within a single science and between sciences. A science works by abstraction, and critical realism points out that such abstraction relates to the real stratification in nature and in society.

They are not subjective classifications of an undifferentiated empirical reality, but attempts to grasp (for example, in real definitions of forms of social life already understood in a pre-scientific way) precisely the generative mechanisms and causal structures which account in all their complex and multiple determinations for the concrete phenomena of human history.[23]

---

21  Bhaskar 1998. Emphasis added.

22  A. Wright 2013, 11.

23  Bhaskar 1998.

Stratification resists reductionism. Higher levels depend on and emerge from lower levels, but this does not mean that higher levels can be fully explained by lower levels or reduced to them.

## Judgmental rationality

Critical realism with its epistemological relativism recognizes that there are different theories of the world we share in common. In OT studies, for example, we find different theories that may be complementary, but we also find different theories that are *in conflict*. Take the Sinai event, for example. Clearly, a view of Sinai according to which YHWH actually met the Israelites there and spoke to them directly and through Moses is in conflict with the view that the Sinai narrative is an imaginative projection from centuries later as Israelite scribes sought to construct a history for Israel. As with Kuhn's examination of different paradigms, the question emerges of whether or not we can adjudicate between such conflicting accounts, especially if they emerge out of different paradigms, as is generally the case.[24]

This is a complex issue and raises difficult questions such as how a scholar (or scholars) comes to embrace a particular paradigm. Critical realists argue that the stratified nature of reality enables us to provide a means of rationally assessing conflicting theories:

> However, if the relation between the theories is one of conflict rather than merely difference, this presupposes that they are alternative accounts of the same world, and if one theory can explain more significant phenomena in terms of its descriptions than the other can in terms of its, then there is a rational criterion for theory choice, and a fortiori a positive sense to the idea of scientific development over time . . . In this sort of way critical realism claims to be able to combine and reconcile ontological realism, epistemological relativism and judgmental rationality.[25]

We find a similar emphasis in the work of Philip Rieff, who argues that with good theory the facts, as it were, rise up to meet it. In my view, especially in relation to the OT, the capacity to explain more significant phenomena will rarely be decisive, but it certainly lays down the gauntlet. An alternative paradigm will need to account better for the phenomena of the OT than

---

24   cf. Bartholomew 2020.
25   Bhaskar 1998.

the regnant paradigm of historical criticism, while drawing on its very real strengths and insights.

## Meta-reality

Intriguingly, Bhaskar's critical realism took an explicitly spiritual turn. Bhaskar's spiritual turn was met with some strong resistance, and with time he came to refer to it more cautiously as the philosophy of meta[beyond]-reality. His doctrine of stratification, with the concomitant notion of the universe moving forward, opened up a view of the universe for him as a totality, which raised the questions of being as such and the meaning of life. Bhaskar rejected the modern occlusion of such questions. He came to argue that critical realism lays the groundwork for and even necessitates its development into a philosophy of Self-realization and ultimately of God-realization. 'God' is conceived non-personally as the ultimate 'categorical structure of the world', the 'causally and taxonomically irreducible' ground and truth of being 'on which the rest of being is unilaterally, existentially dependent'.[26] The meaning and purpose of life exist as a potential waiting for realization. With the opposition to his spiritual turn, Bhaskar's philosophy of meta-reality takes out the 'necessitates' from his earlier approach: it now becomes only one possible development.

## Summary

Bhaskar's critical realism can be summarized as follows:

- It is *realist*: the world we encounter has a discernible shape that is real and can be known truly.
- The world is stratified or layered.
- It is *critical*: knowers bring different epistemologies to bear on this objective world.
- A criterion for evaluating different approaches to knowing this world is the extent to which they account for the stratified nature of the world.

# (c) Critical realism and the Old Testament

Ben Meyer and N. T. Wright have argued for the relevance and fecundity of critical realism in relation to NT studies. Alister McGrath, Andrew Wright

---

26   Quoted in A. Wright 2013, 23.

and others have argued for its importance in systematic theology. In my view, critical realism has great potential for OT studies, both in helping us to make sense of the way we have been making sense of the OT and in finding fresh ways forward for making sense of the OT. In relation to the former point, we have noted above the similarities between positivism in literary studies and historical criticism, as well as attending briefly to creative anti-realism and OT studies. In this section, we will attend to the latter point of how critical realism helps us to understand our task of understanding the OT.

## The reality of the Old Testament

The Jewish and Protestant HB/OT canon is made up of 39 books. As we have seen in Part 1, contemporary discussions in textual criticism debate the extent to which there is an *Urtext* underlying the manuscripts we possess. As we argued in that section, Eric Tully's insight that contemporary textual criticism *operates downstream of redaction criticism* is a profound insight. It alerts us to the fact that, ironically, the notion of 'postmodern textual criticism' is a result of or flows from historical criticism. As the OT text has been excavated to ever more layers, eventually it has come to seem as though it never bottoms out and that OT texts are fluid all the way down. At this point, positivism and postmodernism in OT studies join hands.

In contrast, we have argued that Ancient Israel possessed a view/s of what constituted a text and that, while it is by no means a simple task, textual criticism should be seen and practised as the attempt to provide us with texts that are as close to the *Urtext* as possible. The challenges raised by textual criticism today are difficult, but the degree of fluidity is often overstated, and with most of the OT we have definite texts with clear textual boundaries, as we will see in subsequent volumes in this series.

From a critical realist perspective, the important point to note is that the OT exists *independently of us* as a collection of books from Ancient Israel and it is this entity that we are seeking to understand. At certain points in history the OT texts as we know them came into existence – however hard it may be to be precise about such points – and they have an intransitive ontological status in relation to us as interpreters. Paul Ricoeur expresses this well: 'What the interpreter says is a resaying that reactivates what is said by the text.'[27]

Even the most postmodern readings inevitably work with some sense of the text as given. For example, to deconstruct an OT text one must be able to

---

27  Ricoeur 1991, 2007, 124.

identify the aporia in the text when it is read along the grain. Ideological critiques of the OT have to assume that there is within the OT an expression of genuine ideologies calling for critique. And so on.

## Stratification

Critical realism's notion of stratification enables us to move beyond asserting the reality of the OT, towards beginning to articulate ontological elements of the texts we encounter. The OT texts come to us as Hebrew or Aramaic *literary wholes*. It is as such texts that they manifest their powerful communicative capacity, as discussed in relation to Sanders in Part 1.

As literature, these texts embody a poetics which we encountered in our discussion of Kawashima in Part 1. Indeed, as Meir Sternberg pointed out to me in a conversation, it is *through their poetics* that we hear their message. Undoubtedly, there are sources underlying the OT books, but stratification helps us to be aware that, as real as the sources behind the text may be, we should not make the mistake of equating the sources or earlier versions of 'the text' with the texts in the literary form in which we receive them.

This means that we have to take the reality of the OT texts as literary texts with the utmost seriousness. It is always possible that a 'text' is so broken and incoherent that we conclude that it is not a literary whole after all, but this should be as a last rather than a first resort, especially bearing in mind that any reconstruction of sources or earlier versions of a text is almost always speculative unless we discover such earlier versions. As literary texts, they require that we also attend to what they are about – their reference – and their message. In Chapter 1 we made the case that three strata in particular are fundamental to any analysis of the OT: the literary, the historical, and the kerygmatic or theological. All the OT texts are profoundly religious, and stratification and Bhaskar's notion of meta-reality again remind us that we need to take this dimension seriously and not assume that it can be reduced to natural causes, cultural context and the like.

## The knower

Although I am not partial to the term 'epistemological relativism' because it easily implies that one epistemology is as good as another, it does alert us to the fact that knowing is always something done by humans and that it can never be separated from the humanity and historical situatedness of the knower. It is this that philosophical hermeneutics has so clearly foregrounded. We often think that the challenge to understanding the OT is that it is from so long ago,

Figure 3 **The Old Testament and its reader – both embedded in history**

written in Hebrew and Aramaic in cultures so very different from our own, and so on. This is all true, but an equally important insight is that *just as the OT is embedded in history, so too are we as the readers of the OT.* We can depict this as shown in Figure 3.

A contribution of postmodernism has been to alert us to the fact that all knowers operate within some *tradition* of knowledge. This is part of our historical situatedness and is thus unavoidable. One of the myths of modernity has been the view that modern knowledge is untraditioned. Calvin Seerveld depicts this evocatively: a devil follows a person walking through the snow, carefully erasing the person's footprints so as to support the illusion of operating outside any tradition![28] We now know much more clearly that the Enlightenment and post-Enlightenment traditions are just that, traditions, just as much as the variety of Christian or Islamic traditions are traditions. Alasdair MacIntyre has done seminal work in this regard, alerting us to the nature of traditions, their variety and their unavoidability. He shows how

> all reasoning takes place within the context of some traditional mode of thought, transcending through criticism and invention the limitations of what had hitherto been reasoned in that tradition; this is as true of modern physics as of medieval logic.[29]

MacIntyre acutely observes in this regard that:

> To recognize this [the relationship between virtues and traditions] is of course also to recognize the existence of an additional virtue, one whose importance is perhaps most obvious when it is least present, *the virtue of having an adequate sense of the traditions to which one belongs or which confront one.*[30]

---

28   Seerveld 2012.
29   MacIntyre 2007, 222.
30   MacIntyre 2007, 223. Emphasis added.

As long as the myth of neutrality and a view from nowhere continues to inhabit OT studies, the virtue of being aware of one's tradition and of other options needs to be foregrounded as of primary importance.

Similarly, Gadamer in Part 1 of his *Truth and Method* attends to how we know an artwork.[31] We can and should analyse the work in terms of its composition, use of pigments, style and so on, but such *methodological* analyses only make sense within a large conversation with the work. According to Gadamer, we understand or get to know an artwork when we open a dialogue with the work, a dialogue which goes back and forth until we reach a point of the fusion of horizons. In this dialogue we do not set aside our prejudices (pre-judgements); indeed, growth in knowledge is only possible on the basis of them. *Inter alia, they* enable us to discern that which is other in the work and cause us to reflect critically on our prejudices.

The fact that knowledge is inherently traditioned accounts to a significant extent for the conflict in interpretations of the OT. Meyer notes in relation to NT interpretation:

> The root of our deepest divisions is not lack of evidence. It is the fact of opposed horizons and, above all, of irreducibly opposed horizons, as a moment's reflection on the public controversies will suggest and as sustained reflection will confirm. Irreducibly opposed horizons are a massive human reality labyrinthine in its consequences, leading some to champion as true and good what others with equal sincerity repudiate as false and evil.[32]

N. T. Wright provides a degree of nuance to such a position, correct as it is, by noting that there is something like a sliding scale when a basic story/ies from one group encounters a basic story/ies from another group.[33] At one end of the scale is direct confirmation, at the other end direct confrontation. Of course, there are many positions between these two ends. A confrontation between basic stories could lead to abandoning one for the other; alternatively, one could try to construct a new basic story that makes sense of the total picture as it is now perceived.

---

31   Gadamer 1989.
32   Meyer 1989, 81.
33   Wright 1992, 42.

The reader of the OT thus only ever inhabits one point of view of this corpus of writings, although one's point of view will be deeply related to the communities of which one is a part. As MacIntyre observes: 'I am part of their story, as they are part of mine. The narrative of any one life is part of an interlocking set of narratives.'[34]

There is no god's-eye view – in the deist sense of the term – available.[35] Nor, *contra* Kant, is there one mental grid through which all rational people interpret the phenomena of the world. Humans interpret the world through a grid formed both by their nature as humans and by their nurture, or the way in which the narrative of their life has unfolded. Interpretation through some such grid is unavoidable. For any perception or acquisition of knowledge to occur, some pre-theoretical and tacit point of view is necessary.

As will I, N. T. Wright reaches for the concept of 'world view' to name the lenses through which we interpret the world. Intriguingly, 'world view' is making something of a comeback in OT studies, including Jewish theories of education.[36] However, as is so often the case, it is used to refer to the Egyptian world view, or the Babylonian one, but hardly ever to the world view of the interpreter, as Wright and I choose to use it in addition to those other ways.

# 3 Verification?

As we saw above, critical realism argues that we can make judgements between different epistemological approaches. An important question is: can we do this in relation to the OT?

Verification of a reading of the OT will always be inseparably related to what we actually do with the OT, which will also be integrally related, albeit unconsciously,[37] to what we think should be done with the OT. If, for example, we think that the primary thing to be done with the Pentateuch is to analyse its sources, then the test will be the extent to which we do this successfully. Given that we do not have the sources and that proponents of this approach continue to disagree, it is hard to see how such readings could in any way be strongly

---

34  MacIntyre 2007, 218.

35  See Wright 1992, 36.

36  Vernoff 1986.

37  I say 'unconsciously' because it is perfectly possible to work away within the regnant paradigm in OT studies without giving much conscious attention to this question.

verified. I recognize that this is unlikely to deter source critics of the Pentateuch. As Wright notes:

> as always, the proof of the pudding remains in the eating. There is no
> such thing as 'neutral' or 'objective' proof; only the claim that the story
> we are now telling about the world as a whole makes more sense, in its
> outline and detail, than any other potential or actual stories that may be
> on offer.[38]

For source critics, the story they tell makes best sense of the Pentateuch and
thus it is likely that they will continue to tell and develop this story.

The reader should note that I am not dismissing source criticism out of
hand. Because of the intransitive ontology of the OT text, any serious reading – and source criticism is nothing if not serious – will foreground data
that must be taken into account. At the conclusion to this volume we will
revisit the issue of historical criticism, and I refer the reader to our discussion there.

For now, it will suffice to remind the reader of our discussion in Chapter 1 in which we recognized the exceptional communicative power of the
OT and that what we should do with it is to listen so as to hear it with its full
acoustics. The test of our reading will then be whether or not it enables us to
do so. The proof of the pudding will be, as it were, in a different kind of eating! Source criticism may well play a part in this broader goal, but its track
record thus far makes me somewhat sceptical, at least of source criticism as
typically practised. In my opinion, historical criticism has not yet come to
grips adequately with the literary turn in OT studies and it is here that stratification comes to the fore as a serious contender for verifying a reading of
the OT. If it can be agreed, as we have argued above, that history, literature
and theology are key strands or strata in OT texts, then priority would be
given to readings that successfully take into account and integrate all three
of these dimensions.

This may seem obvious, but in OT studies as a whole it is not. Berlinerblau
says that:

> Old Testament research is an ideational hybrid, a mixing and matching
> of completely disparate, perhaps mutually exclusive, ways of thinking the

---

38   Wright 1992, 42.

world. Perched on the massive superstructures of this peculiar epistemological base the most self-conscious biblical exegete is aptly described by Saul Bellow's poignant depiction of the soul in modernity: 'poor bird, not knowing which way to fly.'[39]

In my view – and that of Plantinga[40] – this is not something to be celebrated or simply accepted but rather a sign of a discipline in a profound crisis. It is ironic that scientific, neutral historical criticism has led OT studies into such a dire situation. In contrast, *integrality* should be a criterion of OT study.

Wright lists the following as criteria that count in NT studies:

- simplicity of outline;
- elegance in handling the details;
- the inclusion of all parts of the story;
- the capacity of the story to make sense beyond its subject matter.

All of these are relevant to OT studies as well. Perhaps one word that could be used to sum up these criteria is 'integrality', in the sense of wholeness. If our concern is to listen to the OT with all its acoustics, then the extent to which our reading allows us to hear the OT in its totality becomes an important criterion.

# 4 Conclusion

In one way or another, all OT study seeks to know the OT. However, the great diversity of things done with the OT in OT studies today alerts us to the fact that *knowing the OT* is far from as simple as it may seem. Very different epistemologies are at work in OT studies, alas, often unconsciously. In this context the student of the OT does well to explore what knowledge of the OT entails and to be conscious of the 'cone' on which their work is taking place – to refer back to our opening illustration of the ice cream cone.

We have argued that a critical realist theory of knowledge holds great promise for OT studies in a variety of ways. It allows us to assert the objectivity of the text of the OT while recognizing the effect of different approaches that scholars bring to it. We found the stratified nature of reality an important insight and

---

39    Berlinerblau 2002, 281. The quote is from Saul Bellow, *Mr. Sammler's Planet* (New York, NY: Penguin, 1969, 1970), 1.

40    See the Preface.

related this analogously to the three major strands in the OT, strands that any reading of the OT should account for. In the next chapter we will focus on the literary dimension of the OT and world view, and explore what insights critical realism provides in this area.

# 3

# Narrative, literature, reading and world view

## 1 Introduction

Critical realism alerts us to the epistemological *diversity* – I far prefer this term to 'relativism' – among knowers of the OT. Following MacIntyre, we could say that scholars read and study the *same* OT out of *different* traditions; following N. T. Wright and myself, we could say they operate from different world views or basic stories about the world. The storied nature of traditions and world views brings us firmly on to the terrain of narrative.

In recent decades a host of philosophers and theologians have drawn our attention to the vital role of narrative and story. For our purposes, two insights are of central importance. First, we understand ourselves and how to act in the world through narrative. Second, at the deepest level we understand our world through narrative.

The OT is full of examples of this; suffice it here to refer to one fecund case. An important part of the stories by which we understand ourselves and our world is *memory*, and in a recent, creative work Culp argues that story, ritual and song are the three vectors of memory in Deuteronomy.[1] Deuteronomy 26.1–11 is a fascinating example of a law in which we see the combination of ritual and story in the shaping of the narrative out of which the individual Israelite *and* the people as a whole are to understand the world and live in it.[2]

**26** When you have come into the land that the LORD your God is giving you as an inheritance to possess, and you possess it, and settle in it, [2] you shall take some of the first of all the fruit of the ground, which you har-

---

1   Culp 2020.

2   On the use of the second-person singular and plural in v. 1 see Christensen 2002, 636. The shift back and forth between the first-person and the second-person plural is noticeable throughout as the ritual weaves the identity of the individual and the people together. Historical critics have, by comparison, often used the difference between the second-person singular and plural as a criterion for different redactions.

vest from the land that the LORD your God is giving you, and you shall put it in a basket and go to the place that the LORD your God will choose as a dwelling for his name. ³You shall go to the priest who is in office at that time, and say to him, 'Today I declare to the LORD your God that I have come into the land that the LORD swore to our ancestors to give us.' ⁴When the priest takes the basket from your hand and sets it down before the altar of the LORD your God, ⁵you shall make this response before the LORD your God: 'A wandering Aramean was my ancestor; he went down into Egypt and lived there as an alien, few in number, and there he became a great nation, mighty and populous. ⁶When the Egyptians treated us harshly and afflicted us, by imposing hard labour on us, ⁷we cried to the LORD, the God of our ancestors; the LORD heard our voice and saw our affliction, our toil, and our oppression. ⁸The LORD brought us out of Egypt with a mighty hand and an outstretched arm, with a terrifying display of power, and with signs and wonders; ⁹and he brought us into this place and gave us this land, a land flowing with milk and honey. ¹⁰So now I bring the first of the fruit of the ground that you, O LORD, have given me.' You shall set it down before the LORD your God and bow down before the LORD your God. ¹¹Then you, together with the Levites and the aliens who reside among you, shall celebrate with all the bounty that the LORD your God has given to you and to your house.

Prior to entering the land, the Israelites were not farmers, and thus their vocational understanding of themselves as farmers in the land needed to be consciously shaped and reinforced through such rituals as this of the offering of the first fruits. Imagination is a key element in entering a story, and one needs to imagine the effect on an Israelite of this ritual and his or her participation in it year in and year out.

A major emphasis of the law is that 'God is the source and true owner of the land's produce'.[3] The idea of the land and its produce as gift recurs a number of times: in verses 1, 2, 3, 9, 10, 11. This may seem obvious, but in the ANE context, in which the fertility of the land and the gods were intertwined, it is distinctive and vitally important. YHWH is the giver and he is identified with the 'God of our ancestors' (vv. 3, 7). The person making the offering is an active participant in the ritual and is required to speak in summary fashion in verse 3 and in a more elaborate fashion in verses 5–10. In both cases the person rehearses the story which explains and interprets the offering he or she is now

---

3  Christensen 2002, 636.

giving. The story is told in such a fashion that it embeds the person firmly in the story and makes it his or her story. Note '*our* ancestors' in verses 3 and 7, and '*my* ancestor' in verse 5; the use of the first-person plural in verses 6–9; and the shift to the first-person singular in verse 10 as the story is brought right into the present moment. In Augustine's *Confessions* one is struck by how, as he tells the story of his conversion, he repeatedly addresses God directly so that his story becomes prayer. We find a similar phenomenon here and see it especially in verse 10 in which the person addresses YHWH directly. Deuteronomy 26.1–11 thus provides us with a luminous example of the role of story in our understanding of ourselves, the world and how to act. Alas, these are not aspects that commentators typically attend to.[4]

Alasdair MacIntyre's work has been seminal in foregrounding the centrality of narrative and story in human life. MacIntyre is a philosopher and ethicist, and he says this of the question 'How am I to act?'

> the key question for [human beings] is not about their own authorship; I can only answer the question 'What am I to do?' if I can answer the prior question 'Of what story or stories do I find myself a part?'[5]

To act consciously is to act with an understanding of the world, and such an understanding is narratival. Mark Wallace notes that, for Paul Ricoeur, another leading philosopher of narrative:

> Everyone needs a story to live by in order to make sense of the pastiche of one's life. Without a narrative a person's life is merely a random sequence of unrelated events: birth and death are inscrutable, temporality is a terror and a burden, and suffering and loss remain mute and unintelligible.[6]

Similarly, the twentieth-century missiologist Lesslie Newbigin remarks that all of human life is shaped by some story: 'The way we understand human

---

4   Gerhard von Rad (1966) is well known for his attention to the Credos in the OT, including the one in Deut. 26.1–11. His argument that Sinai and the giving of the law are not mentioned in this passage seems to me a false trail. Deuteronomy as a whole is premised on the giving of the law at Sinai, of which this law is an example, so that one is entirely justified in assuming the giving of the law at Sinai in the narrative recital.

5   MacIntyre 2007, 216.

6   Wallace 1995, 11.

life depends on what conception we have of the human story. What is the real story of which my life story is a part?'[7]

# 2 Stories and narrative

MacIntyre has focused in particular on the role of narrative in human life and we will focus on him in this respect. Ricoeur has done particularly important work on the narrative–literature relationship and thus we will attend below to him in this regard.

MacIntyre points out that there are two major obstacles to viewing human life as a whole. First, there is the social problem: modernity divides up each life into parts, each one of which has its own styles of behaviour and norms.

> And all these separations have been achieved so that it is the distinctiveness of each and not the unity of the life of the individual who passes through those parts in terms of which we are taught to think and to feel.[8]

Second, there is the philosophical problem: analytic philosophers tend to think atomistically about human behaviour. The way in which actions derive their nature from the context of our lives as a whole is alien to modern thinking. A life is more than a series of episodes and sequences. Sharp separations between the individual and the roles he or she plays occlude life as a unity, and not least, one suspects, among OT scholars.

MacIntyre has developed a virtue ethic, and any assessment of virtues wants to know how a virtue appears in a variety of situations. Thus, 'the unity of a virtue in someone's life is intelligible only as a characteristic of a unitary life, a life that can be conceived and evaluated as a whole'.[9] This concern with virtues and the unity of a human life backs MacIntyre into our view of what it means to be a self:

> it has become necessary to say something of the concomitant concept of selfhood, a concept of a self whose unity resides in *the unity of a narrative* which links birth to life to death as narrative beginning to middle to end.[10]

---

7  Newbigin 1989, 15.
8  MacIntyre 2007, 204.
9  MacIntyre 2007, 205.
10  MacIntyre 2007, 205. Emphasis added.

When we attempt to evaluate and characterize human behaviour, '[w]e cannot, that is to say, characterize behavior independently of intentions, and we cannot characterize intentions independently of the settings which make those intentions intelligible both to agents themselves and to others'.[11] Narrative is a synonym for such settings so that some kind of narrative history becomes essential to understand human action.

The same is true for speech, according to MacIntyre. In this respect he turns to *conversation* and explores what is involved in understanding what is going on if he is standing waiting for a bus and the young man standing next to him suddenly says, 'The name of the common wild duck is *Histrionicus histrionicus histrionicus*.'[12] Only within a narrative can we make sense of this statement. 'The most familiar type of context in and by reference to which speech-acts and purposes are rendered intelligible is the conversation.'[13] MacIntyre states:

> I am presenting both conversations in particular then and human actions in general as enacted narratives. Narrative is not the work of poets, dramatists and novelists reflecting upon events which had no narrative order before one was imposed by the singer or the writer; narrative form is neither disguise nor decoration. Barbara Hardy has written that 'we dream in narrative, day-dream in narrative, remember, anticipate, hope, despair, believe, doubt, plan, revise, criticize, construct, gossip, learn, hate and love by narrative' in arguing the same point.[14]

MacIntyre thus turns to narrative from a variety of directions: from how to act, from how to understand the actions of others, from virtue and from conversation and speech. He notes therefore that:

> A central thesis then begins to emerge: man is in his actions and practice, as well as in his fictions, essentially a story-telling animal. He is not essentially, but becomes through his history,[15] a teller of stories that aspire to truth.[16]

---

11   MacIntyre 2007, 206.

12   MacIntyre 2007, 210.

13   MacIntyre 2007, 210.

14   MacIntyre 2007, 211.

15   The self as becoming is a central theme in Kierkegaard. See Bartholomew and Swart, eds, 2021.

16   MacIntyre 2007, 216.

If we humans tell stories and enact them, then to some extent we are also authors of our stories and can therefore be held responsible for them. However, this is only in a limited way:

> we are never more (and sometimes less) than the co-authors of our own narratives. Only in fantasy do we live what story we please. In life, as both Aristotle and Engels noted, we are always under certain constraints. We enter upon a stage which we did not design and we find ourselves part of an action that was not of our making.[17]

The self finds its identity through participation in communities such as the family, the local neighbourhood, the church, the village, the town, the city and the nation. This does not mean that the self is locked in to such identities, but they provide the base narrative from which to begin. Apart from some particular moral orientation there would be nowhere to begin. The search for the good develops from such particularity. However, we never ultimately escape from particularity. Escape into a realm of universal maxims is a modern illusion. Thus, '[t]he narrative of any one life is part of an interlocking set of narratives'.[18]

Narrative is indispensable in giving an account not only of the self but also of any society, including our own: 'there is no way to give us an understanding of any society, including our own, except through the stock of stories which constitute its initial dramatic resources. Mythology, in its original sense, is at the heart of things.'[19] As we seek to understand the OT and Ancient Israel in its ANE context, narrative thus becomes an indispensable tool for excavating the different ways in which Israel and the surrounding nations understood themselves; in turn, this enables us to compare and contrast such self-understandings in relation to Israel and the OT.

# 3 Traditions

MacIntyre connects his narratival understanding of the self and its unavoidable relationship to community with *tradition*: 'I find myself part of a history and that is generally to say, whether I like it or not, whether I recognize it

---

17 MacIntyre 2007, 213.
18 MacIntyre 2007, 218.
19 MacIntyre 2007, 216.

or not, one of the bearers of a tradition.'[20] Tradition and narrative are thus deeply intertwined, and narrative not only illumines how we act but also how we think. For MacIntyre, living traditions include a history of conflict and disagreement: 'A living tradition then is an historically extended, socially embodied argument, and an argument precisely in part about the goods which constitute that tradition.'[21] However, just as traditions can flourish, they can also decay and disintegrate. What causes a tradition to decay?

> Lack of justice, lack of truthfulness, lack of courage, lack of the relevant intellectual virtues – these corrupt traditions, just as they do those institutions and practices which derive their life from the traditions of which they are the contemporary embodiments.[22]

## 4 Traditions and paradigms

Clearly, what MacIntyre calls a tradition is related to Kuhn's notion of paradigms, discussed above. Indeed, MacIntyre engages directly with Kuhn. According to MacIntyre, an *epistemological crisis* develops when a gap opens up between 'seems' and 'is' and the relation between the two starts to break down. To share a culture involves sharing a tradition/s: 'It is to share schemata which are at one and the same time constitutive of and normative for intelligible action by myself and are also means for my interpretations of the actions of others.'[23] MacIntyre notes that '[p]hilosophers have often been prepared to acknowledge this historical character in respect of scientific theories; but they have usually wanted to exempt their own thinking from the same historicity'.[24]

However, one can become aware of alternative and rival schemata, leading to an epistemological crisis. For MacIntyre, rather than this generating a revolution, an epistemological crisis is resolved by constructing a new narrative in the context of which the criteria of truth and understanding are reformulated. Thus, real progress is possible, but, asks MacIntyre, from where does one begin and what are the narratives from which we set out? Following Bruno Bettelheim, MacIntyre looks at human development and argues that we

---

20  MacIntyre 2007, 221.
21  MacIntyre 2007, 222.
22  MacIntyre 2007, 223.
23  MacIntyre 1997, 139.
24  MacIntyre 1997, 141.

begin with myth, with the fairy tales with which the child engages. Through such stories children learn how to engage with and discern order amid social reality.[25] With time, children mature from myth to an adult account of reality, one which may eschew narrative – as is the case with so many moderns – or one which embraces narrative along the lines of the philosophers Vico and Hamann. As MacIntyre remarks: 'Philosophy is now set the same task that had once been set for myth.'[26]

In much modern – and postmodern – philosophy, narrative has not fared well. Why, asks MacIntyre, do philosophers from Descartes onwards place so little importance on narrative? We might ask the same question about modern OT and ANE studies. According to MacIntyre, René Descartes radically misdescribes his notorious crisis in which he found himself doubting everything. He presents his experiment with doubt as if his doubt lacks any background, as contextless doubt, but this is simply not the case. If he really knew nothing then he would not know how to start on a path of radical doubt. However, as is so often the case with modern thinkers, his tradition goes unrecognized. As Gilson has pointed out, Descartes's language is tradition-laden and his sentences and phrases often come from his school textbooks. He works with a view of knowledge as analogous to vision while simultaneously setting knowledge against sense-experience.

The idea that scholarship – and remember we are thinking of OT scholarship in particular – always operates out of a tradition is a penetrating insight and one we do well to ponder. Descartes was one of the major philosophers at the outset of modernity, and his rationalism was hugely influential and continues to resonate today. Seeing his rationalism within the larger context of the tradition within which he thought goes a long way to helping us understand it more fully and evaluate it more precisely. Exactly the same is true of OT study. As with Descartes, much modern OT study is presented as contextless, as untraditioned, the implication being that it is simply neutral, objective, scientific study of the OT, but this is simply not the case. In order to understand the different approaches in OT studies and to evaluate them properly, a sense of the traditions within which they are operating is essential.

Not least because of the extent to which scholarly traditions in OT studies go unacknowledged, the reader might wonder if the above is really the case. Let me therefore provide an example by looking at some comments made

---

25  Bettelheim 1976, 74–5.
26  MacIntyre 1997, 143.

by one of the fathers of modern OT study, namely Julius Wellhausen (1844–1918), who, among many other things, articulated and established the JEDP theory of Pentateuchal sources. Wellhausen's response to David Friedrich Strauss's notorious *The Life of Jesus, Critically Examined*, in which Strauss argues that the miraculous in the NT is myth, is revealing with respect to philosophical influence on biblical study or, in MacIntyre's language, the extent to which such study operates in a tradition. Wellhausen wrote:

> Because Strauss showed and acknowledged himself to be a child of Hegel in his concept of myth, his book was judged simply as an extension of so-called Hegelianism. Biblical criticism, however, did not in general develop under the influence of philosophical ideas ... Philosophy does not precede, but follows [biblical criticism], in that it seeks to evaluate and to systematise that which it has not itself produced. The authors – who were friends – of the two great theological works of 1835 [Strauss's *Life of Jesus* and Vatke's *Biblical Theology*] were certainly Hegelian. But that which is of scholarly significance in them does not come from Hegel. As Vatke is the disciple of, and the one who brings to completion the work of, de Wette, so Strauss completes the work of the old rationalists. The true value of the *Life of Jesus* lies not in the philosophical introduction and concluding section, but in the main part which in terms of its extent exceeds the others by far.[27]

In my opinion, *contra* Wellhausen, it is greatly to Strauss's and Vatke's credit that they acknowledge the traditions out of which they think about the Bible. This enables us to evaluate their work with the whole picture in view. But note Wellhausen's critical move at this point. Biblical criticism – of the sort practised by Wellhausen and his contemporaries – and that which is of value in Strauss's and Vatke's work is *not* traditioned, not informed by philosophical ideas. It is important that we not let words such as 'philosophical ideas' obscure what is going on here. Philosophy deals with the big issues, including the nature of reality (ontology), how we know (epistemology) and what it means to be human (anthropology), as well as topics such as the nature of religion (philosophy of religion). Taking into account what philosophical ideas deal with, it is absurd to think that biblical criticism is untraditioned; it always operates out of some view of the world, out of some epistemology, out of some view of what it means to be human and out of some view of religion. Strauss and Vatke

---

27    Quoted in Perlitt 1965, 204.

were well aware of this, but, like Seerveld's devil referred to above, Wellhausen erases the tracks of the tradition/s out of which modern biblical criticism emerged, wanting us to think that it is just neutral, objective, scientific scholarship. This view continues to be perpetuated today, as is seen, for example, in the common view that a religiously informed reading of the OT is certainly traditioned, but mainstream, post-Enlightenment readings of the OT are not. In this way, like Descartes, Wellhausen occludes the tradition within which he is working and presents his scholarship as neutral, objective and scientific. If we are to work out what to do with the OT today, we need to see this occlusion and resist it. Only then will we be in a position to evaluate Wellhausen and modern OT criticism fully, appropriating the insights and discarding the baggage.

MacIntyre attends to a crisis in a tradition but approaches it very differently from Kuhn. He argues: 'The criterion of a successful theory is that it enables us to understand its predecessors in a newly intelligible way . . . It recasts the narrative which constitutes the continuous reconstruction of the scientific tradition.'[28] In this way, far from a new form of the tradition being incommensurate with the previous form, the new one enables us to understand the old one *better*. MacIntyre differs from Kuhn also in seeing conflict as inherent in traditions. Indeed, for MacIntyre, a conflict of interpretations is at the heart of a tradition.[29] It is only a degenerate tradition that defends itself from being put into question by rival traditions. Among other examples, MacIntyre lists liberal Protestantism as an example in this respect. He says:

> Notice that all three kinds of tradition – religious, political, intellectual – involve epistemological debate as a necessary feature of their conflicts. For it is not merely that different participants in a tradition disagree; they also disagree as to how to characterize their disagreements and as to how to resolve them. They disagree as to what constitutes appropriate reasoning, decisive evidence, conclusive proof.[30]

For MacIntyre, a tradition embodies the narrative of an argument, and when a tradition decays and breaks down it is only recovered by an argumentative retelling of the narrative inherent in the tradition. According to MacIntyre, reason

---

28  MacIntyre 1997, 146.

29  MacIntyre 1997, 146.

30  MacIntyre 1997, 146.

always operates within a tradition; traditions simply are the bearers of reason.[31] To put a tradition into question requires a tradition from which one can do so.

MacIntyre agrees with Kuhn in subordinating scientific to historical reason. He argues that, although not referenced, Kuhn is dependent on Polanyi, and Kuhn, like Polanyi and like Burke, sees paradigms or traditions as inherently conservative. They fail to see the omnipresence of conflict in living traditions, and thus are unable to explain the transition from one tradition to another. For Kuhn, and this is where MacIntyre thinks he goes wrong, every relevant area of rationality is affected by disagreement. For MacIntyre, this is a misdirected Cartesian view of rationality. It is when the link between narrative and tradition, and theory and method, is lost sight of that philosophy of science encounters insoluble problems.

MacIntyre identifies two ways in which we transition from one tradition to another. First, generally others have already made this journey and so we can learn from and follow them in this respect. If the old paradigm has lapsed into incoherence then a new narrative must be constructed which provides a new way of understanding the subject domain as well as explaining what went wrong with the previous paradigm. 'To evaluate a theory, just as to evaluate a series of theories . . . is precisely to write that history, that narrative of defeats and victories.'[32] This means that we can indeed compare theories and have rational dialogue between them:

> the best account that can be given of why some scientific theories are superior to others presupposed the possibility of constructing an intelligible dramatic narrative which can claim historical truth and in which such theories are the subject of successive episodes.[33]

## 5 Conclusion: Narrative, tradition and Old Testament studies

Our attention to MacIntyre's work on narrative reveals that his argument and narrative as a topic are *complex*. Humans enact in their lives a narrative; their lives can only be understood within a narrative; how to act is determined by the narrative one sees oneself as part of; a person's narrative is individual but

---

31    MacIntyre 1997, 147.

32    MacIntyre 1997, 154.

33    MacIntyre 1997, 156.

inherently communal; traditions are constituted of narratives and all reasoning takes place within a tradition; and so on. Amid the immense amount going on in MacIntyre's account, how can this help us with our project? In my view, an account of narrative such as that of MacIntyre illumines:

- the *work* of OT scholarship;
- the *world* studied by OT scholarship.

## (a) The work of Old Testament studies

As MacIntyre points out, especially since Descartes there has been a sustained attempt in modernity to see scientific scholarship as untraditioned. This has a real parallel in modern OT studies. We saw how Wellhausen sought to deny the role of philosophy *preceding* or informing OT analysis; it could follow on from the results of OT studies but not inform them. We find a similar view in James Barr's comments and in John Barton's argument that theology must be excluded from biblical criticism; it can follow but cannot inform exegesis. The illusion this creates is that historical criticism of the OT as it has been practised is untraditioned. When some believing scholars insist on bringing their religious convictions into OT studies, this is then seen as ideological and unhelpfully traditioned.

However, MacIntyre helps us to see that *all scholarship is traditioned.* Post-Enlightenment OT scholarship of Wellhausen's sort is as traditioned as postmodern readings of the OT. To allude to another of MacIntyre's works, the question for OT scholars becomes not whether to work in a tradition or not, but rather *Whose Tradition? Which Rationality?*[34] MacIntyre argues that a tradition which resists questions is in decay. Of course, as long as OT scholars thought they were not traditioned, it is somewhat understandable that they would resist questions about the particular paradigm within which they worked. However, now that such a view has been exposed as an illusion, we should expect OT scholars to become aware of the tradition within which they work, to be willing to open it to scrutiny, and to acknowledge that alternative traditions are at work within OT studies. This would create the space for a healthy plurality in OT studies, allow different traditions to come to full expression within the discipline, and so allow for real dialogue to take place so that we can assess which tradition makes best sense of the data of the OT.

MacIntyre is right, in my view, that as with Kuhn, historical analysis of the different traditions in a discipline is logically prior to scientific criticism.

---

34   MacIntyre 1988.

This means, for example, that all OT scholars would benefit enormously from attending to *how to tell the story of OT studies*, as this will indirectly but clearly reveal a great deal about the particular paradigm/s they inhabit, as well as alternative traditions in the history of OT studies. It will be through such tellings of the story of OT studies that we will be able to understand different scholars' understandings of the world and of the OT. In other words, having scholars tell their story of the history of OT studies will bring their own traditions to the fore since their traditions will manifest themselves in the way they tell the story, thereby enabling those traditions to be scrutinized.

MacIntyre's approach also resonates with a critical realist approach in that it holds out hope that scholars from different traditions in OT studies can and should communicate with one another and that we should not settle too quickly for the view that different traditions are simply incommensurate. Indeed, MacIntyre suggests that argument and contestation are normal parts of a living, healthy tradition, and that a new or better paradigm needs to be able to account for the strengths and weaknesses in alternative paradigms. Amid such cross-tradition talk, I find MacIntyre's explication of the virtues of a healthy tradition particularly helpful. While doing my PhD, I worked on literary theory and attended literature conferences which were often parades of postmodern theory. Surrounded by the wild pluralism of postmodernism, it was tempting to give up altogether on the goal of truth in one's scholarship. Sertillanges, *The Intellectual Life*,[35] helped me to recover the aspiration towards truth as a central virtue in my work, and aiming for the truth about the OT seems to me an indispensable virtue in OT studies.

## (b) The world studied by Old Testament studies

Whereas the Enlightenment tradition with its disregard for narrative widens the gap between ANE societies and our own, narrative helps to close that gap while allowing real difference to come to the fore. ANE cultures are full of stories, and it will be apparent just how relevant is MacIntyre's statement to our project when he says that 'there is no way to give us an understanding of any society, including our own, except through the stock of stories which constitute its initial dramatic resources. Mythology, in its original sense, is at the heart of things.'[36] Narrative becomes a vital way into an understanding of ANE societies, including Israel and the OT, as well as that of our own societies which also possess their own stock of stories whereby we navigate our ways in

---

35  Sertillanges 1960.

36  MacIntyre 2007, 216.

the world. ANE myth thus becomes of major interest and potential insight, as does an analysis of what Israel does with ANE myth.

The OT cannot be reduced to narrative, but it is extraordinary and noteworthy just how much of the OT has a narrative shape to it. As is well known, Genesis to Kings has a narrative shape to it as a whole, traversing the journey from creation to exile. Chronicles traverses a similar journey. Apart from Jonah, most prophetic books have far less of a narrative shape, but they are always embedded at the outset in the narrative history of Israel. And a surprising development in recent decades in the study of the Psalter and Proverbs is that these books are not random collections but appear to be designed to have something of a narrative shape. The Psalter, for example, seems to be deliberately arranged in five books to mirror the five books of the Pentateuch, suggesting that the Psalter will instruct us in how to respond to God's involvement with Israel and how to live as his people. Psalms 1 and 2 (God's *torah* and the individual, and God's *torah* and the nations) are contained within an inclusio – 'Blessed' – indicating they are the introduction to the Psalter as a whole. The 'kingship of YHWH' psalms in Book IV appear to be the centre and answer to the problems exposed in the Psalms, and 145–150 are a growing, resounding, concluding staircase of praise. Similarly, Proverbs moves from its introduction, via the ABCs of wisdom in Proverbs 1—9, via sections in which wisdom is far more nuanced, to a crescendo in the image of the valiant woman in Proverbs 31, an extraordinary picture of wisdom in real life.

In these and many other ways – not least the hundreds of smaller stories within the larger story of the OT – narrative is central to the OT and offers an important way in which to explore it, both in its ANE content and in how it might relate to contemporary culture.

# 6 Narrative, literature and reading

## (a) Introduction

Sometimes the things that we take for granted reward fresh scrutiny. Reading (the OT) is one such thing. Within the regnant paradigm of historical criticism in OT studies, reading is easily reduced to the application of critical methodologies, and much the same can be said of the smorgasbord of postmodern approaches. What has receded, one might say, is close *reading* of the OT text/s as a text/s. And, of course, if much of the OT has a narrative shape, then reading the OT will include close attention to it as narrative.

# (b) What is a text and what do we do when we read one?

N. T. Wright notes that:

> Protests . . . against the postmodern readings of the Bible are likely to be
> ineffectual. Unless, that is, those who care about serious reading of [the
> Old Testament] set about exploring ways in which to articulate a better
> epistemology, leading to a better account of what happens when a sacred
> text is being read, a better account of what happened when a sacred text
> which purports to be historical is being read, leading to a better account
> of what happens when [the Old Testament is] being read. Any philosoph-
> ically minded literary critics looking for a worthwhile life's work might
> like to consider this as a possible project.[37]

According to Wright, we need a critically realist account of reading.

I need therefore to make no apologies about entering into some of these
areas that Wright calls us to attend to. We read (OT) *texts*, and thus, in order to begin to grasp what is going on in reading, we need to pose the question 'What is a text?' At this stage we are approaching the subject *etically*,
that is, from our own, twenty-first-century perspective. In later sections and
in subsequent volumes we will need to ask *emically*, that is, from inside the
perspectives of the ANE world views, if our approach fits with the ANE and
Ancient Israel.

Paul Ricoeur, one of the major theorists of literature and narrative in recent
decades, suggests the following as a preliminary definition of a text: 'a text is
any discourse fixed by writing'.[38] But is 'discourse' a synonym for 'speech'? Is
a discourse simply speech fixed in writing? Ricoeur's answer is 'no'. He does
not deny the sociological and psychological priority of speech over writing,
but nevertheless argues that we go astray if we think of a text simply as *speech
fixed in writing*.

Ricoeur compares the speech event with the writing event and argues that
fixing a discourse in writing occupies the place of speech so that 'a text is really a text only when it is not restricted to transcribing an anterior speech, when
instead it inscribes directly in written letters what the discourse means'.[39] For
Ricoeur, this 'occupation' of the place of speech is confirmed by the *reader's*

---

37  Wright 1992, 61. Text adjusted to refer to the OT, whereas Wright refers to 'the gospels'.
38  Ricoeur 1991, 2007, 106.
39  Ricoeur 1991, 2007, 106.

*relationship to writing.* The reader occupies the place of the interlocutor, but there is no direct dialogue as in a speech event. Ricoeur overstates the case in my view, but his point is nevertheless clear: 'the book divides the act of writing and the act of reading into two sides, between which there is no communication.'[40] This does not, however, mean that Ricoeur dispenses with authorial intention. He asserts that 'what comes to writing is discourse as intention-to-say and that writing is a direct inscription of this intention'.[41]

Writing maintains discourse and makes it available individually and collectively for memory, but there is more to a text than this. In speech the referent – that about which one speaks – is immediately available via the context, whereas with a text, reference via the immediate context is intercepted. This interception is important, not least because it creates the space for the quasi-world of texts or literature and their interrelationships. With the writing of a text the nearness of the speaker to his or her own speech is replaced by a far more complex relation of the author to the text. For Ricoeur, the task of reading is to fulfil the reference of the text.

In dialogue with Dilthey, Ricoeur explores the relationship between the *explanation* of a text and the *interpretation* of one. Ricoeur argues for an approach which holds the two closely together. Explanation attends to the structural dimensions of the text. It takes its approach not from the natural sciences but from linguistics and attends to the structural features of a text as analogues of language in discourse: to elements of the text such as actants, actions and narration. As such, explanation remains within the text as text and within the suspense of the text that awaits its fulfilment in reading. 'The narrative remains to be assembled as a whole and put back into narrative communication. It is then a narrative that a narrator addresses to an audience.'[42] Explanation and interpretation thus get at two ways of reading. The second one – reading as interpretation – is the real aim of reading. 'Reading is like the execution of a musical score; it marks the realization, the enactment, of the semantic possibilities of the text.'[43] Reading fulfils the discourse of the text in a way similar to that of speech. Indeed, the text as writing awaits and calls for a reading. 'If reading is possible, it is indeed because the text is not closed in on itself but opens out onto other things.'[44]

---

40  Ricoeur 1991, 2007, 107.
41  Ricoeur 1991, 2007, 107.
42  Ricoeur 1991, 2007, 117.
43  Ricoeur 1991, 2007, 119.
44  Ricoeur 1991, 2007, 118.

Reading involves appropriation, enhancing self-understanding. Reading involves a struggle against cultural distance to make one's own what was alien to oneself. However, for Ricoeur, explanation and interpretation are porous to one another, which he demonstrates through an examination of Levi-Strauss on myth. Thus, Ricoeur places appropriation of the text at the outer limit of the hermeneutic arc, lest it be seen as simply imposing the reader's meaning on to the text. For Ricoeur, 'the intended meaning of the text is not essentially the presumed intention of the author, the lived experience of the writer, but rather what the text means for whoever *complies with its injunction*'.[45] Indeed, 'for the exegete, to interpret is to place [oneself] in the meaning indicated by the relation of interpretation that the text itself supports'.[46] The result is that '[w]hat the interpreter says is a resaying that reactivates what is said by the text'.[47]

## (c) Moving forward

Wright is correct, in my view, to call for close attention to epistemology and reading, not least in relation to the OT, with which our project is concerned. In my view, Ricoeur, George Steiner and others provide excellent resources which approximate such a critical realist perspective on texts and reading. Acknowledging the complexity of the discussion of Ricoeur above, how does Ricoeur help us in this respect?

(i) He alerts us to *the difference between a speech event and a* text-*ual event*. This enables us to avoid the naive realism of thinking that reading – not least OT texts – is as straightforward as a conversation with my neighbour. In terms of our communicative hermeneutic above, this means that reading, not least the OT, cannot be simply conceived of as *direct* communication between author and reader. However, as noted above, I think Ricoeur overstates his case when he says that there is 'no communication' between the act of writing and the act of reading. A text is inherently communicative, but Ricoeur is right that its manner of communication is different from that of a speech event.

(ii) Ricoeur enables us to retain a nuanced view of *authorial intention*. He helpfully steers us away from Schleiermacher's view that our aim in interpretation is to know the mind of the author better than the author knows it, but without landing us among postmodern notions of the death or complete irrelevance of

---

45  Ricoeur 1991, 2007, 121. Emphasis added.

46  Ricoeur 1991, 2007, 122.

47  Ricoeur 1991, 2007, 124.

the author. As we will explain below, a variety of scholars, including Ricoeur, have proposed nuanced views of authorial intention that avoid the positivist error of reading for information about the author while focusing attention on reading for what the text and thus the author/s actually says.

(iii) In a way that is similar to critical realism, Ricoeur helps us to respect the integrity and autonomy of the text while also taking into account the reader's role in bringing the text to fulfilment. Explanation of the text involves attention to the building blocks of the text, building blocks which are objectively present in the text. Interpretation – closing the cultural distance between oneself and the text and making the text one's own – follows on from explanation with appropriation at the outer end of the hermeneutical arc. The goal of reading remains a resaying of what is said by the text.

In this way, Ricoeur enables us to avoid common errors in reading the OT. Believers read the OT for God's address but often naively ignore the building blocks of the text – what Ricoeur calls 'explanation' – in the process. On the left and the right scholars, by contrast, often fail to arrive in the arc of their analysis at 'interpretation', namely making what the text is about their own. Some Evangelical OT commentaries, for example, contain much helpful discussion about the people, events and places referred to in OT texts, but fail to attend to the fact that OT historical narratives are written for people living after such events and it is the message for later generations that the text is about. I remind the reader of Sanders' perceptive analysis of the unprecedentedly powerful communicative nature of the OT. Any reading which does not end up wrestling with this is surely woefully incomplete.

## (d) A hermeneutic of love

Wright provocatively and helpfully proposes that we need a hermeneutic of love or what we might call an 'agapic' hermeneutic. At least in parts of the NT, *agapē* refers to a type of love that affirms the other, sees the other for what he/she is without reducing the other to oneself. The otherness of the other is retained even as one's subjectivity is fully engaged. 'In the fact of love, in short, both parties are simultaneously affirmed.'[48] Comparably, Moi argues for reading as a practice of acknowledgement. 'Acknowledgement requires attention, which Iris Murdoch defines as a "just and loving gaze."[49]

---

48  Wright 1992, 64.

49  Moi 2017, 6. Moi draws on the later Wittgenstein to develop an 'ordinary language' approach to reading, which we will return to in the conclusion of the following section.

What might this mean for hermeneutics? In my view, George Steiner and Jean-Louis Chrétien are exceedingly helpful in this respect.

## Language undergirded by real presences: George Steiner's *courteous hermeneutic*

Steiner connects directly with Wright's call for a hermeneutic of love in his definition of true criticism and reading as a 'debt of love'. By contrast, he notes that he has 'felt our age and climate to be one of *invidia*, of the sneer'.[50] Steiner explores in detail what has gone wrong with reading in our time, and we will explore his analysis of this as well as his proposal for a courteous hermeneutic.

### What has gone wrong? Our 'secondary city'

Language is at the heart of George Steiner's wide-ranging work,[51] and he has insisted on exploring the transcendent roots of views of language and the humanities. In *After Babel* and *Real Presences* Steiner articulates an expressivist view of language, one that is indebted to Heidegger but develops in a very different direction from those of Derrida and other postmoderns who also draw on Heidegger.[52] The title *Real Presences*, with its allusion to the Eucharist, indicates Catholic influence, mediated to an extent by Heidegger, but Steiner's theological commitments also separate him from Heidegger.

*Real Presences* is a remarkable book in which Steiner approaches – enters? – the portals of theology in order to address the current state of literature. Steiner argues that a 'secondary city' of endless critical theoretical engagement turned in on itself has developed which prevents us engaging with the major literary works themselves. As one of my readers noted, it is worth emphasizing this point because it resonates with so much of what we experience in OT studies today, namely, endless applications of different methods to the OT but rarely in the service of that goal of interpretation to which Ricoeur refers.

Steiner's diagnosis is that we have lost a sense of the transcendent and that if we wish to re-engage with the great works of literature we need an understanding of the real presences they embody as undergirded by divine presence. Rightly understood, hermeneutics is 'the enactment of answerable

---

50    Steiner 1994, 276.

51    · Steiner 1994, 281. As Krupnick (1994, 46) says: 'His single great theme has been the status of language and the humanities in the wake of the political bestiality of our century.'

52    Steiner (1994, 277) confesses that he is 'utterly persuaded by Heidegger's finding that we are guests of Being, transient dwellers in a temporality and "throwness" entirely beyond our grasp, and that this condition makes of us the custodians of language and of certain values and astonishments in the face of life itself'.

understanding, of active apprehension'.[53] Steiner identifies theological reasons for our strange preference for the secondary, in our case for method and all sorts of analysis rather than actual reading and listening. We shy away from confronting the real presence or the absence of that presence. In the context of our secondary city, we embrace the one who can secularize the mystery, real presence and the call of creation![54] Steiner argues that theory is valuable but always reductive, and is best understood as narratives of moments of illumination in interpreting texts.[55] The obsession with theory in our secondary city is impatience systematized, an impatience that has taken on nihilistic urgency.

Steiner's analysis of how we have reached this point is fascinating. For most of history it was understood that there was a covenant between word and world so that being is sayable, that is, the nature of the world and of texts such as the OT can be adequately expressed in language. However, in our time of the 'after-Word', that covenant has been smashed, and the consequences are serious. Steiner tracks the breaking of this covenant to the period from the 1870s to the 1930s. '*It is this break of the covenant between word and world which constitutes one of the very few genuine revolutions in spirit in Western history and which defines modernity itself.*'[56]

For Steiner, once the covenant between word and world was broken, something like Derrida's deconstruction had to appear. Arguments can be made against deconstruction, but deconstruction lives comfortably with these, and according to Steiner we need to ask what happens if we engage with theology and metaphysics seriously.[57] Steiner

---

53  Steiner 1989, 7. See Steiner 1989, 9, for his emphasis on performance and on ingestion of the text so that it becomes part of the pacemaker of one's consciousness.

54  Steiner 1989, 39.

55  Steiner 1989, 86.

56  Steiner 1989, 93. Emphasis original. Steiner (1989, 96) tracks this momentous development in Mallarmé's view of language as embodying 'real absence' and in Rimbaud's deconstruction of the first-person singular, in his '*Je est un autre*'. Mallarmé rejects the 'covenant of reference', instead arguing that non-reference is the true genius of language. Roland Barthes (1986, 50), author of the notorious 'The Death of the Author', asserts: 'For Mallarmé, as for us, it is language which speaks, not the author; to write is to reach . . . that point where not "I" but only language functions.' 'Where Mallarmé alters the epistemology of "real presence" (theologically grounded) into one of "real absence", Rimbaud posits at the now vacant heart of consciousness the splintered images of other and momentary "selves"' (Steiner 1989, 99). Steiner discerns four great streams of the 'after-Word' that followed: that of Wittgenstein, post-Saussurean linguistics, psychoanalysis (Freud, Lacan) and the indictment of language in *Sprachkritik* (Fritz Mauthner, Karl Kraus). For Steiner, Nietzsche's 'death of God' and Freud's secularization of the psyche are but footnotes to the break in the covenant between word and world signalled by Mallarmé and Rimbaud. The sort of view of language we find articulated in and performed by Derrida must follow: 'In a time of epilogue and after-Word, a critique such as deconstruction *must* be formulated' (Steiner 1989, 120). Emphasis original.

57  Steiner 1989, 134.

chooses not to waste time on polemic: because what Paul Ricoeur calls 'the dismantled fortress of consciousness' is not to be 'restored or made foolproof by replacing this or that fallen brick' . . . He sees with absolute clarity that the most essential repudiation lying at the heart of the whole deconstructive enterprise is a theological repudiation, and thus, as he feels, the one kind of faith (in unfaith) may only be countered by another kind of faith.[58]

A perfectly legitimate question would be: 'Well, what kind of faith does Derrida operate out of?' This is a complex question that merits a long response. Suffice it here to make two points. First, postmodernism and Derrida's thought is as traditioned as other thought. The only concern is: what is its tradition? Second, several scholars have noted an affinity between Derrida's deconstructionism and Gnosticism. Milbank moves in this direction when he states: 'if Derrida can give a gnostic hermeneutic of the human text in the light of the gnostic logos, then we should have the confidence to give a Christian hermeneutic in the light of the real one.'[59]

In Part 3 of *Real Presences*, Steiner sets out his alternative approach. It remains unclear what form Steiner's faith actually took. What is clear is that in response to what Plantinga calls the 'creative anti-realism' of postmodernism, Steiner argues that in order to retrieve a form of realism (*Real* Presences) that will allow us to take with full seriousness the presences (Real *Presences*) we find in great literature, art and in the OT, we need a grammar of creation. Indeed, and quite remarkably, for Steiner, Derrida's nihilism confronts us with a stark choice: either 'In the beginning was the Word' or nihilism! In line with critical realism, for Steiner, a grammar of the world as creation allows us to cut through the secondary city of incestuous criticism, to recover the covenant between word and world, and to entertain the great works of art, literature and the Bible for what they are. What might such 'entertainment' look like in practice?

## A courteous hermeneutic
Steiner uses the metaphor of *courtesy* in order to elaborate on his approach:

the phenomenology of courtesy would organize, that is to say quicken into articulate life, our meetings with each other, with the beloved, with the

---

58   Scott 1994, 4.
59   Milbank 1997, 79.

adversary, with the familiar and the stranger . . . Classically, where branch and leaf are highest, *cortesia* qualifies the last ambush or the final tryst which is the possible venue – the coming, the coming to a place – of God.[60]

We lay a clean cloth on the table when we hear the guest at our threshold. In the paintings of Chardin, in the poems of Trakl, that movement at evening is made both domestic and sacramental.[61]

What we must focus, with uncompromising clarity, on the text, on the work of art, on the music before us, is an ethic of common sense, a courtesy of the most robust and refined sort.[62]

Courtesy of this exquisite sort grants the object of interpretation priority over the reader, thus reversing the misdirection of our secondary city. A courteous hermeneutic means we approach a text initially with *trust*. Our guest may become antagonistic, but to open the door we simply have to gamble on trust.[63] For Steiner, the passage towards meaning inevitably involves attention to context, and, although this is unbounded, it 'does not mean that intelligibility is either wholly arbitrary or self-erasing. Such deduction is nihilistic sophistry.'[64] Indeed, the dialectic of context reminds us of the limits of theory. The historicity and particularity of texts remains important even as we welcome them now. A good reading is never final, but that is quite different from the postmodern alternative of presence or absence.

In art and literature we encounter the other, and Steiner grounds this in the transcendent:

So far as it wagers on meaning, an account of the act of reading, in the fullest sense, of the act of the reception and internalization of significant forms within us, is a metaphysical and, in the last analysis, a theological one. The ascription of beauty to truth and to meaning is either a rhetorical flourish, or it is a piece of theology . . . The meaning of meaning is a transcendent postulate. To read the poem responsibly ('respondingly'), to be answerable to form, is to wager on a reinsurance of sense. It is to wager on a relationship . . .

60   Steiner 1989, 148.
61   Steiner 1989, 149.
62   Steiner 1989, 149.
63   Steiner 1989, 156.
64   Steiner 1989, 163.

between word and world, but on a relationship precisely bounded by that which reinsures it.[65]

Steiner's theological critique of literary and hermeneutical developments is remarkable. The literary turn in OT interpretation in the 1970s onwards brought with it many rich developments, as we have noted. Steiner has not written much on biblical interpretation, but in his review of *The Literary Guide to the Bible*, which was edited by Alter and Kermode and heralded the arrival of literary approaches to all the books of the Bible, he foregrounds with unerring precision the theological weaknesses of some literary approaches to the Bible:

> The question is: Does this 'Literary Guide' help us to come to sensible grips with the singularity and the overwhelming provocations of the Bible – a singularity and a summons altogether independent of the reach of current literary-critical fashions? Does it help us to understand in what ways the Bible and the demands of answerability it puts upon us are like no others? Of this tome . . . a terrible blandness is born . . . We hear of 'omelettes,' of 'pressure cookers,' not of the terror, of the *mysterium tremendum*, that inhabits man's endeavours to speak to and speak of God . . . The separation, made in the name of current rationalism and agnosticism, between a theological-religious experiencing of Biblical texts and a literary one is radically factitious. It cannot work.[66]

Steiner's critique of the *Literary Guide to the Bible* provides a clue as to how interpretation of the OT may differ from the interpretation of other books. Steiner tends to treat all 'great works' as canonical in a similar fashion, but his comments about the peculiar provocations of the Bible point in a different direction. It is surely true that to read the OT without making these provocations a focus is reductionistic. Here, in my view, progress is made towards the approach recommended by Tom Wright – to understand theologically how words work – and how we read text and *sacred* texts such as the OT in particular.

Steiner's courteous hermeneutic is rich and fertile and goes a long way towards helping us to know how to approach the OT. For Steiner, true criticism and reading is a 'debt of love', whereas our age, Steiner feels, is one of '*invidia,*

---

65  Steiner 1989, 216.
66  Steiner 1988, 96–7.

of the sneer'. In Steiner's approach the text is given priority and the reader's first priority is 'answerable understanding'. Texts, we might say, do have rights, and although the right method cannot guarantee the correct reading, if we approach them courteously we can be hopeful that texts will yield their treasures. Steiner rejects the binary opposites of determinacy and indeterminacy, leaving us a rigorous, hopeful and humble hermeneutic.

As with our opening discussion of OT boundaries, it is intriguing once again to see how the theological dimension of the OT comes to the fore. Steiner alerts us to the theological dimension *in* the OT and the theological dimension *and* the OT. In terms of the latter, for Steiner, Derrida's view of interpretation confronts us with either nihilism or 'In the beginning was the Word'. If we are to do justice to the real presences in OT texts, that is, if we are to retain a sense of their otherness, we require a grammar of creation. In terms of the former, a literary approach to the OT which fails to attend to and be informed by God's address is inadequate.

## Chrétien's costly and wounded reading

One of the most exciting developments in philosophy today is that of the new French Catholic phenomenology. Chrétien addresses biblical interpretation in his *Under the Gaze of the Bible*.[67] As with Steiner, Chrétien attends to the personal appropriation of the (biblical) text, in line with Ricoeur. However, Chrétien's is an overtly Christian reading with a focus on the Bible as a sacred text. Just as Ricoeur notes that reading leads to self-understanding, Chrétien asserts that 'to learn to read . . . teaches us also to read ourselves, to decipher ourselves as we decipher, according to a perspective that wasn't ours to begin with'.[68] Chrétien suggests that this image of the text as a mirror probably has its origins in the Bible (James 1.23) and Augustine, before being deployed for literature as a whole.

Chrétien proposes that we approach Scripture *to allow ourselves to be read*. He characterizes such a reading as:

- a costly reading: it requires something of ourselves;
- an exposed reading: it requires vulnerability;
- a wounded reading: it can arrest us and wound us;
- a reading which requires lively patience and active self-discipline that relinquishes our arrogance.

---

67  2015.
68  Chrétien 2015, ix.

Chrétien suggests that we allow Scripture to define the 'today' of reading the Bible today. He appeals to the letter to the Hebrews in this respect, noting his response:

> When I read the Bible this way and receive it as a missive in which my name is traced with the sympathetic ink of grace, the today of my living attention enters the temporal dimension of which this writing itself speaks, that is, the sacred story. As small and narrow as may be the door of my reading, which causes me to enter into that which it speaks of, as insignificant as may be the flame of my today, it is still into the sacred story that I am placed, and to it henceforth that I belong as long as I listen. A French mystic of the eighteenth century said it well: 'The story of all the moments that flow is the sacred story.'[69]

Here Chrétien connects with the narrative shape of the Bible and with the story it tells us as the true story of the world which, following Newbigin, we are called to indwell.

However, Chrétien is clear that this book that addresses us so powerfully – see Sanders above – has not come to us by means of an angel speaking a divine language. This letter to me has arrived via many secretaries, copyists, translators, porters and mail carriers 'who are called Israel and the church'.[70] We cannot and should not dissociate ourselves from this messy history through which the Bible has reached us today:

> The history of the reading, translation, and interpretation of the Sacred Books is itself an integral part of the sacred story, on condition that we not forget that not only saints figure in the sacred story, nor sacred acts, and that it is a perpetual struggle between life and death, word and deafness, justice and injustice – which continues today. This polyphony, here again, is inscribed in the Bible itself, since the Good News, the Gospel, does not reach us only in a single narrative but according to four versions, thus calling by nature for confrontation, comparison, interrogation, interpretation. What is plural calls for the plural in the service of the Unique.[71]

---

69   Chrétien 2015, 2–3.

70   Chrétien 2015, 3.

71   Chrétien 2015, 3–4.

Chrétien's evocative work reminds us that for Jews and Christians the Hebrew Bible / Old Testament is far more than another ANE text, but is, in some way, sacred and special, capable of reading us and bringing us in a unique way to self-awareness. However, as with Ricoeur, such interpretation is not set against explanation, nor should it be.

## (e) Text, authorial intention and a close *reading* of the Old Testament

It is no coincidence that Steiner's courteous hermeneutic is analogous to entertaining a *human* guest. Art and literature are human creations and forms of communication. As such, they merit at least the same respect and courtesy one shows in a human interaction. Of course if we sever the link between humans and art and literature, all this changes, and not for the better.

Although, in my view, postmodernism is in decline, one of its legacies is precisely such a severing, namely the doctrine of the death of the author so that attending to questions such as 'What is the author trying to tell us here?' or 'How does what the author says here relate to what she wrote elsewhere?' is unacceptable. In terms of a communicative hermeneutic there is much at stake here, since intentionality foregrounds what we are after in interpretation, namely the communicative trajectory. Thus, we need to attend to the role of authorial intention in OT interpretation, and to something of the journey from positivism to postmodernism in this respect. The debate about authorial intent emerged as a reaction to positivism in literary theory, with its use of the text to excavate insights regarding the author.

New Criticism (NC) developed in the USA in literary studies as a reaction to positivism. In literary studies the view developed that literary scholarship as a system of knowledge has its own aims and methods, focused on the particular characteristics of literature. Richards located the key to the autonomy of literary studies in the response of the reader, distinguishing between the referential and emotive functions of language. The value of literature is to be found in the latter, its effect on the reader. For Richards, good literature has a jarring, disruptive effect, causing the reader to work to reconcile conflicting values. Richards' lasting contribution to NC was an emphasis on the very close reading of texts. However, it was T. S. Eliot who influenced NC away from affectivity to the objective reality of the poem. The conflict and reconciliation of opposites was not to be located in the mind of the reader but in the poem itself. Complexity – a literary text is often full of tensions – *and* coherence characterize literary texts, and mature works are resistant to quick solutions. In this way, NC shifts the focus of literary study to the literary text itself:

> The natural and sensible starting-point for work in literary scholarship is the interpretation and analysis of the works of literature themselves. After all, only the works themselves justify all our interest in the life of an author, in his social environment and the whole process of literature. But, curiously enough, literary history has been so preoccupied with the setting of a work of literature that its attempts at an analysis of the works themselves have been light in comparison with the enormous efforts expended on the study of the environment.[72]

Criticism from this perspective attends above all else to the text, to its form and structure:

> Only one who will explain without looking to the right or left, above all without inquiring what is before and what is after, only he will fulfil his obligations to the creation, and only he will refrain from undermining the sovereignty of literary study.[73]

Wimsatt's and Beardsley's 'intentional fallacy' and 'affective fallacy' are two of the best-known products of NC.[74] These scholars acknowledge that '[t]he words of a poem ... come out of a head, not out of a hat', but they reject intention as a standard by which to interpret a poem; the intentional solution is a romantic error. We cannot access a poet's intention.[75] Moreover, a literary work is in the public domain and thus not just the private creation of an individual. The author's life and experience are of historical interest but do not and should not determine the meaning of his or her work. What is in the text itself is what counts, and that is available to any reader who is familiar with the language and culture of the text. Thus, the place of authorial intention in literary interpretation is curtailed. The 'affective fallacy' refers to Richards' type of approach; it too is rejected.

---

72 Wellek and Warren 1963, 139.

73 Staiger, quoted by Weiss 1984, 6.

74 See Lodge, ed., 1972, 334–58.

75 Weiss (1984, 13–17) notes that since Socrates the role of intention in interpretation has been disputed. Occasionally, poets themselves have confessed that they did not fully understand their intentions in creating a poem. Weiss suggests that intentionality is intellectual, whereas poetry touches on affective areas neglected by intellect.

In his rich and creative engagement with NC and the HB/OT, Weiss recognizes the New Critics' refusal to allow external, causal factors to control interpretation, but notes that there is a diversity of opinion among New Critics about the role of historical background. Some completely reject it, whereas others reject it as the only method. Wellek and Warren's *Theory of Literature* is a fine example of the latter.[76] About one sixth of *Theory of Literature* deals with the extrinsic approach, compared with two thirds devoted to the intrinsic approach. Clearly, they do not simply reject the extrinsic approach. Even when it comes to intentionality, their position is nuanced. As they say: 'There can be no objections against the study of "intention", if we mean by it merely a study of the integral work of art directed towards the total meaning.'[77]

As we reflect on the OT as literature, it is intriguing to take note of the New Critics' resistance to the paraphrase of a literary work; it can never equate to the work itself. Hence, Brooks' essay 'The Heresy of Paraphrase'.[78] The properties which constitute a work of literature as a unity are dramatic – my preferred term is 'organic' – and not logical, so that the form–content dichotomy often applied to works of literature is invalid. This restricts the value of source criticism:

> That ancient text which gave the push to the artist was at the most some raw material in the hands of the creator but in no sense the source of his creation. This new creation . . . springs completely from the poet's mind and soul. Therefore Knight asserts that the expression 'source' is only a misleading metaphor.[79]

Even if a literary work is constructed from other sources, in its present form it is an integral unity and must be analysed as such. The literary work is always greater than the sum of its sources. Tate notes just how hard critics find it to focus on the literary work itself:

> For some reason critics have a hard time fixing their minds directly under their noses, and before they see the object that is there they use a telescope to scan upon the whole horizon to see where it came from. They are wood

---

76  Wellek and Warren 1963.

77  Wellek and Warren 1963, 149. This approximates to what Sternberg (1985, 9) calls 'embodied intentionality'.

78  In Brooks 1975, 92–214.

79  Weiss 1984, 24.

cutters who do their job by finding out where the ore came from in the iron of the steel of the blade of the axe that Jack built.[80]

Analogously to Steiner's courteous hermeneutic, for New Critics '[t]he true interpretation is the outcome of that fortunate occasion when the interpreter does not subjugate the creation but is subjugated by it'.[81] Close, attentive reading of the text is by far the best key for unlocking the literary text.

Literary criticism has moved on in an immense variety of ways since NC, but NC's method of close reading proved fertile in OT studies and continues, in my opinion, to be of great value. As I have observed, the literary turn in OT studies challenged historical criticism in a whole variety of ways. However, before it could be fully absorbed, the postmodern turn was upon us with its wild pluralism. Now, with postmodernism in decline, there is a danger that we relapse into historical criticism as practised before the literary turn. In my view, we need to return to the literary turn and find helpful ways forward from there. In this respect I find Weiss's approach a wonderfully fruitful resource.

Published in Hebrew in 1962, Weiss's *The Bible from Within* develops a New Critical approach to the HB/OT as the key to resolving the distorting influence of what he calls 'historicism' on HB/OT studies. The general definition that Mandelbaum proposes for historicism fits with Weiss's use:

> Historicism is the belief that an adequate understanding of the nature of anything and an adequate assessment of its value are to be gained by considering it in terms of the place it occupied and the role it played within a process of development.[82]

Weiss's work is particularly interesting since his 1962 version was revised, enlarged and updated for the English edition of 1984.

Weiss coins the expression 'total interpretation' for his method of interpretation of the poetry of the HB/OT.[83] It is 'total' in that it aims to grasp the totality of the literary text through its formal elements. A method must fit with its object, and Weiss argues that the internal method of 'total interpretation' is the appropriate method for interpreting HB/OT poetry.

---

80  Tate 1955, 333.

81  Weiss 1984, 19.

82  Mandelbaum 1967, 24. What Weiss calls 'historicism' is equivalent to what Wellek calls 'positivism'. 'Historicism', even more than 'positivism', is a notoriously slippery word. See Mandelbaum 1967, 24.

83  Weiss 1984, 27.

Akin to Sternberg's approach, Weiss seeks to tease out the balance between historical data and attention to the text itself. Biographical and philological data certainly have their place, but they can only confirm an interpretation and not replace it. Weiss argues that form criticism is too indebted to historicism and uses an outdated understanding of form.[84] The limitations and problems of historical criticism have to be faced; however good its intentions,

> [t]his method seems now to have come to the point where its deficiencies are becoming more obvious than its merit. The keys which have been cut and shaped with such care certainly opened a door; but the door only seems to lead into another room with a door which is locked, and the lock on that door the keys do not fit. And the room we have got into is plainly not the heart of the building, but only another antechamber.[85]

Indeed, according to Weiss, historical criticism as practised is not actually truly historical because of its distorted view of the relationship between literature and history. For Weiss, literature will only yield its secrets if approached *as literature*. A major strength of Weiss's approach is his concern to test it in actual interpretation of the HB/OT. A method, he asserts,

> can only be tested and proved in practice. If the results it produces appear to be *eis*egesis instead of *ex*egesis, then a thorough philological-critical examination of the text should point up the inadequacy and illuminate the source of the error.[86]

As we note above, the proof of the pudding is in the eating!

Weiss's approach appropriates the insights of NC and a close reading of the text but without abandoning historical background and authorial interpretation. A comparable, magisterial approach is that of Meir Sternberg. Sternberg reads the HB/OT very closely as literature but is critical of literary approaches to the HB which treat the text as autonomous, and he discerns the influence of NC here. For Sternberg, seeing narrative technique as part of the text itself means that we have to take the *historical* construction of the text seriously if

---

84 See Weiss 1984, 47–64, for a thorough critique of Gunkel's form-critical approach in relation to Ps. 23.1 .

85 Gardner as quoted by Weiss 1984, 64.

86 Weiss 1984, 73. Emphasis original.

we are to take the functional purpose of biblical narrative seriously.[87] Sternberg similarly examines Wimsatt's and Beardsley's intentional fallacy and concludes that their attack was directed not so much at authorial intention as at speculative dependence on *external* intention. When it comes to the HB/OT, we know virtually nothing about the external intention of authors and thus we have to rely on indications from the text. This focus on *objectified or embodied intention* Sternberg regards as crucial:

> such intention fulfils a crucial role, for communication presupposes a speaker who resorts to certain linguistic and structural tools in order to produce certain effects on the addressee; the discourse accordingly supplies a network of clues to the speaker's intention.[88]

Taking authorial intention seriously in this way means that source criticism and narratology should not be situated in opposition to each other. There is, of course, a large cultural gap between the authors of the HB/OT and us, but that does not mean we should not try to overcome it. 'Once the choice turns out to lie between reconstructing the author's intention and licensing the reader's invention, there is no doubt where most of us stand.'[89] Written as it is in Ancient Hebrew and Aramaic, the historical nature of the HB/OT is unavoidable. However, the nature of the source criticism we employ needs close attention, and Sternberg is critical of much that goes by the name of source criticism. There is a tension between source and discourse, but Sternberg appeals for a partnership between the two; he argues that the two cannot but work together; neither one has the primacy over the other.

It is often assumed that the HB/OT as a religious text is in opposition to the HB/OT as a literary text. For Sternberg, this represents a false antithesis and he notes that in the ancient world highly poetic and literary material was regularly religious and attended to for instruction. 'The question is how rather than whether the literary coexists with the social, the doctrinal, the philosophical.'[90] Representation should not be set in opposition to evaluation, although the extent to which such elements dominate will vary. It is only if the Bible is ideological in an extreme type of didactic that it would be unacceptable to read it seriously as literature. However, 'if biblical narrative is didactic,

---

87  cf. Weiss 1984, 66: 'We would hardly deny that "a poem is at the same time a linguistic document and an historical source".'

88  Sternberg 1985, 9.

89  Sternberg 1985, 10.

90  Sternberg 1985, 35.

then it has chosen the strangest way to go about its business. For the narrator breaks every law in the didacticist's decalogue. Anything like preaching from the narrative pulpit is conspicuous for its absence.'[91] The Bible presents its message by means of narrative, and the two, narrative technique and message, should not be set against each other. Indeed, it is through the poetics of the HB/OT that we gain access to its message.

A vital point Sternberg makes is that the poetics of narrative is by no means confined to literature: 'What determines literariness is not the mere presence but the dominance of the poetic function, the control it exerts over all the rest.'[92] Narrative techniques are as much present in the historical biblical narratives as in fictional texts, and the presence of these techniques does not compromise the texts' historical or ideological–theological nature.

Although their focus is different, Weiss's and Sternberg's work complements each other's, and they land in the same place. Sternberg has focused in particular on the poetics of the HB/OT and, if the proof of the pudding is in the eating when it comes to close reading of the OT, it would be hard to argue that his work has been anything other than spectacular.

# (f) Conclusion

In the wake of postmodernism – which has always been only one among several views, albeit a loud and influential one – we are witnessing a recovery of authorial intention as central to the interpretation of texts.[93] Moi, for example, draws on Stanley Cavell's work and on Wittgenstein to argue for a recovery of intention in literary studies. Moi notes of Elizabeth Anscombe's philosophical work that she understood intentions *retrospectively*, whereas so much discussion of intention begins with the mental act of the author. For Anscombe, the question of intention follows from an action, and Moi asks what happens to intentions if we think of a text as *a kind of action*.[94] She follows Cavell in articulating a view similar to that of Sternberg's embodied intentionality:

> 'Intention,' Cavell writes (in Anscombe's spirit), 'is no more an efficient cause of an object of art than it is of a human action: in both cases it is a way of understanding the thing done, of describing what happens'.[95]

---

91  Sternberg 1985, 37–8.

92  Sternberg 1985, 40.

93  cf. Burke 1992.

94  Moi 2017, 203.

95  Moi 2017, 203.

An advantage of thinking of texts as actions is that this foregrounds the vital issue of responsibility for what is written. 'Intentions matter for the question of responsibility, including political responsibility.'[96] Moi wrote part of her book in Norway in 2011 in the context of Anders Behring Breivik's detonation of a bomb in Oslo and his slaughter of 69 men and women on the small island of Utøya. She notes how this dreadful act challenged Norwegians' view of language. Anders Johansen, a professor of non-fiction, wrote that:

> We no longer immediately dismiss as naïve serious attempts to make words conform to reality. For many of us, it has been crucial to find ways to say something true about what happened, in a language that is accurate both to facts and emotions.[97]

Here we see how political realities push scholars to revisit the covenant between word and world.

Thus, a chastened form of authorial intention is eminently defensible and fits well with our critical realist framework. It confirms that when reading OT texts, our focus should be on their communicative trajectory or embodied intentionality. Our examination of the various forms of reaction to positivism in literary theory alerts us to the vital importance of interpretation, attending above all to the text as we have received it in our interpretation. The turn to the text embodied in NC and other strands of literary theory has been productive in alerting us to the fact that it is the text as we receive it that needs to be the focus of interpretation. An immediate effect of such a focus is to reconfigure how we think about source and form criticism of the OT.

Source criticism is sometimes referred to as literary criticism, but far, far too often the move to an analysis of sources *bypasses* a close reading of the text as a work of literature. This is a major problem – indeed a major error – and in this regard the literary turn in OT studies should have provoked a crisis, but before the literary turn could be fully appropriated the postmodern turn was upon us, so that historical criticism has remained the default mode in mainstream OT studies. Literary texts, we have discovered, are complex and their coherence is often organic rather than logical. OT texts need first to be listened to carefully and rigorously explored as works of literature before it is concluded that they are naively incoherent so that speculative sources can relatively easily be discerned and become the focus of

---

96   Moi 2017, 204.
97   Quoted in Moi 2017, 222.

attention rather than the text as we have received it. As we saw earlier, a remarkable fact of OT literature is the highly developed poetics we find in it. However we account for this, it argues strongly against simplistic readings of OT texts leading quickly to source analysis.

As we have seen, attention to the text itself as a literary entity resists a causal approach to sources. The literary text is always more than a product of its sources and we need a revised account of source criticism, along the lines proposed by Sternberg. Similarly, Weiss has argued that *form criticism*, as developed and practised by Gunkel, stems from the historicist approach to literature and needs revision. For Weiss, Gunkel's misguided view of interpretation comes to full expression in his form criticism as an external approach which interprets texts as historical data rather than as literary works of art. Form criticism bears a superficial resemblance to NC, but its view of form is quite different and is mechanical or abstract. For Gunkel, form criticism is genre criticism, involving attention to the linguistic form, a set of moods and thoughts and a *Sitz im Leben* which determine both content and the form. Weiss argues, however, that no OT genres can be identified by such formal criteria.

Intriguingly, in terms of our earlier discussion of text criticism, Weiss attends to its challenge directly. He asks: is there a text reliable enough for close reading?

> The question recurs, then, even more urgently than before, whether close reading is appropriate for Biblical exegesis. And the answer is emphatically in the affirmative, precisely *because* of the situation we have outlined above. Total Interpretation goes hand in hand with textual criticism; both strive to interpret (and, when necessary, to emend) the text on the basis of *ex*egesis, while assiduously avoiding *eis*egesis. The intensive focus on the text itself – Total Interpretation – is the only reliable guide for textual criticism. M. Greenberg has emphasised this point in slightly different terms: 'To avoid premature text-alteration, *exegesis and text-criticism must proceed together, each illuminating the other. The exegete*, whose task is to interpret the text in hand, *must work on the hypothesis that every element in the text has significance – contributes to the meaning of its context . . .*'[98]

Once we see with Eric Tully that textual criticism operates downstream from redaction criticism, we can see just how helpful is Weiss's perspective, for

---

98  Weiss 1984, 70–1. Emphasis added.

redaction criticism depends on identifying redactional layers in a text but far too often without doing the literary reading of the whole first.

Weiss also asks if we can isolate the whole work, the literary unit. We need to be cautious in this respect, but

> [t]he hermeneutic circle which encompasses every literary interpreter confronts the Biblical critic in the particular matter of determining the limits of the literary unit. And this is the 'circle': on the one hand, close attention to the details of the work (syntactic, stylistic, etc.) in their functional coherence clarifies the whole structure, simultaneously delimiting the unit and assuring its integrity; on the other hand, comprehension of the presumed unit as a whole facilitates the understanding of the meaning and function of the details. The two processes support and sustain each other; each one is both the cause and the effect of the other, and neither takes precedence.[99]

In my view, Weiss's work calls for far more attention than it has received. It enables us to get behind and beyond the wild pluralism of the postmodern turn and to start to explore anew the implications of the literary turn for OT studies and historical criticism. Weiss himself observes that:

> If Biblical scholarship were to embrace Total Interpretation, insisting that one should read what is written in the text, all that is written there, and only what is written there, it would soon become clear that many dearly-held 'higher-critical' theories are mountains suspended by a hair – utterly lacking textual support.[100]

What has also emerged, particularly in relationship to Sternberg, is that we should not pit *literary against historical or theological*. A way in which OT scholars have resisted taking full account of the literary turn is through setting literary approaches as just another one of many different methods for reading the OT, so that we need never enquire how the different methods fit together. However, as we noted above, integrality is a criterion for verifying a reading of the OT, and this must include the interrelationship of the historical, literary and theological in OT texts. An example of the importance of this is found in any treatment of the historical narratives. As Ricoeur, Sternberg, Halpern and others have noted, the same poetics is found in fiction as in historical writings

---

99  Weiss 1984, 71–2.
100  Weiss 1984, 72.

so that the literary nature alone of OT historical narrative does not decide its historicity. The way we distinguish the difference is in terms of *the aims of the author*, another reason why some sense of authorial intention is crucial.

# 7 Literature

Our exploration of authorial intention has already taken us into the field of literature. In this section we will focus on deepening our understanding of how literature works, attending in particular to the work of Paul Ricoeur. Defining literature is not easy, but it does not help to classify all writing as literature. The manual for how to operate my washing machine, for example, would not, in my view, qualify as literature. What then makes literature *literature*? I propose that we think of literature as *written imaginative representation* of aspects of the world. Art in its diverse forms is also representative, but only literature uses the medium of writing for representation.

## (a) Paul Ricoeur

Similarly, Ricoeur reaches for the term 'mimesis', which carries a wide range of meanings, including representation, when he addresses the issue of literature. He attends to the issue of mimesis and literature in his work *Time and Narrative*, especially in volume 2. He explores the way in which narrative is foundational to the world and how humans live in it. For Ricoeur, the semantic innovation in narrative and metaphor originates from the productive imagination with its capacity to schematize. 'The plot of a narrative . . . "grasps together" and integrates into one whole and complete story multiple and scattered events, thereby schematizing the intelligible signification attached to the narrative taken as a whole.'[101]

There is, according to Ricoeur, an 'incipient "configuring" or "emplotting" process that is the experiential foundation of the human capacity to write literature and history'.[102] Ricoeur notes that the 'seeing as' which is the power of metaphor and of narrative could be the revealer of a 'being-as' on the deepest ontological level.[103] Ricoeur's hypothesis is that

between the activity of narrating a story and the temporal character of human experience there exists a correlation that is not merely accidental

---

101  Ricoeur 1984, x.

102  Stiver 1996, 137.

103  Ricoeur 1984, xi.

but that presents a transcultural form of necessity. To put it another way, *time becomes human to the extent that it is articulated through a narrative mode, and narrative attains its full meaning when it becomes a condition of temporal existence.*[104]

Literature and history-writing share a representative or *mimetic* function, and in *Time and Narrative* Ricoeur distinguishes three levels of mimesis. The incipient aspect is identified in level 1. Emplotment is constructed upon this pre-understanding.

**Mimesis 1** alerts us to the fact that the plot of a narrative is rooted and grounded in a pre-understanding of the world, of action, of the world's structures, of its symbolic resources and its temporal nature. For Ricoeur, the plot presupposes *and* transforms this pre-understanding.

> We may sum up this twofold relation between narrative understanding and practical understanding as follows. In passing from the paradigmatic order of action to the syntagmatic order of narrative, the terms of the semantics of action acquire integration and actuality. Actuality, because the terms, which had only a virtual signification in the paradigmatic order, that is, a pure [potential] capacity to be used, receive an actual [*effective*] signification thanks to the sequential interconnections the plot confers on the agents, their deeds, and their sufferings. Integration, because terms as heterogeneous as agents, motives, and circumstances are rendered compatible and work together in actual temporal wholes.[105]

Ricoeur is cautious about whether we can assert that the world itself has a narrative structure. He does assert that action can never be ethically neutral[106] and he recognizes in action temporal structures that 'call for narration'.[107]

> I shall not push my analysis of the temporal elements of action to the point where we could rightfully speak of a narrative structure, or at least of a prenarrative structure of temporal experience, as suggested by our ordinary way of talking about stories.[108]

---

104  Ricoeur 1984, 52. Emphasis original.
105  Ricoeur 1984, 56–7.
106  Ricoeur 1984, 59.
107  Ricoeur 1984, 59.
108  Ricoeur 1984, 59–60. See Ricoeur 1984, 60–4, 85–6.

Ricoeur finds Heidegger's notion of temporality most helpful on this issue: 'Narrative configurations and the most elaborated forms of temporality corresponding to them share the same foundation of within-time-ness.'[109]

**Mimesis 2** opens up the kingdom of the 'as if' and has a mediating function deriving from the dynamic character of the configuring operation of emplotting. Plot mediates in three ways:[110]

1  It draws a diversity of events or incidents into a meaningful, intelligible story so that we can always ask of a story what its 'thought' is.
2  It brings together a variety of factors such as agents, goals, interactions, means, fearful incidents, reversals and so on. Indeed, for Ricoeur, at the heart of plot is 'concordant discordance'.[111]
3  It mediates by its temporal characteristics in both a chronological or episodic sense[112] and by grasping together the incidents into a temporal whole.

Through its mediation between event and story, plot brings to the paradox of temporality, which was foregrounded by Augustine, a solution. Following a story involves moving through the incidents and reversals towards the 'conclusion' of the story. The conclusion provides an 'end point' from which the story can be seen as a whole:

> To understand the story is to understand how and why the successive episodes led to this conclusion, which, far from being foreseeable, must finally be acceptable, as congruent with the episodes brought together by the story. It is this 'followability' of a story that constitutes the poetic solution to the paradox of distention and intention. The fact that the story can be followed converts the paradox into a living dialectic.[113]

Mimesis 2 requires a third stage which Ricoeur also sees as mimesis and which corresponds to what Gadamer terms 'application'.[114] **Mimesis 3** relates to ways in which the world of the text and that of the hearer/reader intersect.

---

109  Ricoeur 1984, 64.
110  Ricoeur 1984, 65–6.
111  Ricoeur 1984, 66.
112  See Ricoeur 1984, 67–8, for how emplotment presents temporal features directly at odds with the episodic dimension.
113  Ricoeur 1984, 67.
114  Ricoeur 1984, 70.

The journey from Mimesis 1 to 3, via 2, is not, for Ricoeur, a vicious circle but an endless spiral. The act of reading schematizes emplotment. Following the insights of Roman Ingarden and Wolfgang Iser, who view the written work as a 'sketch for reading', Ricoeur finds a significant role for the reader in interpretation, as a result of which a world is opened up in front of the text, which the reader is invited to explore. For Ricoeur, this is akin to Gadamer's fusion of horizons.[115]

## Implications

Ricoeur's theory of how narrative, and thus literature, operates is fecund. It foregrounds a series of important issues for our project.

(i) Ricoeur is more cautious on this issue than is MacIntyre, but he nevertheless connects mimesis and thus narrative and literature with the way the world is. Ricoeur is reluctant to conclude that ontologically the world exhibits a narrative shape, but he alerts us through Mimesis 1 to the connection between mimesis and the shape of the world. His view certainly does not represent a strong realism, but in certain ways it is realist, nevertheless. Narrative and literature, we might say, are not in Ricoeur's view alien to the ways of the world.

(ii) As with our tentative definition of literature, Ricoeur recognizes the role of imagination in the production of literature. Events and characters do not simply present themselves to us so that literature merely mirrors reality. Rather, the narrative has to be constructed with a plot and so on.

(iii) This imaginative construction is not unique to fiction. If we call the building blocks of narrative its *poetics*, then history-writing and fiction are both characterized by the same range of poetics. So, for example, the fact that OT narratives tend to be very sophisticated in their poetics does not settle the question of whether they are intended to tell us – among other things – what happened or whether they are fictional or legends. As is widely recognized nowadays, it is the aim of the author/s that is determinative.

(iv) Mimesis 2 strikes me as similar to, or at least a vital part of, Weiss's internal analysis of a text. This also relates back to Ricoeur's distinction between explanation and understanding.

---

115  Ricoeur 1984, 77.

(v) Ricoeur's emphasis on the role of discordance in literature is important. It reminds us just how careful we have to be before we conclude that a literary text is so incoherent and 'broken' that we have to posit underlying sources in order to account for the state of the text as we receive it.

(vi) Mimesis 3 embodies a very important insight for OT interpretation. As the reader engages with an OT text/s, a world is opened up in front of the text which the reader is invited to indwell and to explore. It is this world that is potentially transformative and it is this world which needs to be analysed in terms of the historical ways in which the text refers to the world. This resonates with Chrétien's notion of allowing the Bible to inform our understanding of our 'today' and of indwelling the biblical story as our story. Another way of putting this, using Ricoeur's language, would be to say that reading the Bible as authoritative means that we approach the world opened up by the text as trustworthy and true, and thus are intentional about allowing it to be transformative.

(vii) Ricoeur notes that the end point of the narrative provides a place from which the whole can be seen. Similarly, René Girard refers to the end of a work of literature as the temple of truth.[116] Now, of course, we do not have such an end in the OT. The narrative of the OT ends in an unfinished, open way, looking forward with hope to further acts of God. Both northern and southern kingdoms go into exile and some of the southerners return, but the reconstructed Israel is a shadow of its former self.

From a Christian perspective, the story of the OT is completed or fulfilled in the Christ event and ultimately in the consummation of the kingdom of God. This raises in acute fashion the boundaries of what we attend to in this project and whether or not the NT shapes or should shape our reading of the OT. We discussed this issue above in relation to N. T. Wright and Paul. We do need to respect what Childs refers to as the 'discrete witness' of the OT. At the same time, the gospel is an explosion of good news, casting its light in all directions, so that we would be foolish to ignore the light it casts on the OT.

As every OT scholar knows, the forward look of the OT is complex as the prophets leverage a variety of OT traditions in order to alert their hearers to what is still to come. Clearly, knowing how the OT is fulfilled illuminates the OT in all sorts of ways, and in this sense Ricoeur and Girard are surely right

---

116  Girard 1965, 307–8.

about the end as the temple of truth. We do, however, need to remember that NT eschatology differs from Jewish eschatology in that with Jesus the end has come and yet is still to come. There is thus an awful lot still to be revealed, including about the OT. Furthermore, something cannot be fulfilled if the fulfilment is simply imposed on it. There is thus a delicate balance to be struck between respecting fully the discrete witness of the OT and letting one's reading be illuminated by the NT. Paul's approach, as set out by Wright, seems to me exemplary in this respect.

# 8 World view

Stories come in all shapes and sizes. Were we to meet and want to become friends, sooner or later we would find ourselves saying to each other, 'Tell me your story.' If we wanted to get at the larger story our friend indwells we might ask questions such as 'What, for you, is life about?' or 'What, for you, does it mean to be human?' Note that our friends may not have thought about such issues but will probably realize, on reflection, that they live out of a certain answer to these questions. World views *can* be held unconsciously. Larger stories, or what are called metanarratives or grand stories,[117] address the fundamental questions of life and aim to provide a normative perspective on life as a whole. They describe the basic nature of the world and provide us with direction as to how to live in the world. 'World view' refers to these larger, comprehensive stories that humans tell about the world, and our interest lies in the world view/s of the OT and what it looks like in comparison to the world views of the surrounding ANE nations.

It is intriguing to note how 'world view' crops up in recent literature on the ANE and the OT. For example, critical as she is of *The Intellectual Adventure of Ancient Man* by Frankfort et al., Rochberg nevertheless notes that:

> For all the deficits of its theoretical framework from a contemporary point of view, *The Intellectual Adventure* raised *the fundamental question of worldview* – namely, how what we call natural phenomena, and the external world in general, was construed by the literary elite in Near Eastern antiquity.[118]

---

117 Some scholars distinguish between modern metanarratives and the sort of grand story or world view we find in the Bible. In my opinion, a simple way round this is to say that there are different types of world view.

118 Rochberg 2016, 43. Emphasis added.

Jonathan Z. Smith highlighted the use of 'world view' in Judaic studies.[119] Writing in 1986, Vernoff, in a fascinating chapter worthy of close attention, identifies 'world view' as an emerging direction in religious and Judaic studies. He observes that

> any largely *self-conscious* and thus *choice-making* entity, collective or individual, will need *some* orientation to reality, which entails formation of a worldview; and worldviews accordingly provide the matrices for all group and individual systems of reality manifest in societies, cultures and persons.[120]

Insightfully, Vernoff notes how the social sciences suppress the scholar's personal world view in the name of objectivity. However:

> Fully understanding *worldviews themselves*, on the other hand, requires that a scholar become precisely and vividly *aware* of his or her own worldview *as* worldview – that is, as fulfilling the universal *subjective* human need for orientation – in order to have an empathic, cognitive, and critical touchstone for fathoming the worldviews of others; and this is requisite even if one's personal worldview invokes the authority of science itself.[121]

As we will see below, Mark Smith in his work on translatability and the OT uses 'world view' repeatedly but without ever defining it. In examples such as this, 'world view' tends to be used without much precision. Within the Evangelical Christian tradition there has been a sustained interest in, and thus literature on, world view.[122] Before we get to that, it is worth exploring something of the history of the term 'world view'.

## (a) The origins and use of the term 'world view'[123]

'World view' is a translation of the German word *Weltanschauung*. It was coined by the Enlightenment philosopher Immanuel Kant in his 1790 publication *Critique of Judgement*. *Weltanschauung* is not developed as a concept in Kant's philosophy, and it was Schelling (1775–1854) who gave it its familiar

---

119  Vernoff 1986, 17.

120  Vernoff 1986, 18.

121  Vernoff 1986, 19–20.

122  See Goheen and Bartholomew 2008.

123  The history of the term 'world view' has been mapped in detail in several German articles. In English the definitive treatment is that by Naugle (2002).

meaning of how humans understand and interpret the world around them.[124] The Enlightenment shifted the starting point in philosophy from *ontology* – the nature of the world around us – to *epistemology* – how *we* go about knowing something so that we can trust the results of the knowing process. From a theological perspective this was a major shift. The Enlightenment, and Kant in particular, turned the medieval order on its head with 'man' and not God now firmly in the centre. 'World view' thus has a provocative beginning, nestled as it is in the turn to human autonomy evident in Kant's and other Enlightenment philosophies. As Naugle rightly notes: 'Kant's Copernican revolution in philosophy, with its emphasis on the knowing and willing self as the cognitive and moral center of the universe, created the conceptual space in which the notion of worldview could flourish.'[125]

And flourish 'world view' certainly did. In the first two decades of the nineteenth century, 'world view' entered the vocabulary of German theologians, philosophers and poets, and from them it spread to other disciplines such as history (Ranke), music (Wagner) and physics (von Humboldt). Throughout the nineteenth century, world view established itself as a major companion concept alongside philosophy. From Germany it spread through European academia and then to the UK and to the USA, reaching the zenith of its reputation at the start of the twentieth century when large numbers of books and articles used the term in their titles.[126]

The origin of world view in German philosophy is important to note. Certainly, its roots are in a time when German post-Enlightenment philosophy flourished as never before:

> In a development, powerful alike in its intensity and extent, the German mind during the short span of four decades (1780–1820) produced a wealth of systems of philosophical *Weltanschauung*, gradually projected on all sides, such as has at no other time been compressed within so narrow a space; and in all of these the thoughts of preceding philosophy combine to form characteristic and impressive structures.[127]

Hegel (1770–1831), whose philosophy is the high point of this time in German philosophy, makes substantive use of world view, and differs from Kant

---

124 Heidegger (1982, 4) describes Schelling's understanding of world view as 'a self-realized, productive as well as conscious way of apprehending and interpreting the universe of beings'.

125 Naugle 2002, 59.

126 Naugle 2002, 62.

127 Windelband 1901, 529.

in his stress on *history*. In Kant's idealism there is a single set of determining categories in rational minds by which humans interpret the world. Thus, although Kant believed that we cannot know the world as it is in itself, the make-up of the human mind makes a single view of the world possible and the goal of scientific endeavour. For Hegel, however, there are a variety of forms of consciousness, of world views that manifest themselves in history. Once a sense of the great diversity in history was added to the notion of world view, it became apparent that there are a variety of world views. Sooner or later, this would raise the question of *how* we know or even *whether* we can know which is the right world view. The conjunction of history and world view would thus raise the problem of relativism – do we all just have different world views or is there one right way to view the world? Since others have reviewed the history of world view in detail and we cannot do that here, we will limit ourselves to taking note of the use of 'world view' by key philosophers whose use of the term bears on our appropriation of it in Christian thought and practice.

World view and life view played an important role in the philosophy of the Danish Christian philosopher **Søren Kierkegaard** (1813–55). To understand Kierkegaard's philosophy it is important to note that he lived at a time in Denmark when most Danes thought they were Christians merely because they lived in 'Christian' Denmark. Kierkegaard calls this 'Christendom' because it is reminiscent of the time during the Middle Ages when Christianity was the official religion of the West so that merely by living in Europe you were tempted to think you were a Christian. It is a bit like a mouse thinking it is a biscuit/cookie simply because it is in the biscuit tin! As a result, Kierkegaard worked tirelessly and creatively to distinguish genuine Christian experience from nominal Christianity. For example, he wrote many of his books under pseudonyms with funny names such as Johannes Climacus, and Johannes de Silentio (John the silent one), in order to push readers to work out for themselves what they believed. World view and life view are part of his arsenal of concepts which he uses to make his point. In opposition to the Christendom of his time, he stressed that:

> A lifeview is more than a pure idea or a sum of propositions held fast in abstract neutrality; it is more than experience which as such is always atomistic, it is namely the transubstantiation of experience; it is an unshakeable certainty in oneself which has been won by all [of one's] experience.[128]

---

128 Quoted in Naugle 2002, 76.

'Transubstantiation' is the term for the Catholic doctrine of the Lord's Supper in which the bread and wine *become* the body and blood of Christ. With this evocative metaphor, Kierkegaard asserts that a world view is *not* just assent to theological propositions but involves a transforming encounter with Christ. For Kierkegaard, this is not arrived at easily and inevitably but involves struggle and suffering.

Not everyone, according to Kierkegaard, achieves a life view but only those who experience a type of illumination which radically changes their life. Kierkegaard was a strong opponent of the Hegelianism of his day which was widely accepted among his fellow Christians and was very abstract and intellectual. He insisted that a life view is the antithesis of the sort of abstract, philosophical system of Hegel which failed to transform people's lives and to bring them into existential encounter with the living Christ. Naugle sums up his approach: 'The serious pursuit and development of a *livanskuelse* [life view], in short, is the true love of wisdom, and ought to replace the comedy of abstract thought.'[129]

An important theorist of world view is the German philosopher **Wilhelm Dilthey** (1833–1911). Like Hegel, he recognized that taking history seriously meant that the establishment of a rational ontology[130] which was true everywhere and always was a fruitless project:

> In the vision which encompasses the earth and its whole past the absolute validity of any individual form of life, constitution, religion or philosophy vanishes . . . [T]he development of historical consciousness destroys faith in the universal validity of any philosophy which attempts to express world order cogently through a system of concepts. Philosophy must seek its inner coherence not in the world but in man.[131]

Under the influence of the theory of evolution, Dilthey saw history as flux and change with no God-given order shaping its unfolding. Such an approach to history 'knows only of constant leave-taking, never again to find a permanent home'.[132] Little wonder that once an understanding of a world view as

---

129 Naugle 2002, 81.

130 Dilthey (1976, 142) defines a metaphysic (= ontology) as follows: 'Once a world-view is elevated into a scientifically justified conceptual scheme which lays claim to universal validity, metaphysics comes into being. History proves that, wherever it occurs, metaphysics has been anticipated by a religious development, influenced by poetry and affected by national conditions.'

131 Dilthey 1976, 135.

132 Smit 2002, 313.

originating in the human mind was joined together with historicism – the view that history is full of change and flux – relativism was not far off. In place of ontology, Dilthey set out his theories of world views.

Dilthey stressed that world views emerge out of life and human experience: 'Thus every genuine world-view is an intuition which springs from our involvement in life.'[133] He discerns various strata in the development of a world view. As people struggle with the enigmas of life, different approaches develop; '[s]uch attitudes towards life, the innumerable nuances of responses to the world, form the lower stratum for the formation of world-views.'[134] In the higher strata, understanding plays a formative role.

Ontological systems which major on the higher strata of world views resist their origin in life and experience and seek to evade it, but Dilthey is adamant:

> To start with, every metaphysician, confronted with the enigma of life, begins disentangling the skein, as it were, from a particular point; this point is determined by his attitude to life itself and determines the particular structure of his system.[135]

The result of this origin of world views in life is that there are many different world views which compete with one another. Dilthey does not think that this diversity will ever be solved with one world view emerging as the winner, because at their roots world views are 'unprovable and indestructible'.[136] World views are largely the product of faith and emerge out of the dynamic flow of life, which is unrepeatable.[137] Amid the inevitable diversity this entails,[138] Dilthey, however, stressed that world views are not only influenced by many different ingredients; they also manifest an identical structure that reflects an inherent order in the psyche of human beings:

---

133 Dilthey 1976, 146. Dilthey (1976, 141) is clear: 'World-views are *not* products of thought. They do not originate from the mere will to know. The comprehension of reality is an important factor in their formation, but only one. They emerge from our attitude to, and knowledge of, life and from our whole mental structure.' Emphasis added.

134 Dilthey 1976, 137.

135 Dilthey 1976, 146.

136 Dilthey 1976, 141. Dilthey (1976, 141) asserts that '[t]he struggle of world-views among themselves has not decided any essential point. History selects among them but their great types persist side by side autonomous, unprovable and indestructible.'

137 Dilthey (1976, 139–40) mentions a variety of factors that enter into the formation of a world view: climate, race and nationality, historical developments, individual experience, alterations in science, etc.

138 Dilthey (1976, 147–54) discerns three main world views: naturalism, idealism of freedom, and objective idealism.

All world-views, if they seek a complete solution of the enigma of life, invariably contain the same structure. This structure always takes the form of a system in which questions about the meaning and significance of the world are answered in terms of a conception of the world. From this an ideal, a highest good and supreme principles of conduct are deduced.[139]

It is not hard to see how Dilthey's approach raised for many the spectre of relativism, although Dilthey himself denied that his approach implied such a conclusion. Dilthey notes that all world views are oriented towards valid knowledge, but his approach certainly foregrounded the question of just how solid ground was to be found for knowledge that could be trusted as true; that is, it focused the epistemological challenge in an acute way.

As Naugle demonstrates, the concept of world view has spread to almost all disciplines nowadays: sociology (Mannheim, Berger and Luckmann), psychology (Jung), science (Polanyi with his notions of personal knowledge and the tacit dimension, Kuhn with his influential notion of 'paradigm'), cultural anthropology (Kearney, Redfield) and others. This does not of course mean that its value goes uncontested. Naugle, for example, discusses the strong opposition of the philosopher Donald Davidson to such conceptual schemes.[140]

From this overview of the history of the development of the 'world view' concept, several points should be noted.

First, it must be recognized that once we take world views seriously we are confronted with their *plurality* and *competitiveness*. Again and again in modernity, world views try to assert their neutral objectivity and deny their status as world views, but, as has become clear, every world view has its own 'prejudices'[141] and, as Dilthey notes, their foundations rest on *faith* rather than rationally proved assertions. Also, world views are not easily or at all reconcilable. They may overlap in all sorts of ways because they all seek to make sense of the world common to all, but inevitably they aim to tell *the* story of the world from their perspective and as such are incommensurable. This harkens back to our explication of critical realism. The world is common to us all, but the perspectives we bring to it vary and the result is different and competing world views.

---

139 Dilthey 1976, 137–8. Dilthey (1976, 140) notes that '[a] common human nature and the arrangements by which individuality is produced are vitally related to reality which is always and everywhere the same; life always shows the same sides'. He (1976, 140) speaks of the 'regular structure of world-views'.

140 Naugle 2002, 162–73.

141 Or pre-judgements. 'Prejudices' means only that each world view orients itself towards the world in a particular way, not necessarily that these prejudices are wrong.

McGrath follows Barth in his wariness of 'world view' and states:

This leads me to suggest that, rather than committing itself to any particular world-view, Christian theology should use or appropriate as many world-views and forms of language as are appropriate to explicate the truth of God's Word *without* allowing itself to enter into a relation of dependence upon them.[142]

Elsewhere, I have explored Barth's opposition to world view and find it far from compelling.[143] He is similarly wary of philosophy and would, in my view, be wary of the very critical realism McGrath finds so helpful. McGrath also, in my opinion, fails to take account of the comprehensive nature of a world view; it aims to tell the truth about the world so that the use and appropriation of as many world views as possible – a common, British, eclectic approach – does not escape world view but embraces a particular one that celebrates eclecticism.

Second, we should note, strange as it may sound, that our view of world view will itself depend on our world view. If, for example, we think with some philosophers that a world view is the crowning achievement, the final goal, of philosophy, then we will be dismissive of pre-theoretical world views. In my view, Dilthey is right to note that world views arise *out of* life and lived experience. I also agree with him that there is something about humans and the world which means that there are structural similarities in the variety of world views. Dilthey relates this to a common psychic structure in humans. This may well be so, but, as I will argue below, the deeper source of this common shape to world views is, from an OT perspective, the heart or religious centre of the human being and the discernible shape of the world.

Third, I welcome Kierkegaard's emphasis on the need to own one's world view at a personal and existential level. I disagree with Kierkegaard that not everyone has a world view – world views may be held unconsciously and it is part of being human to be oriented towards the world in a particular way. Thus, indwelling some world view is inescapable.

In this respect the Romanticist use of world view as 'a set of beliefs that underlie and shape all human thought and action'[144] is important. Tarnas

---

142  McGrath 2002, 201. Emphasis original.
143  Bartholomew 2017, 119–20.
144  Heslam 1998, 89.

acknowledges the common ground between Romantics and Enlightenment thinkers; both were 'humanist', but

> [w]hereas the Enlightenment temperament's high valuation of man rested on his unequaled rational intellect and its power to comprehend and exploit the laws of nature, the Romantic valued man rather for his imaginative and spiritual aspirations, his emotional depths, his artistic creativity and powers of individual self-expression and self-creation.[145]

Romanticism thus alerts us to a danger that appropriation of world view has often fallen into, namely that of reducing a world view to a set of rational propositions, thereby succumbing to an arid rationalism that may be academically insightful but lacks heart and vision and life. The Romanticists rightly alert us to the fact that a world view is a vision for life and that it is an extension of the whole person and community. A world view is a deep part of a person's psyche and is constituted *inter alia* by one's culture and emotions and not just by one's reason. This helpfully raises the issue of the different elements that constitute a world view and alerts us to the danger of reducing a world view to a series of intellectual propositions.

Kierkegaard and the Romantics also remind us that while delineation of a world view may indeed be the crowning achievement of a philosophy – although Kierkegaard himself was very wary of systems – world views come into play from the outset in our lives *and* in our academic endeavours. It is not just that we work *towards* a world view but that inescapably we work *from* world views.

Fourth, we need to take seriously the Enlightenment baggage that comes with the concept of world view. We noted above that Kant's idealism created the context in which world views could flourish. This is because Kant stressed in his idealism, and in reaction to realism and empiricism, that we cannot know the world as it actually is; we always interpret the world through a grid and only know it *as interpreted*. For Kant, if we operate rationally, we all interpret it through the same grid and should come to the same conclusions. But, once concede that different rational people interpret the world in very different ways and thus take history seriously, and the question is raised of whether or not world view is an inherently *relativistic* concept. This is particularly the case if one concedes to an evolutionary or historicist view of history, as does

---

145 Tarnas 2010, 367.

Dilthey.[146] The Christian philosopher Alvin Plantinga traces the view of post-moderns that we create our world/s back to its origin in Kant's idealism and anti-realism. Does any appropriation of world view not therefore play right into postmodern relativism?

And indeed it should be noted that, in the hands of philosophers such as Nietzsche (1844–1900), Foucault (1926–84) and other postmoderns, world view or similar concepts do lead to wild relativism. Nietzsche, who has come of age in postmodernism, acutely discerned the breakdown in metaphysics and objectivism in philosophy and of course had little time for Christianity. He celebrated the multitude of world views and perspectives on the world and gave up on any possibility of knowing truly about the world. Developing the Kantian notion of the creative mind, he saw that human minds were creative-ly and ceaselessly active in constructing views of the world – indeed in his opinion human health and well-being requires a world view in order to make sense of and survive in the world. But, for Nietzsche, these world views are just human constructions; they are only imaginary constructs of the world of human aspirations and desires. 'Nietzsche . . . positions himself at the controls of a train that, having entered a tunnel, will never emerge into the light. With his will as the headlight, the train plunges ever deeper into a cavernous noth-ingness.'[147] As Naugle rightly notes: 'A complete perspectivism is at the heart of Nietzsche's philosophy.'[148]

Lyotard famously explains postmodernism as 'incredulity towards meta-narratives'.[149] 'Metanarrative' is another word for a grand story or world view, albeit with a particular, modern focus. Like other postmoderns, Lyotard recognizes the diversity of world views but believes that any such all-encompassing perspectives are simply passé and no longer believable. Again we are mired in the morass of relativism with no possibility of 'true Truth', as Francis Schaeffer liked to refer to it.

Thus, any contemporary appropriation of world view will need to attend closely to the fact that world views emerge out of lived experience in hist-ory. Indeed, how we think about *history* will decisively shape our approach to world views. Clearly, in our late-modern context, afloat in historicism as it is, relativism is a real danger if it is truth that we are after. As with knowledge, we need a critical realist view of world views.

---

146 In assessing the value of world view as a Christian concept, one's philosophy of history is crucial. For a Christian view of history and a valuable critique of Dilthey's historicism see Smit 2002.

147 Sire 2015, 29.

148 Naugle 2002, 102.

149 Lyotard 1984, xxiv.

# (b) Definition of a world view

In the literature on Christian world view, definitions abound. Mike Goheen and I define a world view as '[a]n abstraction of the basic beliefs of a shared grand story, rooted in a faith commitment, which gives shape and direction to the whole of our individual and corporate lives'.

All world views are at base given expression in a grand story of one sort or another. Thus, much modern science tells a grand story of the big bang, the evolution of the cosmos, the appearance of human life and the gradual winding down of the universe. It appears that we need a grand story in order to make sense of the smaller stories of our lives and cultures. As Ecclesiastes 3.11 says, God has put eternity – that is, a sense of beginning and end, a sense of being part of a larger story – in our hearts, in the very core of our being, so that as creatures we require some larger story in order to understand our own story/ies.[150] We are wired, as it were, to find meaning in our lives through being part of a larger story that gives purpose and direction to our lives and explains our world.

Grand stories are inevitably 'shared' because of the communal nature of humanity, an emphasis clearly articulated by MacIntyre in his analysis of narrative and tradition. All of us are raised in the context of some grand story even if our family and society is unconscious of this. Even Western individualism, with its stress on the freedom of the individual, is an approach to life that is shared ironically by millions in the West today.

Embedded in all grand stories are *beliefs* about the world, answers to questions such as: 'What is the nature of the world?' 'Who are we?' 'What is wrong with the world?' A world view is not about highly theoretical philosophical or theological doctrines but about 'basic beliefs'. The beliefs that make up a world view are foundational. They deal with concerns of ultimate importance, such as what life is all about, what it means to be human, where we are, how we tell the difference between right and wrong, what happens at death, the problem of evil, and so on and so forth. It is important to note that, for us, these basic beliefs are *not* philosophical concepts but are beliefs embedded firmly in a 'shared grand story' and forming a framework in the sense that they hang together in a coherent way. In German, 'world view' is clearly distinct from 'philosophy', and this is an advantage because a world view is *pre-theoretical*. By 'pre-theoretical' we mean that the basic beliefs are not conceptually tight and theoretically honed as is the case in traditional philosophy.

---

150  See Bartholomew 2009 on Eccl. 3.11.

These beliefs give shape and direction to the whole of our lives, both individual and corporate. A world view not only describes the world for us but also tells us how to live in the world. The beliefs in a grand story will also affect every aspect of our lives and not just how we think. If, for example, we believe that God has created us male and female and that marriage is his provision for companionship, then we will regard marriage as a great gift and the context for sexual expression and the nurturing of children. Apart from such a belief, we might approach sex as simply a means for pleasure, to be enjoyed as we do a good meal, whenever and however we like.

And it is vitally important to realize that grand stories and world views shape not just our individual lives but the lives of nations and all the public dimensions of life as well. World views have legs and they run into history, embracing individuals, societies, nations. In the South Africa in which I grew up, a grand story of apartheid – a world view according to which whites were superior to blacks – took root, and was deliberately worked out in every area of South African life. Whites went to different and much better schools than blacks; it was legally immoral for a white to marry a black; by law, whites lived in different areas from blacks; the best jobs were reserved for whites; and so on and so forth. Unbelievable in retrospect but very telling in terms of the way in which a world view is comprehensive – it affects not only our individual lives but that of our communities and nations as well. National Socialism in Germany is another example of the comprehensive effect of a world view. Belief in the superiority of the Aryan race and the inferiority of Jews had catastrophic consequences, as modern technology was used efficiently to murder six million Jews and others. At an individual and corporate level, our world views shape our lives far more than we often realize.

The core beliefs in a grand story hang together to form a whole – they are like the scaffolding around a building or the skeleton of a fully embodied human. And they can be abstracted – lifted out – from the grand story to provide a more systematic expression of the grand story, and for us this is precisely what constitutes a world view. A world view is an abstraction, a lifting out of the basic beliefs of a grand story in order to foreground its coherence and to enable us to understand the implications of our or someone else's grand story more fully.

Readers might question whether or not all world views – everyone has one – are rooted in a 'faith' commitment. This is, I think, correct, and it is an aspect of a world view that Dilthey articulates. However, it is important to realize that a faith commitment may not involve, for example, the Trinitarian God, or Allah or YHWH. Roy Clouser is helpful here in defining a religious belief as

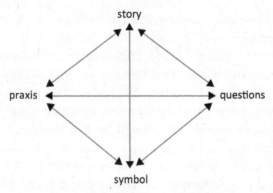

Figure 4 **Elements of a world view**

a belief in that on which everything else depends, but it itself does not depend on anything else.[151] To use Plantinga's terminology, such a belief is properly basic, and while we may be able to provide good reasons for it, our belief does not require reasons. From this perspective, a secular ideology such as Marxism, for example, believes (as a faith commitment – it cannot be proved) in the materiality of the world as properly basic.

We can set out the interacting elements of a world view as shown in Figure 4.[152]

As we have seen above, humans make sense of their world by *story*. Here we are thinking of large or grand stories which provide meaning in life and insight as to how to live. A world view is a level of abstraction from such a grand story, identifying the *core beliefs* of the story and how they hang together. World views, like narratives, are always lived, and thus praxis enters into any analysis of an individual's or a group's world view. Generally, world views are communal and so praxis includes culture and society. Humans enact their most important values in rituals and symbols, and so an additional way to get at a group's world view is through an analysis of these.

Hopefully, by now it is becoming clear just how fertile a tool world view could prove to be for an analysis of the cultures surrounding Israel in the ANE and of Israel herself and her sacred literature, the OT. Texts that may to some seem of little interest, namely ANE stories of the gods, now move to the forefront as the stories people told in order to comprehend the world in which they lived. Excavating ANE world views in this way also allows real comparative

---

151  Clouser 1991.
152  cf. Wright 1992, 124.

work to be done between Israel and the OT and the ANE, to discern both similarities and differences.

It is important to note that not only do we find world views in the ANE and the OT but we ourselves inhabit world views. Above, we defended the fact that a world view rests on a faith commitment of some sort or another. Again and again in our journey thus far, we have seen how theology comes to the fore. Here is another such case, and in a later section we will need to attend to how theology can and should function in our approach to the OT and its origins.

# 4

# History in/and the Old Testament and the Ancient Near East

## 1 Introduction

A central element in any world view is what we make of history. In my *God Who Acts in History: The significance of Sinai*,[1] a prequel to this work, I attend to a puzzle. Jewish scholars in particular, but also Christian, assert that Sinai is at the heart of the HB/OT, but many then proceed to say that we can have no idea whether Sinai happened or not. Speech Act Theory alerts us to the fact that a speech act can and will misfire if certain conditions are not met. Thus, the poignant question arises of whether one can retain the extraordinary message and theology of Sinai without the Sinai 'event' having ever taken place. Any attempt to work out what to do with the OT today simply has to wrestle with the question of the OT and history.

The issue of history has, however, become controversial and exceedingly complex in OT studies. Historical criticism has bequeathed us a legacy by means of which each part of the OT and parts of parts of parts must be individually assessed in terms of possible historicity. In one sense, of course, we *have to* assess different parts of the OT in terms of historicity. Genesis 1—11, for example, is very different from the famous court narrative in Samuel. And the exodus, the Sinai event and the role of Moses need to be attended to discretely, albeit in an interrelated fashion. However, the fragmentation of the OT that historical criticism has led to leaves us with shards and little sense of how they fit together. Thus we need to begin afresh with the question of the nature of history and how a critical realist perspective might orient us in relation to the OT. In this way, we will begin with an etic approach, as it were, but in the course of this series of books we will need to immerse ourselves in the actual texts of the OT.

---

1 Bartholomew 2020.

# 2 The nature of history

Augustine famously said of 'time' that we all know what it is until we stop and ask ourselves, 'Just what is time?' The same can be said of history. It is a concept that we all work with, but when we stop and ask about it in more detail it turns out to be complex.[2] Any assessment of the OT and history does well to explore carefully what we mean when we speak of the OT and *history*.

## (a) The complexity of history

A moment's reflection reveals that history is far more complex than 'what happened in the past'. History always involves some telling, some *narrating* of the past – this is how we access the past – and in the process the historian has to be extremely *selective*. If one reflects for a moment on the millions or billions of things that occur in one day in one place, one starts to see just how selective the historian has to be. In this respect, history is no different from other sciences. All disciplines have to zoom in on a particular aspect of reality and limit their focus in order to give deep attention to a particular number of things. A critical question thus becomes: 'What aspects of reality do historians focus on?' One answer to this question by the Dutch philosopher Dooyeweerd is that the historical aspect of reality is about 'formative power', the opening up of the potentials latent within society. Doubtless, we could think of other answers, but Dooyeweerd is helpful here in alerting us to the fact that all history-telling and -writing uses a lens to filter much out and to bring key elements into focus.

The selectivity of history-writing alerts us to the fact that the historian always writes from a *point of view*; it is simply impossible to do otherwise. For example, a Marxist historian would pay particular attention to the role of economics in history. Of course, individual historians may argue that they simply write history as they were taught to do so by the guild, but, as we have become increasingly aware, 'the guild' never writes history from nowhere but itself has a perspective/s from which it practises history; it is traditioned. It is not uncommon nowadays to find books on *the history of historical scholarship*, books which alert us to the variety of ways in which history has been practised. The Wiley-Blackwell *Companion to the Philosophy of History and Historiography* has 17 categories under the heading 'Part IV: Classical Schools

---

2  Philosophy of history and of historiography is a complex subject with a vast literature. See Bartholomew 2015; 2022 and 2024, in French and forthcoming in English respectively.

and Philosophers of Historiography and History',[3] giving us some idea of how complex historiography, the writing of history, has become.

If history-writing is always far more than 'what happened', it is never less than this. 'What happened in the past' is too comprehensive to define what we mean by history, but the difference between history and fiction is that history-telling refers to actual people and events that existed and took place in the past, and good history *intends* to tell us truly about such events and people. Here again a critical realist perspective is helpful. In this sense, history-telling is never less than about what actually happened. Sternberg points out that

> history-writing is not a record of fact – of what 'really happened' – but a discourse that claims to be a record of fact. Nor is fiction-writing a tissue of free invention but a discourse that claims freedom of invention. The antithesis lies not in the presence or absence of truth value but of the commitment to truth value.[4]

He notes that the difference between truth value and truth claim is of foundational importance. Bad historiography does not amount to fiction. 'For if fiction contrasts with fact, it contrasts even more sharply with fallacy and falsity, which are value judgments passable on factual reporting alone. Falling between fallacy and falsity, therefore, *bad* historiography is bad *historiography*: no more, no less.'[5]

## (b) History-writing as literature

It might be thought that style or poetics could help us distinguish fiction from history, and it is common to find OT scholars moving in this direction. Hendel, for example, notes that '[t]he memory of Abraham, while authoritative in terms of genealogical prestige, is also fictional and problematic in its *literary representations*'.[6] Apparently, the 'literary representations' enable us to see that much of the narrative about Abraham is fictional. However, this is simply not the case. Ricoeur and others argue that historical narrative shares its literary poetics with fiction so that the poetics of a text alone is not decisive

---

3  Tucker, ed., 2009. The 17 are: Ranke, Scientific Historiography, Darwin, Logical Empiricism and Logical Positivism, Jewish and Christian, Muslim, Vico, Kant and Herder, Hegel, Neo-Kantian, Marx, Collingwood and Croce, Phenomenology, Jan Patočka, Hermeneutics, Postmodernism, End of the Cold War.

4  Sternberg 1985, 25.

5  Sternberg 1985, 25. Emphasis original.

6  Hendel 2005, 38. Emphasis added.

for determining whether a text is historical or fictional narrative.[7] Sternberg observes that '[t]here are simply no universals of historical vs. fictive form'.[8] He refers to Alter's characteristics of fiction, especially individuation and realistic psychology, thematic shaping, play of language and conscious artistry. For example, for Alter, through 'the privilege of fictional invention' the David cycle develops 'history into fiction' through means such as imaginative dialogue and characterization.[9] Esther's fairy-tale plot and schematic neatness show it to be a 'comic fantasy'.[10] Sternberg quotes Henry James's reference to the house of fiction as possessing a million windows, and notes that for some windows the characteristics invoked by Alter, Schneidau and the Gunkel school, for example, look attractive. Alas, other windows of the house of fiction refer to their opposites. 'To say the very least, historiography as well as fiction is a house of a million windows, but all giving on the real world.'[11]

## (c) Narrative and historiography

As we reflect on historiography as literary,[12] *narrative* moves front and centre. Ricoeur notes that:

> The cognitive function of narrativity seems to me, taking everything into account, better recognized if it is linked to the phase of historical discourse representative of the past. Our problem will be to understand how the configuring aspect of emplotment gets articulated through the modes of explanation/understanding placed in the service of the representation of the past. To the extent that representation is not a copy, a passive *mimesis*, narrativity will suffer no *diminutio capitis* [diminished capacity] from being associated with the properly literary moment of the historiographical operation.[13]

Thinking of history in terms of narrative rightly evokes the idea of history as a narrative or story told by the historian about aspects of the past. Such an ap-

---

7    Ricoeur 2004. See our discussion above.

8    Sternberg 1985, 30.

9    Alter 2011, 41–2.

10   Alter 2011, 38.

11   Sternberg 1985, 28.

12   Ankersmit (2009, 207) notes that 'contemporary philosophy of language is condemned to remain a mere torso without legs and arms for as long as its practitioners stubbornly persist in their present disregard of narrative. Historiographic narrative is the best point of departure to remedy this lacuna.'

13   Ricoeur 2004, 186.

proach goes back to antiquity: Quintilian (*c.* AD 35 – *c.* AD 100) observes that 'historia scribitur non ad probandum sed ad narrandum [history is written in order to narrate, not in order to prove]'.[14]

In the second half of the twentieth century the issue of narrative played a major part in discussions of historiography, stemming from unease with an exclusive focus on explanation,[15] which failed to account for the history work as a whole text. Narrative stressed that a work of history-writing is more than its component parts; it cannot be reduced to explanatory truth. One needs to discern at least three layers in history writings: the statement of individual facts, explanation and the narrative as a whole. Ricoeur connects the literary dimension with the third stage in particular, but rightly notes the selective elements in all stages. Indeed, facts and explanation make sense within narratives.

Two approaches have come to the fore in narrative and historiography, namely the philosophical and the literary. Ankersmit points out that, '[n]evertheless, so-called "narratology" – a branch of literary theory specially devised to deal with narrative – has only rarely been appealed to by narrativist philosophers of historiography (Herman 2005)'.[16] In philosophy the central issue has been whether to take *a realist or a nominalist approach*, whether history-writing tells of the past as it was or whether its narrative-telling is largely underdetermined by the individual facts. Mink represents the nominalist option: he denies 'the idea that there is a determinate historical actuality, the complex referent for all our narratives of "what actually happened," the untold story to which narrative histories approximate'.[17] David Carr and Paul Ricoeur critiqued Mink's position (shared by Arthur Danto, Hayden White and Frank Ankersmit) from a phenomenological point of view, arguing that narrative inheres in life. For Danto, however, '[u]nity and continuity are the product of narrative synthesis and do not mirror the features of an object existing in the past itself'.[18]

## (d) Postmodernism and historiography

Not surprisingly, bearing in mind that postmodernism took root in literary theory, narrative approaches to history-writing have also been taken in a

---

14    This approach was developed by nineteenth-century German (Ranke, Droysen), French (Barante, Michelet) and British (Carlyle, Macaulay) historians.

15    cf. the 'covering law' model of the 1950s and 1960s.

16    Ankersmit 2009, 201.

17    Ankersmit 2009, 202.

18    Ankersmit 2009, 205.

radically postmodern direction. Postmodernism developed in literary studies (while structuralism was still in vogue, Derrida famously gave his lecture on post-structuralism) and then extended into a critique of Western culture as a whole, hacking into many of the central pillars of post-Enlightenment thought. Christopher Norris argues that

> literary theory, through its colonizing drive into other disciplines, bids fair to reverse that entire movement of progressive or enlightened critique which has sought to establish adequate protocols for the discrimination of truth from falsehood, of factual from fictive or historical from mythic modes of utterance.[19]

Hayden White wrote:

> in general there has been a reluctance to consider historical narratives as what they most manifestly are: verbal fictions, the contents of which are as much invented as found and the forms of which have more in common with their counterparts in literature than with those in the sciences.[20]

If, as Munslow says, '[t]he past is not discovered or found [but rather] created and represented by the historian as a text, which in turn is consumed by the reader',[21] where does this leave history-telling?

At the heart of postmodern debates about history is the extent to which historiography can represent the past accurately through narrative. Proponents invoke the interpretative and hermeneutical element in historiography and many draw extremely radical conclusions from these characteristics. Munslow, for example, proposes that 'history is best viewed epistemologically as a form of literature producing knowledge as much by its aesthetic or narrative structure as by any other criteria'.[22] 'All such narratives make over events and explain why they happened, but are overlaid by the assumptions held by the historian about the forces influencing the nature of causality.'[23]

---

19  Norris 1994, 114.
20  White 1978. Quoted in Ankersmit 2009, 205.
21  Munslow 1997, 178.
22  Munslow 1997, 5.
23  Munslow 1997, 10.

# (e) Critical realism and historiography

Postmodernism is helpful insofar as it alerts us to the inevitable input of the historian into historiography and the literary nature of the historical text. However, its tendency to reduce, to the point of obliterating, the gap between fiction and history is profoundly unhelpful. There is an enormous amount at stake in maintaining the distinction between historiography and fiction; indeed, we need to retain the dimension of *discovery* in history-writing, discovery of what actually happened. Gertrude Himmelfarb's *On Looking into the Abyss: Untimely thoughts on culture and society*[24] is a helpful antidote in this respect. She notes that history encounters monsters that live in the abyss. Whereas moderns were aware of the dangers of the abyss, postmoderns tend to play around the abyss, unaware of the dreadful dangers that lurk therein. It has been argued that the twentieth century was the most brutal in history, and unspeakable events such as the Holocaust resist any attempt to collapse the divide between history and fiction. With Sternberg, we need to hold fast to the truth claim of historiography and to hold historians to that claim. How then do we distinguish history-writing from fiction? It is the intention of the author that is determinative, whether or not we judge the product to be good or bad history-telling. As Bruce Halpern observes: 'whether a text is history, then, depends on what its author meant to do.'[25] Of course, if with postmoderns we think that authorial intention is irrelevant and anyway cannot be discerned, then we are in real trouble in distinguishing between fiction and history.

Nevertheless, there is an undeniable constructive element to history-writing, and a critical realist perspective enables us to retain a strong emphasis on the reality of the past outside and beyond any tellings about it, and on the point of view of historians as well as their selectivity and development of a narrative of the past. A poignant question in adjudicating between what we refer to above as realist versus nominalist accounts of history is that of the extent to which the world does indeed have a narrative shape so that narrative connects with and fits with the way the world is. A postmodern historicist would clearly reject any such view, and a major scholar such as Martha Nussbaum observes that few of us even believe in any sort of teleology to history nowadays. However, in his fine book, Gordon Graham argues that one of the strongest contenders for philosophy of history today is that of providence, so that we may not need to take Nussbaum's comment too seriously.[26] Here I

---

24  Himmelfarb 1994.

25  Halpern 1988, 8.

26  Graham 1997.

find MacIntyre's stronger sense of the connection between narrative and reality even more helpful than that of Ricoeur. Human lives comes to expression and find meaning in narratives, we understand our nations and events by telling their stories, world views are at the deepest level storied in shape, and so we could continue. All of this seems to me to confirm that the world is story-shaped. Inevitably, a decision on this issue will back one into one's world view, and, from a Christian perspective with a Bible that is, as Eugene Peterson expressed it, a sprawling capacious metanarrative, there are good reasons to affirm that narrative does indeed inhere in and reflect reality. (Critical) realism here trumps nominalism.

# 3 The Old Testament and history

An effect of historical criticism is to send the OT scholar down a thousand rabbit holes with no promise of ever arriving at the desired destination. Working on a book on the doctrine of creation, and trying hard to engage rigorously with Scripture, I vividly remember encountering the following sort of statement from major OT scholars: 'Genesis 2 is never again mentioned in the Bible.' Not only is this untrue, but for the theologian who is attempting to engage with Scripture seriously it functions as a sign to take a long detour with no promise of the detour's ability to get one back on track. The temptation is either to ignore the detour sign and proceed straight ahead or to relinquish serious engagement with Scripture, because at point after point one faces such detour signs resisting the sort of synthesis fundamental to theology.

And it is much the same with history and the OT. I enjoyed reading Hendel's well-written *Remembering Abraham: Culture, memory, and history in the Hebrew Bible*.[27] However, when it comes to the OT and history, it is worth reflecting on where such work leaves us. In order to unpack how elements such as narrative, poetics, world view and theology influence our view of the OT and history, we will attend closely to Hendel's work in this section.

As I found time and again in my earlier work on Sinai, Jewish (and Christian) scholars so often stress the vital importance of the HB/OT narrative for Jewish identity but are extremely reluctant to affirm the historicity of even the largest building blocks. Hendel is no exception. To his credit, Hendel draws on the work of Sternberg and the older, evocative work of Yerushalmi, but he maintains that 'history does not come neat or plain in these

---

27  Hendel 2005.

writings; the Hebrew Bible consists in large part of interpretations and reflections on history – more a midrash on the times than the times themselves'.[28] Hendel notes that:

> In the case of ancient Israel, the imagination that flows into the construc-
> tion of a cultural identity is, at least in part, preserved for us in the biblical
> portrayal of Israel's origins. The most important of these imaginative
> constructs are the stories of the Exodus-Sinai-Wanderings period, related
> in the books of Exodus through Deuteronomy.[29]

These stories amount to a national biography and are, as such, 'a *historical*
engine for the construction of cultural identity'.[30] Hendel is alert to the vital
role of narrative, understanding how Israel's identity is shaped by its grand
narrative. Inevitably, this is followed by a major disclaimer: 'Even if some or
many of these formative events did not really happen in the way that they are
told, they were – and still are – felt and understood to be a shared memory of
a collective past.'[31]

Abraham is the father of the nation of Israel in the HB/OT, and Hendel
evokes his role well: 'The landscape of Israel – which is one of God's promises
to Abraham – silently attests to Abraham's memory.'[32] However:

> The memoirs of Abraham and the narratives about him in Genesis obey
> this condition of tribal genealogies – they involve the present in the past
> and look to the past as a model and warrant for the present. The remem-
> bered past is not merely a glorified projection of the present, but a confla-
> tion of past and present in which history, folklore, and ethnic self-fash-
> ioning are thoroughly entangled.[33]

The very landscape of Israel may attest to the memory of Abraham, but '[t]he
memory of Abraham, while authoritative in terms of genealogical prestige,
is also fictional and problematic in its literary representations'.[34] As Hendel
states: 'In my understanding of the text and the historical facts, the patriar-

---

28  Hendel 2005, 6.
29  Hendel 2005, 7.
30  Hendel 2005, 7. Emphasis added.
31  Hendel 2005, 8.
32  Hendel 2005, 33.
33  Hendel 2005, 35.
34  Hendel 2005, 38.

chal narratives of Genesis are a composite of historical memory, traditional folklore, cultural self-definition, and narrative brilliance.'[35] Indeed, when it comes to the patriarchs, '[w]e do not know when or if any of these persons ever existed in history'.[36] Hendel asks:

> When is the patriarchal era? In the most obvious sense, it is the time forever recreated in the biblical narrative of Genesis 12—50. This era consists of myth and memory, mingled in a way far more compelling than ordinary history. It is an era in sacred time.[37]

On the exodus Hendel is alert to its foundational importance: 'The story as a whole defines the collective identity and ethnic boundaries of the people, providing a common foundation for social and religious life.'[38] Some of us think that when a nation's biography locates its origins in brutal slavery it has the ring of historicity about it, but not so Hendel: 'The Egyptian Empire was crumbling during the early decades of Israelite culture, and it is no surprise that the settlers defined themselves, at least in part, as former victims of an oppressive regime.'[39] It is not necessary to understand the plagues as real events; rather, they may reflect communal memories of actual plagues in Egypt: 'A devastating epidemic in the late fourteenth century, interpreted as an act of divine punishment, may be distantly recalled in the story of the Egyptian plagues.'[40]

On Moses, R. Smend's work is cited by Hendel with approval, according to which we can only be sure of two facts about Moses: his Egyptian name and his unlikely marriage. 'Everything else about Moses' life is so interwoven with narrative motifs and religious ideology that it is impossible to disengage the history from the tradition.'[41] However, these two facts are not unhelpful; they alert us to a possible mediatorial figure so that '[a] historical figure named Moses may have been transformed into the savior and mediator of all Israel, perhaps generalized from the memory of a smaller group'.[42]

What are we to make of such work? First, clearly it leaves us in a hopeless situation in terms of ever recovering the history of Ancient Israel. But why is

---

35  Hendel 2005, 46.
36  Hendel 2005, 47.
37  Hendel 2005, 55.
38  Hendel 2005, 72.
39  Hendel 2005, 62.
40  Hendel 2005, 72.
41  Hendel 2005, 67.
42  Hendel 2005, 72.

this the case? Second, what Hendel says of Moses' life gives the game away: *narrative motifs and religious ideology* prevent us from taking these narratives as history-telling. Presumably, if there were just no narrative motifs and no religious ideology – that is, if we could just get narrative and God out of the picture – we would be in a far better position historically!

Now, we have already seen that the presence of narrative motifs simply cannot be a deciding factor in terms of the historicity of OT narrative. History-writing shares such poetics with fiction, and the presence of poetics does not for a moment decide the issue. But what should we make of 'religious ideology'? Clearly, for Hendel, this moves the Moses narratives beyond the pale of history-telling. But, of course, this is nothing new. It is the quintessential modern move of removing God to the margins and beyond so that we can secure true knowledge on the basis of our autonomous selves. However, this is the move that the HB/OT resists with all its might from beginning to end, so that in order to pull off such a move we have to set ourselves intentionally and deliberately against the overarching perspective of the HB/OT.

Wright observes that:

It is not the ancients who were deceived about the nature of history, living in a pre-modern age and not knowing what critical thought consisted of. It is we who, in the Enlightenment's rejection of reliance on *auctores*, 'authorities' in a multiple sense, have come to imagine ourselves to be the first to see the difference between subjects and objects, and so have both misjudged our forebears and deceived ourselves.[43]

Remarkably, for Sternberg, it is precisely the ideology of the HB that leads him to a very different conclusion from Hendel, namely that the HB aims to tell history. In Sternberg's view of the HB, '[t]he product is neither historicized fiction nor fictionalized history, but historiography pure and uncompromising'.[44] For Sternberg, everything points this way: the obsession with memory of the past and its relevance for the present among the Israelites and Israel's uniqueness in this regard in the ANE – such factors confirm that the historical narratives of the HB/OT make a strong historical truth claim. 'Were the narrative written or read as fiction, then God would turn from the lord of history into a creature of the imagination, with the most

---

43  Wright 1992, 85.
44  Sternberg 1985, 35.

disastrous results.'[45] Sternberg's approach is by no means uncontested! But it demonstrates well how our assessment of the 'religious ideology' shapes our view of the OT as history.

It is worth pausing at this point to make sure we understand what is going on here, using terms from our previous chapter. Sternberg examines the poetics of the HB/OT inductively, seeking to allow his theory to arise from the data of the HB/OT. From this perspective he argues that the HB/OT sees the story it tells as history. Using the language of world view, we could say that the literature of the OT embodies a world view according to which the major events of the HB/OT actually happened. In my view this is correct, and one would be hard-pressed to argue otherwise.[46] What happens in OT studies is that the modern reader studies the OT through the lens of his or her world view. In the process, a dialogue or confrontation emerges between the world views, albeit unconsciously. If the reader of the OT espouses a post-Enlightenment world view then it brings certain baggage with it, baggage such as there is no God, or if there is a God we cannot know anything true about him, and we certainly should not bring any kind of religious belief into our OT scholarship because that would undermine its objectivity. In the name of objectivity and truth, the OT, embodying a very different world view from this, is read through the lens of a post-Enlightenment world view, and, not surprisingly, the results look a lot like the post-Enlightenment world view. For example, when Hendel refers to the 'times themselves', I expect what he means is the times in which Israel existed as they would be understood through the grid of a post-Enlightenment world view.

Again and again the post-Enlightenment world view tries to pass itself off as neutral, scientific and objective, with religious world views as inherently biased and ideological. What could be more neutral and objective than the 'times themselves'? To come to grips with this as we read the OT, it is absolutely crucial to realize that the post-Enlightenment world view is as traditioned as a modern, believing Jewish world view or a modern, Christian, believing world view. We should no longer allow such a world view to be assumed; it needs to be argued for, or at the very least declared out front and in the open. Once this is done, it will become clear that a modern, Christian world view, for example, will approach the same data in the OT potentially in a very different way from that of Hendel. This is not for a moment to deny the major progress in so many areas generated by the Enlightenment. Nor is it to deny that there

---

45  Sternberg 1985, 32.
46  See Chapter 8, section 6, in this respect.

can be dialogue between OT scholars of different world views. For example, the issue of whether or not the poetics of a text determines whether it is fiction or not can be rigorously investigated, as has been done by Sternberg, Ricoeur and others. It is, however, to assert that there are fundamental and deep differences between a modern Christian world view and a post-Enlightenment one, and they influence in a major way how one reads the OT and, in this context, assess it as history.

An important predecessor of Sternberg in this respect is Erich Auerbach in his classic – but largely neglected by OT scholars – *Mimesis*, which we discussed above. *Mimesis* is a fascinating work and not least because it is 'ideologically unintelligible without the Christian doctrine of Incarnation'.[47] From Genesis 22, the narrative about Abraham's journey to Moriah to sacrifice Isaac, Auerbach comments in general on the biblical stories. Intriguingly, he notes that the Elohist aimed not primarily at realism but at *truth*, as noted above. Auerbach argues that the OT presents *universal history*. It is clear from Auerbach's work that in the Bible the literary, the historical and the theological are intertwined. What needs to be noted is that the best literary work on the Bible has foregrounded the issue of history and the Bible's unique insights in this respect.

Remarkably, other writers, some of whom Hendel cites, find in the OT a revolutionary view of history which allows history to come into focus as such for the very first time. And, what is more, they connect this revolution with precisely that religious ideology which Hendel finds so very unhistorical. We turn now to examples of such work, which will back us into the question that lurks behind our work and that of scholars such as Hendel, namely the question of God.

# 4 History from the perspective of the Old Testament

It is intriguing to note how *The Intellectual Adventure of Ancient Man* (*IAAM*), published in 1946, is receiving fresh, albeit critical, attention.[48] Irwin, who writes the four chapters on 'The Hebrews' in this volume, recognizes the religious dimension of Israel's view of history. Speaking of special divine action (SDA), he notes: 'But all this by its occurrence became historical; it was part

---

47  Said 1953, 2003, xi.

48  Rochberg, for example, rightly critiques *IAAM* for not attending to the full corpus of Babylonian texts. However, this does not undermine many of the other substantial insights in *IAAM*.

of man's career, rather of the story of God and man, for that was the Hebrew's concept of history.[49] He argues that the people of Israel possessed a philosophy of history and that, with it, they brought something radically new into the world: 'in this way they were bringing into existence a new thing . . . one goes all the way to Nicholas of Damascus[50] to find anything deserving of comparison with this aspect of Hebrew historiography'. In Israel's view of history the will and purpose of God is on one side, humans with their purposes and independence on the other.

> Here is the great conviction of Israel's thinkers. History is not the meaningless clash of human passion that it may sometimes seem or yet the plaything of blind force; God is ruler of all, and he is shaping events to his far-off purpose . . . History is a tale of progress![51]

According to Irwin:

> In Israel's philosophy of history there entered human culture a new idea that was destined to have far-reaching results all the way down to our own days . . . [P]hilosophy of history as the Hebrews conceived and developed it had never been known in all the centuries of the great civilizations which preceded them.[52]

Israel's history is told from a specific point of view and for a specific purpose; nevertheless, for Irwin, it is great history. As per Genesis 1—10, Israel's history is uniquely set in a world setting. For the OT, history has meaning; it looks back to the origins of life and forward to a future. Life is surveyed *sub specie aeternitatis*, allowing the OT to affirm Israel's significance in history. Israel's history-tellings 'manifest that high feeling for narrative which is the remarkable quality of the Hebrew literary genius'.[53]

For Irwin, the limitations of OT history are apparent. It fails to attend to economic and social forces. Its greatest weakness is lack of critical appraisal, and at times it simply relates miraculous and legendary material, such as in

---

49   Irwin 1946, 321.

50   64 BC – 4 BC. Nicholas's writings include a universal history from the time of the Assyrians to his own day.

51   Irwin 1946, 323.

52   Irwin 1946, 322.

53   Irwin 1946, 321.

the Elijah–Elisha narratives.[54] Nevertheless, '[i]t was no accident that the su-premely religious people of all times were likewise our first great historians'.[55]

Herbert Butterfield (1900–79) was Regius Professor of History and Vice-Chancellor of the University of Cambridge. He was one of the major historians of the twentieth century and also a Protestant Christian. In his The Origins of History[56] he has an exceptional chapter entitled 'The Originality of the Hebrew Scriptures'. In the two chapters leading up to this one, Butterfield deals with the ANE. And then he observes:

> [S]uddenly, one finds oneself confronted with what must be the greatest surprise in the whole story. There emerges a people not only supremely conscious of the past but possibly more obsessed with history than any other nation that has ever existed. The very key to its whole development seems to have been the power of its historical memory . . . Everything hung on men's attachment to a single event that could never be forgotten.[57]

This nation is, of course, Ancient Israel. The single event: the exodus.

In normal circumstances one would expect that the Israelites would have adopted the gods of the people living in the land they entered, as citizens of the ANE were prone to do if they moved from one culture to another; the Israelites' resistance to accepting the religion of the Canaanites, according to Butterfield, comes through their view of history:

> The tradition of the children of Israel seems to have begun with an emphasis upon the exodus from Egypt . . . Either in the course of that story itself or through the masterstroke of an historical genius, the Exodus came to be particularly associated with a Promise which kept hope alive in the wilderness and seemed fulfilled when the Israelites entered the land of Canaan. This was combined with the stories of the hopes that had been held out to the patriarchs. It seemed that the whole history of the people had been a history based on the Promise . . . All this implied a

---

54 This is Irwin's view. A case can be made that the OT is well aware of economic and social forces, and, personally, I do not regard the miraculous material in the Elijah–Elisha narratives as obviously legends.

55 Irwin 1946, 321. Emphasis added.

56 Butterfield 1981.

57 Butterfield 1981, 80–1.

further bond, fastening men's minds on history, and connecting religion with history.[58]

Of the exodus, Butterfield observes: 'It is difficult to think of any other event in history which had so powerful an effect on the mentality or the tradition of a people.'[59] He notes how in Deuteronomy 26.5–10 the cycle of seasons is associated with a unique event, and how in Deuteronomy 6.20–23 the exodus is the motivation for obedience.

The renewal of the Sinai covenant in Joshua 24 performed for the Israelites the function of epic in other peoples and, according to Butterfield, this seemed to relieve Israel of the need for an elaborate mythology.[60] The prophets identify actual events as part of God's judgement, and look towards the future. Something like the idea of progress in history as predominantly linear appears in the OT; history is irreversible and unrepeatable. In the context of its view of history Israel is depicted as having a unique mission, and '[t]his is the first appearance of the idea of the "historic mission" of a nation'.[61] Indeed, the concepts that characterize the religion of Israel – promise, covenant, judgement, national mission – are concepts particularly associated with history.

Among the great empires of the ANE there is no hint of anything like the history of a nation. Israel provides us for the first time with something we can call the history of a nation. Remarkably, the Israelites seem to have reached a consciousness of history without having to go through the intermediate stages that made other countries so slow to appropriate history. Israel's depiction of its past is often unpretentious:

Yet it was among these people – for whom the past was not a golden age at all but was a thing to escape from – that somebody had the idea of producing a history of the nation and turning it into a great theme.[62]

'Ancient Israel provides, therefore, a pocket-size example of the very rise of historiography.'[63] Butterfield works with the state of play in OT scholarship of his day. He describes J as a historian of genius. Of the Davidic court narrative

---

58  Butterfield 1981, 87.

59  Butterfield 1981, 81.

60  Butterfield 1981, 84.

61  Butterfield 1981, 89. The missional element of the OT is far too often neglected by missiologists, let alone OT scholars. However, it only makes sense within a certain view of history.

62  Butterfield 1981, 94–5.

63  Butterfield 1981, 95.

he asserts that '[t]he ancient world, at least down to the time of the Greeks, produced no historical narrative that was more distinguished than this'.[64]

Another extraordinary work is that by the former professor of Jewish history, culture and society, Yosef Yerushalmi, appropriately titled *Zakhor* (Remember).[65] Yerushalmi notes that in primitive societies only mythic time is real, and refers in this respect to Eliade's *The Myth of the Eternal Return*. He observes that '[i]n the metaphysics and epistemology of some of the most sophisticated of Far Eastern civilizations, both time and history are deprecated as illusory, and to be liberated from such illusions is a condition for true knowledge and ultimate salvation'.[66] Herodotus is commonly referred to as 'the father of history', but Yerushalmi points out that Herodotus has no concept of universal history. He perceptively notes that '[i]f Herodotus were the father of history, the fathers of meaning in history were the Jews'.[67] Indeed, '[i]t was ancient Israel that first assigned a decisive significance to history and thus forged a new world-view whose essential premises were eventually appropriated by Christianity and Islam as well'.[68]

For the Ancient Israelites, the heavens declare the glory of God, but it is especially in and through history that God revealed his will and purpose. Israel's knowledge of God emerges not from the result of speculation; rather, '[i]t emerged out of an intuitive and revolutionary understanding of God, and was refined through felt historical experiences'.[69] However it actually came about,

> [s]uddenly, as it were, the crucial encounter between man and the divine shifted away from the realm of nature and the cosmos to the plane of history, conceived now in terms of divine challenge and human response. The pagan conflict of the gods with the forces of nature, or with one another, was replaced by a drama of a different and more poignant order: the paradoxical struggle between the divine will of an omnipotent Creator and the free will of his creature, man, in the course of history; a tense dialectic of obedience and rebellion . . . With the departure of Adam and Eve from Eden, history begins, historical time becomes real, and the way back is closed forever.[70]

---

64  Butterfield 1981, 98.
65  cf. Ricoeur 2004, 397–401.
66  Yerushalmi 1989, 6.
67  Yerushalmi 1989, 8.
68  Yerushalmi 1989, 8.
69  Yerushalmi 1989, 8.
70  Yerushalmi 1989, 8.

In Ancient Israel, the people's rituals and festivals are no longer repetitions of mythic archetypes; instead, they evoke the past. 'Far from attempting a flight from history, biblical religion allows itself to be saturated by it and is inconceivable apart from it.'[71]

In the patriarchal narratives, we read of the 'God of the ancestors', that is, the God who acts in history. 'For here as elsewhere, ancient Israel knows what God is from what he has done in history.'[72] Memory is crucial to Israel's faith and thus to its very existence: 'Only in Israel and nowhere else is the injunction to remember felt as a religious imperative to an entire people.'[73] The Red Sea can be crossed only once and Israel's encounter with God at Sinai is singular. Israel is not told to become a nation of historians. Rather, '[i]t is above all God's acts of intervention in history, and man's responses to them, be they positive or negative, that must be remembered'.[74] As does Butterfield, Yerushalmi notes that Israel's history is not focused on heroic national deeds; indeed, many narratives deflate national pride.

Yerushalmi is insightful in recognizing that memory in Ancient Israel flowed through several channels, including ritual and recital. He says of the ritual in Deuteronomy 25.5–9: 'This is capsule history at its best.'[75] Indeed, for Yerushalmi, the fundamental biblical conceptions of history were forged not by historians but by priests and prophets, and the need to remember overflowed into actual historical narrative. 'In the process, and within that varied Hebrew literature spanning a millennium which we laconically call "the Bible," a succession of anonymous authors created the most distinguished corpus of historical writing in the ancient Near East.'[76]

As Yerushalmi observes, this is an amazing achievement. Religion goes hand in hand with history-writing: God is the true hero of the OT and yet Israel wrote history on an unprecedented scale. Like Butterfield, Yerushalmi asserts that parts of the OT historical narratives are poetry and legend. Nevertheless, they have a firm anchorage in historical realities. He says of the Council of Jabneh that '[f]or the first time the history of a people became part of its sacred scripture'.[77]

---

71  Yerushalmi 1989, 9.
72  Yerushalmi 1989, 9.
73  Yerushalmi 1989, 9.
74  Yerushalmi 1989, 11.
75  Yerushalmi 1989, 12.
76  Yerushalmi 1989, 12.
77  Yerushalmi 1989, 15.

# 5 Conclusion

On all accounts, large parts of the OT are *not* historical narrative. We have the corpus of wisdom books (Proverbs, Job, Ecclesiastes), collections of the sayings of prophets, poetic books such as the Song of Solomon and the Psalms. In the Old Testament, historical narrative constitutes Genesis[78] to 2 Kings and 1 and 2 Chronicles, Ezra, Nehemiah, Esther and Daniel.[79] History remains indispensable for the non-historical narrative parts of Scripture since they were produced in particular cultural and historical contexts, and archaeology, studies of ancient culture and many other aspects of historical studies can illuminate their meaning. However, when it comes to the topic of the Bible and history, the focus is on the historical narratives in the OT and the extent to which they *intend* to narrate what actually happened.

If study of the OT and history is to move forward we need to break free from the atomistic approach of historical criticism, endlessly assessing fragments in terms of possible historicity. How might we do this? Our preceding discussion has yielded many insights.

First, we need to attend closely to the nature of historiography. All history-writing is selective and from a point of view. Second, we need to affirm the ontology of history; history is about what happened in the past and it needs to be discovered. Third, we need to really take on board the literary nature of history-writing. Fourth, we need to explore the possibility that Israel's faith allowed history to come to the fore in an unprecedented fashion. Fifth, we must make the connection between this revolution and Israel's view of God. Sixth, we must become conscious of the ways in which the world view of the reader, always traditioned, influences an investigation of this topic.

We saw in our examinations of the OT as literature that the question of God keeps coming to the fore. Intriguingly and tellingly, the same has happened in our examination of the OT and history. For Hendel, the religious ideology in OT texts counts against their being historical. For Sternberg, by comparison, the HB's/OT's view of God compels us to take the historical narratives of the OT seriously as history. Sooner or later, both literature and history back us into the question of God, or what we might call the 'theological nature' of the OT. It is to this question that we now turn.

---

78    In a later volume we will address the special challenges of Gen. 1—11.
79    The genre of Esther and Daniel is, of course, contested.

# 5

# Theology, authority and the Old Testament

## 1 Introduction: From literature and history to theology

In our previous discussion we have seen how the historical and the literary dimensions of the OT are fundamental to our interpretation of it. However, we have also seen how, despite being ignored by scholars time and again, the theological dimension insists on pushing its way to the surface.

We began with a description of Israel as a God-trodden land. Attention to the different descriptions of the land in the OT alerted us to just how important it is to take the literary dimension seriously in this respect, following Wazana's creative work. Wazana helpfully identifies three dimensions of the HB/OT text, namely the historical, the literary and the ideological. Unfortunately, she attends least to the ideological, whereas this appears to play a major role in descriptions of the land.

Sanders foregrounds the unique communicative dimension of the HB/OT in the ANE but remains deeply committed to naturalistic explanations. Even though he notes how OT narrative and the other genres of the OT are framed by *prophecy*, at the heart of which is the phrase 'Thus says YHWH', he still fails to attend to the God or theological dimension of the HB/OT. Refreshingly, Kawashima's attention to the literary dimension of the OT leads him to the theological. Similarly, we saw how Auerbach's and Sternberg's attention to the OT as literature connects with the theological, and it is the theological that leads both of them to affirm the historicity of the OT. Kawashima reaches for the insights in *IAAM* to argue that Israel's doctrine of God enabled something unique to take place in the nation's literature. Herberg, and others, argue that the HB/OT uniquely among ANE literature allows history to come to the fore, and in *IAAM* Irwin connects this specifically with Israel's view of God.

For better and for worse, much of modernity, especially that dominant strand known as the radical Enlightenment, has been deeply opposed to allowing religion a role in the acquisition of knowledge. Sanders perceptively notes that biblical criticism is a child of modernity. I am not proposing that we react by becoming pre-modern. However, the fact that time and again we have seen the theological dimension of the OT pushing itself to the surface and calling for attention means that we cannot simply accept the Enlightenment or post-Enlightenment paradigm/s as the only one/s within which serious OT study can be executed. As we have argued, we can now see that the post-Enlightenment paradigm within which much OT study has been carried out is only one paradigm among others and it is as traditioned as any other paradigm. Of course, it is perfectly possible and acceptable for an OT scholar to work within this paradigm, but the critique of this paradigm has reached the point where it needs to be argued for, rather than just assumed. Postmodernism has savaged major planks of the post-Enlightenment approach, but has also left key elements such as human autonomy in place and signally failed to provide a constructive alternative. The result is that as we move beyond postmodernism, post-Enlightenment historical criticism easily becomes the default mode in the absence of other alternatives. In my view, this is unacceptable. What is required is delineation of a new paradigm/s for OT studies which retains the gains of historical criticism and subsequent developments in OT studies, and allows us to see their strengths and weaknesses.

In the West, modernity dealt with religion by privatizing it and thus marginalizing or eradicating it from the great public spheres of life such as university education and, in our case, OT studies. Built into this is a doctrine of progress where objective, scientific scholarship evolves beyond primitive religious belief, which, in any case, would inevitably die out as we continue to advance. However, the expected 'twilight of the idols', to allude to Nietzsche and Mark Lilla, has been postponed.

Doubtless, staunch defenders of the Enlightenment tradition within OT studies will find Lilla's comments disturbing. At one level there is little to be done about that. In the West, mainstream OT studies will undoubtedly continue to be practised within the post-Enlightenment tradition to a great extent. However, if Lilla is right, then this tradition is *not* the only choice available to us. There is also the option of the Judeo-Christian tradition, and it is this tradition that the theological dimension of the OT pushes us to explore, rooted as it is in the HB/OT. There will, of course, be other options to explore. As we saw above, Bhaskar's critical realism eventually took a spiritual turn, but a distinctively Eastern one rather than a Judeo-Christian one. However, that it took a spiritual turn is significant and, at the very least, similarly opens up the possibility that OT studies might also take a 'spiritual turn'.

The revival of religion in the majority world is accompanied by a hardened secularism within parts of the West, so that polarization within OT studies is a lived reality for most of us believing OT scholars. Because world views are by their very nature antithetical, to an extent this deep division is unavoidable. However, it will be unfortunate if it becomes overly entrenched and exclusive on all sides. Believing OT scholars need to be alert to the fact that a hardened secularism will have a vested interest in obscuring the choice available to us that Lilla sets out so very clearly.[1] One way for believing scholars to engage with this hardened secularism is to cooperate actively with majority-world OT scholars, who do their work amid the global renaissance of religion and thus are less likely simply to assume the post-Enlightenment world view. A much healthier way forward in the West is a pluralist option in OT studies which allows room for different world views or traditions to come to fruition so that real comparisons can begin to reveal which approaches make best sense of the data of the OT.

# 2 The Old Testament and theology

If Israel is a God-trodden land, the OT is a God-trodden book. From beginning to end, God is the central character. It is therefore ironic that the theological dimension of the OT is the one that much mainstream, modern OT study finds least acceptable. But what do we mean when we speak of 'theology' in relation to the OT?

'Theology' is a term with many levels of meaning. It can refer to basic beliefs as well as to the scientific discipline of theology. We have already discussed the concept of 'world view', and in terms of basic beliefs world view is extremely helpful. Humans express their world views at a pre-theoretical level through stories or narrative, and world view identifies the central, basic beliefs in such narratives and their interrelationship.

## (a) The dominant religious dimension of the Old Testament

It is important to note that rarely does the OT offer us truth in a propositional form; instead, it tells stories and provides us with other genres of literature. As our previous discussions showed, this is a common way then and now to express one's world view, and so it should come as no surprise. As we begin to reflect on the interrelationship between the literary, the historical and the

---

1  See the discussion of Lilla in Chapter 1, section 6(b).

theological dimensions of the OT, we should note that the theological or religious dimension is far and away *the dominant one*, and thus it profoundly colours how the other two operate. In his critical realist articulation of theology, van Huyssteen perceptively notes that:

> As an ancient Near Eastern book composed of many books with divergent literary forms ... and as a book that has to be interpreted according to its own nature ... the Bible now stands before us as a book of faith with a nonnegotiable religious dimension. If that book is to be understood according to its own character, no contemporary hermeneutics can dismiss its religious dimension.[2]

Sarna, in his assessment of the book of Exodus as history, opts for the descriptor *historiosophy* (wisdom history) as a way of articulating the dominant religious dimension while retaining the historical dimension. In terms of our threefold cord of history, literature, and theology or kerygma, all this means that the theological or kerygmatic dimension is the most important one.

The dominance of the religious dimension relates to Sanders' evocation of the unique communicative nature of the HB/OT. I am somewhat reluctant to describe this as *theological* since in almost all its uses 'theological' refers to beliefs, either at the basic level or at the most sophisticated level, as well as at intermediate levels. In my view, the most appropriate word for this communicative dimension is 'kerygma' or 'kerygmatic'. As Meir Sternberg reminded me in a conversation some years ago, while this may be true, with narrative texts one always arrives at the kerygma via the poetics of the narrative. Nevertheless, it remains true that the OT is primarily concerned not to relate history or to produce literature[3] but to articulate a message to the Israelites about God and his relationship to his people and his world.

The historical narratives of the OT are also never written for the participants it discusses but always for those living after the events described. We can call this the *rhetorical trajectory* of the narrative books of the OT. Take 1 and 2 Kings for example. As is often noticed, the narrator keeps the focus on the particular king's relationship to God, with major other aspects of the king's reign generally ignored. Girard argues that the ending of a piece of literature is the 'temple of truth', as noted above, and in this respect 2 Kings 17.5–23 is the interpretative crux for the book as a whole. This section contains a lengthy

---

2   Van Huyssteen 1989, 192.

3   cf. George Steiner's critique of *The Literary Guide to the Bible* cited above.

reflection on why the northern kingdom went into exile, and it is noteworthy that it includes a discussion of Judah as well in 17.19–20. Kings as a whole is clearly written for Israelites living after the northern and the southern kingdoms had gone into exile.

Another way of getting at this is through Ricoeur's useful distinction between the world of the text, the world behind the text and *the world opened up in front of the text*. Kerygma relates most closely to the latter, and it is through the world opened up in front of the text, which the reader is invited to indwell, that we gain a sense of the world view of the particular book and consequently of the OT as a whole. Of course, the possibility exists that the OT articulates not one but multiple world views, and we will have to attend to this as we explore different aspects of the OT in subsequent volumes. There is also the issue that the world view/s of the OT develops, and this progressive aspect will also need to be kept in view.

The ANE and the OT is awash with stories and rituals which embody participants' perspectives on the world. Narrative and world view thus prove to be vital tools for accessing the world views of the nations of the ANE as well as that of Israel. In Part 3 of this volume we will turn to an analysis of the world views of the nations of the ANE, apart from Israel. At this level, theology is concerned with the role of the gods in the world view and how it shapes the whole. Such an approach enables us to take seriously an emic approach to both the ANE and Ancient Israel.

## (b) The world view of the reader

A vital hermeneutical insight is that it is not only the Ancient Israelites, the writers of the OT and the ANE nations that possess world views, but also contemporary OT scholars. World views easily remain unconscious since they are like lenses or glasses through which we view the world, so we readily assume that this is simply how the world or the OT is. This is one reason why people like me, who wear glasses, lose them so easily. As proverbial academics, when we are looking for them we sometimes discover, to our surprise, that they are sitting securely on our noses! It requires a conscious effort to become aware of one's world view and to take a close look at it.

Once we realize that the post-Enlightenment world view is traditioned, and that there are other contenders for our world view today, then it behoves us to take the time to become conscious of our world view, to become aware of how it shapes our work on the OT and to be ready and willing to give a critical account of it. As we saw from Lilla above, 'the actual choice contemporary societies face is not between past and present, or between the West and "the rest."

It is between two grand traditions of thought, two ways of envisaging the human condition.[4] If the Enlightenment and the post-Enlightenment tradition is one option, the Judeo-Christian perspective is another. Of course, within each of these there are multiple variants and we must guard against oversimplifying our analysis.

## (c) The shape of a Christian world view

There is not one Christian world view – there are several, and they will relate to contemporary OT studies in different ways.[5] You will recall that Mike Goheen and I define a world view as follows: '[a]n abstraction of the basic beliefs of a shared grand story, rooted in a faith commitment, which gives shape and direction to the whole of our individual and corporate lives'.[6] The following key aspects of the Christian world view need to be noted.

*(i) The Christian world view involves a shared grand story.* In this respect it is noteworthy that as a whole the Bible has the shape of a grand, sprawling, capacious metanarrative, as Eugene Peterson describes it. Scripture is authoritative for the Christian world view and it is the grand narrative of Scripture in which a Christian world view seeks to be grounded.

The story is about the Creator and his creation, about humans created in the *imago Dei*, made for relationship with God and to be royal stewards of God's good creation by caring for and developing the potentials of the creation. The material reality and time are real, but neither is ultimate or independent since they depend on God for their existence. Humans can realize themselves only in and through history. Furthermore, as Herberg asserts:

> Biblical faith . . . [i]n its essentials . . . defines a three-phase pattern in which the present 'wrong' and contradictory existence of man and society is seen as a falling away from the original 'rightness' of God's creation, and as destined for restoration and rectification in the final fulfillment of the kingdom of God.[7]

All human history is encompassed within the range of this metanarrative: 'its purpose is universal, though its center – the crucial revelatory,

---

4 Lilla 2007, 2008, 13.

5 cf. Bartholomew 2017, ch. 4, for a detailed discussion of the major Christian world views.

6 In terms of the basic shape of a Christian world view, I am in substantial agreement with N. T. Wright. See Wright 1992, 132–7.

7 Herberg 1976, 39.

community-creating event (Exodus-Sinai in Judaism, Calvary-Easter in Christianity) – is particular.'[8] From a Christian perspective, God acts in history, especially through Israel and climactically in Jesus Christ, to rescue his creation and lead it to the goal he always intended for it.

***(ii) The basic beliefs that are central to this narrative can be identified and abstracted from the story to provide the building blocks for a world view.*** Utterly central to the Christian world view is God, creator and redeemer. The entire creation depends for its existence on God, but God himself is not dependent on anything else. God thus transcends the creation but is also immanently involved with it and in it.

As is regularly noted, God is rendered in narrative and evoked through the use of a whole range of *metaphors*. Amid positivism, and going all the way back to Aristotle, metaphor has been thought to be unscientific and ornamental, so that scientific statements need to be free of metaphor. However, recent decades have seen a revolution in studies of metaphor under the name of 'cognitive metaphor', and this shift has also deeply penetrated philosophy of science. Metaphors can and do refer, and there is no reason why the network of metaphors in the OT for God should not work together to refer accurately to God, to render him truly. Metaphors play a formative role in theories, including theological ones, and we will need to attend to the relationship between OT metaphors for God and the construction of theological theories.

Image, in the *imago Dei*, is, for example, itself a metaphor, bringing together God and humankind – a surprising association in the context of Israel – in order to spark an insight into the nature of what it means to be human. In terms of how metaphor works, image alerts us to major differences between humans and God, as well as remarkable similarities. God is creator; humankind is not. God is sovereign over history; humankind is not. And so on. There has been immense theological discussion on the nature of the similarities, which, broadly speaking, can be divided into functional and ontological ones. In my view, the *imago Dei* is both functional and ontological. In Genesis 1, the functional seems to be the focus, with humans presented as God's under-stewards with responsibility for developing and caring for the creation. In order to do this, humans need to be a particular type of creature, such as rational, linguistic, social and so on; hence the ontological nature of the image.

Neither creation nor the *imago Dei* commits one to a particular view of origins, although they do rule out an atheist account of evolution. Where the

---

8  Herberg 1976, 39–40.

*imago Dei* is particularly helpful when it comes to scholarship is that it alerts us to the fact that humans are designed by God with appropriate faculties to know and understand the world around them.[9] According to a Christian world view, evil stems from human free will and the rebellion of the first couple through a quest for human autonomy. Evil is privative and not inherent to the creation. The answer or solution is God's redemptive work in Israel and climaxing in Christ.

We have moved fast over the territory of the basic beliefs inherent in a Christian world view.[10] These can be and should be developed in far more detail and can be developed theoretically in the direction of both philosophy and systematic theology. We have seen, with the literary and historical dimensions of the OT, that our project requires etic and emic analyses of these. The same is true of the theological dimension. We are concerned in this project to attend to OT origins and the question of God. In the process, we will need an emic understanding of the view/s of God from within the OT as well as a robust doctrine of God. What makes this complex is that these etic and emic approaches are deeply intertwined.

## (d) The Old Testament and the doctrine of God; the doctrine of God and the Old Testament

### The Old Testament and the doctrine of God

The complexity of the relationship between the OT and the doctrine of God can be articulated as follows. First, Colin Gunton and others have pointed out the debilitating error made by theologians in neglecting the Old Testament and privileging instead Greek philosophy for developing a view of God.[11] Gunton notes that the long neglect of the Old Testament has been detrimental to Christian faith, most obviously in the history of anti-Semitism but more basically in the reduction in our understanding of the immensity of the gospel. For Gunton, '[t]his is no more truly the case than in the treatment of the being of God, that most central of doctrines'.[12] To use the language of etic (*our* view of God) and emic (the view of God within the OT), we could say that the former has become unhelpfully loosened from the latter.

---

9  cf. Alvin Plantinga's argument that naturalistic evolution cannot account for reliable epistemic capacities in humans.

10  For more detail see Goheen and Bartholomew 2008.

11  I discuss this in more detail in my *God Who Acts in History*.

12  Gunton 2002, 4–5.

Where our doctrine of God, and our view of creation, are developed from Greek philosophy rather than the Old Testament, unhelpful dualisms often result, dualisms such as: creation versus that which negates the creation, abstract versus material, immanent versus transcendent, all of which have implications for how we conceive of God, divine action and the OT. By contrast, the Old Testament alerts us to the fundamental distinction as *that between creator and the created*. For all the genuine insights of Greek philosophy, the position one adopts at this foundational point has implications for major elements that relate to divine action and the OT: one's doctrine of God, whether we can know God truly, the nature of language, whether and how we can know the world truly, and so on.[13]

Central to Gunton's critique of much of the theological tradition is its inadequate *doctrine of creation*, again an area where the witness of the OT is crucial.[14] Dionysius and his followers, according to Gunton, situate timeless, metaphysical causality over against the temporal and economical depiction of God's action in his world. In this way, the spiritual or intellectual is set against the materiality of creation, whereas this is a false dichotomy: the true distinction is between Creator and the created.

There is thus a major need to put the Old Testament back into the heart of our theologies of God, creation and divine action. We will need to explore how the Old Testament shapes our view of God, and how this is related to a biblical view of creation and divine action. This nexus of *God–divine action–creation* is of fundamental importance to our doctrine of God and how we think of God in relation to the OT.

## The doctrine of God and the Old Testament

Thus, second, God in/and the OT needs renewed attention because God himself is neglected in much Old Testament study. John Barton argues that the bracketing out of 'questions of theological truth' is 'methodologically essential' for biblical criticism.[15] Such questions follow on from a critical reading of the OT but should not inform it. Liberal OT study is characterized thus by the exclusion of God as a formative factor in our study of the OT. Evangelical scholarship less so, but even here we find a reluctance to allow the doctrine of God to play a full role. In his *On the Reliability of the Old Testament*, Kenneth

---

13　All of this is discussed in Gunton 2002.

14　The doctrine of creation in the OT is controverted and there is a tendency nowadays for theologians to anchor *creatio ex nihilo* in the Gospels.

15　Barton 2007, 164.

Kitchen, for example, is clear: 'In this little book we are dealing with matters of history, literature, culture, *not* with theology, doctrine or dogma.'[16] In recent Pentateuchal studies, we have seen a welcome recovery of what one might call the 'criterion of similarity', namely, reading the OT against its ANE environment.[17] What is missing from this is the criterion of dissimilarity, obviously of vital importance if we believe that the main character in the OT is YHWH, actively at work among his ANE people, Israel, and that it is God's action amid Israel that accounts for the distinctive contribution of the OT.

Indeed, it is only when the role of God in Israel is given its full force that the unique contributions of the Old Testament come to the fore. One hears little of this nowadays and has to reach back, for example, to an important but neglected work, namely *IAAM* (which, as we have seen, is garnering renewed, albeit critical, attention), to get a sense of the radicality and comprehensive nature of the OT's contribution, and this not least to the intellectual life.[18]

Irwin, for example, argues that although Israel's thought world is shaped by the cultures of the ANE:

> Israel yet far transcended them and attained a world of thinking and of concepts much like our own ... [T]he boundary between the ancient world and the modern is to be traced ... in the pages of the Old Testament.[19]

From the OT with YHWH at the centre, we learn that the world may be understood in personal terms. Israel demonstrated her critical capacity in the searching critique of the thought world of her context.[20] Israel's de-divinization of nature did not lead the nation away from the natural world as in much Greek and some medieval philosophy: 'Nowhere in the ancient East do we

---

16   Kitchen 2003, 3. Emphasis original. Note that I understand this as an apologetic move, but it is remarkable to think that one could write 662 pages on the reliability of the Old Testament without dealing with God. Provan, Long and Longman (2003) are more nuanced but still clear: 'what we have to say about the history of Israel is not *determined* by these [theistic] beliefs, even though it is *bound up* with them' (Provan, Long and Longman 2003, 103). Emphasis original. I affirm the value of such a project but think that the history of Israel will be deeply influenced by, indeed bound up with, one's view of God and historical revelation.

17   Berman 2017; Walton and Sandy 2013.

18   In my view, a major source for the contribution of the OT to intellectual life remains Henri Frankfort et al., 1946. Raaflaub, ed., 2016 has sought to redo this volume for today, but it falls far short of the original.

19   Irwin 1946, 224.

20   Irwin's (1946, 234–54) analysis of the OT's critical and rigorous engagement with the world views of those surrounding Israel bears on Gunton's point above about the vital importance of allowing our view of God to be shaped by the OT.

find such sublime concepts and descriptions of nature as in Israel.'[21] The place of Babylon in the history of science is receiving fresh attention,[22] but Irwin points out that especially in Second Isaiah we find one of the earliest clashes of science and religion; Isaiah responds to Babylonian astrology by articulating 'the wonders of the infinite intelligence which not alone established these wonders but holds them in their proper relations'.[23] And so we could continue. In a chapter titled 'Man in the World', Irwin argues that Israel understood and articulated natural law apart from and prior to Greek influence. Irwin finds Israel's treatment of history remarkable and wonders 'whether later interest in world history is not directly the heir and consequence of the Old Testament'.[24]

When God is given his rightful place in the OT, the full dimensions of its message are allowed to come to the fore, with all sorts of implications for public and intellectual life. The complexity of the issues at stake here should not be underestimated. There is, for example, an inevitable hermeneutical circle between developing a model of *God–divine action–creation* from the OT and allowing such a model to inform our reading of the OT. Among other things, this alerts us to the role of concepts and thus of philosophy and theology in such a model.[25] As with N. T. Wright's Christian Origins and the Question of God, the aim is to develop a hermeneutic that allows the full range of the kerygma of the Old Testament to be heard, including, not least, its contribution to public and intellectual life.

# 3 A critical realist theology

In our exploration of knowledge we argued for a critical realist paradigm. Now we need to extend this to an understanding of systematic theology. We will use Wentzel van Huyssteen's work as a dialogue partner for this discussion. For van Huyssteen, a critical realist account of theology evokes a theology which remains true to the Christian tradition and to the basic metaphors of that tradition – its origins are located in the archetypal sources in religious experience – but is also valid in its appeal to reality and current philosophic and scientific concerns. Indeed, a major element in his work is opening up a dialogue

---

21  Irwin 1946, 244.

22  Van De Mieroop 2016; Rochberg 2011; 2016; etc.

23  Irwin 1946, 251.

24  Irwin 1946, 319; cf. Herberg 1976, ch. 1.

25  For my 'tree of knowledge' model for the relationship between Scripture and the disciplines, see Bartholomew 2015, ch. 13. This model sees philosophy and theology as foundational disciplines but represents an ecology of scholarship with feedback loops operating throughout.

between philosophy of science and theology. As we have already seen in this work, attention to developments in philosophy of science is indeed valuable for our project. According to van Huyssteen, if theology fails at any of these levels we will need a new and better model. Van Huyssteen affirms Polanyi's statement that '[o]ur believing is conditioned at its source by our belonging';[26] nevertheless, the quest for criteria of theology's rationality remains valid: 'the question of rationality leads theology directly to the question of criteria that would also be valid from a philosophy of science point of view.'[27]

Van Huyssteen defines theology as 'an attempt to reflect as authentically and creditably as possible on whatever we have, through our religious commitment, come to know and experience as God's revelation'.[28] He engages deeply with philosophy of science and argues that theology, like science, develops models which turn metaphoric language into theoretic concepts. The latter are creative conceptual constructions so that there is an inevitable plurality in the Christian tradition.

Van Huyssteen develops three criteria for a critical realist theology, as follows.

## (a) The reality depiction of theological statements

Van Huyssteen is rightly *not* concerned here to try to prove the existence of God. This is an assumption of faith. *Reformed epistemology*, associated with Alvin Plantinga and Nicholas Wolterstorff in particular, has argued that the believer is warranted in taking belief in God as properly basic. One important way in which Plantinga and Wolterstorff came to this position was through meta-epistemology, namely stepping back to survey the epistemologies that have been at work in much modern scholarship. This reveals that *classic foundationalism* has commonly been the epistemology of 'choice', but there are few if any good reasons for it, and it should be rejected. According to Plantinga, it is not that there are no good reasons for belief in God, but they are not required for the believer to take belief in God as epistemically basic. This insight is of vital importance. Believing OT scholars do not need to keep 'proving' the existence of God according to epistemological criteria provided by others before they can assume belief in God as a formative element in their scholarship. The Christian OT scholar is rationally justified in assuming such belief and setting it to work in his or her scholarship.

---

26  Van Huyssteen 1989, 144.

27  Van Huyssteen 1989, 144–5.

28  Van Huyssteen 1989, 144.

What van Huyssteen is concerned to do is to show, especially in relation to philosophy of science, that there is no reason to regard theological statements as unscientific or irrational. We are justified in taking theological statements to refer to that reality which is God, while being intensely aware that theological statements are provisional and partial models which cannot begin to encompass God. The rediscovery of the centrality of metaphor in lived experience and in theorizing is central to this argument. Religious language is highly metaphoric, and 'our religious language is the only valid line of access to the reality of God to which we are committed through faith'.[29] While it is true that '[t]heology, as the very specific reflection on Christian experience and the relationships thereof to the religious dimensions of our culture, certainly has a rather unique nature which sets it apart from most other forms of scientific reflection',[30] for both theology and science their objects of belief lie beyond literal description, making the use of metaphor constitutive of any theorizing. For both science and theology, their descriptions are always tentative and provisional, but, following a critical realist line, what we are provisionally conceptualizing really exists. As van Huyssteen states:

> In theology, critical realism will imply, on the one hand, a model of rationality where theological concepts and models are indeed provisional, inadequate, and partial, but, on the other hand, also necessary as the only way of referring to the reality that is God, and the reality of His relation to humanity . . . The metaphoric language of the biblical text, as well as the dominant models we have formed from this, represent aspects of the reality of what Christians believe are in no way directly accessible to us.[31]

Van Huyssteen affirms the foundational role of the biblical text, but, of course, theology as a systematic discipline always moves creatively beyond the Bible in its development of models that indirectly describe reality. 'This means that something new and valid is being said about reality which the user of the model believes describes it better, more appropriately, than competing views.'[32] The Bible has provided believers with metaphors so basic as to be indispensable, and we should not dismiss such language as unscientific or

---

29  Van Huyssteen 1989, 147.
30  Van Huyssteen 1989, 155.
31  Van Huyssteen 1989, 158.
32  Van Huyssteen 1989, 157.

non-referential: 'the metaphoric language of theological models and theories can therefore be seen as referential and as reality depicting. This can be achieved without falling back into a naïve-realist, unrevisably descriptivist position'.[33] As Soskice points out, it is absurd to regard religious language as *only* describing human experience; this defeats its whole purpose.[34] Van Huyssteen also argues that theological models should be ecumenical, which fits well with this project.

The Bible and tradition must play a central role in theological models, but so too must context. In terms of contextuality, van Huyssteen refers to religious experience, the Church and the academic context of theological reflection. He notes that 'religions may also be seen as comprehensive interpretive frameworks based on myths or narration and, as such, often strongly ritualized'.[35] Theology must include plausible interpretation of the tradition, but the Church and tradition cannot be the exclusive context:

> In its broadest sense, theological reflection may be seen as *scientific engagement*, from whatever point of view, with the long-standing Christian tradition and the way the Bible – as the classic document of Christianity – has provided and still provides a basis for reflection on what that religious tradition holds to be its central truth, namely, that the true God finally revealed Himself in Jesus Christ.[36]

Of the theologian's self-concept, van Huyssteen observes that 'the first priority for any form of Christian theology is to be finally and radically theocentric'.[37] Indeed, van Huyssteen argues that it would be irrational of a Christian theologian not to accept the reality of God's existence. Theology strives through critical realism to make its language more lucid to illuminate the mystery of God's presence in everyday reality. For our project, the current state of mainstream OT studies and the understanding that the post-Enlightenment tradition is just that, a tradition, are key contextual elements in calling for an attempt to map out a new paradigm in which the reality of God is taken with full seriousness.

---

33　Van Huyssteen 1989, 161.

34　Van Huyssteen 1989, 159.

35　Van Huyssteen 1989, 164.

36　Van Huyssteen 1989, 170. Emphasis added.

37　Van Huyssteen 1989, 171.

## (b) The explanatory success of theological models

A second criterion for theological models in critical realist mode is their capacity to explain. To explain what? Anything that strikes us as unusual, so that if a theory offers a solution we should give it maximal scope by applying it as widely as possible. The Bible should play a central role in such models. It is a classic, a book of faith with 'a radical religious dimension'.[38] The metaphors we use to describe the Bible remain valuable, metaphors such as the word of God, inspiration and so on. 'A scriptural conception is a model and, as a theory, a structured way of looking at the Bible.'[39] Theological models cannot and should not be reduced to emotional responses; they generate these because they claim to explain something, to refer.

In terms of our project we can, for example, refer to the explanatory limits that historical criticism has run up against. God is the central character in the OT, and the OT has profoundly shaped the history of Christian theology, and yet, if we are to follow John Barton and the post-Enlightenment tradition, theology should never be part of biblical criticism. These issues raise a host of questions and, in terms of our project, the question will be whether or not taking theological models of divine action seriously in OT studies, instead of distorting OT interpretation, in fact has better explanatory power than interpretative approaches which exclude such data.

## (c) The constructive and progressive nature of theology

This relates closely to the above criterion. Theology needs to be constructive in the development of models and progressive in enabling us to engage with the problems presented to us *today*. For example, an obsolete theory of the Bible as Scripture may lead to a new theory. Tom Wright's creative proposal for how to conceive of the authority of the Bible today seems to me an excellent example of such a move.[40] However, as regards the progressive nature of theology, van Huyssteen nuances the challenge in a way that connects directly with our project, noting that hermeneutics cannot ignore the religious dimension of the Bible. Reinjecting theology into OT studies, as I am proposing, is a way of insisting that we do not ignore its religious dimension.

For van Huyssteen, the authority of the Bible should not be equated with historical accuracy, although in many cases the question of historicity remains

---

38  Van Huyssteen 1989, 177.

39  Van Huyssteen 1989, 179.

40  Wright 1991. This article is readily available on the internet <https://ntwrightpage.com/2016/07/12/how-can-the-bible-be-authoritative>. In our *The Drama of Scripture*, Mike Goheen and I have sought to develop this approach in a narrative biblical theology.

important. This relates, of course, to our discussion of history and the OT above.

# 4 Conclusion

We have seen time and again how readings of the OT push the issue of theology to the surface. Taking theology seriously is vital for this project in all sorts of ways.

- It positions us to explore the world view of the ANE nations and of Ancient Israel emically and to take their views of the divine seriously.
- There are multiple levels of theology, and at the world-view level we can identify the basic beliefs that are fundamental to the world views of the ANE, beliefs which are strongly oriented to the divine. In the next section we move on to explore the major world views of the ANE and in the process will attend to the basic beliefs embedded in them, and this will, of course, include their view of the divine.
- At a basic level this will enable us to compare and contrast world views and to start to see what the OT's perspective looks like in relation to the world views of other ANE nations.
- OT scholars also indwell world views and, as I have argued at length in my *God Who Acts in History: The significance of Sinai*, it is not a question – *contra* Barton – of whether religion should play a formative role in OT studies but of which religion and how. If OT scholars, such as Barr and Barton, continue to indwell the post-Enlightenment perspective on reality, then this is a paradigm that will need to be argued for. However, as Lilla so evocatively explains, it is not the only world view on offer. The Judeo-Christian world view/s provides a major alternative, and it is within this world view that this project situates itself.
- A critical realist approach rejects the post-Enlightenment view that religious language is meaningless and to be kept out of scientific scholarship. Drawing on van Huyssteen's work, we have seen that there is nothing about the language of the OT or of theology that prevents us from taking it as meaningful, scientific and referential. However, this does not mean that there are no criteria for its rationality, and the onus is on us to show that injecting theology into OT studies reaps major explanatory rewards and attends insightfully to many of the puzzles in contemporary OT studies.

- The OT is a fundamental part of Christian Scripture and is, as such, normative for theology. However, we have seen that the relationship between the OT and theology is complex. We need to reinject the OT into our doctrine of God, *and* we need models of God and divine action to inform our reading of the OT. Both moves are essential and we will need to negotiate this circularity further down the line.

For now, we turn to immerse ourselves in the world views of the ANE with an eye in particular on how they conceive of the divine in relation to the world.

# Part 3

# THE WORLD VIEWS OF THE ANCIENT NEAR EAST

The peoples [of the Ancient Near East] had always deferred, and referred, to God or the gods in all things, going back to time immemorial . . . The gods' looming presence in the ancient Near East has, of course, some practical consequences . . . [H]ow someone thinks about God . . . has very much to do with how that person conceives of himself or herself, and more precisely, how such a self conceives of itself fitting into the world. (Theodore Lewis)[1]

---

1   Lewis 2020, 10.

# 6

# Ancient Near Eastern world views

## 1 Introduction

Above we identified, following Wright, four interacting elements in a world view: story, praxis, core beliefs and symbol. Although there is still much we do not know about the ANE, the archaeological gains of the last century and a half are vast, as is the amount of scholarship on the cultures of the ANE, thus putting us in an ever-expanding, albeit challenging, position to articulate the variety of world views in the ANE as well as their commonalities. Within monotheistic traditions whose adherents are 'people of the book', it is tempting to focus just on core beliefs in order to articulate world views. However, Wright's analysis is helpful in drawing attention to other key embodiments of a world view, elements which are front and centre in the ANE.

For example, take the view of royal authority or politics in Ancient Egypt. As we will see below, there are texts, titles and iconography to be explored, and developments over time in the ideology of the pharaoh, but one should not overlook the great *symbol of the pyramids*. 'The Step Pyramid started life ambitiously enough, as a huge mastaba tomb, built in stone to last for eternity. It rose in one single step, towering above the king's burial chamber, a mountain of stone to replicate the primeval mound of creation.'[1] This is the first time in history that we know the name of the architect of such a royal monument, one Imhotep.[2] His creativity and vision was extraordinary, and he oversaw the development from a one-stepped mastaba to a four-stepped pyramid and finally to a six-stepped one, the highest building of this time. 'His innovation marks the beginning of the Pyramid Age, and it had far-reaching effects.'[3] Construction on this scale required administrative efficiency at a level never before experienced in Egypt, and led to the creation of the post of vizier, the person in charge of the government, reporting only to the pharaoh. The Joseph narrative in Genesis indicates that it was to this position that Joseph

---

1  Wilkinson 2010, 54.
2  See Wilkinson 2003, 111–13.
3  Wilkinson 2010, 55.

was appointed. The royal court became increasingly professional, opening it up to talented individuals from wider sections of society. It is a mantra of a theology of place that 'we form places and places form us'. Wilkinson comparably observes: 'As Egypt embarked on pyramid building, the pyramids were building Egypt.'[4]

It is hard to conceive of more powerful symbols than the pyramids. Until the building of the Eiffel Tower in AD 1889, the Great Pyramid of King Khufu (r. 2545–2525 BC) remained for 44 centuries the highest building in the world. Clearly, this is a great symbol, but what is it a symbol of? The pyramids were tombs, albeit of the pharaohs, and thus symbolize death. This in itself is astonishing and hard to imagine in our contemporary Western societies. However, they were far more than symbols of death. Wilkinson entitles his chapter on the pyramids 'Heaven on Earth'. He notes the vastness of Pharaoh Khufu's Great Pyramid, constructed on an area of 13 acres (5.25 ha) and built of 2.3 million blocks of stone, each weighing more than 1 ton (1,016 kg) on average. In the course of a ten-hour day, the builders would have had to set in place a block every two minutes. Monumentality was not new in Egypt, but the pyramids were an innovation and Wilkinson notes that they were accompanied by a transformation in the understanding of the relationship between the pharaoh and the people.

The change manifested itself in the king's titles. Khufu's father, Sneferu (2575–2545 BC), oversaw the building of the geometrical pyramid. For his 'Horus name', the most symbolic element of the royal titles, Sneferu adopted the expression *neh maat*. As we will see below, *maat* is a major element in the Egyptian world view, encompassing truth, justice and creation order. Wilkinson notes that:

> Sneferu was announcing nothing less than a new model of kingship. For him, the exercise of power was no longer confined to dispensing justice. The king's word was the law because the king himself was the law. If this smacked more of divine than human authority, that was the point.[5]

To complement this title, Sneferu adopted another, *netjer nefer*, meaning 'the perfect god'. This claim to deity was embodied in the way in which Sneferu's pyramid and its complex were constructed, built, in contrast to monuments of the Third Dynasty, along an east–west axis, consciously and intentionally

---

4   Wilkinson 2010, 55.

5   Wilkinson 2010, 58.

mirroring the sun's journey across the heavens. 'As "the perfect god," the king was publicly associating himself with the supreme divinity and source of all life.'[6] Pyramid-building reached its zenith with the Great Pyramid of Khufu. The narrow shafts leading from the burial chambers to the outer edge of the edifice are noteworthy. They open out on to the stars, key elements in Egyptian state religion. 'Khufu's pyramid was nothing less than a way of uniting heaven and earth for the everlasting well-being of the king.'[7]

Clearly, royal ideology underlies the profound symbolism of the pyramids. But were these monumental building projects favoured by the populace, bearing in mind the arduous labour involved? Scholars disagree. If they were not about national pride, what was their motivation? 'The uncomfortable answer is that it was the ultimate projection of absolute power.'[8] Wilkinson says of the Great Pyramid that:

> At its most stark, the structure represents the untrammeled exercise of political and economic control; at its most inspirational, it represents a unique episode in human history. It is this combination of the sinister and the dazzling that gives Khufu's monument its enduring fascination.[9]

As we embark on an examination of the world views of the ANE, the pyramids are instructive. Attention to them as a symbol has led us into reflection on death, politics and royal ideology, extraordinary inventiveness and accomplishments in vast building projects grounded in precise science under the absolute power of the king, the role of the pharaoh as lawgiver, as well as into the religious aspects of the pyramids. If the pyramid is meant to symbolize the creation mound, and if the pharaoh was regarded as divine, then we are pushed into an examination of the stories and core beliefs of the Ancient Egyptians. This brings us up against the thorny topic of *myth*, since it is in their myths and stories that we find such core beliefs articulated, and we will attend to myth below before we dig in to the actual world views on the ground in the ANE.

For now, it is worth noting from this initial foray into Ancient Egypt the fertility of an examination of the world view of the ANE for our understanding of the OT. The role of the vizier, for example, casts an interesting light on Joseph's role in Egypt, a source of much discussion among OT scholars whether

---

6   Wilkinson 2010, 61.

7   Wilkinson 2010, 72.

8   Wilkinson 2010, 71.

9   Wilkinson 2010, 65.

the narrative is regarded as historical or not. The architectural achievements of the Ancient Egyptians remain rightly a cause for wonder. Israel came on the scene much later but would produce no great, comparable architectural achievements. Indeed, to a major extent the OT world view is set *against* that of Egypt, and especially in regard to the absolute power and deity of the pharaoh. Bellah notes that 'king and god emerged together in archaic society and continued their close association throughout its history'.[10] When it emerges in Israel, however, kingship is awash with suspicion, and (uniquely in the ANE) YHWH, and not the king, is the lawgiver par excellence. As we will see later in this book, such differences yield a very different world view.

It is also worth noting how ANE world views may (re)shape our understanding of world view. James Sire has done exceptional work on world view over many years and I am deeply indebted to his work. His book *The Universe Next Door: A basic worldview catalog* is now deservedly in its sixth edition.[11] Over the years, he has continued to develop his set of diagnostic questions to foreground a world view. In the sixth edition he has seven diagnostic questions. Intriguingly, politics is not one of them. In the ANE, politics is utterly central, by comparison, to every ANE world view, as we will see. Perhaps this is one way in which the ANE can push us to look anew at the key elements of a world view.

# 2 Myth in the Ancient Near East

> Mythic (narrative) culture is not a subset of theoretic culture, nor will it ever be. It is older than theoretic culture and remains to this day an indispensable way of relating to the world.
> (Robert N. Bellah)[12]

As we enter into the world views of the ANE, we immediately run into a vast range of stories of the gods and thus of 'myth'. This is no simple topic. In his *Theorizing About Myth*, Robert Segal discusses 13 main theories and nine others. He observes furthermore that it is hard to compare theories of myth because to do so is 'ineluctably to compare theories of the broader categories,

---

10   Bellah 2011, 266.
11   Sire 2020.
12   Bellah 2011, 280.

themselves as varied as the physical world, the mind, society, culture, literature, and religion'.[13] In his *Myth: A very short introduction*, Segal proposes that:

> What unites the study of myth across the disciplines are the questions asked. The three main questions are those of origin, function, and subject matter. By 'origin' is meant both why and how myth arises. By 'function' is meant both why and how myth persists. The answer to the why of origin and function is usually a need, which myth arises to fulfil and lasts by continuing to fulfil. What the need is, varies from theory to theory. By 'subject matter' is meant the referent of myth. Some theories read myth literally, so that the referent is the straightforward, apparent one, such as gods. Other theories read myth symbolically, and what is symbolized are most often natural phenomena or human attributes.[14]

Edward Tylor (1832–1917) read myth literally; myths are about gods and not human beings, and they are meant to be taken literally and not metaphorically. They explain how the gods control the physical world, but do not provide an evaluation of their actions. For Tylor, myth is thus replaced by science, whereas for Eliade, Bultmann, Jonas and Jung, myth is compatible with science. They revision either the function of myth so that it does not explain the world, or its subject matter so that it does not refer to the actual world.

William Robertson-Smith (1846–94), a prominent nineteenth-century Scottish OT scholar, pioneered the myth–ritual school, agreeing with Tylor that myth is a primitive explanation, but of ritual and *not* of the world. For him, myths arose once the mainly naturalistic reasons for rituals were forgotten. James Frazer provided the classic formulation for the myth–ritual school. For Frazer, myth is secondarily a primitive explanation of the world but primarily a ritualistic means of securing control of the world. For Jung, myth is not about the external world but about the mind, which projects itself on to the world. Through myth we can access human archetypes. Campbell develops a romantic theory of myth as an indispensable resource of wisdom about humans and ultimate reality. 'Tylor is thereby the quintessential nineteenth-century theorist of myth. The quintessential twentieth-century ones are A. R. Radcliffe-Brown and Malinowski, who pursue function, and Bultmann and Hans Jonas, who pursue significance.'[15]

---

13    Segal 1999, 1.

14    Segal 2015, 1–2.

15    Segal 1999, 152.

Our concern is, of course, with ANE myth, especially in relation to the Old Testament. With Tylor we affirm that ANE myths are meant to be taken literally. The ANE was awash with gods – it was polytheistic through and through – and inhabitants of the ANE would have been surprised to hear that the gods might not exist. Barr notes in this respect that *correspondence* is at the heart of ANE mythology:

> Myth always maintains a secret correspondence or hidden harmony of some kind between gods and man, gods and nature, man and nature, the normative primeval and the actual present. The correspondence is . . . not merely figurative but ontological.[16]

In an uncertain world, myth provided an explanation for why the world is the way it is, and also showed people how to navigate it successfully as a vital resource for wisdom. Myth is functional and as such is an essential means for maintaining human life in the cosmos. Ritual is central to ANE myth in actualizing the relationship to reality which myth evokes and in gaining control over the world, thus drawing in magic. The origin of myth is shrouded in mystery and, while it certainly includes projection on to the world, it is too easy for moderns to dismiss the religious dimension of myth in this way. We cannot explore this in detail, but we will need to draw from theology of religions to provide some inroads in this area.

In the Preface to volume 2 of his *Philosophy of Symbolic Forms*, entitled 'Mythical Thought', Ernst Cassirer reflects critically on the relationship between philosophy and myth after Kant.[17] Kant's idealism appears to mark a break between myth and science, with myth relegated to the realm of illusion and thus now transcended and forgotten. From this perspective, mythical thinking is replaced by autonomous, rational, scientific thinking and should therefore be abandoned as a primitive stage in humankind's development.

Midgley, by comparison, asserts that:

> We are accustomed to think of myths as the opposite of science. But in fact they are a central part of it: the part that decides its significance in our lives. So we very much need to understand them.

---

16   Barr 1959, 5–6.
17   Cassirer 1955.

> Myths are not lies. Nor are they detached stories. They are imaginative patterns, networks of powerful symbols that suggest particular ways of interpreting the world. They shape its meaning.[18]

Clearly, *much will depend on how we define myth*. Symbols suggesting patterns for interpreting the world are different from literal belief in the immense pantheon of gods of the ANE. Intriguingly, even in this respect some in our post-Christian West are arguing for the polytheism of societies such as those of the ANE as a more helpful theology of religions than the 'coercive monotheisms'. Where Midgley's comments are helpful in our project is that even if we, as does the OT, reject the reality of the thousands of gods of the ANE, the symbolism they yield for understanding the world of the various ANE peoples, and their consequent accomplishments, remains to be seriously investigated.

In the ANE literature in which I have been immersed, it is rare to find ANE myths evaluated through the lens of a theology of religion. Tylor's point, noted above, that in myths the gods are not evaluated continues to intrigue me, not least because it is mirrored in so much contemporary work on the ANE, which seems reluctant to evaluate ANE myths and world views. For our work, which seeks to retrieve YHWH as utterly central to an understanding of the OT, a theology of religion clearly remains important and cannot rest easily with Midgley's assertion that myths are not (ever) lies.[19]

In his fascinating book *The Faith of the Outsider*, Spina begins by affirming in essence what we have referred to above as the Mosaic distinction. 'In the Bible's macro-story . . . exclusivity is at the heart of the biblical message.'[20] Within the metanarrative of the Bible, the motif of exclusivity is simply unavoidable, as the theme of YHWH's election of Israel makes clear. 'Theologically speaking, Israel is the only game in town! At least, that's the way the Old Testament consistently presents the picture.'[21] The fact that Israel's God had a personal name, YHWH, was not at all unusual in the ANE, '[b]ut the difference for Israel, as it is portrayed in the Old Testament, was the radical belief that its god, YHWH, was the only living god and therefore the only divine being deserving of worship

---

18  Midgley 2003, 7.

19  Interestingly, the analogy of the relationship between Israel (OT) and the nations of the ANE and how this relationship is viewed in the NT has become a central motif in recent *inclusivist* theologies of religion. For a very useful explication of such views, see the work by my former colleague, Adam Sparks (2010).

20  Spina 2005, 9.

21  Spina 2005, 5.

and obedience'.[22] However, YHWH's election of Israel was neither because of her merits – 'This explains why Israel is portrayed in the Bible in such stupendously unflattering ways'[23] – nor for her only; the OT is clear that Israel's election is God's mechanism for including all nations as part of his people.

The centrality of exclusivism and election in the OT make the OT texts that concern outsiders so intriguing. Spina defines an 'outsider' as 'any person or group that has not been specially chosen by God to be the vehicle of the world's restoration and reconciliation'.[24] Spina engages in this respect in close readings of the stories of Esau, Rahab, Naaman, Jonah, Ruth, and the woman at the well in the NT. He rightly notes that such outsider stories are not incidental to the witness of the OT, but serve to nuance the motif of exclusivity and to enhance the emphasis on God's grace. Indeed, it is precisely the OT emphasis on the uniqueness and sovereignty of YHWH that makes such outsider texts possible, and they serve as a reminder that an OT theology of religions is never one of simple rejection.

Sparks notes that profitable avenues in a theology of religions awaiting further research are the 'function of truth and general revelation in non-Christian religions. The relationship between general and special revelation, and the possibility of other "modalities" of special revelation also warrants further research.'[25] The Mosaic distinction means that the OT's critique of idolatry is very strong. However, its doctrine of creation whereby all humans live in the same world, subject to the same creation order brought into existence by YHWH, means that all humans of all religions respond to God's general revelation, albeit in distorted ways. This has important consequences for how we approach ANE myth. In philosophy, Wolters asserts that when we encounter idolatry we need to do two things.[26] First, we need to be conscious of the idolatry. Second, and this is the really important insight, it is at the point of idolatry that we are likely to find the most poignant insights. Wolter's approach to the history of philosophy is eminently transferable to and helpful with our engagement with ANE myth. In our engagement with ANE myth we need critically to be aware of how it differs from the world view of Israel / the OT, *and* the insights into the world it provides.

Myths come to us mainly in story form. Segal notes that

---

22   Spina 2005, 5.

23   Spina 2005, 7.

24   Spina 2005, 9–10.

25   Sparks 2010, 287.

26   Wolters 1981.

myths undeniably tell stories rather than give arguments. But this difference in form need scarcely mean a difference in function. Plato, Plotinus, and other ancient critics of myth as story take for granted that the function of myth is the same as that of philosophy.[27]

However, as Ballentine points out, not all ANE myths come in story form; they include poems, proverbs, prophecy, letters, epitomes, inscriptions and iconography.[28] Nevertheless, as we will see, narrative remains fundamental to ANE myth, and here our earlier work on narrative and world view comes into its own. Narrative is foundational to the world views of both ancients and moderns, and world view allows us to access the world views of the nations of the ANE emically, while retaining room for an etic analysis. World views aim to tell the true story of the world and in this respect are exclusive. Barr notes that:

> Myth has to be seen as a totality within the relevant cultural group . . . [T]he effect of myth upon the consciousness of a people is seen only when we realise that it was the mythology as a totality which both shaped and expressed its mind.[29]

Myth strives after a total world view; it strives to interpret all that is significant:

> Mythology is not a peripheral manifestation, not a luxury, but a serious attempt at integration of reality and experience . . . Its goal is a totality of what is significant to man's needs, material, intellectual and religious . . . Myth is then a total world outlook.[30]

## 3 Myth in the Old Testament

When it comes to myth and/in the OT, we encounter a bewildering range of views. Perhaps the strongest view of the OT/HB as anti-myth is that of Yehezkel Kaufmann. His view exemplifies what Assmann refers to as the

---

27  Segal 1999, 150.
28  Ballentine 2015, 2.
29  Barr 1959, 3.
30  Barr 1959, 3.

Mosaic distinction. The HB does not deny the existence of other gods; instead it ignores them.[31]

> There is no evidence that the gods and their myths were ever a central issue in the religion of YHWH. And yet this religion is non-mythological ... It is precisely this non-mythological aspect that makes it unique in world history; this was the source of its universal appeal.[32]

Kaufmann argues that the pagan myths of the ANE were transmuted by Israel:

> Originally conceived of as mythological beings, born of the primordial realm, divine in their essence, these monsters [i.e. beasts featuring in pagan myths] became in Israel creatures of YHWH, who rebelled against him. This transformation reflects the peculiar Israelite conception of the demonic realm as a whole.[33]

Kaufmann sums up his view as follows:

> In sum then, the biblical religious idea, visible in the earliest strata, permeating even the 'magical' legends, is of a supernal God, above every cosmic law, fate, and compulsion; unborn, unbegetting, knowing no desire, independent of matter and its forces; a God who does not fight other divinities or powers of impurity; who does not sacrifice, divine, prophesy, or practice sorcery; who does not sin and needs no expiation; a God who does not celebrate festivals of his life. An unfettered divine will transcending all being – this is the mark of biblical religion and that which sets it apart from all the religions of the earth.[34]

Similarly, G. E. Wright argues that 'the God of Israel has no mythology'.[35]

In what remains a rigorous and perceptive view of myth in the OT, Childs asserts that '[t]he unique elements of Biblical thinking can best be seen by contrasting them with mythical thinking'.[36] For Childs, God has made himself known in the total experience of Israel: 'In saga, in legend, the broken myth,

---

31  Kaufmann 1960, 20.
32  Kaufmann 1960, 20.
33  Kaufmann 1960, 63.
34  Kaufmann 1960, 121.
35  Wright 1950, 26.
36  Childs 1962, 73.

through these unhistorical vehicles as well as through the historical, Israel articulated her understanding of her existence.'[37] He argues that:

> The Old Testament's 'history of redemption' (*Heilsgeschichte*) is the life of Israel. The demythologizing of mythological traditions is also a definite part of this history. Naturally, it is our decision of faith whether or not we want to take our standpoint with Israel and see her experience as a genuine encounter *with God* rather than just an encounter with herself.[38]

Childs examines a range of OT texts in which mythical elements are discerned, and he is well known for his analysis of how the OT 'breaks' ANE myth through the ways in which it appropriates them. Childs identifies as a characteristic of ANE myth an emphasis on 'Urzeit-Endzeit' and he finds the presence of this in the OT compelling.[39] However, the witness of the OT is that 'the structure of reality is not determined in a series of primeval acts, but rather a new reality came into being through the redemptive activity of God working in her history'.[40] This is evident, for example, in the Israelite cult, in which we do not find simple identity; rather, the new preserves the form of the old so that the passing of *chronos* (time) has significance.

Barr's position is similar to that of Childs. He too uses the metaphor of breaking: 'The main thesis of this paper is, then, that in Israel the correspondence pattern of mythology was broken.'[41] In Israel's thought we find a 'radical departure' from mythical thought. 'It is not too much to say that the main battle of the Hebrew faith is fought against the confusion of human and divine, of God and Nature.'[42] This confusion was a particular problem in Canaanite Baalism, which may provide the *Sitz im Leben* in this development of Israelite thought. Fragments of myth remain in Israelite thought, but 'Israelite thought is a totality with its own centre', and the fragments must be understood in relation to this centre. The importance of history for Israel enforced this difference from mythology so that '[i]t is thus perhaps possible to say that the central position in Israel is occupied by history rather than myth, and that such survivals of myth as exist are

---

37  Childs 1962, 103.
38  Childs 1962, 103.
39  On myth and eschatology in the OT cf. Barr 1959, 9–10.
40  Childs 1962, 78.
41  Barr 1959, 7.
42  Barr 1959, 7.

controlled by the historical sense'.[43] If we ask how this interest in history developed in Israel, we are 'probably forced back on Israel's own confession to the centrality of the Exodus and the events surrounding it'.[44]

Mark Smith, by comparison, asserts that 'the Baal cycle expresses the heart of the West Semitic religion from which Israelite religion largely developed'.[45] Bernard Batto says of his book *Slaying the Dragon: Mythmaking in the biblical tradition*:

> The thesis upon which this book is predicated is that myth is one of the chief mediums by which biblical writers did their theologizing. Rather than trying to read myth out of the Bible as many in the past have done, I intend to demonstrate that myth permeates virtually every layer of biblical tradition from the earliest to the latest. Texts from all periods and of virtually every literary genre reveal that biblical writers borrowed old myths and extended their meanings in novel ways for the purpose of expressing new theological insights.[46]

Batto defines myth as '*a narrative (story) concerning fundamental symbols that are constitutive of or paradigmatic for human existence*'.[47] Of the exodus, Batto concludes that the styles of the various traditions describing Israel's escape from Egypt compel us to conclude that we are dealing with a tradition that owes as much to myth as to history – if not more to myth than history. Apart from fresh archaeological discoveries, whatever historical core the exodus had is now lost to us.[48]

Schutte asserts that:

> The Psalms, and indeed all the texts of the Bible, were written against the background of a mythical worldview, where everything that we would call supernatural would be considered entirely normal. This worldview understands its environment as a three-story universe of gods and goddesses that include a heaven, an earth and an underworld, and where God speaks directly to humans. Such a worldview is what I would call the perfect setting for myth, but not in the sense that it would indicate

---

43   Barr 1959, 8.
44   Barr 1959, 8.
45   Smith 1994, xxvii.
46   Batto 1992, 1.
47   Batto 1992, 11. Emphasis original.
48   Batto 1992, 126.

a primitive, unsophisticated story or an 'untrue' fable. Rather, myth is a language: one in which divine and human actors can interact, and one that sets the world as a stage where the encounter with God, nature and human kind is reflected.[49]

As we have noted above, much depends on how one defines myth and what one thinks about it. Batto's definition is similar to that of Midgley, quoted above, and from her perspective science and post-Enlightenment thought *do not* escape myth. Schutte's points alert us to the fact that much also depends on our view of God and divine action. In our modern world it has become commonplace to believe that we can only find truth – including the truth about the OT – if we bracket out religion and divine action. In my opinion, it is precisely such a view that the OT contests, and the wager of this volume is that it is only as we take YHWH with full seriousness that we will discover the truth of the OT, and the truth about our world and ourselves.

Clearly, the relationship between the OT and ANE myth is contested. In the following parts of this volume we will revisit this issue as we explore divine action in the OT and the view of God in the OT. For now, it is worth noting that if all talk of God and the divine is myth then evidently the OT is awash with it, but so too is theology and much philosophy of religion. Indeed, Batto's definition is so broad that it easily encompasses all world views, including post-Enlightenment ones. I am reminded here of Clouser's point that all world views ultimately depend on religious beliefs, with such beliefs defined as that on which everything else depends while it depends on nothing else. Clearly, however, such a broad definition as that of Batto does not get us very far in our engagement with the mythology of the ANE. The nations of the ANE believed in and told stories about thousands of different gods and it is this phenomenon that we are referring to when we speak of myth. There are certainly mythical elements in the OT, but the OT uniquely and unequivocally asserts belief in the one God YHWH, and with Childs and Barr it then becomes interesting to see what the OT does with the mythical elements in its texts. Try as one might – and as we will see, scholars really do try! – it is hard to get away from the fact that something very different is going on with the OT view of God in comparison to the hundreds of gods of the ANE peoples and their mythologies.

As we move now to attend to the world views of the different nations in the ANE, their particular mythologies will come to our attention.

---

49   Schutte 2007, 1.

# 4 The world view/s of Ancient Egypt[50]

## (a) Introduction

The OT locates the origins of Israel as a people in Egypt, where they grew in numbers and stayed, according to Genesis 15.13, for 400 years. The dominant figure in the Pentateuch, apart from YHWH, is Moses, and according to Exodus 2 he was adopted into the royal Egyptian household and would have received an excellent education there. Kass observes that when it came to Israel's liberation:

> leadership must come from someone who had been raised to rule. Moreover, if he is to be a leader for God's Way, such a ruler would need to know not only how to be a leader of men (and not, like Joseph, largely an administrator of things). He would also need to be prepared *intellectually*, to learn about the world and the powers that rule it, especially should there be competing claims regarding knowledge of what is highest; that is, of the divine.[51]

Ironically, the great leader who would confront Pharaoh in the name of YHWH, and lead Israel out of Egypt, is incubated within Pharaoh's own palace. However, '[b]ecause Israel is to be the anti-Egypt, it is important to discover what Egypt is: its worldview, its politics, its way of knowing, its gods'.[52] Doubtless, Moses benefited greatly from his Egyptian upbringing, but he would also need to learn how God's way differed from that of this great empire. One of the many insights of Kass's *Founding God's Nation* is his tracking of Moses' development and formation once he left Egypt. To discern Israel's difference from Egypt, Moses would need to know the Egyptian world view intimately, and so do we as readers of the OT. As Kass notes about the contest between YHWH/Moses and Pharaoh embodied in the plagues: 'It is a contest of ideas and worldviews – about god, man, and nature; about rulers and ruled; and about knowing itself'.[53]

The historicity of the Moses narratives in Exodus is contested by many historical critics, but at the very least the *literary* witness of the OT ought to be

---

50  On the current state of Egyptology see Wilkinson, ed., 2008.

51  Kass 2021, 45. Emphasis original.

52  Kass 2021, 136.

53  Kass 2021, 139. On epistemology in Exodus see the very useful chapter in Abraham 2021, 97–110.

taken seriously as the context against which to understand Israel as a people. The name 'Egypt' occurs some 546 times in the OT, an indication of its influence on the thought world of Israel. And, as we have seen above, the symbolic dimension of Egyptian religion was exceptionally powerful and would have been unavoidable for inhabitants of Egypt.

According to the timeline of those who take the historicity of Moses and the exodus seriously, the Israelite sojourn in Egypt and Moses' life would have fallen in the period of the New Kingdom (c.1567–1085 BC). In terms of the development of Egyptian religion, this was a highly formative period in which implicit theology was increasingly complemented by explicit theology.[54] It was a time of political and economic expansion and one in which the pharaohs abandoned the pyramid complex of the Old and Middle Kingdoms, expanded old temples and built many new ones. Temple construction reached its heights under Amenophis III (1391–1353 BC) and Ramesses II (1290–1224 BC).[55] Wilkinson notes that:

> If the Amarna Period[56] can only be seen as a decisive downturn for the fortunes of most of Egypt's cults, the following Ramessid era was characterized by recovery and unprecedented growth. Rameses II . . . is credited with building more temples than any other monarch in Egyptian history.[57]

The latter is often regarded as the pharaoh at the time of the exodus.[58] What, we might ask, did the world view/s of Egyptians look like and how might Israelites have experienced it?[59]

## (b) Characteristics of the Egyptian world view

*First, the Egyptian world view was thoroughly and comprehensively religious.*

Indeed, Egyptians were renowned for being deeply spiritual: Herodotus observed of the Egyptians that '[t]hey are religious excessively beyond all other

---

54    This is Assmann's (2001) language.

55    Wilkinson 2000, 24–5.

56    The Amarna period was the brief time of the triumph of a form of monotheism in Egypt, as we will see below. King Akhenaten moved his capital to Akhet-Aton, now called Amarna. See Seyfried, ed., 2012; Kemp 2012.

57    Wilkinson 2000, 25.

58    Durham 1987, xxv; Berman 2020, 43–75.

59    On *Private Life in New Kingdom Egypt* see Meskell 2002.

men';[60] and 'temple of the whole world' and 'image of heaven' are phrases used of Egypt in *Asclepius* 24.[61] For Ancient Egyptians, all of life was religious and, as with the Israelites and the other ANE nations, it is anachronistic to impose a modern sacred–secular dualism on their way of living.[62] 'The influence of religion was everywhere. The most prominent features of the built landscape – temples and tombs – served as sacred space, and so much of the immense material legacy of the culture – coffins and mummies, statues, figurines, amulets, and papyri – are manifestations of religious beliefs',[63] as we saw with the pyramids above.

However, as with the Israelites, one can distinguish between the cultus and the rest of life; in OT language we would speak of cult and covenant, with the cult as part of the covenant. As with Israel, the boundary between cult and the rest of life is thoroughly porous, with cult having everything to do with the rest of life. Apart from Akhenaten's brief revolution, which we will attend to below, Egyptian religion was *polytheistic* so that the Egyptians the Israelites encountered would have been devoted to the local god/s who ruled over and dominated the city formed in relation to the god's temple. 'For the believer, every deity is a separate figure with unmistakable features, among which are certain characteristics that are shared with no other deity.'[64] Hornung notes that:

Any sort of contact with the world of the Egyptians silences one question, that of the existence and reality of these gods. Egyptian religion lived on the reality that gods exist, and this certainty pervaded all of Egyptian life. If we remove the gods from the Egyptians' world, all that remains is a dark, uninhabited shell that would not repay study. The gods are part of Egyptian reality and hence are for us at the least historical realities that should be taken seriously . . . In order to understand the forces that circumscribe the very closed and homogeneous world of the Egyptians, we must inquire after their gods and employ all our conceptual armory in order to seek out the reality of these gods – a reality that was not invented by human beings but *experienced* by them.[65]

---

60   Herodotus, *Histories*, II, 37.

61   Assmann 2001, 17.

62   Thus, Teeter (2011, 4) notes that '[o]ne could easily argue that there was no "secular" realm in Egypt because all aspects of the society and culture were outgrowths of religion'.

63   Teeter 2011, 197.

64   Hornung 1982, 143.

65   Hornung 1982, 251. Emphasis original.

Thus, any attempt to articulate the Egyptian world view/s simply has to take the gods with utmost seriousness.

In the nineteenth and twentieth centuries, Egyptologists' understanding of Egyptian religion went through various permutations, from being trumpeted as basically monotheistic to an appropriate recovery of its strongly polytheistic nature.[66] We need to explore how Egyptians thought about the gods or a single god, whether or not they identified and worshipped an impersonal power behind their many gods, and whether or not their gods can be seen as forerunners of monotheism. 'Such questions as these mark the beginning of a laborious road that must be traveled by anyone who seeks a correct answer.'[67] However, this is no easy task. Wilson observes that:

> The way of the Egyptian was to accept innovations and to incorporate them into his thought, without discarding the old and outmoded. This means that it is impossible to find in ancient Egypt a system in our sense, orderly and consistent.[68]

Furthermore, as we will see below, it was not unusual for different descriptions of phenomena, including the gods, to be presented side by side even though they contradict one another.

*Second, the Egyptian world view was deeply shaped by Egypt's geography.*

Indeed, the distinctiveness of Egyptian religion and world view is related to the country's geography. The Egyptians were acute observers of their unique geography, dominated by the Nile, desert and the sun, as well as its wildlife, and this finds expression in their view of the gods and the world.

As we noted earlier in this book, Egypt was relatively isolated from other cultures, unlike Israel, for example. As a result, their land in its relative isolation was the focal point of their world view (see Map 6 overleaf). For example, Egyptians were regarded as people; foreigners were not.[69] This is not to deny Egyptian hospitality, abundantly evident in the Joseph narrative in Genesis. Once foreigners had become integrated into Egyptian culture, they were regarded as 'Egyptian' and able to rise to the highest positions in the land. Understandably, Egyptians understood other nations from their own

---

66   See Hornung 1982, 15–32.
67   Hornung 1982, 31.
68   Wilson 1946, 33.
69   Wilson 1946, 33.

perspective. Egypt experienced very little rainfall; the annual flooding of the River Nile provided them with the water needed to make their agricultural land fertile. They thus saw other nations as having the Nile falling from the skies!

The Nile and the sun dominated Egyptian life, and both loomed large in Egyptian religion. Bearing in mind the small amount of rainfall Egypt experienced, the dominance of the sun is striking. Not surprisingly, the Egyptians viewed the sun as a god integrally related to the daily birth, journey and death

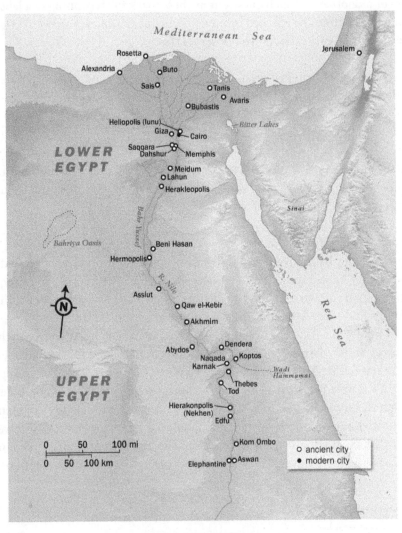

Map 6 **Ancient Egypt**
(© Baker Publishing Group)

of the sun. The sun dominated the Egyptian psyche. The personification of the sun's power, the sun god was supreme and creator. In this respect, Egypt's theology was a solar theology. The Fifth Dynasty was the apogee of solar religion. In the sun temple of Neuserre, there is a relief-decorated corridor called the *Weltkammer* (world room) containing huge numbers of images of animals, birds, and watercourses filled with fish. The reliefs depict all the events characteristic of each season, showing that the sun god is lord of seasons and provisions.

Herodotus aptly described Egypt as 'the gift of the Nile'.[70] The Nile made the very life of Egypt possible. The Nile Valley is surrounded on both east and west sides by extensive desert. 'This belief in the coexistence of opposites was characteristic of the ancient Egyptian mind-set, and was deeply rooted in their distinctive geographical surroundings.'[71] Wilkinson observes that the Nile has shaped 'over the course of generations their [the Egyptians'] most fundamental philosophical and religious beliefs'.[72] As we will see, according to Egyptian accounts of origins, in the beginning there was a watery chaos, personified by **Nun**: 'The great god who creates himself: he is water, he is Nun, father of the gods.'[73] A later creation story describes the primeval waters as threatening and scary, and indeed the Nile with its annual inundation, to say nothing of predators such as crocodiles, could be both life-giving and destructive, as the ancient concern to measure the inundation with a Nilometer bears witness.[74]

The annual rebirth of the Nile in the form of its flooding was a major event. The summer rains fell on the Ethiopian highlands, causing the Blue Nile – one of two tributaries that come together to make up the Egyptian Nile – to swell and sending a torrent of water downstream. In early August, the coming inundation was visible in the south, and shortly thereafter the flood arrived. With great power the Nile burst its banks, with water flowing over the floodplain. The amount of water spread this phenomenon along the whole Nile Valley. For several weeks, the water flooded the agricultural lands but also deposited fertile silt, and once the waters subsided the soil emerged, watered and fertilized, ready for cultivation. Egypt's agricultural productivity, indeed her survival, depended on this annual inundation. If the inundation was too great or too small, the effects could be catastrophic for food production. Generally, however, the inundation was moderate.

---

70  Herodotus, *Histories*, II, 5.
71  Wilkinson 2010, 15.
72  Wilkinson 2010, 15.
73  Quoted in Wilkinson 2010, 15.
74  Wilkinson 2014, 41.

Furthermore, the slightly convex shape (by cross-section) of the Nile Valley ensured that the valley was particularly suited for irrigation, both naturally and artificially.[75] The floodplain also divides naturally into flood basins, each able to be managed by the local population. In Ancient Egypt one could only survive near the Nile, and this proximity enabled the first king, Narmer, to unite Egypt under a single leader.

It is easy to see, therefore, why the Nile was a central metaphor for the Egyptians. According to an early creation story, Nun's waters recede to foreground a mound of earth, just as the floodwaters would recede. **Atum**, the creator god, emerges with the mound, his name signifying both 'totality' and 'nonexistence'.[76] Wilkinson observes the political implications of such religious doctrine:

> The message was clear and unambiguous: if Atum was the first king as well as the first living being, then created order and political order were interdependent and inextricable. Opposition to the king or his regime was tantamount to nihilism.[77]

In the history of temple-building in Ancient Egypt, each temple modelled itself on this ancient myth, building on a sacred mound in an attempt to recreate the world. This link between cult and creation is notable. Studies of the Priestly source in OT studies have been especially fertile in opening up the link between cultus and creation in the OT.[78] Navigation north or south on the Nile required sails positioned differently, and in tombs and with the sun god two boats are provided.

Not surprisingly, crocodiles were feared in Egypt, and **Sobek**, the great and ancient crocodile god of Egypt, was understood as both dangerous and a source of fertility. The Nile was thought to result from his sweat.[79] Sobek was linked to the sun god **Re** and was a symbol of the pharaoh's power. Intriguingly, Kass proposes that the *tannîn* of Exodus 7.8–9 is the crocodile, noting that '[t]urning a staff of authority into a crocodile is thus a most fitting wonder to create in front of Pharaoh'.[80] If this is correct, then even as Moses and Aaron

---

75  Wilkinson 2010, 16.
76  Wilkinson 2010, 17.
77  Wilkinson 2010, 17.
78  See Morales, ed., 2014.
79  Wilkinson 2003, 218–19.
80  Kass 2021, 134.

are presenting their credentials to Pharaoh the battle lines are being drawn, and drawn in ways that Pharaoh would understand. A major theme of Exodus is knowledge, and particularly knowledge of YHWH. The ensuing plagues will function as 'the curriculum for the Lord's educational purposes', and 'Pharaoh – exposed as *merely* King of Egypt – will become the most distinguished witness to the existence and superiority of Y-H-V-H God of Israel'.[81]

Amid the uniformity, perhaps monotony, of the Egyptian landscape animals stood out, and Wilson notes of the falcon floating in the sky, the jackal moving along the desert margins, the crocodile submerged in the mudflats, and the muscular bull that:

> These beasts were forces going beyond the normality of landscape; they were forces which transcended the minimal observed nature of animals. They therefore took on high relief in the scene and were believed to be vested with mysterious or inscrutable force related to an extra-human world.[82]

In a huge variety of ways, animals play a central role in the depiction of the gods.

In his *Complete Gods and Goddesses of Ancient Egypt*, Wilkinson has sections on avian gods, reptile, amphibian and fish gods, and invertebrate and insect gods. One of Egypt's most ancient gods was **Horus**, commonly depicted as a falcon. Horus was the lord of the sky, a solar god, the god of kingship, and came to be worshipped as the son of the goddess **Isis**.

> From the earliest Dynastic Period the king's name was written in the rectangular device known as the *serekh* which depicted the Horus falcon perched on a stylized palace enclosure and which seems to indicate the king as mediator between the heavenly and earthly realms, if not the god manifest within the palace as the king himself.[83]

Intriguingly, in Ezekiel 17 both the king of Babylon and the pharaoh of Egypt are depicted as a 'great eagle'. The same word for eagle (נֶשֶׁר) is used in Exodus 19.4 to describe how YHWH brought the Israelites out of Egypt to himself. Bearing in mind that for Egyptians the sky was alive with gods, and Horus was the lord of the sky and closely connected with kingship, it is likely that Exodus 19.4 with its reference to how YHWH carried the Israelites out of Egypt like an

---

81  Kass 2021, 131. Emphasis original.

82  Wilson 1946, 40.

83  Wilkinson 2003, 201.

eagle with its young on its back is, among other things, an anti-Egyptian motif. Even amid the god-ridden skies over Egypt, YHWH can act with impunity; it is he and not Horus or Pharaoh who is the true king.

As Teeter notes:

> The Egyptians were visually oriented and were tremendously keen observers of their environment. Their worldview was based entirely on concrete principles that they could see around them ... their response to their world was based entirely on their observed reality.[84]

Teeter suggests we might categorize them as the most rational of people, but perhaps *empirical*, in a pre-theoretical sense, is the more appropriate word.

> The contrast between the Egyptian mind and the Greek mind is startling. With their tradition of adversarial discussion, the Greeks would debate one theory against another to reach a new, single synthesis – a process that was alien to the Egyptians, who, through accretion, would layer one possible solution on another without discarding any.[85]

A great achievement of the Egyptian world view was its longevity. 'For more than three thousand years, the Egyptians maintained generally the same outlook on the world, making theirs one of the most conservative and unchanging societies yet known.'[86] However, this left Egypt with a static world view and one that prevented a concept of history and development from appearing, as Assmann points out. They looked back to the primeval era as one of perfection, and religion served to maintain the world or to restore it to this original state.

*Third, the Egyptian world view embodied particular, Egypt-centric views of the cosmos.*

As we noted above, Egypt's isolation, as well as a strong sense of her distinctiveness and superiority, kept the focus of her cosmology on the land of Egypt, with her cosmology projected from it. The Nile and the sun were key compass points in this respect; she took her geographical orientation from the Nile, but referred to the east from where the sun was resurrected each morning as *ta-netjer*, namely 'God's land'. The rising of the sun relates to life, and

---

84   Teeter 2011, 9.
85   Teeter 2011, 13.
86   Teeter 2011, 13.

evening and darkness to death. Even the animals worship the sun as it rises each morning. To enter into the Egyptian world view, we need to imagine seeing the sun each day as the god Re who had once again died during the night and risen yet again.

Egypt's concept of the world developed incrementally over approximately 3,000 years. Furthermore, as we have seen, Egyptians were quite comfortable with differing perspectives of an entity, and this is also true of their cosmology. For example, when it came to the question of what held up the sky, Egyptian myths provide a whole variety of answers: posts, walls, a god, a goddess with her feet and arms touching the earth, or a cow! Following Wilson, we will choose a single picture to evoke Egypt's view of the cosmos.[87]

According to one picture, the earth was viewed as a flat platter with a corrugated outer edge. The flat inside of the platter is the land of Egypt; the rim refers to the mountains and thus to the other nations. At its heights Egypt was 'the world's premier civilization',[88] and this Egypt-centric world view is a far cry from Israel's Table of the Nations, as discussed above. The earth floated in the primeval waters (Nun) below. The sun died each evening as it entered the waters and was reborn each morning out of Nun. A boat was given to the sun for the day and for the night, with crews of gods to power the boats. The Nile poured forth from caverns fed by Nun. Symmetry is a major characteristic of Egyptian thought, and Nun, as the waters, not only was under the earth but also encircled the earth. Above the earth was the inverted platter of the sky, and once again in terms of symmetry there was a counter-heaven under the earth. As noted above, there are a variety of images for what supported the sky, namely posts to carry it, **Shu** the air god, the underbelly of a celestial cow, and so on. The stars and moon form part of the sky. The circumpolar stars were especially prominent and were associated in the early mortuary texts with the place of the dead, and of the god **Dat**. With the development of the sun mythology, Dat moved to the underworld from the northern part of the sky. Clearly, for Egyptians the world was awash with gods.

*Fourth, the Egyptian world view included stories of creation.*

The people of Egypt accepted not one creation myth but several different accounts. According to one story, a mound or primeval hillock (the *benben*) emerged from Nun. As per our earlier comments, this too is a projection from

---

87   Wilson 1946, 44–9.
88   Kass 2021, 130.

nature since such mounds would appear in the Nile. According to one version, 'the great cackler', a phoenix-like bird, settled on the mound and its cries broke the silence and heralded the beginning of life.[89]

According to a second version, the god Atum appeared on the mound. He was self-created; he 'became, by himself'.[90] From the Pyramid Texts we learn that Atum created the first gods, Shu and Tefnut, through masturbation.[91] According to other sources, he created them through his spit. Shu (air) and Tefnut (moisture) gave birth to earth (Geb) and sky (Nut). Through procreation Geb and Nut gave birth to two couples: Osiris and his consort Isis, and Seth and his consort Nepththys.

> These represent the creatures of the world, whether human, divine, or cosmic . . . [I]n this ruling family of the gods we have a creation story implicitly. Atum, the supercharged vacuum, separated into air and moisture. As if in the operation of the nebular hypothesis, air and moisture condensed into earth and sky. Out of earth and sky came the beings that populate the earth.[92]

In yet another version Nofertum, the first god, came forth out of a water lily which itself emerged out of Nun.

We lack a specific account of the creation of humankind. Some myths explain that the ram god Khnum formed humankind on his potter's wheel. Intriguingly, one text describes humans as made in the image of god, a reminder of Genesis 1.26–28:

> Well tended are men, the cattle of god. He made heaven and earth according to their desire, and he repelled the water monster (at creation). He made the breath (of) life (for) their nostrils. They are his images that have issued from his body. He arises in heaven according to their desire. He made for them plants and animals, fowl and fish, in order to nourish them. He slew his enemies and destroyed (even) his (own) children when they plotted rebellion (against) him.[93]

---

89  Teeter 2011, 12.

90  Wilson 1946, 53. *ANET*, 4.

91  cf. *ANET*, 6: Re says, 'I planned in my own heart, and there came into being a multitude of forms of beings, the forms of children and the forms of their children. I was the one who copulated with my fist, I masturbated (xxvii I) with my hand' ('The Repulsing of the Dragon and the Creation').

92  Wilson 1946, 54.

93  Urk. 1.232. Wilson 1946, 55.

Wilson draws particular attention to an inscription called the Memphite Theology.[94] The elements related to creation in this inscription are present in other Egyptian texts, such as the ones we have been looking at, but 'only in this text were they brought together into a broadly philosophical system about the nature of the universe'.[95] This inscription, now held in the British Museum, is on a worn-out stone with the name of a pharaoh who reigned *c.*700 BC. This pharaoh claimed to be copying a much earlier inscription, which Wilson takes to be correct. The text takes us back to very early in Egyptian history when the first dynasties established their capital at Memphis. It forms part of an apology for the primacy of the god Ptah and his home, Memphis.

According to Wilson, this text comes as close to articulating a philosophical view of creation as was possible in Egyptian thinking, with its emphasis on creation by speech and thought, again a reminder of Genesis 1.1—2.3. The Memphite Theology assumes details we refer to above, namely, Atum's emergence out of the primeval waters and the creation of his Ennead, a group of nine gods. 'In place of discarding them as competitive, it wishes to subsume them into a higher philosophy'.[96] This elevated philosophy asserts innovation through ideas and production through speech acts. Thought and speech are deities in the earliest Ancient Egyptian literature, normally Hu and Sia. In the Memphite Theology these two powers are taken materially as the heart (for thought) and the tongue (for speech), and both are related to the activity of Ptah, who is equated with Nun. 'Thus it was discovered and understood that his (Ptah's) power is greater than (that of the other) gods. And so Ptah rested after he had made everything, as well as the divine order.'[97] Wilson's 'the divine order' is literally 'the word of the god'. As he notes:

> 'the divine order' implies that the gods have a system into which all the created elements should fit as soon as created. The context enumerates the created elements: gods, fortunes, food, provisions, towns, districts, etc. . . . What can this mean other than the directive order?[98]

---

94  *ANET*, 4–6.
95  Wilson 1946, 55.
96  Wilson 1946, 56.
97  Wilson 1946, 59.
98  Wilson 1946, 59. See also Pardee 2012.

Closely related to 'divine order' is the concept of *maat* and the goddess Maat. Order, truth and balance in the cosmos are embodied in *maat*. Teeter notes that:

> The goddess represented the divine harmony and balance of the universe, including the unending cycles of the rising and setting of the sun, the inundation of the Nile River, the resulting fertility of the land, and the enduring office of kingship; she was considered to be the force that kept chaos (*isft*), the antithesis of order, from overwhelming the world.[99]

Maat thus tied personal behaviour to maintaining the order of the world. 'There is punishment for him who passes over its [*maat's*] laws.' 'Do *maat* so that you may endure upon Earth.'[100] *Maat* has long been of interest to some OT scholars since it provides an intriguing parallel to creation order, as taught, for example, in Genesis 1.1—2.3. However, in the OT, creation order is not personified as a god but is related to YHWH's creation; nor is it connected integrally to the king.

Frankfort is adamant that the pharaoh was regarded as a god: 'Pharaoh was no mere despot holding an unwilling people in slavery. He ruled in the strictest sense by divine right; and any attempt to describe the Egyptian state irrespective of the doctrine of Pharaoh's divinity would be fatuous.'[101] Similarly, Wilson observes that 'the king of Egypt was a god and he was a god for the purposes of the Egyptian state'.[102] Teeter refers to the king as partially divine. What all agree on is the close relationship between the king and *maat*. The social order was part of the cosmic order: 'The laws of nature, the laws of society, and the divine commands all belong to the one category of what is right.'[103] But this could not be taken for granted and the king was responsible for maintaining *maat*. Obeying him was thus also vital for the maintenance of cosmic order and may account for there being so few periods of unrest in Egypt's very long history. The king's relationship to *maat* is clearly evidenced in the ritual of the goddess Maat's presentation to the other gods by the king, a ritual which embodied the commitment of the king to uphold *maat*.[104] Maat was also pervasive among the gods. Hornung notes: 'Through creation gods and

---

99  Teeter 2002, 189. In Redford, ed., 2002.
100 Teeter 2002, 189. In Redford, ed., 2002.
101 Frankfort 1948, 1975, 31.
102 Wilson 1946, 71.
103 Frankfort 1948, 1975, 54.
104 cf. Teeter 1997.

men acquire a common task: to maintain their existence, which has an end, against the unending non-existent and together to build a living order that allows space for creative breath and does not become atrophied.'[105]

*Fifth, the Egyptian world view contained a pantheon of humanlike gods.*

Leitz notes that if we are after an overview of Egyptian deities and demons, it is wise not to let ourselves get bogged down in detail. Apart from the 50 to 100 major gods, there were many thousands of minor ones.[106]

The Egyptian word for 'god' is *ntr*, pronounced *netjer*, once vowels are added. It is written with a hieroglyphic sign whose normal form is that of a staff bound with cloth. Other pictograms for 'god' are a hawk on a carrying pole and a squatting god. There is also a series of pictograms of animal-like and anthropomorphic gods. However, neither the pictograms nor the etymology or original use of *ntr* helps us to understand the nature of Egyptian religion.[107] Other terms for gods are *b'w*, which always refers to an active, visible side of the divine person, and *shm*, commonly translated as 'power' but which came to mean 'image' of a god in the New Kingdom.[108]

The gods of Egypt were like humans in that they were created, lived, grew old and died. Indeed, all Egyptian gods are born. Even the 'god' who was the mother or father of the gods himself emerged at creation from the primeval ocean, Nun, which 'precedes' the gods: 'in Egypt one cannot speak of a true transcendence that would raise a deity above space, time, and fate and extend his being into the realms of the absolute and limitless.'[109] The phrase 'who came forth from Nun' is used to refer to the council of the gods as a whole, as well as to individual gods. However, four pairs of gods are identified as part of the primeval chaos: Nun and his consort Naunet, Huh and his consort Hauhet, Kuk and his consort Kauket and Amun and his consort Amaunet.[110]

Egyptian theology has a clear doctrine of creation, but the view that one god creates the others does not in any way imply monotheism.[111] References to the creator god could be to Ptah, Re, Amun or Atum, or to any god worshipped as creator. All gods are born, but not all gods are equal. The Egyptian pantheon was ordered genealogically. 'Like men, the gods die, but they are not dead.

---

105 Hornung 1982, 216.
106 Leitz 2004, 393. See Wilkinson 2003.
107 Hornung 1982, 33–42.
108 Hornung 1982, 62.
109 Hornung 1982, 191.
110 Wilson (1946, 52) equates this with Gen. 1.2.
111 Hornung 1982, 150.

Their existence – and all existence – is not an unchanging endlessness, but rather constant renewal.'[112] As Hornung observes:

> the Egyptian gods are . . . 'neither unbegotten nor imperishable.' They begin with time, are born or created, are subject to continuous change, age, die, and at the end of time sink back into the chaotic primal state of the world.[113]

The gods were finite; only a few had power outside a town, a nome, a region.[114] Generally, the gods' efficacy decreased as distance increased, so that travellers prayed to local gods. The gods could be male or female and in some cases androgynous. Darkness was a boundary of the ordered world, and even the creator god of all could not simply pass this boundary. In the New Kingdom the sun god achieved more universal pretensions, a development which came to approximate monotheism in the Amarna period.

Early in his reign, Pharaoh Amenhotep IV began to formulate a significantly new theology. His temples at east Karnak were unusually dedicated only to the **Aten**, an embodiment of the new vision. In this new vision, Aten is seen as the sole god and this is related to the singularity of the sun disc. In earlier Egyptian thought, anyone could 'know' the gods, but the knowledge of Aten came to be reserved for the king alone. 'The constant reminders that the king was "unique" in his solo communication with the Aten are among the most striking and troubling aspects of this new theology.'[115] Thus, devotion to the god/s became absolute loyalty to the king. Akhenaten's 'monotheistic' revolution failed, but it had a profound effect upon Egyptian theology and played an important role in foregrounding the tension between one god and the many. However, Egyptian religion remained polytheistic. Assmann argues that Akhenaten's monotheism was historical but did not last, whereas Moses was not historical but the Mosaic distinction lasted. As we will see below, once YHWH and his action in history is retrieved, the historical figure of Moses comes strongly into view again. What is more, whereas Akhenaten's revolution enhances autocracy, the Mosaic distinction democratizes the image of God (Gen. 1.26–28) and thoroughly subverts notions of the absolute authority and deity of the king.

---

112  Hornung 1982, 160.

113  Hornung 1982, 165, referencing J. G. Griffiths, *Plutarch's De Iside et Osiride* (Cardiff: University of Wales, 1970), 150–1.

114  Hornung 1982, 166.

115  Teeter 2011, 187.

For most of its history Egyptian religion was dominated by practice rather than theory. Assmann identifies 'divine presence' as the main theme of Egyptian religion, and he defines this as 'the area of activity and the conceptual horizon of both divine care and human religious activity and experience. Its specific dimensions thus determine both the concept of the divine and the forms of religious experience.'[116]

*Sixth, local cultic practice, especially of the temple, was central to the Egyptian world view.*

The practice of polytheism does not easily lend itself to metanarratives, and Assmann is wary of extending myth into narrative when it comes to the Egyptian gods. However, some overarching narrative is unavoidable and the Ancient Egyptians did indeed have an account that explained the existence of temples, gods in them, cities and the king. In the Book of the Heavenly Cow, an explanatory myth found in several New Kingdom royal tombs, the present condition of the world is depicted in relation to a heavenly cow and multiple gods. In the myth, the present condition is contrasted with the original situation 'when humans and gods were (still) together'.[117] According to Ancient Egyptian religion, in the earliest, primordial times the gods dwelt on earth with humankind. As a result of a revolt by humans – 'Then the people devised a plot against Re' – judgement begins to be executed on humans – the daughter of Re 'returned after she killed the people in the desert' – but then Re regrets his decision to destroy humans. Sky and earth are separated, as the sky – the heavenly cow along which the sun travels – is lifted up by the god Shu – the god of the air separating earth and sky – and his eight assistants. The gods removed themselves to the heavens, and humans were left to their own fate. Shu became mediator between earth and heaven, and the state and the cult emerged as compensation for the relegation of the divine to the sky. The state (king) and temples were introduced to sustain the relationship between the gods and humans. Gods were thus encountered in everyday life through the king and the cult.

Egypt was packed with temples and thus gods. Temples dominated the landscape and every sizable town had several. The edges of towns were dominated by tomb chapels. 'The presence of deities in these temples was conceived of as more intense and personal, and less symbolic, than in other

---

116  Assmann 2001, 7.
117  Assmann 2001, 113.

religions.'[118] Egyptian gods were seen as resident on earth in their respective temples so that Egyptian religion was thoroughly this-worldly. Assmann notes that:

> The demise of Egyptian civilization as a semantic universe was a direct result of the advent of the redemptive religions. To the very end the unshakeable convictions that informed Egyptian theology . . . were that man is at home in the world, that human participation is essential to the divine scheme of sustaining the world, and that the unending task of reconciling the human and the divine is the true source of worldly coherence and continuity. The longing to be redeemed from this world instead of being piously incorporated into it was completely alien to Egyptian thought.[119]

Most of the surrounding land that constituted *the city* belonged to the temple so that the gods were like lords of the manor. 'The dual props of the economy were land held by the temples and land held by the state, and there was often no clear division between them.'[120] As we will see, the wealth of the temples and the priesthood in Egypt form a stark contrast with the land-lessness of the Levitical priesthood in Israel. City and local deity were thus inseparable, as the Egyptian city names demonstrate, names such as 'city of Thoth', 'city of Amun' and so on. Assmann refers to this as Egypt's 'city god theology'.[121] 'For the ancient Egyptians, the concept of a city was thus first and foremost determined by religion.'[122] To live in a city meant to live in proximity to the city's god. This tied not just deities but also citizens to a particular locality. Egyptian temples but not their cities were surrounded by walls. The temples did not pay taxes to the state, 'for there was no economic or conceptual separation of church and state'.[123] Indeed, upon the coronation of the king the rituals were enacted before the deities of the land and they acknowledged him as their representative. Temple complexes were also government, commercial and scholarly centres.

The city was characterized by temples and especially by the chief temple. This becomes evident when we think of how the castle-like temples with high

---

118  Assmann 2001, 18.

119  Assmann 2002, 424–5.

120  Teeter 2011, 4.

121  Assmann 2001, 18.

122  Assmann 2001, 19.

123  Assmann 2001, 19.

fortress-like walls[124] and towers loomed over the flat land, and were thus visible from afar. They dominated all other cultural and architectural manifestations. The temple of Amun at Karnak is the largest religious building ever constructed.[125] Temples served different functions in Egypt: as houses of the gods; as mortuaries; and some as fortresses, administrative centres and royal retreats.[126] For Egyptians, the gods lived in their castles on their primeval mounds, so that it was possible to think of Egypt as a single large temple, the 'temple of the entire world'.

The temple itself was part of a large temple complex. In Egyptian, *pr* referred to the total temple complex, the totality of a deity's possessions. In contrast, *hwt-ntr* referred not to the divine household as a whole but to the god's house. The actual temple was built of sandstone as was typical of sacred buildings, which included tombs; buildings filling the remaining space were made of sun-dried bricks and constituted the magazines that belonged to the temple as an economic concern. We cannot always be sure of the extent of the properties belonging to the temple, but they could be vast: the *pr* of Amun covered 590,000 acres (238,750 ha).

In principle, the king or pharaoh was the officiate in the cult. Thus the walls of temples are full of depictions of the king executing his religious duties. In practice, however, a very large group of Egyptians functioned as full- or part-time priests. 'Priests were an omnipresent feature of the Egyptian society and economy, and few people who appear in the written record lack a priestly title.'[127] The priests were *hmw-ntr*, servants of the god, and they lived on the divine offerings. The personnel of a temple consisted of about 10 to 20 people who had homes inside the temple enclosure,[128] but there were also lay priests, comprising a group about ten times the size of the official priests, and these served only periodically and lived outside the temple enclosure.

Not surprisingly, the architecture of the temple was laden with meaning. Assmann reminds us that the plan of temples changed over time and indeed a succession of temples is known in one particular place.[129] Historically, the temple was an ever-growing organism, and its development can be traced

---

124 New Kingdom temples best embody a fortress.

125 Wilkinson 2000, 6.

126 Wilkinson 2000, 7.

127 Teeter 2011, 17.

128 cf. Teeter (2011, 17) who notes that Ancient Egypt had no 'monastic' orders. Priests lived in the villages, married, had children, were occupied in other professions, etc. Most served part-time. On types of priests and their duties see Teeter 2011, 19–27. Women played a less active role than men in the cultus. The priesthood was often hereditary.

129 Assmann 2001, 39.

from huts onwards to, for example, the various stages of the temple of Satis at Elephantine. Assmann points out that it is best to begin a study of Egyptian religion with later, especially Ptolemaic temples, which manifested a clearly defined type. Their ground plan was thought to be derived from a primeval temple designed by the creator god at the beginning of the world.

Assmann examines the temple of Horus at Edfu.[130] Two parts stand out: the monumental pylon (gateway) at the entrance, and at the opposite end the innermost part of the sanctuary. The inner sanctuary or centre is surrounded by five 'layers':

- a corridor;
- a ring of 13 rooms opening off three sides;
- another corridor;
- an outer corridor;
- the external wall of the temple.

To the south of the inner sanctuary there are five rooms and five connecting doorways. Then there are:

- an anteroom, known as the hall of the Ennead because the deities who dwelled in the ring of chapels opening off this corridor were gathered there before the chief god;
- an offering room;
- the inner hypostale hall;
- the great hypostale hall, the hall of appearances;
- a collonaded court.

In the move from the exterior to the interior rooms, space becomes smaller, floors become higher and ceilings become lower with concomitant increasing darkness.

The architecture was designed to insulate the inner holy of holies with screens so that the profane, impure and evil were prevented from penetrating the protective layers around the sanctuary. Cult statues must at all costs be protected from contamination from the outside. Indeed, the nearer to the exterior, the more people were allowed access; movement from the outside in was governed by ever stricter rules of purity. Assmann does, however, point

---

130 Assmann 2001, 31.

out that 'the concept of screening and isolation of the holy, as expressed in the centralizing concept of spatial ordering, is a typically late concept'.[131]

As the architecture of the temple indicates, the image of the deity and the cult were at the very heart of Egyptian religion. Everything rested on the cultus and thus on the daily routine of the cult: according to Assmann, 'nowhere else in the world was so much done for the divine, or so continuously'.[132] Assmann elucidates the concept of the image in relation to action. Cult statues were understood to have two natures: one divine and one material, one above and one below humankind: 'As creators of these statues, humans are reminded of their own divine origin, and by piously tending and worshipping them, they make the divine at home on earth.'[133]

The sky was the home of the gods, and thus the theme of *descent* was central to the cultus. The *ba* (spirit or soul) of the god alights on his *sekhem* (statue/image). Once the *ba* filled the statue it became the physical form or *ka* of the deity.[134] Assmann uses a variety of terms to evoke this descent: uniting, fraternizing, embracing, installation, indwelling. The gods did not 'dwell' on earth; instead, they repeatedly installed themselves in their images. Examples of this are the ritual of Uniting with the Sun in which portable statues were carried up to the temple roof to be bathed in the sun and thus become full of the god. A comparable ritual is that of the Opening of the Mouth so that the *ba* entered the statue. However, it should not be thought that the god was thereby confined to the statue: it could burst out at any time. The statue was not conceived of as the image of the deity but as the body itself. From an Egyptian perspective the cultus involved a genuine relationship – and not just a symbolic one – with the deity, as the daily rituals make clear.

Daily rituals and festivals constituted the heart of the cultus. The extant temples have lost their original colour: originally the carved scenes on the walls were painted in bright colours, with red, blue, green, white and yellow pigments, a riot of colour and drama. The god resided in the temple in two forms: as a cult statue and as a portable processional barque. During a festival, which provided ordinary people with an opportunity to be involved in the cultus and of which there were hundreds,[135] the temple doors were opened and the god processed outside. This turning to the outside sanctified the world outside.

---

131  Assmann 2001, 33.
132  Assmann 2001, 41.
133  Assmann 2001, 41.
134  Teeter 2011, 44.
135  cf. Teeter 2011, 56–75.

The god's processional route extended beyond the temple; there would, for example, be a sacred avenue leading to the river, and other avenues to other sacred places. Assmann notes that this blurring of inner and outer boundary constituted a festival. In the history of Egyptian religion, oracular deities spoke through moving so that in Egypt oracles were connected with festivals. The procession of gods actualized the land in its social aspect. Related to this is the fact that no deity was the sole occupant of his or her temple.

The gods were attended to constantly. In every temple the daily ritual offering was performed three times each day. In a temple a priest woke up, greeted, worshipped, purified, anointed and dressed the cult statue in carefully ritualized behaviour.[136] The god was also provided three times daily with a huge variety of foods.

Assmann discerns four major aspects of the cultus:

- It involved personal service to the lord of the temple.
- Intriguingly, it was conceived of as an interaction between deities in which the priest assumes the role of deities. Assmann refers to an example in which, when meat is placed on the fire,

The breast is the eye of Horus,
the leg is the testicles of Seth.
As Horus is satisfied with his eye,
as Seth is satisfied with his testicles,
so is the god satisfied with his meat.[137]

- The ritual and speech performatively accomplished the transposition of the cultic events into the divine realm. Much has been written about the cosmological significance of temples in later periods: the floor represented the earth; the ceiling the sky which was decorated with stars. Columns assumed a plant-like form. Thus, while viewed from outside the temple seemed separated from the world, viewed from within it embraced the whole world so that '[t]he temple was an image of the cosmos, and the god who dwelled in it was a universal god'.[138]
- It was polytheistic, being carried out in the framework of divine constellations.

---

136  cf. Assmann 2001, 48, for the first nine acts of the morning clothing ritual.
137  Assmann 2001, 49.
138  Assmann 2001, 37.

The extent to which the pharaoh was regarded as divine is contested, as noted above. Frankfort argues that he was; Teeter refers to him as partially divine. Either way, the king had his own cult, and there are extraordinary examples of kings making offerings to themselves.[139]

*Seventh, in the Egyptian world view, personal religion played an important part.*

Teeter notes that '[t]he Egyptians had an intensely personal relationship with their gods whom they constantly approached with prayer, offerings and requests for assistance'.[140] Parts of the temples were open to the public, and chapels were often built around temples, one variety of which was known as a 'chapel of the hearing ear', where anyone could go to pray. However, Egyptians could contact their gods outside the temples through village shrines, stelae, figurines which functioned as votive offerings, and such like.

As the architecture of Ancient Egypt reveals, death loomed large in the Egyptian psyche. 'Egypt is obsessed with decay and death – two massive and most unwelcome natural facts. It is culturally preoccupied not with morality but mortality: with the natural goods of life, health, fertility, ageless bodily beauty, and, especially, longevity.'[141] Kass suggests that this obsession with mortality casts an interesting light on Pharaoh's question in Genesis 47.8 when he asked Jacob about his age.[142] In verse 9 Jacob, wisely, describes his 130 years as 'few and hard'! The pyramids are the most obvious example of the Egyptian focus on death, but so too are the vast number of tombs cut out of the hillsides of the Nile Valley. Construction of one's tomb generally began once one had regular employment and thus the resources for the project. Work on the burial place often continued for the rest of one's life so that a common claim was: 'I made this tomb while I was alive.'[143] Despite this visual and practical closeness to death, it was not welcomed or taken lightly by Egyptians. Elaborate rituals and processions were associated with funerals, although practices varied depending on one's wealth and position in society.[144] Tombs generally consisted of a below-ground burial chamber and an above-ground chapel where offerings could continue to be made for the deceased. Communication with and prayers to the dead were possible. Embalming of the corpse took some 70 days, after which the coffin

---

139  Teeter 2011, 51.
140  Teeter 2011, 76.
141  Kass 2021, 136–7.
142  Kass 2021, 137.
143  Teeter 2011, 123.
144  cf. Teeter 2011, 119–47.

and other boxes containing innards removed through embalming were processed to the tomb. The procession enacted a ritual drama led by the priests which represented the deceased person's journey to the west and union with the gods. At the entrance to the tomb the priests performed the Opening of the Mouth ritual on the deceased to restore life to him or her. Tomb paintings, utensils, figurines and offerings were intended to provide the dead with all they would need in their new life, which was conceptualized much as the Egyptians experienced daily life.

*Eighth, the Egyptian world view yielded a particular view of society.*
Egyptian society was grounded in religious institutions and in the absolute rule of the pharaoh:

> According to pharaonic ideology, the maintenance of cosmic, political, and natural order was unthinkable without the king, who served as the crucial lynchpin that held together not only Upper and Lower Egypt, but also the disparate worlds of gods and men.[145]

Even today, a cruise on the River Nile encounters myriad temples and representations of Pharaoh. The temples and the statues and representations of Pharaoh drove home two messages relentlessly: 'The king is the aggressive defender of his people, and the king is the only mortal who is on the same plane with the divinities and who may enter into relations of reciprocity and affection with them.'[146]

Morris examines three monuments from early Egypt to analyse the royal ideology: the Narmer Palette and two maceheads that predate the Early Dynastic period. She notes that these three, more than any extant monuments of that time, evoke the roles of the king. King Scorpion is known mainly through the one macehead; it is probable that he reigned just before Narmer. Significantly, Narmer's macehead and palette were discovered beneath the floors of the temple of Egypt's god-king, Horus. Their size is extraordinary, as befits a god. In Egyptian iconography Pharaoh continued to grasp a mace hundreds of years after it had become obsolete in warfare. These monuments were intended to be seen by the gods, but the scenes are of dramatic rituals that communicated, through their actual performance, foundational ideological concepts.

---

145 Morris 2013, 33.
146 Morris 2013, 34.

The size and placement of these monuments evoke the status of the king as far above the highest official: 'Whatever his posture or placement, the message is unambiguous: the king towers above humanity. The same rules that bind flesh and blood do not apply to him.'[147] Such artistic chicanery was adopted by virtually all following kings. In a literary work, Sinuhe tells of his audience with Senusret, providing us with a sense of how Pharaoh was viewed in this period:

> I found his Majesty on the great throne in the portal of electrum. Then I was stretched out prostrate, unconscious of myself in front of him, while this God was addressing me amicably. I was like a man seized in the dusk, my soul had perished, my limbs failed, my heart was not in my body. I did not know life from death.[148]

In the Old Kingdom there is some evidence that Pharaoh was regarded as not only a god but a great god. Morris observes of the portrayal of Narmer in his macehead that his role in world creation is evoked. Intriguingly, scent played a role in discerning the presence of a god, and pharaohs were sure to exude the fragrance of Horus. The dependence of Pharaoh on the gods is also evident in the four standards portrayed in the monuments.

> The other symbols that topped the remaining two standards also may be interpreted on multiple planes. The 'cushion' was known as the king's *nḥn*, most convincingly argued to be his placenta and thus the materialized presence of his spiritual twin (i.e., *ka* – Blackman 1915).[149]

It is likely that Horus was thought to enter the king at his coronation, and in this ritual the king received a shepherd's crook, symbolizing the pharaoh's role as caretaker of humanity. Morris notes of the two major festivals of kingship that 'all the leading figures of the terrestrial and celestial realms came together to pay their respects to the king, to give him gifts, and to receive gifts in return'.[150] Royal edicts for sculpting new statues of the gods and for founding temples abound, and here too we find evidence for the special status of the pharaoh. The Narmer Palette used to be read as depicting the unification

---

147  Morris 2013, 40.
148  Parkinson 1997, 40. Quoted in Morris 2013, 40.
149  Morris 2013, 45.
150  Morris 2013, 56.

of Upper and Lower Egypt, but it probably evokes the king as a fighter and punisher of Egypt's external and internal enemies. 'Royal smiting, which was the fate reserved for the most socially important individuals of a conquered people, was likely also a publicly staged event, replete with its own abasement and horror.'[151]

Morris concludes:

If it remains somewhat unclear whether the first kings of Egypt were thought of as deities incarnate, the protective hovering vulture god-dess on the Narmer macehead, the multiple supportive appearances of Horus, the dual depictions of the celestial cow-goddess that flank the king's name on the palette, and the shrines engraved in the background of scenes on the two maceheads make it quite clear that the king was under the protection of the deities and in an intimate relationship with them. Indeed, until the mid-2nd millennium the king was as a rule the only mortal portrayed directly interacting with the gods, much less enfolded in their embrace, as many of the kings prior to that point were commonly depicted.[152]

Similarly, Bellah observes that:

However variously the relation between the divine and the human was figured in archaic religions, the role of the king was always central. Even when, as in Egypt, piety had become democratized and private devotion was widespread, the formation of religious community depended on kingship ... Only when Christianity had decisively replaced the ancient religion could the vestigial role of pharaoh be abandoned altogether.[153]

In a culture awash with the gods, *magic* also played a role in Egyptian soci-ety. But since religion pervaded life, it is hard to know exactly what constitut-ed magic in Ancient Egypt.[154] According to Teeter:

It is best, then, to consider magic in ancient Egypt as a valid and ac-cepted – although a clearly distinguishable – part of religious belief. In

---

151  Morris 2013, 51.
152  Morris 2013, 44–5.
153  Bellah 2011, 246.
154  cf. Teeter 2011, 162.

a culture in which regular communication with the gods was natural, what we view as magic was just another means through which humans could effectively communicate with deities to seek protection from illness or from enemies.[155]

Magicians are clearly referenced in Egyptian literature,[156] and, for example, wands of a bronze snake were part of their magic, comparable to those used by Moses and Aaron in their confrontation with Pharaoh.

*Ninth, the Egyptian world view provided for ethics and values.*

**Historical development.** The Egyptian Empire lasted for longer than any other empire in history and thus it is hard to generalize about its beliefs and ethics. Wilson notes that '[h]ere it is not possible to compound out one nice generalization to cover two thousand years of history'.[157] In order to demonstrate his point, he proposes we visit two tombs of two viziers, one from *c.*2400 BC and one from *c.*600 BC.

The first is located close to the Step Pyramid at Saqqara. The rooms exude life in all its fullness. The vizier is depicted in various ways:

- spearing fish as his servants trap a hippopotamus;
- supervising the catching and butchering of cattle;
- overseeing the ploughing and harvesting of the fields, the metalworkers and carpenters, and the building of boats in preparation for his funeral service;
- overseeing the punishment of tax offenders;
- watching children play.

Wilson comments: 'Non-spiritual and active life is the full account of this tomb. This is his monument for eternity; this is how he wants to be remembered; this is the good life which he wishes to extend into eternity.'[158] It is easy to see how such a vision fits with Bellah's argument that '[t]he apparent Egyptian preoccupation with death was in reality a preoccupation with life'.[159]

---

155   Teeter 2011, 163.
156   cf. Teeter 2011, 169, for a photograph of one.
157   Wilson 1946, 93.
158   Wilson 1946, 94.
159   Bellah 2011, 233.

It should also be noted that this vizier would not have described such a life as 'non-spiritual'. This is to import a modern sacred–secular distinction that would have been alien to Egyptian thought.

Our first vizier lived during the Old Kingdom; our second, whose tomb is only 330 feet (100 m) or so from the first,[160] lived during the late period c.600 BC. In this tomb the teeming life of the earlier one has gone. Magic and ritual texts cover the walls. A few pictures are found of the vizier in the presence of the god of the dead. 'The life of this world is completely lacking; the funeral services and the world of the dead are the only concerns of this man.'[161] Wilson observes that this is the heart of the challenge in describing Egyptian ethics. At one extreme we find an emphasis on life, the materiality of the world, and activity; at the other an emphasis on death, contemplation and religion. He discerns two major periods: the earlier optimistic and energetic period and the later submissive, yet hopeful one, with a drawn out transition between the two.[162]

Wilson traces this development as follows. In the Old Kingdom there was a sudden flowering of culture epitomized by the building of the Great Pyramid of Giza by the architect Khufu-onekh. Accompanying this architectural flowering was the intellectual development inherent in the Memphite Theology and the scientific insights in the Edwin Smith Surgical Papyrus. Wilson says of this period that humankind was regarded as sufficient in and of itself. The gods were out there, to be sure, but the world was good not just because the gods made it so, but because humankind was in control. For Egyptians, the world 'was not completely devoid of god'[163] because the order for the world had been laid down by the god or gods.

Insofar as ethics are concerned, there is a focus on table etiquette and administration in which the *ka* of the person is particularly relevant. The *ka* was the part of the person that sustained one's individuality; it could also be the divine force within one which governed one's activity. The *ka* could also be a person's god. Wilson notes: 'We are here referring to the Old Kingdom, when the gods of the pantheon were more remote from common man, although not necessarily from his intermediating *ka*.'[164] Wilson finds support for the autonomy of the individual Egyptian during the Pyramid Age in the spatial

---

160 Wilson 1946, 94.
161 Wilson 1946, 94.
162 Wilson 1946, 94.
163 Wilson 1946, 96.
164 Wilson 1946, 97.

decentralization of the nobles' tombs. Earlier, they were built close to the god-king whom the nobles served; with time, they were moved to people's home districts, an individualistic trend. According to Wilson, in this earlier time securing the great benefits of life was not dependent on a slavish reliance on the gods. Humans were accountable to the pharaoh, to the creator god and to their own *ka*, but they were neither sycophantic devotees of a particular god nor particularly accountable to Osiris, who later became ruler over the dead. Affluence gave the Egyptians confidence that they could enjoy life now and that this enjoyment could be extended into the afterlife.

Wilson finds the ethos of this period embodied in The Instruction of the Vizier Ptah-hotep,[165] a text which he calls the 'gospel of the "go-getter," the bald rules for a young man who is on the make'.[166] Ptah-hotep contains pragmatic instructions for an official about how to speak and conduct himself in the administration – for example at a dinner party thrown by a superior – so as to succeed. 'A success visible to all men was the great good. These were the supreme values of the Old Kingdom, and they continued in value throughout Egyptian history.'[167]

As long as all was well, such values could be sustained. However, the Old Kingdom collapsed into a time of chaos in which the old principles seemed to be swept away. Some people embraced scepticism and despair, and we learn that the crocodiles of the Nile were sated through suicides. In one document, a suicidal Egyptian reflects on his impending death with his *ba* or soul.[168] He proposes to kill himself by means of fire. This life is rejected in preference to a future life of blessedness. An alternative attitude was that of hedonism: 'Pursue a holiday (mood) and forget care!'[169]

Wilson argues that it is during the Middle Kingdom that Egypt reached moral heights in the quest for the good life. He sees this in the decline in materialism and the move towards an emphasis on social action as *the* good, with an increasing sense that good things are available to all. Wilson identifies a coffin text[170] that only occurs in this period as remarkable, for in it the supreme god sets out the purposes of creation.[171] Wind and water are created for everyone; bearing in mind the inundation of the Nile and its role in Egyptian

---

165 In Pritchard, ed., 2011, 343–6.

166 Wilson 1946, 98–9.

167 Wilson 1946, 100.

168 Wilson 1946, 102.

169 Wilson 1946, 103.

170 Coffin texts are funeral spells inscribed on coffins.

171 *ANET*, 7–8: 'All Men Created Equal in Opportunity'.

agriculture, equal access to water means equality of opportunity. Every person is made like the next person, evoking an egalitarian society. Humans were not created to do evil, but their hearts led them astray. Human hearts were made such that they would cease from 'forgetting the west', the place of eternal life, with the result that divinization became available to all and not just the king.

> These were important changes of this period, the democratization of the next world and closer attachment to the gods. All men might now enjoy eternity in the same terms as had the king alone in the previous period ... Whereas only the dead king had become Osiris in the earlier period, now every deceased Egyptian became the god Osiris.[172]

However, such divinization was by no means automatic. It depended on successfully navigating a post-death judgement by a tribunal of the gods. Lorton comments:

> It is essential to note the emergence in Egypt of a concept of a Judgment of the Dead, which is first mentioned in the Middle Kingdom ... Among the misdeeds that the deceased claims not to have committed are murder, telling lies, stealing food, appropriating land, adultery, and cursing a god.[173]

Tomb biographies are also relevant here, reporting good behaviour such as 'I spoke *ma'at*, I did *ma'at*',[174] and so on.[175] Here *maat* comes into its own, and is, for example, the theme of 'The Eloquent Peasant' dating from this time.[176] This emphasis on *maat* 'permitted an age of real social consciousness, in which the psychological and moral basis was the belief that every man is the careworthy creation of the god'.[177] Also of ethical import are the texts of local leaders from Upper Egypt during the First Intermediate period. They provide us with an insight into effective leadership. Lorton notes that '[t]hese leaders seem to have been persons of extraordinary ability and outstanding civic virtue'.[178]

---

172 Wilson 1946, 107–8.

173 Lorton 2004, 515.

174 Lorton 2004, 515.

175 Tomb biographies originated in the Old Kingdom. *RAW*, 515.

176 Fisher 2015.

177 Wilson 1946, 109.

178 Lorton 2004, 515.

Wilson discerns a major transition in the Second Intermediate period after the Middle Kingdom between the eighteenth and sixteenth centuries BC. Again the central government collapsed, but now an additional factor was present, namely the incursion of the Hyksos, leading to a real awareness of potential threats from the outside and of the vital need for security. It became necessary to expand Egypt's empire in order to extinguish any threat, and the support of the gods was essential in this regard. A result was that:

> The previously modest temples in Egypt grew in physical size, in personnel, in land, and in total property, until they became the dominating factor in Egyptian political, social, and economic life. It has been estimated that, after the Empire had had three hundred years of active life, the Egyptian temples owned one out of every five inhabitants of the nation and owned almost one-third of the cultivable land.[179]

In terms of the individual, there was a concomitant shift from individualism to a type of nationalism. One should submit to society and anticipate better things in the world to come. 'There was thus a shift from an enjoyment of this world to the promise of the next world. That will explain the contrast between those two tombs which we outlined previously'.[180] With this went a new emphasis on concern for the poor; one's wealth and position in the hierarchy were not as important as proper relations with one's neighbour. 'Silence' is associated with the marginalized poor but now becomes a virtue of all, including the gods.[181] This silence is related to a fatalistic determinism that took hold. Ironically, Breasted describes the period of the late empire as an 'age of personal piety'.[182] Wilson explains: the Egyptian

> saw that his own personal god, who showed him mercy in his weakness, was also little and weak like himself. He saw that the great gods of Egypt, the national gods, were rich, distant, powerful, and demanding . . . He turned from a lusty appreciation of this life to means of escape from this life.[183]

---

179 Wilson 1946, 112.
180 Wilson 1946, 113.
181 Wilson 1946, 114–15.
182 Breasted 1912, 1972, 344–70.
183 Wilson 1946, 118.

*Maat.* In a short article on 'Ethics and Law Codes' in Ancient Egypt, David Lorton intentionally spends most of his time on what we can learn about ethical conduct in Ancient Egypt. However, at the conclusion he turns to *maat*, discussed above. He writes:

> Since ethics is a widespread human phenomenon, while *ma'at* was a concept peculiar to ancient Egypt, it was deemed best here to begin by discussing the surviving sources and what they have to tell us about ethical conduct, proceeding next to the religious framework within which ethical concerns were placed, and finally to the concept of *ma'at*.[184]

He adopts this strategy to protect comparative interests but rightly notes that this risks downplaying the role of religion. He concludes as follows:

> In fact, from what has survived from ancient times, there is every chance that if we had some means of asking an educated Egyptian to tell us about ethical conduct, he would begin with *ma'at* and the necessity of serving its interests by saying and doing it, for reasons ranging from individual survival in the afterlife through maintaining social order and cohesion to preserving the very fabric of creation itself, which was, at least hypothetically, in ever-present danger of dissolving back into the watery chaos of precreation.[185]

*Law codes?* Unlike for the empires and nations of Mesopotamia, we possess no extant law codes from Egypt. Either they did not survive, or they have not yet been discovered, or there was something about Egypt that precluded their production. If Egypt did not produce law codes it is most likely because of the absolute and divine or semi-divine nature of the pharaoh, which made them unnecessary. Frankfort notes that '[t]here were few codified laws because the pharaoh was the highest judge in the land and all laws emanated from him'.[186]

*Gods.* As we noted above, the Egyptian gods were all too human even with their greater powers. Within the Judeo-Christian tradition we are familiar with the theme of the *imitatio Dei*. This is not a theme that comes to the fore in Egyptian literature, but it is hard to imagine how Egyptians could worship their gods without attending to their behaviour and being drawn in to follow

---

184  Lorton 2004, 515.
185  Lorton 2004, 516.
186  Teeter 2011, 4.

it.[187] Nowadays, it is common to find polytheism celebrated as a tolerant alternative to monotheism, but attention to the behaviour of Egyptian gods hardly provides support for such a view. It is also common to find Egyptian religion and ethics lauded as exemplary. However, Toby Wilkinson expresses a growing sense of unease in this respect.[188]

**Not all good.** Certainly, thousands of gods were tolerated, but it needs to be remembered that these gods were all too human, and, as a god or semi-divine, Pharaoh held absolute power. And such power was not always wielded magnanimously. In the initial reigns of the First Dynasty, for example, the scale of funeral sacrifices of humans was large. Hundreds of individual Egyptians were slain to fit out the retinue of the dead king for the next life. In the late twentieth century, Flinders Petrie excavated seven tomb-pits in the Royal Necropolis at Umm el-Qaʿab in the western desert a few miles beyond Abydos. Petrie identified the tombs as royal and dated them in the First Dynasty. Each tomb is surrounded by smaller pits large enough for one individual, most probably for individuals sacrificed at the time of the royal funeral. The earliest of these royal tombs has around 338 'subsidiary burials' alongside it.[189] Analysing comparable death-pits at Ur, Wooley argued that the individuals sacrificed there, dying with the person whose funeral it was, went willingly or at least passively to their deaths. Dickson argues that only members of the lowest orders were sacrificed in this way:

> At Ur, neither royal spouse nor royal offspring seems to have accompanied the king or queen in the grave; noble courtiers, high temple officials, viziers, and generals do not appear to have been required to attend the royal personage in the afterlife.[190]

The scale of such human sacrifices declined as the First Dynasty wore on.

## (c) Conclusion

Religion dominates Egypt's world view. It is an immanent type of religion in which the myriad gods are part of the creation and projections from the experience of the Egyptians of their world. This, as we will see, is very different from the world view which emerges among the people of Israel, in which

---

187  See our comments in this regard in Part 4 on YHWH as servomechanism.
188  Wilkinson 2010.
189  Dickson 2013, 322.
190  Dickson 2013, 321. Cf. Morris 2013, 52.

YHWH transcends the creation. Understandably, because of their oppression in Egypt, the Israelites remember Egypt primarily as 'the house of bondage'. However, the picture in the OT is far more nuanced than that. Egypt's exceptional hospitality to the Israelite refugees from famine enabled them to survive and to flourish and grow exponentially. Even amid genocide, Moses ended up being educated in Pharaoh's household and thus profoundly shaped by Egyptian culture. And we must not forget the extraordinary longevity, and cultural and material achievements, of the Egyptian civilization.

In Exodus, when things come to a boiling point for the Israelites in Egypt it is in the area of *politics and social life*, key elements in a world view. In an autocracy of the Egyptian sort, life is fine when the pharaoh 'knows Joseph', but not fine when a new pharaoh arises. Pharaoh's authority was absolute, and thus politics and law were always precariously balanced on the whim of one man who was also perceived as 'divine', utterly apart from ordinary Egyptians. It is the brutal oppression of the Israelites and the genocide initiated by this one god-man that arouses YHWH's ire and results in his confronting Pharaoh and liberating the Israelites. Kass remarks: 'Where people think that human life is unendowed and only a powerful man can be a god to men, slavery – the absence of freedom in *all* its forms – is the only logical outcome.'[191] In Egypt, politics could not be separated from religion, and the OT discerns in the clash with Egypt a clash with the view of the divine and how this manifests itself societally. Kass asserts that 'Egypt lacks any real politics (rule addressed to the souls of men). Administration and technology, not law and governance, are supreme.'[192] In a footnote he argues that in this way Egypt anticipated the dreams of Marx and Engels who anticipated an end to politics and the state, to be replaced by 'the administration of things'. 'In Egypt, as in our own lifetime, that dream turned into a political nightmare, producing not liberation but despotism and massive human suffering.'[193]

# 5 Mesopotamia

Egypt is relatively self-contained, undoubtedly one reason why its world view remained stable for so very long. Mesopotamia is surrounded, and to an extent contained, by five seas: the Mediterranean, the Red Sea, the Persian Gulf, the

---

191  Kass 2021, 139.

192  Kass 2021, 138.

193  Kass 2021, 629, n. 11.

Caspian Sea and the Black Sea. Perhaps more significant than these seas are the two major rivers that run through Mesopotamia, namely the Euphrates and the Tigris, from which Mesopotamia ('between the rivers') gets its name. Diverse geographies – from the marshes in southern Iraq, to the basalt deserts of Syria and Jordan, to the snow-capped mountains of Iran – and its sprawling, capacious nature allowed Mesopotamia to become home to a variety of cultures, and empires, all of which inevitably interacted with one another. Roaf notes that:

> The variety of habitats in close proximity allowed different ways of life to exist in constant contact with each other, a factor that may have led to a cross-fertilization of ideas and stimulated the remarkable technological, scientific and social advances of the ancient Near East.[194]

The danger is that, as Robson observes,

> Mesopotamia . . . is all too often used as a catch-all term to refer to a large area over a vast period of time . . . There is a resultant temptation to over-generalise from single instances and to downplay geographical and chronological difference.[195]

We will see that the danger of over-generalization is present even within smaller groupings such as Sumer. This generalization is also seen in the tendency for writers to treat Mesopotamian religion as a unity. Whereas there are undoubtedly common elements, it is becoming clearer that there was also considerable diversity among Mesopotamian groups. Porter notes, for example, of Assyria that '[i]n religion as well, the Assyrians developed their own approach, borrowing gods and religious literature from the earlier Sumerians and Babylonians, but incorporating these in a system of belief and practice that although largely derivative, *was nevertheless distinctive*'.[196] In order to minimize this danger of generalization, we will attend to the major ANE world views, namely the Sumerian world view, the Hittite world view, the Assyrian world view, the Babylonian world view, the Aramean world view, the Phoenician world view, the Canaanite world view and the Persian world view, while remaining sensitive to the fact that within these groups there was often more than one

---

194  Roaf 1990, 19. Cf. Roaf 1990, 20–1.

195  Robson 2019, 1–3.

196  Porter 2000, 213. Emphasis added.

world view in place, as well as important continuity among the world views of Mesopotamia. Readers should also note that this list is far from comprehensive. There are many other groups in the ANE, and this chapter could expand exponentially. Space, limited expertise and the limits of what we know about many cultures of the ANE prohibit that!

Of course, the history of Mesopotamia and the Levant stretches way back beyond the Sumerians into the mists of time, and even as we push back behind Sumeria we become aware of just how right Roaf is to note that ANE study is still in its early stages.[197] ANE scholars demarcate the Natufian period (*c*.11,000–9300 BC), the Proto-Neolithic period (*c*.9300–8500 BC), the Aceramic Neolithic period (8500–7000 BC), the Neolithic period (7000–4000 BC) and then on into the time of the Sumerians which is where our analysis begins. Intriguingly, the oldest buildings in the Ubaid period (*c*.6000–4000 BC) were shrines or temples.[198] The major shift from villages to cities probably took place in the early and middle Uruk periods (*c*.4300–3450 BC). While religion goes back as early as our sources, it is in Uruk in the late Uruk period that we find our earliest-known written documents. Scholars have concluded that the language in the texts from late Uruk was probably Sumerian. The Uruk period (*c*.4000–3100 BC) ended in the final quarter of the fourth millennium. While we learn about a culture's or people's world view from far more than their writings, writings play an indispensable role, and the origin of writing marks a major breakthrough.[199]

# 6 The Sumerian world view

The significance of Sumer is evoked by the title of Kramer's book *History Begins at Sumer: Thirty-nine firsts in man's recorded history*. In his Preface, Kramer notes of Sumerian culture that all the landmark achievements of human culture are already present: politics, education, literature, philosophy, ethics and law, agriculture and medicine. However, geographically and historically, Sumer was distant from Israel (see Map 7 overleaf). Whereas, according to the narrative of the OT, the influence of Egypt on Israel was direct, the connection with Sumer is indirect, but nevertheless significant.

---

197  Roaf 1990, 18–56.

198  Lisman 2013, 6. There is some debate about the oldest temples in the world. See, e.g., <www.dainst. blog/the-tepe-telegrams/tag/sculptures>. These carved images at Göbelki Tepe would predate Uruk III by some 5,000 years.

199  See Roaf 1990; Algaze 1993, 2005; 2008; Glassner 2003.

Sumer and the Sumerian language and literature influenced ancient Near Eastern culture in a formative way. This is due in no small part to the fact that they were the originators of many of the cuneiform cultural and scribal traditions that dominated much if not all of the fertile crescent for almost two millennia.[200]

Already in 1959, Kramer had identified 15 themes or motifs common to the Bible and Sumerian literature: creation out of a primeval sea, humankind fashioned out of clay and given the breath of life, creation by command and fashioning, paradise, the Flood, rivalry motifs (cf. Cain and Abel in Gen. 4), the Tower of Babel, the organization of the earth, the idea of the personal god, law and law codes, ethics and morals, divine retribution, the plague motif, the suffering of the righteous and the bleakness of the netherworld.[201]

Politically, Sumeria was made up of multiple city states, including Nippur, the important religious centre Uruk, Ur and Eridu. Some of these cities, such as Nippur and Uruk, in particular go back to the urban revolution in the Uruk and Jemdet periods (4300– 2900 BC) when cities first developed in Mesopotamia, with concomitant societal changes in terms of governance, accumulation of wealth, taxation, and the building of great monuments, not least temples. The first example of writing comes from Uruk from c.3300 BC, an extraordinary achievement. Out of this came the cuneiform script:

The cuneiform script, first evolving in southern Mesopotamia, was adopted as the writing system of the Sumerian city-states. It then passed to a succession of other Near Eastern states, from the Akkadian and Ur III empires in late M3[202] through the Middle and Late Bronze Age kingdoms of Mesopotamia and Syria, the Middle and Late Bronze Age Anatolian-based kingdom of Hatti and well down into M1[203] BC, when it served to record the exploits of Persian Achaemenid kings.[204]

In the early part of the Early Dynastic period (c.2900–2334 BC) each city state was governed by a king whose authority was limited by that of the

---

200  Averbeck 2002, 121.

201  Kramer 1963, 269–300.

202  M3 = third millennium BC.

203  M1 = first millennium BC.

204  Bryce and Birkett-Rees 2016, 48.

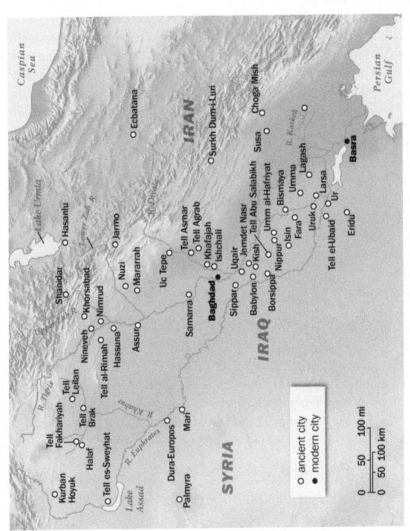

Map 7 **Sumeria**
(© Baker Publishing Group)

priesthood. Some of the kings became absolute rulers and sought to extend their rule over other city states through force.[205] Brisch notes that:

> The early Mesopotamian concept of a royal dynasty was closely tied to the city that was its power base; this differs strongly from modern conceptions of royal dynasties, which are mainly defined through blood ties . . . [K]ings stated that their rule was legitimised through divine favour.[206]

'Sumerian' is derived from an Akkadian word; the Sumerians themselves referred to their country merely as *kengir* (native land) and themselves as the *saggiga*, meaning the 'black-headed people'.

## (a) History of scholarship

Sumerian views of the origin of the universe, of the gods and of humankind are very complex and have recently been scrutinized afresh by Lisman through a rigorous re-examination of all the relevant texts.[207] Lisman notes the importance of Kramer, Jacobsen and van Dijk in the development of our understanding of these areas.

**Samuel Noah Kramer** (1897–1990) did seminal work in relation to our concerns.[208] He sums up the creation concepts of the Sumerians as follows:

i  The bottom line of reality for the Sumerians was the *primeval sea*. The Sumerians may well have understood it to exist eternally.

ii  The primeval sea gave birth to the *cosmic mountain*, made up of heaven and earth united.

iii  Understood as gods in human form, *an* (heaven) was the male, and *ki* (earth) the female. Through their sexual union the air god Enlil was born.

iv  Enlil as the air god separated heaven from earth. *An* carried off heaven, but Enlil carried off his mother *ki*, the earth. The union of Enlil and *ki* sets things up for the arrangement of the universe, the creation of humankind and the development of civilization.

---

205 Bryce and Birkett-Rees 2016, 65.
206 Brisch 2013, 2017, 117.
207 See Lisman 2013, 2, for his starting points and distinctives.
208 See Kramer 1961, 1972, 30–75: ch. 2, 'Myths of Origins'.

It would make our life a lot easier if Kramer's summary had withstood subsequent investigation. As we will see, Kramer's summary remains useful, but recent scholarship has complicated the picture considerably.

Kramer argues that it is the introduction to 'Gilgamesh, Enkidu, and the Nether World' that gives us the most significant information about the Sumerian understanding of the creation of the universe.[209] Recently, in a dissertation focused exclusively on 'Gilgamesh, Enkidu, and the Nether World', Gadotti appears to have taken the rug out from under Kramer's feet, as it were, with the following argument:

> Upon closer scrutiny ... it emerges that, similarly to the prologues to the debate poems, all the cosmological prologues attested in Sumerian literature are specific to the composition they introduce and are in no way meant to be cosmologies in the same way as, for example, the Akkadian 'Enūma Eliš.[210]

One appreciates Gadotti's attention to 'Gilgamesh, Enkidu, and the Nether World' as a literary whole, but there is no reason why the specificity and integration of prologues into their compositions should not simultaneously provide us with cosmological information. Indeed, the combination of both elements is precisely what we would expect. Lambert asserts that 'one-sentence myths and allusions have as much importance as lengthy epic-style narratives'.[211]

Commenting on 'KAR 4: The Creation of Humanity (4.90)',[212] Averbeck alerts us to the more nuanced view that has gained ground when he points out that:

> There is disagreement among scholars about how to understand all this. Speculation abounds but, basically, it appears the ancient Sumerians reasoned that, initially *an* 'heaven' and *ki* 'earth' were an inanimate pair. There is no explanation given for the origin of this pair. They appear to be the starting point for creation in the Enlil/Nippur tradition, in contrast to the watery abyss starting point in the Enki/Eridu tradition ... cf. Gen 1:2.[213]

209 Kramer 1961, 1972, 37. For the text see <https://etcsl.orinst.ox.ac.uk/section1/tr1814.htm>.
210 Gadotti 2014, 8.
211 Lambert 1980–3, 219. Quoted in Lisman 2013.
212 For text and commentary see *COS* IV, 333–40. Cf. Clifford 1994, 49–51.
213 Averbeck 2018b, *COS* IV, 334.

The idea that there were two different traditions about origins – Enlil/Nippur and Enki/Eridu[214] – among the Sumerians originated in particular with van Dijk. He distinguishes between the cosmic motif and the chthonic (belonging to the underworld) motif.

According to the *cosmic motif*, the universe consists not of separate entities but of a whole in interdependence. In support of this motif, van Dijk appeals to the cosmic marriage of heaven and earth – which fertilized the earth, and from which gods, humans and plants arose – found in the earliest Sumerian literature, and to the genealogies of the gods, found, for example, in the Nippur List.[215] Enlil's main temple was situated in Nippur. Primarily on the basis of the Nippur List, van Dijk identifies the following 'stages' in creation:[216]

- There is a pre-existing universe, with the world in embryonic form, in which the gods of basic culture reside. Van Dijk likens this to a primeval city of gods.
- An (heaven) comes forth as lord of the city.
- An marries Ki (the cosmic marriage of heaven and earth).
- Heaven separates from earth.
- The great gods *emerge* (emersion) through the union of heaven and earth.

The *chthonic motif* is associated with Eridu, and is so named because the god Enki/Ea creates life on the earth by inseminating or inundating it from the underground waters through rivers and canals. According to van Dijk, the separation of heaven and earth does not belong to the Eridu view of the origins of the world.

Van Dijk argues that there are two views of the origin of humans in Sumerian texts: that of *emersion* and *formation*. The latter fits with the chthonic motif. In 'Enki and Ninmah',[217] Namma, Enki's mother, gives life to humans after having *formed* their image in clay. With the cosmic motif, however, humankind emerges through the union of heaven and earth, that is, through emersion. Van Dijk discerns a twofold relation in Sumerian anthropology: 'On the one side man is a slave of the god; on the other side there is a family

---

214 Nippur was the home of the god Enlil, and Eridu was the home of the god Enki.

215 Lisman 2013, 10. For the list see *SLT* 122–4.

216 Clifford 1994, 21.

217 <https://etcsl.orinst.ox.ac.uk/section1/tr112.htm>.

relationship: man has been created from the semen of the god or even from his blood, the immortal principle of life.'[218]

The origin of humans has been further pursued by Pettinato.[219] In his 1971 monograph he pursues two questions: why were humans created and what does it mean to be human? On the former question the texts are clear: 'Der Mensch wurde erschaffen, um zu arbeiten, und zwar um die Götter von ihrer schweren Arbeit zu entlasten. [Man was created to work and to lighten the heavy workload of the gods.]'[220] Pettinato discerns two concepts of the origins of humans in Sumerian texts; following van Dijk, he refers to *emersion* and *formation*. According to the former, humankind sprouts forth out of the earth once An has impregnated Ki. Having been impregnated, Ki bears the gods, humans and animals. Initially, humans are like animals; only in a second phase do they attain the instruments of culture. Finally, they become fully human by a gift from the gods. The origin of humans by formation is related to the Eridu genealogy of the gods. Enki creates everything without the agency of An. Humans are made by Enki and Namma by forming clay.

Most recently, the data for Sumerian views of origins has been re-examined by **Jan Lisman** (2013). The data is limited and the arguments complex. Lisman concludes that:

i   In Sumerian mythology the cosmos is represented repeatedly by *an-ki*. In third-millennium texts there is no mention of the separation of An and Ki, but the marriage and intercourse between them is to the fore. Old Babylonian texts alone mention the separation.

ii  'The common goal for the creation or civilization of mankind is the same in all stories, and may be formulated as: man has to care for the gods, to take over the tasks originally carried out by the gods, and to provide the gods with food and drink.'[221]

## (b) The Sumerian world view and the origin of the cosmos

The third-millennium texts all mention the presence in primeval times of *an* and *ki*. Cosmogony begins with their presence, but no indication is given of their origin; they are just there. The circumstance around their presence

---

218  Lisman 2013, 16.
219  Pettinato 1971. For the critique of Pettinato see Lisman 2013, 19–20.
220  Pettinato 1971, 21. Quoted in Lisman 2013, 17.
221  Lisman 2013, 69.

ranges from the absence of the sun and the moon to the presence of storm and gale. The latter may be metaphorical, as may be the shouting of *an* and *ki*, a metaphor for sexual intercourse. The interaction of *an* and *ki* is depicted variously, as we will see below: they shout, they unite, they lie together. Intercourse is clearly depicted. In preparation for the latter and for marriage, they beautify themselves. By contrast with the third-millennium texts, the separation of heaven from earth is described in three of the four second-millennium texts Lisman examines.

Below we will explore some of the key Sumerian texts dealing with the origin of the cosmos.

## Ukg 15 (AO 4153) (Lagash, c.2400 BC)[222]

This is a fascinating text which in column iii clearly sets the events in primeval times:

> in the long-ago, in a bygone year,
> the sun did not get up early,
> the moon did not appear all along.[223]
> (lines 2–4)

In column ii it is stressed that the gods Enki, Ninki, Enlil and Ninlil did not yet exist, but *an* and *ki* are present. *An* is '*en*', either the adjective 'exalted' or the noun 'lord or high priest'. He is called '*šul*', that is, a young man. He is virile and in the prime of his life. *An* and *ki* are shouting, a metaphor for exuberant sexual intercourse. 'It seems as if these lines [in column ii] say: at the moment of the courtship and intercourse of **an** and **ki** these gods are *not yet* present, but as a consequence of this event they will be and in this order.'[224]

Column i describes the irrigation of the earth:

> He has lowered the inlets of the irrigation channels in it,
> in order to make earth appear in luxuriance:
> a garden, moist and cool;
> water has filled the holes in the earth.[225]
> (lines 2–5)

---

222 For the correct order in which to read this text see Lisman 2013, 27–30. For text, translation and commentary see Lisman 2013, 230–5.

223 Lisman 2013, 27.

224 Lisman 2013, 29. Boldface and italic emphasis original.

225 Lisman 2013, 27.

'Because of the climate of Mesopotamia it is quite understandable that a moist and cool garden must be an ideal situation, almost "heavenly".'[226] Lisman cross-references this description to a parallel one in 'Enki and the World Order',[227] in which Enki fills the River Tigris through ejaculation. He thus argues that the motif here of the inundation of the earth is also a sexual metaphor, that is, it results from the coupling of An and Ki.

In summary:

- *an* and *ki* (heaven and earth) are present in the beginning;
- no other gods are present;
- there is courtship and creative sexual intercourse between *an* and *ki*;
- water reservoirs and vegetation come into being;
- there is indirect evidence for the origin of gods from the intercourse of *an* and *ki*.

## The Barton Cylinder (Nippur, *c.*2300 BC)[228]

Column i clearly refers to primeval times with the word 'remote' (*rí*) occurring six times in the first six lines. *An* is shouting with *ki* and *ki* is shouting with *an*, probably, as above, a metaphor for sexual intercourse, and thus a reference to cosmic courtship. In column ii 11 of the Barton Cylinder 'the *muš-ĝír*-snake' is mentioned, and in column ii of *IAS* 174 we also find a mention of a snake 'inside Ningal'. The snake probably functions here as a fertility symbol. Of course, one cannot but be aware of the comparable presence of the snake in Eden in Genesis 2—3.

## NBC 11108 (Ur III, *c.*2000 BC)[229]

This text is the closest to a pure cosmological text: 'Until now there has been no evidence of a single pure Sumerian cosmogonic text.'[230] We find *an* and *ki* occurring in line 1:

> The mighty An lighted heaven, earth he
> darkened, he looked at the netherworld.

---

226 Lisman 2013, 29.
227 Lines 250–9.
228 For text, translation and commentary see Lisman 2013, 236–42.
229 For text, translation and commentary see Lisman 2013, 243–50.
230 Lisman 2013, 37.

The centre of this composition is line 6: '(but) as wife he had not taken her.'

The many negatives make it clear that we are in primeval times before the origin of the gods, culture and ritual, and the mighty *an* lights up heaven in the activity preparing for his marriage to *ki*. He is 'wearing luxuriance in the residence' (line 8). Line 6 is the only place in the texts being examined in which *ki* is clearly referred to as *an*'s prospective wife, and it is literally in the centre of the story. That heaven is lightened and earth darkened probably refers to the lack at this stage of the development of earth; this will follow from *an* and *ki*'s marriage and sexual union. The absence of culture and living beings (lines 2–4) and the absence of the Annuna, the offspring of *an* and *ki*, is explained by the fact that the gods of heaven are not yet present. 'The marriage is considered as the starting-point, the *sine qua non*, for everyone and everything: gods, people and culture. But until that moment there was nothing but **an** and **ki**.'[231] *An* and *ki* are both referred to in this composition as animate and inanimate.

It will be evident from the above that many of the details of the Sumerian world view are complex and contested.[232]

## (c) The Sumerian world view and the origin of the gods

One of the oldest texts, *IAS* 114,[233] tells us more about the origin of the gods than any other third-millennium text. After referencing *an* and *ki*, there is a statement about Enki and Ninki, the ancestors of Enlil, who brought a group of seven gods into existence, of which Enlil is the youngest brother. Ukg 15 refers to *an* and *ki* during their courtship and implies by negation that their union allows Enki and Ninki to appear. Lisman suggests that:

Both groups are named after each other in these cases, but the fact that there is no direct mention of **an-ki's** parenthood of Enki-Ninki, may be a strong suggestion that Enki and Ninki – Lord Earth and Lady Earth – the

---

231 Lisman 2013, 38–9.

232 Averbeck 2003b summarizes the Sumerian view of creation as follows:
1. At one time, heaven and earth were united.
2. Some of the gods existed before the separation of heaven and earth.
3. The heaven god An carried off heaven, but the air god Enlil carried off the earth.
4. Nammu is 'the mother, who gave birth to heaven and earth'. This implies that heaven and earth are a product of the primeval sea.
5. Heaven and earth united were a mountain whose base was the bottom of the earth and whose peak was the top of heaven.
6. The air god Enlil separated heaven from earth.

233 For text, translation and commentary see Lisman 2013, 225–8.

pair that have brought forth septuplets and later Enlil, originated or developed from **ki**/earth alone before the separation of **an-ki**.[234]

## (d) The Sumerian world view and the origin of humankind

In the third-millennium texts the origin of humans is not mentioned. This changes in second-millennium texts, but humankind is described in different ways. In some texts they were at first like animals until the gods needed them and then they were inspirited to become civilized. We see this, for example, in 'The Debate between Grain and Sheep'.[235] This text begins in primeval times: 'When Heaven had caused the mountain range of **an-ki** to bring forth the Annuna gods...' The many negations that follow this opening statement accentuate the view that the world is not static and also describe what we may expect in the future once the Annuna gods are in existence. In this respect the negations are fascinating because they provide us with a view of what really mattered to the Sumerians in the world, things such as weaving from thread, goats and their offspring, barley of various sorts, clothing, eating bread. Humankind is referred to but in a primitive, animal-like stage in which '[t]he people moved on all fours' (line 23). Towards the end of this text the Annuna 'inspirit' humankind, and this enables them to become civilized and thus provide the service and food the gods need. 'For the sake of the sweet substance of their pure udder they have inspirited mankind' (lines 35–36). Once again, the comparable motif of God's breathing into the nostrils of the man of dust in Genesis 2.7 is noteworthy.

The creation of humans by formation is found in 'Enki and Ninmah'.[236] The first two lines are not fully extant and thus are somewhat unclear.[237] They appear to refer to the separation of *an* from *ki*, thus making the birth of the gods possible, and the assignment of gods to various forms of work, such as digging out canals and scratching the clay (lines 10 and 11). Meanwhile Enki, 'the one with great wisdom, the creator among all the existing gods' (line 12), is sleeping! The gods weep and lament at the work they have to do. Namma takes their message to Enki and he sets things in motion for humans to be created from clay. As Namma says to Enki: 'when you have created those who will take over the work of the gods, let them [the gods]

---

234  Lisman 2013, 72.

235  See Lisman 2013, 256–82, for the text, translation and commentary.

236  For the text, translation and commentary see Lisman 2013, 293–309.

237  Lisman 2013, 51.

loose their basket' (line 23). In line 30 Enki says to his mother Namma, 'My mother, when the creature which you have suggested exists, fasten the carrier basket of the gods to him.' In comparison with this story, in Atrahasis, the eighteenth-century BC Akkadian epic, which begins with 'When gods were "man,". . .'[238] and goes on to describe their labour, a god is slaughtered and his blood and flesh is mixed with clay to create humankind. This motif is unknown in Sumerian literature:

> I think that anyone familiar with Sumerian mythology will agree that the scene of general mayhem . . . somehow does not go together with the well-ordered system of divine relations projected by Sumerian religious sources. The same is true of seals . . . showing the mutilation and death of a mountain-god, for the slaughter of a god is likewise a motif that is foreign to Sumerian mythology.[239]

Clay is also used by Enlil in 'The Song of the Hoe' to create humans.[240] Enlil separates the heaven from the earth, in contrast to 'Gilgamesh, Enkidu, and the Nether World', where An takes the heavens and Enlil takes the earth. In line 6 the creation of the 'first-born', that is, humankind, is announced but no reason is given. This action is carried out in lines 19–20: 'he placed the first of humankind in a brick-mould.' The first human was created with clay which was placed in a brick mould. Lisman argues that the brick mould is a metaphor for the womb.[241] Once mature, the human breaks open the mould, his metaphorical womb. He appears as a human, 'black-headed one' (line 21), that is, a Sumerian. That Enlil created a prototype is confirmed by the Annunas' request for 'a black-headed people' (line 25). Probably through the instigation of Enlil, Ninmena, the Sumerian mother goddess, takes responsibility for the procreation of the humans. She is the one who gives birth to the *en*, the king, but also to 'loyal and strong' people who 'provide for the daily rations of the gods' (lines 26 and 31).

## KAR 4[242]

This text begins with the time after *an* and *ki* had been separated. From line 2 it appears that this separation was a condition for the mother goddesses to

---

238  Lisman 2013, 54.

239  Steinkeller 1992, 246–7. Quoted in Lisman 2013, 52.

240  For the text, translation and commentary see Lisman 2013, 324–9.

241  Lisman 2013, 59.

242  For the text, translation and commentary see Lisman 2013, 330–46.

live in heaven. From line 7 we can infer that the mother goddesses gave birth to the Annuna gods, who prepared the earth in order that cult places could be established. Heaven and earth are clearly shaped; even the Tigris and the Euphrates are mentioned. Enlil asks 'what can we change? what can we create?' (line 15), which leads on to a discussion of creating humankind. Two gods answer, proposing that the gods Alla and Illa be slaughtered in order to make humankind grow.[243] Then:

> Let the work assignment of the gods be its [humankind's] job
> to establish for ever the boundary ditches;
> to take in hand the hoe and the pannier;
> planning the houses of the great gods, befitting an exalted
>     shrine,
> (and) meadows,
> to establish for ever the boundary ditches;
> to put in order and to consolidate the ditches;
> to increase all kinds of plants for the estates in the four
>     corners . . .
> (lines 21–8)

On the reverse, lines 7 and 8, we read:

> The feast for the gods is completed,
> when cold water is poured out,
> and when the large abode of the gods is suitable for an exalted
>     shrine.

## (e) The Sumerian world view and paradise

The Sumerian myth 'Enki and Ninhursag' is referred to by Kramer as a 'paradise myth'.[244] The purpose of the myth is unclear and we do not know its date. However, the story is situated in Dilmun, a land and a city. Dilmun was the island of Bahrain, renowned as a trading centre and for its dates.[245] The description of Dilmun has paradisical overtones and thus may provide us with

---

243 Lisman (2013, 63, 337–8), however, agrees with Steinkeller that theomachy, the slaughter of the gods, is unknown in Sumerian mythology.
244 Kramer, *ANET*, 37.
245 See Crawford 1998; for the complexities of the story as a whole see Postgate 2010.

an insight into what Sumerians viewed as the ideal or 'unfallen' state. Dilmun is described as:

- pure and clean ('clean' is repeated three times);
- most bright;
- the place where the god Enki lay with his wife, Ninsikilla;
- a place where the raven does not cry;
- a place where the ittidu-bird does not cry out;
- a place where the lion does not kill;
- a place where the lion does not snatch the lamb;
- a place where there is no kid-eating wild dog;
- a place where the widow is unknown;
- a place where the dove does not droop its head;
- a place where there is no sickness;
- a place where people do not get old;
- a place where there is no lament;
- a place of water, and sweet waters in particular;
- a fertile place of abundant agriculture.

Clearly, there are similarities here to the OT's view of Eden with its verdant pastures, and its eschatology such as the wolf lying down with the lamb in Isaiah 11.6.

# (f) The Sumerian world view and creation order

## Enki and the World Order (EWO)[246]

We have seen how Egypt's world view was shaped by her geography. The same is true of Sumer, which becomes clear when we explore the Sumerian view of world order. Averbeck notes that '[f]rom the perspective of the Sumerian literary corpus, EWO provides perhaps the most natural point of departure for gaining a comprehensive view of the Sumerian world order'.[247] EWO is a long and fairly well-preserved mythological composition. It divides into four sections:

i  Lines 1–60: The author offers third-person praise to Enki.
ii  Lines 61–139: Enki praises himself twice.

---

246  For translation and commentary see *COS* IV, 340–51.
247  Averbeck 2003a, 29.

- Lines 61–85: Enki tells how Enlil commissioned him and gifted him with the '*me*'s – literally 'he put the *me* in my hand' – and *nam-tar*, which refer to the cultural components that constitute Sumerian culture, and the power to control destinies.
- Lines 86–139: Enki proposes to journey through Sumer by barge in order to establish order and thus prosperity in the land. There is a surprising shift to third-person narrative in lines 131–2:

> To the one who has no city, to the one who has no
>     house;
> (to) the Marta nomads he granted livestock as a gift.

- This sentence is repeated in lines 248–9 and thus functions as a framing device. 'This has implications for our understanding of the literary composition as it now stands, and also for the composer's understanding of the boundaries and fringes of the Sumerian homeland. The first part of the journey ends on the geographical and/or sociological fringes of the homeland. It ends with the Martu.'[248]

iii  Lines 140–386: This central part of the work recounts Enki's journey through Sumer.

- Lines 140–249: In the first part Enki begins with Sumer as a whole, and Ur in particular, and travels from there to the surrounding areas of Magan, Meluḫḫa and Dilmun.
- Lines 250–386: Enki returns to the homeland, and in a series of 12 cycles he designates specific gods to take responsibility for a variety of functions so as to maintain world order.

iv  Lines 387–471: Inanna complains to Enki that she has not had any special function assigned to her and he responds.

Scholars are divided among themselves as to whether EWO describes the origin of the world, is a description of how the Sumerian world functioned, a combination of the two, or something else.[249] Averbeck rightly notes that the

---

248  Averbeck 2003b, 762–3.
249  Averbeck 2018a, *COS* IV, 341.

first two are not mutually exclusive in ANE terms. He refers to lines 451–2 near the end of the composition:

Now, surely the heart has overflowed its banks;
let the land (of Sumer) restore its (fertile) soil.
The heart of Enlil has surely overflowed its banks;
let the land (of Sumer) restore its (fertile) soil.

Averbeck notes that there are important similarities between these lines and the opening lines of Gudea Cylinder A i 5–9. He writes:

The multiple correspondences between these two compositions suggest that the primary concern of EWO was the *restoration* of world order in Sumer, or perhaps the reflex of that, the need to *maintain* that world order against erosion, whether physical alluvial erosion or other kinds of socio-cultural erosion of their civilization and its resources.[250]

Either way, EWO provides us with a lens through which to view the Sumerian understanding of world order initiated through creation.[251] According to Averbeck:

Basically, EWO programmatically sets forth the fundamental environmental, ecological, technological, economic, architectural, pastoral, and industrial occupations and conditions that were the foundations of life in ancient Sumer. It begins with the lifeline of ancient Sumer, the watercourses of the Tigris and Euphrates rivers, the swamps and lakes that arose in connection with them, all the way down to the sea in the south (i.e., the Persian Gulf), and even the importance of rainfall (cycles 1–4). In turn, these rivers provided for the possibility of irrigation agriculture, which involved the work of digging canals and ditches, working the soil and planting crops with plows and teams of oxen, and the growth and harvesting of barley, lentils, and other crops (cycles 5–6). The making of bricks and the use of them in the construction of buildings, domestic and otherwise, fills out the basic foundations of life in ancient Sumer (cycles 7–8). Enki's work then turns to the highland and lowland plains,

---

250  Averbeck 2018a, *COS* IV, 350. Emphasis original.
251  On EWO and ritual see Averbeck 2018a, *COS* IV, 341.

the places of wild game and pastoral activity – the place of the shepherd as opposed to the farmer (cycles 9–10).[252]

The prosperity arising from all these resources presents the need to identify the boundaries between the city states in the alluvium (cycle 11) and to establish the textile industry which was foundational to trade (cycle 12). The latter was based on the pastoral activity of the plains. The cycles are not presented as exhaustive: 'Nevertheless, the twelve cycles provide a general picture of the ancient Sumerian homeland and its ecosystem.'[253] As Averbeck notes: 'EWO stands out as a composition in which the conceptual analogies between the worlds of the gods and men are especially evident.'[254]

EWO thus provides us with insight into daily life in Sumer and into how the Sumerians saw the gods as related to the order of their world, which they conflate with the whole of the creation. The Euphrates and the Tigris were central to and fundamental for Sumeria, and in cycle 1 Enki ejaculates to fill these two rivers with life-giving water: 'Like a wild bull, he ejaculates to fill the Tigris with the flow of life-giving water'.[255] Repeatedly through the cycles, once Enki has set things in motion he puts a god in charge of each particular area, in this case Enbilulu. Enki's insemination of the rivers enables sweet wine and barley to be produced for the people, for the temple of Enki, known as Enkur, and for the palace. There is a particular emphasis on the Tigris in cycle 1, and Averbeck notes how recent students have foregrounded its importance.[256] Cycles 1–3 move from north to south attending to water and its benefits. In cycle 2 the marsh regions are established, the source of reeds, fish and fowl,[257] and thus of crafts such as reed matting, and the vocations of fisherman and fowler.

Cycles 4–6 deal with rain and the appointment of the canal inspector Iškur. The great rivers were essential for life but also posed a threat from flooding. Thus, irrigation through the building of canals was necessary to contain and capture the flood. Sumerian culture was basically agrarian, and cycle 5 deals with the establishment of farming and farmers, of working fields

---

252  Averbeck 2018a, COS IV, 341.

253  Averbeck 2018a, COS IV, 342.

254  Averbeck 2003b, 761.

255  Averbeck 2003a, 30.

256  Averbeck 2003a, 31.

257  cf. The Disputation between Bird and Fish; The Heron and the Turtle; The Home of the Fish; and Nanše and the Birds.

with ploughs and yokes of oxen.[258] Enkimdu is put in charge of this area of culture. Summers were too hot for crops in Sumer and thus winter was the growing season. In cycle 6 the agricultural fertility goddess Ašnan is put in charge of crops.

Cycles 7 and 8 deal with the building of houses and other edifices, attending to the making of bricks with the hoe and the brick mould. The gods Kulla and Muš̌dama are put in charge of this area of life.[259] Building makes urbanization possible. Cycles 9 and 10 move from the area around the river basin to the plains, distinguishing between the highland plain and the lowland plain. Cycle 11 attends to the whole region and the boundaries of the city states, as well as the building of temples for the Annuna gods. Utu the sun god, god of the underworld and divine judge, is put in charge of this order. Cycle 12 deals with the textile industry as the province of women.

## (g) The Sumerian world view and temples

The Sumerian view of world order as explicated in EWO is clearly a projection of life as the Sumerians experienced it. At the same time, it is clear that religion and the gods relate to all of life, including every aspect of culture and worship. Any kind of sacred–secular dichotomy is alien to the Sumerian world view. Temples, where the gods lived and were served, were central to Sumerian life.

The Gudea Cylinders[260] provide us with one of the most important ANE compositions dealing with temple-building. Hurowitz identifies a fivefold structure in ANE accounts of temple-building:[261]

  i  the decision to build, including divine sanction;
  ii  preparations for the building: materials, workers, laying the foundations;
 iii  the construction process;
 iv  prayers of dedication and associated festivities;
  v  divine promises and blessings for the king.

In the Gudea Cylinders there is a sentence that is repeated five times at central breaks in the narrative: 'The faithful shepherd Gudea had come to know

---

258  cf. The Disputation between Summer and Winter; The Farmer's Instructions; The Disputation between the Hoe and the Plough.
259  The Gudea Cylinder provides details on planning and building houses, especially temples.
260  See Edzard 1997.
261  Hurowitz 1992.

what was important, (so) he proceeded to do it'.[262] This results in a sevenfold structure:[263]

   i  the initial dream and its interpretation;
  ii  incubation of a second dream;
 iii  the construction of the new Eninnu, the temple of the warrior god Ningursu;
 iv  furnishing, decorating, supplying and praising the temple complex;
  v  preparing for the induction of Ningursu and his consort, Baba, into the new Eninnu;
 vi  induction of Ningursu and Baba into the new Eninnu;
vii  housewarming celebration of the induction.

This structure presents the temple-building as a ritual process: 'Ritual actions and processes saturate and structure the text.'[264] Unlike the clear divine commands about how to build the tabernacle (Exod. 25—40), 'Gudea had to pry the specific desires and plans for the temple out of the heart of the deity for whom the temple was to be built (i.e. Ningursu, the patron deity of Lagash)'.[265]

Based on his work on the Gudea Cylinders, Averbeck identifies 15 parallels with temple-building in the OT:[266]

- the close relationship between temple-building and fertility, abundance and prosperity;
- the association of royal wisdom with temple-building;
- the need for divine approval;
- the importance of following the divinely revealed plan in every detail;
- the commitment of the ruler;
- the levying of labourers and materials;
- the importance of the first brick;
- the significance of laying the foundation;
- building a temple on a mountain or raised platform;
- laudatory descriptions of the temple;

---

262  Averbeck 2002, 117.
263  Averbeck 2002, 117.
264  Averbeck 2002, 118.
265  Averbeck 2002, 118.
266  Averbeck 2002, 119–20.

- announcement of the completion and the invitation of the deity to indwell the temple;
- the seven-day temple dedication festival;
- the relationship between social justice, equity and purity, and temple-building;
- the connection between temple-building and the blessings and responsibilities of kingship.

## (h) The Sumerian world view and ethics and law codes

Although we know that earlier law codes existed, the Sumerian Code of Ur-Nammu (c.2050 BC) is the earliest extant law code we possess. Kramer reports how he happened across this law code in 1952:

> In all probability I would have missed the Ur-Nammu tablet altogether had it not been for an opportune letter from F. R. Kraus, now Professor of Cuneiform Studies at the University of Leiden in Holland . . . His letter said that some years ago, in the course of his duties as curator in the Istanbul Museum, he had come upon two fragments of a tablet inscribed with Sumerian laws, had made a 'join' of the two pieces, and had catalogued the resulting tablet as No. 3191 of the Nippur collection of the Museum . . . Since Sumerian law tablets are extremely rare, I had No. 3191 brought to my working table at once. There it lay, a sun-baked tablet, light brown in color, 20 by 10 centimeters in size. More than half of the writing was destroyed, and what was preserved seemed at first hopelessly unintelligible. But after several days of concentrated study, its contents began to become clear and take shape, and I realized with no little excitement that what I held in my hand was a copy of the oldest law code as yet known to man.[267]

In 1965, additional tablets were found in Ur, enabling 30 of the 57 laws to be translated and reconstructed. A further copy found in Sippar contains slight variants.

Below is a list of ANE legal codes in chronological order:

- Code of Urukagina (2380–2360 BC); Urukagina was the king of the city states of Lagash and Girsu; although not extant, his reforms to deal with corruption are referred to as the first legal code in history;

---

267  Kramer 1981, 52–5.

- Code of Ur-Nammu, king of Ur (*c*.2050 BC);
- Laws of Eshnunna (*c*.1930 BC);[268] these laws are named after Eshnunna, the place where they originated, north of Ur on the River Tigris;
- Codex of Lipit-Ishtar of Isin (*c*.1870 BC);[269] according to the Sumerian King List, Lipit-Ishtar was the fifth king of the First Dynasty of Isin;
- Babylonian laws / Code of Hammurabi (*c*.1790 BC);
- Hittite laws (*c*.1650–1100 BC);
- Law of Moses (thirteenth to sixth century BC);
- Assyrian laws (*c*.1075 BC).

The Code of Ur-Nammu is our oldest known law code.[270] We know that earlier codes such as that of Urukagina existed, but Ur-Nammu is our earliest extant text of a law code. It is some three centuries older than the Code of Hammurabi. As noted above, the first copy of the code, discovered in two fragments at Nippur, was translated in 1952 by Kramer. According to the preface, the laws come from Ur-Nammu of Ur (2112–2095 BC) who was the first ruler of the Third Dynasty of Ur.

The prologue, in a way typical of Mesopotamian law codes, invokes the deities for Ur-Nammu's kingship, Nanna and Utu, and decrees 'equity in the land':

> After An and Enlil had turned over the Kingship of Ur to Nanna, at that time did Ur-Nammu, son born of Ninsun, for his beloved mother who bore him, in accordance with his principles of equity and truth . . . Then did Ur-Nammu the mighty warrior, king of Ur, king of Sumer and Akkad, by the might of Nanna, lord of the city, and in accordance with the true word of Utu, establish equity in the land; he banished malediction, violence and strife, and set the monthly Temple expenses at 90 *gur* of barley, 30 sheep, and 30 *sila* of butter. He fashioned the bronze sila-measure, standardized the one-mina weight, and standardized the stone weight of a shekel of silver in relation to one mina . . . The orphan was not delivered up to the rich man; the widow was not delivered up to the mighty man; the man of one shekel was not delivered up to the man of one mina.[271]

---

268 See Yaron 1988.
269 See Steele 1948.
270 cf. 'Sumerian Laws', YBC 2177, in *ANET*, 525–6.
271 cf. *ANET*, 523–5.

The code provides insight into the social hierarchy during the 'Sumerian Renaissance'. Below the *lugal* ('great man' or king), everyone belonged to one of two categories: the *lu* or free person, or the slave (male, *arad*; female *geme*). The son of a *lu* was called a *dumu-nita* until he married, becoming a 'young man' (*gurus*). A woman (*munus*) transitioned from the status of a daughter (*dumu-mi*) to a wife (*dam*), then, if she survived her husband, a widow (*nu-ma-su*) who was free to remarry. The laws are arranged in the casuistic form of 'If . . . then . . .', a pattern that is followed in most later codes.

## Laws

As we come to other law codes below, we will not provide their text. As this is our first extant law code, we include it so as to get a taste for ANE law. Among the surviving laws from the Code of Ur-Nammu are the following:

1. If a man commits a murder, that man must be killed.
2. If a man commits a robbery, he will be killed.
3. If a man commits a kidnapping, he is to be imprisoned and pay 15 shekels of silver.
4. If a slave marries a slave, and that slave is set free, he does not leave the household.
5. If a slave marries a native (i.e. free) person, he/she is to hand the firstborn son over to his owner.
6. If a man violates the right of another and deflowers the virgin wife of a young man, they shall kill that male.
7. If the wife of a man followed after another man and he slept with her, they shall slay that woman, but that male shall be set free. (§4 in some translations)
8. If a man proceeded by force, and deflowered the virgin female slave of another man, that man must pay five shekels of silver. (5)
9. If a man divorces his first-time wife, he shall pay (her) one mina of silver. (6)
10. If it is a (former) widow whom he divorces, he shall pay (her) half a mina of silver. (7)
11. If the man had slept with the widow without there having been any marriage contract, he need not pay any silver. (8)
13. If a man is accused of [*translation of word disputed; some interpret as 'sorcery . . .'*], he must undergo ordeal by

water; if he is proven innocent, his accuser must pay three shekels. (10)

14. If a man accused the wife of a man of adultery, and the river ordeal proved her innocent, then the man who had accused her must pay one third of a mina of silver. (11)

15. If a prospective son-in-law enters the house of his prospective father-in-law, but his father-in-law later gives his daughter to another man, the father-in-law shall return to the rejected son-in-law twofold the amount of bridal presents he had brought. (12)

16. If [*text destroyed* . . .], he shall weigh and deliver to him two shekels of silver.

17. If a slave escapes from the city limits, and someone returns him, the owner shall pay two shekels to the one who returned him. (14)

18. If a man knocks out the eye of another man, he shall weigh out half a mina of silver. (15)

19. If a man has cut off another man's foot, he is to pay ten shekels. (16)

20. If a man, in the course of a scuffle, smashed the limb of another man with a club, he shall pay one mina of silver. (17)

21. If someone severed the nose of another man with a copper knife, he must pay two thirds of a mina of silver. (18)

22. If a man knocks out a tooth of another man, he shall pay two shekels of silver. (19)

24. [*text destroyed* . . .] If he does not have a slave, he is to pay ten shekels of silver. If he does not have silver, he is to give another thing that belongs to him. (21)

25. If a man's slave woman, comparing herself to her mistress, speaks insolently to her, her mouth shall be scoured with 1 quart of salt. (22)

26. If a slave woman strikes someone acting with the authority of her mistress, [*text destroyed* . . .]

28. If a man appeared as a witness, and was shown to be a perjurer, he must pay 15 shekels of silver. (25)

29. If a man appears as a witness, but withdraws his oath, he must make payment, to the extent of the value in litigation of the case. (26)

30. If a man stealthily cultivates the field of another man and
    he raises a complaint, this is, however, to be rejected,
    and this man will lose his expenses. (27)
31. If a man flooded the field of a man with water, he shall
    measure out 3 *kur* of barley per *iku* of field. (28)
32. If a man had let an arable field to (another) man for
    cultivation, but he did not cultivate it, turning it into
    wasteland, he shall measure out 3 *kur* of barley per *iku*
    of field. (29)

What do we learn from this code about Sumerian values? Murder, robbery, adultery and rape[272] were capital offences, and thus regarded as particularly heinous. Theft of property is on the same level as taking a life and committing adultery, a notable contrast with OT law. Intriguingly, this code imposes monetary fines for bodily damage in comparison with the later *lex talionis* ('an eye for an eye') articulated by Babylonian law. However, as we will see below, as with other ANE law codes the actual function of this code in legal practice is contested. In practice, judges were often far more lenient and financial penalties tended to dominate.

## Proverbs

A world view not only describes the world but also prescribes how to live and navigate life in the world. In other words, a world view facilitates wisdom among its adherents. In the OT we have the well-known wisdom books as well as wisdom motifs scattered across its literature. Intriguingly, '[t]he Sumerian proverb collections are the oldest substantial corpus of written documents testifying to the secular thinking of ancient man'.[273] They are dated to the Isin-Larsa period (*c.*1900–1800 BC) and are most likely school tablets. The earliest-known proverbs come from the Early Dynastic proverb collection (EDP) and the Early Dynastic versions of Šuruppak's Instructions.[274] These texts came to light through a discovery in 1963 and 1965 at Tell Abu Salabikh, 93 miles (150 km) south-east of Baghdad, of a collection of clay tablets. These earlier proverbs support the notion of a living oral tradition of Sumerian proverbs between *c.*2600 and 1800 BC. Sumerian proverbs

---

272  But cf. YBC 2177, 7–8, in *ANET*, 526.
273  Alster 1997, iii.
274  Alster 1997, xvi.

reflect agriculture, animal husbandry and the many jobs within Sumerian society. Other topics include:

- the daily routine of a woman;
- family relationships;
- the good man;
- the liar;
- legal proceedings;
- fate;
- the palace;
- the temples and their gods;
- historical and ethnic allusions.[275]

Proverbs are rooted in tradition and, according to Alster, Sumerian proverbs are inherently conservative. Alster claims of the early proverbs, and by implication of the Sumerian ones, that they

> testify to the contemporary existence of a completely secular attitude toward social behavior . . . So a safe conclusion is that the 'mythopoetic' way of thinking was restricted to the religious sphere of life and applied to the telling of myths and the participation in rituals, but it was not the normal attitude toward daily life.[276]

A similar approach has been taken to the earliest strata of proverbial wisdom in the OT. In my view, this is simply wrong. The sacred–secular dichotomy is a modern invention and it is unimaginable that Sumerians would have held the views of the gods they did and then imagine that reason and observation are somehow divorced from the gods. We know from Sumerian administrative and economic texts that the Sumerians were capable of rational, instrumental thinking, of discerning cause and effect, but, as with proverbial wisdom, they would have seen this as integrally related to how the gods made the world. Alster also argues that the Sumerian proverbs were not 'expressions of intellectual systems'.[277] It is hard to know what to make of such a statement. Proverbs arise at the intersection of a value system and observation; they are

---

275  Alster 1997, xxiii.
276  Alster 1997, xviii.
277  Alster 1997, xiii.

not empirical alone, and thus they express the world view of their adherents in a profound way.

## (i) Conclusion

The fecundity of the Sumerian world view should not be underestimated. Its achievements were monumental and exercised a profound influence on the whole of the ANE. If I were to reach for one crowning symbol of Sumeria, it would be a clay tablet with cuneiform writing on it. Of course, there are many other symbols that vie for contention, especially those that made possible and emerged with the development of cities, to say nothing of the great temples the Sumerians built. It remains intriguing that king and cult emerge from the mists of history together, and we see that clearly in the Sumerian city states. The beginning of writing is epochal and *inter alia* makes possible the fascinating writings we have referred to above. Here in Sumer, civilization emerges, as it were, and politics, economics and organized religion take shape, and a vast literature of stories of the gods, law codes and proverbs appears.

As in Egypt, king and temple were dominant institutions in Sumer; indeed, in Uruk, which was the first city, the temples dominated.

> It is thus no surprise that the head of the temple organization was the head of the state. His powers extended into the economy and probably other aspects of life, but his authority derived from his association with the city's patron deity.[278]

Unlike in Egypt, the king was generally not regarded as divine. This, as Frankfort notes, is an important distinction between Mesopotamia and Egypt with a few exceptions which we will come to below. Although he is not a god, the autocratic character of the king remains in place, as ruler and lawgiver. Israel is the great ANE exception to the idea of law issuing forth from the king; the king as the source of law is clear from the Code of Ur-Nammu. This 'code' and the proverbial wisdom from Sumeria are, of course, of great interest to OT scholars. There continues to be debate about the function of such 'codes' and in particular whether or not they represented and were normative for the actual practice of law. As we will see, Hammurabi's code was not normative. Neither, it appears, was the Code of Ur-Nammu, despite its casuistic ('If . . . then . . .') form. Indeed, the Sumerians invented the casuistic style of law. The Sumerians also invented

---

278  Van De Mieroop 2016, 283.

the legal contract. Jacobsen referred to 'primitive democracy' in Mesopotamian societies like those of Sumer.[279] The description has fallen out of favour, but there were mediating assemblies in the city states, and Van De Mieroop makes the point that kings needed the support of both gods and the populace to rule.

As with all the ANE world views we will examine, the gods are many and they are portrayed in quintessentially human ways, and immanent to the creation. The complexity of the stories will not have escaped the reader's notice. As with Egypt, '[a]ltogether, the texts do not yield a standard cosmogony [an account of the origin of the universe]. Ancient Near Easterners apparently did not expect a single coherent account, tolerating different versions of the beginning of the world.'[280] Clearly, *an* and *ki* were central to the Sumerian world view and were both gods *and* places; here, one cannot but be struck by the difference between Sumerian myths and the prosaic nature of Genesis 1.1 in which heaven and earth are simply places created by God. The human nature of the gods results in a projection of human understanding on to them so that, just as procreation of human children is through intercourse, so sexual intercourse emerges as a key means by which the gods, the world and later humans come into existence. Particularly in contrast to the Babylonian world view, the stories of origin appear mainly peaceful and lack the violence of Babylonian accounts.

The Sumerians' rich and evocative view of world order is clearly related to their own geography, but what must not be missed is once again how religion and the gods relate to every aspect of the people's social, working and political lives. Indeed, their concept of world order celebrates the richness of created life. As moderns, we instinctively relate temples to worship, and that is certainly part of the cultus of the Sumerians. But the human nature of the gods means that they also need to eat and to be cared for, and this is a major aspect of the temples. With the differentiation of creation, the gods also have to work; in fact, a major reason for the creation of humans is to relieve the gods of work so that they can relax and enjoy life. In the Israelite world view, work is also a central part of what it means to be human, but the Sumerian view of humans, despite some notable similarities, is a far cry from the dignity and nobility of the *imago Dei* of Genesis 1.26–28 which lacks any sense that humans are created in order to relieve Elohim of work. Moreover, Genesis never sees the Israelite as the quintessential human, unlike, for example, the Sumerian myth describing the production of Sumerian 'black-headed ones' through a mould.

---

279 Jacobsen 1946.
280 Clifford 1994, 15.

# 7 The Hittite world view

## (a) Introduction

In OT studies, many of us will have come across the Hittites in our exploration of *covenant*. Israel was unique among ANE nations in understanding the relationship between YHWH and the people as a whole as a covenant. However, in her depiction of this relationship she drew from the language of international treaties. In 1954, Mendenhall proposed that remarkable similarities existed between Hittite treaties of the fourteenth and thirteenth centuries BC and the Sinai covenant in Exodus.[281] This sparked a vigorous debate, and some scholars argued that the articulations of the Sinai covenant in Exodus and Deuteronomy are closest to later Assyrian treaties.[282] Clearly, this debate has implications for the historicity of Moses and the Pentateuch.

The word 'Hittite/s' occurs some 34 times in the OT, especially in Genesis and Exodus, referring in these contexts to inhabitants *inside* the land of Canaan.[283] The Old Kingdom of the Hittites and then the Hittite Empire existed to the north-east of Mesopotamia in Anatolia, a considerable distance from Israel. However, chronologically, the Hittites are far closer to the Israelites than are the Sumerians. The Hittite Empire ceased to exist in 1175 BC, some 175 years before the birth of King David, and just as Israel was emerging as a nation.

Until 1834, we had no idea such a people group as the Hittites even existed. Charles Texier, riding on a donkey on the rough road near the village of Boghazköy in north-east Mesopotamia (Anatolia) that year, came to some ancient ruins there while in search of a Roman city.[284] Set out in straight lines, the massive blocks of stone belonged to a huge temple complex, from the Hittite Empire. The miles-long fortification wall interspersed with massive, carved gates had once protected the capital of the Hittites. The relief carved into the walls of a rocky outcropping called Yazılıkaya to the north-east of the ruins 'held the key to the religious beliefs of an entire civilization'.[285] Thus began our discovery of the Hittites, triggered by a discovery of their great symbols.[286]

---

281  Mendenhall 1955.

282  Berman 2011; Levinson and Stackert 2012.

283  The Hittites of the Bible are most likely related to the Iron Age Neo-Hittite (Luwian) city states in what is now south-east Turkey and northern Syria.

284  See Collins 2007, ch. 1, for the history of the discovery of the Hittites.

285  Collins 2007, 1. Yazılıkaya is positioned about 1.25 miles (2 km) north-east of Hattusa.

286  For a sense of the richness of Hittite culture see Doğan-Alparslan and Alparslan, eds, 2012.

The Old Kingdom of the Hittites is dated *c*.1700–1400 BC and the Hittite Empire itself *c*.1400–1175 BC. Excavations in the key cities of the Hittites have proved fertile; the Boghazköy (Hattusa) archives alone have produced more than 30,000 cuneiform tablet fragments.

## (b) Geography and history

The centre of the Hittite Empire was in Anatolia, but it extended into the north-east corner of the Mesopotamian basin where the Anatolian peninsula is geographically diverse (see Map 8). There are fertile river valleys in the west and a high semi-arid plateau in the east. To the north and to the south there are narrow coastal plains backing in to the Mediterranean Sea in the south and into the Black Sea in the north. Communication took place through narrow mountain passes or by means of ships.

The peoples who established themselves in Anatolia were just as diverse as its geography. The result is that the cultural development of Anatolia is the story of many civilizations. Hittite is an Indo-European language, as are Luwian and Palaic. It is likely that peoples speaking these languages penetrated Anatolia sometime in the third millennium BC. Anatolian history begins at Kaneš where the Assyrians established a colony of merchants at the onset of the second millennium BC,[287] one among some 40 trading posts covering central Anatolia, leaving behind thousands of business records.

Written documents and other material remains show that in the early centuries of the second millennium BC this trade became institutionalized and expanded to cover all of Anatolia, mainly through the efforts of Assyrian traders. These merchants established a trading network based on the exchange of tin and fabrics from northern Syria and northern Mesopotamia with minerals from Anatolia. The Assyrian merchants lived in settlements they called *kārum*, a word meaning 'harbour' and referring in this case to places providing facilities for caravans when they halted, which they established on the edge of Anatolian cities.[288]

The capital city of the Hittites was Hattusa, chosen as such by Hattusili I *c*.1650 BC, most likely because of its strategic location.[289] Collins describes Hattusa as '[a] city fit for gods and kings'.[290] The architectural achievement of the Hittites was considerable and Schachner points out that:

---

287 See Roaf 1990, 113, for a map showing the route most likely taken by Assyrians travelling from Assur to Kaneš. The same map shows the extensive trade routes developed by Assyria in this area.

288 Schachner 2012, 152.

289 Schachner 2012, 155.

290 Collins 2007, 33.

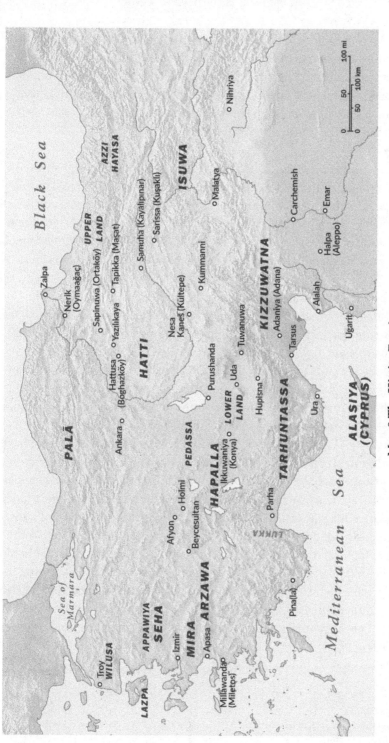

**Map 8 The Hittite Empire**
(© Baker Publishing Group)

Both the monumental architectural techniques and indicators of their functions demonstrate that structures of this kind had functions closely related to the Hittite concept of the state, and by symbolizing state power played a key role in the formation of the ideological foundation of Hittite culture, a shared mentality, a common identity, and, perhaps most important of all, the legitimacy of kingship.[291]

Hattusa is some 93 miles (150 km) to the north of Kaneš and is situated at the southern end of the Budaközü Valley next to a stream that has cut deeply into the rocks, forming a natural citadel. From the citadel the entire city is visible. In the northern part lies the oldest area of the city, where the great temple was situated. Here lived the storm god and the sun goddess. Positioned where it was, the great temple was as central to the commerce of the city as its religion.

As one moves southward through the city, the ground rises towards the Upper City, also a temple district. Thirty temples have been excavated here.[292] The city is surrounded by major fortifications with impressive gates.[293] Gates provided passageways and were also central to festivals; in addition, they served to safeguard the gods in the city, and the cultured city life set up by the king on behalf of the gods, from chaos outside.[294] Stone and water were sacred to the Hittites, so that the many rocky outcrops took on particular importance to them. By the citadel, two large pools functioned as a reservoir.

Hattusili I (r. c.1650–1620 BC) is the first Hittite king for whom we have historical evidence. He was able to trace his genealogy back two generations. It was most probably he who made Hattusa the royal centre and developed an administrative infrastructure that remained of fundamental importance for the state. This was facilitated *inter alia* by the state's adoption of cuneiform. Hattusili conducted campaigns to the north, into Syria in the southeast where lay vital trade routes, to the west into the Arzawa lands and to the east into Hurrian territories. At home his reign fostered a rich literature, including myths, historiography, rituals and the Hittite law code, and he also established the *pankus*, a legal assembly whose job was to witness and enforce royal proclamations and agreements, and to judge criminal offences of high status.

---

291  Schachner 2012, 160.
292  Collins 2007, 35.
293  See Schachner 2012, 162, for photographs of the Lion Gate on the west side of the Upper City.
294  Schachner 2012, 159.

During the second half of the sixteenth century BC, the Hittites adopted a creative new way of developing settlements. Kuşakh (*Kuşaklı*), for example, was developed according to a specific plan. New settlements incorporated large granaries and dams, making them a formidable economic force. Huttasa was likewise expanded into a metropolis, well equipped to function at an international level. Additional temples were built; more than 24 are found along well-planned streets at the heart of the Upper City. As the Hittites came into contact with Syrian and Mesopotamian cultures and witnessed their architecture, they too began to build symbolic, monumental structures in their capital. The development of the palace demonstrates that they developed a style all their own.[295] For example, a viaduct enabled the king to ride on his chariot right into the palace.

A recurring problem in the Old Kingdom was that of succession. Telipinu (1500–1425 BC), for example, succeeded to the throne through a bloodless coup. He instituted reforms to prevent the endless infighting in the Hittite court. He also concluded Hatti's first treaty with Isputahsu, ruler of the kingdom of Kizzuwatna to the south-east. The Hittites were under threat from all sides. Things moved in a more positive direction when Tudhaliya II became king c.1400 BC. Indeed, he can be credited with founding the Hittite Empire.[296] Tudhaliya II decisively defeated the Assuwan confederacy in the west. However, the Kaska invaded from the north, a move effectively blocked by Tudhaliya II, only to be challenged by the kingdom of Mittani in northern Syria. The pressure remained on the Hittites, and during Tudhaliya III's reign things came close to collapse through the 'concentric invasion'. The kingdom was attacked from all sides and Hattusa was burned. Tudhaliya III recovered some of the lost territory, and this recovery was taken further by Suppiluliuma I (c.1350–1320 BC). Suppiluliuma I formed multiple treaties that brought the vassals and appanage kingdoms firmly under his rule.

Whatever successes his predecessors may have had, through this system of alliances and the appointment of his sons Shari-Kushuh and Telipinu to administer his Syrian holdings, which now included Ugarit, Nuhasse, Qadesh, and Amurru, Suppiluliuma went beyond mere conquest to establish for the first time a sustainable Hittite empire.[297]

---

295  Schachner 2012, 165–71.
296  Collins 2007, 42.
297  Collins 2007, 49.

Here we see how important stable international relations were for the Hittites, and the vital role of the treaty in bringing some order to those relationships.

During the reign of Muwatalli II (c.1290–1273 BC), Egyptian power re-asserted itself. After a campaign to the west, Muwatalli moved the capital to Tarhuntaşsa ('[city] of the storm god'), appointing his brother as governor of the Upper Land. He brought the statues of the gods and manes (venerated spirits) of the ancestors there. 'Recently arguments have been put forward in favor of an above all religiously inspired move to a city wholly dedicated to the cult of a single deity, the Stormgod of Lightning.'[298] Ramesses II (r. 1279–1212 BC) of Egypt sought to regain control over Syria-Palestine and this led to a major battle between Egypt and the Hittites at Qadesh. Ramesses failed in his objectives, and the border between Egyptian and Hittite control in this region was re-established where it had been for generations past. During the reign of Tudhaliya IV (c.1237 BC), Assyria became a significant threat, effectively seizing lands controlled by the Hittites. Under Suppiluliuma II (c.1207 BC) the Hittite Empire entered its last days. His obsessive building of religious monuments was most likely a sign of his desperation.

Internal dissension, the effect of famine, and external pressures led to the final collapse of the empire. By the eighth year of Ramesses III of Egypt (1175 BC), the devastation was complete.

## (c) Religion

The impressive architecture and material remains of Hattusa and the other Hittite cities powerfully evoke Collins' point that:

> Religion animated every facet of life in Hatti. This simple truism applied equally to the king and to his subjects and explains why texts of a religious character constitute by far the largest percentage of the documents recovered from the Boghazköy-Hattusa libraries.[299]

These texts are state documents and not devotional materials. They were written to aid the courtiers in organizing the king's religious duties and regulating the cultus. They are thus a rich source for understanding the religious life of the Hittites.

---

298 Van den Hout 2012, 35.

299 Collins 2007, 157. The literature is immense as in so many areas of ANE studies nowadays. The reader will see that I have drawn particularly on Collins, a very useful one-volume work. But see also the multiple works and projects of Daniel Schwemer; Alice Mouton 2015 and her many other publications (available online at <https://fr.art1lib.org/g/ALICE%20MOUTON>); Ada Taggar-Cohen 2014; etc.

## Creation

Unlike with the Sumerians, we lack material about cosmogony and cosmology in Hittite texts. However, allusions to various cosmological ideas are found in texts of various genres. In 'The Song of Ullikummi', Ullikummi is hidden away in the netherworld, positioned on the right shoulder of Ubelluri. As long as Ullikummi stays there, Teshub cannot defeat him. Thus:

> Ea spoke to the Primeval Gods, 'Hear my words, O Primeval Gods, who know the primeval words. Open again the old, fatherly, grandfatherly storehouses. Let them bring forth the seal of the primeval fathers and with it reseal them. Let them bring forth *the primeval copper cutting tool with which they cut apart heaven and earth*. We will cut off Ullikummi, the Basalt, under his feet, him whom Kumarbi raised against the gods as a supplanter (of Teshub).'[300]

The motif of the severing apart of heaven and earth is similar to the motif of the separating of heaven and earth that we found among the Sumerians. In a ritual fragment we read: 'The crescent moon rose, the darkness (bore) the Earth, the lightness bore the stars.'[301] In prayers we learn how the sun god crosses the gate of heaven and arises from the sea. *KUB* 29.1, a ritual text, tells how in primeval times the gods built a palace and established the kingship. In Bo 3617 (*CTH* 433), another ritual text, the client recites:

> When they took heaven and earth, the gods divided (it) up for themselves, and the underworld deities took the land beneath the earth for themselves. So each took something for himself. But you, O River, have taken for yourself purification, the life of the progeny, and procreation(?)[302]

Art may also provide insight into Hittite views of the cosmos. The relief of the rock monument at Eflatun Pinar represents the cosmos:

• The main gods of the land are surrounded by symbols of the earth (mountain deities) and of the heavens (winged sun deities).

---

300 Hoffner 1990, 59. Emphasis added.
301 Collins 2007, 191.
302 Collins 2007, 191. Collins suggests we may have here eschatology similar to 2 Sam. 7; Isa. 9; 11.

- In between and on either side of the seated gods are supernatural creatures and bull-men. Their raised arms support the winged discs above the gods.
- Holes in the rock beneath the mountain deities show that water was once channelled between them and between the seated deities, evoking the confluence of rock and water. Water was a channel to the netherworld beneath the earth.

## Official religion

Religion was deeply intertwined with politics among the Hittites. Gods were adopted and introduced as was politically expedient. The Hittites were polytheists: 'May the thousand gods give you life', wrote a scribe to his father and mother who lived in Tapikka.[303] Collins asserts that:

> Polytheism by definition precludes religious dogma and orthodoxy, and the religion promoted by and for the Hittite ruling elite reflects the expansiveness inherent in such a system even as it accommodated reforms initiated by individual kings to promote favored cults.[304]

Gurney notes that Hittite religion had two aspects: the local cults, and the state religion of the king based on Hattusa.[305]

> At the national level the king took over these services as supreme High Priest of the realm, and the texts of the royal library reveal how conscientiously the kings of the later Empire discharged their duties on behalf of the nation.[306]

A vast number of priests – and priestesses – attended to the daily care of the gods. Some priests were cult specific; some were specific in relation to spheres of duty. The anonymity of the priests relates to the fact that the cult was state sponsored. As far as we know, being a priest was a full-time job among the Hittites.

## Places of worship

Schwemer observes that:

---

303  Collins 2007, 173.
304  Collins 2007, 158.
305  Gurney 1977, 1.
306  Gurney 1977, 1.

The divine sphere forms an integral part of the Hittite landscape; mountains, rivers and rocks are regarded as numinous powers, as are the sea, the sun and the storm. The gods inhabit the various regions of the cosmos and the land, but, at the same time, they reside in houses built for them by mortals whose relationship to their divine lords is conceived on the analogy to that of a slave to his master. The people take care of and provide for the gods whose contentment and favourable presence are considered to be essential for the prosperity of the land.[307]

Temples were pervasive among the Hittites. Within the Hittite territory each substantial village and town possessed at least one temple with cult personnel. The image of the god was located in the cella or main shrine. Hattusa's temple had two inner chambers, one for the sun goddess and one for the storm god. Interestingly, ordinary people were not allowed into the temple to worship.[308]

Sacred precincts were often located on rocks or mountains, some of which functioned as open-air sanctuaries, such as Yazılıkaya, referred to above. Gods were also represented by standing stones (*huwasi*); each one belonged to a specific deity. Schachner observes that:

> Hittite sacral architecture has its own style that is easily distinguishable from that of other cultures. As well as the distinctive plan features, the large windows in the cult rooms show that Hittite temples were used in a very different way from those of neighboring cultures, and that their form of worship also differed significantly.[309]

Intriguingly, in the Hittite temple of Ain Dara huge footprints have been carved into the temple threshold, inviting the god to enter.[310]

## Festivals

Not surprisingly, the Hittite year was punctuated with religious festivals.[311] Overall, more than 80 Hittite festivals are recorded. In one, the king restrains

---

307 Schwemer 2012, 432.
308 Collins 2007, 161.
309 Schachner 2012, 164.
310 See Schwemer 2012, 436, fig. 4.
311 There is a large body of festival texts. We possess c.9,500 tablets and fragments from Hattusa alone.

the goddess.[312] As we would expect, many festivals related to changes in the agricultural year. Examples are:

- the festival of the crocus;
- the festival of 'haste', which would keep the king and his entourage on the road for weeks (the spring and autumn festivals included celebrations at the many temples in Hatti, but the royal entourage would also journey to local cult centres);
- the spring *purulli* festival, which focused on the regeneration of life at the start of the agricultural year, coinciding with the flowering of the AN.DAH.ŠUM plant[313] and the opening of storage vessels; *inter alia* the storm god's victory over the serpent was enacted.

The 'liturgies' of the festivals are spelled out in detail in the festival texts. Sacrifices and libations were offered to the gods, and music and singing accompanied the rites in the temples. Statues were processed so that many different parts of the city were incorporated into the rites. 'Dance, play, acrobatic performances, and athletic competitions formed part of the festivals.'[314]

The cultus and politics were thoroughly intertwined with festivals, which were designed to embed allegiance to the king and thus to secure national unity. The king would gather his elite for major festivals, and thus 'the cult and its festivals played an important role in forging a common identity among the elites of the Hittite state and reinforced compliance with royal authority'.[315] Hittite religion and festivals were subject to external influence, but the major festivals remained unchanged until the end of Hittite history.

In the sacrificial cult it could not be assumed that the gods would participate. Elaborate rites of attraction were enacted to entice the gods and draw them in to the rituals, including feasts and colourful textiles (cf. the reference to big footprints on the threshold of a temple above). Blood sacrifice was common and had to involve only the very best animals. Unique among the Hittites was the practice of the king's toasting of the god; literally, he would 'drink the god'. Sacrifices were both public and private. In a ritual for the storm god of Kuliwisna the head of the household would take up the bronze knife and put it on the jugular vein of the bull and the ram. He

---

312 Collins (2007, 164) relates this to Jacob's experience of wrestling with God.

313 An alliaceous plant, such as onions and other alliums.

314 Schwemer 2012, 437.

315 Schwemer 2012, 437.

did not actually perform the slaughter, but this action signified that it was done on his behalf.[316]

## Communicating with the gods

The gods were utterly central to Hittite life and everything depended on retaining their good favour. For example, favour had to be maintained with the chthonic gods lest all sorts of evil seep out from the underground realm. As we would expect, therefore, there were multiple ways of communicating with the gods. Thus, there were rituals for oracles, questions which received a 'yes' or 'no' answer; augury; snake oracles; and the interpretation of dreams.[317] Collins notes that:

> Symbol (KIN) oracles are distinctly Hittite in origin and involved the manipulation of symbolic tokens with names that represented personages (Heart of the King, Enemy, Storm-God) or concepts (Wealth of the Land, Emptiness, Desire). The 'active' tokens (perhaps an animal?) took one or more 'passive' tokens and gave them to a third symbolic object, known as the 'receptive' token. For example: 'His Majesty will go up (on campaign) into the Haharwa mountains and will spend the night there. If we have nothing to fear regarding his person, let (the oracle) be favorable. The "gods" stood up and took "fire" and "great sin." They were given to "the overseer." (Result:) Unfavorable.' The tokens were either positive (e.g., Rightness, Good, Will) or negative (e.g., Enemy, Evil, Failure), and the overall outcome was determined by the balance of positive tokens to negative ones. The tokens could also be customized to the subject of the specific inquiry.[318]

The Hittites did not, however, rely heavily on prophecy.

Magic rituals for therapeutic purposes and to avert evil were performed in the temples and in homes.[319] In one of these rituals, the evil afflicting the person was transferred on to a mouse in the following way. Tin was tied on to the client's right hand and foot. It was then removed and tied to a mouse, which was then chased away and assigned to the two demons who needed to be appeased. The following words were said: '*I have taken away the evil*

---

316 Collins 2007, 165.
317 On dreams see Ünal 2012b, 476–91.
318 Collins 2007, 167–8.
319 On magic rituals see Schwemer 2012, 437–46. Cf. Collins 2007, 188.

*from them, I have wrapped it around a mouse. Let this mouse carry it through high mountains, deep valleys, on long roads! . . . Zarniza, Tarpatašša, you take it!'*[320]

Personal prayers requested divine action in difficult situations brought about by the anger of a god. Common elements in such prayers were:

- a call to gain the god's attention, accompanied by ritual acts;
- a hymn of praise and adoration;
- a request for the god's favour;
- a plea against an accusation.

## The Hittite pantheon[321]

The Hittites are well known for their international treaties, and in later treaties the order is fixed, with only minor variations from the treaty established by Suppiluliuma I with Hukkana of Hayasa. Gurney draws attention to the treaties as the best place to access the Hittite pantheon, reminding us again of just how intertwined were religion and politics: 'Both the treaty lists and the prayer present virtually the complete Hittite pantheon, but the treaty lists are manifestly a compilation made for this particular purpose.'[322] The pantheon thus revealed is as follows. At the head: the Sun God of Heaven (the god of justice) and the Sun Goddess of Arinna. There is a long list of weather gods: De Martino notes that the storm god (Tarhuna) was the primary deity of the Hittites.[323] He caused storms, and thus lightning and thunder were his attributes. He provided rain to make the land fertile, essential for the life of the Hittites. His consort was a female sun goddess. It may be that the god of justice is listed first in the treaties because of their legal concern.

The Hittites were proud of their vast pantheon, which had evolved through expansion and assimilation:

Hittite religion is an amalgam of beliefs, cults and traditions drawn from different regions and cultures. In the 13th century a process of assimilation was carried out and gods were grouped in homogenous 'circles' (*kaluti*) according to their origin, function and attributes.[324]

---

320 Quoted in Schwemer 2012, 441, 444. Emphasis original.
321 See van Gessel 1998–2001. Cf. the reliefs of gods at Yazılıkaya in De Martino 2012, 411.
322 Gurney 1977, 6.
323 De Martino 2012, 412.
324 De Martino 2012, 410.

The gods were usually depicted in human form. The Hittites drew on daily, agricultural images in order to understand the world. Consequently, many of their gods were associated with and depicted by animals.

The gods were conceived of in thoroughly human terms. In order to survive they required food; the deeds of other gods could affect them badly, and in all of this they manifested diverse emotions. No one god was wholly good. They could make mistakes and could be deceived. They differed from humans in terms of their power and wisdom, but even these varied among the gods.[325] In the cultus the schedule for the gods was akin to that of any royal. They arose, bathed, dressed, ate, held court and enjoyed being entertained.

In our modern West it is hard to imagine just how deeply Hittite life was pervaded by religion. Collins notes that:

> Human ambition could achieve no greater purpose than to serve the gods well, as a good servant served his or her master. The pious could hope to be rewarded with a life free of illness and hardship. Humans and deities also depended on one another for survival. The gods needed the sustenance provided by humans in the daily cult. Thus Mursili II reminded the gods, 'but if the gods, my lords, [do not remove] the plague [from Hatti], the makers of offering bread and the libation pourers will keep on dying. And if they too die, [the offering bread] and the libation will be cut off from the gods, my lords. Then you, O gods, [my lords], will proceed to hold the sin against me.' At the same time, humans were dependent on the beneficence of the deities who controlled the forces of nature that ensured agricultural bounty and the growth of the herds.[326]

## Death and afterlife

The Hittites both cremated and buried their dead. The cemeteries are simple, but remains of animals, food and pottery indicate that burials were accompanied by appropriate rituals. The soul of the deceased was thought to journey to the underworld, a bleak, muddy place. The deceased person's mother would emerge from the underworld to accompany her child on this journey; hence, death was referred to as the 'day of the mother'. If ordinary Hittites thus faced a reduced existence, it was not so for the kings. The king's soul ascended to heaven and there he was accepted among the gods. Unlike the

---

325  Collins 2007, 174.
326  Collins 2007, 177.

simple cemeteries, royal tombs had estates and personnel to ensure the ancestor cult was maintained.

## (d) Society and kingship

Hittite culture was predominantly agrarian. Thus, their world view was focused on such issues as the fertility of the land and the maintenance of the natural order. Famine, for example, could be devastating.

Prior to the thirteenth century BC, the idea of kingship was embodied in Hattusili I. The campaigns he embarked on created the expectation that the king should be a military figure and a militant one. Hattusili portrayed himself as a ferocious conqueror, writing: 'In a matter of days I crossed the Ceyhan River and overthrew (?) Hassuwa like a lion with its paws.'[327] Hattusili's heir was expected to follow his example, since 'the god [will install only] a lion in the place of the lion'.[328]

Kingship was a divine appointment, but the king was not a god. Indeed, the gods owned the land:

> May the Tabarna, the king, be dear to the gods! The land belongs to the storm-god alone. Heaven, earth, and the people belong to the storm-god alone. He has made the Labarna, the king, his administrator and given him the entire Land of Hatti. The Labarna shall continue to administer with his hand the entire land. May the storm-god destroy whoever should approach the person of the Labarna, [the king], and the borders (of Hatti)![329]

The king was the chief priest of the national god and thus played a vital role in the major festivals and ceremonies. The sun goddess was supposed to run before the king when he headed into battle.[330] The throne god Halmasuitt was the patron of the office of the king.

Although the king was not a god, as in Egypt, Hittite society was thoroughly hierarchical, and blessing on the king meant blessing on the land. Comparably, if things went badly for the land then the king would be held responsible.

---

327  *KBo* 10.2 ii, 17–19. Collins 2007, 92.
328  Collins 2007, 92.
329  Quoted in Collins 2007, 93.
330  Collins 2007, 93.

# (e) Law and society[331]

Hittite law is known from laws, edicts and court records. The primary judge was the king, whose verdict was absolute. He presided – or at least his representatives did – over cases of capital punishment and complicated judgements. The second in power was the *dugud*, whose verdict could also not be contested. Every settlement had a council of elders and military governors who heard cases.

Our most important source for Hittite law is The Laws.[332] Excavations have yielded two series of legal tablets that include 200 clauses or paragraphs. Paragraphs in series 1 begin 'If a man . . .'; in series 2 'If the vineyard . . .' The earliest surviving version dates back to the Old Kingdom *c*.1650 BC. The law tablets lack a prologue or epilogue. Bryce describes The Laws as 'a plain straightforward secular document'.[333] Similarly, Collins observes that the Laws are entirely secular, unlike the Hammurabi Code and the covenant code of the OT. Given the pervasiveness of religion in Hittite society, this seems strange, and Dinçol is surely right when he comments:

> Law tablets do not contain a prologue and an epilogue, which makes it impossible to determine which king is the author or how he obtained the right to legislate from the gods. Since other texts mention the Sun God as the bringer of justice, it was he, who must have charged the king for this task. A prayer text addresses him as follows: *'O Sun God! You are the one who settles the customs of the countries.'* As a judge, the god is also designated as . . . 'the righteous lord of the judgment.' Hittites believed that the gods were just lords that did not allow injustice done even to a 'speechless' animal like cattle.[334]

Like Mesopotamian law, Hittite law is casuistic in form. In comparison with other Mesopotamian law, Hittite law was compensatory rather than retributive or vengeful. Personal responsibility was generally upheld, but in certain cases a father could lend his children to compensate for his crime. 'For almost every crime including murder compensation was proposed, which could be belongings, animals, land, slave, even a family member.'[335] The laws deal with a range of topics, including murder, kidnapping, pollution, marriage, burglary, violation

---

331  See Dinçol 2012.

332  Hoffner 1997.

333  Bryce 2002, 34.

334  Dinçol 2012, 524. Emphasis original.

335  Dinçol 2012, 525.

of contracts, and inheritance. Bryce points out that a fundamental characteristic of them is that all subjects of the state have the right to legal redress. He writes:

> It is this which provides us with one of The Laws' defining features. Its concern was much less with the elite elements of Hittite society than with the little people of the state – the villager injured in a tavern brawl or in a dispute with his neighbour over boundaries, the small farmer seeking to buy some pigs or a small orchard, the hired labourer, the herdsman, the cattle rustler, the slave, the local romeos and lotharios, the participants in family weddings, the partners in mixed and common law marriages.[336]

However, citizens are clearly distinguished from slaves, and

> most of the clauses which deal with slaves probably have little to do with the rights or welfare of the slaves themselves. Nowhere is there any reference to what a master may or may not do to his slave – which may well indicate that this was a matter with which the law was not concerned, reinforcing the notion that a master's power over his slaves was absolute. What apparently *was* subject to some legal control was the legal redress a third party could expect if someone else's slave committed an offence against him. In such a case the law clearly discriminated between slaves and free persons.[337]

As with so much ANE law, a crucial question is how these laws functioned in practice. Bryce argues that '[t]he Laws must with few exceptions have been intended to guide rather than to prescribe, allowing considerable discretion to the local judicial bodies'.[338]

An important aspect of law among the Hittites was the treaty. 'The treaty, however, signals a new attitude on the side of the Hittites. The power of diplomacy and the written word came to be preferred over that of military domination as far as possible.'[339] Collins argues that:

> The reciprocal, multicentered worldview reflected in the Hittite treaties is unique in the ancient Near East, and it is further demonstrated in the

---

336  Bryce 2002, 38.
337  Bryce 2002, 53.
338  Bryce 2002, 37.
339  Van den Hout 2012, 26–7.

Hittites' use of borders as a means of reward and punishment. The Hittite kings used the treaties to define the boundaries of the vassal state, entrusting territory to the faithful and taking it away from the rebellious.[340]

As we noted above, there is a debate about the extent to which the Sinai covenant as depicted in Exodus and Deuteronomy is modelled on Hittite or later treaties. In 2012, Kenneth Kitchen and Paul Lawrence published a massive three-volume work setting out the full extent of ANE documentation relating to *Treaty, Law and Covenant*.[341] In the Introduction, Kitchen notes that a reason why Mendenhall's proposal, referred to above, was not taken sufficiently seriously is that he had not surveyed the evidence comprehensively. Over some 25 years Kitchen, and then Kitchen and Lawrence, laboured away at this task, resulting in their massive work.[342]

In their conclusion in *Part 3: Overall Historical Survey*, Kitchen and Lawrence note the important role played by the Hittites in developing and formalizing the treaty form: 'Under Suppiluliuma I, this new overall form was in effect canonized into a highly consistent schema, with but few variations'.[343]

> Thus, for two full centuries (c. 1380–1180 B.C.) throughout the Near East, the conventions for the content and layout of interstate treaties remained remarkably uniform (but not mechanically so), with only minor but visible variations. These were the norms for all participating states and communities – until the whole political framework suddenly disappeared virtually overnight (and forever, politically) with the fall of Hatti and disruption of the Levant involving the onset of foreigners ('Sea Peoples' and others) around 1180.[344]

Kitchen and Lawrence are acutely aware of the implications of this conclusion for OT studies. They explain how the source-critical approach to the Pentateuch developed and assert that:

> On behalf of scientific accuracy, firstly, it has perforce (and embarrassingly) to be made clear to 'non-initiates' in these matters that the vast

---

340 Collins 2007, 111.

341 Kitchen and Lawrence 2012a; 2012b; 2012c.

342 The late-second-millennium Hittite treaties are set out in Kitchen and Lawrence 2012a, *Part 1: The Texts*, 365–654, and make for fascinating reading.

343 Kitchen and Lawrence 2012c, 251.

344 Kitchen and Lawrence 2012c, 252.

acreage of 300 years' worth of imposing and elaborate theories . . . enjoy[s] no tangible or visible means of support. Not in any library, archive, or ancient text-find (like, e.g., the Dead Sea Scrolls) has any copy or MS ever been found, of any separated form of documents J, E, or P, (or D, other than canonical Deuteronomy). They are all, without exception (and remarkable to have to relate), 'dream-children', born exclusively out of the versatile minds and imaginations of the gifted 'critics' in whose learned volumes they are so ably elaborated. These 'documents' and their variants have no other physical existence, outside of the pages of their creators and discussants.[345]

For Kitchen and Lawrence, the endless source-critical analysis of the OT that continues to this day is a case of the emperor having no clothes.

We have referred above to Kitchen's a-theological methodology, and Kitchen and Lawrence reaffirm such an approach in this work:

> our approach is to treat *both* our main corpus and the biblical items in exactly the same way, even-handedly, without privileging either texts or particular views on them in either case. **No** appeal to, or assumption of, any theological viewpoint(s) is either made or assumed in this work.[346]

As the reader will be aware by this point, while I value Kitchen and Lawrence's exhaustive work, in my opinion such an a-theological approach has value but is theoretically naive.

## (f) Conclusion

For those of us who love OT studies, as do I, once we see that in the Bible, as in these nations of the ANE, religion relates to all of life, cultures such as that of the Hittites become quite fascinating. As with the other ANE nations, Hittite culture was predominantly agrarian, and for the Hittites nature was alive with gods, something that it is hard for urban Westerners to begin to grasp, removed as we are from nature. Archaeology reveals a highly sophisticated culture; for example, the ceramic pottery produced by the Hittites – for both cultic and common use – is often aesthetically remarkable.

The Hittite Empire is dated to the fourteenth and thirteenth centuries BC, and these were the very centuries in which the oppression of the Israelites in

---

345 Kitchen and Lawrence 2012c, 260.

346 Kitchen and Lawrence 2012c, 260, n. 12. Boldface and italic emphasis original.

Egypt, Moses, the exodus and the Sinai event are dated, assuming they are historical. Ramesses II led the confrontation with the Hittites and he was probably one of the pharaohs referred to in Exodus. If during this time Moses was being raised and educated in Pharaoh's court, he would undoubtedly have heard all about the Hittites and their clash with the Egyptians, as well as witnessed the typical pharaonic refusal to acknowledge defeat, always maintaining 'the big lie' of perpetual victory. If Moses' education was as rigorous as I suspect it was, then it is likely too that he would have been inducted into the treaty form canonized by the Hittites.

The Hittite world view is typically polytheistic with the typical ANE view of the gods as larger-than-life humans. The gods depend on the Hittites for their very survival, and the king and the Hittites depend on the gods for theirs. This co-dependence underlies the absolute authority of the king as the mediator between the people and the gods. An intriguing motif in the Hittite view of the gods is the need people felt to attract their attention. Of course, if humans had relieved the gods of hard labour then it is not altogether surprising that the deities needed to be attracted by the Hittites' service of them. This is a very different attitude from the other-person centredness of Elohim and YHWH in the OT.

The crucial role of the Hittites in the development of the treaty tradition of the ANE brings us on to the terrain of relationships between nations, what we nowadays call international affairs. If Egypt was relatively isolated, neither the Hittites nor the Israelites were shielded from other powers. The multicentric world view reflected in the treaties reminds us of the multicentrism in the Table of the Nations, as discussed in Chapter 1. However, there the similarity ends. If the Hittites shared, as they seem to, the cosmology of the Sumerians, a marked difference from the city states of Sumeria is the centralized political and military power of Hatti. Indeed, it is this that facilitates and leads to the Hittites' celebration of war, conquering and defeats, and results in changes in organization and administration, leading not least to the use of treaties to maintain their power. As with Sumeria, law issues forth from the king, and in volume 2 of this series we will return in detail to ANE law in relation to that of the OT.

# 8 The Assyrian world view

We move now on to the terrain of the great empires of Mesopotamia, empires that would impinge powerfully and directly upon the nation of Israel. We have already seen the role of Assyria and Egypt in the downfall of the

Hittites, and once Assyria reached the zenith of her power, no part of the ANE would escape her attention. Nineveh was one of the great cities of Assyria; indeed it was here that King Sennacherib established his capital. An example of how Assyria looms in the mind of Ancient Israel is the small but fascinating book of Jonah. Grasp the Assyrian world view and one might well find oneself siding with Jonah as he flees to Tarshish in Spain, seeking to put as much distance as he can between himself and Nineveh – and Zion! Many of the worst practices of empire move to the fore with Assyria. Sargon II famously said: 'I left behind a terror never to be forgotten.' How could YHWH possibly have mercy on such a people? Has he gone mad? Intriguingly, it is the fall of Nineveh that would mark the end of the Assyrian Empire.

## (a) History

The city of Assur shares the name of Assyria's great war god Aššur,[347] and it is here that Assyrian history begins, with the establishment of Assur early on in the third millennium BC, in all likelihood as a centre of commerce for the Sumerian cities in southern Mesopotamia. Saggs notes that:

> The biblical implication, that the Assyrians were Semites with Sumerian cultural influence as primary, is substantially in accord with the evidence of archaeology and cuneiform texts, though ethnic and cultural influences from other groups, such as Hurrians and Indo-Aryans, are also discernible.[348]

Indeed, in the mid third millennium BC onwards, Assur was regularly appropriated as part of larger states in the south. After the collapse of the Sumerian Third Dynasty of Ur c.2000 BC, Assur once again became an independent city state. Her inhabitants spoke Assyrian, later called 'Akkadian', but nowadays both Assyrian and Babylonian are generally described as dialects of Akkadian. The cuneiform script was used for writing in both languages; with time, their languages became more clearly divergent.

Aššur and the city of Assur are inseparable. The god personifies the rocky outcrop towering above a bend of the River Tigris. The crag rises some 130 feet (40 m) above the Tigris Valley. Aššur's shrine was at the top of the crag and became the heart of the city and later of the entire land of Aššur. It

---

347 We will follow the common solution of referring to the god as Aššur and the city as Assur.
348 Saggs 1973, 156.

was known by several names: Eamkurkurra (The House of the Wild Bull of the Lands) in the early second millennium; Ehursagkurkurra (House of the Mountain of the Lands) in the later second millennium; and Ešarra (House of the Universe) in the first millennium BC. This was the one and only temple of Assur, and the city's residents cared for it as such until its destruction in c. AD 240.

After achieving her independence, hereditary local rulers governed the city. However, they did not describe themselves as kings, as had their overlords from Akkad and Ur. Instead they proclaimed: 'Aššur is king and Silulu is representative of Aššur', as an inscription from one ruler in the early second millennium BC expressed it. From this perspective, Aššur was the sovereign king and it was in his name and as his representative that the ruler governed. Even in the seventh century BC, King Aššurbanipal (668–631 BC) still resorted to this expression in a hymn to the god: 'Aššur is king, Aššur is king, and Aššurbanipal is his representative!' Intriguingly, the representative of Aššur shared his power with the citizen body in the city assembly and with an official, chosen each year, called a *līmum*, the name of whom was used to date the year (e.g. 'when Ennam-Aššur was *līmum*' for 1760 BC). Such a tradition of collective government or 'primitive democracy' is attested elsewhere in the ancient world, as noted above.

From the eighteenth century BC onwards, Assur came again under the control of larger regional entities such as the Hurrian kingdom of Mitanni, and Babylonia, but retained a strong cultural identity. Mitanni's power declined in the fourteenth century BC, releasing Assur to attend to her own development. Her rulers used this time to establish Assur at the heart of a territory that today covers most of northern Iraq. Assur, Nineveh and Arbela formed a triangle that made up the heartland of a state that would subsequently govern much of the Middle East. When new areas were appropriated as provinces, their inhabitants were considered to be 'Assyrians', a label justified by their contribution to the worship of Aššur. By the late thirteenth century BC, Assyria ruled over most of Mitanni's former holdings, a considerable achievement. Saggs observes that '[t]he foundations of the later power of Assyria were laid in the thirteenth century, the last independent Hurrian kingdom, Hanigalbat, being incorporated into Assyria'.[349]

At the end of the second millennium and the beginning of the first millennium, Assyria faced a considerable threat from the Arameans. During

---

349 Saggs 1973, 157.

Tiglath-pileser I's reign (1116–1076 BC), the Arameans were able to penetrate into Assyria, taking cities and collapsing lines of communication.

> The Aramaeans thus came to achieve historical significance at the end of the second millennium and the beginning of the first millennium B.C., at which time a cluster of independent Aramaean states arose... The climax of the Aramaean threat to Assyria came during the century spanning the turn of the millennium when Assyria reached a nadir under Ashur-rabi II (1012–972 B.C.) and Tiglath-Pileser II (936–935 B.C.).[350]

In the period 934–827 BC, several Assyrian kings worked to recover the lands lost. Aššur-dan II (r. 934–912 BC) was the first to engage in repeated military campaigns in this respect. However, it was Aššur-dan's son, Adad-nerari II, who campaigned to the north (against tribes), to the east (against the Arameans) and to the south (against the Babylonians). He conducted some eight campaigns against the Arameans, opening the way to the Euphrates, which he crossed in 899 BC. In this way, these two kings established the foundation for the Assyrian Empire, which was the very first true empire in the world.

By the middle of the ninth century BC Assyria had regained its former size, and later kings repulsed the Arameans, with the final blow dealt by Tiglath-pileser III (744–727 BC) who reduced the Aramean states to Assyrian provinces. The leading of military campaigns and conquering of other nations became a characteristic part of Assyrian kingship, and the Assyrian army continued to press towards the west, finally reaching the Mediterranean Sea. This leads us into the emergence of the Neo-Assyrian Empire.

The political organization of Assyria was transformed with the establishment of Kalhu as the centre of the empire and with the programme of relocating populations to serve the interests of the state maximally. Kalhu is c.43 miles (70 km) from Assur, c.37 miles (60 km) to Arbela and c.22 miles (35 km) to Nineveh. Travel between these cities was, therefore, a relatively easy journey.[351] Between 879 and 706 BC, Kalhu dominated Assyria as its political centre. The palace gateway was given the name 'Palaces of joy which bear abundance and bless the king who made their structure everlasting', demonstrating that Kalhu was conceived of as the centre of the world and not just of the Assyrian Empire. Up until Sargon II, Kalhu was the primary residence of all

---

350  Malamat 1973, 137–8.
351  The excavation of Kalhu was begun in November 1845 by Austen Henry Layard.

the kings, until Sargon II moved his court to his new capital of Dur-Šarrukin in 706 BC.

With the accession of Aššurnasirpal II in 883 BC we find records of booty and tribute from the conquered territories. Another characteristic of Assyrian conquest was the practice of massacre and pillage, deporting and resettling large elements of the conquered populations. As mentioned above, Sargon II would famously say, 'I left behind a terror never to be forgotten.' Holloway notes that:

> Like the advertising juggernaut in the modern world, the Assyrians adroitly exploited public spectacle. The stock theater of cruelty included the 'live' flaying of traitorous vassals transported to the capital cities, and other mutilations and staged degradations. Symbols of foreign sovereignty, such as city fortifications, palaces, temples and their contents, royal families and their representations, were subject to destruction, death, and deportation in semiotically charged rituals of conquest . . . There should be no mistaking the visceral reaction intended by the torching of an enemy's temple and the destruction or deportation of its divine images. While 'iconoclasm' in the sweeping sense of the Byzantine 8th-century ban on icons or anti-Catholic Puritan fury vented against images and sacramentals had no parallel in the Assyrian Empire, the targeted destruction of cities, temples and divine images tapped into the same reservoir of communicative degradation and ritual elimination that strikes directly at national cohesiveness.[352]

Military and brutal expansion was central to the Assyrian Empire. However, when it came to any defeats, it was a bit like a Rolls Royce having problems: they simply did not occur. According to their inscriptions, the Assyrians never ever were defeated in battle.

The resettlement of local populations facilitated Assyrian control and prevented local leaders from easily stirring up opposition to Assyria. Of course, it also affected Assyria as displaced populations brought their languages, cultures and gods with them. On the basis of royal inscriptions it is estimated that a whopping 4,400,000 people, plus or minus 900,000, were resettled between the mid ninth and the mid seventh centuries BC. This made immense expertise available to the Assyrians from all over the place, and by the start of

---

352 Holloway 2002, 194.

the seventh century BC the major Assyrian cities of Nineveh, Kalhu and Assur were home to experts from across the known world.

Ironically, this policy *inter alia* facilitated the rise of Aramaic as a dominant language. In the first millennium BC, Aramaic was the most commonly spoken language in the Assyrian Empire. The army was the vehicle for Assyrian domination, and it grew in size from 60,000 during Aššurnasirpal II's reign to a massive 200,000 by the start of the seventh century BC. In royal inscriptions from the first millennium the Assyrian army is referred to as the 'Hosts of the god Aššur', evocative of the description of YHWH as 'the Lord of Hosts'.

Aššurnasirpal II expanded the city of Nimrud to make it the administrative hub of the Assyrian Empire, also building temples, including one dedicated to Ninurta. The name of the palace entrance was 'Justice Gates, which fairly judge the rulers of the four quarters of the world, when they come bearing tribute from the mountains and the sea to their King, their Lord'.[353] Ninurta maintained world order, and,

> [t]hrough association with Ninurta, Assyrian kings reinforced their claims to world-wide domination. They were deemed the favourites of Ninurta, 'the one who controlled all the quarters with his strong might.' The name Ashurnasirpal indeed means 'Ashur is the custodian of his son, Ninurta.' And Ashurnasirpal II's new temple for the god in Nimrud remained the most important sanctuary until the fall of the Assyrian empire in 612 BC.[354]

Aššurnasirpal II's son, Shalmaneser III, continued the policy of aggressive and brutal expansion. An inscription dated to the late 850s BC lists the cities conquered by Shalmaneser along the upper Tigris. It notes that he 'massacred many of its inhabitants, carried off booty, erected a tower of heads before the city and burned young boys and girls'.[355] Resistance to Assyria called forth campaigns, and ultimately Syria and Palestine were brought under Assyrian rule. Tiglath-pileser III structured them as provinces, under appointed governors or rulers. In 729 BC he entered Babylon and was crowned there as king. Cotterell observes that:

---

353 Cotterell 2019, 67.
354 Cotterell 2019, 68.
355 Cotterell 2019, 71.

Tiglath-pileser III ranks as one of the most industrious Assyrian kings for, with the exception of a single year, he campaigned every year he was on the throne. Not only was the organization of the army greatly improved in terms of weaponry and supply, but the empire itself was better administered and more secure. Tiglath-pileser III also paid attention to internal communications, by making sure there were fresh mounts at staging posts for messengers carrying official letters. The Royal Road, as the imperial relay system was called, connected an unprecedented expanse of territory, from the Mediterranean coast to the Zagros mountains, from the upper reaches of the Tigris to the Persian Gulf. When the Assyrian empire disintegrated at the end of the seventh century BC, the Royal Road did not.[356]

Three decades of territorial expansion meant that *c.*700 BC Assyria ruled over the territory from the Mediterranean shore to Hamadan (Ecbatana) in what is now Iran, and from Cappadocia to the Persian Gulf. A later king, Sennacherib (r. 705–651 BC), established his capital in Nineveh with magnificent new buildings. Esarhaddon adopted a more conciliatory approach to Babylon, including rebuilding the temple of Marduk. This allowed him to focus attention elsewhere, such as on conquering Egypt. Assyria's empire was vast, but

[o]verreach had already put a severe strain on its empire, which was compounded by an increasingly restive nobility. It took surprisingly little to expose Assyria's vulnerability to determined foes: the fall of Nineveh in 612 BC would mark the end of a once mighty empire.[357]

It was only in the late seventh century BC, when in 614 BC the city of Assur was captured and the temple of Aššur destroyed by the emergent Babylonians, that the death knell sounded for Assyria. In 612 BC, the then capital Nineveh was lost and the last rightful king, Sin-šarru-iškun, died defending his city and empire. Until then, the Assyrian Empire was unrivalled as the political, economic and cultural power of the Middle East and the wider eastern Mediterranean region. Upon Assyria's defeat by the Babylonians, most of the peoples from its heartland were resettled in Babylonia, where Nabopolassar and his successor Nebuchadnezzar developed their capital Babylon into an imperial centre, rivalling the great cities of Assyria. Those cities, such as Kalhu,

---

356  Cotterell 2019, 78.
357  Cotterell 2019, 83.

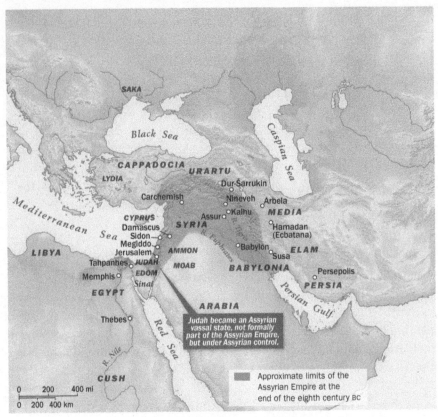

Map 9 **The Neo-Assyrian Empire**
(© Baker Publishing Group)

Dur-Šarrukin and Nineveh, were not maintained and their irrigational systems fell into disrepair.

The Assyrian Empire was immense and could understandably claim world dominion (see Map 9). As such, it was the paradigm for the successive empires, the Babylonian, the Persian and the Roman. Ideology, infrastructure and innovation enabled Assyria to retain control for some three centuries. Its ideological, infrastructural and organizational innovations provided the basis and template for the successor states. For example, speedy communication was essential in a vast empire, and a network for communication was carefully planned in the ninth century, becoming known as the 'King's Road'. After the demise of Assyria it was maintained. Representatives of the king needed to be able to act in his name, and all magnates (senior officials) of the empire were given a signet ring engraved with the imperial emblem showing the king killing a lion. This enabled them to function on behalf of the king.

# (b) The gods

The gods were utterly central to and pervasive in the life of the Assyrians in a way that is hard for us to imagine today. Discerning the will of the gods and their favour was, for example, central to military strategizing and foreign policy.

## Aššur

The pre-eminent god of the Assyrians was Aššur. In lists, he precedes gods mentioned with him. As noted above, his name is the same as that of the city Assur. His temple was there and was the main centre of his cult; indeed, 'the evidence shows that the god Assur is the deified city'.[358] It is likely that Aššur was initially a city god and that it was particularly as the Assyrian Empire developed that his role expanded. The importance of Aššur is evident not only in the god lists but also in the coronation prayers in which he is central to royal ideology.

Over time, elements of the theology of Babylonia were appropriated to fill out the nature of Aššur. In the second millennium, for example, he comes to be equated with Enlil, a prominent figure in the Babylonian pantheon. In the Sargonic period, Assyrian scribes adopted the practice of writing his name as AN.ŠÁR, thereby, according to Livingstone, achieving an ideological coup. Aššur is not listed in the Babylonian pantheon, but in one Babylonian theogony Anšar and Kišar (literally 'whole heaven' and 'whole earth') precede the senior gods Enlil and Ninlil. By naming Aššur 'Anšar', Aššur was made to appear as the head of the Babylonian pantheon. Following the sack of Babylon in 689 BC, there was an attempt to develop a cult in Assyria in which Aššur played the role of Marduk. Assyria established a vast empire, and wherever outposts were established, areas were set up where Aššur was worshipped. However, it seems the Assyrians did not require local cults to be replaced. Leaving them intact enhanced the propaganda of the empire that the local gods had failed their citizens.

As much as the Assyrians drew on Babylonian theology, the Assyrian view of the gods is also distinctive. Porter points out that during a century of discussion about whether the gods were viewed as one or many in Ancient Mesopotamia, scant attention has been given to the Assyrians. They are commonly considered to represent the religion of Mesopotamia in general.[359] As noted above, they did appropriate much from the Babylonians,

---

358 Livingstone 1999, 108.
359 Porter 2000, 211.

but they formed their own culture from what they gleaned and their religion is distinctive. Aššur, as mentioned, was far and away their primary deity and the head of their pantheon. Intriguingly, Aššur was not worshipped outside Assyria and is different from most Mesopotamian gods. The Assyrians also attached greater importance to Nabû than to his father Marduk, leader of the gods in Babylon. They worshipped various local forms of the goddess Ishtar, including one who was the patron of ecstatic prophecy, never a central element in the cult of Ishtar in Babylonia. As Porter observes: 'Such distinctive aspects of belief and practice make it clear that Assyrian religion was not entirely typical of Mesopotamian religion as a whole and requires its own independent evaluation.'[360] Similarly, Cotterell notes that, '[a] part from Ashur, the deity after whom they were named, the Assyrians worshipped the same gods as the Babylonians, but they did not always attach the same ideas to them'.[361]

We noted above Esarhaddon's re-establishment of the temple of Marduk in Babylon. What is fascinating is how stressed he was about this process. He asked:

Whose right is it, O great gods, to create gods and goddesses in a place where no man dare trespass? The task of refurbishment which you have given me is difficult. The making of cult statues is yours, it is in your hands.[362]

His concern centred on the creation of cult statues. Cotterell points out, however, that:

Mesopotamian peoples did evolve a method of ensuring that a cult statue was correctly created: that it was 'born in heaven, made on earth'. The special ritual and incantations involved were called by the Babylonians *mis pi*, by the Sumerians *kaluhuda*, meaning 'mouth washing'. It was akin to the Egyptian ritual used in workshops where divine statues were carved. Obviously the aim was to credit the gods with the process of manufacture, which is why the craftsmen who actually made the images symbolically cut off their hands with knives of tamarisk wood. They also disclaimed any responsibility for the work they had done. How seriously Esarhaddon

---

360  Porter 2000, 213.

361  Cotterell 2019, 195.

362  Cotterell 2019, 197.

approached the return of Marduk's cult statue, and those of other gods to Babylon, is evident in the festivities which marked their journey from Ashur to Babylon. Every half kilometre, piles of brushwood were lit as the procession passed; while every two kilometres, a bull was sacrificed.[363]

## (c) Temples and worship

The relationship between the gods and the Assyrians, as throughout Mesopotamia, was what we might call co-dependent. Cotterell points out that:

> Humanity's need for the protection and love of the gods, as expressed in prayers and hymns of praise, was complemented by the need on the part of the gods for humanity as their servants, to build and maintain their temples, and to feed and clothe their cult statues. In their inscriptions, Babylonian and Assyrian kings boasted of how they served the divine meal, consisting of food not generally consumed by ordinary people. Indeed, surviving instructions outline the proper times and manner of preparing and serving the divine meal each day in Babylonian and Assyrian temples.[364]

It was, of course, a great privilege to serve Aššur and he was assured of a daily feast. Andrae discovered some 650 clay tablets in part of Aššur's temple complex. The tablets contained the records of four successive temple administrators, who were in charge of arranging Aššur's meals in the twelfth and early eleventh centuries BC.[365] The many different ingredients that constituted his meals were delivered from all parts of the empire, perhaps impractical but *symbolically* crucial. The empire was the realm of Aššur, and all his subjects had to play their part in his service. Refusal to do so was an act of treason. As the gods were thought to eat their meals by smelling, the 'leftovers' could then be shared out.

The temples and their cult objects were made and maintained by expert craftsmen. Some gods had their own temples (e.g. Ishtar, the goddess of sex and battle), but, as Assyria expanded, more and more gods were brought into Aššur's temple, partially as a result of the Assyrian policy of 'godnapping'. The list of gods living in Aššur's temple had become so long by the first millennium

---

363  Cotterell 2019, 197–8.
364  Cotterell 2019, 133.
365  Radner 2015, 17.

BC that a text that is nowadays called the Divine Directory of Aššur was written to set out the topography of the temple. By being hosted by Aššur, these gods acknowledged, for all to see, Aššur's sovereignty. It is not hard to see the powerful symbolism at work here. Even when the administrative centre of the empire was moved – to Kalhu in 879 BC, to Dur-Šarrukin in 706 BC and finally to Nineveh c.700 BC – the cultus of Aššur in Assur was maintained with all provinces involved. Because the king was the chief priest in Assyria, the priests did not have the same degree of independence as in Babylonia.

## (d) One god or many?

Intriguingly, a significant debate has been waging among Assyriologists as to whether or not Assyrian religion was monotheistic. On the surface Assyria appears to have been thoroughly polytheistic. The great god-list known as *AN* (= *Anum*) lists, for example, some 1,970 gods. However, Saggs in his survey of the culture and history of Assyria argued that some Assyrian texts manifest an 'incipient monotheism' provided one understand that although there are many gods they are 'aspects of one God', with the result that 'ultimately all divinity is one'.[366]

The strongest proponent of Assyrian monotheism is Parpola. He claims that

it is a mistake to regard Assyrian religion as *exclusively*, or even primarily, polytheistic. On the contrary, belief in the existence of a single omnipotent god dominated the Assyrian state religion, royal ideology, philosophy and mystery cults to the extent that Assyrian religion in its imperial elaboration, with all its polytheistic garb, must be regarded *as essentially monotheistic*.[367]

For Parpola, the great gods are only attributes and powers of the one, supreme god, Aššur. Their independence is illusory. In the imperial propaganda Aššur is the creator and lord of the universe: he is

the creator of himself, the father of the gods, who grew up in the Abyss; the king of heaven and earth, the lord of all the gods who emanated . . . the supernal and infernal gods and fashioned the vaults of heaven and earth, the maker of all the regions, who lives in the [pur]e starlit heave[ns].[368]

---

366 Saggs 1984, 204.
367 Parpola 2000, 165. Emphasis original.
368 Quoted by Parpola 2000, 170.

Aššur is both transcendent and immanent.

There are nine other great gods in the Assyrian pantheon and the case for Assyrian polytheism rests mostly with them. They are:[369]

- Anu: the god of heaven;
- Ea: the god of wisdom, also described as the creator of everything;
- Sîn: the moon god;
- Shamash: the sun god and in particular the divine judge;
- Marduk, the son of Ea, raised to be king of the gods and the one who maintained cosmic order;
- Ishtar: goddess of beauty and love;
- Ninurta/Nabû: a warrior god and lord of the stylus;
- Adad: god of thunder;
- Nergal: king of the earth.

Parpola argues that each god has a distinct function or office related to particular powers. All were related to one another by birth. He explores these great gods as a council, a family, as numbers, as a body, as a tree, as garments of Ishtar, as colours – all of which enables Parpola to argue that the gods are powers or attributes of Aššur. He concludes that

> the heavily monotheistic 'bent' of Assyrian religion appears to have been a genuinely Assyrian development. The system of divine numbers that formalized the doctrine of the unity of the divine powers, the sacred tree in its triadic elaboration, as well as the equation 'God' = '(all) the gods' appear only with the emergence of the Middle Assyrian empire in the fourteenth century BCE.[370]

Porter has responded to Parpola's proposal in detail. She has offered, for example, an alternative interpretation to Parpola's view that the stylized trees represent Aššur as 'all the gods'.[371] She acknowledges that Assyrians thought of the divine as both singular and plural and asserts the need to investigate this further. Because of Assyrian borrowing from southern Mesopotamia, it is vital to try to attend to texts that are clearly and distinctively Assyrian. In her 2000 chapter, Porter focuses first on a range of artefacts, a survey that supports the

---

369  For more detail see Parpola 2000, 15–79.

370  Parpola 2000, 206.

371  Porter 1993.

view that 'the Assyrians, from the time of their rise to power in the fourteenth century BCE until the fall of their empire in the late seventh century BCE, believed in and worshipped a large number of Gods'.[372]

She then moves on to focus on hymns and ritual texts – which provide the clearest data for views of the gods – and here fails to find evidence of monotheism: 'the texts that I have examined reveal a concept of divinity that is consistently polytheistic, one that reflects belief in the existence of many independent gods.'[373] However, she does note a certain tendency in the relatively small number of texts that are thought to embody a view of the divine as singular:

> they suggest that despite a fundamental belief in the multiplicity of the divine, some Assyrians felt a powerful attraction to one or another single god and in some cases envisioned that god as a particularly intense locus of divine power.[374]

In other words, there is a degree of ambivalence in the Assyrians' response to the multiplicity of the divine.

W. G. Lambert proposed that monotheism was espoused by a few thinkers in Mesopotamia but this was a late theological development.[375] To explore this view, Porter attends to 'singular' Assyrian texts chronologically. She begins with the *tākultu* ritual texts which set out the performance of royal food offerings. The unusual juxtaposition of two divine names – there are 11 or more pairs almost always including Aššur, for example Aššur-Ishtar – 'implies a concept of Aššur as an unusually powerful god, a singularly potent locus of divine power who embodied qualities and powers usually attributed to several gods'.[376] The crucial issue is how we interpret the link, and Porter proposes that the first god is being likened to the qualities of the second one. However, '[w]hile this represents an unusually intense focus on the powers and person of one particular god, neither text nor ritual is in the least monotheistic in the image of divinity it presents'.[377] The two *tākultu* ritual texts together list some 246 names of gods, so that:

---

372 Porter 2000, 223. Cf. Porter 2000, 224–8.

373 Porter 2000, 217.

374 Porter 2000, 228.

375 See Porter 2000, 229, n. 31.

376 Porter 2000, 237–8.

377 Porter 2000, 238.

Although the *tākultu* texts reflect some sense that a single god could be a focal point where divine powers were concentrated, the texts' dominant image of divinity is nevertheless characterized by a multiplicity of divine forms and a division of divine powers among numerous independent divine beings.[378]

Above we referred to Parpola's attention to the gods as a body. In a hymn to Ninurta, the god's body is described as made up of other gods – for example 'your neck is the god Marduk' – and several scholars find here an indication of monotheism.[379] The text seems to be a revision of a text going back to the twelfth century BC. Our reading of the text hinges on the interpretation of the word *ilu* which labels each body part of Ninurta. The term *ilu* refers to the spectrum of forms and powers associated with each deity. 'An Assyrian *ilu*, in short, was not a "god" in our sense, but a set of related but not completely congruent phenomena and qualities, only one of which was imagined as a divine person.'[380] Furthermore, the structure of the poem makes Ninurta's absorption of the other *ilus* into himself highly unlikely. However, '[t]he Ninurta hymn is the only clearly Assyrian text to focus to this degree on the qualities and powers of one god at the expense of other gods'.[381]

Porter also attends to a hymn to Marduk in which he is depicted as incorporating into himself powers of other gods. For example, 'Sîn is your divinity, Anu your sovereignty, Dagan your lordship, Enlil your kingship'.[382] 'As with the Ninurta hymn, the text's equation of other *ilu*s with Marduk has the effect of representing him as god par excellence, one who incorporates the powers and roles of the greatest gods of the pantheon.'[383] However:

the prayer to Marduk does not reflect a concept of divinity as embodied in a single powerful god who replaces and eliminates all other gods, but reflects instead a tendency to *focus* from time to time on one god in a context that remains explicitly polytheistic.[384]

---

378  Porter 2000, 239.

379  See Porter 2000, 240, n. 49.

380  Porter 2000, 247.

381  Porter 2000, 252.

382  Porter 2000, 253.

383  Porter 2000, 253.

384  Porter 2000, 254. Emphasis original.

# (e) The king and Aššur

When the king entered the temple of Aššur for his coronation, the chant of the priests was: 'Aššur is king! Aššur is king!' Even as the new king assumes power, his role is clearly distinguished from the kingship of Aššur. At his coronation the king did not become a god; he did not become part of the Assyrian pantheon. Holloway points out that:

> The state, in creating a monarch, signifies through the implied *vox populi* that the divine imperial will to expand the borders of the Land of Aššur is as one with the earthly king. It implies that his exercise of diplomacy, military force and administrative acumen shall magnify the Assyrian Empire, and, in context of ritual and imperial culture, communicates that the ideology of the new king shall satisfy the tutelary god and the people of the Land of Aššur. The paradox of an earthly king who incarnates the imperial will-to-power of Aššur is the ideological fulcrum to three centuries of Neo-Assyrian foreign relations.[385]

Van Driel notes that texts from building inscriptions indicate that in the Middle Assyrian period the gods used to visit the king's palace, most likely annually and all together. However, there are few signs of this in the Neo-Assyrian period.[386]

It would seem, therefore, that the king was in no way regarded as divine in Assyria. However, recent debates have blurred, even erased, this distinction. Parpola, whose view of Assyrian monotheism we discussed above, argues that just as Aššur is seen as a tree, so too is the king. This equation, according to Parpola, means that the king was the 'human incarnation of the almighty God, Aššur'.[387] He writes:

> The king's 'consubstantiality' with God, implicit in his identification with the tree, constituted an article of faith of central importance to Assyrian religion and imperial ideology. As a 'perfect man,' the king was not only God in human form, whose government represented the 'kingdom of heaven' upon earth, he was the very cornerstone of man's salvation.[388]

---

385 Holloway 2002, xv.
386 Van Driel 1969, 166–7.
387 Parpola 2000, 190.
388 Parpola 2000, 192.

Parpola's is an extreme view and we noted above the critique of his view of the tree. Generally, it is agreed that the Assyrian kings were not regarded as divine, but clearly the king shared a special relationship with Aššur. A question that has received new attention is whether the kings' images in temples were ever worshipped, another way of getting at the status of the king. Cole and Machinist, for example, have argued against the general view that royal worship did in fact take place.[389]

Holloway points out that:

The Neo-Assyrian royal titularies, narrative inscriptions, astrological prognostications and unctuously flattering correspondence hammer away at the theme of the unique proximity of the king to the divine realm and extol his god-like powers. The kings were summoned pre-natally to kingship, suckled by goddesses, warned by eclipses and other portents of imminent personal hazards, and succored by upbeat, motherly prophecies uttered by goddesses. Kings like the gods strode into battle surrounded by the *melammu*, a radiant, terrifying nimbus devastating to foes, occasionally represented by a halo of stars surrounding deities in glyptic art, and kings embodied god-like wisdom and could be characterized as the very image of the gods. The kings were not members of the state pantheon, but they dwelt in closer physical and ontological proximity to the gods than any other mortals, and that ideological fact had implications for their role in the temple beyond that of beloved priest of Aššur.[390]

Neo-Assyrian kings never built temples for their own worship. In Assyrian iconography the gods are clearly distinguished and the king is depicted as a servant of the gods, and not as a god himself. And so, for example, in the Aššur temple Esarhaddon proclaims: 'I set up an image of my majesty in an attitude of prayer to their divinities, to implore constantly for my life'.[391] Many of the statues of Gudea were made to be put in temples and to receive sacrifices, and yet the king is portrayed as a worshipper and servant of the gods.[392]

---

389  Holloway 2002, 78.
390  Holloway 2002, 181–2.
391  Holloway 2002, 184.
392  Holloway 2002, 184.

Nevertheless, Mesopotamian kings were worshipped in temples, and it would appear that the Assyrians simply followed this tradition. Holloway argues that

> in light of the millennia-old tradition of offering sacrifice to images of Mesopotamian kings and the role played by the ᵈṣalam-šarri in the Assyrian cultus, we should seriously entertain the notion that the Balāwāt bronzes and the Nimrūd liturgical setting preserve visual relics of the *limited* divine honors commissioned and received by the kings of the Neo-Assyrian empire. And I do underscore the qualification 'limited.' The hermeneutical stumbling-block of kings who are not gods but at the same time are kings who have divinized images that receive sacrifice in temples and abroad, may be fruitfully reconsidered through the use of DINGIR in Neo-Assyrian god-lists and ritual texts.[393]

The Assyrian kings magnified their role and position by spending great sums on the construction of images of themselves and placing these adjacent to images of the gods.

> The presence of the royal image as votary in the god's sanctuary both speaks to a need for the god's munificence and also testifies to a special relationship between the ruler and the divine. It makes manifest a ruler's privileged mediating role between the gods and the people, a status sanctioned in the Mesopotamian cosmology . . . the royal image is affective, and serves to reinforce the hierarchical order that privileges the ruler through its very presence in the shrine. The ruler's image in the god's shrine is not only the result of his special status, it also works to establish that special status.[394]

Indeed, by (at least) the seventh century BC, royal ideology saw the king as a being quite separate from ordinary humans and superior to them. In a literary text about the creation of humankind, the gods fashion the king in a separate act after having already created human beings:

> Ea (god of wisdom) opened his mouth to speak, saying a word to Belet-ili (goddess of creation): 'You are Belet-ili, the sister of the great gods; it was

---

393 Holloway 2002, 189. Emphasis original.
394 Holloway 2002, 91, quoting Winter 1992.

you who created man, the human (*lullû amēlu*). Fashion now the king, the counsellor man (*šarru māliku amēlu*)! Gird the whole of his figure so pleasingly, make perfect his countenance and well formed his body!' And Belet-ili fashioned the king, the counsellor man.[395]

# (f) Law and ethics

Surprisingly, we have no law codes from the Middle Assyrian period or from the Neo-Assyrian period. I say 'surprisingly' because the Assyrians would have been well aware of the Code of Hammurabi, for example. As Radner points out:

> No collection of laws from the Neo-Assyrian period is known to us. If a text of this kind had ever existed, it seems highly likely that it would have been part of Assurbanipal's famous library in Nineveh. But neither in Nineveh nor in twenty-three excavated sites located in different parts of the empire have archaeologists succeeded in unearthing so much as a fragment of such a text. In addition, in none of the numerous Neo-Assyrian texts is the existence of a collection of laws hinted at, making it implausible to argue that such a text had existed, written on perishable material such as wooden writing tablets or scrolls of leather or papyrus.[396]

However, we do have a collection of 14 tablets from Middle Assyria that are known as Middle Assyrian Laws (MAL). To access Neo-Assyrian law we have to draw on private legal documents, royal decrees, letters, and reliefs from the palaces.[397] The topics dealt with in Assyrian law are typical ones across the Ancient Near East, and in volume 2 of this series we will attend to law in detail.

In the MAL, the death penalty is imposed for a variety of offences. The *lex talionis* was practised, for example, in relation to sodomy. Mutilation of the face and body was also carried out. A married woman who knowingly committed adultery merited the death penalty, as did the rapist of a married woman who resisted his attack. A woman who practised self-inflicted abortion was impaled and denied burial. The punishment for murder, however,

---

395 Quoted in Zamazalová 2011, 313.

396 Radner 2003, 883.

397 Radner 2003.

was decided by the head of the family of the victim. He could seek blood vengeance (according to *lex talionis*) or compensation.

Women had few rights, with the husband the absolute head of the household. There were limits on what a husband could do to his wife, but he was free to whip her, pull out her hair and crush her ears! He could also take more than one wife and could sell his wife.

In relation to Neo-Assyrian law, which would also have been true of Middle Assyrian times, Radner points out that:

> The king, as the chosen representative of the gods, was the head of the state and thus the head of the administration. His power was absolute, restricted only by his being answerable to the gods as the ideal king who was supposed to exercise a just rule.[398]

Every official was personally appointed by the king, and certainly on occasion he looked to the gods for wisdom. In terms of the lower ranks, the king relied on the advice of his officials.

In comparison to Middle Assyrian law, Neo-Assyrian law seems to have relied to a much lesser extent on the death penalty:

> Although there is no evidence from the legal texts for judgments imposing physical punishment on the offender, the case of a cook who stole temple property shows that not only political offenders such as traitors or rebels were tortured, maimed, and/or killed, practices well known from the royal inscriptions. In a letter to the king, the cook is reported to have died as a consequence of the beating he received as punishment for his crime. The context of a memorandum from Nineveh recording the names of persons who were tried and subjected to severe physical punishment is unknown.[399]

Polygamy was rare but not completely unknown in the Neo-Assyrian period. Murder, robbery, and theft of and damage to property were dealt with by compensation, although in the case of murder, if compensation was unavailable, blood vengeance could be sought.

---

398  Radner 2003, 886.
399  Radner 2003, 906.

# (g) Creation

The Neo-Assyrians were well acquainted with the Babylonian late-second-millennium *Enuma Elish* and the Epic of Gilgamesh. They held a similar view of the origins of the world, although, as noted above, with their gods as primary players. Originally, there was a watery chaos out of which the gods emerged, and the gods created the world. We will attend to these cosmogonies in detail in our discussion of the Babylonians.

# (h) Conclusion

With the Assyrian world view, we move firmly on to the terrain of imperial ideology, leading to Israel's experience of a tormented geography, as Brague evocatively describes it. Assyria would end up taking the northern kingdom of Israel into exile. According to the OT narrative, this is not the first time the Israelites have come up against such power. Embedded deeply in their memory should be the confrontation between the divine pharaoh and YHWH, when they were completely disempowered as slaves but nevertheless triumphed because of YHWH's assistance. Brueggemann speaks evocatively of the 'totalizing silence' engendered by Pharaoh's brutal, oppressive rule. The cry of the enslaved Israelites changes everything:

> The cry changes circumstances for the slaves, for the shut-down slaves have been changed by voiced possibility. The cry changes matters for Pharaoh, because now the reductionism of manageable technology and administrable labor have been altered by the fresh insistence that the slaves are not mere statistics but are named historical agents.[400]

Of course, the cry changes everything because it is heard by YHWH and he acts on the Israelites' behalf. As the Neo-Assyrian Empire emerged on the scene, the question became: on whom will Israel depend – now as a nation – when the imperial screws are tightened? Alas, the northern kingdom elected not to own her memory but to enter into the machinations of international relations, a disastrous move.

Politics and religion remain as intertwined as ever in the Assyrian world view. Empire requires centralization, and this is found in Aššur and his representative the king. However, Assyrian religion remains thoroughly polytheistic. If we have not noticed this already, religion is no guarantee against imperial brutality but is perfectly capable of undergirding it. In an imperial context

---

400 Brueggemann 2021, 3–4.

where the king is the law rather than being under it, the stage is inevitably set for the worst forms of brutality in the lust for power, with the full support of the gods.

In our discussion of the view of the land early in this volume, we noted how Weinfeld and Wazana relate the encompassing view of the land to the Neo-Assyrian imperial ideology of world rule. However, according to Wazana, Assyrian imperial descriptions refer to past events whereas '[b]iblical promise traditions are just that: a promise to be fulfilled in the future, that is, Israel's vocation'.[401] Thus, in the OT, '[t]he spatial merisms in promise terminology reflect a land that has no borders at all, only ever-expanding frontiers; they are referring to universal rule, using stock terminology typical of Neo-Assyrian royal inscriptions'.[402] For Assyria *and* Israel, the vision of world rule is monocentric, but in very different ways. We explored above the uniqueness of the Table of the Nations, and world rule within the OT certainly includes coming under YHWH's rule but as a means of blessing the nations and respecting their particularity.

# 9 The Babylonian world view

## (a) Introduction

Spectacle and wonder are at the heart of imperial world views, whether in the building of the most impressive structures or in the flaying of conquered warriors. In few places is this element of wonder as clearly in view as in the rebuilding of the Ishtar Gate and the Processional Way in Babylon by Nebuchadnezzar II (r. 604–562 BC). The reconstruction of the Ishtar Gate in the Pergamon Museum gives us some idea of the impression the architecture must have made on a person passing through this entrance.

> Entering this city through this portal, a visitor was first confronted by ferocious lions patrolling the Processional Way and then by majestic bulls and fierce *mušhuššu*-dragons (a composite being with the head and scaly body of a snake, the front paws of a lion, and the back legs of a bird of prey) who stood guard on the walls of the Ishtar Gate itself . . . These high-relief yellow and white animals stood out from a lapis lazuli-inspired blue background. Each animal was made of dozens of molded,

---

401  Wazana 2003, 70.
402  Wazana 2003, 71.

kiln-fired, and glazed bricks, assembled like the pieces of a puzzle ... The monument's overall technical virtuosity made it an especially spectacular work of art.[403]

We have foregrounded the importance of symbol in a world view, and the sensory experience generated by the Ishtar Gate should not be underestimated. The enlarged eyes of the animals are notable: 'It is possible, therefore, that the white rims of the animals' eyes were a representational device intended to capture and convey what Winter has termed "intense" or "augmented" viewing – that is, the experience of "wonder."'[404] Nebuchadnezzar himself wrote: '*I filled those gates with splendor for the wonder of all people.*'[405]

Wonder, certainly, but also fear and terror, a very real sense of what Rudolf Otto called the *mysterium tremendum*. Even in their reconstructed form, the animals, representing the gods of Babylon and her power, seem to watch one through their enlarged eyes as one walks along the path. If we can step out of our post-Enlightenment shoes for a moment, we can imagine a visitor, himself or herself thoroughly religious, being utterly overwhelmed by the gods and power of the Babylonian Empire. This, of course, was just the impression the structure was intended to create.

The Babylonians were renowned for their literary, scientific, artistic and religious innovations. They also bring us into close contact with Israel and, notoriously, took Judah into exile in 587 BC. However, their history extends a long way back before that, and we need to review this history in order to get a sense of their influential world view.

## (b) History

'Babylonia' refers to southern Mesopotamia, and as such it has a very long history. Situated where it was, it was wide open to the influx of different peoples, unlike Egypt. Indeed, it was only by the close of the fifteenth century BC, when the Kassite ruler was called 'King of Babylonia', that we can without anachronism refer to *Babylonia*. The great achievement of the Kassites was the development of a nation under a king with clear borders comparable to those of Hammurabi's empire and maintained as such for centuries. From now on, Babylonia remained a unified entity.

---

403  Amrhein and Knott 2019b, 25.
404  Amrhein and Knott 2019a, 146.
405  Amrhein and Knott 2019b, 25. Emphasis original.

It is the Old Babylonian period, the Middle Babylonian period (1595–1155 BC), the Early Neo-Babylonian period (1155–800 BC) and the Neo-Babylonian period (800–539 BC) that are of most interest to us. As Bryce observes:

> Our journey will take us from the Old Babylonian kingdom of Hammu-rabi through the period of the second great Babylonian kingdom, ruled by the Kassites, and then through a long period of relative insignificance until Babylon shines forth more splendidly than ever as the capital of the Neo-Babylonian empire. This was when Nebuchadnezzar II (604–562) became the Near Eastern world's most powerful king.[406]

However, we will not understand these periods if we do not journey back, albeit briefly, beyond them into the origins of Babylonia. Samuel Kramer, as we noted above, wrote a book entitled *History Begins at Sumer*, and, of course, Sumer is located in southern Mesopotamia, as we have seen. It was here in the fourth millennium BC, prior to the invention of writing, that a number of developments took place – urbanization and concomitant architecture, the invention of metallurgy and the wheel, the emergence of certain art forms, the development of commerce and trade – which signal the move from 'prehistory' to history. Writing probably developed more or less simultaneously across a region broader than Sumer. However, Sumerian is the first clearly identifiable language written in syllabic cuneiform, and Uruk is the best example of this development of writing.[407] Sumerian culture forms an indispensable background to Babylonia, and readers are referred here to our earlier discussion of the Sumerian world view. Many Babylonian works are versions of Sumerian texts.

However, there is evidence that in northern Babylonia the population at this time was Semitic and formed something of a contrast with the Sumerian south. The Old Semitic language of these peoples came to be called 'Akkadian', the language which would be used widely across Mesopotamia and beyond for nearly two millennia. Sargon I unified north and south *c.*2300 BC.

Religiously, certain Semitic deities were elevated to new positions in the pantheon; this was especially true for Semitic Ishtar, who was associated with Sumerian Inanna. Of note here is Sargon's daughter Enḫeduanna, whom he installed as high priestess of the moon god Nanna at Ur. Gifted

---

406 Bryce 2016, 5–6.
407 Arnold 2004, 17–18.

with remarkable literary ability, Enḫeduanna is the first poet in history known by name.[408]

Sargon's grandson Naram-Sin is credited with developing the united kingdom into an empire, and he is also the first Babylonian ruler to be seen as a god, an unusual phenomenon among the Babylonians. Arnold suggests that this may have been related to the need for a patron deity for Akkad and the Akkadian Empire thereby linking heaven and earth with Babylonia and her social and political life.

The Legend of Sargon is intriguing with its parallels to the narrative of Moses' birth:

I am Sargon the great king, king of Agade . . . My mother, the high priestess, conceived me, she bore me in secret. She placed me in a reed basket, she sealed my hatch with pitch. She left me to the river, whence I could not come up. The river carried me off, it brought me to Aqqi, drawer of water. Aqqi, drawer of water, brought me up as he dipped his bucket. Aqqi, drawer of water, raised me as his adopted son. Aqqi, drawer of water, set (me) to his orchard work. During my orchard work, Ishtar loved me. Fifty-five years I ruled as king. I became lord over and ruled the black-headed folk.[409]

Sargon is also accredited with naming the city of Babylon 'Babylon'.[410] We do not know the earliest meaning of 'Babylon', but '[t]his ancient and now obscure name for the city gave rise to an Akkadian form, created through popular etymology, *bāb-ilim*, "Gate of God," which then assumed a Sumerian equivalent, **ka-dingirra**, also meaning "Gate of God"'.[411]

A Neo-Sumerian 'empire' arose again under Ur-Nammu's son and successor, Shulgi. He developed a massive administrative infrastructure, established a standing army, set up scribal schools, distributed land to loyal members of the military, and established innovative ways of record-keeping and a new calendar. Like Naram-Sin, Shulgi was worshipped as a god.

The second millennium BC brings us into the Old Babylonian period. The 400 years that followed the Neo-Sumerian period were dominated by the

---

408  Arnold 2004, 24.
409  Quoted in Arnold 2004, 26.
410  Arnold 2004, 32.
411  Arnold 2004, 2.

Amorites, who came to control the major cities of Mesopotamia. They established new centres, the most important of which were Isin, Larsa, Eshnunna and Kish in southern Mesopotamia, Mari and Assur to the north, and Qatna and Aleppo in the north-west. Significantly, one Amorite by the name of Sumuabum established a dynasty at Babylon in 1894 BC, a development that heralded the vital role Babylon would come to play.

The sixth ruler of this new dynasty was **Hammurabi** (1792–1750 BC).[412] Initially when he became king, Hammurabi was one ruler among many in southern Mesopotamia. He devoted his early years as king to religious and legal reforms, the latter culminating in his final years in his famous law code.[413] He began by cancelling debts that were outstanding. 'A good king took care of the gods and their temples',[414] and Hammurabi attended to the well-being of the patron deities of the cities under his rule. He also did his best to ensure that his people were secure from attack. However, having reigned for 28 years, within some four years he brought the whole of southern Mesopotamia under his rule, a move that would 'fundamentally change the political configuration of the Middle East'.[415] Hammurabi's five sons and successors ruled after his death for a century and a half, but the Kassites soon made their appearance, and the death blow was dealt by the Hittites in 1595 BC when they captured Babylon. However, as Van De Mieroop notes, something fundamental shifted during Hammurabi's reign:

> Babylonia never became a region of city-states again, but metamorphosed into a large territorial state with a single capital city whose rulers had varying degrees of control over the countryside. No competing city-states were ever to emerge again. That was the most lasting consequence of Hammurabi's rule in political terms.[416]

As Hammurabi rose to prominence, so did Babylon. In the prologue of Hammurabi's code, it is the gods Anu and Enlil who 'named the city of Babylon with its august name and made it supreme within the regions of the world'. These gods also granted Marduk supreme power and provided Hammurabi with his name: 'Thus the prologue creates an ideological nexus of city, deity,

---

412  There is a debate about whether his name was Hammurabi or Hammurapi. For the different meanings see Arnold 2004, 42.

413  For the text see Pritchard, ed., 2011, 155–79.

414  Van De Mieroop 2005, 13.

415  Van De Mieroop 2005, 14.

416  Van De Mieroop 2005, 39.

and king, which demonstrates the importance of Babylon during what has come to be known as the Old Babylonian period.[417] Likewise, in the *Enuma Elish* Marduk proclaims that he built and named Babylon to be a residence for his fathers: 'I shall call [its] name [Babylon], (meaning) "Houses of the Great Gods."'[418]

Hammurabi is particularly well known as a lawgiver because of the black stela with his law code engraved on it. This monument was probably set up after Hammurabi's thirty-eighth year of rule.[419] It has three parts:

- *A prologue.* This is about Hammurabi's relationship to the gods. In the first person, Hammurabi explains how the gods made him king, he lists them, and then he tells how he provided for their well-being.
- *The epilogue.* Also in the first person, this section speaks of Hammurabi as the quintessential just king, 'the king of justice', and calls upon the gods to curse those who do not follow Hammurabi's precepts.
- *The laws.* The 275–300 laws are introduced with the note that it was Marduk who commanded Hammurabi to maintain justice and truth. The laws are casuistic with the punishment phrased as a command. There is a coherence to the list of laws dealing progressively with legal proceedings (paragraphs 1–5), property offences (6–25), ownership of land and buildings (26–65k), financial arrangements (65l–126), women, marriage and inheritance (127–94), assault (195–214), professional fees and responsibilities (215–40), agriculture (241–67), costs of hire (268–77) and slaves (278–82).[420]

Hammurabi's law code articulates a literal *lex talionis*. Indeed, many of the penalties are extremely harsh: around 30 times the death penalty is prescribed, including for stealing temple or palace property. However, social standing affects the penalties. Scholars continue to debate the purpose of the code. The code is based partially on older law codes, it is not comprehensive, and there is scant evidence that it was used by courts in Hammurabi's time. Hammurabi identifies two audiences in the epilogue: his contemporaries and the future kings. Van De Mieroop argues that '[s]omeone who felt wronged could thus find solace that justice would prevail in the end'.[421] However, it is hard to find

---

417  Arnold 2004, 32.

418  Arnold 2004, 32.

419  Van De Mieroop 2005, 100–1.

420  See Van De Mieroop 2005, 103–4.

421  Van De Mieroop 2005, 110.

this persuasive if the code bore little resemblance to justice as exercised in Babylonia. Of particular interest to readers of the OT are the many parallels between Hammurabi's casuistic laws and laws in the OT.

It is likely that it was also during the Old Babylonian period that the Epic of Gilgamesh (EG) – titled, as was common in the ancient world, with the opening words, namely 'He who saw everything' – was edited from various Sumerian stories into a continuous, fresh narrative. The EG recounts the story of the ancient king of Uruk, Gilgamesh, and his rebellion against death upon the loss of his friend Enkidu. Through many travels and experiences, Gilgamesh returns home to accept his mortality, the theme of the work. At a critical point the barmaid Siduri tells him:

Gilgamesh, where do you roam?
You will not find the eternal life you seek.
When the gods created mankind
They appointed death for mankind,
Kept eternal life in their own hands.
So, Gilgamesh, let your stomach be full,
Day and night enjoy yourself in every way,
Every day arrange for pleasures.
Day and night, dance and play,
Wear fresh clothes.
Keep your head washed, bathe in water,
Appreciate the child who holds your hand,
Let your wife enjoy herself in your lap.[422]

When the Babylonian version of the EG was first published by George Smith in 1872, it caused a sensation because of the story of the Flood in the eleventh tablet. Gilgamesh meets an immortal man, one Utnapishtim. He was warned of a divine plan to flood the world and gained immortality by escaping death in a large reed boat with his family and pairs of animals. Not surprisingly, Utnapishtim is known as the 'Babylonian Noah'.

A significant prophetic literature also developed in the Old Babylonian period.[423] In addition, major progress was made in mathematical and astrological studies.

---

422  Quoted in Arnold 2004, 51. The parallels with Ecclesiastes are notable.
423  Arnold 2004, 57.

The Middle Babylonian period (1595–1155 BC) spans some four and a half centuries, during which time Babylonia was dominated by the Kassites, who filled the vacuum left by Mursili I after he quickly withdrew to Hatti. They brought stability to the region for four centuries under a monarchy with a geographical extent comparable to that of Hammurabi's empire. Arnold notes that, '[w]hile the Kassites will represent virtually no break from the Old Babylonian period *culturally*, important *political* differences will be obvious, reflecting the beginning of an internationalism that will change the course of ancient history permanently'.[424] The Kassites embodied a strong nationalism and focused the wealth they achieved on infrastructure, religious and royal. Literature flourished amid the stability, and it is likely that the so-called Babylonian Job, a text beginning 'Let me praise the lord of wisdom', was written during this time. The main character suffers many things and seeks to find the reason (theodicy). He explores many options, only to come to see that the source of his problems is the god Marduk himself.

As we move from the thirteenth to the twelfth century BC, astonishingly 'nearly every city in the eastern Mediterranean world collapsed in ways that appear from archaeological and textual evidence to have been rather sudden and cataclysmic'.[425] This catastrophe was, however, accompanied by significant cultural developments: the alphabet, a new form of writing, spread outside the Levant and made communications far more accessible; Syria, the Israelites and the Philistines emerged; and soon Assyria would achieve world domination, not least through repeated clashes with Babylonia (see 'The Assyrian world view').

The Isin Dynasty ruled over Babylonia from 1157 to 1026 BC. The fourth king in this dynasty, Nebuchadnezzar I (1125–1104 BC), avenged the sacking of Babylon by the Elamites in the course of which they took the statue of Marduk prisoner and carted him off to Susa. Nebuchadnezzar launched an unexpected attack and brought Marduk back home! This event seemed to have resulted in an elevation of Marduk to the supreme god. A text from this period calls him 'king of the gods'.[426]

Around 911 BC a new group emerged in the south, the Chaldeans, who were destined with time to become a major player in Babylonia. From 814 to 811 BC, Assyria invaded Babylonia year after year for four years. With the seizure and deportation of two of her kings in 813 and 812 BC, Babylonia approximated anarchy. During the early years of this Early Neo-Babylonian period, the major

---

424 Arnold 2004, 62. Emphasis original.
425 Arnold 2004, 76.
426 Arnold 2004, 80.

works of literature were standardized into a corpus, sometimes referred to as a 'stream of tradition'.[427] This included the famous *Enuma Elish*, the Babylonian creation epic. In it Tiamat, the powerful salt-water god, conspires with her husband and 11 divine monsters she created to threaten the other gods. The fearful gods persuade Marduk to enter into combat with her, promising loyalty if he is successful. He *is* successful and uses her corpse to create the world, and the blood of her husband to create humankind to do the hard work in the universe so the gods can rest and enjoy life. The city of Babylon becomes Marduk's resting place. The New Year festival now came to focus on Marduk. All the gods were required to come to Babylon and share in the celebration of Marduk's kingship.

During the first millennium BC, major empires dominated Mesopotamia: the Assyrian Empire, the Persian Empire and latterly the Greek Empire. The Neo-Babylonian Empire falls between the Assyrian and the Persian. While relatively short, 'the grandeur of the empire, especially under Nebuchadnezzar II, and its legacy in the biblical and classical sources, left an indelible mark on subsequent history, making this one of the most important and interesting periods of ancient Babylonian history'.[428]

By the mid-eighth century BC the Chaldeans had become serious contenders for power in Babylonia, ready to fill the vacuum as Assyrian power declined. The first Chaldean king was Eriba-Marduk, later described as the 're-establisher of the foundation(s) of the land'.[429] His reign concluded shortly prior to 760 BC. Nabonassar (747–734 BC) was the next prominent king. During his reign, scribes began to keep far more precise records of events.

> The Neo-Babylonian Chronicle series, a valuable new historiographic source for this period, records outstanding events of each year beginning with the reign of Nabonassar. Greek astronomers recognized the 'Nabonassar era' as a turning point in the history of science, and the term 'Chaldean' came to mean 'astronomer' in Hellenistic times.[430]

Nabonassar was not a Chaldean, but Mukin-zeri, who assumed the throne in 731 BC, was. Tiglath-pileser III deposed him and assumed the throne of Babylonia himself. Tiglath-pileser's son inherited the dual kingship, but a

---

427  Arnold 2004, 82.
428  Arnold 2004, 87.
429  Arnold 2004, 89.
430  Arnold 2004, 89.

Chaldean named Merodach-baladan seized power in Babylonia and held on to it for a decade. He was ousted by Sargon II in 710 BC. For the following century, Assyria exerted considerable effort to maintain control of Babylonia. Upon Esarhaddon's death (c.668 BC) the Assyrian Empire was divided between his sons, with Aššurbanipal (668–627 BC) made king in Assyria, and Shamash-shum-ukin (667–648 BC) king in Babylonia. However, sibling rivalry destroyed this arrangement and led to a bloody civil war. Assyria regained control but at great cost, and emerged weakened. Upon Aššurbanipal's death, Nabopolassar (625–605 BC) seized control of Babylon and established the Neo-Babylonian Empire (see Map 10 overleaf). The Medes captured Assur, and Nabopolassar arrived late on the scene and made a treaty with Cyaxares, the Median king.

Nabopolassar increasingly entrusted power to the crown prince, Nebuchadnezzar II (605–562 BC). Nebuchadnezzar defeated the Egyptians at Carchemish in 605 BC, and swiftly seized the throne when Nabopolassar died in the same year. Arnold notes that 'Nebuchadnezzar quickly fell heir to most of the former territories of the Assyrian Empire'.[431] Resistance in certain areas continued, including in Palestine. Nebuchadnezzar laid siege to Jerusalem, capturing it in 597 BC. King Jehoiachin and other members of the Judean royal household were taken off to Babylon, and Zedekiah was appointed in Jehoiachin's place (2 Kings 24.17). Zedekiah sided with the Egyptians against Babylonia, and in 586 BC Jerusalem and the Temple were razed, and most of the population was deported.

> [Nebuchadnezzar's] empire surpassed Hammurapi's in geographical dimensions, and his inscriptions reflect a royal ideology different from those of his father, Nabopolassar . . . A new Babylonian imperialism emerged in which hegemony became the means by which the king could fulfil his obligation to rebuild, refurbish, and supply Babylonia's cult centers; the king became the protector of all humanity; and the city of Babylon became the economic and administrative center of the world.[432]

Nebuchadnezzar developed Babylon into the greatest city in the ancient world, spread over some 2,000 acres (809 ha). The great walls of the city

---

431  Arnold 2004, 92.
432  Arnold 2004, 96.

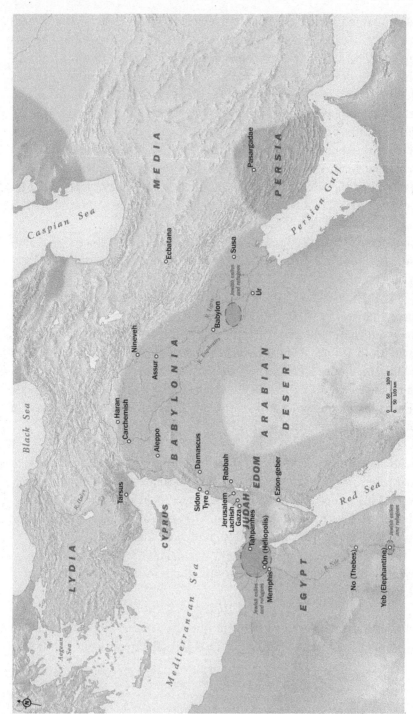

**Map 10 The Neo-Babylonian Empire**
(© Baker Publishing Group)

contained eight gates, each named after a deity. The Ishtar Gate,[433] referred to above, was approached by a street paved white and red, while the surface of the gate was covered with bricks of blue enamel. At points, the street by which one approached was 65 feet (20 m) wide, and walls rose on either side up to 40 feet (12 m) high. Nebuchadnezzar would accompany the statue of Marduk along this street each spring at the time of the New Year festival. Late in his reign, Nebuchadnezzar built a massive new palace for himself with its famous hanging gardens. 'A well-attested Babylonian document, the Topography of Babylon, which is essentially a scholarly compendium glorifying the city as a religious center, lists ten quarters of the city, each with its own temples and landmarks.'[434]

Nebuchadnezzar was succeeded by three ineffectual heirs: his son Ameel-Marduk (561–560 BC), his son-in-law Neriglissar (559–556 BC) and Neriglissar's son Labashi-Marduk (556 BC). Nabonidus (556–539 BC) usurped the throne. Remarkably, he sought to make Sîn, the moon god, head of the pantheon, thereby demoting Marduk. However, in October 539 BC, Babylon fell to Cyrus and the Persians.

## (c) Marduk, the Babylonian pantheon, and creation and humankind

Abusch points out that Marduk was originally a Sumerian name, meaning 'the calf of the storm'. During the Old Babylonian period he was a local god of Babylon, the son of Enki/Ea, and a junior deity in the Babylonian pantheon. As such, he was particularly associated with the fertility of the land through water, rain and storms. However, with his rise he 'became the god and master of the Babylonian national state and the supreme god and absolute ruler of the universe'.[435] The *Enuma Elish* (*EE*) tells the story of Marduk's rise to supremacy among the gods and his establishment of Babylon as his city and thus the centre of the world.

The recognition of Marduk as the supreme god was a new religious idea that depended upon a radical shift in thinking about the state. What was required was not only a different centre, but also a new conception of the

---

433  See Amrhein, Fitzgerald and Knott, eds, 2019.

434  Arnold 2004, 98.

435  Abusch 1999, 545. For the Babylonian map of the world with Babylon at the centre, see Finkel and Seymour 2008, 67.

cosmic and political world as a world-empire revolving around one central city.[436]

It is regularly pointed out that the *EE* should not be thought of as *the* Mesopotamian creation story – even in Babylonia, as we will see, there were others – or even as a creation story since it is really about the rise of Marduk. While this is true, a narrative can perform multiple speech acts at once, and there is a great deal that we learn from the *EE* about the Neo-Babylonian view of the gods, of Marduk in particular, and about creation and humankind. Babylonia covers a long period of history, and religious ideas developed over that time. For the Neo-Babylonian period, the *EE is* an important source for the Babylonian view of creation and humankind.[437] Our copies of the *EE* do not precede the first millennium BC and we cannot be sure of its date of origin.

The hero of the work is Marduk, who is celebrated again and again in the narrative. This is perhaps seen most clearly in the final section of the *EE*, which proclaims and explains Marduk's 50 names.[438] Clearly, the present form of the text relates to Marduk's rise to pre-eminence in the Babylonian pantheon, and the rise of Babylon, as discussed above. Arnold notes that:

> The epic thus reflects an era when the city of Babylon had risen politically and even replaced Nippur as the traditional locus of divine power in the world and a new sense of nationalism had emerged with Babylon at the center of a world empire. The reign of Nebuchadnezzar I (especially the return of the statue of Marduk from Elam) spawned a flurry of literary activity celebrating the elevation of Marduk, and it seems likely that this is when the epic was composed, although it no doubt relied on earlier hymnic-epic materials.[439]

The importance and influence of the *EE* is confirmed by the role it came to play in the New Year festival at Babylon each year. The New Year festival can be traced back to the times when it was celebrated in Ur in the Neo-Sumerian period, but it achieved far greater significance and symbolic clout in the Neo-Babylonian period. The festival was celebrated in Babylon in Nissanu

---

436 Abusch 1999, 546.

437 For the full text see Foster 2005, 436–86. He entitles it 'Epic of Creation'. *Enuma Elish* is the Akkadian title taken from the first two words.

438 *EE* in Foster 2005, 473–86.

439 Arnold 2004, 83.

during the vernal equinox; it lasted 12 days and on day four the *EE* was read out. Prior to this development, celebrations took place at a variety of cities and in relation to diverse deities. Now all the gods travelled to Babylon to celebrate Marduk's kingship. Rituals included prayers to Marduk, a cleansing of his temple, recitation of the *EE*, and the ritual enthronement of Marduk referred to as 'taking the hands of Bel'.

Marduk's main sanctuary was the heart of Babylon consisting of the lower temple Esagila and the high ziggurat Etemenanki, the foundation platform of heaven and earth, with the processional street running between the two. Marduk's statue was kept in Esagila, which operated as his royal palace and a reception site for visiting deities. It was surrounded with all the necessary amenities. The ziggurats built by the Assyrians were modest structures whereas Etemenanki was huge, much larger than the grand palaces. It took 43 years to build, some 17 million bricks, and was begun by Nabopolassar in response to instructions from the gods after he defeated Assyria, and completed by Nebuchadnezzar. At its base it was 980 square feet (91 sq. m), giving rise to a structure probably over 230 feet (70 m) high.[440] A temple sat at the top, but it is unclear what it was used for. Leick observes that '[t]he building therefore anchored the whole city within cosmic parameters'.[441] She also notes that 'here, where heaven and earth were connected, where gods hovered in elevated security above the city, the hub of the state could be contemplated as a cosmic pillar assuring continuity and renewal'.[442]

Although the *EE* celebrates Marduk as supreme, as king, as sovereign, the religion it embodies is thoroughly polytheistic. *Theomachy* – the quarrelling and battle of the gods – is central to it, with Apsu initially conspiring with Tiamat against the gods because their noise prevented rest, sleep and peace in the interior of heaven. However, Ea catches wind of the plot, puts Apsu into a deep sleep and murders him. The magnificent Marduk is formed out of the corpse of Apsu.

However, Marduk's activity and that of other gods similarly prevents the gods from sleeping and resting, and they appeal to Tiamat to deal with him:

Think of our burden, our eyes are pinched,
Lift this unremitting yoke, let us sleep![443]

---

440 Finkel and Seymour 2008, 38. See Finkel and Seymour 2008, 43, for a reconstruction of the ziggurat.
441 Leick 2001, 262. Leick (2001, 265) argues that the temple atop the ziggurat was a symbolic space.
442 Leick 2001, 265.
443 *EE* in Foster 2005, 443.

Tiamat raises up the male god Qingu and gives him the 'tablet of destinies', namely, power and great authority to deal with Marduk and the troublesome gods. Again Ea intervenes, and amid an assembly of gods Marduk is promised sovereignty and supremacy if he defeats Tiamat. 'Marduk is king!' the gods shout in jubilation, and Marduk sets off and successfully and brutally slays Tiamat. He tramples on her, crushes her skull with his mace and slices open her arteries. Although they have superhuman powers and are divine, the gods are portrayed as embodied, needing sleep and rest. They are also eminently capable of some of the worst human emotions and behaviours, such as resentment, secret plotting against others, and terrible violence. All of this appears to be normal in the divine world.

The *EE* begins 'When on high . . .', an introductory phrase that is often compared to Genesis 1.1 translated as 'In the beginning when . . .' As is common in ANE discussions of creation, the origins of the universe are referred to by negations, in this case to the fact that neither heaven nor the netherworld had been *named*. The primeval ocean, consisting of Apsu (fresh water) and Tiamat (salt water), is the original reality, from which the gods are brought forth. Thus, Van De Mieroop is misleading when he says that the *EE* 'relates how the universe *evolved from nothingness* to an organized structure with the city of Babylon at its center'.[444] Early in Tablet 1, Anšar and Kišar – 'the totality of heaven and earth'[445] – are formed.

However, the *EE* has no problem in repositioning Marduk as *the creator of heaven and earth*. He inspects Tiamat's carcass and splits it in two, making heaven and earth. There is no conception here of an ontological gap between divinity and creation; both are from the same stuff. Heaven is for the gods. Marduk makes night and day, the sun, the moon and seasons, and his temple on earth where he will establish his reign, named Babylon, 'Houses of the Great Gods'.[446] Babylon, and Marduk's temple in particular, is the centre of the cosmos for both gods, nations and humans.

As with the creation, so too humankind is made out of a god. The traitor Qingu is slain, and humans are made from his blood. The purpose of the creation of humans is clear and reiterated: 'They shall bear the gods' burden that those may rest.'[447]

---

444  Van De Mieroop 2016, 4. Emphasis added.

445  Foster 2005, 439, n. 4.

446  *EE* in Foster 2005, 468.

447  *EE* in Foster 2005, 469.

# (d) Epistemology

As we have noted, the ANE is currently being revisited in relation to the history of science.[448] This is certainly true of Babylonia. It is easy to dismiss the extensive treatment of Marduk's 50 names at the end of the *EE*, but Van De Mieroop attends to precisely this discussion at the outset of his *Philosophy Before the Greeks: The pursuit of truth in Ancient Babylonia*.[449] He notes of the names that:

> These present a work of explanatory philology so complex that later Mesopotamian commentators provided clarification in order to show how these analyses came about . . . Most scholars paid little attention to the passage . . . until Jean Bottéro unlocked its structure and showed its significance in 1977.[450]

Van De Mieroop argues that writing and textuality are central to Babylonian epistemology. He notes that 'Babylonian scholars grasped reality through its written form'.[451] The Babylonian language, which alongside Assyrian was a dialect of Akkadian, was written in cuneiform. Cuneiform, named after the wedge shape of its signs, was invented by the Sumerians between 3400 BC and 3300 BC, an extraordinarily significant invention. Glassner notes that:

> Between the thirty-fourth century B.C. and the first centuries of the common era, cuneiform was used to write a dozen different languages from the Mediterranean to the Iranian plateau and from the Black Sea to the Arabian peninsula. Some of those languages were Indo-European (Hittite and Old Persian), others Semitic (Akkadian, Eblaite, and Amorite). Yet others were not part of any known language group and in addition have no relation to each other, such as Sumerian, Elamite, and Hurrian; this fact alone makes the understanding of its origin important.[452]

Van De Mieroop maintains that *writing*, and not just language or speech, is the key to Babylonian epistemology. The Babylonian world view was god-centred,

---

448 Multiple works are appearing in this area. See, e.g., Robson 2019, ch. 1.
449 See also Charpin 2010.
450 Van De Mieroop 2016, 7–8. Bottéro 1977.
451 Van De Mieroop 2016, 9.
452 Glassner 2003, 2.

but the gods had created writing as the tool for understanding and naming the world, so that the world had to be interpreted as though it were a text. In place of Descartes's *cogito ergo sum*, Van De Mieroop proposes 'I read therefore I am' for the Babylonians.[453] Through the analysis of names in the long final section of the *EE*, 'Marduk was connected to agriculture, wisdom, warfare, and other areas of life – every aspect of civilization came into being at the time of creation through this naming process'.[454] And thus it is through names that the secrets of the cosmos are unlocked. Naming is, of course, also central to the creation narratives in Genesis 1—2, but in a far less mystifying way than in Babylonia.

Within OT studies it is generally assumed that long oral traditions underlie biblical texts. Surprisingly, Van De Mieroop argues that while '[f]ew scholars of ancient Mesopotamia have addressed the question explicitly . . . those who have done so have concluded, against standard opinion, that the oral tradition did not have primacy over the written one'.[455] Of course, oral traditions cannot be accessed as such, but the Mesopotamians granted primacy to the written. 'There is no evidence at all from Mesopotamia that oral communication was considered superior to writing or that there was an oral tradition independent from the written one.'[456] The Mesopotamian concept of authorship of texts was different from ours. At least three people functioned as the author of a text: the originator of the text, the owner and the scribe who transmitted the text. There was a fluidity to transmission as scribes generally did more than just copy the text. Van De Mieroop argues that each stage of a text was equally valid, lending itself to considerable intertextuality. 'Babylonian texts invite the discovery of their own genealogy.'[457]

Close observation was an important part of the Babylonians' epistemology, but their epistemology was not empirical.[458] The gods and the world had to be interpreted through the lens of texts. And their sense of textuality was complex. The scribal, literate culture of Babylonia[459] was bilingual, treating Akkadian and Sumerian as parallel, interchangeable languages, what they evocatively called 'the languages of the meeting of each other'. Babylonians

---

453  Van De Mieroop 2016, 10.

454  Van De Mieroop 2016, 9.

455  Van De Mieroop 2016, 16.

456  Van De Mieroop 2016, 19.

457  Van De Mieroop 2016, 27.

458  Van De Mieroop 2016, 189–93.

459  Van De Mieroop (2016, 15) uses 'Babylonian' to refer to the bilingual Sumerian–Akkadian literature produced by people in southern Mesopotamia for the duration of cuneiform.

exploited the polysemy this opened up to the full in their quest for true knowledge of the world.

In his examination of Babylonian epistemology, Van De Mieroop attends to word lists, omen lists and laws.[460] The close and vast attention to *word lists*, the sort of phenomenon we saw at the end of the *EE*, is unique to southern Mesopotamia. Word lists are also the first works in world history.[461] 'Babylonian lexicography was a scientific activity intended to foster understanding of the world. Its practitioners gave structure to reality.'[462] By the early second millennium BC the collections of word lists were huge, attempting to capture every word in Sumerian. The number of words runs to tens of thousands and includes fantasy words of no practical value. In the twenty-fourth century BC, scribes in Ebla (Syria) introduced bilingualism, occasionally inserting Eblaite translations after the Sumerian word. In the early second millennium, in Babylonian scholarship bilingualism became the norm, with every Sumerian word accompanied by its Akkadian translation. In this Old Babylonian period further innovations were made to the lists: readings were spelled out in syllables (hence they are called 'syllabaries'), and grammatical elements and parts of words were explicated. During this period, Babylonian cuneiform was used way beyond southern Mesopotamia. In the first millennium a further innovation in lexical materials was the commentary, providing synonyms, variants, etymology, and quotations from canonical texts.

By the ninth century BC, Babylonian had become the lingua franca across most of the ANE. Assyria played a key role in preserving the culture of Babylon, and, in his seventh-century library in Nineveh, King Aššurbanipal[463] sought to bring together all earlier written knowledge. Babylonia was the major source for these texts: 'The content of most of Ashurbanipal's seventh-century BC library and scholarly texts derives from southern Mesopotamian sources composed and written long before, during the Old and Middle-Babylonian periods of the second millennium BC.'[464] The majority of the scholarly texts (lexical, religious, magical, mythological, historical) are in Babylonian Akkadian. About 3.5 per cent of the Babylonian materials comprises lists. These lists present us with the best versions of nearly all such lexical lists from Mesopotamia.

---

460  For a sense of the history of Babylonian epistemology see Van De Mieroop 2016, 193–215.
461  The Uruk tablets date from the late fourth millennium BC.
462  Van De Mieroop 2016, 41.
463  See Finkel 2018.
464  Finkel 2018, 86.

When Babylon became the dominant empire, temples and the palace promoted and supported such lexical activity:

> An investigation of all scholarly materials from later Babylonian libraries shows that their aim was to keep together the entirety of Sumerian and Akkadian wisdom, and lexical texts were an integral part of that encyclopedic project. Marduk's temple library in Babylon, which existed continuously from the mid-seventh to the mid-first centuries BC, must have contained a treasure trove of scholarly materials, including all current lexical texts.[465]

Van De Mieroop argues that such lists are the key to understanding Babylonian philosophy. As the lists developed, their creative potential was fully exploited so that they are rightly referred to as an easily missed form of art. Each entry – the horizontal level or syntagm – made sense in itself. However, entries were also linked to one another – the vertical or paradigmatic dimension. Syntagms had fewer than ten parts; paradigms could run to thousands. For the Babylonian lexicographers, by far the greatest challenge was how to organize the lists. Although very close observation of the world played a central role in the Babylonian acquisition of knowledge, the lists do not reflect an empirical epistemology. 'They are not the product of scientific inquiry into reality, but studies of the written word.'[466] There is a logic behind the order of lists, but it is motivated by many different concerns: thematic, semantic, phonetic and graphic. The lists are literary in their exploitation of analogy, alliteration, polyphony – words can be pronounced in various ways – and homophony.

> The general principle that dictated the elaboration of entries was pointillism[467] ... Knowledge was cumulative, in the sense that each entry in the list could be comprehended only when seen in the context of the other, closely related, entries surrounding it.[468]

The lists thus yield knowledge, but knowledge mediated through the Babylonian world view with its high view of writing.

---

465  Van De Mieroop 2016, 51.
466  Van De Mieroop 2016, 65.
467  The blending of small dots or points to yield a whole.
468  Van De Mieroop 2016, 72.

*Divination* ranked high among the Babylonians as the means by which to discern what the gods were up to. The literature associated with this is the *omen lists*, which Van De Mieroop describes as 'the height of Babylonian epistemology, as they provide the most detailed evidence on the hermeneutical systems behind knowledge – albeit of something we do not consider knowable'.[469] Amid the uncertainties of life, divination was essential. Humans knew only the present and this in part, whereas the gods knew the past, the present in its fullness and the future.

And the gods needed humans, just as humans needed the gods. From the Babylonian Flood Story (the Epic of Gilgamesh), we know how dependent the gods were on humans for food and drink, and thus they, like humans, could be bribed. Of course, the gods needed to tell the truth, and rituals contain appeals to them to do so. Fortunately, the messages from the gods were to be found everywhere.

> Just as the king spread his power from the center to the edges of the state through a highly developed capillary administrative network which transmitted his written orders to his subjects, so the gods used writing to make known to humanity the fate which they had fixed for each individual. For the gods, however, the only writing tablet large enough for their expression was the universe itself.[470]

Most of the texts preserved about divination relate to the king, whose success depended on the gods. Experts in divination and the related texts were thus well represented at the palace. In Aššurbanipal's vast library more than 50 per cent of the texts relate to divination. 'In Babylonia, the text came before the divinatory act, and reading techniques used for the cuneiform script fully informed the interpretation of ominous signs.'[471]

Like a detective, diviners were attentive to the smallest traces as signs from the gods. These were found throughout the whole of the universe. The form of omens follows from this; they read like legal clauses with the typical casuistic 'If . . . then . . .' form. What is controversial is the rationality informing the move from *if* to *then*. Some scholars, such as Bottéro, have argued that empirical observation underlies the complex system of divination.

---

469  Van De Mieroop 2016, 88.

470  Manetti quoted in Van De Mieroop 2016, 136.

471  Van De Mieroop 2016, 91. On the history of divination in Babylonia see Van De Mieroop 2016, 98–112.

Van De Mieroop finds this unlikely: 'When we look at omens as expressions of inferential logic, it becomes irrelevant whether or not their content was possible. They function at the level of metaphysical rather than physical possibility.'[472] Divination goes back to the origins of history, but divinatory *lists* were an invention of the early second millennium BC. Like the lexical lists, omen texts exploit literary possibilities and function at the syntagmatic and paradigmatic levels. Although the rationality of the omens escapes us, they do manifest a coherent rationality.

The third list genre that Van De Mieroop attends to is that of *law*, which, unlike omens, was restricted to daily life in the state, which was governed by the king. The 'If . . . then . . .' casuistic structure of Babylonian law is common to the ANE. In the ANE, kings and not gods issued laws, and law 'codes' contain lists of laws. Israel is unique in this respect in that law is issued by God.[473] The list nature of Babylonian law means that, like lexical and omen lists, it can be analysed at the syntagmatic and paradigmatic level. Context is important, as is similitude, and in Babylonian law the groupings demonstrate two underlying principles: opposition and pointillism. Connections between successive laws are real, even if difficult to grasp from our perspective: they may relate to societal practices, societal hierarchy or word associations.

As discussed above, the function of law codes is controversial and problematic. Omen texts were used in the practice of divination, but this does not seem to have been the case with legal texts: 'no law paragraph was ever quoted in preserved legal writings, which are very extensive for the Old Babylonian period and include court decisions.'[474] Van De Mieroop argues that the law codes were treatises on law but not legislation. He relates Hammurabi's Code to the king's wisdom:

> The code was not just a confirmation of royal justice, but also a work of the king's wisdom. It required wisdom to know what is true, and the code was the epistemological tool that gave true insight into the law.[475]

Long before Plato, Hammurabi claimed to be the philosopher-king. Hammurabi acknowledges his indebtedness to the sun god Shamash for insight into truth, but the pronouncements are his own.

---

472  Van De Mieroop 2016, 116.

473  Van De Mieroop 2016, 151.

474  Van De Mieroop 2016, 172.

475  Van De Mieroop 2016, 175.

Van De Mieroop opposes the view of Babylonian epistemology as empiricist:

> Rather than searching for an elusive core of real entries derived from empirical scholarship in all of these lists, is it not more logical to regard them as the products of written creativity, fully composed by scholars who set out to investigate language, divination, and law? This work was purely rational and based on concepts the ancient scholars intuitively knew to be true and which they expanded through logical deduction.[476]

They certainly were highly observant, but they observed through the lens of the written text. Van De Mieroop notes Sapir and Whorf's controversial view that a world view emerges out of a particular language, but argues that when it comes to Babylon we must look to writing rather than language as the key: 'The Babylonians did not create order in the universe by investigating its component parts; they created order in lists and applied the results to the universe. The text preceded reality.'[477]

## (e) Historiography

Van De Mieroop notes that ANE historiography, including that of Babylonia but with the exception of Israel, as noted above, lacks the overarching narrative aspect of modern history-writing. This is by no means to say that ANE societies lacked any historical interest. In this respect we can distinguish between records of events close to their time and chronographic (recording of time intervals) texts.[478] The former consist of annals, royal building accounts and royal inscriptions. It is rare for such records to refer to events before the reign of the particular king.

Chronographic texts record events that preceded the writer. Primarily, they are made up of lists, such as king lists including the length of a king's reign, and lists of the year names, perhaps with notes about military campaigns. Clearly, these are invaluable for history *from above*, but Van De Mieroop notes that most historical writing from Mesopotamia consists of annals and chronicles rather than narratives. In the West, 'we have arrived at an equation of narrative with history, which might be more intuitive than rational, but still governs our appreciation of the historical sources and their authors'.[479]

---

476  Van De Mieroop 2016, 190.

477  Van De Mieroop 2016, 221.

478  Van De Mieroop 1999, 25–7.

479  Van De Mieroop 1999, 81.

Ironically, in the light of Van De Mieroop's emphasis on writing as so central to the Babylonian world view, he notes in his *Cuneiform Texts and the Writing of History* that, apart from written records, historical memories could have been preserved in visual and oral ways, most of which elude us. Our sources provide very limited capacity for what is nowadays called 'history from below'. Ordinary people are often reduced to a name on a list. However, we can reconstruct to a degree how they were organized and rewarded for work, and how they suffered. Liverani sees the lack of large-scale narrative historiography as an advantage when it comes to writing the histories of the ANE:

> we lack an ancient historiography able to provide a sort of guideline for our reconstruction. This substantial, yet not total, lack is, however, a useful aspect. It forces the reconstruction of a guideline from a responsible evaluation of the sources, rather than encouraging a lazy reliance on pre-existing guidelines that are often unrealistic, biased, and reductive.[480]

While this may be true for the modern scholar, it still alerts us to the limits of ANE historiography.

Thompson and Holm do, however, point out that:

> The historiography of the New Babylonian Empire from 626 B.C. until its destruction by Cyrus in 538 B.C., when the country was reduced to a Persian province, produced the best historical work of any cuneiform people. This is the *Babylonian Chronicle*. In the form in which it has come down to us it was written in the twentieth year of Darius the Great (ca. 500 B.C.), but it was copied and revised from an earlier exemplar. Not all of it has survived. What we have covers the years 745–668 B.C., but almost certainly it must have extended down to the fall of Assyria in 612, and perhaps later. The Babylonians were superior to the Assyrians in the production of period history, for the Assyrians made each reign of their kings a separate unit of time. In clear statement of facts the *Babylonian Chronicle* is a model.[481]

## (f) Conclusion

If the Sumerian view of the origins of the world is peaceful, that of Babylon is definitely not. Violence of a horrific sort among the gods is woven into the

---

480 Liverani 2014, 5.
481 Thompson and Holm 1942, 12.

fabric of the origins of the creation. And, as is typical of the ANE, humans are made to relieve the gods of their burdens. The world view of Babylon facilitated remarkable developments, including architectural, legal and scientific ones. The centrality of writing to the Babylonian world view is significant, and brings into question the common view among mainstream OT scholars that long periods of oral tradition by necessity preceded the production of the OT texts. Indeed, in the Sinai narrative, YHWH himself is depicted as writing the Decalogue (Exod. 31.18), and it is worthwhile in the light of Babylonia to reflect on what effect such a tradition had on the Israelite view of writing in relation to speech and oral tradition. The tradition of law in Babylon is noteworthy and central to the case that law 'codes' such as that of Hammurabi did not actually function practically as texts for judges.

# 10 The Aramean world view

## (a) Introduction

The number of nations and people groups in the ANE is vast, and as more and more knowledge becomes available we could expand this chapter exponentially. Our modest aim, however, is to dig into the major world views that impinged on Israel in the OT in order to get a sense of the world the Israelites inhabited and to which they responded. In the remainder of this chapter, we will attend to the Arameans, the Phoenicians, the Canaanites and the Persians. If one were looking for a symbol of the Arameans, I would choose their language, Aramaic, which became hugely influential in the ANE and made its way into small parts of the OT. The Arameans were, as we have seen, a thorn in the side of the Assyrians, and when the Assyrians deported them to different places, of course they took their language with them, and it ended up becoming the lingua franca of the first millennium BC in the ANE.

## (b) History and geography

In our discussion of Assyrian history we noted how the Arameans emerged as a threat to Assyria and how they met their ultimate demise at the hands of the Assyrians. Lipiński traces the history of the Arameans back much earlier, from the last third of the second millennium until their incorporation into the Neo-Assyrian Empire.[482] Aram is known as a place name as early as the twenty-third century BC. However, it was only towards the end of the

---

482  On the history of the Arameans see also Reinhold 2016; Younger 2016.

second millennium BC and the start of the first that a group of Aramean states emerged. Their threat to Assyria reached a high point early in the first millennium BC.[483] The earliest-known reference to the Arameans apart from the OT comes from the period of Tiglath-pileser I (1116–1076 BC).

The Arameans did not occupy one area but inhabited clusters of cities spread around Syria,[484] south-eastern Anatolia and Mesopotamia. Lipiński discusses a number of groupings.

*Laqe.* This group did not exist before 1000 BC. It was a tribal confederacy made up of 12 places or rulers. Lipiński thinks that the parallel to Israel with her 12 tribes is no coincidence. Although the view of early Israel as a confederacy has fallen out of favour, Lipiński intriguingly argues that 'the basic thesis of M. Noth remains valid and cannot be questioned seriously,[485] although it is not fashionable nowadays'.[486] There is no indication that Laqe had a central shrine. It was constituted of Arameans and North Arabic clans in a loose confederation that was never under a single ruler. It was probably only made part of the provincial system of the Assyrians in Tiglath-pileser III's reign.

*Nisbis and the Temanites.* Nisbis was at the heart of an Aramean state. It was established in the tenth century BC and grew around a Semitic shrine of stones. Strategically situated as a trading town on the main road from Upper Mesopotamia to the west, Nisbis proved to be a formidable enemy of the Assyrians. In 896 BC, Adad-nirari II conquered it.

*Other prominent cities and states.* Gozan was the capital of the northern Syrian state established in the tenth century BC. It became an Assyrian province under Aššurbanipul *c.*870 BC. Arpad was the capital of another north Syrian state. Founded in the ninth century, it was conquered by Aššurdan II, thus removing its threat to Assyria. Bet-Zammani was a tribal state that developed between the thirteenth and ninth centuries BC. In 879 BC, Aššurnasirpal II integrated it into the Assyrian Empire. Bet-'Adini was an Aramean clan and tribal state situated in the Middle Euphrates. It was conquered in 856 BC.

---

483 But see Younger 2016, 35–6.

484 On the history of ancient Syria see Bryce 2014.

485 Martin Noth, *The History of Israel* (London: A&C Black, 1958). Noth argued that after their settlement in Canaan the Israelite tribes were organized like a Greek amphictyony.

486 Lipiński 2000, 77, n. 4.

## (c) The Arameans and the patriarchs

Deuteronomy 26.5 contains this well-known confession: אֲרַמִּי אֹבֵד אָבִי (my father was a wandering Aramean), seeming to indicate an Aramean origin for Abraham and the patriarchs. Lipiński discusses the meaning of אֹבֵד (wandering) at length and argues that the traditions of the patriarchs fit well with the tenth century BC:

> The biblical tradition assuming the parentage of the Hebrew patriarchs with the Aramaeans of the Ḥarrān area is thus explainable in the historical context of the 10th century B.C., especially if one reckons with the possible influence of royal scribes of Aramaean descent, whose family was native from the Ḥarrān region. The other tradition, which links Abraham's clan with Ur of the Chaldees, is obviously more recent, since the city of Ur could not be called 'Ur of the Chaldees' before the foundation of the Neo-Babylonian empire in the 7th century B.C. One should admit the long proposed view that this second tradition originated among the Judaeans exiled to Babylonia.[487]

Such a date is far later than the traditional dating of the patriarchs. We will explore the religion of the patriarchs later in this volume.

## (d) Religion

We do not know a great deal about the religion of the Arameans.[488] Clearly, they were polytheists. There is also evidence that they practised an ancestral cult. One intriguing characteristic of their worship is that they had a cult of 'betyls' or standing cultic stones.[489] Lipiński discerns parallels in Genesis 28.18, 22; Judges 9:6; and 2 Kings 10.26–27.[490] These stones were aniconic,[491] and a betyl would be connected to a deity so that we find sayings such as 'the Betyl of God' (El), and 'Baal is a betyl', the latter being a reference to the main god of the Arameans, Hadad.

We can identify the following major deities among the Arameans.

---

487 Lipiński 2000, 74–5.

488 Lawson Younger is working on a book on this.

489 On this terminology see Doak 2015, 78–101.

490 Lipiński 2000, 600.

491 They contained no form of the god. See below for a more detailed discussion of aniconism.

'*Attar.* A male, astral deity who provided fertility through rain. 'Since 'Attar represents the generative power of the sky, which fructifies the earth with moisture of rain, his consort should be the earth dried up by the summer heat.'[492] 'Attar is identified with the Eblaite and Moabite god Chemosh[493] in the astral triad of the ninth century BC (*KAI* 181 lists Chemosh ten times).

*Il (El).* Herrmann notes: 'In the Phoenician, Aramaic, Punic and Neo-Punic inscriptions the noun '*l* is generally used as appellative in the sense of "god, godhead" or as adjective "divine" ... Yet, El was also used as proper name, e.g. when El is mentioned alongside other gods.'[494]

*Resheph.* A god worshipped in northern Syria since the third millennium BC. The great kingdoms of Ebla in Syria were largely earlier than the Arameans: the first kingdom was destroyed in 2300 BC, the second lasted from 2300 to 2000 BC and the third from 2000 to *c.*1600 BC when Ebla was destroyed by the Hittite king.[495] Resheph was very popular among the Eblaites. He is also attested in the Ugaritic world, the Phoenician–Punic world, and among the Egyptians.[496] In ritual texts from Ugarit he is the underworld deity, guarding access to the netherworld. He is a god of battle and disease, both dangerous and benevolent.

*Sîn or Sahar.* The moon god. Stol notes that '[i]n Mesopotamia, the Sumerian and Babylonian moongod, Nanna/Sîn, was venerated everywhere, but Ur remained the centre of his cult'.[497] The last king of the Neo-Babylonian Empire, Nabonidus, gave Sîn exalted names such as 'king of the gods' and 'god of gods'. Among the Arameans, intriguingly the sun god was not as prominent as in other parts of the ANE.[498]

---

492  Lipiński 2000, 611.

493  See Müller 1999.

494  Herrmann 1999, 276–7. Herrmann provides two examples of the latter in Aramean inscriptions. In the eighth-century BC inscription of Panamuwa I, king of Sam'al (*KAI* 214), the following gods are listed: Hadad, El, Resheph, Rakib-el and Shamash. They are Panamuwa's benefactors, giving him the kingship and ensuring the welfare of his domain. In the first stela of the eighth-century BC Aramaic Sefire inscription which sets out the treaty between the kings of KTK – an unidentified kingdom – and Arpad (*KAI* 222), El is mentioned with Elyon and other gods. Lipiński argues that 'Attar dethroned Il as chief god, and although he is still mentioned he is preceded, as above, by Hadad, the storm god. '*l* is, according to Lipiński, the most common theophoric element in the personal names of Arameans in the first millennium BC.

495  On Ebla see Matthiae 2021.

496  Xeller 1999, 700–3.

497  Stol 1999, 783.

498  Lipiński 2000, 625.

**Hadad.** The storm god and head of the Aramean pantheon in Syria and in south-east Anatolia. Macrobius thought Hadad meant 'One, One', but most likely his name meant 'thunderer'.[499]

> It is in the 9th century when the Arameans are settled in the western marshes of the Assyrian empire, in Syria and in parts of Anatolia, that Hadad's dominant role can be documented. A clear bifurcation had taken place in the use of the names Ba'lu and Hadad. Ba'lu – biblical Ba'al – is now confined to the Canaanite god, worshipped in the Phoenician cities and their colonies, and mentioned often in the OT, while Hadad is best known as the god of Damascus, and was also called by the epithet *Rammānu* 'the thunderer' (vocalised *Rimmôn* in 2 Kgs 5:18).[500]

In the agricultural economies of the ANE a great deal depended on the fertility of the land, and Hadad was the god who provided irrigation and fertility, and thus prosperity. He was seen as merciful but also as a god of judgement. He was also a god of war, and in a recent Aramaic inscription from Tel Dan (*IEJ* 43) he is described as going before the king – most likely Hazael – in battle and securing victory for him.[501] In an inscription from Hinjirli (*KAI* 214, 215), Hadad is given credit by Panamuwa I for being with him since his youth, making him king and granting him the 'sceptre of succession'. In response, Panawuma constructed a temple for Hadad and set up a statue of him on a stela.

Il is the most common theophoric element in Aramaic personal names of the first millennium BC,[502] but Hadad is also common in the onomastica. Samalian inscriptions list Hadad with a triad of gods: El, Rakib-el and Shamash, to which Resheph can be added in various positions. Lipiński argues that 'the divine triad of Šam'al was conceived as a three-man chariot team with a team commander, a driver, and a "third-man" or squire'.[503]

## (e) Conclusion

Intriguingly, the Arameans emerged as a force to be reckoned with around the same time as the emergence of Israel. The politics of the Arameans is noteworthy, and the confederacy of 12 groups that constituted Laqe alerts us to the different forms that politics took in the ANE and, at least, provides an interesting parallel to the 12 tribes making up Israel.

---

499  Greenfield 1999, 378.

500  Greenfield 1999, 379.

501  Greenfield 1999, 379–80.

502  'Theophoric' means the names contain the name/s of a god.

503  Lipiński 2000, 615.

# 11 The Phoenician world view

If one were looking for a symbol of the Phoenicians, I would propose a boat or ship. Israel was not a seafaring nation, making the alacrity with which

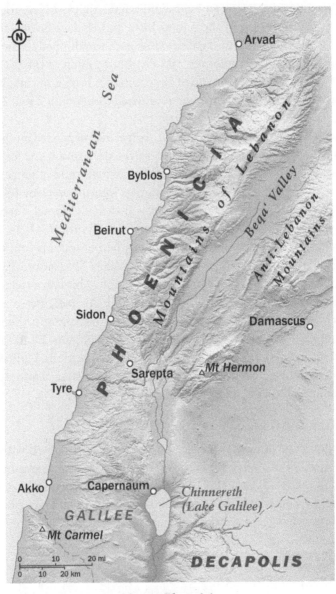

Map 11 **Phoenicia**
(© Baker Publishing Group)

Jonah leapt aboard the first available ship to Tarshish in Spain surprising and indicative of his desperate desire to escape Assyria and Zion. Phoenicia was, however, the quintessential seafaring nation. As we will see, Phoenicia's geography constrained her opportunities for development but provided her with important harbours, and seafaring meant immense opportunities for trade and wealth (see Map 11).

Woolmer begins his book *The Phoenicians* by noting that among the nations of the ANE the Phoenicians probably had more impact on the Mediterranean and yet they are little understood.[504] They occupied a narrow strip of coastland and never became an empire; in fact they were constituted of a number of independent city states. Nevertheless, they shared a language, and were merchants par excellence united in their maritime expertise and interests. This commonality allows us to think, albeit cautiously, in terms of Phoenician civilization.

A major challenge in exploring the Phoenicians (*c*.1500 BC – *c*.300 BC) is that they left very little written legacy.[505] A result is that we can only describe their world view to a limited extent, as with the Arameans. Furthermore, the Phoenicians did not self-identify as such, with their city being the primary locus of their identity. Thus the question of their common identity is a moot one. Woolmer uses the term 'Phoenician' as 'short-hand to denote a specific group of Levantine city states that were connected by their geographic location, had a common interest in seafaring and maritime commerce, and shared a small number of cultural characteristics'.[506]

## (a) Geography

The Phoenician city states were located in a narrow coastal strip extending from what is now northern Israel through to Lebanon and on into the south of Syria. Most agree that the island of Arwad represents their northernmost point, but it is debated as to whether Tyre, Akko and Mount Carmel, or even Ashkelon, represent their southernmost border. Woolmer settles for an area ranging from Akko in the south to Arwad in the north (see Map 11). Their geography meant that the Phoenicians were confined within the Mediterranean Sea on the west and the Lebanon mountain range on the east, which rose to more than 9,800 feet (3,000 m) at its highest; thus they had limited opportunity for political expansion but were well served by harbours that facilitated

---

504 For example, they played a major role in the dissemination of alphabetic writing.

505 On sources see Woolmer 2017, 12–21. He (2017, 16) notes that the OT is the most expansive source but is unreliable and biased. See also Peckham 2014.

506 Woolmer 2017, 6.

seafaring. As our map of Phoenicia demonstrates, although her coastline was jagged and rocky, lacking deep estuaries, her multitude of natural harbours alongside the calmness of the Mediterranean Sea, and weather that was predictable and mild, meant that her geography was ideal for extensive trading by ships.[507] By building their cities close to the harbours and the coast, or on islands, the Phoenicians were able to control the valuable trade routes between the western and eastern Mediterranean. They also developed substantial navies and they wisely 'exploited to the greatest possible extent the small areas of arable land under their control' for agriculture, also becoming experts at irrigation.[508]

## (b) History

The area we call 'Phoenicia' has a history that reaches back at least as far as the tenth millennium BC. However, the general consensus is that it was c.1200 BC, in the Early Iron Age, that Phoenicia as a distinct entity emerged. As with the rest of the ANE, cultic activity stretches back to the earliest origins. Jar burials typified the Early Bronze Age, and while most of these jars, found at Byblos, lacked expensive jewellery and goods, some 20 jars did contain high-valued goods, indicating a stratified society. Indeed, '[s]ocial stratification was to be a consistent feature of Phoenician culture and can be identified in all of the major cities and overseas settlements'.[509] Woolmer identifies the following classes: royalty, nobility, middle class, working class and servant class.[510] In the Middle Bronze Age the preference for burial had shifted to rock-hewn tombs of various types situated away from settlements. By this time, villages and towns were to be found scattered along the coastline every 9–12 miles (15–20 km). Towards the conclusion of the Middle Bronze Age, temple-building grew steadily with Byblos containing the densest concentration of sanctuaries. The 'Temple of Obelisks' is the best preserved of these, built upon the remains of an older temple that was destroyed through a fire in the late third millennium BC.[511]

The items found in graves demonstrate that crafts and metalworking flourished. Phoenicia would become well known for its trade, and the stability of the Middle Bronze Age enabled the coastal cities to set up intricate

507  Woolmer 2017, 10.

508  Woolmer 2017, 82.

509  Woolmer 2017, 24.

510  Woolmer 2017, 64.

511  Woolmer 2017, 25–6.

trade networks across Egypt, Anatolia, the Levant and Mesopotamia. In the Late Bronze Age, Phoenicia came under Egyptian and then Hittite control, but her cities continued to be successful trading entities. Phoenicia recovered from the crisis at the end of the Bronze Age faster and better than many, under the looming shadow of Assyria. 'The Early Iron Age was therefore a period of commercial expansion for the coastal cities of Phoenicia, both at home and overseas. This period of prosperity also resulted in the emergence of urbanisation, an important innovation that would be synonymous with the Phoenicians',[512] as seen in the major cities of Tyre, Sarepta, Sidon and Byblos.

Tyre rose to particular prominence under King Hiram I (969–936 BC), mainly through exploiting trade routes and establishing trade agreements such as that with King Solomon (1 Kings 5.1–18), according to which Hiram would provide building expertise and materials, and Solomon would supply food products and silver. Hiram and Solomon also joined forces in seafaring expeditions (1 Kings 9). 'Hiram and Solomon profited greatly from these joint ventures, enabling them to spend lavishly on monumental construction projects.'[513] While Solomon had the Temple built in Jerusalem, Hiram engaged in multiple building projects: the reconstruction of the harbour of Tyre, the construction of several shipyards, enlarging Tyre by connecting the two islands of which it was constituted, and building a palace, a public market and temples. Hiram's successors, including Ithobaal I (c.887–856 BC), followed Hiram's policies, as seen for example by the marriage of Ithobaal's daughter Jezebel to King Ahab of Israel. Such marriages between royal houses were designed to cement and secure trade advantages. Woolmer comments: 'The discovery that a significant number of Phoenician craftsmen, architects and merchants were living and working in Israel at this time (particularly in the cities of Samaria, Hazor and Megiddo) suggests that Ithobaal's policy was successful.'[514]

Amid the resurgent Assyria, Phoenicia's significance as a centre of trade played to her advantage, provided cities remained loyal to Assyria, which they did not always do. King Luli of Tyre (729–694 BC), for example, followed an anti-Assyrian policy which led eventually to Sennacherib's decision to deport many of Tyre's people to Nineveh. Woolmer notes Sennacherib's shrewdness in this respect and points out that '[i]n the short term the damage to the city's

---

512  Woolmer 2017, 34.
513  Woolmer 2017, 36.
514  Woolmer 2017, 38.

economy must have been devastating and it is this weakened and humbled Tyre that the Israelite prophet Isaiah (23:1–17) sings about in his great oracle against the city'.[515]

With the triumph of the Babylonians, after Nebuchadnezzar destroyed Jerusalem in 587 BC, he moved on to bring the Phoenician cities under his control, initiating a 13-year siege of Tyre in c.585.

> The reign of Nebuchadnezzar and his successor was to have a severely detrimental impact on Phoenician commercial ventures. Babylon's annexation of southern Palestine, Trans-Jordan and Cilicia denied the Phoenicians access to the highly lucrative south Arabian and southern Anatolian trade networks, while commercial interactions with Egypt and Israel had been significantly curtailed.[516]

With the demise of Babylon, and the emergence of the Persian Empire, Phoenicia's commercial role and her navy played yet again to her favour. Persia needed their navy and, provided they remained loyal, the Phoenician cities were granted 'managed autonomy'.[517]

The Phoenicians seized the opportunities that Persian rule provided. In the final quarter of the sixth century, they recreated their trade links in Mesopotamia, introduce new trade links in the heart of Persia, and later competed with the Greeks to control the markets in Egypt and the Mediterranean. Alexander the Great recognized the strategic importance of the Phoenician cities, and most submitted to him with minimal resistance. Tyre later sought to rebel and was brutally put down in 332 BC.

## (c) Kings and society

The Phoenician entities were dynastic monarchies. Intriguingly, unlike other ANE nations, they did not celebrate and record their exploits in monuments. Nevertheless, Phoenician kings exercised sovereign power. As with kingship across the ANE, Phoenician kings were seen as having been granted their position by the gods, and were held responsible for justice and called upon to mediate the divine in their cities. The king was the commander both of the military and of the navy. Kings were shepherds of the people: 'kings were also directly responsible for administering justice on behalf of the gods who were

---

515  Woolmer 2017, 43.

516  Woolmer 2017, 46.

517  Woolmer 2017, 47.

believed to have established law and order in the universe.'[518] As we have seen again and again in the ANE, final and absolute legal authority rested with the king. Generally, a king's name included his god's name, thus embodying the inseparable link between government, politics and the gods. Each king had a personal deity and functioned as a chief priest in that deity's temple. Woolmer notes that, '[a]lthough there is no evidence to suggest that Phoenician kings ever had themselves formally deified, occasionally some seem to have confused divinely granted authority with divinity itself'[519] (cf. Ezek. 28.1–2). However, as Doak observes:

> [A]t Phoenician sites the relationship between king and priesthood seems to have been particularly noteworthy . . . The close identification between the king and the local cult could then stand in close politico-religious union with the primary deity of the city, further elevating the ruler and strengthening the local identity. Aubet (2001, 148–49) goes so far as to state that, in the case of Tyre, 'the king and the god Melqart are at once the incarnation of the same institution, the state.' If the Tyrian king claimed outright divinity . . . which would have been a rare move in the ancient Near Eastern world but with better parallels in Egypt – then the biblical prophet Ezekiel clearly directs his mockery at the institution (Ezek 28:2).[520]

Kingship was generally hereditary. Cities also contained councils and assemblies which played a part in governance.

As a language, Phoenician was part of the West branch of Central Semitic languages. It became distinct from Aramaic and played a formative role in the ANE in developing an alphabet.

## (d) Religion

As with much of Phoenician life, the paucity of literary texts makes it hard to be definitive. Ugarit, from which texts abound, provides an important parallel, but Woolmer notes that:

> As the Ugaritic texts are far more extensive than the cursory inscriptions found in Phoenicia, it is tempting to place undue importance on this ma-

---

518  Woolmer 2017, 59.

519  Woolmer 2017, 60.

520  Doak 2015, 18. Cf. Ribichini 1999, 564–5.

terial: however, the substantial differences between the two corpora mean that it is impossible to assume simple continuity between the religions of Ugarit and those of Phoenicia.[521]

Ugarit is chronologically earlier than Phoenicia and geographically distinct.

Religious practices evolved over time, although there is disagreement as to whether they did so slowly or suddenly at critical moments. Woolmer argues that Hiram's 'revolution' involved his enlargement and renovation of the temples of Melqart and 'Ashtart (Astarte). Melqart was Hiram's personal god. Phoenicia shares much with Mesopotamian religion.

> However, the recording of divine names, such as El, Ba'al, 'Ashtart or Reshef, in documents that are chronologically and geographically diffuse, does not mean that the characteristics and fundamental features of these deities remained unchanged. Although some aspects of Phoenician religion clearly retained a sense of continuity with the past and with wider Canaanite traditions, the individual city pantheons and cults that emerge in the Iron Age are largely the product of an autonomous development process.[522]

According to Woolmer, during the first millennium an emphasis on her religious autonomy came to dominate Phoenicia. Even when she experienced the oppressive influence of the great empires, this was sustained.[523]

There was a two-level hierarchy within the pantheon of each Phoenician city. The top tier contained a male and female deity who were local and closely related to the monarchy. The other deities occupied the lower level in the pantheon. The top tier of gods comprised the patron gods of the king and the city, but not necessarily the chief god/s, a position sometimes occupied by El. The upper levels of the gods in major Phoenician cities were as follows.

In **Tyre**, Melqart and Astarte were the major gods. Melqart means 'king of the city',[524] and he was the royal patron, a warrior god, as well as a god of fertility and of maritime activity.[525] 'Melqart represented the all-pervasive power of

---

521  Woolmer 2017, 104.

522  Woolmer 2017, 107.

523  Woolmer 2017, 108.

524  Ribichini (1999, 563) notes that Melqart is also a chthonic god and 'the city' could be a euphemism for the underworld, called 'the great city', and not Tyre.

525  On the issue of depictions of Melqart and aniconism see Doak 2015, 92–5.

the monarchy and was considered to be the divine personification of the ideal Phoenician king.'[526] According to Ribichini:

> Epigraphical, archaeological and classical records prove also that Melqart had a remarkable role in the religious ideology of the commercial expansion of Tyrians westward throughout the Mediterranean world, and that his cult was very popular in all Phoenician colonies, from Cyprus to Malta, from Carthage to the whole of North Africa, from Sardinia to Iberia (Cadiz esp.)[527]

Astarte, the Queen of Heaven, was a royal patron, a celestial and maritime goddess, a warrior and associated with fertility.

In **Sidon**, Eshmun and Astarte were the primary gods. Eshmun was a local variant of Baal. He was a dynastic patron and especially associated with healing. His name means 'oil'.

In **Byblos**, Baal and Baalat Gubal were the primary gods. Baal is thought to be Resheph. He is menacing. Baalat Gubal shared some of the features of Astarte but was a goddess in her own right. She was a dynastic patron, and associated with fertility, birth and seafaring. Several texts refer to an 'Assembly of the Holy Gods of Byblos' (*KAI* 4, 10).

**Berytus** (**Beirut**) is said to have been founded by El, who bestowed the patronage on Poseidon, the god of the sea, and the seven Cabiri (great ones). The main deity at **Sarepta** was Tanit-'Ashtart, either fused into one goddess or representing both goddesses.

Within Phoenician religion there is a tradition in which the male god dies and rises again: Eshmun at Sidon, Adonis at Byblos and Melqart at Tyre. It is possible that this is what Elijah is referring to when he taunts the prophets of Baal to awaken their god (1 Kings 18.27). This resurrection was related to agriculture, as was the festal calendar, which was lunar and cyclical. The New Year festival was particularly important, and we know, for example, that on such an occasion Hiram had an effigy of Melqart placed on a giant raft, set alight and cast adrift. In the ritual, the king and his consort assumed the roles of Melqart and Astarte. Singers and dancers played an important part in cultic rituals and feasts. The priesthood was also central to divination, with extispicy an important way of hearing the will of the gods. Ecstatic prophecy and the giving of oracles were also a part of Phoenician religion.

---

526  Woolmer 2017, 113.
527  Ribichini 1999, 564.

In the Phoenician cultus there were priests and priestesses. They were professional clergy with the chief priest closely associated with the palace. The priesthood appears to have been hereditary, and among the normal cultic duties priests were responsible for keeping the library up to date and maintaining it. Sacred prostitution was widespread among the Phoenicians, perhaps with a view to enacting the gods' fertilizing of the land, or as a means of giving thanks to the gods or to raise funds for the cultus. Phoenician temples followed ANE traditions of sacred space. They could be enclosed or open, and groves, caves, rivers and streams were also often seen as sacred places. Phoenicians held to a doctrine of the afterlife, lived in the underworld.

## (e) Aniconism

An intriguing discussion that has developed among scholars of Phoenicia in recent decades is the extent to which an aniconic strand is present in Phoenician religion.[528] Defining iconic and aniconic is no easy matter.[529] Doak's working definition of aniconism is 'a representational style that systematically (i.e., not inadvertently) avoids specific kinds of figural representation, most specifically anthropomorphic images of the deity or deities'.[530] There is no question that Phoenicians produced iconic – as opposed to aniconic – representations of their gods: 'Amid the many ambiguities about Phoenician identity and the problems of locating aniconism in the material record, we can be sure of one thing: Phoenicians produced anthropomorphic images of their deities.'[531]

Doak examines three lines of evidence. The first is that of stelae, pillars, standing stones and betyls. Stelae were common across the ANE, used for various purposes. Doak discerns three interpretations of stelae: as tomb markers, as memorials or representations of the dead, and as somehow performing a cultic function.[532] He concludes from his analysis of the stelae that in Phoenicia they functioned according to some kind of 'iconographic code'.

The question of the aniconic status of any particular stele must be kept open, yet even funerary use suggests a ritual context of memory and

---

528. For an overview of the discussion see Doak 2015, 69–73, which includes the work of J. J. I. Döllinger, George Rawlinson, Sabatino Moscati, Eugene Stockton, Gioacchino Falstone and especially Tryggve Mettinger.

529 See Doak 2015, ch. 3.

530 Doak 2015, 34.

531 Doak 2015, 41. See Doak 2015, ch. 4, and note our discussion above.

532 Doak 2015, 83–4.

cult; there seems to be no clear preference for the nonfigural materials over the figural, but rather we find a continuum of types, ranging from the fully iconic, to isolated and schematic symbols, to the aniconic. This continuum is not evolutionary, but seems to represent simultaneous strategies, and we must take care to see the nuances of anthropomorphism where they may appear even in very simple motifs (such as the bottle idol).[533]

The second source of evidence is that of shrines with aniconic objects or empty shrines. Miniature or model shrines have generated considerable discussion. Size presents its own challenges and limitations, and, not surprisingly, the issue of whether such miniature shrines represent actual shrines and even their images remains contentious. Doak concludes about the shrines that

the aniconic or 'empty' shrines offer a distinct and indisputable nonfigural *possibility* . . . [W]e simply cannot be certain about the relationship of these shrines to 'official' temple or larger shrine settings or whether the shrines once housed material, figural images.[534]

Third are thrones with aniconic objects and thrones that are empty. The data for empty thrones runs up against the same challenge as miniature shrines, namely, how to be sure that they were originally empty.

Doak compares the aniconism of Phoenicia with that of other cultures, including Israel, and acknowledges that '[o]f all the complex examples of aniconism from the ancient world we have been considering thus far, ancient Israel is apparently the only group that offered a textual explanation for an image prohibition'.[535] Intriguingly, Hendel[536] locates the origin of this Israelite emphasis in her early wariness of kingship. In the ANE, king and god were so closely intertwined that once the image of one – the king – was rejected, so too was the image of the other. Mettinger, by comparison, argues that Israelite aniconism was not original to Israel but was rather an 'inherited convention of religious expression which only later formed the basis for theological reflection'.[537]

---

533 Doak 2015, 101.

534 Doak 2015, 108. Emphasis original.

535 Doak 2015, 130–1.

536 Hendel 1988; 1997, 225–8.

537 Mettinger 1995, 195.

This makes for a fascinating discussion and, as so often in this book, the question of divine action emerges again. Hendel and Mettinger seek naturalistic explanations of Israel's 'distinctiveness' without ever considering the possibility that God spoke at Sinai and addressed this issue.

## (f) Conclusion

Phoenicia's small and restricted land mass is comparable to that of Israel. Both existed in constrained geographies and were vulnerable to the great powers. However, Phoenicia's maritime expertise is distinctive and allowed trade and the economy to move front and centre, with commerce enabling the development of cities and maximal development of her lands. The Phoenician cities were polytheistic and the king was integrally bound up with the cult, as we have seen again and again in the ANE. The aniconic strand in Phoenician religion is notable but still significantly different from what we find in the OT, not least because of Phoenicia's polytheism.

# 12 The Canaanite world view/s

## (a) Introduction

If one thinks that Israel emerged within Canaan and that there was no major exodus from Egypt and conquest of the land, then the Canaanite world view becomes the primary influence on Israel. In my view, there *was* a long sojourn in Egypt, and there was an exodus and a profound formation of Israel through YHWH's revelation of himself at Sinai and the ratification of the Sinai covenant. All of that happened *before* Israel conquered and indwelt the land, and thus one would not expect the Canaanite world view to exert nearly as dominant an influence on Israel.[538] However, once in the land, the Israelites embarked on a wholly different way of life, one which the Canaanites knew well but which the Israelites did not, and thus we would be foolish not to take the Canaanite world view seriously. Within Israel, for example, as the stories of famine in the land in the OT make clear, rainfall and fertility of the soil could be a matter of life and death. Among the Canaanites Baal was the great god of fertility, and worship of him would remain a perennial temptation for the Israelites.

---

538 Of course, according to Genesis three generations of the patriarchs had exposure to Canaanite culture.

# (b) Ugarit

Ugarit evokes one of the major ways in which our knowledge of the ANE has exploded in recent decades. A port city in northern Syria, Ugarit, occupied from the seventh millennium BC onwards but with its zenith occurring from the mid-fourteenth to the start of the twelfth century BC, was rediscovered in the late 1920s. This truly remarkable find began in March 1928 when a farmer ploughing a field uncovered the slab of a burial vault. After a first archaeological campaign, archaeologists excavated a tell called Ras Shamra some 2,600 feet (800 m) to the east of the coast. Remnants of a large temple of Baal were uncovered,[539] as well as a stela dedicated to Baal Zaphon, and a temple dedicated to Dagan. Many objects were discovered with the temples, such as ship's stones used as anchors and dedicated to Baal, works of art and limestone stelae. One of the latter is known as the 'Baal of lightning'. Many, many tablets began to emerge through this and subsequent excavations. Unlike the tablets, which are from the Late Bronze period, the 'Baal of lightning' stela was dated to the Middle Bronze period.

> The way in which the god is represented on the stele confirms the portrait of Baal that emerges from a reading of the myths inscribed on the tablets dating back to a period more than half a millennium later than the stele. This is evidence that the main deity of the city of Ugarit was represented in art and mythology with a high degree of continuity for a long time. The same continuity in the religion of Ugarit is also evident in the use of the temples of Baal and Dagan until as late as the twelfth century B.C. The foundations of these temples were laid in the beginning of the second millennium.[540]

After 1939, excavations uncovered the large royal palace, containing ivories depicting the royal theology of Ugarit. Many administrative and diplomatic texts were unearthed here. Given the city's situation between the Hittites to the north and the Egyptians to the south, such diplomatic texts provide insights into the international challenges Ugarit faced during its zenith before it suddenly collapsed at the start of the twelfth century BC. 'The city was ruined at the height of its prosperity.'[541]

---

539 Much of the Baal Cycle is about Baal's quest for a temple.
540 Caquot and Sznycer 1980, 3.
541 Caquot and Sznycer 1980, 4.

# (c) Religion

As we would expect from Ugarit's location and trade, its religion manifests broad influence: 'different cults had to some degree merged together at Ugarit, a datum that is confirmed by the liturgical tablets, in which offerings made to Dadmish and Ishhara are mentioned together with sacrifices made to the native gods.'[542] Nevertheless, '[t]he fact remains ... that the Ugaritic religion was quite distinct from the religions of the Nile Valley, Anatolia and the islands of the Aegean Sea'.[543] As we will see below, the extent to which the religion of Ugarit can provide us with insight into 'Canaanite' religion is debated. Caquot and Sznycer take a minimalist position when they remark: 'All we can derive from them [i.e. Ugaritic excavations] is a sample of the religions of the city-states in the second half of the second millennium.'[544] They do, however, go on to say that:

> This sample ... is unique and rich. Only the Bible can rival the Ras Shamra texts as a complete source of information about so many aspects of religion, myths, rites and expressions of religiosity, in the case of the Bible for the first millennium B.C.[545]

**El** was the head of the Ugaritic pantheon, as is evident, for example, in the myth known as 'Birth of the Gods'.[546] In this story, El encounters two women on the seashore, one of whom is Athirat. El is old and thus impotence is a problem – described graphically in the story – but his marriage to Athirat is consummated and two astral deities, Shahar and Shalim, as well as many other gods, are born. El is not only the father of the gods but also 'the father of men',[547] from which title we can assume that he created humans when he fashioned the earth. Ugarit has not provided us with anything like the detailed cosmogony embodied in the *Enuma Elish*. El brought order to the earth and also resolved conflicts between gods and in politics.

> According to the legends, El was the source of royal power, not simply at Ugarit, but everywhere. He derived his authority from his great age. He had an old man's white hair and white beard and because he was so

---

542 Caquot and Sznycer 1980, 16.
543 Caquot and Sznycer 1980, 6.
544 Caquot and Sznycer 1980, 7.
545 Caquot and Sznycer 1980, 7.
546 Gordon 1949.
547 'Creator of creatures' in the Baal Cycle. Pritchard, ed., 2011, 114, 129.

old he had sufficient wisdom to carry out his functions as a moderator and supreme authority. This wisdom was not, however, expressed in cool impartiality.[548]

If age brought wisdom for El, it also brought imperfections, notably his impotence. Iconographically, El is depicted as a bull with powerful horns whereas the active and somewhat impetuous Baal is a bull-calf. El is depicted standing whereas Baal is seated. El is passive whereas Baal is active, often scarily so.

**Baal**, the son or grandson of El – he is described as begotten by El but also as Dagan's son[549] – was above all else the storm god. The major source for our knowledge of Baal at Ugarit is the so-called Baal Cycle. 'Baal' is a title rather than a name, meaning Master or Lord. Baal's real name was Hadad.[550] 'Unlike El, who dwelt in a distant place in the middle of the river that surrounds the inhabited world,[551] Baal was close to man.'[552] Agriculturally, the irrigation of the land was a matter of life and death, and Baal was pre-eminently a god of water. Baal was thought to dwell on Mount Zaphon, a mountain some 5,800 feet (1770 m) high that dominates Ras Shamra:

> The water that is gathered in the clouds at the summit of Zaphon . . . falls down in the form of rain and penetrates into the dried bowls of the earth, from where it rises again and reforms clouds. In this mythical transposition, a phenomenon which is natural but always risky, because of the constant threat of drought, is changed into a heroic exploit undertaken by the god Baal, who sacrifices himself in his devotion to men and is swallowed without resisting by Mot.[553]

In the mythology of Ugarit, Baal is challenged by **Mot** (Death) and submits to death, but not before having sexual intercourse with a cow and thus providing for fertility.[554] El and the whole of humanity mourn Baal's death. Part of Baal's corpse remains and the goddess **Anat** requests it from Mot. In the confrontation Anat kills Mot and Baal is restored to life, and he replaces Mot on his throne. Baal fights with the sons of Athirat and defeats **Yam** (Sea).

---

548  Caquot and Sznycer 1980, 12.
549  Both occur in the Baal Cycle.
550  See Baal Cycle. Pritchard, ed., 2011, 132.
551  See Baal Cycle. Pritchard, ed., 2011, 116.
552  Caquot and Sznycer 1980, 13.
553  Caquot and Sznycer 1980, 13.
554  Baal Cycle. Pritchard, ed., 2011, 124–6.

Baal is thus credited with fertilizing flocks and herds; graphically, he is described as being able to have intercourse with a heifer 77 and 88 times. Baal was considered well able to protect Ugarit; he was generous and benevolent but also impetuous.

The goddesses of Ugarit are portrayed in a less flattering light than the major gods. Anat helps Baal, but she is impulsive and is depicted as relishing massacres: 'Unlike Baal, she has no respect for her father, the god El, and does not hesitate to threaten him with violence when he does not give in to her demands at once.'[555] **Athirat** (of the sea) is likewise ambitious and corrupt. The sun goddess **Shapash** is the messenger of the gods and the link between the living and the dead.

The god **Kothar** (capable one) is pre-eminently skilful as a goldsmith, blacksmith and architect. He builds Baal's temple/palace.[556] He is portrayed as living in distant and fabulous countries. **Athart** (**Astarte**) is a goddess who was highly regarded in antiquity but in Ugarit is colourless and uninfluential. Considering his temple, we might expect **Dagan** to be a major deity at Ugarit, but it was probably recognized that he was a foreign god. Like Baal, he was a storm god. The motif of the assembly of the gods is found at Ugarit,[557] but it most likely consisted of a group of anonymous deities.

Many liturgical and ritual texts have been excavated from Ugarit.[558] Sacrifice was central to and common in the Ugaritic cultus, and texts are replete with a technical vocabulary for the variety of sacrifices.[559] There was a vast cultic staff, but we do not know precisely how it was organized.[560] Two ritual texts admonish men and women to make sacrifices because they have 'sinned'.[561] One appeals to its hearers to lift up their eyes to Baal and to offer to him their firstborn.

> This seems to have been a religious practice in which a child was sacrificed – in principle a royal child – to appease the anger of the god that was

---

555 Caquot and Sznycer 1980, 14.

556 See the Baal Cycle. Pritchard, ed., 2011, 119–20.

557 See the Baal Cycle, e.g. Pritchard, ed., 2011, 115.

558 Pardee 2002.

559 See Pardee 2002, 222–5.

560 See Pardee 2002, 232–3, for unanswered questions, namely, the actual form of each cultic act; the economics of the cultus; since nearly all the rituals relate to royal ideology how the cultus functioned for ordinary citizens; what meaning the Ugaritians assigned to the offerings and rituals, etc.

561 Caquot and Sznycer 1980, 17.

manifested in the danger threatening the city. (There is evidence that this practice existed among the other Semitic peoples.)[562]

It appears that the king played a central part in the cultic life of Ugarit, not least because the ritual texts nearly all relate to the king in one way or another.

> The king's superhuman status, which was the result of his function in society, was common to all monarchies of the Ancient Near East. What is more, it is the monarchy in general that was regarded as superhuman rather than individual kings, who were seen to be simply the transitory recipients of a kingship bestowed by the gods on a human family. Every true monarchy in the Ancient Near East was hereditary and this principle was certainly accepted at Ugarit.[563]

The king acted as an intermediary between the gods and the citizens of Ugarit, representing the people to the gods, and the gods to the people. In the period of its zenith, some eight kings ruled over Ugarit in succession.

Recently, Tugendhaft has analysed the Baal Cycle as a profound piece of political–royal theology. He notes that it was written when the Hittites to the north were under great pressure from the Assyrians (see above). The response of the Hittites was to dig in and strengthen their royal ideology. Tugendhaft argues that the author of the Baal Cycle does something very different:

> It is curious . . . that in the contemporaneous Ugaritic poem known as the Baal Cycle, the hero is never said to enjoy divine favor. Rather, Baal's two enemies, Yamm and Mot, are the ones repeatedly designated as 'beloved of El.' And yet despite their beloved status, both Yamm and Mot are defeated. Unlike the Hittite king, Baal wins victory without divine approval.[564]

In this way:

---

562 Caquot and Sznycer 1980, 18. But cf. Pardee (2002, 233) who observes that 'no certain reference thereto [child sacrifice] appears in the Ugaritic texts (the reference to a "firstborn" sacrifice in text 13 [RS 24.266:31] does not necessarily refer to a human firstborn)'.

563 Caquot and Sznycer 1980, 19.

564 Tugendhaft 2018, 4.

the Baal Cycle offered its audience a means to take a critical stance toward contemporary political institutions and opened a space for them to reflect upon the workings of power, authority, and legitimacy. The poem offers less a *reflection of* its world than a guide for *reflecting upon* it.[565]

I am not persuaded by Tugendhaft's reading, but it certainly reminds us of the centrality of royal ideology in Ugarit and the ANE.

Pardee notes similarities between the cultus of Ugarit and the Bible, and differences. The similarities he notes are as follows:

- There is a similarity of *vocabulary* in terms such as those for sacrifice, altar, peace-offering, presentation-offering and burnt-offering, as well as a similarity in relation to sacrificial victims. However, a common vocabulary does not necessarily imply a common ideological meaning and matrix. Furthermore, several terms in the Bible and in the Ugaritic texts are not found in the other.
- The OT condemns child sacrifice and, according to Pardee, there is no evidence for it at Ugarit.
- Neither culture sacrificed dogs or pigs.
- Both refer to the use of perfumed oil.
- Both stress bodily purity, but in the Ugaritic texts this is only in relation to the king.
- The basic architectural vocabulary is the same.
- Neither corpus manifests evidence of a fertility cult.
- In neither was the *marziḥu*, a group with a patron god, a primary cultic institution.
- In neither is there clear reference to a New Year festival.
- In neither is there substantial influence from the Akkadian language or from Mesopotamian religion.

The differences he flags are as follows:

- The *genres* in the respective literatures are different. Most Ugaritic ritual texts are either prescriptive texts or poetic ones that reflect on phenomena external to but related to the cultus. In addition there are deity lists, memorial and *ex voto* inscriptions, and divinatory texts. However:

---

565 Tugendhaft 2018, 6. Emphasis original.

Despite certain superficial similarities, the biblical texts are quite different: the cultic texts reflect a reasoned literary presentation of what are described as the historical situations in which the Israelite cult was prescribed by God to Moses and in that literary context many details as well as certain theological motivations were provided – both categories of information are almost entirely lacking in the Ugaritic texts. The cultic psalms show certain formal similarities to some of the Ugaritic poetic texts, but the themes, in particular the mythological and narrative elements of the historiolae, are vastly different. With the exception of the traditions regarding the Urim and Thummim, explicit divinatory material has virtually been eradicated from the Hebrew Bible, as have incantations.[566]

- As Pardee observes, by far the most obvious difference is the ubiquitous presence of the Ugaritic pantheon compared with the HB/OT. We discuss this further below, but as Pardee notes, 'the fact remains that there are only traces of polytheism visible in the Hebrew Bible in contrast with the full-blown Ugaritic polytheism'.[567]
- The archaic features of Israelite religion reflect southern Canaanite religion, whereas the comparable features in Ugarit reflect Amorite links.
- Ugarit, unlike Israel, is significantly influenced by Hurrian elements.
- Certain Ugaritic rites find no parallel in the HB/OT and so too with Israel.
- Some organs used in Ugaritic sacrifice do not occur or do not have the same meaning in the HB/OT.
- The donkey sacrifice of Ugarit is not found in the HB/OT.
- Incense is not specifically mentioned in Ugaritic texts.
- It is likely that most of the wine mentioned in text 58 (RS 19.015) was drunk by participants. Leviticus 10.9, by contrast, forbids priests from drinking wine.
- The regular offering of textiles as clothing for the deities or priests – perhaps both – is lacking in the HB/OT.
- Some architectural terms differ, and clearly the multiplication of sanctuaries related to Ugarit's polytheism differs radically from the centralized view of worship we find, for example, in Deuteronomy.

---

566 Pardee 2002, 235.

567 Pardee 2002, 236. In n. 16 (p. 242) Pardee asserts that he finds little support in Ugarit for de Moor's (1997) theory of a crisis of polytheism at the end of the Late Bronze Age.

- The cult calendar of Ugarit is lunar compared with the seven-day week characteristic of the HB/OT.
- In Ugarit, unlike Israel, the king was central to the cultus and thus had to traverse the boundary between sacred and profane repeatedly. Pardee notes perceptively that the term for the king's return to the profane alerts us to the fact that whatever sacredness was connected with his being king, it was not the same as the sacredness of the cult.[568]
- In Ugarit, unlike in Israel, the centrality of the king obscures the role of other cultic personnel.
- The intervention of the ancestors and calling on them was a key element in Ugaritic religion, but it is opposed by the HB/OT.

## (d) Ugarit and Canaanite religion

The inhabitants of Canaan did not refer to themselves as 'Canaanites'. It is a word applied to them by outsiders, as with 'Phoenicians'. Furthermore, historically the word 'Canaanite' has a variety of references.[569] As noted above, Ugaritic culture came to a sudden end at the start of the twelfth century BC. There is thus not just a geographical but also a historical gap between Israel and Ugarit. Therefore, the extent to which Ugarit can be taken to represent the Canaanite world view is, not surprisingly, contested.[570] It is not clear, for example, if Ugaritic is a Canaanite language. Lewis notes that it is clearly not Aramaic, but is either a northern Canaanite dialect or a descendant of an 'Amorite' dialect. In his judicious assessment of Ugaritic as Canaanite, Lewis asserts:

> most importantly for the present discussion, we come to a cultural and religious definition. Without doubt, the vast corpus of literature (and iconography) from Ugarit presents us with the clearest picture of 'Canaanite' religious culture as it has been customarily defined. For example, thanks to texts of varying genres (mythological, ritual, administrative) and numerous divine figurines and other cultic artifacts, Ugarit presents us with the fullest assemblage of Canaanite deities universally recognized as Canaanite from other sources (i.e., Phoenician, Punic, Egyptian, Amarna Canaanite, the Hebrew Bible, epigraphic Hebrew, Moabite, Edomite, Ammonite).[571]

---

568  Pardee 2002, 239.
569  See Woolmer 2017, 2–3; Smith 2001; Lewis 2020; etc.
570  The works of Rainey, Na'aman, Pardee, Tropper, have provided important clarifications.
571  Lewis 2020, 261.

Lewis discerns a continuity in the pantheon in Late Bronze Age Ugarit and the West Semitic gods of Late Bronze Age Egypt, Amarna Canaanite cults, and the Iron Age religions (Phoenician, Israelite, Moabite, Edomite, Ammonite), for which he reserves the label 'Canaanite'. However, '[t]his is not to say that each of these cultures did not develop their own preferences (and novelties) with regard to the makeup of their regional pantheons and which deities played which roles'.[572]

Lewis argues that Ugaritic religion is of vital importance for understanding key motifs and elements of Canaanite religion found in the HB/OT, themes such as the combat myth (or *Chaoskampf* traditions), and poetic conventions such as parallelism, phraseology, poetic formulae and stock literary type-scenes. Parker goes so far in this respect as to speak of a pre-biblical narrative tradition. We referred to the shared cultic vocabulary noted above, and this is allegedly 'so exact and precise etymologically that one cannot deny a shared cultural legacy'.[573] Nevertheless, according to Lewis, '[i]t is certainly the case that each of these cultures developed different religious practices and imbued many of these religious terms and deities with different ideologies'.[574] As an important example, he observes that '[t]he royal cult of Judean kings never comes close to matching the pageantry of the Ugaritic king as chief religious officiant (e.g., KTU 1.41, 1.119)'.[575]

Mark Smith adopts a similar approach in his *Origins of Biblical Monotheism: Israel's polytheistic background and the Ugaritic texts* (2001). He writes:

> This book represents a synthesis that focuses not so much on specific deities as on the concepts that the ancients used to understand them. In other words, I am interested not only in describing Israelite monotheism but also in examining the conceptual unity and coherence of its religious congener, Israelite polytheism, as well as the religious unity expressed in the polytheism revealed in the largest cache of relevant extra-biblical texts, namely the myths and rituals from the ancient city of Ugarit (modern Ras Shamra).[576]

---

572 Lewis 2020, 261.
573 Lewis 2020, 263.
574 Lewis 2020, 263.
575 Lewis 2020, 264.
576 Smith 2001, 5.

# (e) Conclusion

The Canaanite world view is polytheistic but with El and Baal as dominant gods. Unlike the Sumerian world view, but as with the Babylonian, violence among the gods is central to the emergence of the world and humans. As we will see below, there is much discussion among OT scholars about the relationship between El and YHWH. What is clear is that the Canaanite gods are viewed, as in the rest of the ANE, in human terms, and a motif such as the impotence of El is never one that we find in relation to YHWH. Baal, of course, plays a considerable role in the OT, and worship of him is clearly identified as a major temptation for the Israelites. King and cult are interwoven in Canaan, unlike in Israel, and the practice of child sacrifice, if it existed, is noteworthy and repulsive. Overwhelmingly, the Canaanite world view is set against that of Israel in the OT, but ways in which Israel drew from the Canaanites should not be overlooked. Ugaritic poetry developed an advanced poetics and it is likely that Israel was influenced by it. The motif of the assembly of the gods is also one we find in the OT, but, as always, the proof of the pudding is what is done with it.[577]

# 13 The Persian world view

## (a) Introduction

Embedded in world views are beliefs and ideas, and these ideas have a habit of developing legs and running into history. This is certainly true of the Persian world view. Once the Persians defeated the Babylonians and the Persian (Achaemenid) Empire emerged, it was the Persians' different understanding of how empire should operate that allowed Israelites to return to Judea and to rebuild the walls and the Temple.

Kass notes that eating is that most political of acts,[578] and in Esther, set in the heart of the Persian Empire, feasting plays a central role. And, indeed, feasting is an appropriate symbol of the Persian Empire. The Greeks were amazed at the King's Dinner, at which truly vast amounts of food were consumed. Athenaeus commented: 'One thousand animals are slaughtered daily for the king; these comprise horses, camels, oxen, asses, deer, and most of the smaller animals; many birds also are consumed, including Arabian ostriches – and the creature

---

577 See, for example, our discussion of Ps. 82 below, which I argue is an example of broken myth.
578 Kass 1994, 1999.

is large – geese, and cocks.'[579] An immense consumption of alcohol accompanied such dining. The result was that a visit by the king and his entourage – and these visits were not uncommon – even for a single meal represented an enormous challenge for the hosts. At different scales this emphasis on feasting extended throughout Persian society, with the types of food demarcating one's social position. This characteristic of the Persians was well known and could be manipulated to their advantage. For example, when Cyrus first attacked the Massagetae, his army set out a great feast and pretended to retreat. The Massagetae attacked, became drunk on the 'abandoned' wine and were then defeated by the Persians.[580]

## (b) History

The Persian Empire established by Cyrus II and his successors is also referred to as the Achaemenid Empire, because of the kings' supposed ancestor Achaemenes, who was said to have founded the dynasty. The Achaemenid Empire lasted from c.550 to 330 BC and the name 'Achaemenid' serves to distinguish it from the following eras in Iranian history. For our purposes we will use 'Persian' and 'Achaemenid' as synonyms. As with the other people groups we have explored, the Persians have a long history prior to the emergence of the Persian Empire under Cyrus II.[581] The Persian Empire originated in the western Zagreb mountains after Cyrus united the Medes and the Persians under his rule. Cyrus conquered Babylon in 539 BC. He built a new palace and garden at Pasargadae, establishing an architectural and aesthetic style that would resonate for the coming centuries. '"Palaces" characterized by many-columned halls and formal gardens with symbolically charged layouts, watered via elaborate channels, and spatial layouts emphasizing open air and movement set Pasargadae apart from both normal life and from the palaces of earlier Mesopotamian kings.'[582] Indeed, with time, the gardens or 'paradeisoi' were exported around the Persian Empire and became a means of establishing its presence, ideology and power.[583] Here, as in the ANE, the garden is an urban phenomenon, and this is one reason why Eden in Genesis 2—3 should

---

579  Ath. 4.145e. Quoted by Dusinberre 2013, 116. See Dusinberre 2013, ch. 4: 'Eating and Drinking with Class and Style'.

580  Waters 2014, 52.

581  This prehistory pushes us back into groups such as the Mittanites, the Elamites and the Medes. For an introductory history see Waters 2014. For a detailed history see Briant 2002; and for sources see Kuhrt 2007, 2010.

582  Dusinberre 2013, 9. See also Silverman 2016, 178–83.

583  Dusinberre 2013, 54–6. It is notable that 'paradeisoi' is a Persian loanword found in Ecclesiastes.

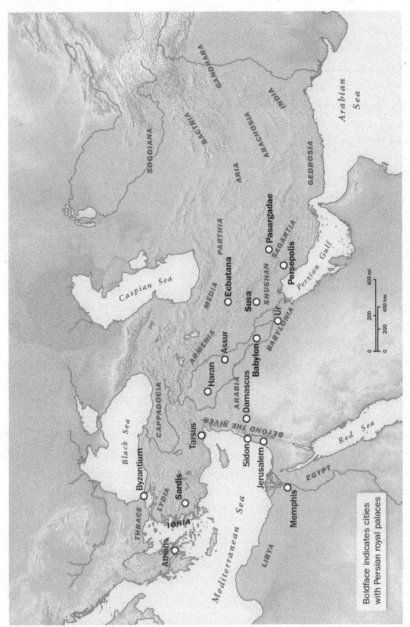

**Map 12 The Persian Empire**
(© Baker Publishing Group)

Boldface indicates cities
with Persian royal palaces

perhaps not be thought of as a pristine wilderness but rather as urban in character. Cyrus's building also parallels the sort of experiment Qohelet embarks on in Ecclesiastes.

Cyrus was succeeded by Cambyses, his son, who brought Egypt into the vast Persian Empire. Under Darius I (c.522–486 BC), who usurped the throne and built a new palace at Susa, the empire expanded maximally, encompassing an unprecedentedly large territory, as evident in Map 12. 'The empire encompassed within its boundaries twenty-three distinct subject peoples, who spoke different languages, worshipped different deities, lived in different environments, and had widely different social customs.'[584] Darius's son Xerxes (486–465 BC) was succeeded by Artaxerxes I (465–424/3 BC), and '[u]nder Artaxerxes I and his son Darius II (423–404) the empire remained stable and powerful, the wealthiest and most powerful sociopolitical entity on earth'.[585] After a long period of nearly 200 years, the Persian Empire was brought to an end by the invasion of Alexander the Great in 334 BC.

## (c) Kings and governance

Royal ideology was thoroughly interwoven with the gods in imperial iconography, and the king was regarded as way above ordinary mortals:

> An elaborate court-ceremonial served to stress the fact that he was elevated above ordinary mortals . . . When ushered into the presence of the king . . . one had to do obeisance to him by throwing oneself prostrate before him, and kissing the ground.[586]

Different views have been held as to whether or not the king was regarded as divine. Kuhrt observes that:

> The royal declarations are suffused with the sense of the king's dependence on the gods. He himself is part of the divine creation and it is his duty to strive to maintain it. Gods are invoked to protect Persia's land and people, the empire and royal constructions. While the king stands in a privileged relationship to the divine sphere, he is certainly not himself a god.[587]

---

584 Dusinberre 2013, 8.
585 Dusinberre 2013, 12.
586 Widengren 1973, 345.
587 Kuhrt 2007, 2010, 473.

Empires require that rulers assert power and control, and the Persian kings did not default in this respect. What is noteworthy, however, is their means of doing this. Deported peoples were allowed to return home, as were their gods, and the different parts of the empire were allowed lingual and religious autonomy provided they remained loyal to the empire.

> The policy followed by Cyrus regarding the deported ethnic groups and their deities meant a new attitude in the history of the Ancient Near East. His policy of toleration was dictated by political reasoning which implies that with him politics counted for more than religion.[588]

However, the king's god-given role in maintaining order in the universe belies such a separation of politics from religion.

## (d) The gods

Wiesehöfer notes that '[h]ardly any subject has led to as many arguments among scholars as the religious beliefs of the Achaemenid rulers (and their Iranian subjects)'.[589] For example, the relationship between Achaemenid religion and the far older Zoroastrianism remains contested. This lack of agreement is related, at least in part, to the fact that the Persians, unlike the Babylonians, passed on their myths orally. Artaxerxes II (404–359 BC)[590] reformed the liturgical calendar and named the months after gods, among whom were:[591]

- Ahura Mazda, the chief god of the Zoroastrian pantheon; he was good, true, wise and powerful, but his power was limited by his evil adversary;
- Mithra, a god with solar dimensions and also the deity of the contract;
- Anahita, the goddess of water and thus fertility;
- Arta, associated with truth and order;
- Humban, an Elamite god connected especially with the king.

In line with the toleration of the Persian kings, Persian religion was polytheistic and eclectic. In the famous Cyrus Cylinder, Cyrus II credits Marduk with appointing him king over Babylon and never refers to Ahura Mazda. However,

---

588  Widengren 1973, 319. But see Fitzpatrick-McKinley 2016; and Agut-Labordère 2016.
589  Wiesehöfer 1996, 2001, 94.
590  See Shannon 2007 for the Achaemenid kings and the gods they worshipped.
591  Wiesehöfer 1996, 2001, 94. On Achaemenid religion see Wiesehöfer 1996, 2001, 94–101.

Cyrus's pluralism was restricted by his royal followers. Garrison discerns an upward tendency in Persian religion and argues that "'[a]scension," then, may be the defining characteristics of the numinous, the divine, and the royal'.[592]

## (e) Conclusion

The Persian Empire comes at the end of the OT narrative, facilitating the return of the Israelites to Judea and the rebuilding of Jerusalem. However, Jerusalem would never recover the glory of its past and, on the whole, this is a time of decline and submission to the reign of foreign powers. However, among mainstream, historical-critical scholars this is seen as the creative time of the emergence of the OT. As Anderson states: 'Recent years have seen a growing consensus among scholars that the formative years for the writing and editing of the Hebrew Bible was the Persian period, even if monarchic-era source material was used in some books.'[593] While it is certainly possible that books of the OT were edited into shape during this period, such an assessment depends on a history-of-religions approach which locates the most creative times at Israel's low points, ignoring the high points of revelation. Davies captures this perspective well in his assertion that the view that monotheism

> was imposed or created in a single moment – at Sinai, or in a religious reform, or during the experience of deportation to Babylonia – is perhaps unduly influenced by the theological preference for the role of divine self-revelation and the assumption that Jewish monotheism is the earliest manifestation of that belief. But sudden changes of theology do not occur – or will not persist – unless there exist strong cultural currents that support and sustain them.[594]

Of course, it is always possible that genuine divine revelation could generate major cultural currents!

# 14 Evaluation

I must begin by noting how fascinating I find the world of the ANE. Too much Christianity has followed modernity in privatizing religion with the result that it is reduced to 'the spiritual', namely the institutional Church and evangelism.

---

592  Mark Garrison quoted by Dusinberre 2013, 208.

593  Anderson 2106, 9. See also Bautch and Lackowski, eds, 2019.

594  Davies 2016, 24.

ANE religion, including that of Israel, utterly resists such privatization. It is a type of religion that takes us deeply into every aspect of culture: worship and cultus, certainly, but also architecture, the development of cities and writing, law, politics, economics, science, sexuality and family life, agriculture and commerce, travel, empires and international relations, and so very much more. This is life in all its glory and horror, and if we are to unmute the OT then this comprehensive nature of religion, including that of the OT, simply has to be recovered. It is in this world that the OT speaks with unprecedented power, and the argument of this series is that it is as we listen to it in *this* context that we will hear it speak in this way.

With the possible exception of Akhenaten and the sun god, the ANE is thoroughly polytheistic. It is awash with gods and they are consistently portrayed in human terms, and reveal themselves to a significant extent as cultural and geographical projections. A co-dependent relationship exists between the gods and the people. To survive, the gods must eat and be cared for, and humans are there to provide for the gods and in most cases to relieve them of the burden of work. Needless to say, this is not a very dignified view of the human person or of work, and it is notable in many of the cultures of the ANE how the boundaries between nature, animals, humans and the gods are blurred. At the same time, the gods are far more powerful than humans – this is what distinguishes them as gods – and humans need them if they are to survive and flourish.

Philosophically, the ANE world views embody an *ontological monism*. Nature, animals, humans and gods are all part of the same (monistic) reality. James Sire identifies this question as a key component of a world view: what is the bottom line of reality? In the ANE it is never the gods but rather the primeval waters or some such equivalent. It is out of such a substrate of pre-existent matter that the gods emerge, and they too live and die. This monism militates against breaking out of a cyclical view of the world and means that, although some of the ANE cultures produced important historical documents, they were unable to develop an overarching view of history in development.

Among humans the king always stands apart, mediating the relationship between the gods and the people, and is in some cases viewed as a god. Inevitably, the king plays a central role in the cult so that politics and religion are joined at the hip. The stratification of ANE society reflects this hierarchy, with slaves at the bottom of the pile. Law in the ANE is *always* connected with the king from whom it issues forth. Of course, this is in response to the gods, but the king as the quintessential lawgiver marks a major contrast with Israel in which YHWH and not the king is the lawgiver. Death looms large in ANE world views, as the pervasive presence of mortuary cults confirms. Rituals were in place to facilitate the move through death to what lay beyond.

If the ANE world views constrain development in certain ways, as they undoubtedly do, we must not ignore the extraordinary achievements they made possible. Temple and king appear to emerge together out of the mists of history, and the ANE world views facilitated the emergence of civilization, the development of cities and agriculture, the origin of writing and the creation of a vast and complex body of literature in a range of genres, extraordinary scientific achievements, architectural feats that we still do not fully understand to this day, the emergence of law and law codes as well as wisdom and wisdom literature, a range of political models, and so on. Israel, as we noted at the outset, emerged late on the international scene in the ANE. She was therefore able to assume these developments and establish her own life with its distinctives within the context of the great achievements that preceded her. And, just as the early Church had to draw on its surrounding culture and intellectual developments in order to craft its world view, so too Israel drew on her environment as she crafted hers. Thus, as we should expect, there is much similarity between the world view of Israel and those of her neighbours. Many motifs are shared in common, but it will always be necessary to scrutinize carefully what Israel does with such common elements as she positions them within her world view.

# 7

# God and the gods of the Ancient Near East

## 1 The Mosaic distinction and translatability

In previous chapters we have explored the diverse world views amid which Israel came into existence. For all their many differences, they were all polytheistic. By stark contrast it appears that Israel acknowledged only one God, YHWH.[1] However, it is not unusual nowadays for it to be argued that monotheism was a late development in Israel. How, then, are we to think about YHWH in relation to the gods of the ANE?

### (a) The Mosaic distinction

Assmann has made a major contribution in identifying what he calls *the Mosaic distinction* between true and false religion, although this does not mean that he recommends it.[2] Assmann argues that Akhenaten first made this distinction but he was quickly forgotten, whereas the memory of Moses has remained and been hugely influential:

> Moses is a figure of memory but not of history, while Akhenaten is a figure of history but not of memory. Since memory is all that counts in the sphere of cultural distinctions and constructions, we are justified in speaking not of Akhenaten's distinction, but of the Mosaic distinction.[3]

The Mosaic distinction was radical in the polytheistic ANE. Polytheism with its differentiated pantheons provides for 'techniques of translation'

---

1  There has been extensive discussion about monotheism in/and the OT. See, e.g., Anderson 2015; Cataldo 2012; Gnuse 1997; Hurtado 2015; MacDonald 2012; Moberly 1992; 2020; Sekine 2014; Smith 2001. Schmid (2019, 294) argues that explicitly monotheistic views of God are found for the first time in P and Second Isaiah, i.e. not before the Persian period.

2  The words 'monotheism' and 'polytheism' are not older than the seventeenth century AD (Assmann 2004, 17), but of course this does not mean that the concepts were not understood much earlier.

3  Assmann 1997, 2.

between gods so that religions had a common ground, a 'common semantic universe':[4]

> they functioned as a means of intercultural translatability. The gods were international because they were cosmic. The different people worshipped different gods, but nobody contested the reality of foreign gods and the legitimacy of foreign forms of worship. The [Mosaic] distinction I am speaking of simply did not exist in the world of polytheistic religions.[5]

Gods had names with meanings, and a particular god was associated with stories, hymns, rituals and so on. 'This character makes a deity comparable to other deities with similar traits. The similarity of gods makes their names mutually translatable.'[6] For example, the sun god in one culture was easily recognizable in the sun god of another culture even if the names and the cultural contexts differed. In our discussion of the Babylonian world view above we noted the central role of bilingual lists in Babylonian and thus ANE culture. It is here that we find literal translatability, with god-names sometimes listed in multiple languages. Assmann refers, for example, to the explanatory list *Anu sa ameli*, which lists the god's name in Sumerian and Akkadian and then the function of the god.[7] He locates the origin of this practice in international treaties in which equivalence in function and rank was crucial. Thus, '[i]ntercultural theology becomes a concern of international law'.[8]

However, the Mosaic distinction renders all other gods as false gods and it distinguishes clearly and radically between YHWH and other 'gods', so that it is simply impossible to find an equivalent to YHWH among the thousands of gods of the ANE. Assmann argues that in the OT monotheism is based on revelation and not on evidence.

> The distinction between true and false refers, in its ultimate meaning, to the distinction between god and the world. Revolutionary monotheism worships an extramundane or transcendent god, whereas the deities of both polytheistic and evolutionary monotheism create and animate the

---

4   Assmann 2004, 24.

5   Assmann 1997, 3.

6   Assmann 2004, 24.

7   Assmann 2004, 24–5.

8   Assmann 2004, 25.

world from within and constitute its life. These religions may be termed 'cosmotheism,' because they worship the world as a divine being.[9]

Assmann notes that the basic distinctions of a culture are generally given expression in a grand narrative. Israel's dependence on revelation is closely associated with memory, writing, transmission and canon. In Israel, her grand narrative is that of the exodus myth set out in Exodus–Deuteronomy. It is both narrative and normative, and is symbolized by the opposition between Egypt and Israel. Egypt is the place of images of the gods, and such images are forbidden to Israel in the law code flowing out of the exodus. Opposition to idolatry or paganism is Israel's first priority. Assmann points out that:

> Both the story and the law code are symbolically expressive of the Mosaic distinction. The story is more than simply an account of historical events, and the Law is more than merely a basis for social order and religious purity. In addition to what they overtly tell and establish, they symbolize the distinction. Exodus is a symbolical story, the Law is a symbolical legislation, and Moses is a symbolical figure. The whole constellation of Israel and Egypt is symbolical and comes to symbolize all kinds of oppositions. But the leading one is the distinction between true religion and idolatry.[10]

True religion versus idolatry; this is the Mosaic distinction. Geographically, Israel and Egypt were proximate, but in the map of memory they are utterly distinct. By 'the map of memory' Assmann does not mean the past as it happened but rather the past as it came to be remembered by Israel, what he calls her *mnemohistory*. For Assmann, this distinction cannot be accounted for in evolutionary ways but is a revolution. It necessitates revelation: 'The truth can only come from outside, by way of revelation.'[11] And, we might say, as noted above, that it necessitates an 'outside', a radical distinction between God and the world as creation.

Belief in one true God, YHWH, brings with it all sorts of consequences, and Assmann helpfully elaborates on some of these. He argues, for example, that in biblical monotheism idolatry becomes psychologized into the new concept of *sin*. With this emerges the concept of the inner, the inner person, with religion

---

9   Assmann 2004, 29. For assessments of revolutionary monotheism see Pongratz-Leisten, ed., 2011.
10   Assmann 1997, 4.
11   Assmann 1997, 7.

becoming a matter of heart and soul. In his *Symbolism of Evil*, Ricoeur, with his hermeneutic of explanation and understanding, also foregrounds how the OT opposition to ANE mythology brings sin into focus. He is adamant that, as people of science, we cannot believe in an historical fall of Adam.[12] Nevertheless, for Ricoeur the myth of Adam retains great symbolic power. It renders theogony and the tragic god, so common in the ANE, impossible. Negatively, '[c]onflicts and crimes, trickery and adultery are expelled from the sphere of the divine: animal-headed gods, demigods, titans, giants, and heroes are ruthlessly excluded from the field of religious consciousness'.[13] Positively, it allows the accusation of humans – 'the same theology that makes God innocent accuses man'[14] – and thus sin, repentance and the possibility of mercy to move to the fore.

Assmann argues further that OT monotheism foregrounds what one believes rather than keeping the attention on how to respond to the gods. Justice moves to front and centre. It is a distortion and caricature to assert that polytheistic cultures were unconcerned with justice, but cult and law were separate, with law associated with the king. 'But it is true that no other god than YHWH or Allah ever acted as legislator. The idea of justice is divine, but the formulations and promulgation of specific laws [in polytheistic cultures] is the task of the king.'[15]

In his many books, Assmann writes about the history of this revolutionary monotheism in the West. Intriguingly and correctly, he argues that during the Enlightenment

> Spinoza's (in)famous formula *deus siva natura* [god or nature][16] amounted to an abolition not only of the Mosaic distinction but of the most fundamental distinctions, the distinction between God and the world. This deconstruction was as revolutionary as Moses' construction. It immediately led to a new appraisal of Egypt. The Egyptians were Spinozists and 'cosmotheists.'[17]

---

12  Ricoeur 1967, 235.

13  Ricoeur 1967, 239–40.

14  Ricoeur 1967, 240.

15  Assmann 2004, 30.

16  For Spinoza, god or nature could be used interchangeably; they are the same. See Bartholomew 2020 for a detailed analysis of Spinoza.

17  Assmann 1997, 8.

As I explain in my *God Who Acts in History*, Spinoza, with his pantheistic monism – nature and God are the same – was hugely influential on the radical Enlightenment and on the rise of historical criticism of the OT. What Assmann helps us to see is that Spinoza moved away from a world view grounded in the Mosaic distinction to one comparable to those of the ANE nations we have examined above, in which the divine and the world are all part of the same thing. If nothing else, this should alert us to the fact that the emergence of historical criticism cannot be seen simply as the triumph of neutral, objective science.

## (b) Translatability

When I first encountered this issue, I found the meaning assigned to 'translatability' confusing. Thus, it is important to note what Assmann – and Smith (see below) – does *not* mean by translatability. He does not mean the borrowing of concepts or motifs from ANE religions to express the character of YHWH, for which we have ample evidence in the OT, as in Psalms 29; 48.3, for example. He defines translatability more narrowly as *the recognition of the reality of other gods and the interchangeability of gods among the nations*.

Mark Smith engages with Assmann's account of the Mosaic distinction in detail and critically. Since a great deal is at stake in this debate, we will examine Smith's position in detail and then evaluate it carefully.

Smith analyses the words used in the ANE for a god and concludes that, whereas in the Middle Ages all creatures were thought to receive their being from Being itself, namely God, in the ANE *ĕlōhîm* and its related terms were conceived of in terms of power and powers.[18] In response to Assmann's religious interests, Smith refreshingly acknowledges his own. He notes that, in recent generations, '[i]n biblical studies there seemed to be an unwritten rule that religious experience was to be avoided precisely because it seemed to partake of the confessional, and thus was not an element of serious scholarship'.[19] Smith, as a Roman Catholic, seeks to take theology *and* a history-of-religions approach seriously. He calls this his 'double-lenses'. He references his Catholicism but describes it somewhat unusually as a type of incarnational Christianity in that he senses God through the creation and not outside it. He taught in Catholic institutions but now teaches in a department of Hebrew and Judaic studies.[20] He works on the Bible, and in extrabiblical

---

18  Smith 2008, 14. See also Smith 2011.
19  Smith 2008, 31–2.
20  Since then, Smith has joined the teaching staff of Princeton Theological Seminary.

areas. In short, he writes: 'Duality is a basic feature of my personal and intellectual horizon.'[21]

A central element in Smith's engagement with Assmann's Mosaic distinction is that the biblical data is far more complex than Assmann takes account of.[22] Hendel leans on Balaam's comment in Numbers 23.9 about Israel to agree with Assmann:[23]

> For from the top of the crags I see him,
>> from the hills I behold him.
> Here is a people living alone,
>> *and not reckoning itself among the nations!*

Smith, by comparison, argues that this poetry may not be as early as is sometimes suggested and, furthermore, it may point to Israel's self-reliance rather than affirming the Mosaic distinction. In fact, according to Smith, the Balaam narrative as a whole *supports* translatability. As a non-Israelite, Balaam recognizes the god of Israel, and Numbers recognizes him as a prophet. 'Balaam himself was recognized cross-culturally by Israel, as seen in Numbers 22–24, and by non-Israelites as indicated by the extra-biblical Deir 'Alla inscription that bear[s] his words.'[24] Smith concludes that, as '[a] prophet who crosses cultural and religious boundaries, Balaam is a quintessential figure of translatability'.[25]

## (c) Translatability in the Old Testament

Through a close examination of specific biblical texts, Smith argues that *we find both translatability and untranslatability in the OT*. It is especially in texts from the pre-exilic period that we find evidence for translatability. Smith relates this to the background of Late Bronze Age treaties and letters in which the gods of both sides to agreements are acknowledged. He comments on the passages that we will attend to below:

> What these biblical passages represent is a form of translatability, specifically a component in a monarchic period worldview that sees the various

---

21  Smith 2008, 33.

22  Pongratz-Leisten (2011, 2) notes that Assmann 'is primarily interested in the later reception of ancient texts – that is, a history of memory, rather than the historical information provided by the texts themselves'.

23  Hendel 2005, 9.

24  Smith 2008, 129.

25  Smith 2008, 129.

chief gods of the nations who stand more or less on par with one another. These deities have been called national gods, and they figure in an international religious worldview (or, what might perhaps be called a 'world theology').[26]

According to Smith, in this perspective or world view, each nation had its own national god and to a significant extent these gods operated on a par with one another.

**Genesis 31.43–55.** In this narrative, Laban and Jacob form an alliance and in the process they invoke their gods: the god of Abraham and the god of Nahor. Jacob swears by the fear of his father Isaac. Smith argues that the meal in verse 54 brings the two deities together. They, together, act as guarantors of the agreement. The god of Abraham is Abraham's family or patron god, and the same is probably true of the god of Nahor. Although Jacob and Laban come from the same family, the agreement takes place across languages, namely Hebrew and Aramaic. For Smith, this text contains the sorts of elements common to texts of translatability, with its recognition of the reality of the other god alongside one's own.

**Judges 3.20.** Ehud, the judge, says to King Eglon in this verse: 'I have a message from Elohim for you.' Here again Smith discerns translatability since the god that communicates could be shared by both parties.

**Judges 7.** Gideon is assured by YHWH that he will be triumphant in battle, but if he is cautious he should go down to the enemy's camp with his servant and hear what the troops are saying. He does so and overhears a story of a dream. In verses 13–14 a non-Israelite narrates an authentic dream involving the Israelite god, and a second non-Israelite interprets it correctly in relation to the action of Elohim, an interpretation understood by Gideon, who translates it into his own 'culturally specific expression for divinity', YHWH.[27] The author views non-Israelites as being able, through their experience, to understand a revelation from YHWH.

**Judges 11.** Smith discerns the same ideology at work in verse 24 with the reference to 'your god Chemosh' and in verse 23 'YHWH, the God of Israel'.

---

26  Smith 2008, 119.
27  Smith 2008, 109.

The deity of each party is named, in a comparable way to what we find in international relations as expressed, for example, in the Amarna letters: 'we have a representation of the explicit recognition of deities of the parties across cultures. In addition, we have the implicit equation of the two deities based on their comparable roles as national warrior-gods.'[28] The world view in verse 23 differs from that in verse 27 in which Deuteronomistic material has been added to represent the exclusive Iron Age religious world view of only YHWH.

*1 Kings 20.* This chapter recounts the wars between King Ahab and the Arameans under Ben-hadad. From verses 23 and 28 Smith argues that the author depicts the Arameans as recognizing YHWH in ways with which the Israelites were familiar. Thus, here again he discerns a cross-cultural recognition of deities, or translatability.

*2 Kings 1.* Smith argues that the dialogue related to Ahaziah's injury presupposes that divine enquiry can be addressed to both YHWH and a Philistine god so that translatability is implicit in this narrative. The author 'prefers Israel's own god for the task'.[29]

*2 Kings 3.27.* This is a strange and horrific verse. When the king of Edom sacrifices his firstborn son, 'great wrath came upon Israel', causing the Israelite army to withdraw. Smith argues that this narrative recognizes divine power apart from YHWH.

Even within the Deuteronomistic history, Smith finds vestiges of the older world view in which YHWH was Israel's national god.

*1 Samuel 26.18–20.* As Saul seeks to kill David, and David spares Saul's life, David refers to his enemies' words to him in verse 19: 'Go, serve other gods.' Smith argues that here YHWH is seen as the national god; to leave Israel is to leave the inheritance of YHWH (cf. Exod. 22.20).

*1 Kings 18.* The polemic of Elijah in this chapter is often read as a quintessential monotheistic text, but Smith argues that we can see in it an older, pre-Deuteronomistic form of competition between major gods: 'The story's

---

28 Smith 2008, 111.
29 Smith 2008, 115.

critique of Baal indicates, even as it rejects, a cross-cultural acceptance of Phoenician Baal, championed by his prophets, alongside Yahweh.'[30] Smith foregrounds the importance of geography in this discussion, with the area between the coastal region and the Transjordan presented as one of conflict between national gods.

*2 Kings 5.* This passage tells the story of the Aramean general Naaman and his healing from leprosy through the ministry of Elisha. He takes soil from Israel back to Aram with him but requests that he will be forgiven when he has to bow down to the god Rimmon with the king. Elisha tells him: 'Go in peace' (v. 19). Smith argues that verse 17 is not about monotheism but is a pledge to Israel's national god and involves the exchange of one national god for another with exceptions allowed.

*2 Kings 17.26.* Smith argues that the expression 'the law of the god of the land' understands each nation to have a main god.

It has long been recognized that much of the OT discourse about gods is polemical, but Smith argues that even in the Deuteronomistic rejection of other gods we see an acknowledgement of their existence. Thus, the problem in 1 Kings 11.7, where Solomon is described as building places of worship near Jerusalem for foreign gods, may not be idolatry so much as religious dissonance. Likewise, the Deuteronomistic editing of Judges works with a representation of translatability (see Judg. 2.11, 13; 3.7 which reference the gods of the nations). Again, for Smith, the proclamation of YHWH's greatness by foreigners (see Exod. 18.11; Josh. 2.10a; cf. 11b) implicitly acknowledges the existence of other national gods. Smith wonders if we might imagine comparable statements by Israelites about the gods of other nations.[31]

## Rejection of translatability in the Old Testament

Smith does think that we find the Mosaic distinction in the OT but it is a late development. And even such texts dramatize what they reject, thus implicitly acknowledging the development.

---

30   Smith 2008, 123.
31   Smith 2008, 127.

**Psalm 82.** This is a fascinating psalm due to its engagement with the ANE motif of the divine council, probably with Ugaritic literature in the background.[32]

> In short, Psalm 82 calls for an end to translatability. It is evident that Psalm 82 presupposes, even as it disputes, an older worldview of the nations each headed by its own national god. The translatability expressed in the worldview is acknowledged at the same time that it is being rejected.[33]

According to Smith, Psalm 82 starts with YHWH as a national god but ends with him as the God of the entire world.

**Deuteronomy 32.8–9.** This is the first of two main cases of what Smith calls 'censorship' in the OT. The other is Genesis 14.22. Smith argues that censorship has not yet been adequately investigated. In Deuteronomy 32.8–9 Elyon apportions the boundaries of the nations, with Israel being YHWH's portion. According to Smith, 'here is the national world view presupposed by the older reading of the verses and the rejection of its implied polytheism in the larger context of the poem'.[34] He maintains that 'Deuteronomy 32.8–9 reflects an old version of the divine founding of the world known in broader West Semitic tradition, one that is otherwise eclipsed in the biblical record by Israel's specific foundational traditions'.[35] However, such a view is censored in verse 39, and such censorship is also implied in verses 17 and 21. For Smith, the composer did not intend any affirmation of polytheism in this text.

**Deuteronomy 6.4.** This famous text might be thought of as the quintessential text of monotheism, but Smith argues otherwise. אֶחָד (one) can be translated in a variety of ways, and he notes that whether it is translated as for Israel as a whole, as the only god for Israel, or as unique, all of these translations depict YHWH only as the main god for Israel. The Shema of Deuteronomy 6.4 is, however, referenced in Zechariah 14.9 and here it clearly refers to monotheism.

*For Smith, the biblical data indicates that Israel clearly developed a doctrine of non-translatability, but it was not an original feature of her faith.* It only emerged at the end of the monarchy, in the exilic period and beyond. The crucial questions are: how and why did it develop? El and Yahweh came to be iden-

---

32   See Mullen 1980. He (1980, 284) concludes that 'the major source of influence upon the council motif in early Hebrew literature comes from Canaan and not from Mesopotamia'.

33   Smith 2008, 139.

34   Smith 2008, 141.

35   Smith 2008, 142.

tified with each other, and the tradition as it developed championed only one god for early Israel. According to Smith, '[i]n the wake of this development, the tradition generated a foundational myth that early Israel only had a single deity and thus other deities were "new gods" or "other gods"'.[36] We see this, for example, in Deuteronomy 32.17, and in Deuteronomy 32.1–43 we witness the identification of YHWH with Elyon, the assertion of there being only one God, and the view that other gods were not known by Israel.

## One-god world views

For Smith, Israel was not unique in her development of a one-god world view. Neo-Assyrian influence was an important aspect of Israel's development in this respect. The emergence of the Neo-Assyrian Empire changed the situation drastically in the ANE. Small states such as Israel and Judah were overwhelmed by ruthless imperial power so that parity of gods simply no longer made sense. The emergent monotheism in Israel is related to this power differential.

In Smith's view, Israel's development of a one-god doctrine of YHWH must be seen against the background of Assyria's development of a one-god doctrine of Aššur and Babylon's one-god doctrine of Marduk. Aššur and Marduk were respectively seen as the single god at the top of the hierarchy who underlies the realities of the other gods and is not translatable into them. Polytheism remained in place, but the view of the top god was new. For Smith:

> It was in this period that Israel's own 'one-god' expressions took the form of monotheistic declarations and representations of reality. Israel constructed its own monotheistic 'one-god' formulations perhaps under the larger atmosphere of Mesopotamian 'one-god' expressions.[37]

Earlier, we discussed Parpola's view of Assyrian religion as expressing monotheism, and Smith quotes Parpola to the effect that in Deuteronomy 13 YHWH has assumed the place of Assyria's great king. Smith asserts: 'While ancient Israel evidently constructed its expressions of monotheism in response to the larger discourse of divinity taking place in the ancient Near East in this period, the result is as notable for its difference as for its similarity.'[38] Smith is cautious of Parpola's use of 'monotheism' for Assyria since

---

36  Smith 2008, 149.
37  Smith 2008, 159.
38  Smith 2008, 165–6.

clearly her polytheism remained in place. He finds Voegelin's term 'summode-ism' more helpful, which expresses the view of one god as head of a pantheon of gods. However, out of this one-god view Israel developed a distinctive approach: 'While Marduk has all other names as his own, Jeremiah 16.21 presents the name of Yahweh as demarcated from all other names.'[39]

The contrast between Marduk and YHWH is made explicit in Second Isaiah (Isa. 40—55). In Isaiah 40.18, 25; 46.5 we see the polemic against other gods. 'Israel's monotheism emerged in the context of its lack of power in the face of empires, perhaps as a form of resistance to them.'[40] As in Ugarit, as noted by Sanders above in Part 1, we find in Israel the development of a vernacular literature. However, in Ugarit we find a retention of Akkadian classics, whereas in Israel, motifs and plotlines are borrowed but not under the aegis of translatability.

It is in the Persian period of Israel's post-exilic experience that Smith locates the development of a corpus of sacred texts which *inter alia* involved the reinterpretation or censorship of some older texts.[41]

Indeed, it is important for understanding 'biblical censorship' to note that there was a vast range of deities in ancient Israel and the Bible and *the monotheism of the Bible is an outcome of a long historical and textual process, not simply the perspective that guided all of its authors.*[42]

With Morton Smith, van der Toorn and Dever, Smith locates the development of this national literature among the priestly scribes, which fits with P's position as the latest Pentateuchal source.

Smith revisits the motif of censorship in this context. He attends to the manuscript differences of Deuteronomy 32.8–9. All the manuscript witnesses understood the poem as monotheistic (cf. vv. 17, 21, 39), but verses 8–9 drew on an older polytheistic tradition according to which El and Asherah had 70 nations.

However, the composer of Deuteronomy 32 had implicitly effaced this polytheistic notion that had been inherited from Israel's old literary

---

39  Smith 2008, 176.
40  Smith 2008, 179–80.
41  cf. Schmid 2019, 281–3.
42  Smith 2008, 187. Emphasis added.

heritage, by combining it with statements that expresses (*sic*) divinity in more exclusive terms ('no-gods' in verses 17 and 21 as well as verse 39).[43]

According to Smith, '[w]e might say that these later scribes were perceptive in sensing the old polytheism pushing through the monotheistic veneer of the author's formulation'.[44]

In terms of censorship, Smith also attends to **Genesis 14.22** in which Abram replies to the king of Sodom and refers to God as 'YHWH, El Elyon, creator of heaven and earth'.[45] Again Smith attends to the different textual witnesses and notes that the addition of YHWH demotes El Elyon. 'With the picture of Yahweh and El Elyon in the past reconfigured, the story of Israel with respect to other gods was in turn reconfigured. The potential "hermeneutical power" of this correlation in divinity was considerable.'[46] It is in the new monotheistic foundational narrative produced in the post-exilic period that we find the strongest element of censorship. As in Nehemiah 8.8, it is the priestly scribes, the Levites, who write, read and interpret, engaging in what Smith calls *scripturalizing*, which 'aimed at a harmony of worldview'.[47]

It was thus in the Persian period that the Israelites' view of God continued to develop along the trajectory from a national god, to an empire god, to the world god. Amid radical shrinkage of her political influence and domain, Israel radically enlarged the terms of YHWH to world-historical transcendence. 'The notion of its national deity was generalized not only geographically as the god of the universe . . . it was correspondingly generalized across time, as the god, the only god of this Israel's history.'[48]

> It was further expressed in religious teaching (Torah) reserved for and by this people, that not only asserted these claims about this one deity and this one people, but also conveyed its reality as the one authoritative collection emblemized in the one authoritative figure of Moses as remembered in it.[49] Various aspects of this worldview had enjoyed a long history that reached well back into the pre-exilic period . . . The particular highlighting and interweaving of these aspects largely represented a

---

43  Smith 2008, 197.
44  Smith 2008, 211.
45  My translation.
46  Smith 2008, 215.
47  Smith 2008, 221.
48  Smith 2008, 224.
49  Smith (2008, 224) references here Eckart Otto 2006.

post-exilic innovation. It was an innovation cloaked in the august robes of hoary antiquity, precisely the hallmark of the religious traditioning process.[50]

Before the exile, cultural production largely flowed from the monarchy, but this creative process is located in the priesthood.

# 2 Evaluation

*(a) Translatability.* It is to Smith's credit that he engages with Assmann's proposal in detail. Assmann is, of course, an Egyptologist, whereas Smith is an OT scholar. Assmann's proposal needs to be investigated through close attention to the OT text, and this is what Smith does. The question is: just how compelling is Smith's reading of the texts in which he discerns translatability?

In **Genesis 31** we find multiple names of God: YHWH, Elohim, angel of God, God of Bethel, God of your father, the God of my father, the God of Abraham, the Fear of Isaac. We also find references to Laban's household gods, notoriously stolen and hidden by Rachel. Fokkelman comments on Rachel's hiding of the *tĕrāpîm* and her excuse of menstruation:

> Suspense turns into malicious pleasure at the deadly fun made of the *terafim*: they are only to be 'saved' by a menstruation. This means that they are as unclean as can be, in this new position they come near functioning as . . . sanitary towels.[51]

Smith argues that the covenant engaged in by Laban and Jacob amounts to the recognition of translatability by both partners, and thus by Israel as reflected in this text. Sarna, by comparison, references Joshua 24.2 and asserts: 'It is highly significant that in response Jacob ignores Laban's formula and invokes only the "Fear of his father Isaac."'[52] What Smith fails to do here or elsewhere is to attend closely to the *literary* nature of the text as a whole, highlighted by Fokkelman, in which this account of a covenant is narrated. Once we do so, the data becomes more complex and far less patent of Smith's reading.

---

50   Smith 2008, 224.

51   Fokkelman 1991, 170.

52   Sarna 1989, 222.

Laban refers to two gods: the god of Abraham and the god of Nahor, followed by a plural verb. The reference to his household gods confirms that he is a polytheist. Jacob, however, swears by 'the Fear of his father Isaac'. Köckert asserts that '[n]o definite interpretation can be given' for this expression.[53] He reviews the different proposal for the meaning of 'Fear' and states:

> If, because of the philological problems, one does not want to interpret *paḥad* as 'thigh', it is advisable to start from *paḥad*'s original meaning 'terror' as attested in Hebrew and to interpret the phrase *paḥad ʾābîw* ... in the context of Gen 31 ... In the narrative, the introduction of *paḥad ʾābîw* is prepared for by the nocturnal appearance of Jacob's family god in vv 24 and 29. In fact, this is about the fear with which the god threatens Laban to the advantage of ... Jacob and his kin. In confirming the terms of the contract with an oath to the *paḥad ʾābîw* (v 53), Jacob will draw the fear upon himself ... if he breaks the contract.[54]

In the OT, 'the Fear of Isaac' is found only in Genesis 31.42, 53. In verse 42 Jacob tells Laban that 'the God of my father, the God of Abraham and the Fear of Isaac' had protected him. This alludes back to Laban's dream referred to in 31.29. There are multiple intertextual allusions to other parts of Israel's history in 31.42.[55] '[S]ent me away empty-handed' and 'saw my affliction' (cf. Exod. 3.7) evoke the exodus narrative.

> With this concentration of phraseology associated with the exodus, and especially with the call of Moses in Exod 3, the designations 'God of my father Abraham and the fear of Isaac' seem particularly at home (cf. Exod 3:6, 15, 16; 4:5).[56]

In Jacob's dream referred to in 31.10–13, God says: 'I am the God of Bethel', a reference to Genesis 28.10–22, in which God/YHWH reveals himself to Jacob with the words: 'I am YHWH, the God of Abraham your father and the God of Isaac' (28.13).

Clearly, the narrative of Jacob and Laban in Genesis 31 is told from a post-Sinaitic perspective in which the God of Abraham, Isaac and Jacob is identified

---

53  Köckert 1999.

54  Köckert 1999, 330–1.

55  Wenham 1994, 277–8.

56  Wenham 1994, 278. See Wenham 1994, 278, 266–9, for the literary structure and the variety of source-critical views of Gen. 31.2—32.3.

with YHWH, quintessentially the God of Sinai.[57] It is also an integral part of the broader narrative of Laban and Jacob, and recent source critics see this section as predominantly from J. Equally clear is the motif of the theft of the household gods, their apparent proximity to menstruation, and Jacob's swearing by the Fear of Isaac whereas Laban swears by two gods. As the narrative is told, it is Elohim and 'the God of our father' who speaks to Laban, and the fact that Laban's gods can be stolen hardly places them in a flattering light. From the narrative it would appear that Laban, Jacob and certainly the narrator have different views of divinity. Entering into a covenant would necessitate Laban's invocation of his gods, but a covenant does not necessitate translatability, and the narrative is a long way from affirming that because of this, Jacob, and thus the narrator, affirm the reality of each family's having its own equally real gods. Once we take the literary nature of Genesis 31 seriously, Smith's case for translatability is incorrect. Of course, one can attempt to reconstruct a story behind the narrative as we receive it, and then argue that in it different gods are presented as equally legitimate, but this is speculative and does not deal with the literary shape of the narrative as we receive it. Such an approach would also leave us with two contradictory accounts of the event.

This is also clearly true of **Judges 3.20**. The Ehud narrative (Judg. 3.12–30) is carefully crafted literature. Irony abounds, for example, in the name 'Ehud', meaning 'Where is the glory/majesty?' As Beldman observes:

> Thus, Ehud's name does raise a particularly pertinent question: Where is the glory in a context where God's people are bringing their tribute/offering not to the feet of their true King at the place where his glory dwells (at that time, the tabernacle) but to the feet of a foreign king![58]

Deceit is a major motif in the narrative, and Ehud's use of 'Elohim' is designed to appeal to Eglon and to draw him into the plot; it is not necessarily a statement of Ehud's belief or that of the narrator.

In **Judges 7** we find a motif that recurs in the OT (cf. Jonah; Job), namely, YHWH's activity is not confined to Israel, the reverse of how Smith reads the narrative. The issue of kingship is central to the Gideon narrative, and 'Yahweh went to great lengths to remove any doubt that he was the ultimate source of Israel's deliverance'.[59] The Midianite's dream comes from Israel's God, as

57  See Wenham 1980, 161–95.
58  Beldman 2020, 74.
59  Beldman 2020, 123.

does the interpretation. Far from this confirming the view that YHWH was Israel's national god, this narrative alerts us to his freedom to operate outside of Israel.

It may be that in **Judges 11** Jephthah does recognize deities across cultures. Even if we concede this, it far from resolves the issue. How, from the narrator's perspective, are we to view Jephthah? Block, for example, argues that this episode is full of ambiguity.[60] Beldman notes that 'Jephthah musters all of his rhetorical and logical skills in the hopes that he can avoid a military confrontation with the Ammonites'.[61] As a diplomat, therefore, Jephthah could be appealing to the Ammonite king in terms of the latter's *own* understanding, without necessarily affirming it himself. Alternatively, Jephthah could be affirming such a view, but it is one rejected by Judges as a whole. Of course, Smith sees the perspective of the whole as stemming from the Deuteronomistic editor.

Again and again, attention to the narrative context in which the verses Smith refers to occur makes his reading of them dubious. Sweeney, for example, notes of **1 Kings 20** that '[v]erse 1 introduces a self-contained narrative that relates Ahab's defeat of Ben-Hadad and the condemnation of Ahab for releasing Ben-Hadad and concluding a treaty with him'.[62] Verses 23 and 28 have to be read within the context of this narrative, which is strongly critical of Ahab. Sweeney notes of the servants' proposal to the king of Aram in verses 23–25 that it

> caricaturizes pagan perspective insofar as they propose that Israel's victory must be due to the fact that YHWH is a god of the mountains. This assumption contradicts the Israelite understanding that YHWH is the G-d of all creation (see 1 Kgs 17–19) and that YHWH will grant Ahab victory.[63]

Ahab recognizes Ben-hadad as a 'brother', a legal term in parity treaties. Ahab himself may well have held the view of other gods that Smith finds in this passage, but in the narrative as a whole Ahab's recognition of Ben-hadad is roundly condemned. In verses 35–43 Ahab is sentenced to death by a prophet because of his failure to eliminate Ben-hadad.

---

60   Block 1999, 364. Referred to in Beldman 2020, 146.
61   Beldman 2020, 147.
62   Sweeney 2007, 237.
63   Sweeney 2007, 243.

Similarly with Ahaziah in **2 Kings 1**. Ahaziah seems to have held the view Smith finds here, but Ahaziah is condemned for it. Sweeney sums up verses 2–17 as follows: 'Elijah's condemnation of Ahaziah following his accident emphasizes YHWH's power to punish Ahaziah for his apostasy.'[64] **2 Kings 3.27** is a strange verse. However, Sweeney says of it:

The notice, 'and great wrath was upon Israel' (Hebrew, *wayĕhî qeṣep gādôl ʿal yiśrāʾēl*) is frequently understood as a reference to Chemosh's wrath that then plays a role in Israel's defeat. Although the term *qeṣep*, 'wrath,' generally describes YHWH's anger 'against' (ʿal) wrongdoers (see Num 18:5; Deut 29:27; Josh 9:20; 22:20; Cogan and Tadmor 47), the phrase here can hardly refer to wrath directed 'against' Israel. Such an interpretation requires that YHWH's oracle concerning the defeat of Moab would remain unfulfilled and thereby raises doubts about its legitimacy. There is otherwise no indication in this narrative that YHWH's oracle is to be considered as false. The reference to anger must be read as 'upon' (ʿal) Israel, that is, Israel became angry at the sight of Mesha's sacrifice of his son, and consequently withdrew from Kir Haresheth. Israel/Jehoram – and not YHWH – would be responsible for the failure to achieve victory over the Moabites. The scenario provides a parallel to the wilderness tradition – for example, the Israelite spies refused to accept YHWH's guarantees of victory and suffered as a result (Num 14).[65]

In **1 Samuel 26.18–20** it is David's enemies who exhort him to leave Israel and go and serve other gods. Here again we do find the view Smith discerns, but it is hardly recommended by the narrative. Smith's reading of **1 Kings 18**, furthermore, turns its message upside down. There was surely acceptance of Baal in Israel, as championed by Jezebel, but this is precisely what the confrontation is all about. As Sweeney observes: 'First Kings 18:17–46 demonstrates YHWH's efficacy as master *of creation* and Israel over that of the Phoenician deities Baal and Asherah.'[66] As Bronner shows, again and again the Elijah–Elisha narratives show that the powers thought to belong to Baal actually belong to YHWH.[67]

---

64  Sweeney 2007, 269.
65  Sweeney 2007, 284–5.
66  Sweeney 2007, 226. Emphasis added.
67  Bronner 1968.

**Psalm 82** is a fascinating psalm which has generated considerable dis-cussion.[68] John Dominic Crossan refers to it as 'the single most important text in the Christian Bible'.[69] This psalm is certainly aware of the Canaanite council of El, but the central question is what it does with this motif. König makes Psalm 82 central to his discussion of 'mocking the gods' in the OT.[70] In Canaanite mythology El convened the council of the gods, but in Psalm 82.1, according to König, YHWH (God) has replaced El as the chair![71] Astonishing-ly, the gods are put on trial, found guilty and given the death penalty because they have not provided justice, and this especially for the weak and the needy. Such injustice threatens the very foundations of the creation (v. 5b). The psalm concludes with an appeal to God to bring justice to the earth 'for all the na-tions belong to you!'

Thus, what might at first appear to be an acknowledgement of the existence of other gods turns out to be an example of broken myth[72] and a strong state-ment of exclusivism:

> the Lord took over the presidency of the council of gods, and did it in such a way that El was eliminated and no longer appeared in the picture. Other Old Testament traditions, in which the Lord takes over the name El, should be interpreted in this light. It is not the merging of the Lord with one or another god named El, but an elimination of El, with the Lord taking over his place and functions.[73]

This is evident also from the basis of God's legal case against the gods, namely, their failure to provide justice. In the ANE, justice and law were the provenance of the king rather than of the gods. The gods had power but, in general, the king issued laws. Brague observes that:

> The Bible avoids representing the king as legislator. The one lawgiver is God. That idea was an unparalleled novelty in the ancient Middle East, where only the king made laws. The Torah has no real parallel in those ancient civilizations. The God of Israel replaces the Oriental king in the

---

68  See White 2014, 24–33; Moberly 2020, 93–123; Bartholomew, 'YHWH, the Gods of the ANE and Law: An Engagement with Psalm 82', forthcoming; and the major commentaries and secondary sources.

69  Crossan 1998, 575.

70  König 1982, 11–13.

71  See White 2014, 27–9, for the different views of v. 1.

72  See above.

73  König 1982, 12.

role of lawgiver. Hence the predicates attributed to the pharaoh in Egypt are reserved for God alone in Israel.[74]

The author of Psalm 82 depicts all of this exquisitely, provocatively and imaginatively[75] in poetry, leveraging the motif of the council of El in order to break it and to make his point about YHWH. The name YHWH does not occur in Psalm 82 – Psalm 82 is part of what is called the Elohistic Psalter – but the point is crystal clear. In the process, the author subverts the Canaanite world view rather than affirming its belief in multiple gods.

**Deuteronomy 32.8–9** is part of the Song of Moses (31.30—32.44), which functions as a witness (Deut. 32.46) to the renewal of the covenant or as a warning following on from the renewal of the covenant (Deut. 29—30).[76] The emphasis, as established from the outset in verses 1–6, is on YHWH's goodness to Israel but her unfaithfulness. 'In sum, the song is meant to serve as a mnemonic in Israel that will perpetually warn the people of the dangers of disloyalty.'[77] The dominant metaphors for God are as a rock and as a father so that what is specifically in view is YHWH's relationship with Israel. Verse 7 issues a call to remember, elaborated on in verses 8–9. The object of remembrance in verse 7 has often been thought to be the events of the exodus. However, Culp notes that 'scholars now tend to identify the reference with primeval events of the Bible, such as the parceling of land in Gen 10–11, and not the exodus'.[78] Remembrance of the exodus and the primeval events are not, of course, mutually exclusive. However, verse 8 fits with this, particularly if it has Genesis 10—11 and the Table of the Nations in view. It needs to be remembered that in context the focus of verses 8–9 remains on YHWH's particular relationship with Israel. Bearing in mind that the song takes 'the people on a whirlwind tour of [their] relationship with Yahweh',[79] it is not surprising that verses 8–9 are compact and succinct, leaving much unsaid and assumed.

In verse 8 God is referred to as 'Elyon', Most High. Elnes and Miller note of 'Elyon' that:

---

74  Brague 2007, 49.

75  The imaginative dimension of Ps. 82 cannot be overstressed. There is an (alternative) motif of the council of YHWH in the OT, but in Ps. 82 the author *imagines* the council of the gods of Canaanite myth.

76  On the meaning of 'witness' see Culp 2020, 177. Culp (2020, 177) notes that 'the song then serves as a kind of transformer; it readies the agents and agencies for their new roles in Israel's future'.

77  Culp 2020, 180.

78  Culp 2020, 179.

79  Culp 2020, 183.

In the present form of the biblical text, the term is understood as an epithet for Yahweh, the God of Israel. It is possible, however, as some have argued, that the epithet may conceal a reference to a separate deity, possibly an older god with whom Yahweh came to be identified.[80]

White argues that in the song 'Yahweh starts out as one of the "sons of God," but is transformed by the narrative into a chief God, which would make it similar to Psalm 82'.[81] However, the song is already well under way, with its main themes clear, by the time we get to verses 8–9. 'Elyon' may well be a borrowed term, but in context it clearly refers to YHWH (cf. vv. 16–17, noted by Smith). Craigie observes that:

> In vv. 8–9, the sovereignty of God over all men and nations is expressed, but it is stated in such a way as to emphasize his particular concern for his chosen people . . . The title [Elyon] emphasizes God's sovereignty and authority over all nations, whereas in relation to his own people he is called Yahweh or Lord (v. 9). All nations received their inheritance and had their boundaries fixed by this sovereign God (v. 8), whose role was in no way restricted to the sphere of Israelite life and history (see also Ps 74:17).[82]

The different names for God in verses 8 and 9 make sense in terms of the narrative logic of the poem, as does the כִּי at the start of verse 9 if it is emphatic, translated as 'Indeed'.[83]

What has occasioned considerable debate is the expression לְמִסְפַּר בְּנֵי יִשְׂרָאֵל (according to the number of the sons of Israel) in the MT and its textual variants. The LXX reads 'Elohim' instead of 'Israel', that is, 'sons of God' or 'sons of gods'. Earlier, we discussed the Table of the Nations in Genesis 10 and noted that the total number of nations listed is 70, the same number as constituted Jacob's family. From this perspective the MT may be the original reading, drawing attention to the symbolic and real relationship between Israel and the nations. Certainly in verse 8, בְּנֵי אָדָם (sons of Adam) parallels the expression בְּנֵי יִשְׂרָאֵל (sons of Israel). Alternatively, 'sons of God' could be an expression for the members of the divine council and/or God's 'holy ones' in Deuteronomy 33.2–3. Thus, there are various persuasive options apart from seeing verses 8–9

---

80   Elnes and Miller 1999, 293.
81   White 2014, 37.
82   Craigie 1976, 379.
83   Craigie 1976, 378, n. 19.

as containing unredacted vestiges of a different world view with each nation having its own god.

**Deuteronomy 6.4** has indeed been referred to as 'the fundamental mono-theistic dogma of the OT',[84] but Smith argues that it references YHWH as the one main god for Israel. The verse is:

שְׁמַע יִשְׂרָאֵל יְהוָה אֱלֹהֵינוּ יְהוָה אֶחָד

⁴ Hear, O Israel: The LORD is our God, the LORD alone.

The primary debate is over the meaning of אֶחָד (one/alone). Zechariah 14.9 reads this verse as teaching monotheism and that is certainly consistent with it. However, the emphasis in context is not that YHWH is the one main god for Israel, but that Israel is the one main people for YHWH. As such, Israel is called to be absolutely faithful to this God. YHWH is singular and unified, and Israel is to be singular and unified in her allegiance to YHWH. As has been noted, the great theme of Deuteronomy is one God, one people, one land.

Smith's attention to texts is welcome; however, again and again we have seen how he fails to read the texts referred to with close attention to their literary nature. We saw above that the literary dimension of the OT is one element of the threefold cord that is essential to an OT hermeneutic, and a criterion for validating readings of the OT will be the extent to which the literary, historical and theological are integrated. In my opinion, the sort of readings Smith pro-poses fail this test. Above we have noted as well how revealing intertextuality can be. With Psalm 82 we saw how the historical, literary and theological can combine to provide a fresh insight into what Psalm 82 is doing. Postmodern-ism challenged the hegemony of historical criticism but without providing an alternative paradigm. Thus, as it has waned, historical criticism has remained in place as the default mode of OT studies. At many points Smith's argument reflects this in its dependence on the identification of sources or redactional layers in texts without noting or investigating how a literary reading might challenge such speculative reconstructions.

*(b) One god?* Smith finds a parallel to Israel's one-god world view in Neo-Assyrian (Aššur) and Babylonian (Marduk) religious developments. The sorts of views Smith leans on are ones we have already discussed under the Assyrian world view. Porter assesses such views and concludes, for example, of Aššur,

---

84   Craigie 1976, 169, referencing Rupprecht 1964.

that 'even he remains one god among many, confirming the Assyrians' inerad-
icable belief in the multiplicity of the divine'.[85] This makes Smith's view of the
comparability between movements in ANE cultures and Israel's construction
of monotheism far less persuasive. The irony in Smith's position should also
be noted. In his view, it is their experience of *empire* that pushes Assyria and
Babylonia towards a one-god world view. By contrast, Israel is said to move in
the same direction as she experiences *catastrophe and exile and diminution.*

*(c) World view.* A fascinating aspect of Smith's 2008 book is his use of the
word 'worldview', which is pervasive throughout the book. Alas, it is never
defined and nor does it occur in the Index. One result of this unconscious use
of a word which, as noted above, has a significant history is that Smith is able
to set out a developmental view of Israel's move towards monotheism without
flagging contradictions. However, the contradictions or alternative, contradictory world views are real. A world view which sees YHWH as one national god
among a multitude of others is very, very different from a world view whose
bottom line is that YHWH alone is God. The one cannot, in my view, be blurred
into the other as part of a traditioning process. These two different world views
compete in such a way that is irreducible. This is not, of course, to say that a
polytheist cannot become a monotheist or to deny that we might have in the
OT moves from implicit to explicit monotheism, but it is to say that a polytheist would need to *become* a monotheist, and we would need to account for this
radical transformation in perspective or world view.

*(d) Duality.* World view can also be leveraged in an assessment of Smith's
approach. He is refreshingly candid about his own religious commitments,
as noted above, something that we still see far too little of in the OT guild.
Smith is helpfully alert to the 'unwritten rule' in modern biblical studies that
religious experience is to be avoided. Smith refers to his own approach as a
double-lenses one which seeks to take theology and history of religions seriously, arguing that they can enrich each other. Smith acknowledges his Catholicism but, as noted above, describes it unusually as an incarnational Christianity that senses God through the creation rather than outside it.

Smith sees 'duality' as a feature of his approach, but duality is hard if not
impossible to integrate into a coherent world view. What is noticeable is that
nowhere in his analysis of how Israel's 'construction' of monotheism developed does Smith *ever* invoke or refer to *divine action*, leading one to wonder

---

85   Porter 2000, 269.

what view of God Smith works with. Perhaps this reflects Smith's immanent understanding of Catholicism, but his affirmation of theology would lead one to expect some reflection on revelation as a key element through which Israel comes to know God. The Catholic *Dei Verbum*, for example, states clearly that:

> Through the patriarchs, and after them through Moses and the prophets, He [God] taught this people to acknowledge Himself the one living and true God, provident father and just judge, and to wait for the Savior promised by Him, and in this manner prepared the way for the Gospel down through the centuries.[86]

Alas, neither this nor any critical engagement with it is to be found in Smith's writing, so that his work represents a history-of-religions approach rather than a theological one, with any place for divine action replaced by development, traditioning, Israelite 'construction', the ANE influences and so on. Doubtless, all of these are important elements, but the elephant in the room is God. Smith notes that '[in] our time, the very use of God-language is under siege',[87] but, in my view, it seems to remain under siege in Smith's assessment of translatability.

*(e) Historical-critical bias.* As has become typical of historical criticism, P is seen as post-exilic and the source of Israel's most profound insights at the point where Israel was at a very low ebb. I have noted elsewhere the strangeness of such a view, for we would expect a literature to emerge at high points of Israel's existence rather than when she was in such a forlorn state. By 'high points' I mean times of major divine action and revelation such as the exodus and Sinai events. The reason for so much of this is that even the *possibility* of divine action gets bracketed out, and Smith's approach is no exception. Nowhere, for example, does he discuss the Sinai event and its influence on Israel's view of God as expressed in the OT.

*(f) Modern bias.* Smith is conscious that our modern answers are not always better than ancient ones. The following quote is the epigraph for Smith's Chapter 4 and is also discussed in his Epilogue: 'Culture hides much more than it reveals, and strangely enough what it hides, it hides most effectively from its

---

86  <www.vatican.va/archive/hist_councils/ii_vatican_council/documents/vat-ii_const_19651118_dei-verbum_en.html>.

87  Smith 2008, 337.

own participants.'[88] The question becomes: what does the modern guild of OT studies hide from its practitioners? As I seek to argue in this volume, for all its advances it hides a great deal. Are there, we might ask, ways in which the editors of the OT might be better informed and more insightful than us moderns? Here I provide one example.

In his useful analysis of the religion of the patriarchs, Wenham concludes that the patriarchs worshipped the Semitic high God El. He notes that:

> The writer of Genesis identifies the patriarchs' El with Yahweh and prefers to use the latter term when describing divine activity, yet in reporting the words of God to the patriarchs he uses Yahweh very sparingly suggesting that he wanted to transmit the traditional form of the promises, not create divine words *ex nihilo*.[89]

Such a view is anathema to many modern OT scholars, but *what if* the author/s of Genesis was right? The use of 'El' acknowledges that YHWH came to the patriarchs wrapped in their cultural and religious idioms, but the narrator insists that the one they encountered as El was in fact YHWH.

# 3 Conclusion

When I began work on translatability it was with a sense of just how complex is this issue. It *is* complex, but having worked on it I am struck by this fact: so much of what we find in the OT depends on how we approach it. We arrive at the meaning of OT texts *through their poetics*, and this alerts us to the importance of the literary strand in OT interpretation. The recovery of the Bible as literature, from the 1970s onwards, has radical and far-reaching implications for historical criticism. Alas, before the literary turn could be fully appropriated, the postmodern turn was upon us, and this has meant that as the postmodern turn retreats, historical criticism has remained the default mode of mainstream OT scholarship. Above, we have seen, again and again, how taking seriously the literary shape of texts calls into question results that are dependent on historical-critical analysis.

It is important to note that one cannot have it both ways. One way the OT guild has handled the literary turn is to see reading the OT as literature as one among a smorgasbord of methods. From this perspective, the historical

---

88   Hall 1959, 1981, 29. 1959 edn quoted by Smith 2008, 187, 334.
89   Wenham 1980, 184.

critical is one, the literary another, and so on. The problem with this is not only that the different methods produce contradictory results but also that you cannot read the Bible historically apart from taking its literary shape seriously, and you cannot analyse its literary nature without being conscious that this is historical, ANE literature that you are analysing. Whether acknowledged or not, the literary, historical and kerygmatic are interwoven, and any approach which ignores this is destined to assume, albeit unconsciously, positions on the other strands.

We have engaged with Smith in detail because he engages critically with Assmann's notion of the Mosaic distinction, defending in the process a move in the OT from polytheism – for that is what it is, with YHWH being Israel's god among many other national gods – to monotheism very late in the history of Israel. Smith's work is helpful in that it allows us to take a close look at the textual evidence in the OT proffered for such an approach. As will be clear from our assessment of it above, I do not find Smith's case persuasive.

In a sense this section has been an important ground-clearing exercise, showing that the sort of evidence used against the Mosaic distinction is not persuasive. However, we now need to move on to the positive portrayal of YHWH in the OT in order to fill out our understanding of the Mosaic distinction with biblical content.

Part 4

# THE GOD WHO APPROACHES

# 8

# God in/and the Old Testament: the living God

## 1 Introduction

Having defended the Mosaic distinction against many of its criticisms, we now turn to attend to YHWH himself, as he is portrayed in the OT. There are many different ways to approach the question of God in the OT. An obvious way would be to focus on the 6,288 uses of the name YHWH. However, the revelation of God as YHWH is particularly associated with the events of the exodus and Sinai, and thus we will begin not with YHWH but with the *logically* prior description of God as 'the living God'.

## 2 The living God

Many of us may be familiar with the evocative expression 'the living God', from the NT. In fact, it is more common in the OT and it is very instructive. אֱלֹהִים חַיִּים / אֵל־חַי (living God) occurs 15 times in the OT, two of which are in Aramaic sections of Daniel (6.21, 27(20, 26)).[1] Related to this, however, is the oath formula 'as YHWH lives' (חַי־יְהֹוָה), which occurs some 67 times. In all of the former passages, God is referred to as 'ēl or Elohim, as above. By comparison, 'ēl or Elohim only occurs twice in oath texts, namely in Job 27.2 and 2 Samuel 2.27.[2]

Mettinger notes that:

YHWH went from Sinai to Canaan; this step introduced a new, highly dramatic section in God's 'biography.' It is a chapter that deals with a fascinating trial of strength between YHWH and the gods of Canaan; and

---

1   Note the informative context of these references, namely Daniel's impending death by being thrown into the lions' den.
2   See Mettinger 1988, 91, for the data.

the God of Israel emerged from this trial with three new names written on his banner: 'the living God,' 'the King.' And 'YHWH Sabaoth.'[3]

In Canaanite religion, and in the Baal Cycle in particular, the myth of the dying and rising god, of Baal and Mot, is central. This myth involves a projection of the seasons of agriculture on to the world of the gods. It is possible that Elijah's mocking of Baal in 1 Kings 18.27 as asleep and needing to be awakened refers to this myth.[4] Widengren argued that YHWH is portrayed similarly in the OT,[5] pointing to similarities between phrases such as 'YHWH lives' and 'mightiest Baal lives', as well as references to God sleeping (Ps. 78.65–66).

However, the OT nowhere claims that YHWH has died. Only in Habakkuk 1.12 is death connected with YHWH and here such a possibility is negated (לֹא נָמוּת?). In terms of YHWH and the Canaanite background, Hosea 1.10 and following are important. In 1.10 it will be said of those of whom it was said לֹא־עַמִּי (not my people) that they will be בְּנֵי אֵל־חָי (children of the living God). In 2.7(5) and 2.18(16) the Israelites are judged for their idolatry in the quest for agricultural fertility. Mettinger notes of this contrast between YHWH and Baal that it yields a profound insight about the difference between YHWH and Canaanite Baal. YHWH was *not* a projection from below of seasonal changes on to the world of the gods. He is elevated above the world of the changing seasons and has ruled the process of history from the very beginning. As such he can use destruction and droughts for his purposes. Activities assigned by Canaanites to Baal and Mot were combined in YHWH.[6]

According to Mettinger, the vegetation myth expressed the basic character of Canaanite religion, but

> [w]hen we examine the Old Testament's expressions about 'the living God' of Israel against this background, our attention is drawn to an important feature of Israel's faith: *history* comprised the radius of action of 'the living God.' In several passages it is the special quality of 'the living God' that he intervenes in history; he manifests himself on the arena of salvation history.[7]

---

3  Mettinger 1988, 82.

4  Mettinger 1988, 84. See Mettinger 1988, 84, for references to the burial and resuscitation of the god in Phoenician inscriptions.

5  Widengren 1955.

6  Mettinger 1988, 85–6.

7  Mettinger 1988, 86. Emphasis original.

In Joshua 3.10–11 God is referred to as the living God in relation to his action in history in driving the Canaanites out of the land. In verse 11 his role as 'the Lord of all the earth' (אֲדוֹן כָּל־הָאָרֶץ) is foregrounded, perhaps a deliberate and polemical alternative to Baal, who is described in the Baal Cycle as 'lord of the earth'.

In the David and Goliath narrative in 1 Samuel 17, David in verse 26 speaks of 'the armies of the living God' (מַעַרְכוֹת אֱלֹהִים חַיִּים). Mettinger detects in verse 46 a polemical allusion to Baal's threshing of Mot and leaving his body available to the birds of the air: 'I will give the dead bodies of the Philistine army to the birds of the air and to the wild animals of the earth, *so that all the earth may know that there is a God in Israel*' (וְיֵדְעוּ כָּל־הָאָרֶץ כִּי יֵשׁ אֱלֹהִים לְיִשְׂרָאֵל). In contrast with the Baal Cycle, this text speaks about God intervening in history as the living God. Mettinger acknowledges the close parallel between the expression 'YHWH lives' as in Psalm 18.47(46) (חַי־יְהוָה), for example, and 'mightiest Baal lives', but the contexts of these expressions differ radically: 'Once again it is in the field of history in which "the living God" is manifest.'[8]

The metaphor of God sleeping is found in the Psalms (e.g. Ps. 78.65), but, as Mettinger notes, here, as opposed to in the Baal myth, it is not related to renewing the vegetation but to God acting in history to vanquish his enemies.[9] Generally, such language is found in laments, with the metaphor of God sleeping used to call on him to act in history (cf. Ps. 44.24–25(23–24)). Mettinger thinks that the language about God awakening and sleeping may derive from the Baal Cycle but it is now put to different use. 'These texts nowhere speak of God's death; what they offer us are expressive metaphors for God as the *Deus absconditus*, the hidden God, the God who "hides himself" (Isa 45:15).'[10] We must therefore reject Widengren's thesis. Indeed, according to Mettinger, '[a]mong the divine names used by Israel's neighbors it is difficult to find anything comparable'.[11]

Jeremiah 10.10a is an evocative verse with three major descriptions of YHWH:

וַיהוָה אֱלֹהִים אֱמֶת הוּא־אֱלֹהִים חַיִּים וּמֶלֶךְ עוֹלָם

But the LORD is the true God;
    he is the living God and the everlasting King.

---

8   Mettinger 1988, 88.

9   Mettinger 1988, 89.

10  Mettinger 1988, 89.

11  Mettinger 1988, 90.

YHWH is the true or genuine God, he is the living God, and he is the king for ever. In Jeremiah 10.1–16 the Mosaic distinction is clearly articulated – לֹא־כְאֵלֶּה חֵלֶק יַעֲקֹב (not like these [the idols] is the portion of Jacob, v. 16) – and in the process a further, obvious aspect of YHWH – his being the living God – comes to the forefront. The lifelessness of the idols of the nations – וְלֹא־רוּחַ בָּם (there is no breath in them, v. 14) – is referred to repeatedly in this passage, forming a stark contrast with YHWH as the God who is alive. For all the ingenuity of the craftsmen involved in sculpting the idols and overlaying them in fine metals and clothing, they are unable to move (v. 4), to speak or to walk (v. 5), and thus are not to be feared. The well-known word from Ecclesiastes *hebel*, here meaning 'vacuous', is used to describe the cultic laws of the peoples – כִּי־חֻקּוֹת הָעַמִּים הֶבֶל (for the statutes of the people are *hebel*, 10.3). NRSV translates חֻקּוֹת as 'customs', but it more likely has the meaning of statutes or laws and in context these clearly relate to the cultus. An obvious point that is too often missed must be noted here. As the living God, YHWH is well able to move and to speak.[12] Jeremiah 10 also clearly emphasizes YHWH as creator.

It may be, as Mettinger proposes, that contact with Baal and his myths led to the description of YHWH as the living God, but the picture of YHWH in Jeremiah 10 alerts us to the fact that from the earliest times contact with this God would have alerted the Israelites to the fact that he is alive, that is, the living God. The patriarchs encountered God as living, and certainly the confrontation with Pharaoh, the exodus and the Sinai event, as well as the fact that God dwelt among his people in the tabernacle, would all have left the Israelites in no doubt whatsoever that YHWH is the living God. Of course, much of the historicity of these events is doubted by many OT scholars, and the question of God is too often bracketed out of OT scholarship.

For our purposes, and the reason we began with God as the living God, is that this description foregrounds God as *the one who acts in history*, as we have seen above. He speaks, he moves and he acts in history, and this acting is placed, at least by Jeremiah but also in many other places, in the context of his being the Creator.

Such language is, of course, anthropomorphic, and Lewis points out just how common *anthropomorphisms* are in relation to God in the OT: 'overall, anthropomorphic descriptions of Yahweh are ever present.'[13] Apart from genitalia, the OT has no reservations about describing YHWH in human terms.

---

12  See Bartholomew 2020 for an examination of the view that God cannot speak.
13  Lewis 2020, 289.

According to Lewis, J presents YHWH in strongly anthropomorphic terms whereas P stresses YHWH's transcendence. J speaks of YHWH as:

- forming Adam out of clay (Gen. 2.7);
- planting the garden of Eden (Gen. 2.8);
- walking in Eden (Gen. 3.8);
- making garments (Gen. 3.21);
- sealing the door to the ark (Gen. 7.16);
- smelling an aroma (Gen. 8.21);
- and so on.

If we juxtapose this mountain of anthropomorphism with the aniconic tradition in the OT, and the places where authors reflect more critically on anthropomorphism – Lewis refers to Numbers 12 and Ezekiel in particular – then it is not too surprising that Lewis discerns considerable diversity of emphasis in the OT. He relates this primarily to the development of the diverse traditions of the OT over centuries. In my view, other explanations are more persuasive.

There is no doubt that the OT unreservedly uses anthropomorphic language for God. Such language is, however, regularly juxtaposed with the aniconic tradition in the OT. Exodus 20.2–4 is one of the strongest expressions of aniconism but is surrounded in 19—24 and beyond by descriptions of God in anthropomorphic terms, not least in relation to divine action. Are we to discern diverse emphases here or complementary ones? In my opinion they are complementary. The aniconic tradition resists the danger of extrapolating from the anthropomorphisms to the view of God as a giant human being. The anthropomorphisms, by comparison, resist extrapolating God's refusal to allow images of him towards transcendence *without* immanence. Anthropomorphic language allows for an emphasis on and the embrace of God's deep involvement in human affairs and in his world.

From an OT perspective, anthropomorphic language for God should not be too surprising. The aversion to anthropomorphic language for the divine that we find in Maimonides and parts of the classical theist tradition stems from a philosophical view of God as so 'other' that such language becomes inappropriate and primitive. Once, however, we embrace the OT view of creation, we expect continuity between God and his creation, and not least between God and his image-bearers, namely humans. From an OT perspective, humans are as they are because God has made them thus, and this making is good.

To know God, we need not 'just' divine action but also interpretation of it, and such interpretation inevitably resorts to anthropomorphisms and metaphors. Indeed, *our knowledge of God stems from such action and its interpretation*, and thus we begin our exploration of the God of the OT from this perspective, rather than, for example, beginning with philosophical speculation such as we find in Aquinas.[14]

# 3 Historical narrative and the living God of the Old Testament

If God is the living God who acts in history, then it is, of course, to the historical narratives of the OT that we need to look to find out what such action looks like. Alas, these narratives have been challenged and subverted again and again in relation to divine action. In my *God Who Acts in History*, I examine Spinoza's and Kant's dismissal of the historical narratives as significant for our view of God, and show that they arrive at such a view not through careful examination of the narratives but simply through reading them through the lens of the philosophy of religion and a philosophical view of God. The question thus arises of whether there is a far better doctrine of God available that is informed by the OT and can inform our reading of the OT. In my view, Gunton is exceptionally helpful here.

In Chapter 5 we discussed both the OT and the doctrine of God *and* the doctrine of God in the OT. These two elements are integrally and dialectically related. I say 'dialectically' because if we are to read the OT through the lens of a Christian world view then we need to bring to our reading a robust sense of God, that is, a doctrine of God. However, as we noted in Chapter 5, there is at the same time a great need for our doctrine of God to be informed by and reformulated through input from the OT. This circularity or dialectic is unavoidable, and in this section we will use Gunton's critique of the sort of classical theism typical of Aquinas to show how taking God as the living God reformulates our view of God, and thereby provides us with a rich doctrine of God that we can bring to our reading of the OT, not least the historical narratives. Part of our argument in this book is that we must take the theological or kerygmatic dimension of the OT seriously, and thus I make no apology for this foray into historical theology, strange and complex as it may strike the reader! I will try to make the argument as clear as I can.

---

14   See Bartholomew 2020.

Aquinas's doctrine of God in his *Summa Theologica* is that of classical theism or 'perfect being' theology. Perfect being theology makes two assumptions about God:

- God is the most perfect being;
- human reason is able to and should use philosophy to explain God as the most perfect being.[15]

Gunton is a well-known critic of classical theism.[16] Intriguingly, he identifies a major weakness in its doctrine of God and in the post-Reformation hybrids of it in their failure to take the OT sufficiently seriously. 'It is when Christian theology becomes dependent on the philosophers' speculations rather than on the equivalent Old Testament polemics against paganism that the troubles begin.'[17] For Gunton it is a tragedy, almost a crime, that the OT was pushed aside by classical theism in favour of Greek philosophy as the basis for our doctrine of God. This is particularly the case when it comes to the divine attributes or how we think about God.

Gunton points out that in the OT we already find a strong polemic against the pagan anthropomorphisms of Israel's surrounding nations, and that theology gets into trouble when it depends on philosophical speculation rather than such OT polemics. As a symptom of there being a problem with classical theism, Gunton highlights the fact that prior to the Reformation there was no substantial treatment of God's holiness, a characteristic of God that it could be argued is central to any biblical/OT account of the divine attributes, and one to which we will come below.[18]

Central to Gunton's critique of classical theism is its inadequate *doctrine of creation*, again an area where the witness of the OT is crucial, albeit contested.[19] Pseudo-Dionysius and his followers with their preference for negative theology situate timeless, metaphysical causality over against the temporal and economical depiction of God's action in his world, thereby undermining the OT emphasis on God as the living God who acts in history. In this way, the spiritual or intellectual is set against the materiality of creation and the comprehensive witness of the OT gets seriously reduced, whereas

---

15  Rogers 2000, vii.
16  See Bartholomew 2020 for a much fuller discussion.
17  Gunton 2002, 6.
18  cf. Brunner 1949, 157–82.
19  See Ashford and Bartholomew 2020.

this is a false dichotomy: the true distinction is between Creator and the created. The material, from this perspective, is as spiritual as the abstract and intellectual.

Gunton naturally agrees with classical theism that metaphors describing God in terms of created things – rocks, fortresses, lions and so on – have to be treated as metaphors. The difference emerges in what we make of them theologically. If our language must be purified of reference to material things then it will be rationalized and all references to the created world will be demythologized. A theology of language should recognize that words are part of God's good creation, and that God has empowered certain humans to use words to speak truthfully about God. Barth notes that:

> The further we move away from the witness of the Holy Scriptures to the sphere of general conjectures about God, so much the purer, we think, is the air of thought, i.e., so much the less do we need the anthropomorphisms which are found to be particularly suspect. But, if it lets itself be guided by its object, theology ought to try to evade these anthropomorphisms least of all.[20]

Insightfully, Barth observes that abstract concepts are just as much anthropomorphic as those developed from concrete, material perception. Gunton also, in true Reformed manner, alerts us to the need to take the effect of the fall of human reason seriously, as well as the influence of redemption on reason.

Classical theism manifests an excessive reliance on sight, whereas, for Gunton, '[w]e do not see God, but we are given to know his essence, who and what he is'.[21] Gunton argues that to think of God mainly in terms of intellect, an emphasis we see in Thomas, results in a conception of God at odds with the biblical rendition of God according to which God is mainly known *through his particular acts in history*, that is, as the living God. God certainly does not lack intellect, but his intellect is grasped in relation to wisdom, through practical intellect directed towards involvement in the world.

For Gunton, 'an adequate doctrine of creation will affirm that the creator makes a world that is other than he, but not opposed to him – apart from sin, that is. The negative theology runs the risk, if not more, of identifying existence with fallenness.'[22]

---

20  Barth, *CD* II/1, 222.
21  Gunton 2002, 37.
22  Gunton 2002, 47.

Classical theism tends to restrict its focus to cosmology rather than attending to the divine economy. Thomas sets up his framework in the Five Ways through a general philosophical analysis with the rest flowing logically. According to Gunton, such an approach is in danger of collapsing into Spinoza's pantheism or Kant's idealism. If the negative way is pushed, one ends up with the unknowable God of Kant. 'In certain essential respects, Kant's theology is but that of Aquinas radicalized. Kant is the fate of the negative theology transposed into a mechanistic world.'[23] To see God as pure intellect risks denigrating the materiality of creation and takes the focus away from the knowledge of God that comes to us through the narratives of God's involvement with Israel, climaxing in the Incarnation.

In our discussion above we have seen the growing recognition in OT studies of the myriad ways in which the OT polemicizes against the world views and deities of surrounding nations. Gunton thus rightly points out that it was not only the Greeks who developed critiques of anthropomorphic gods but also the Israelites, and the latter is very different from the Greek approach grounded in cosmological philosophy. The Israelite version proceeds largely by assertion and not by negation. Gordon Wenham and others have shown how this is the case in Genesis 1—2, in which the author not only says no to pagan world views but also provides a positive, constructive view of God, of his power, sovereignty, creativity and goodness. Gunton argues that the flood saga in Genesis 6—9 can and should be read as an account of God's immutability in Barth's sense of God's constancy. Like Genesis 1—2, Genesis 6—9 is also directed polemically against alternative, pagan accounts, in this case of the Flood.

Following Barth, Gunton proposes that we start with revelation and the divine economy and then ask what the divine attributes look like in this context and how they relate to the traditional concept of classical theism.

> Thus, while the first question concerns the relation of God's act and his being, the second is about his being and, accordingly, the attributes which are revealed in action. If God is in his act, then the questions are essentially the same, or different aspects of the same.[24]

In Scripture God is truly rendered to us narratively and creedally: in the narratives of his actions and in the creed-like summaries of those actions.

---

23   Gunton 2002, 53.
24   Gunton 2002, 77.

Both need to be attended to closely. Neglect of the narratives neglects the historical contexts of God's actions; neglect of the creedal statements risks losing touch with the being of God. A Trinitarian starting point means that for Gunton we must confess that *God is knowable*:

> Therefore what may seem, in the light of much of the Christian tradition, to be an outrageous claim must be made: that it is part of the Christian claim to truth that human beings are given to know the being of God.[25]

God is unknowable only in the sense that we cannot provide a fully rational account of his being. We can agree with Thomas that God is known only by his effects, but only if his effects include historical revelation. 'Salvation depends on the unflinching affirmation that the God who meets us in the Son and the Spirit is the only God there is.'[26] Humans are open to God not primarily because we have intellect but because, like God, we too are persons. We should not drive a gulf between the Trinity of the divine economy and a God who lurks behind the divine economy who may be very different from the Trinity. In other language, the immanent and the economic Trinity must be held together, affirming that God is eternally this way.

This discussion takes us into the deep waters of philosophy and theology in relation to the doctrine of God. Our purpose in introducing this discussion at this point is to underscore our approach to the question of God in the OT through the insight from above, namely that YHWH is *the living God who acts in history*. The significance of this must not be missed. As complex as is the above argument, it should be clear to the reader that the sort of doctrine of God Gunton articulates builds on just such a foundation, and allows us to expect God's action in history as the living God and as the means by which we come to know him. This orients us towards historical narrative of divine action in the OT in a particular and positive way, and one that is very different from those of Spinoza and Kant, major figures in the origin of historical criticism.[27] Of course, it means even more that we need to do very hard work on these narratives.

Gunton argues that when classical theism is radicalized, one approaches the unknowable God of Spinoza and Kant. What needs to be noted, in relation to their contributions to the development of historical criticism of the OT, is that

---

25  Gunton 2002, 111.

26  Gunton 2002, 93.

27  See Bartholomew 2020.

both Spinoza – with his pantheistic monism – and Kant – with his religion of morality – unashamedly bring their doctrines of God to bear on how they read the OT.[28] In both cases, this leads to a marginalization and denigration of historical narratives of divine action without ever making an argument for such an approach to the OT narratives. Of course, if they can do that, why cannot we bring the sort of doctrine of God articulated by Gunton to bear on the OT and read it through such a lens?

Despite repeated denials that historical criticism is shaped integrally by philosophy (of religion), the evidence overwhelmingly confirms that it is. De Wette, for example, often regarded as the father of modern biblical criticism, read Kant voraciously before going to the University of Jena and, having been converted to the Kantian paradigm, spent his life trying to rethink religion and the OT within that context. When one examines Spinoza and Kant in this respect, as I do in detail in my *God Who Acts*, a remarkable insight comes to the fore. Spinoza and Kant rejected historical narrative and its importance in the OT not because they carefully analysed it and found it wanting, but because they read it through the grid of their philosophical systems, pantheistic monism in Spinoza's case, and idealism in Kant's case.

Our discussion above of God as the living God shows that the OT itself resists such a move, and pantheistic monism and Kantian idealism are not the only philosophical shows in town. Reject the lenses that they bring to the OT, embrace a different view of God and religion such as that of Gunton, and the role of history in the OT is wide open for discussion once again. Alvin Plantinga, for example, has argued, against Kant's creative anti-realism, that it is not we who are ultimately creative, but God. And, of course, nothing could be further from Spinoza's concept of God, whom he equates with nature in a determinist system, than the living God of the OT. As we will see below, Plantinga is a luminary amid a remarkable renaissance in Christian philosophy and there is every reason both philosophically *and* theologically to retain a commitment to divine action in history as we approach the OT.

# 4 The living God and metaphor

The OT portrayal of God is metaphorical through and through. Aristotle is well known for his view of metaphor as ornamental so that metaphorical language can always be replaced with literal language. The implication of this

---

28  See Bartholomew 2020; 2015; 1998.

is that theoretical, scientific language must be purified of all metaphor. Such an approach would make us wary of trusting the OT depiction of God and incline us towards a classical theist perspective. However, the recent decades of intense study of metaphor have revealed that metaphor is far more than ornamental or a mere literary trope. All language contains metaphors, including that of scientific and philosophical theories. Thus, and this is a very importance consequence, the fact that God is depicted in the OT with a great variety of metaphors by no means renders such depictions unreliable. In their own way metaphors refer, and the metaphors of God in the OT yield a rich and true knowledge of him.[29]

It is important that we understand how metaphors work. Cognitive linguistics defines metaphor as 'understanding one conceptual domain in terms of another conceptual domain'.[30] The source domain is the one we draw from in order to understand in new ways the target domain. In the light of this new understanding Goodman defines metaphor as follows:

> Briefly, a metaphor is an affair between a predicate with a past and an object that yields while protesting . . . Where there is metaphor, there is conflict . . . Application of a term is metaphorical only if to some extent contra-indicated.[31]

If recent studies have subverted the literary versus metaphorical distinction, a danger of 'all language is metaphorical' is to reduce everything to metaphor and thus metaphor to nothing. Distinctions need to be made between different types of metaphorical language and not least in relation to literary texts. Lakoff, Turner and Gibbs explain that poets use a variety of devices to create unusual language and images, devices such as extending, elaboration, questioning and combining.[32] To these Kövecses adds personification, image metaphors, and megametaphors or extended metaphors.[33] As Semino and Steen note: 'While the formalist view of metaphor as linguistic deviation can no longer be sustained, the idea that some metaphorical expressions are more foregrounded than others remains highly relevant, and is not at all incompatible with more recent cognitive approaches.'[34]

---

29  See our discussion of critical realism and theology in Part 2 above.
30  Kövecses 2010, 4.
31  Goodman 1976, 69.
32  Lakoff and Turner 1989; Gibbs 1994.
33  Kövecses 2010, 55–9.
34  Semino and Steen 2008, 238.

Semino and Steen also note that some scholars have drawn attention to the way in which an author's use of metaphorical patterns reflects the individual's world view.[35] Context has also come to be seen to be vital for metaphor.

Megametaphors are found primarily in literary texts. 'They are large-scale metaphors . . . "behind" a text that underlie other, more local metaphors (called 'micrometaphors'). Their cognitive function is to organize the local metaphors into a coherent metaphorical structure in the text.'[36] Metaphor is the building block of world construction, and in Proverbs 1—9, for example, a world view is evoked through the repetition of metaphors: the two types of love, the two paths or ways, the two women – Lady Folly and Lady Wisdom – and the culmination of 1—9 in the two houses (Prov. 9) with the two invitations and the two meals. Such world construction generally operates with a 'root' or basic metaphor, and a variety of root metaphors have been proposed for the world construction in Proverbs.[37] The root metaphor organizes and provides for the coherence of the 'surface' metaphors.

This leads us on to a megametaphor for YHWH, namely as the king.

## 5 YHWH as king

Mettinger poses the question 'What is the center of the Old Testament understanding of God?' He responds: 'Although this question is not an easy one to answer, nevertheless the idea of the Lord as "King" can stake a claim to a position of importance.'[38] He notes the metaphorical nature of this description of God and argues that it functions as a root metaphor which opens out into a network of other metaphors, namely those associated with the Temple, the heavenly court, the armies of God and the Day of YHWH.

The kingship of the Lord, then, provides an organizational matrix for a whole cosmos of ideas. This understanding of God lies beneath the surface of numerous texts, even of some that do not use 'king,' 'to rule,' 'throne,' and so forth.[39]

---

35   Semino and Steen 2008, 239.

36   Kövecses 2010, 325.

37   cf. Pepper 1942.

38   Mettinger 1988, 92.

39   Mettinger 1988, 93.

Mettinger rightly rejects the view that YHWH as king is a projection from the Israelite monarchy; it precedes the emergence of kingship in Israel.

Mettinger attends to the period of the judges in particular and explores the Baal Cycle as background for this evocative metaphor. In the Baal Cycle both El and Baal are referred to as king, but whereas El's kingship is more static, Baal's is more dynamic. Israel's literature lacks anything like the Baal myths, but she utilizes pieces of the mosaic – motifs such as victory over chaos, acclamation of Baal as king and the building of a palace for Baal. According to Mettinger, when we examine the OT in the light of the Baal Cycle we uncover a deep, structural dimension that illuminates some OT texts with a surprising coherence. YHWH as king is at the heart of this structure and this in three ways: YHWH's battle against the forces of chaos, YHWH's kingship which is established through fighting and defeating evil, and YHWH's temple, the visible sign of his rule. Mettinger uses this analysis to open up the OT root metaphor of YHWH as king.[40]

One thing that the metaphor of YHWH as king maps on to the domain of God is that kings go into battle, as we have seen again and again in our review of the world views of the ANE. YHWH enters into battle, and Mettinger identifies three major areas of battle.

First, he speaks of *YHWH's creation battle*. He notes that in Psalm 74.12 the statement that 'God my King is from of old' is followed by this type of battle in verses 13–17. 'In other words, the text presents God as a king in battle with the forces of chaos. Through its very existence and by virtue of its beauty and purposeful design, the creation proclaims God's victory over chaos.'[41] Mettinger foregrounds the importance of the noun גְּעָרָה (rebuke) and the verb גָּעַר (to rebuke) in this sort of passage (cf. Ps. 104.7). In Psalm 104.26 we appear to have a conscious demythologization of the monsters of chaos: 'In brief, Leviathan has been reduced to the more modest dimensions of a household pet; this is no doubt an example of the Israelite demythologization of a Canaanite motif, which has been realized with rare humoristic appropriateness!'[42]

Second, Mettinger attends to the *Zion battle*. In Psalm 24.1, 7, 9 God's creation and his entrance into the Temple are juxtaposed, and in verse 8 YHWH is described as 'mighty in battle'. The word for temple can also be translated as 'palace', and indeed the Temple's architecture and furniture imply it is such, and Psalm 24 is full of royal imagery. Psalm 48, which celebrates YHWH

---

40   Mettinger 1988, 97.

41   Mettinger 1988, 98.

42   Mettinger 1988, 99–100.

as king and Mount Zion as his city, contains the phrase normally translated as 'Mount Zion, in the far north'. Mettinger argues that it is better translated as 'Mount Zion, the heights of Zaphon'. As we saw above, Mount Zaphon was the home of Baal to the north in Syria, but in Psalm 48 the name has been intentionally applied to Zion, the mountain and temple in Jerusalem.

Psalm 46 is well known for its exhortation in verse 10: 'Be still'. The verb used here (הַרְפּוּ) is sometimes used in the OT with the meaning of 'let your hands fall' (cf. 2 Sam. 24.16) and Mettinger proposes that it might have that meaning here: 'This would then be an admonition to acknowledge the senselessness in attempting to resist the God who possesses ultimate power, as he is the battling King.'[43]

In summary, Mettinger observes of the metaphor of YHWH as king that '[i]t is logical to assume that this root metaphor was especially cultivated in the milieu of the temple, which would help to explain its occurrence in the Psalter and related literature'.[44] Mowinckel's theory[45] that such texts – Psalms 47; 93; 96—99 in particular – in the OT relate to an autumn enthronement festival in Jerusalem comparable to the Babylonian New Year festival is disputed.[46] Mettinger agrees that YHWH is not portrayed as a dying and rising god, but finds the basic elements of Mowinckel's thesis persuasive. He agrees with Mowinckel that יְהוָה מָלָךְ in such psalms should be translated as 'YHWH has become king' and that this is related to cultic ritual. In these psalms in which we find the motif of YHWH's kingship and Zion linked, we also find the motif of the struggle with the peoples, the nations. Mettinger points out that '[t]he motif of the battle with the people implies the "historicization" of the chaos battle'.[47]

Third, Mettinger attends to the *exodus battle*. In Psalm 114, which celebrates the exodus from Egypt, the retreat of the sea and the River Jordan are related to the presence of YHWH. So too in Psalm 77 the exodus is evoked vividly in relation to the waters and the deep (vv. 16–20). In the Baal Cycle we find, comparably, a battle with the sea and the river; however, 'in the biblical texts there is no mention of mythical primeval time, but of God's actions in the history of his people'.[48] Mettinger notes of Psalm 77 that we find in it a re-enactment of God's struggle with the chaos waters:

---

43  Mettinger 1988, 103.

44  Mettinger 1988, 104.

45  Mowinckel 1922.

46  See Mettinger 1988, 119–22. He reviews Mowinckel, Barth, Kraus but draws on Welten 1982 in particular.

47  Mettinger 1988, 105.

48  Mettinger 1988, 105.

The adaptation of the battle motif to the exodus leads to an interesting double exposure of creation (battle motif) and salvation (exodus). This in turn sheds a special light on the biblical miracle: when God acts miraculously, it is as Creator.[49]

If the battle against chaos is historicized in the OT, it is also *eschatologized* in the Day of YHWH. In what is called the Isaiah Apocalypse of Isaiah 24—27, chapter 24 contains strong language describing YHWH's battle against the earth as well as the host of heaven (24.21). There follows in 25.6–8 an exquisite description of the eschatological feast: 'the characterization of the eschatological meal is to be read in the light of the words about the Lord as King. The festivity on Mount Zion is God's coronation banquet!'[50] Mettinger rightly notes that all such language of YHWH's becoming king does not imply that there was a time when YHWH was not king. It evokes instead the fact that in the last days he will dramatically reveal his kingship before all.

Mettinger clearly argues that creation is seen in the OT through the lens of the battle against chaos. However, he is cautious when it comes to articulating the history of the motif:

> I think it is wise to leave open the question whether the motif, as used in Israel, was from the outset connected with the idea of creation. It appears, however, that such a connection is later displayed in texts such as Psalms 74 and 89.[51]

In my view, the battle motif is far more clearly related to the exodus and to God's acts *within* the creation than to *the act of creation itself*. The link between creation in the OT and the *Chaoskampf* motif originated with Gunkel, but it has been questioned in recent times.[52] Undoubtedly, the battle motif blends into and is set in the context of God as the powerful Creator, but this is importantly different from arguing that the act of creation itself is depicted as a battle against chaos. In Psalm 89, for example, the battle language of verses 9–10 is immediately connected with God's creating in verses 11–12, but the battle is against the enemies of David and the Davidic covenant in history. Similarly, in Psalm 74 the battle language of verses 13–15 leads into creation in

---

49  Mettinger 1988, 107.

50  Mettinger 1988, 110.

51  Mettinger 1988, 115.

52  Scurlock and Beal, eds, 2013.

verses 16–17, but the battle itself is about YHWH's past actions in history when he defeated Israel's enemies.

# 6 Psalm 93: YHWH as king: a world view and a view of history

Mettinger's rich analysis alerts us to the fact that while the metaphor of YHWH as king has important parallels in Canaanite religion, an important difference is its *historicization*. YHWH exercises his kingship, *inter alia, by acting in history* as the living God. In this section I follow Hendrikus Berkhof in his *Christ the Meaning of History* by attending to Psalm 93 as one of the royal psalms which embodies an important stage in what Berkhof refers to as 'a growth in the sense of history' in the OT.[53]

**Psalm 93**
[1] YHWH reigns as king / YHWH has become king, he is robed
    in majesty;
  YHWH is robed, he is girded with strength.
He has established the world; it shall never be moved;
    [2] your throne is established from of old;
    you are from everlasting.
[3] The floods have lifted up, YHWH,
    the floods have lifted up their voice;
    the floods lift up their roaring.
[4] More majestic than the thunders of mighty waters,
    more majestic than the waves of the sea,
    majestic on high is YHWH!
[5] Your decrees are very sure;
    holiness befits your house,
    YHWH, for evermore.

Important points to note from Psalm 93 are as follows:

---

53   Berkhof 1966, 53.

- Verse 1a hopes for a revelation of YHWH's kingship, his might *in the present.*[54]
- Verses 1b and 2 base this hope on YHWH *as creator.* According to Berkhof, 'God repeatedly intervenes triumphantly in order to reveal and confirm his kingship because he has executed his kingship over the earth since creation'.[55]
- In verses 2–4 the 'waters' shout and roar. They are 'the world powers which threaten Yahweh's people and work'.[56] YHWH is mightier than these threats and he continually subdues them. In verse 5 the decrees of his kingship are 'very sure' and the Temple ('your house') is a sacramental indication of the reality that the forces of chaos in history cannot threaten his work.
- 'For evermore' (v. 5) contrasts with the time references in verse 2, and embodies a future perspective so that God's reign, his kingship, is active in creation, in history, with a particular focus on Israel, and looks forward as far as one can imagine.

I learned years ago from John Macquarrie that you can discover a great deal about a group's *world view* from their prayers and worship.[57] This is certainly true of Psalm 93 and the kingship psalms of which it is a part. In Psalm 93, in comparison to most psalms of trust, the focus is on YHWH instead of the one worshipping. However, one can, as it were, turn the telescope round the other way or take a cross-section through the psalm to see the world view it express-es of the worshippers. A world view is, as we have seen, expressed at its deepest level as a story, and especially if we translate verse 1a as 'YHWH began to reign . . .' or as 'YHWH became king . . .' we see that a narrative of YHWH, Israel, the worshipper, the nations and the world underlies this psalm.

For our purposes, what is important is that *within* this story and world view centred on the metaphor of YHWH as king, we find expressed *a view of history.* I am not suggesting that we find here a developed *philosophy* of history but that in pre-theoretical terms we find embodied in this psalm a world view which contains a view of history. Key elements in this are:

---

54 The translation of YHWH *mālāk* is contested. Cf. Mettinger 1988, 120–1, for a defence of 'YHWH has become king'.

55 Berkhof 1966, 42.

56 Berkhof 1966, 42. In v. 3 the Hebrew word the NRSV translates as 'floods' is normally rendered 'river' in English. Cf. Horowitz 1998, 2011, 29–30, for the sort of background in 'The Babylonian Map of the World' that might inform such imagery.

57 Macquarrie 1969.

- **The particular God of Israel, namely YHWH.** Psalm 93 speaks about YHWH (vv. 1, 4) and it speaks to YHWH (vv. 2–3, 5). Clearly, he is utterly central to the world view of the worshippers.

- **YHWH as immanently involved in the life of his people.** 'His house', which I take to be a reference to the Temple and Mount Zion, is in their midst, so that as a Jewish author noted, 'God has an address on earth'![58]

- **YHWH as the transcendent Creator.** Note here how YHWH's transcendence and immanence are held together. He established the world but also has a throne and a house.

- **YHWH as king over history, but opposed within history.** If the rivers of verse 3 and the mighty waters and waves of verse 4 are symbols of powerful opposition to YHWH, then we have in Psalm 93 an understanding of history as contested but always remaining under YHWH's control. Theologically, we have here in a nutshell the doctrine of his providence.

- **YHWH as holy and everlasting but able to be called upon by his people.** Here we see YHWH's immanence and transcendence held closely together, as well as his character as holy.

I am well aware that many who follow me thus far will immediately have questions as to the extent to which we can generalize from Psalm 93's view of history to the rest of the Psalter, let alone the OT as a whole. In my view one can,[59] and in this regard the following points should be noted.

Gerald Wilson, J. Clinton McCann, James L. Mays, Patrick Miller and others have done seminal work in enabling us to understand the Psalter as a rich, textured, vital, literary whole. The arguments are detailed and here I merely note that, as Wilson proposes, Books IV–V of the Psalter are the answer to the 'question' posed in Psalm 89. Book IV is the editorial centre of the Psalter with its primary affirmation of YHWH *mālāk*! Few have articulated this as clearly as James Mays:

---

58 Especially because historical critics see Gen. 1.1—2.4a as from the Priestly writer, scholarship on the cultus of Israel has been fertile in noting the connections between cult and creation. See, e.g., Morales, ed., 2014.

59 cf. Miller 2004, 2007a, 214–25.

The coherence and reference of the psalmic language world is based on a sentence on which all that is said in the psalms depends. Everything else is connected to what this one sentence says. It is a liturgical cry that is both a declaration of faith and a statement about reality . . . The sentence is 'Yhwh malak,' 'The LORD reigns.'[60]

Mays explains that:

The reign of God is God's activity as creator and maintainer of the universe, and as judge and savior who shapes the movement of history toward the purpose of God . . . The psalms are, then, the liturgy of the kingdom of God.[61]

The psalms are vehicles for prayer and worship but are also there to instruct and teach, hence the subtitle of Clinton McCann's excellent book, *The psalms as torah.*[62] Mays, as quoted above, perceptively notes that as a liturgical cry the Psalms are both a declaration of faith and a 'statement about reality'. Embedded in this statement about reality is a view of history, as noted above. According to Mays, 'The words of the psalms are the vocabulary of a particular language world. We must by means of the psalms enter and live in that language world if praise and prayer by their words are to be authentic.'[63] I take it as following logically, therefore, that if we appropriate the Psalter authentically, then *we will adopt its view of history.*

Berkhof's point that Psalm 93 reflects an important stage in 'a growth in the sense of history' in the OT is helpful. In the OT we see what one might call a growing focus emerging in the development of a world view. As a theologian, Berkhof's range over the OT is impressive. Personally, I would place greater emphasis on the narrative from Genesis to Kings and on the remarkable significance for history of Genesis 1.1, about which Herrera argues:

The foundational charter of the philosophy of history is found in one biblical verse: 'God, at the beginning of time, created heaven and earth' . . . This text, as traditionally interpreted,[64] shattered the pagan conception

---

60  Mays 1994, 6.
61  Mays 1994, 7.
62  McCann 1993.
63  Mays 2004, 6.
64  The translation of Gen. 1.1 is vigorously contested. See Ashford and Bartholomew 2020.

of an eternal universe parcelled out in an infinity of cycles. That view was voiced by Berossus, the Babylonian astrologer, who maintained that the universe passes through a number of Great Years with each cosmic cycle reproducing that which had preceded it. The doctrine of creation entailing linear time opened a vast horizon of novel events that took history beyond the limits of the ancient chroniclers. Even Herodotus . . . was imprisoned in a circle.[65]

Central to the view of history the OT commits us to is YHWH, this God as creator, redeemer, ruler, sovereign. How might this change OT studies? In all sorts of ways, but let me provide *an* example. The exclusion of YHWH from OT studies and the adoption of a history-of-religions approach has had a profound effect on studies of the development of the OT canon with an immense amount of energy devoted to trying to work out the *terminus ad quem* of the canonical process. With this has come, ironically, a tendency to see Israel's least vital times – exile and the post-exilic period – as her most creative times in the production of the OT. We will see this immediately below, for example, in Schmid's history-of-religions approach to YHWH.

In contrast, Gunnar Östborn argues in relation to the OT canon:

> As to understanding the question of the assumed canonizations, I should like to stress a matter of importance. There is an opinion, not so seldom advanced, that they are to be regarded as results of certain periods of decline, often, it is true, in a spiritual sense. Nevertheless, even in this case such a view seems to be misleading. I find it more motivated to connect each of these canonizations with a rise of power, and to look upon them as an outcome of ascendancy rather than of wane.[66]

Bringing the statement of reality from Psalm 93 into the picture confirms Östborn's insight. It would, furthermore, reverse our telescope from focusing on the *terminus ad quem* of the canonical process to a focus on the explosion of energy at the point of the *terminus a quo*. If YHWH is for real, if he is the living God and the king, if he can speak and did speak at Sinai, if he continued to speak through the prophets, and so on, then we would approach the issue of the canonical process from a very different perspective from that of a history-of-religions approach. Of course this orientation I am proposing needs

---

65  Herrera 2001, 13.
66  Östborn 1950, 81.

to be worked out in detail in relation to the messy, tough, obscure detail surrounding the history of the OT canon. My point here is one that Stephen Neill makes in relation to NT studies. We need a theology of history, not that it will solve all our problems, but it will create the ring within which solutions may be found.

# 7 YHWH

We come now to the major name of God in the OT, YHWH. As Patrick Miller states, 'the centrality of this deity' and his 'nature and character' are 'at the heart of all the practices of Israelite religion'.[67] Similarly, Lewis points out that our primary data for Israelite religion are centred on YHWH. And, because YHWH is not attested outside Israel, there is not much comparative work to do.

## (a) YHWH and the history of Israelite religion

Despite the assurances by scholars such as Miller and Lewis, disagreement about this mysterious name YHWH continues. Schmid, for example, asserts that:

> In terms of philological history, the etymology of the Yhwh name remains unsettled to this day. To some extent certain is only that it has nothing to do with the Hebrew verb היה (hyh), 'to be,' as suggested by Exod 14. If the divine name has something at all to do with a verbal (and not a nominal) form, then it instead likely arises from the south Semitic hwh, 'fell, blow,' which contains a further indication of the religious historical origins of Yhwh as a storm god.[68]

Mettinger, Moberly and many others, by comparison, agree that if there is one thing we know about the name YHWH, it is that it comes from the Hebrew verb 'to be'.[69]

Although Schmid's German original is entitled *Theologie des Alten Testaments* (Theology of the Old Testament), his approach is that of the history of religions. The difference between Schmid, and Mettinger and Moberly, is related to Schmid's assertion that '[t]he theological explanations of the Bible are to be evaluated in light of their proximity and distance to the religious-historical

---

67  Miller 2000, xviii. Quoted in Lewis 2020, 11.
68  Schmid 2019, 287.
69  Mettinger 1988; Moberly 2020.

evidence'.[70] Schmid acknowledges the ways in which the documentary hypothesis has been challenged but nevertheless states:

> Recent religious-historical scholarship reckons that historical monarchic Israel thought within the normal orientation coordinates of an ancient Near Eastern 'national' religion, and the biblical image of Israel essentially arose from later receptions and interpretations, chiefly from the epochs of Persian-period and Hellenistic Judaism.[71]

Schmid here concurs with Smith that Israel thought of YHWH as a national god during the monarchy.

Schmid appreciates the difficulty of clarifying the history of origins of a deity. He notes that this topic is rarely documented but asserts that when sources address this issue, as in the OT, 'then they in no way display interest in historical illumination'[72] but engage in retrojections or projections from their present understanding. In ways that are comparable to Smith's discernment of earlier layers of belief in OT texts, Schmid claims that the OT contains memories of YHWH as a weather and mountain deity (Judg. 5.4–5; Deut. 33.2; Ps. 68.8–9; Hab. 3.3). Through these hints, '[t]he Bible provides insight into the historically complex process of how one is to think of God'[73] and, for example, of his origin in the south. 'For Deut 33:2 . . . one can assume that the parallelism of "Sinai" and "Se'ir" presents a harmonizing interpretation to reconcile the traditions of the Torah ("Sinai") with the religious-historical memories ("Se'ir").'[74] Schmid notes the centrality of the Sinai theophany in the OT but states: 'It should be maintained, however, that the question of how God reveals himself is determined by certain religious-historical limits.'[75] Lewis similarly concludes that the origin of YHWH is found in the south and is related to a religion of storm gods. Only later did the worship of YHWH connect with that of El Elyon.

Thus, for Schmid, YHWH as a god precedes the existence of Israel. As a god, YHWH has his geographical roots in southern Edomite hill country. Schmid acknowledges that such a view depends on one's view of the origin of Israel. He sides with the theory that she developed through a complex process in Canaan and that her relationship with YHWH emerged between the twelfth and ninth

---

70  Schmid 2019, 279.
71  Schmid 2019, 283.
72  Schmid 2019, 283.
73  Schmid 2019, 285.
74  Schmid 2019, 285.
75  Schmid 2019, 285.

centuries with the result that there is no clear gap between Canaanite and Israelite civilization. In the time of Saul and David, the theophoric elements in names present an uneven picture but they do not witness to monotheism. Canaanite Jerusalem was linked with the solar god, and '[a]s the biblical God, whose roots are as a storm god, becomes solarized over the course of Judaic religious history, he moves into the sphere of a God who creates and guarantees justice'.[76] In relation to monotheism Schmid argues that

> a religion's conception of God is dependent on the particular political circumstances of its circle of devotees, even if the religion . . . is not fully explained by its political circumstances . . . [T]he notion of 'big gods' first develops in socially complex political entities. In monarchies people envision God as king, and the idea of a God ruling over everything presupposes the intellectual influence of empires.[77]

It was the cultural pressure of Assyria that catalysed the development of Israel and Judah into states.

For Schmid, 'the fact that the biblical God bears a name, Yhwh, points to the fact that he arises from a polytheistic context'.[78] Inscriptions that refer to YHWH of Samaria and YHWH of Teman signal the existence of a poly-Yahwism: 'The inscriptions present a picture of the religion of monarchic Israel that is only accessible in mediated fashion in the Bible.'[79] The sort of mono-Yahwism we find in Deuteronomy 6.4 is the end point of a long development. The explicit monotheism we find in P and Second Isaiah should not be dated before the early Persian period.

In my view, a more constructive and less speculative history-of-religions approach is found in Lewis's *The Origin and Character of God*. Lewis says of his book that it is a reference work about God – the god who came to be viewed differently by Jews, Christians and Muslims. He asks, 'Can you imagine a more daunting challenge?'[80] In an interview Lewis explains why the task is so daunting. The ideal investigator would have expertise in working with texts, including: epigraphy, onomastica, textual criticism, Northwest Semitic philology, comparative Semitics, linguistics, source criticism, redaction criticism,

---

76   Schmid 2019, 290.

77   Schmid 2019, 291.

78   Schmid 2019, 293.

79   Schmid 2019, 294.

80   Lewis 2020, 1.

genre theory and literary analyses. Creative archaeological training would also be required, as would expertise in iconography and visual representations. In addition, knowledge of the social sciences would be important, ranging from sociolinguistics and ritual performance to gender theory and spatial theory.[81]

The task is indeed daunting, and certainly this vast range of expertise yields an immense amount, or, to use Lewis's metaphor, a rich distillate with seven evocative flavours. Although the focus is primarily on YHWH, Lewis's range is impressive and he regularly summarizes bodies of complex material even as he carves out his own way through such materials. His work shows how attention to YHWH opens out into a great many areas of the OT, and, as he rightly observes:

> By using divinity, I do not mean to narrow the topic theologically; rather, writing as a historian of religion, I intend to explore divinity as a window to the historical, the sociological, the performance of cult, the ideological, and the aesthetic.[82]

Lewis's rigorous work is a reminder of the validity of a history-of-religions approach alongside that of a theology of the OT. Indeed, in my view, the intriguing question is the relationship between the two, an issue that surfaced earlier in our engagement with Mark Smith.

Lewis notes early on that, '[a]gain, God must be given his due',[83] and, remarkably, he ends his work with a benediction from Psalm 106.48:

> Blessed be Yahweh, the God of Israel,
> from everlasting to everlasting.
> And let all the people say, 'Amen.'[84]

But what does it mean to *give God his due*, not least in OT studies? I have reflected at length on this short statement by Lewis. Indeed, in one sense this entire series is a reflection on what it means to give God his due. Amid all the skills Lewis lists above – and they are very wide-ranging – noticeably absent is any reference to theology or philosophy or faith. Here again, as we have seen so often, YHWH can be exhaustively investigated apart from YHWH

---

81 Lewis, August 2020, <https://bibleinterp.arizona.edu/articles/fascination-challenges-and-joys-being-historian-ancient-israelite-religion>.

82 Lewis 2020, 9.

83 Lewis 2020, 5.

84 Lewis 2020, 699.

himself! As we have repeatedly observed, what we need in an investigation of the OT, let alone of YHWH, is historical, philological and literary, *and theological* expertise. In my view the question of YHWH cannot simply be bracketed out, whether one is busy with the theology of the OT *or* a history of Israelite religion. Clearly, for example, if YHWH did reveal himself at Sinai, then this has radical implications for any history of Israelite religion.

## (b) YHWH's land of origin?

As we have seen, Schmid argues that YHWH originates in the south. Evidence for this is found by scholars in verses such as Judges 5.4–5 – YHWH goes or sets out from Seir, from the area of Edom; Deuteronomy 33.2 – YHWH came from Sinai, dawned from Seir, shone from Mount Paran, came from Meribat-kadesh; Psalm 68.8–9(7–8) – the one from Sinai; and Habakkuk 3.3 – God comes from Teman and Mount Paran. Complementing such data is the theory that 'Moses' embraced YHWH among the Midianites after he fled from Egypt, the so-called Midianite hypothesis. Kass, in his close reading of the text, astutely observes:

> Has Reuel (Jethro) opened Moses up to some form of monotheism and the possibility of a supernatural deity? Or has Midianite theology left Moses perplexed and searching? . . . As with his time in Pharaoh's house, the text seems completely uninterested in Moses's life in Midian before God calls him; for the unfolding story, it matters only that God called Moses and Moses answered.[85]

Lewis concludes that:

> Yahweh's origin seems to be southern, yet many of the garments put onto Yahweh are sewn from northern and inland Canaanite cloth. And yet over time the deity Yahweh would become central to the differentiation process whereby Israel's ethnic boundaries were constructed and maintained.[86]

Schmid finds the southern origin of YHWH concealed in Deuteronomy 33.2, but, once again, such historical excavation and a literary reading are at odds. In this verse Sinai (its only use in Deuteronomy), Seir and Mount Paran are in

---

85  Kass 2021, 60.
86  Lewis 2020, 286.

parallel with one another and, as Craigie observes, '[t]he references to Seir and Paran are in poetic parallelism to Sinai; from a literary point of view, however, it is clear that one specific place is intended in the verse, namely Sinai'.[87] Sinai is the place of the theophany of YHWH, and the content of verse 2b – YHWH is accompanied by myriads of holy ones and his great warriors – suggests the more familiar home of YHWH as heaven.

There are also linguistic and metaphorical issues at stake in this discussion. What does 'the one of/from Sinai' mean, for example? Does it mean literally that YHWH is located geographically at Sinai so that when he appears he literally comes from there? Certainly, YHWH is portrayed as active and on the move, but does not this expression serve as a reminder that YHWH is the God who revealed himself definitively at Sinai, first to Moses in the burning bush and then to the whole of Israel on Mount Sinai, and as such continues to be active among his people? Discerning a geographical location for YHWH in the south because of such expressions seems to me reductionistic and insensitive to the metaphorical language involved.

## (c) The name YHWH

Schmid, as we have noted above, sees the fact that YHWH has a name as indicating that its origin is polytheistic. I do not find this persuasive. If we take seriously as historical the sojourn of the Israelites in Egypt, then they would have had continual exposure to Egyptian polytheism and would have become familiar with gods having names. How else was one to distinguish between the myriad Egyptian gods? As Kass observes:

> The interest in divine names is an especially Egyptian proclivity, for biblical Egypt is the pinnacle of civilization and human ingenuity – celebrating mathematics, astronomy, technology, bureaucratic administration, and a highly elaborate theology. In Egypt the gods are all named, formed, defined.[88]

Moses, having been trained in Egyptian religious ideology, would have understood well in this light that the Israelites would want to know the name of the God on behalf of whom he was speaking.

Many different proposals have been made for the meaning of the name YHWH. As Lewis notes, with all the work devoted to the etymology of YHWH

---

87    Craigie 1976, 393, n. 7.
88    Kass 2021, 70–1.

one might think that deciphering its meaning is the key to Israelite religion. He rightly argues that only a handful of origins are serious possibilities and that the following should be rejected:[89]

- an Egyptian moon god with the name of *Yah* + *we3*, 'one';
- a Proto-Indo-European *Dyau-s*, which enters into Greek as Zeus, into Latin as Jupiter, and into Hebrew as Yaw;
- the Hurrian *ya*, 'god,' plus a *-ha* or *-wa* suffix;
- Yae/Yaue, a deity assumed to have existed, from an undeciphered third-millennium BC inscription from the Indus Valley;
- Mowinckel's proposal for YHWH as a cultic shout, *ya-huwa* ('O He!'), comparable to 'the ecstatic cries of the Islamic dervishes "Allah hu!"'[90]

Instead, Lewis notes that 'the consensus of scholarship is certainly correct that *yhwh* represents a verbal form, with the *y-* representing the third masculine singular verbal prefix of the verb *hyh* "to be"'.[91] A challenge for this view is the w in YHWH where we would normally expect a Y. This discrepancy is explained, according to Mettinger,

> [b]y the assumption that the form of the root underlying the divine Name derives from an evolutionary stage in the development of the language which antedates standard Hebrew. In the Bible itself there is evidence for this earlier form in the ancient words of Isaac's blessing upon Esau (Gen 27:29). Moreover, the corresponding verb in Akkadian, Amorite, and Aramaic has a medial *w*.[92]

It is, however, important to note that the explanation of YHWH in relation to the verb 'to be' rests on the *narrative accounts* in Exodus 3 and 6. As Kass notes: 'the *content* of those mysterious "words" or "names" – they are, to begin with, mere placeholders – gets filled in mainly through watching and listening to His [God's] deeds and speeches, as these are recounted in the unfolding text'.[93] Exodus 3.14 is of particular importance:

---

89   Lewis 2020, 214.
90   Mowinckel 1961, 131.
91   Lewis 2020, 214.
92   Mettinger 1988, 31.
93   Kass 2021, 72. Emphasis original.

וַיֹּאמֶר אֱלֹהִים אֶל־מֹשֶׁה אֶהְיֶה אֲשֶׁר אֶהְיֶה וַיֹּאמֶר כֹּה תֹאמַר לִבְנֵי
יִשְׂרָאֵל אֶהְיֶה שְׁלָחַנִי אֲלֵיכֶם:

[14] God said to Moses, 'I AM WHO I AM.' He said further, 'Thus you shall say to the Israelites, "I AM has sent me to you."'

אֶהְיֶה אֲשֶׁר אֶהְיֶה (I am who I am) occurs nowhere else in the OT. It is somewhat enigmatic and has been interpreted in different ways. The LXX translates it as 'I am he that is' and this provides the basis for Aquinas's universal philosophy of being. Albright, Freedman and Cross argue that YHWH is a causative, meaning 'he who causes to be', thus referring to YHWH as creator. However, nowhere in the OT does the verb 'to be' occur in the causative stem.[94] Lewis assesses this elegant view but finds de Vaux's critique of it decisive. It involves correcting the text of Exodus 3.14 and in the process alters the wordplay at work in this verse. The threefold occurrence of the verbal form (*'ehyeh*) in Exodus 3.12 and 4.12, 15 supports the MT vocalization of 3.14. אֶהְיֶה is the first-person prefix form of the verb 'to be' (cf. Exod. 3.12; 4.12), which is turned into the third-person YHWH when people speak to or address YHWH. McCarthy asserts that in Exodus 3.14–15 'the repeated assonance *'ehyeh* – *'ehyeh* – *'ehyeh* – *yahweh*' has 'tied Yahweh to *hyh* irrevocably'.[95] Of course the question is: in what way?

In Exodus 3 Moses encounters YHWH in the burning bush in the region of Sinai. This encounter parallels Israel's encounter in Exodus 19. Indeed, Greenberg notes that 'it is possible to epitomize the entire story of Exodus as the movement of the fiery manifestation of the divine presence'.[96] LaCocque refers to the burning bush narrative in Exodus 3 as 'an entirely original event within a general context of proclamation followed by popular or individual recognition'.[97] Kass evocatively describes God as catching Moses in a move from wonder to awe. He notes that the extraordinary sight offered 'an especially Egyptian attraction'.[98] We have seen above how strongly the sun featured in Egyptian life and religion, and like the sun the burning bush is radiant and appears to be self-sustaining. 'Someone initiated into Egyptian wisdom would be especially attracted by the ever actively burning (not to say immortal) bush, which would appear to be at least an image,

---

94  See Lewis 2020, 220–2.
95  McCarthy 1978, 316.
96  Lewis 2020, 345; Greenberg 1969, 16–17.
97  LaCocque in LaCocque and Ricoeur 1998, 321.
98  Kass 2021, 62.

if not an actual terrestrial instance, of the eternal divine.'[99] However, what happens next did not fit into any of Moses' philosophical training. The fire *speaks*, and addresses Moses twice by name and with authority! God identifies himself as 'the God of your father (sgl), the God of Abraham, Isaac, and Jacob'. Kass points out that this is 'an answer, please note, that speaks powerfully to any longing Moses may have to know his father, his identity, and his god'.[100] 'Paradoxically', says Kass,

> the awe-struck Moses, stranger in a strange land, is now more at home with himself than he has ever been . . . Moses has been perfectly caught. His Egyptian (indeed, human) orientation to and expectation of the world has been overturned.[101]

God's name YHWH stems from this encounter of Moses with God at the burning bush. It becomes God's proper name. Zimmerli speaks evocatively of 'I am YHWH' as the 'formula of self-introduction' (*Selbstvorstellungsformel*), and asserts that 'the phrase "I am Yahweh" carries all the weight and becomes the denominator upon which all else rests . . . [E]verything Yahweh has to announce to his people becomes an amplification of the fundamental statement, "I am Yahweh"'.[102]

In his fine discussion of YHWH in his dialogue with Paul Ricoeur, LaCocque asserts that אֶהְיֶה אֲשֶׁר אֶהְיֶה is not, contrary to Aquinas and classical theism, a call to ontological abstraction. Indeed:

> most philosophical speculations on the Divine are in need of a radical revision. The philosophical concepts of transcendence, omnipotence, infinitude must be considered *sub specie historiae* [from the perspective of the historical], instead of *sub specie aeternitatis et absoluti* [from the perspective of the eternal and absolute].[103]

The name and this 'explanatory' phrase must support the affirmation 'I will be with you' (Exod. 3.12). As Childs asserts: 'the God of Israel makes known his being in specific historical moments and confirms in his works his ultimate

---

99   Kass 2021, 63.
100   Kass 2021, 63.
101   Kass 2021, 65.
102   Zimmerli 1982, 9.
103   LaCocque in LaCocque and Ricoeur 1998, 324.

being by redeeming a covenant people.'[104] YHWH evokes exclusivity in his relationship to Israel; the name is both theophanic and performative,[105] revealing the ultimate meaning of the redemptive event of the exodus. Sarna emphasizes how the name YHWH is evocative of active dynamic presence so that 'the name Yhwh is clearly action-oriented and not conceptually devised'.[106] Kass notes of the imperfect form of the verb 'to be' in this statement that it 'suggests something not only incomplete and unlimited, but also ongoing, progressing, free and unpredictable; not *static*, but *acting in time*; and "knowable" therefore only through watching "its" deeds and words'.[107]

Kass points out that through the revelation of God as YHWH we gain a vital, indeed revolutionary, insight into how to approach and know God. Knowledge of God

> should be pursued not through inquisitive speech or philosophical speculation (fruitlessly seeking the essence), but through attending to God's commands and deeds, to what God will be *in time*. We should redirect our desire to 'know God' away from philosophy and theology (speech about God) and attend instead to what He reveals of Himself in 'history,' to what *He says* to and *does* for human beings.[108]

Similarly, Zimmerli pays close attention to the use of the formula of self-introduction in Exodus and concludes that:

> One cannot fail to see the conceptually delineated, theologically reflected context of the statements in which the Priestly Writing employs the statement of recognition. Exodus 14 speaks of Yahweh's show of power before the Egyptians as his self-glorification . . . In Exodus 16 we first hear it in Moses' announcement that Israel will see Yahweh's glory. Shortly thereafter Yahweh's glory is visible to the entire people . . . . [T]o know Yahweh does not mean to encounter some part of Yahweh's transcendent being, but rather to recognize his beneficial deed on Israel's behalf.[109]

---

104  Childs 1974, 88.
105  LaCocque in LaCocque and Ricoeur 1998, 316.
106  LaCocque in LaCocque and Ricoeur 1998, 315.
107  Kass 2021, 73. Emphasis original.
108  Kass 2021, 73–4. Emphasis original.
109  Zimmerli 1982, 44.

Thus, as we have seen from scholar after scholar, the name YHWH is tied irrevocably to divine action in history, however one ends up translating אֶהְיֶה אֲשֶׁר אֶהְיֶה.

However, Moberly poses the question:

> If Exodus 3 is not a transcript by Moses of what God said to him on a particular momentous day in the desert . . . but a text whose author, date, tradition history, and relation to Israel's origins cannot be determined with any precision (in line with insights from modern historical-critical work) and a story in which an omniscient narrator gives access to the intentions and words of God and Moses (in line with premodern literary insights), then what follows? . . . Does that mean that a reader cannot seriously engage the narrative world and the subject matter that the text presents? Clearly not . . . Does it mean that the text does not *really* speak of the one God? For many and various theological and philosophical reasons, the short answer is no. Such a conclusion would simply be a non sequitur.[110]

Moberly's language is provocative and I am not sure who would argue that Exodus 3 is a 'transcript' by Moses. We will come below to a nuanced account of revelation and its relationship to historical narrative. One would like to hear more of the theological and philosophical reasons for Moberly's view. The name YHWH alerts us to the fact that he is known through his words and deeds in history, and if, as so much historical criticism seems to believe, there were neither words nor deeds, not least in God's revelation of his name, then the very speech act of the revelation of the divine name appears to misfire. One cannot escape the question of historicity so deftly as Moberly attempts to do.

LaCocque, by comparison, speaks evocatively of the Decalogue as *a legal commentary on YHWH*, and states:

> Now we must shift the emphasis to Sinai as an event, even as the symbolic event par excellence. Strikingly, the formula is closely knit with that event, the paradigm of all subsequent events of the *Heilsgeschichte* [history of salvation], meant, according to their accompanying interpretation, to provoke a decision from their audience . . . Either one rejects

---

110  Moberly 2020, 89–90.

the conviction and its evidence, or one recognizes that God is the Lord, Yhwh, the One who is up to his name.[111]

Indeed:

> The recognition does not come from some conceptual reflection but from an encounter with Yhwh's self-manifestation . . . Similarly, the knowledge/recognition of the lordship of God is no metaphysical knowledge. The Tetragrammaton is no invitation to speculate upon the aseity of God. It does not refer to a divine *causa sui* [cause of itself]; on the contrary, it always takes place within very concrete happenings.[112]

According to LaCocque, the exodus from Egypt that follows is just such a concrete event:

> Within Israel's consciousness, the Exodus inaugurates not only its history as a people . . . but also the world's redemption. The exodus from Egypt is toward the promised Land, the microcosm and 'bridge-head' from where the whole of creation has started its transfiguration into the Kingdom of God. The Exodus is thus *the* event par excellence, the 'V-Day' of history, the day when the world is changed into itself by eternity.[113]

We saw above how Gunton highlights the importance of creation for our understanding of God and divine action. And there are indeed strong creation and Genesis motifs in Exodus. Martin Buber and Franz Rosenzweig pointed out the strong parallels between Exodus 39—40 and Genesis 1—2: Exodus 39.43a//Genesis 1.31a; Exodus 39.32a//Genesis 2.1; Exodus 40.33b//Genesis 2.2a; Exodus 39.43b//Genesis 2.3a.[114] 'While the account of Genesis marks the creation of the world, the creation language of Exodus 39–40 might be viewed as heralding the new creation of Israel's cultic life with its deity.'[115] Zevit has argued that the narrative of the plagues presents them as a judgement of a kind of uncreation, being deliberately modelled on Genesis 1.[116] The creation language in 19—24 fits with the new-creation language of 39—40. 'The major

---

111 LaCocque in LaCocque and Ricoeur 1998, 320.

112 LaCocque in LaCocque and Ricoeur 1998, 322.

113 LaCocque in LaCocque and Ricoeur 1998, 326.

114 Smith 1997, 266.

115 Smith 1997, 266.

116 Zevit 1976.

theme of creation clearly links the beginning and end of the book.'[117] Egypt is thus portrayed as the place of death, judgement and uncreation, whereas life and new creation are initiated at Sinai. Egypt is the place of slavery; Sinai of freedom. 'The freedom from the Egyptians was made complete only by the Sinai legislation.'[118] Smith asserts that:

> It is a gross understatement to say Sinai occupies a central place in the priestly theology of the Pentateuch . . . Sinai became the Mount Everest of priestly theology which looms larger than subsequent cultic sites such as Jerusalem. For the priestly tradition Sinai would represent the site of the definitive covenant and model for cultic recollection in the land. In short, this mountain defines life inside and outside the land.[119]

Like the gods of Egypt, God thus has a name, YHWH. But it is a name unlike other names. Its strangeness and open-endedness alert us to the fact that its content can only be filled in by attending closely to God's action in history and his revelation of himself in this way. And his actions that cluster around the revelation of his name, such as the exodus and Sinai, connect back into his being the Creator and into his purposes for his creation.

## (d) The character of YHWH

One of the attractive features of Lewis's *The Origin and Character of God* is that his focus on YHWH opens out into a detailed investigation of the character and activity of YHWH, namely his representation, YHWH as warrior and parent, YHWH as king and judge, and YHWH as holy. YHWH is particularly associated with Moses and Sinai in Exodus. Indeed, Exodus 6.3 asserts that it is only with Moses and the exodus and Sinai that God reveals himself by his name YHWH. Thus, even as we attend to YHWH, we do need to circle back to how the OT understands God before Exodus 3.6.

## (e) YHWH and the patriarchal narratives

This topic has, of course, generated considerable discussion. Wenham, as noted earlier, examines the use of the divine names in the patriarchal narratives and concludes that the name YHWH is used very sparingly in reporting human and angelic speech, thereby both respecting the names under which

---

117  Smith 1997, 266.
118  Smith 1997, 268.
119  Smith 1997, 306.

the patriarchs knew God and equating their God with YHWH. This confirms the view that God's revelation of himself to Moses as YHWH was new. Wenham notes that the religion of the patriarchs has much in common with later Israelite worship but also important differences:

- First, the use of El rather than the later YHWH is a distinction that is more significant than language alone. 'The exclusiveness, holiness, and strictness of the God of Exodus is absent from Genesis . . . There is an air of ecumenical bonhomie about the patriarchal religion which contrasts with the sectarian exclusiveness of the Mosaic age and later prophetic demands.'[120]
- Second, Baal is completely absent and this testifies to the antiquity of the patriarchal narratives.
- Third is the unmediatedness of patriarchal religion.
- Fourth is the fact that Jerusalem is not mentioned.

Wenham concludes: 'These features of patriarchal religion are compatible with an early second-millennium date for the traditions, but they would be strange if it grew up in the later monarchy period.'[121] Mettinger comparably notes that we do not find a single theophoric name including YHWH among the names of the patriarchs.[122] Pike makes a similar assertion:

a simple survey of the Biblical onomastic evidence yields no Yahwistic PN [proper name] preserved from the time prior to the Israelite bondage in Egypt, nor do such names appear in significant numbers until well into the period of the Judges.[123]

Wenham proposes that since the patriarchs lived away from the central Canaanite cities, it is likely that they began to worship El in Mesopotamia.[124] However, according to Herrmann, '[i]n Ancient Mesopotamia *ilu* is attested as an appellative for deities, though a deity *Il* is not attested'.[125] We discussed above in our treatment of the Arameans the statement in Deuteronomy 26.5: 'A wandering Aramean was my ancestor . . .' and Lipiński states: 'The name

---

120  Wenham 1980, 184.
121  Wenham 1980, 185.
122  Mettinger 1988, 21.
123  Pike 1990, 35. Quoted in Lewis 2020, 226.
124  Wenham 1980, 184.
125  Herrmann 1999, 275.

'Il is the commonest theophorous element in the Aramaic personal names of the first millennium B.C. and it certainly reflects the importance of the cult of 'Il among the early Arameans.'[126] The fullest representation of El is, however, found at Ugarit.[127] 'In about half of the occurrences, El denotes a distinct deity who, residing on the sacred mountain, occupies within the myths the position of master of the Ugaritic pantheon.'[128]

For Wenham, the data supports the view that the patriarchs worshipped the Semitic God El. From his analysis Lewis likewise concludes that the evidence strongly supports the view the Israelites originally worshipped El. Indeed, El is embedded in the very name Isra-el. However, the use of El is more complex than this. The Semitic term 'El' was used both in a generic sense (god) and as a proper name (El), and it is often difficult to discern which is which in particular cases.[129] 'Related to a personal god, the noun has the meaning "the strong one; mighty one; head; chief, leader".'[130] According to Lewis, generally *ilu* [El] in East Semitic (Mesopotamian) culture is used more as a name for deity and to designate spirits rather than as a proper name for a god.[131]

In the patriarchal narratives – and elsewhere – we also find the composite names El Elyon, associated with Salem (Gen. 14.18–22); El-roi, associated with Beer-lahai-roi (Gen. 16.13); El Olam, associated with Beer-sheba (Gen. 21.33); and El-bethel, associated with Bethel (Gen. 31.13; 35.7). Elyon was an adjective common in the West Semitic region, applied to any god regarded as supreme.[132] El-roi, generally translated as 'God of seeing', occurs only in Genesis 16.13. Lewis notes that this name is unattested in cognate cultures, although the idea that gods see the problems of their devotees and provide for them is common. Similarly, El Olam, meaning 'the god of eternity', 'the ancient god' or 'El, the Eternal One', is found only in Genesis 21.33.

El Shadday most likely means 'God of the wilderness'.[133] 'This deity is attested as a theophoric element in Egyptian, Ugaritic, Phoenician and Thamudic personal names from the Late Bronze Age onwards.'[134] In the OT,

---

126 Lipiński 2000, 614. Quoted in Lewis 2020, 83.

127 Lewis 2020, 76.

128 Herrmann 1999, 275.

129 Lewis 2020, 73.

130 Herrmann 1999, 274.

131 Lewis 2020, 74.

132 Lewis 2020, 88.

133 Knauf 1999, 749. Lewis (2020, 102–4) also mentions 'God the destroyer' and 'God of the mountain' as possible meanings.

134 Knauf 1999, 749.

El Shadday alone among the above descriptions is not associated with any particular place. Intriguingly, it is El Shadday that the author of Exodus 6.3 mentions as the name by which God revealed himself to Abraham, Isaac and Jacob. This name for God is found most often in the OT in Job. Lewis comments about Exodus 6.3 that the author seems to be right to describe worship of El Shadday as ancient. As Cross noted in relation to kinship and covenant, the Pentateuch often portrays early Israel better than historical critics often imagine.

Paul Ricoeur rightly identifies the relationship between creation and redemption as a central area in the interpretation of the OT. He notes that:

> For the past few decades, one problem has dominated the exegesis and theology of the Old Testament: what degree of independence is to be accorded the doctrine of creation in relation to the fundamental soteriological affirmation that is assumed to run through both testaments of the Bible . . . Within Christian communities, then, the stakes of this discussion are high.[135]

El is interesting in this respect. In Genesis 14.19, for example, we find the expression לְאֵל עֶלְיוֹן קֹנֵה שָׁמַיִם וָאָרֶץ (El Elyon, maker of heaven and earth). Röllig refers to this narrative as late biblical midrash but with an early core![136] The evidence for El as creator in the ANE is limited. Lewis comments: '*'Ilu* also plays the role of creator, though this conclusion is drawn more from inference rather than from explicit references.'[137] Thus far, we do not have a myth from Ugarit about El's creation of the world. However, Lewis does find such evidence in traces of El in the Hittite myth of Elkunirsha and Ashertu, found in fragments from around the thirteenth century BC. Lewis notes that:

> The name Elkunirsha is evidently the Hittite translator's rendering of 'El, the Creator of Earth' (*'l qn 'rṣ*), an epithet known elsewhere: (1) in the eighth-century BCE Phoenician-Luwian inscription from Karatepe (KAI 26A III: 18); (2) in a partially restored eighth-/seventh-century BCE Jerusalem inscription ([*'l*] *qn 'rṣ*); (3) in late Aramaic texts from Palmyra (cf. too *b'[l]šmwn qnh dy r'h* from Hatra; KAI 244:3); and (4) in a Neo-Punic text from Leptis Magna (Miller 1980).[138]

---

135  Ricoeur in LaCocque and Ricoeur 1998, 31.

136  Röllig 1999, 281.

137  Lewis 2020, 76.

138  Lewis 2020, 81.

It is therefore far from impossible or unlikely that the patriarchs already held a view of God as the Creator. Lewis asserts that El's supremacy was emphasized by referring to him as the creator of heaven and earth. This appellation was well known in West Semitic areas of the Late Bronze and Iron Ages. Creation and sovereignty go together.

In addition to the limited evidence related to El in the ANE in this respect, we saw in our overview of the ANE world views that a view of the gods as creator/s goes back as far as we can go and is already clearly present among the Sumerians. This is important, for example, in the covenants that dominate the Abraham cycle indicating that God is at work recovering his purposes for his creation.

El was worshipped in different contexts and with different nuances in the ANE. In the literature from Ugarit El is portrayed as benevolent and good-natured, as wise and thus a good judge, and as father of the other gods.[139] How, then, did the patriarchs view El; how exactly did they view El, the God of Israel (Gen. 33.20)? There is no indication, for example, that they viewed him as the father of other gods. 'The biblical texts, written and edited in retrospect, present patriarchal religion as monolatrous El worship, but we have few clues as to how this came to be so.'[140] Clearly, as portrayed in Genesis 12—50, the patriarchs did not simply take over the character of El from their cultural surroundings. In typical historical-critical fashion, Lewis observes that, '[a]s with most biblical material, we are faced with the dilemma of uncovering earlier traditions through a later overlay'.[141] We saw above with Wenham, however, how the editors of the patriarchal narratives went out of their way to retain the original El-worship of the patriarchs in their telling of the stories. With the widespread and diverse traditions about El in the ANE, the only way we can discern how the Israelites understood him is to examine the texts of the patriarchal narratives in triadic fashion, that is, using our threefold cord of history, literature and kerygma.

Lewis, as quoted above, in relation to the monolatrous worship of El among the patriarchs, asserts that 'we have few clues as to how this came to be so'. Of course, there is one gigantic clue staring the reader of the OT in the face, but it tends to be disallowed in OT studies. The editors of the patriarchal narratives, while going out of their way to preserve the historical distinctiveness of patriarchal religion, are crystal clear that it is YHWH who was at work in their

---

139  Herrmann 1999, 275.
140  Lewis 2020, 109.
141  Lewis 2020, 92.

midst, forming them into a people worthy of the promise given to Abraham, and then to Isaac and Jacob. Genesis 12.1 is clear that Abram's departure from his country is in response to God's address: וַיֹּאמֶר יְהוָה אֶל־אַבְרָם לֶךְ־לְךָ מֵאַרְצְךָ (And YHWH said to Abraham, Go from your land). Some later Jewish tradition interprets this to mean that Abraham reasoned himself to monotheism, a rationalist rereading of the text that is unable to affirm that God is speaking. The narrator here makes it clear that the voice that came to Abraham was none less than that of YHWH.

In his discussion of the few places in which the name YHWH is used by God in divine speeches in Genesis 12—50, Wenham draws attention to Genesis 15.7 in particular:

וַיֹּאמֶר אֵלָיו אֲנִי יְהוָה אֲשֶׁר הוֹצֵאתִיךָ מֵאוּר כַּשְׂדִּים לָתֶת לְךָ אֶת־הָאָרֶץ הַזֹּאת לְרִשְׁתָּהּ

Then he said to him, 'I am the LORD who brought you from Ur of the Chaldeans, to give you this land to possess.'

Wenham notes that the expression 'YHWH who brought you out' occurs 22 times in the Pentateuch. Every one except here refers to the exodus from Egypt.

> It seems likely that the editor of Genesis was wanting to draw attention to the parallel between Abraham's departure from Ur and Israel's exodus from Egypt. He had to substitute Ur for Egypt in the standard formula. If he had also replaced Yahweh, the name for God usually in the formula, the allusion to the exodus would have become inaudible. He therefore used Yahweh in Genesis 15:7 to make the typological point that the God who brought Abraham out of Ur was the same God who saved Israel from Egypt.[142]

If the narratives about the exodus and Sinai are historical narratives, and if it is demonstrably clear that the authors intended them to be so, then it follows logically that in a text like Genesis 15.7 the narrator is making a literary and theologically sophisticated point that the God of the exodus and Sinai called Abraham and engaged with him and his descendants to form the people Israel. The introduction of the name YHWH signals a new phase in the life of God's people as they become a nation, thus allowing for significant differences in the religious practices of the patriarchs compared with the covenant nation.

---

142 Wenham 1980, 182.

## (f) YHWH as fire and radiance

As I have noted above and elsewhere, once confidence in divine action in history is lost, the most creative periods of Israel tend to be identified as her low points historically, periods such as the exile and post-exilic years. However, once take divine action seriously and then it becomes logical to see the *terminus a quo* as the place of most creativity rather than the *terminus ad quem* of canon formation. Read as historical narrative, it is surprising just how generative and comprehensive Sinai is in its revelation of YHWH.

Lewis notes that in contrast to the anthropomorphisms pervasive in the OT, it also contains abstract images for YHWH. It is certainly true that the aniconic tradition in the OT is highly abstract. Mettinger (1995) provided much needed nuance to the discussion of aniconism, refining broad-brush approaches to differentiate between 'de facto traditions' (indifference to icons, mere absence of images, tolerant aniconism) and 'programmatic traditions' (repudiation of images, iconophobia, iconoclasm).[143] He introduced the terminology of 'material aniconism' (no anthropomorphic or theriomorphic icon of the deity serving as the central cultic symbol) versus 'empty space aniconism' (sacred emptiness such as YHWH invisibly seated on the cherubim). The Decalogue certainly evinces a programmatic aniconic tradition, as well as material and empty space aniconism.

Lewis refers to radiance (*kābôd*) and fire (*'ēš*) as examples of more abstract concepts of YHWH.[144] He notes that fire's numinous dimension is one of the most common images used in the OT to evoke the presence of God. In my view, such concepts are less abstract than *sensory*, and both are clearly on *view* in Exodus and at Sinai.

Earlier we quoted Kass's statement: 'Someone initiated into Egyptian wisdom would be especially attracted by the ever actively burning (not to say immortal) bush, which would appear to be at least an image, if not an actual terrestrial instance, of the eternal divine.' In Deuteronomy 33.16 we find an evocative recollection of Exodus 3.2 in the description of YHWH as 'he who dwells in the bush' (*šōknî seneh*).[145] In Exodus 19 YHWH descends on Mount Sinai in fire, and as a result the mountain is wrapped in smoke (19.18). Thunder, lightning, thick cloud and the sound of trumpet blasts are also associated with this theophany, and these are visceral, sensory realities and not abstract concepts. We are not told whether the mountain, like the bush, was not

---

143 Mettinger 1995, 18–20.
144 Fire is a recurring theme in Sonderegger 2015.
145 My translation.

consumed, but can perhaps assume this to have been the case. Exodus 24.17, using the same verb as Exodus 3.2, may suggest that the mountain, like the bush, was not consumed:

וּמַרְאֵה כְּבוֹד יְהוָה כְּאֵשׁ אֹכֶלֶת בְּרֹאשׁ הָהָר לְעֵינֵי בְּנֵי יִשְׂרָאֵל׃

Now the appearance of the glory of the LORD was like a devouring fire on the top of the mountain in the sight of the people of Israel. (Exod. 24.17)

וַיֵּרָא מַלְאַךְ יְהֹוָה אֵלָיו בְּלַבַּת־אֵשׁ מִתּוֹךְ הַסְּנֶה וַיַּרְא וְהִנֵּה הַסְּנֶה בֹּעֵר בָּאֵשׁ וְהַסְּנֶה אֵינֶנּוּ אֻכָּל׃

There the angel of the LORD appeared to him in a flame of fire out of a bush; he looked, and the bush was blazing, yet it was not consumed. (Exod. 3.2)

In Exodus 24.10, after the ratification of the covenant, the elders and Moses, Aaron and Nadab see the God of Israel but remain untouched, unconsumed. In Exodus 33.3, in the context of YHWH's threatening not to remain among his people, the reason is given: lest he consume them on the way. A different verb for 'consumed' is used here compared with Exodus 3.2.

Fire has many functions in human culture and it also has these in the OT. In Exodus 13.21 the pillar of fire *illuminates* the way of the Israelites by night. A universal aspect of fire is its numinous energy which attracts and repels. At Sinai we witness this experience on steroids, as it were, evoking for the Israelites the god-ness of YHWH, his power and his potential danger to the Israelites. The mountain trembles and so too do the Israelites (Exod. 19.18; 20.18; two different verbs in the Hebrew). Sinai conceals even as it reveals; YHWH comes in thick cloud (Exod. 19.9) and thick darkness (20.21) so that the Israelites might *hear* YHWH speaking but not see him. The thick cloud is a reminder that YHWH is *Deus absconditus* (the hidden God) even as he is *Deus revelatus* (the revealed God). Real intimacy with YHWH is granted only to Moses.

In the Sinai narrative it is this experience of YHWH that is referred to as the 'glory of YHWH'. Exodus 24.16–17 reads as follows:

וַיִּשְׁכֹּן כְּבוֹד־יְהוָה עַל־הַר סִינַי וַיְכַסֵּהוּ הֶעָנָן שֵׁשֶׁת יָמִים וַיִּקְרָא אֶל־מֹשֶׁה בַּיּוֹם הַשְּׁבִיעִי מִתּוֹךְ הֶעָנָן׃ וּמַרְאֵה כְּבוֹד יְהוָה כְּאֵשׁ אֹכֶלֶת בְּרֹאשׁ הָהָר לְעֵינֵי בְּנֵי יִשְׂרָאֵל׃

[16] The glory of the LORD settled on Mount Sinai, and the cloud covered it for six days; on the seventh day he called to Moses out of the cloud. [17] Now the appearance of the glory of the LORD was like a devouring fire on the top of the mountain in the sight of the people of Israel.

This confirms our statement above that YHWH's fire and glory are *sensory* revelations of his presence, rather than abstract concepts about him. Of course, this flows from the perspective that YHWH actually revealed himself in this way rather than being a later projection.

## (g) YHWH as holy

The word 'holy' occurs only once in Exodus 19—24 (19.6), but the reality is everywhere. The theophany to Moses of the burning bush at which Moses is instructed not to come near and to take off his sandals because he is standing on *holy* ground (Exod. 3.5) anticipates the far greater theophany of Sinai. Gammie refers to the 'magnificent theophany at Sinai' and notes how the five major aspects of Rudolf Otto's *The Idea of the Holy*[146] are all present:[147]

- awfulness, power evoking dread, and wrath;
- majesty and unapproachability;
- movement, energy and vitality;
- a sense of the wholly other and mysterious;
- fascination.

Gammie supplements this analysis by foregrounding God's 'glory' or majesty and by noting that Otto fails to identify the fact that God's holiness calls for purity which is attained through separation. Thus, although the word 'holy' hardly occurs in Exodus 19—24, we may justifiably say that Sinai is drenched in God's holiness.

Writing in 1989, Gammie laments the fact that 'the holiness of God in recent years has not itself been the object of theological investigation but has usually been so within the framework of other and more dominant motifs'.[148] Intriguingly, as noted above, Gunton similarly laments the lack of attention to God's holiness in systematic theology. Holiness is a characteristic of God that

---

146  Otto 1950.
147  Gammie 1989, 5–8.
148  Gammie 1989, 74.

should be central to any biblical account of the divine attributes.[149] The OT is also central to any doctrine of the holiness of God, and one wonders if the neglect in OT studies is related to the neglect in theology.

Gammie's lament occurs amid his discussion of holiness and the prophets. He suggests that God's holiness was marginalized by other concepts such as God as the Divine Warrior – foregrounded by von Rad[150] and central to one wing of the Biblical Theology Movement[151] – and the emphasis on God and covenant with the concomitant view of God as the divine suzerain. Gammie identifies three challenges to taking the holiness of God in the OT with full seriousness:

1  It is not a basic and early distinction.[152] Gammie, however, recommends caution here. God's holiness is present in the earliest poetry (Exod. 15.11, 13; 1 Sam. 2.2); it pervades the priestly tradition, Ezekiel and Isaiah, the post-exilic Minor Prophets, and is present in the wisdom traditions.
2  In relation to James Fowler's *Stages of Faith* (1981) it could be argued that attention to God's holiness represents an immature stage of faith. Gammie rejects this.
3  Holiness in the OT may prove difficult for certain ideological approaches.

Gammie quotes with approval Ernst Sellin's statement that '*God is holy*. Herein we touch on that which constitutes the deepest and innermost nature of the God of the Old Testament.'[153]

The origin of YHWH as holy and the diversity of holiness traditions in the OT remain live issues. In his Introduction Gammie notes that he has 'become aware that there is no single doctrine of holiness in the Old Testament but rather a diversity – or, more correctly, a unity within a diversity'.[154] However, as we will see below, taking the Sinai event seriously enables us to see how the different expressions of holiness in the OT come together. God's holiness calls forth purity among the Israelites, and Gammie discerns three streams of purity required in the OT:

---

149  Brunner 1949, 157–82.
150  Von Rad 1991.
151  Gammie 1989, 73.
152  Gammie 1989, 2.
153  Sellin 1936, 19. Emphasis original.
154  Gammie 1989, 1.

1  In the priestly literature the call is to ritual purity.
2  In the prophetic literature the call is to the purity of social justice.
3  In the wisdom literature the call is to purity of individual morality.

More recently, Hugh Williamson has paid major attention to the theme of holiness in the OT, presumably as part of his commentary work on Isaiah. In his commentary on Isaiah 1—5 he asserts that:

> There need be little doubt that the ascription of holiness to Yahweh has as its background the comparable ascription to El in the Ugaritic texts, and that this was also therefore probably predicated of El Elyon in the pre-Israelite Jerusalem cult (note the proximity of holiness to Elyon in Ps. 46.5), whence it would have been transferred to Yahweh sometime after Jerusalem became part of Israel.[155]

Lewis comparably but potentially critically comments: 'The widespread concept of holiness (*qdš*) in multiple Northwest Semitic cultures from the Late Bronze Age forward demands a closer look by historians of Israelite religion, and not just those interested in priestly understandings of ritual and cultic holiness.'[156]

*Contra* Williamson, Lewis asserts that the idea of YHWH's holiness is present in the earliest traditions of the OT. Lewis discusses Exodus 15,[157] Psalm 68 and Psalm 89. Exodus 15 is well known for its celebration of YHWH as 'a man of war' (15.3), that is, the Divine Warrior. However, in verse 11 YHWH is described as 'majestic in holiness', and in verse 13 we find a reference to YHWH's 'holy abode'. In Psalm 68, in which many acknowledge the presence of early traditions, Lewis notes the similarity between verses 8–11(7–10) and Judges 5.4–5. Archaic elements are also found in Psalm 89, and Lewis draws attention to verses 5 and 7 in which we find a reference to the council of the holy ones, and in verse 18 the description of YHWH as the 'Holy One of Israel'. For Lewis, the language of YHWH as holy evolved in Israel and he notes that these three passages confirm that saying YHWH is holy speaks of his being actively and scarily powerful.[158]

---

155  Williamson 2014, 45.

156  Lewis 2020, 575.

157  On the date of the Song of Moses see Childs 1974, 245–7.

158  Lewis 2020, 582.

As has become current in work on the priestly tradition, Gammie helpfully makes the connection between cultus and creation. However, despite his commendation of Sinai as a 'magnificent theophany', Sinai plays a negligible role in his investigation. Williamson simply notes that we need have no doubt that the notion of holiness would have been transferred to YHWH after Jerusalem became part of Israel. This appears to be a typical history-of-religions move. One wonders: transferred by whom and why?

If the narrative of Sinai is historical, then there is every reason for seeing God's pivotal revelation of himself at Sinai as the primary origin of the OT view of his character as holy. Rather than identifying *disparate* OT traditions of holiness, Sinai itself helps us to see how God's holiness manifests itself in different spheres of Israelite life as we would expect in an integrated nation. Preparation for the theophany requires purification and separation, including boundaries of holiness.

Lewis refers to Exodus 19.10–25 as a 'relatively early Israelite tradition' but defers to source criticism in a footnote.[159] He helpfully identifies six elements in the ritual:[160]

- sacred time involving a three-day enactment;
- the washing of clothes (Exod. 19.10, 14);
- abstinence from sex (Exod. 19.15);
- the delimiting of sacred space (Exod. 19.12, 21, 23);
- ritual warnings about divine lethality (Exod. 19.12–13, 21–24);
- the entering into sacred space (with visuals and sound), marked by gradations of holiness as the people remain at the base of Sinai while Moses (and later Aaron) ascends to its summit to meet YHWH.

He summarizes his analysis thus:

To review, the Mt. Sinai narrative in Exodus 19:10–25 is rudimentary when it comes to ritual details, emphasizes the consecration (*qdš*) of people and priest set against a backdrop of divine lethality, and prescribes gradations of sacred space that correlate with social and cultic status.[161]

---

159 Lewis 2020, 608.
160 Lewis 2020, 609.
161 Lewis 2020, 613.

That which is rudimentary at Sinai will be developed in detail in the cultic law. The question is whether this rudimentary approach is a projection back on to Sinai, or whether the rudimentary becomes far more specific with the tabernacle and later the Temple. William Propp evocatively notes that 'the whole purpose of biblical worship, and ancient worship in general, is to bring the human and divine into safe contact'.[162]

Clearly, once YHWH reveals himself as holy, safe contact becomes an issue, and hence the need for a cultus, which serves as something of a diplomatic corps mediating between the holy YHWH and his people. *Logically*, assuming that YHWH did *indeed* reveal himself at Sinai to the Israelites, we would expect cultic holiness to follow immediately and to be a vital part of the life of Israel from this point onwards.

However, Sinai resists restricting holiness to the cultic sphere. As the Holy One of Sinai, YHWH is also the Divine Warrior who rescued his people from Egypt in the exodus (Exod. 20.2). He enters at Sinai into a covenant relationship with this people, and whether the analogy of the Sinai covenant is with earlier Hittite treaties or later Assyrian ones – a topic that we will attend to in volume 2 of this series – clearly covenant evokes the image of YHWH as the great King, ruling over Israel in particular but also over the whole earth (Exod. 19.5). He has brought Israel 'to myself' (אֵלָי) and all the earth is 'mine' (לִי). And at Sinai, holiness flows into the giving of law, essential if the people are to be a kingdom of priests and a holy nation (וְאַתֶּם תִּהְיוּ־לִי מַמְלֶכֶת כֹּהֲנִים וְגוֹי קָדוֹשׁ). In this way, holiness is integrally connected with God as just and righteous.

Deuteronomy 4.6 relates the legal tradition issuing forth from Sinai directly to Israel's wisdom and understanding, and, of course, 'the fear of YHWH' is the foundational principle of OT wisdom, and if one takes Sinai as historical then it is hard not to connect this motif with the Holy One of Sinai. Proverbs, the foundational wisdom text in the OT, does not have much to say directly about holiness, but there are two fascinating verses that do mention holiness. Proverbs 9.10 is an important place where the main theme of Proverbs and thus of OT wisdom is repeated, namely:

תְּחִלַּת חָכְמָה יִרְאַת יְהוָה וְדַעַת קְדֹשִׁים בִּינָה

The fear of the LORD is the beginning of wisdom,
  and the knowledge of the Holy One is insight.

---

162 Propp 2006, 686.

In this verse 'the knowledge of the Holy One' is notably in parallel with 'the fear of YHWH', confirming our point above about the fear of YHWH in Proverbs. Proverbs 30.3 provides a remarkable negative parallel to 9.10 with its use of 'wisdom' and 'knowledge of the Holy One' in parallel:

וְלֹא־לָמַדְתִּי חָכְמָה וְדַעַת קְדֹשִׁים אֵדָע

I have not learned wisdom,
nor have I knowledge of the holy ones (Holy One).[163]

It is instructive how the Sinai event enables us to hold integrally together the different streams of the OT. We have not commented on Sinai and prophecy, but clearly the basic premise of prophecy, namely divine speech and communication, is utterly central to Sinai. Indeed, it is in YHWH that the unity of the different genres of the OT is to be located. Once relinquish YHWH as unified and one (Deut. 6.4), and subvert the very idea of his action in the world, and then the OT collapses into fragments and, somewhat like Humpy Dumpty, it is very difficult to put them back together again. In subsequent volumes we will explore in detail the interrelationship of the different genres of the OT.

## (h) YHWH as all-powerful

In our analysis of the metaphor of YHWH as king, we have already explored some of the ways in which YHWH is portrayed as a divine warrior. Above, we referred to Lewis's analysis of Exodus 15, Psalm 68 and Psalm 89. He notes that in these passages holiness is about the power unique to gods rather than about cultic purity. Exodus 15 and Psalm 89 evoke YHWH's power as supreme, far superior to that of the gods. The connection between holiness and power is integrally related to the OT concept of holy war.

Lewis observes that in comparison to El, YHWH is militaristic. While battle is not alien to the patriarchs (Gen. 14.14–16) and YHWH as warrior is not absent from the patriarchal narratives (Gen. 19.23–26), in general it is true that it is only once the confrontation with Pharoah develops in the biblical narrative that the image of YHWH as Divine Warrior moves front and centre, as is particularly evident in the Song of Moses in Exodus 15, in which YHWH is described as 'a man of war: יְהוָה אִישׁ מִלְחָמָה יְהוָה שְׁמוֹ. Lewis comments:

---

163 In a note, the NRSV indicates that 'holy ones' could be translated as 'Holy One'. In context this seems to me the right translation.

We need not posit a specific historical setting (e.g., an exodus from Egyptian slavery) or sociological setting (e.g., the collapse of the Late Bronze Age) to underscore how the ancients at all times felt the need to believe in a warrior deity who could protect their livelihood. Such a belief was a constant throughout the ancient Near East geographically and chronologically.[164]

He points out that the motif of YHWH as Divine Warrior at a cosmic and historical level is common to the earliest and the latest traditions of the OT. Nevertheless, he acknowledges that the way in which some memories are prioritized over others in the OT is instructive. As regards YHWH as warrior, it was by far the exodus *event* that captivated Israel's imagination. The poetic account of the exodus in Exodus 15.1–18 is often regarded as archaic and as one of the OT's best poems.

Propp similarly notes: 'The story of Israel's flight from Egypt is the most important in the Hebrew Bible.'[165] Friedman, who has recently come out in defence of the historicity of the exodus, notes just how much is at stake in this discussion:

> We have evidence that without the historical anchor of the exodus, we would not have had the rise of the idea of monotheism. And without the experience of that returning group from Egypt, we might not have had the ethic of caring for the stranger.[166]

YHWH's power is seen in his actions, and if the exodus is the paradigmatic display of YHWH's power then it seems to be important that it happened and was in fact a great display of his power. I have italicized 'event' above because so many scholars nowadays repudiate the very notion of the exodus as a historical event. Views of the exodus narrative range from fairy tale[167] to fiction, to historical narrative, with many other views in between.[168]

In the light of Lewis's, Propp's and Friedman's comments above, to say nothing of Exodus 20.2, it is not surprising that the question of the historicity of the exodus remains a live issue. Berman asserts that:

---

164 Lewis 2020, 428.
165 Propp 2006, 795.
166 Friedman 2017, 5.
167 Baruch Halpern. Reported in Friedman 2017, 11.
168 See Levy, Schneider and Propp, eds, 2015.

Were there no Exodus, it would seem, nearly all of Judaism's sacred texts over the centuries would have perpetuated a great lie. In response to the question posed by the child at the Seder meal, 'How is this night different from all other nights?' a father would be obliged to reply, 'Really, my child, there's no difference.' And indeed, at many a contemporary Seder table where questions about the historicity of the Exodus arise, a new figure has emerged: next to the son who knows not how to ask sits the father who knows not how to answer.[169]

In a recent chapter, Berman reviews the debate and makes a persuasive case for the historicity of the exodus. First, against the historicity of the exodus is the lack of supporting evidence. However, Berman notes that the Egyptians named all of their West Semitic slaves 'Asiatics', so that we should not expect to find clear references to the Hebrews or Israelites in Egyptian literature. Second, Berman estimates that 99 per cent of the papyri from Ancient Egypt in the relevant period has been lost, so our sources are inherently limited. Third, archaeological silence about conquests we 'know' to have happened is not unusual. There has been substantial debate about the large numbers said to have left Egypt in the Pentateuch. Berman finds the Pentateuchal evidence for the numbers complex, and finds other places in the Pentateuch where a much smaller number of Israelites is envisaged. He relates the large numbers to *symbolic intent* as a way of flagging the status accorded to tribes.

Much as does Hoffmeier, Berman discerns eight ways in which the exodus narrative reflects late-second-millennium Egypt:

1  There is evidence that West Semitic peoples lived in the eastern Nile Delta (Goshen) for most of the second millennium.
2  Ramesses II (1279–1213 BC) developed a major administrative centre out of mudbrick called Pi-Rameses. The reference in Exodus 1.11 to Pithom and Rameses is possibly to Pi-Rameses.
3  In the exodus narrative, pharaohs are simply called 'Pharoah', whereas in later texts they are referred to by their proper name. This echoes Egyptian practice. From the mid second millennium until the tenth century BC, the title 'pharaoh' was used without the proper name.
4  The national entities in Exodus 15 are found in Egyptian sources shortly before 1200 BC.

---

169  Berman 2020, 43.

5  The narrative of the exodus and subsequent wanderings in the wilderness reflect an accurate knowledge of the eastern Nile Delta, the Sinai Peninsula and Transjordan.

6  Extensive Egyptian fortifications have been discovered along the northern coastal route which Israel is said to have deliberately avoided (Exod. 13.17).

7  Archaeologists have found hundreds of new settlements in Israel from the late thirteenth and twelfth centuries BC, which fit with the arrival there of the liberated Israelites. Significantly, these settlements manifest an absence of pig bones.

8  The mention of Israel in the Merneptah Stela (1206 BC) fits with a gradual conquest of the land as set out in Joshua and Judges.

In Exodus, the power confrontation between Pharoah and YHWH is a major theme of the first half of the book. The tabernacle in the second half of Exodus, and its historical nature or not, has also occasioned debate. An effect of the work of Graf and Wellhausen has been to see the tabernacle as a post-exilic invention to support the fiction of a period of desert wanderings. It remains common to see the depiction of the tabernacle as a retrospective imposition from the perspective of the Temple.[170] Homan, in his rigorous study of tents in the ANE, found his view changing as he studied the evidence:

> Although I began this enterprise as a skeptic, the many parallels collected to the Tabernacle's form and function have convinced me that an elaborate tent served as the focal point for Israelite religion until the completion of Solomon's Temple. If this tent-shrine did not correspond exactly to the description in Exodus 25–27, it came very close.[171]

However, although excavations of Phoenician temples reveal a floor plan very similar to that of the first Temple, it has been harder to find closer parallels to the plan of the tabernacle. Astonishingly, Berman marshals substantial evidence that the tabernacle (Exod. 25—29) is modelled on the camp of Pharoah as depicted in the Kadesh bas-reliefs.

Egypt reached its zenith, as noted above, during the period of the New Kingdom in 1500–1200 BC. Ramesses II reigned from 1279 to 1213 BC. His

---

170  Cross 1947 remains the most influential rebuttal to Wellhausen.
171  Homan 2002, 5.

great achievement was the defeat of the Hittites at Kadesh in 1274 BC. Berman notes that:

> Upon his return to Egypt, Rameses inscribed accounts of this battle on monuments all across the empire. Ten copies of the inscriptions exist to this day. These multiple copies make the battle of Kadesh the most publicized event anywhere in the ancient world.[172]

The texts were accompanied by bas-reliefs showing the battle frame by frame so that the illiterate could join in celebrating Pharoah's victory.

On the bas-reliefs there is a depiction of Ramesses II's throne tent. This camp's length is twice that of its width. At the end of a long corridor, at the centre of the camp, is the entrance to a rectangular tent. The tent is made up of two sections: a 2:1 reception tent and a domed square space which is the pharaoh's throne tent. These proportions mirror the instructions for the tabernacle and the surrounding camp in Exodus 25—27. In Pharaoh's throne tent an emblem bearing Pharaoh's name, and symbolizing his might, is flanked on either side by falcons symbolizing Horus,[173] their wings spread over Pharaoh in protection. In Exodus 25.20 the ark is comparably flanked by two cherubim, whose wings hover over it protectively. God cannot be represented by an image and does not need protection. Hence, instead of falcons and Horus we have cherubim guarding the ark. The four-army division of the Egyptian army would camp on the four sides of Pharaoh's throne tent, and in Numbers 2 we learn that the Israelites camped on the four sides of the tabernacle. Berman notes that:

> The resemblance of the military camp at Kadesh to the Tabernacle goes beyond architecture; it is conceptual as well. For Egyptians, Rameses was both a military leader and a divinity. In the Torah, God is likewise a divinity, obviously, but also Israel's leader in battle (see Num. 10:35–36). The tent of God, the divine warrior, parallels the tent of the pharaoh, the living Egyptian god, poised for battle.[174]

---

172 Berman 2020, 56. Cf. Frankfort (1948, 1975, 55) who notes the difference between the reports of Kadesh and the accounts of the council of war preceding major battles which followed an established literary form: 'Only the Battle of Kadesh is reported in an unconventional manner which finds its correlate in the entirely exceptional way in which it is rendered in the reliefs.'

173 On Horus and Pharaoh see Frankfort 1948, 1975, 36–47. In the light of Horus's expansive wings one wonders if the reference in 19.4 to flying Israel out of Egypt is not a polemical motif against Horus, and thus Pharaoh.

174 Berman 2020, 59. Berman (2020, 59) acknowledges his indebtedness to Homan 2000, 55, n. 12.

Some scholars, of course, interpret this data differently. However, this data provides strong support for the historicity of the tabernacle, and also for its embodying a polemical displacement of Pharaoh as the supreme *power* of the day.

The longest of the inscriptions about Pharaoh's victory consists of 335 lines. A comparison with the dividing up of the sea in Exodus 14—15 reveals a similar plotline. Berman observes that:

> What emerges is that the similarities extend to the entire plotline of the Kadesh poem and that of the Splitting of the Sea in Exodus 14–15.[175] I believe it is reasonable to claim that the narrative account of the Splitting of the Sea (Exodus 14) and the Song at the Sea (Exodus 15) may reflect a deliberate act of cultural appropriation. If the Kadesh inscriptions bear witness to the greatest achievement of the greatest pharaoh of the greatest period in Egyptian history, then the book of Exodus claims that the God of Israel overmastered Rameses the Great by several orders of magnitude, effectively trouncing him at his own game.[176]

In both narratives the army is on the march when attacked unexpectedly by a large group of chariots. In both, the lead character appeals to his god. Amun reassures Ramesses and commands him 'Forward!' Similarly, Moses cries out to YHWH who tells him to command the Israelites to go forward (Exod. 14.15). Ramesses assumes divine powers at this point. In both accounts the king confronts the enemy alone (cf. Exod. 14.14). This feature of both narratives of a victorious leader who works to achieve the loyalty of those he serves in war has no parallel in ANE literature. In both texts the enemy expresses the futility of fighting and endeavours to escape. In both texts the enemy is submerged in water. In panic the Hittites plunged into the river where they were slaughtered by Pharaoh. Both accounts say there were no survivors.

The most remarkable parallel is found in the use of the kings' 'mighty arm'. In Exodus 14.30–31 we read:

וַיּ֨וֹשַׁע יְהוָ֜ה בַּיּ֥וֹם הַה֛וּא אֶת־יִשְׂרָאֵ֖ל מִיַּ֣ד מִצְרָ֑יִם וַיַּ֤רְא יִשְׂרָאֵל֙ אֶת־מִצְרַ֔יִם מֵ֖ת עַל־שְׂפַ֥ת הַיָּֽם׃ וַיַּ֨רְא יִשְׂרָאֵ֜ל אֶת־הַיָּ֣ד הַגְּדֹלָ֗ה אֲשֶׁ֨ר עָשָׂ֤ה יְהוָה֙ בְּמִצְרַ֔יִם וַיִּֽירְא֥וּ הָעָ֖ם אֶת־יְהוָ֑ה וַיַּֽאֲמִ֙ינוּ֙ בַּֽיהוָ֔ה וּבְמֹשֶׁ֖ה עַבְדּֽוֹ׃

---

175  Note that the dividing of the sea also recalls Gen. 1. See Kass 2021, 203.

176  Berman 2020, 60.

[30] Thus the LORD saved Israel that day from the Egyptians; and Israel saw the Egyptians dead on the seashore. [31] Israel saw the great work that the LORD did against the Egyptians. So the people feared the LORD and believed in the LORD and in his servant Moses.

הַיָּד הַגְּדֹלָה 'great work' here (literally 'great hand') and 'great arm' in Exodus 15.16 parallel 'my strong arm' in the Kadesh poem. Berman points out that '"great hand" here and "great arm" in 15:16 are used exclusively only in the Tanakh with regard to the Exodus, a trope found elsewhere only within Egyptian propaganda, especially during the late second-millennium New Kingdom'.[177]

In both accounts, after the victory, praise is offered to the king. In both, the opening stanza consists of three elements: the troops praise the name of the king as a warrior, give him credit for strengthening their morale and exalt him for their victory (cf. Exod. 15.1–3). In both, the narrative goes on to extol the powerful arm or hand of the king. In Exodus 15.6 we find 'your right hand' repeated twice. The Hebrew root for the right hand (יָמִין) is common among other ANE languages, but in other cultures the right hand is related exclusively to grasping or holding.

> In Egyptian literature, however, we find depictions of the right hand that match those in the Song. Perhaps the most ubiquitous motif of Egyptian narrative art is the pharaoh raising his right hand to shatter the heads of enemy captives . . . In no other ancient Near Eastern culture do we encounter such portrayals of the right hand, which resonate closely with the Song and particularly with 15:5: 'Your right hand, O Lord, shatters the enemy.'[178]

In both, the enemies are compared to chaff; in both, the troops declare their king to be peerless in battle; in both, the king leads his troops home while intimidating lands along the way; both end with the king enthroned and his universal reign celebrated. 'The Exodus text focuses on precisely those elements of the Kadesh poem that extol the pharaoh's valor, which it reworks for purposes of extolling God's.'[179] The totality of the parallels makes the relation between the two texts convincing. More generally, Berman notes the common literary

---

177  Berman 2020, 63.
178  Berman 2020, 64–5.
179  Berman 2020, 66.

Egyptian motif of the period of causing the boasting of one's enemies to cease. Remarkably, this is the emphasis of Exodus 15.8–9. 'This concern with silencing the enemy's boastings is distinctly Egyptian, not found in the military literature of any other neighboring culture.'[180]

Intriguingly, Kass finds the view that Moses wrote the Song of the Sea persuasive:

> The text, it is true, does not say that Moses wrote the Song of the Sea. But I have never doubted his authorship. A multitude does not compose. And this multitude would have been incapable of anything as remarkable as this song. Only Moses knew the prophetic messages in the song, especially Israel's coming to the Lord's holy mountain. Only his great and prophetic soul could offer up – instantly and spontaneously – such astonishing poetry . . . In pagan odes of triumph, Cassuto points out, 'The glory of the victory is ascribed to the conquering king, but here there is not a single word of praise or glory given to Moses.' Astonishingly, Moses writes himself out of the song. It is from start to finish a song of praise to, an ode of triumph for, and a hymn of glory about the Lord. Through this song the Lord achieves one of His stated goals: His great glory. Lifted up in song, He gets it from Moses and His people.[181]

As we have often noted, theory is underdetermined by facts. This remarkable parallel can be interpreted in different ways. Berman notes:

> But my own conclusion is otherwise: The evidence adduced here can be reasonably taken as indicating that the poem was transmitted during the period of its greatest diffusion, which is the only period when anyone in Egypt seems to have paid much attention to it – namely, during the reign of Rameses II himself. In my view, the evidence suggests that the Exodus text preserves the memory of a moment when the earliest Israelites reached for language with which to extol the mighty virtues of God, and found raw material in the terms and tropes of an Egyptian text well known to them. In appropriating and 'transvaluing' that material, the Torah puts forward the claim that God has far outdone the greatest achievement of the greatest earthly potentate.[182]

---

180  Berman 2020, 67.
181  Kass 2021, 208.
182  Berman 2020, 69.

Berman's rich analysis goes a long way to showing how justified Israel was in letting her imagination be captivated by the memory of the exodus as the paradigm example of YHWH's power. His analysis is a further reminder of the ways in which the historical, the literary and the theological coalesce in the speech acts of such powerful texts. If, as I do with Berman, we take the exodus as historical, then it is here that we can locate a powerful source for the image of YHWH as the Divine Warrior. It should be noted that, in context, YHWH battles on behalf of oppressed slaves against the utterly autocratic power of Pharaoh. Clearly, one takeaway from the exodus narratives is that YHWH, and not Pharaoh, is the king and all-powerful. An obvious point to note is that YHWH is here portrayed as acting *in Egypt* so that he can by no means be seen as the national god of the Israelites alongside other national gods. Joshua 5.13–15 has always struck me as instructive in this respect. Near Jericho, Joshua encounters a warrior with his sword drawn. Not surprisingly, Joshua enquires whether the man is of the Israelites or for their adversaries. The warrior's reply is telling:

וַיֹּאמֶר ׀ לֹא כִּי אֲנִי שַׂר־צְבָא־יְהוָה עַתָּה בָאתִי

[14] He replied, 'Neither; but as commander of the army of the LORD I have now come.'

Clearly, the warrior's answer is related to the name of God, YHWH Sabaoth (Lord of Armies). Mettinger argues that YHWH Sabaoth was connected with the Temple in particular but traces its origins back to the time of the judges.

> The name itself characterizes the God of Israel as the one who was present in the temple, enthroned upon the cherubim and surrounded by the hosts of heaven. Here the throne conception is the central theological motif: *YHWH Sabaoth is the enthroned and regnant God.*[183]

Doubtless, Sabaoth was connected with the Temple, but it makes more sense to locate its origin and meaning – Lord of the Armies – amid the early periods of Israel's exodus and conquest. As with Moses in Exodus 3, Joshua is instructed to remove his sandals because he is standing on holy ground. Israel is YHWH's people and YHWH is their God, but YHWH is no national deity, never such as to be disposed of at will. He is holy.

---

183 Mettinger 1988, 148–9. Emphasis original.

## (i) YHWH as creator

As has often been noted, creation motifs abound in Exodus. In Exodus 19.5 YHWH states that 'the whole earth is mine', clearly asserting his sovereignty over the entire creation as the Creator, and positioning his work in the exodus and at Sinai in relation to that sovereignty. Furthermore, in 20.11 the Sabbath commandment is related to YHWH's resting after his work of creation. Canonically, redemption is subsidiary to creation. Above, we discussed the ways in which El was conceived of as father of the gods and creator, and we have seen how some doctrine of creation was pervasive across the cultures of the ANE, so that we would expect the patriarchs and Israel to espouse a view of God as creator from early on.[184] Lewis observes that, according to the OT, the ancestors of Israel never worshipped two different gods, namely El and YHWH. YHWH is El (see Pss. 118.27; 150.1).

However, as is well known, von Rad catalysed a debate in this regard, arguing that creation is a subordinate theme to redemption.[185] As noted above, Ricoeur considers this relationship one of the most important issues in OT studies today. Childs refers to creation and redemption as correlates but notes that 'it is highly questionable whether creation was subordinated in principle'.[186] It is particularly in source-critical studies of P that the connection between cultus, YHWH and creation has been foregrounded again and again with rich theological implications.[187] Of course, Wellhausen and most contemporary source critics regard P as late (JEDP).[188] However, there is a minority tradition, represented by Yehezkel Kaufmann[189] and some of his 'followers', that argues that P is early, indeed the earliest Pentateuchal source. At the end of this volume we will revisit what our approach means for historical criticism today.

Clearly, in the Sinai narrative, in Exodus as a whole and in the rest of the OT YHWH is portrayed as the Creator. In the Pentateuch, Genesis 1—3 provides an important clue in this respect. In Genesis 1.1—2.3 the name Elohim (plural) is used for God. The verbs are singular so we cannot read Elohim as 'gods'. Something like a *pluralis majestasis* (a plural of majesty) is in play. What is notable is that in Genesis 2—3, the first major section in Genesis contained within the 'toledoth' – 'generations of' – structure, an unusual name for God is

---

184  See Schmid 1984.

185  Von Rad 1984.

186  Childs 1985, 33.

187  See Morales, ed., 2014.

188  See, e.g., Schmid 2019, 109–13.

189  Kaufmann 1960.

used, namely YHWH *Elohim*. Why? The point is to make clear, even as the narrative focuses on God in relationship with the first couple and then on Abraham and his descendants, that YHWH, the covenant relational God, is also the Creator God, Elohim.

## (j) YHWH as king, lawgiver and judge

Throughout the ANE, kings played an important role as judges in the judicial system. Intriguingly, in the OT the word 'judge' is applied to God only 11 times (Gen. 18.25; Judg. 11.27; Job 23.7; Pss. 7.12; 9.5; 50.6; 58.12; 75.8; 94.2; Isa. 33.22; Jer. 11.20), although the concept of YHWH as judge is widespread. Brettler notes that '[i]t is difficult to determine the extent to which God's role as judge may be studied within the metaphor "God is king"'.[190] Nevertheless, he does explore this aspect of the king-metaphor in relation to God. Of the above verses, Isaiah 33.22 is the most evocative and rich theologically:

כִּי יְהוָה שֹׁפְטֵנוּ יְהוָה מְחֹקְקֵנוּ יְהוָה מַלְכֵּנוּ הוּא יוֹשִׁיעֵנוּ

> For the LORD is our judge, the LORD is our ruler,
>   the LORD is our king; he will save us.

YHWH is here designated as judge, ruler, king and saviour!

We have seen above that in the ANE, while the gods are related to justice, it is always the king who is the lawgiver and who promulgates the law. It is here that we encounter a remarkable contrast with Israel. Brettler notes that:

> In contrast to ancient Near Eastern law 'codes,' such as Hammurabi, no text explicitly mentions the Israelite king as the promulgator of an extensive body of law. It is quite possible that the Pentateuchal law collections, which show remarkably little interest in the royal court, developed independently of the king.[191]

Brague makes the point concisely: 'The Bible avoids representing the king as legislator.'[192] Unique to the OT is the view that YHWH himself promulgates the law. He is the lawgiver par excellence.

---

190 Brettler 1989, 113.
191 Brettler 1989, 109.
192 Brague 2007, 49.

The one lawgiver is God. That idea was an unparalleled novelty in the ancient Middle East, where only the king made laws. The Torah has no real parallel in those civilizations. The God of Israel replaces the Oriental king in the role of lawgiver. Hence the predicates attributed to the pharaoh in Egypt are reserved for God alone in Israel.[193]

This would have come as a shock to the average ANE citizen, let alone a ruler. It should not and must not be taken for granted. In the context of the ANE, as Brague observes, there was nothing about 'divine law' that was obvious, self-evident and thus a natural development. 'Divine law' presupposes the existence of 'the divine' (singular) and of social power expressing itself in terms of laws. Its emergence thus requires a two-sided historical development: societal power expressing itself through laws and divinity having appeared which is able and willing to provide the normativity required.[194]

Of course, the OT has a great deal to say about law, and we will attend to law in detail in volume 2 of this series. For now, we note the theological and practical significance of such an emphasis. As Brague observes, we should not underestimate the significance of law in the OT for understanding God and OT ethics. 'The idea of divine law implies that *human action, in its full breadth, receives its norm from the divine.*'[195]

Within the political, the juridical is not necessarily connected to the divine. Ancient China, for example, had a well-developed system of law, but there was never ever the suggestion that a written law was of divine origin.[196] In the civilizations of which Western Europe is the heir, Brague identifies three possible paradigms for the triangular relationship between the divine, political power (the king) and the law (see Fig. 5).

- First, the divine can influence the king directly but the law only indirectly.
- Second, the divine can influence the law directly but the king only indirectly.
- Third, a direct relationship exists between the king and the law but leaving the divine apart from the juridical and the political.

Brague finds Ancient Egypt to be the best example of the first, where it is possible that something akin to a state appeared for the first time

---

193  Brague 2007, 49.
194  Brague 2007, 11.
195  Brague 2007, 7–8. Emphasis original.
196  Bodde and Morris 1967, 10. See Brague 2007, 14.

The divine

The law                              The political

Figure 5 **The relationship between God, law and political power**

(1994–1781 BC). He quotes E. Otto's definition of Egyptian laws: they refer to 'a universally valid rule, usually decreed by the king (or a god) and concerning singular and concrete states of fact'; originally, they indicated a punishment. Law here is a collection of cases.[197]

Law was the word of Pharaoh. Meir Sternberg alerted me years ago to the fact that we have discovered no law codes from Egypt. This may relate to Pharaoh's being a god and the source of law. However, things are more complex than that. Papyrus does not last and it is possible that we have not discovered, and probably will not discover, such codes even if they did exist, as some Egyptologists think. Brague perceptively poses the question: did the Egyptians write down laws? Certainly not monumentally, as far as the evidence shows, so if they did, it was on perishable materials. Brague concludes that in Egypt there was never an attempt to organize laws into a code from which principles and thus rules could be developed. Pharaoh may be a god, but this does not make the law divine. Egypt opted for the first possibility above. Brague explores how this relates to the Egyptian concept of *maat*, explored above, noting that in this way Egypt approximated natural law.[198] In general, Mesopotamian societies, unlike Egypt, did not regard the king as divine. Nevertheless, the same first model above is embodied in their view of law: 'the god is not considered as being himself the origin of the enacted laws. The religious and the political are juxtaposed rather than merged.'[199]

The idea of divine law is the second model above, where the divine influences the law directly. Brague refers to this as a short cut; 'divinity applies to the law itself and not to a living person who "makes the law."'[200] Because the law cannot

---

197  Brague 2007, 15.
198  Brague 2007, 16.
199  Brague 2007, 17.
200  Brague 2007, 18.

impose itself unaided, it needs to be legitimated by the divine. 'To describe a law as divine is to refuse to reduce it to the conditions of its formulation.'[201] Brague discerns this model in the view of law in Greece and Ancient Israel.

> Greek divine law is divine because it expresses the profound structures of a permanent natural order; Jewish Law is divine because it emanates from a god who is master of history. In both cases, it is external to the human and transcends the quotidian.[202]

Brague quotes Leo Strauss to the effect that both attend to the problem of divine law but they solve this problem in opposite ways.

None of this is straightforward, and neither is the development of the idea of divine law among the Greeks.[203] The Greek idea of divine law can be traced back to the goddesses of the law and on into the classical period in which the philosophers introduced the concept of 'nature'. This concept called for reconsideration of law: if laws are in opposition to it then they are mere convention; if in accord with it then they are natural law. In the Greek tradition, that which is divine has no origin; it is simply permanent. Gods do not make laws since they too issue forth from the divine. 'All the philosophers in fact tend to neutralize divinity. And the divinity of the laws, according to them, depends on the fact that they come, not from the gods, but from the divine.'[204] Written and divine are mutually exclusive. In the third century, Galen mocked the laws of Moses, not because of their content but because of how they were given without any proof.

As Brauge thus notes, for the Greeks the concept of 'divine law' was familiar, indeed, far more familiar than the notion of a law from God. For the Greeks the adjective 'divine' in 'divine law' did not refer to the origin of law in a god. Instead it referred to a deep, impersonal order immanent within reality. By contrast, as the concept of divine law developed in the post-biblical and medieval eras, 'divine' came to refer to a god external to the world but one who is well able to engage with it.

Brague is clear that 'Ancient Israel revolutionized the relations between the normative and the divine'.[205] He pays scant attention to Sinai and sees the

---

201  Brague 2007, 18.
202  Brague 2007, 18.
203  See Brague 2007, 19–38.
204  Brague 2007, 23.
205  Brague 2007, 42.

critique of kingship in 1 Samuel as a *vaticinium ex eventu* (prophecy after the event). Monarchy was really the only model for the state known in the ANE, but 'only in Israel does a criticism of the very institution of monarchy appear'.[206]

> Israel is distinctive in having conceived of human kingship as not only distinct from divine kingship but even opposed to it. In this fashion Israel planted seeds of democracy that proved just as fertile as the Greek traditions, even though they are cited less frequently.[207]

Torah is thought to have come from YHWH himself, and Brague notes evocatively that the divinity of the law resulted from YHWH's having *written it himself* (Exod. 31.18; 32.16; Deut. 9.10). This anthropomorphism signals deep personal engagement: 'in giving the law, God gives of his own and of himself.'[208] In Israel, Torah replaces the king. We witness here an excarnation of the law. In relation to Deuteronomy 33.5, Brague finds the most profound comment in Judah Halevi: the Torah is the true king of Israel.[209]

This new view of law results in a new view of election. In Egypt the pharaoh was elect; in Israel it is now the whole people: 'The king of Israel is replaced by YHWH in his function as legislator, but he is also replaced by the people as the subject of history.'[210] Whereas the Greeks solved the question of human community in terms of natural sociability, the Israelites did so in terms of historical election. Wisdom is also expanded. In Egypt wisdom is incarnate in the pharaoh; in Israel the people as a whole are invited to become wise (see Eccl. 12.9). Unlike most ancient nations, as a result Israel is not defined geographically, but religiously. 'There are two aspects to that religion. The first is the cult at the Temple of Jerusalem, whose claim to a complete monopoly was finally realized; the second is adherence to the precepts of the law.'[211]

In the Pentateuch, *torah* emerges overwhelmingly in the context of YHWH's entering into a covenant relationship with the people of Israel. This is unparalleled in the ANE, as is the embedding of law in such a narrative context. Brague is thus quite right when he notes that 'the deepest meaning of the law

---

206  Brague 2007, 46.

207  Brague 2007, 47.

208  Brague 2007, 49.

209  Brague 2007, 50.

210  Brague 2007, 30.

211  Brague 2007, 53.

is no less than life with the divinity'.[212] Brague points out the background of 'covenant' in personal covenants between equals and in international law. The similarity between the Sinai covenant in Exodus and Deuteronomy has long been compared to ANE suzerain treaties, whether Hittite or Assyrian. As is well known, in such international treaties the gods are called upon to guarantee the treaty, resulting in a mutual recognition of one another's gods. The gods of the contracting party were 'part of the furniture' of such agreements.

> With the Bible, however, the idea of an alliance of a people with a god first appears, as is the case in Exodus 19–20. This means that *the god who had been the guarantee of the alliance became a partner in it*.[213]

This has radical implications: the people become the god's people and

> [t]he divine no longer hovers far above human history; it enters into the domain of the religious . . . The clauses of the treaty no longer hold any validity in themselves; they are the conditions . . . of a more essential phenomenon, which is the entry into contact with the god, the communion with the divine.[214]

The result, which enables Judah to survive the exile, is that YHWH is by no means constrained by the land of Canaan in the sense of being inherently connected to it. As Brague evocatively notes: 'YHWH is a "floating" god who settles in a territory with his people.'[215]

Apodictic law – of the imperative form 'You shall . . .' rather than the casuistic form of 'If . . . then . . .' – is found throughout law in the ANE,[216] but the Decalogue is unique. Brague asserts that its contents are nothing exceptional, a view we will query below. For Brague, it is the opening of the Decalogue in Exodus 19.1 that transforms it. Brague evocatively compares the Decalogue to the rules for an office building or a house:

> on entering God's domain, one learns something about him . . . we learn that God is the sort of person who, if he were a man, would not kill, would

212  Brague 2007, 58.
213  Brague 2007, 59. Emphasis original.
214  Brague 2007, 59.
215  Brague 2007, 59.
216  Kitchen and Lawrence, 2012c, 267–76.

not steal, and so forth. This is the sense in which the law is, quite literally, a teaching (*torah*) . . . I might say that it cuts you in on the deal . . . The aim of the commandments is not to impose obedience but to provide an entry into the divine mores.[217]

Similarly, Patrick Miller refers to the Decalogue as the ethos of the good neighbourhood.[218] Clearly, YHWH is king, lawgiver and judge. Brague's and Miller's comments remind us that YHWH's *torah* is in no way oppressive but rather an invitation into life with him, life lived according to the grain of creation, for this YHWH is also the Creator.

As mentioned above, Brague asserts that the contents of the Decalogue are nothing exceptional. In my view this is wrong, and nowhere does this become more clearly apparent than in the tenth commandment, which we come to next.

## (k) YHWH and the tenth commandment

There are multiple ways in which the Decalogue is unique: its grounding in YHWH's deliverance of the Israelites from Egypt, its aniconism, its Sabbath law and concurrent view of time, and so on. However, in terms of uniqueness, the tenth commandment merits special attention.

**Exodus 20.17**[219]
You (sgl) are not to desire
   the house of your (sgl) neighbour.
You (sgl) are not to desire
   the wife of your (sgl) neighbour,
   nor his (sgl) servant, nor his (sgl) maidservant,
   nor his (sgl) ox, nor his (sgl) ass,
   nor anything that belongs to your (sgl) neighbour.

The tenth commandment differs from the other nine in that it relates to the subjective attitude of desire and cannot be legislated for, as commentators have noted.[220] Leon Kass rightly notes, for example, that

---

217  Brague 2007, 57.
218  Miller 2004, 2007b, 51–67.
219  My translation ('sgl' means 'singular'). Cf. Deut. 5.21.
220  Durham 1987, 297–8.

if most of the prohibitions in the second table are familiar, the Decalogue concludes in a surprising turn by focusing not on an overt action but on an internal condition of the heart or soul, a species of ardent desire or yearning. The uniqueness of this proscription of coveting is suggested both by its greater length and by the spelling out of the seven things belonging to your neighbor that you not only must not steal but also must not even long for.[221]

Nahum Sarna asserts that:

> The Decalogue thus becomes a self-enforcing code in that its appeal is to the conscience, not to enlightened self-interest, and its enforcing mechanism is the spiritual discipline and moral fiber of the individual, not the threat of penalty that is imposed by the coercive power of the state.[222]

Ten is a symbolic number and the final commandment forms an inclusio with the first one. As Rabbi Goldman notes: 'The Decalogue begins with a right relation to God in the heart and concludes with a similar obligation in respect to man.'[223] Cassuto observes that 'your neighbour' parallels 'your God' in the opening: 'There the essence is the love of God, and here it is the love of one's fellow-man. The two parts are parallel to each other, so also are the two loves.'[224] He astutely notes the positive dimensions of both the opening and closing commandments. As Benedict XVI says,

> the law of God is not to be seen as a concentrate of 'nos' that are an end in themselves, but as the door of access to the great 'yes' that opens up to God and to life. The Commandments are not chains that bind humans, but *an antidote to the seductions, the passions, the unfettered desires that give the illusion of a limitless freedom, while in reality [they] are false conquests that debase existence and make it empty.* Placed in the right perspective, these laws are therefore to be considered as essential references for a life project directed to responsibility, fidelity and love, and therefore

---

221  Kass, Fishbane, Berkowitz, Meilaender, Soloveichik 2013.

222  Sarna 1986, 1996, 142.

223  Goldman 1963, 188.

224  Goldman, 1963, 189.

based on solid and enduring values that generate true freedom and the joy of living.[225]

These points are insightful and widely acknowledged. René Girard's unique contribution is to enable us to see just how radically and powerfully the final commandment shapes the good neighbourhood.

## The gateway of mimetic desire

The sixth to the ninth commandments forbid the most heinous acts of violence towards one's neighbour. The tenth prohibits a desire, not an act. *ḥāmad*, as Durham proposes, is the verb deliberately selected for this commandment. The commandment seeks to slam the gate of covetousness shut, aware that it is the route through which the other commandments end up being broken. Going back up the commandments from the tenth, the order reflects the precept not to harm your neighbour by desire, by word or by action.

Desire is a major theme in twenty-first century philosophy and thought, but Girard argues that the final commandment is far more radical than we generally realize: 'What the tenth commandment sketches, without defining it explicitly, is a fundamental revolution in the understanding of desire.'[226] Leon Kass observes that

> the final injunction *causes us to reflect about the meaning of possession and about the nature of desire and neighborhood.* A man who covets what is his neighbor's suffers, whether he knows it or not, from multiple deformations of his own desire. Not content with his own portion of goodly things, he is incapable of seeing them in their true light: as means to – and participants in – a higher way of life. Moreover, some of the same items occur on both the list of seven partakers in Sabbath rest and in the list of seven 'covetables' – as if to indicate the mistaken direction of the coveter's desire.[227]

Where Girard's work is unique is in his profound exploration of *the mechanics of desire* and thus the *radicality* of the tenth commandment. He notes that, in the Christian tradition, theologians 'speak much of original sin, but they fail to

---

225 Benedict XVI 2014. Emphasis added.
226 Girard 2001, 9.
227 Kass, Fishbane, Berkowitz, Meilaender and Soloveichik 2013, Kindle Locations 623–35. Emphasis added.

make the idea concrete'.[228] Girard's analysis of the mechanics of desire enables us to see concretely just how powerful the tenth commandment is.

The focus of desire is, according to Girard, not so much on objects such as houses, spouses and fields, but on another person, usually our neighbour, just as the tenth commandment asserts 'nor anything that belongs to your neighbour'. Humans are social creatures and thus the model or focus for our desires is our neighbour. Girard's language for this is mimetic desire. If we think about how children develop, it is clear that *mimetic desire* is natural. Children develop by copying (mimesis) the behaviour of their parents and siblings. As Girard states:

> The only culture really ours is not that into which we are born; it is the culture whose models we imitate at the age when the power of mimetic assimilation is the greatest ... Mimetic desire ... is responsible for the best and the worst in us, for what lowers us below the animal level as well as what elevates us above it. Our unending discords are the ransom of our freedom.[229]

In a fallen world, mimesis and desire easily turn to rivalry. Our neighbour can become an idol, which reflects back on the idolization of our autonomous selves. According to Girard, 'The conflicts resulting from this double idolatry of self and other are the principal source of human violence.'[230] Such desire unchecked is contagious, and it contaminates those around us. Like a conflagration, mimetic rivalry can grow and become so intense that we begin to speak falsely about the other, to steal her or his belongings, to seduce the other's spouse and ultimately to murder. The perceptive reader will note that these are *the four commandments preceding the tenth, in reverse order.*

Mimetic desire is the engine of violence, and, in *I See Satan Fall Like Lightning*, Girard examines the crucial role of the tenth commandment in constraining mimetic desire before it catches fire. In this respect, it is revolutionary and, according to Girard, comes to fulfilment in the Gospels, which encourage us to follow (imitate) Jesus in his remarkable handling of desire.

Situated where it is, at the very heart of OT Torah, the final commandment is thus far more radical than it first appears to be. Strategically, it reaches beyond actions through to the heart, seeking to defuse societal violence before

---

228 Girard 2001, 150.
229 Girard 2001, 15–16.
230 Girard 2001, 11.

it sparks and becomes an uncontrollable fire. The Decalogue addresses the people of God as a whole, but its use of the second person singular must be noted. As Philo observed:

> God thought good in proclaiming his ten oracles to address each [person individually] . . . He wishes to teach the readers of the Sacred Scriptures . . . that each single person, when he is law-abiding and obedient to God, is equal in worth to a whole nation . . . even to the whole world . . . [God] wills that no king or despot swollen with arrogance and contempt should despise an insignificant private person.[231]

In this way, the tenth commandment both makes the *individual* accountable for his or her desire and defends his or her interests. Simultaneously, it is wonderfully comprehensive in its focus on the individual household in relationship to other households. In terms of SAT, we might say that its illocutionary force is both individual and communal. Halevi perceptively points out that the tenth commandment

> not only applies to another's property but to coveting that which belongs to God . . . A human being may borrow for his time on earth those things he is given by providence, but he may not consider them as possessions, because they are all gifts.[232]

The common language in the tenth and the Sabbath commandment support this view. As the household is to rest and remember God as creator, so it is to be protected against the conflagration of misdirected desire.

The Decalogue is thus remarkable. It is the key to the good neighbourhood because it inculcates a world view with YHWH at the centre, enabling the Israelites to find their place in healthy relationship with one another. Such an ethos will only survive if the door to misdirected mimetic desire remains closed. It has been argued that the twentieth century was the most brutal in history, a reminder of the importance and radicality of the tenth commandment.

Brague is perceptive in his recognition of how the Decalogue tells us about YHWH. Similarly, André LaCocque refers to the Decalogue evocatively as the exegesis of the name YHWH. Indeed, just as in the NT the Lord's Prayer tells us a great deal about the Lord of the prayer, and just as the Beatitudes in Matthew

---

231 Goldman 1963, 75–6

232 Halevi 1988, 123.

5 tell us a great deal about the king who rules over the citizens of his kingdom, so too the Decalogue tells us a great deal about YHWH. He acts in history to deliver his people from slavery, as God he is appropriately jealous of his people's loyalty and will not tolerate rivals, as the transcendent God he is immanently involved in the creation and concerned with all of life as he has made it, his rhythm of life is healthy and he calls his people to live similarly, the family is his creation and he wants it to flourish, he values human life highly and is faithful in relationship, and he wonderfully respects the otherness of the creatures he has made. What should not be missed in this discussion is the implicit doctrine of the *imago Dei*. This is often thought to be restricted to Genesis 1, but here it is with YHWH's people being fashioned in his likeness, in his image.

What can we say about the antiquity of the Decalogue? The evidence is not without its complexities as, for example, the differences between the Decalogue in Exodus and Deuteronomy make clear. Coogan follows the source criticism of the Pentateuch and concludes that in their present form these versions of the Decalogue are fairly late. However, both leant on an older form of the Decalogue. Coogan concludes:

> In my view, then, the Decalogue is very ancient, older than its expansions in the redacted biblical sources, and the covenant that it formulates, and perhaps even the formulation as ten short commandments, is the essence of the teaching of Moses himself. This would explain its priority in biblical tradition and beyond.[233]

At the centre of OT law we find YHWH. As we conclude our reflections in this area we return to Psalm 82, discussed above. In verses 2–7 we have God's judgement of the other gods. Like a good lawyer, God asks the right questions that reveal his case against the gods. They are accused of judging unjustly and of showing partiality to the rich. Verses 3–4 indicate positively how a god should relate to justice:

- providing justice for the weak and fatherless;
- maintaining the rights of the afflicted and destitute;
- rescuing the weak and needy;
- delivering such vulnerable people from the hand of the wicked.

---

233 Coogan 2014, 49.

Verse 8 is a prayer, calling on God to arise and to *judge* the earth. He will inherit the nations.

Where Psalm 82 is vitally important is in demonstrating that world views have consequences. According to the psalmist, the failure of the gods to deliver justice is catastrophic; it threatens the very creation. This alerts us unequivocally to the vital importance of law and justice in any society if it is to be healthy and to promote human flourishing.

On one issue at least, Liberation Theology is surely right, namely, 'God takes the side of the poor because he is the God of righteousness and justice.'[234] *YHWH is the God of justice,* and as such he exercises what Catholics refer to as a preferential option for the poor. This, I propose, is the answer to the title of Hayes' book, *What's Divine about Divine Law?*[235] In Protestant theology this was clearly expressed by Karl Barth in his treatment of the mercy and righteousness of God:

> For this reason the human righteousness required by God and established in obedience – the righteousness which according to Amos 5:24 should pour down as a mighty stream – has necessarily the character of a vindication of right in favor of the threatened innocent, the oppressed poor, widows, orphans and aliens. For this reason, in the relations and events in the life of His people, God always takes His stand unconditionally and passionately on this side and on this side alone: against the lofty and on behalf of the lowly; against those who already enjoy right and privilege and on behalf of those who are denied it and deprived of it . . . We are all widows and orphans who cannot procure right for themselves . . . According to the Gospel of Luke and the Epistle of James, as also according to the message of the prophets, there follows from this character of faith a political attitude, decisively determined by the fact that man is made responsible to all those who are poor and wretched in his eyes, that he is summoned on his part to espouse the cause of those who suffer wrong . . . The man who lives by faith that this is true stands under a political responsibility . . . He cannot avoid the question of human rights.[236]

A test of a healthy society will, therefore, be the extent to which it in theory (law) and in practice protects the rights and lives of its most vulnerable. As

---

234  Spykman, Cook, Dodson, Grahn, Rooy and Stam 1998, 229.
235  Hayes 2015.
236  Barth, *CD* II/1, 386–7.

with the Lord's Prayer, Psalm 82.8 is a prayer for the in-between times. With its prayer at the end for YHWH to arise and judge the nations, '[t]he liturgical movement of the psalm's recitation holds the "already" and the "not yet" of the LORD's rule in tension'.[237] Mays points out that '[i]t is through law and prophecy, supported by historic interventions against the wicked, that this God manifests identity and rule'.[238] God is already uncovering and condemning the false gods, and '[f]aith must always see the LORD standing in the midst of the gods of the nations and know that to say "Thy kingdom come" is to pray for the death of our gods'.[239]

In her book *What's Divine about Divine Law?* Christine Hayes argues that if an ancient follower of biblical law was asked this question, he or she would answer by indicating its origin in the divine will, 'a will expressed in history rather than nature'.[240] This, in my view, is a distortion of the OT view of law. YHWH is YHWH Elohim, both creator and redeemer, so that his law reflects and runs according to the grain of creation, as he made it. At the same time, OT law is not a collection of timeless, universal principles. Even the Decalogue is clearly situated historically at a certain point in Israel's history. The OT has a strong and unique view of history, and this accounts for the particularity of OT law as well as its paradigmatic character for later times. It is for this reason that the psalmist calls on God to judge the earth and notes that he will inherit the nations. Israel is, as constituted at Sinai, an ANE theocracy in covenant relationship with YHWH. Its legal insights remain invaluable, but they cannot simply be transplanted into modern pluralistic cultures. YHWH remains king, lawgiver, judge, but we will need to work out what that means for us today, drawing on all the many clues provided by the OT.

## (l) YHWH as 'servomechanism'

The above section alerts us to the fact that YHWH's presence in the midst of Israel shapes her society as a whole and in all areas. Israel remains a particular, ANE nation with much in common with her neighbours, but also radically different and distinct, and her difference cannot be reduced to her doctrine of God. To put it differently, her doctrine of God changes everything.

---

237 Mays 2011.
238 Mays 2011.
239 Mays 2011.
240 Hayes 2015, 2.

Our overview of the world views of the ANE demonstrated how king, cult and law are inseparable and dominant in the ANE. However, as we have seen, in Israel it is YHWH who is king and lawgiver. This signals a radically different society from those of the ANE. Instead of a typical ANE hierarchy in which the pyramid ascends to the king and then to the gods, in Israel we have a nation under the rule of and in covenant with King YHWH. This generates an unprecedented *egalitarian* tendency in Israel, in which all, including the king, stand before and are responsible to YHWH.

No one that I am aware of has drawn attention to this characteristic of the OT as strongly as Gottwald,[241] and it is he who speaks of mono-Yahwism as a *servomechanism*. Note that he here speaks of Yahwism rather than YHWH, and in line with his sociological analysis of the OT he tends to reduce YHWH to such a mechanism, whereas we have seen that he is the living God who acts in history.[242] In line with modern views of the origin of Israel, Gottwald primarily reads the OT against a Canaanite background. Nevertheless, through his attention to the social dimensions of Israel and the ways in which Yahwism relates to this – which is what he means by 'servomechanism' – Gottwald foregrounds significant ways in which Israel developed a very different society from those of the ANE. In terms of the egalitarian tendency in the OT, for example, Gottwald makes this important point:

> It cannot escape our attention that, instead of the many gods, Israel projected one God, in symbolic complementarity with the determined way in which, in place of the many strata of Canaanite society, Israel projected a strataless society, which is to say: one indivisible God for one indivisible people.[243]

In Gottwald's language, the *religious* anomalies of OT Israel mirror the *social* anomalies, and vice versa.[244] In addition to this egalitarian tendency, Gottwald identifies the following distinctives of Yahwism and OT Israel.

***An intentional disregard of the underworld.*** Gottwald observes that:

---

241 Gottwald 1979. I was aware of Gottwald's work but am grateful to Chris Wright for nudging me to take a closer look.

242 See Gottwald 1979, 692, for his demythologized definition of Yahwism.

243 Gottwald 1979, 648.

244 Gottwald 1979, 693. Gottwald (1979, 693) notes that the mid-twentieth-century Biblical Theology Movement (BTM) was correct in arguing for Israel's religious distinctiveness but failed to locate this distinctiveness in her social constitution. See below for more discussion of this movement.

Yahweh forbade communication with the dead as Israel forbade the socially enervating and economically draining preoccupation with ancestor worship and memorialization of the dead, practices that were ways of
securing loyalty to the sociopolitical status quo.[245]

Gottwald notes that, through a connection back to what he calls the 'Moses
group', it is possible that Egypt is in view here as the adversary. Such a possibility is highly likely if Israel did indeed live in and then exit from Egypt,
and, as we saw above, Egyptian culture was obsessed with death. The concern
with death in the ANE, and especially in Egypt, had enormous cultic, political, social and economic consequences. In our modern, individualistic West
it is hard to imagine such connections, but an Ancient Egyptian, or someone
raised in the Egyptian court, would have no such problem. It is to Gottwald's
credit that he draws our attention to these connections. In subsequent volumes
we will attend in detail to the OT's approach to death. Suffice it here to note
that the effect of YHWH on Israel is to subvert the obsession with death and
thereby to radically restructure her society.

***The rejection of the sexualization of reality.*** In the OT the imitation of YHWH
is, in my opinion, a strong motif, as we have seen with the Decalogue above. A
lingering question for me has been the extent to which imitation of the gods
played a role in ANE life. It is hard to imagine that it did not, although the gods
are portrayed as larger-than-life, that is, far more powerful, humans. Nevertheless, in this area of the sexualization of reality we do find an imitation of
the gods present in the ANE. Gottwald asserts that:

> Fertility rites and concepts in ancient Near Eastern religion saw the hu-
> man and divine worlds united in a bisexuality that extended from crops
> and herds and flocks through human pairing to the innumerable divine
> couplings of gods and goddesses with their consorts. This sexualization
> of natural and social reality tended to concentrate human energies in
> *microcosmic imitations of the divine energies*. The sexual symbols were
> monopolized by priesthoods and political elites, so that celebration of the
> sexualization of reality was celebration of the ruling system.[246]

---

245  Gottwald 1979, 694.
246  Gottwald 1979, 694–5. Emphasis added.

Gottwald notes that, by comparison, in Israel the locus of the divine was not in reproduction and sexuality but in social order and relations. Within the world view of the OT, we might say, sexuality is resituated so as to avoid both the 'mystical glorification of sex'[247] and the degrading practice of prostitution, the latter generally left to the lower class. Gottwald further argues that the incorporation of women into extended families in early Israel reduced, if not eradicated, prostitution.

It seems to me that Gottwald is right here. In the OT, YHWH, *unlike the gods of the ANE*, is not part of the creation, does not have a wife or consort, is never depicted as engaging in sexual intercourse, is not born and does not die, but transcends the creation and brings into existence humans who are differentiated in terms of gender. All of which ought to make us reconsider the power and social and political implications of a text such as Genesis 1.26–28 in which all humans, male and female, are made in the *imago Dei*. Gender and sexuality are surely part of what it means to be made in God's image, but the primary focus of the image is for humans to *function* as God's royal stewards in caring for the creation, developing its potentials and enhancing God's reputation in his world. All humans, and not just the king, bear these responsibilities, and this leads to a very different view of society, as Gottwald notes.

*A radical reduction of the economics of the cultus.* Out of the mists of antiquity of the ANE, cult and king seem to appear together, and in the ANE king and cult remain closely bound up with each other, as we have seen. In the OT, however, the role of the king is radically downgraded and replaced by YHWH as king and lawgiver, and in the process the place and role of the cultus is also resituated. In Egypt, as we saw, the temples and the priesthood were owners of extensive holdings and thus an economic force to be reckoned with. Strikingly, by comparison, the Levites in the OT are landless. Just as, according to the Decalogue, YHWH's name is not to be manipulated in power games, so too Israel's cultus is not to be manipulated by the elite for economic advantage. Gottwald observes that:

> Yahweh owned all but demanded less economic investment and expenditure from worshippers than was customary in the monarchic-imperial cults of the ancient Near East. This is a dramatic instance of Yahwism's function as a social servomechanism – i.e., as a facilitator of chosen societal ends – since Yahweh's massive symbolic power was marshalled to

---

247 Gottwald 1979, 695.

prevent the old familiar game plan of political manipulation of religion in order to extract surplus wealth from the general populace.[248]

***The production of history for the people.*** The historiography of the OT is distinctive. This is not to say that Gottwald would agree with the approach we have taken to the history of the OT; he is very much a mainstream OT scholar. However, he notes that:

> The differentiating criterion in Israel is that Yahweh's deeds are conceived as stages in the liberation of a whole people within the recent historic past. Elsewhere in the ancient Near East the gods are active chiefly in the deeds of kings, dynasties, ruling classes, city-states, and national entities which are assumed to have rootage in a distant past.[249]

By comparison, in the OT YHWH's great acts are for the whole people and through the whole people. Gottwald draws attention to the symbolic power of the exodus–conquest paradigm and notes evocatively that "'[d]eliverance from Egypt" typified all sorts of "escapes" from Canaanite, Egyptian, Philistine, and Transjordanian political-military domination'.[250] This insight of Gottwald's ties back into Sanders' point that we explored in Part 1, namely that the communicative power of the HB/OT is unprecedented in the ANE.

Replace YHWH as servomechanism with YHWH as the living God, and I think we are closer to the view and truth of the OT. Israel was an ANE nation and the marks of that particularity are clear to see. But YHWH was in her midst, and that radically rearranged her social, political and religious furniture, as it were. The king was demoted, the cultus resituated, sexuality redefined, the potential for an egalitarian culture established, a potent form of history-telling invented, and so on.

Here in the UK, from time to time there are discussions about whether we should remain a monarchy or become a republic. These are interesting and important discussions, but no one imagines that if we became a republic our politics, economics, local church life and so on would be radically changed. However, it was very different in the ANE. Proclaim the name of YHWH – our next section – and the king is demoted (if you even have one), the cultus is resituated, politics shifts; indeed everything changes and is realigned.

---

248 Gottwald 1979, 696.

249 Gottwald 1979, 696.

250 Gottwald 1979, 698.

# (m) Proclaiming the name of YHWH: all YHWH's goodness

The expression 'proclaim the name of YHWH' comes from the narrative in Exodus 34 following Moses' successful intercession in Exodus 33 on behalf of the idolatrous Israelites. Moses' request to see God's כָּבֹד (holiness) is denied, but YHWH makes a promise in Exodus 33.19:

וַיֹּאמֶר אֲנִי אַעֲבִיר כָּל־טוּבִי עַל־פָּנֶיךָ וְקָרָאתִי בְשֵׁם יְהוָה לְפָנֶיךָ וְחַנֹּתִי אֶת־אֲשֶׁר אָחֹן וְרִחַמְתִּי אֶת־אֲשֶׁר אֲרַחֵם׃

¹⁹ And he said, 'I will make all my goodness pass before you, and will proclaim before you the name, 'The LORD'; and I will be gracious to whom I will be gracious, and will show mercy on whom I will show mercy.'

In Exodus 34.5–7 we read:

וַיֵּרֶד יְהוָה בֶּעָנָן וַיִּתְיַצֵּב עִמּוֹ שָׁם וַיִּקְרָא בְשֵׁם יְהוָה׃ וַיַּעֲבֹר יְהוָה
עַל־פָּנָיו וַיִּקְרָא יְהוָה יְהוָה אֵל רַחוּם וְחַנּוּן אֶרֶךְ אַפַּיִם וְרַב־חֶסֶד
וֶאֱמֶת׃ נֹצֵר חֶסֶד לָאֲלָפִים נֹשֵׂא עָוֹן וָפֶשַׁע וְחַטָּאָה וְנַקֵּה לֹא יְנַקֶּה
פֹּקֵד עֲוֹן אָבוֹת עַל־בָּנִים וְעַל־בְּנֵי בָנִים עַל־שִׁלֵּשִׁים וְעַל־רִבֵּעִים׃

⁵ The LORD descended in the cloud and stood with him there, and proclaimed the name, 'The LORD.' ⁶ The LORD passed before him, and proclaimed,

'The LORD, the LORD,
a God merciful and gracious,
slow to anger,
and abounding in steadfast love and faithfulness,
⁷ keeping steadfast love for the thousandth generation,
forgiving iniquity and transgression and sin,
yet by no means clearing the guilty,
but visiting the iniquity of the parents
upon the children
and the children's children,
to the third and the fourth generation.'

This pronouncement of the name YHWH[251] occurs in the narrative of the golden calf incident in Exodus 32—34. Childs says of Exodus 34, in which these verses occur, that '[c]h. 34 is one of the most difficult chapters in Exodus to analyze and opinions differ widely'.[252] The main problem is the relationships of the laws in Exodus 34.10–38 to the Decalogue. He quotes Driver: 'The great difficulty is that one thing is commanded, and another done'. Our focus is on Exodus 34.6–7 in particular, and, not surprisingly, there is a whole range of historical-critical proposals about the origin of these two verses. Dentan, for example, argues that this formula was produced in wisdom circles and later inserted into the Sinai narrative.[253]

Here again, as with Exodus 19—24, literary analysis has turned out to be remarkably fruitful. Brichto, with his insights on episodes, recapitulation and resumptive repetition in OT narrative, subjects Exodus 32—34 to analysis and argues that

> chapters 32–34 of Exodus make up a carefully crafted narrative in the service of a single theme, that every discrepancy is deliberate, that a single author made use of an episodic narrative technique to weave a tapestrylike presentation of a theological principle.[254]

Brichto himself thinks that Exodus 32—34 is a 'philosophical fable or myth',[255] with which I disagree, but his literary analysis is insightful and very helpful in responding to historical-critical problems with the unity and coherence of the narrative.

In Brichto's analysis, 34.5–7 occurs in the eleventh Episode which provides the context and content of YHWH's revelation to Moses.

> The occasion is YHWH's act of grace, his reaffirmation or reinstitution of his covenant with Israel, symbolized by his inscribing a duplicate set of tablets. (Unlike the first set, which were carved as well as inscribed by YHWH himself, these tablets are carved by Moses – perhaps to suggest how important a role has been played by him in winning YHWH over to a renewal of the covenant.)[256]

---

251  cf. 1 Cor. 11.26 for a possible intertextual reference.
252  Childs 1974, 604.
253  Dentan 1963.
254  Brichto 1992, 90.
255  Brichto 1992, 88.
256  Brichto 1992, 107.

Exodus 34.27–34, in which YHWH instructs Moses to 'write down these words', forms the thirteenth Episode in Brichto's analysis. Exodus 34.11–26 form what Brichto calls the second Digression. He notes that all of these instructions, with the exception of two, appear with often identical phrasing in Exodus 23.12–33. The repetition 'is due neither to accident nor to the whimsy of an incompetent editor'.[257] One exception is 34.17 whose relevance in context is obvious. The second exception is 34.19–20, the dedication of the firstborn to YHWH. This points forward to the ordination of the Aaronite priesthood whose dedication to the service of YHWH releases other Israelites from this obligation.

It is these instructions in 34.11–26 that Moses is told to write down in 34.27. Brichto notes that:

> In all probability, this catalogue itself, characterized as the conditions imposed on Israel for the covenant with God, are only intended as an abstract of the fuller instructions which follow in the rest of Exodus as well as in parts of Leviticus and Numbers – hence the lengthy stay on the mountain. The Decalogue itself, as consistently described elsewhere, was inscribed by YHWH himself.[258]

The theophany in Exodus 34 responds to Moses' two queries: in Exodus 33.13 he requests that YHWH show him his ways; in 33.18 he requests that YHWH show him his glory. YHWH's passing before Moses answers the second; his recital of his character, the first.[259] Cassuto explains that in Jewish tradition 33.6–7 are referred to as the Thirteen Attributes of God, a delightful title. *Inter alia* on festival and holy days they are chanted aloud as the Torah scroll is taken out of the ark in preparation for it to be read. These verses are also referred to repeatedly in the OT, for example in Numbers 14.18; Nehemiah 9:17; Psalms 86.15; 103.8; 145.8; Jeremiah 32.18; Joel 2.13; Jonah 4.2; and Nahum 1.3. Widmer asserts that 'Exodus 34:6–7 undoubtedly contains the most comprehensive account of YHWH's nature in the entire Bible'.[260]

The wonderful list of YHWH's attributes can be summed up from the exquisite phrase in 33.19: כָּל־טוּבִי (all my goodness). 'The combination of terms expresses God's absolute and eternal dependability in dispensing His

---

257  Brichto 1992, 109.

258  Brichto 1992, 111.

259  Sarna 1991, 216.

260  Widmer 2004, 169.

benefactions.'[261] Exodus 34.6–7 refers back to the Decalogue and 20.5–6 in particular. The same view of YHWH is in place, but the order of the attributes is reversed as befits the context.[262] The double YHWH[263]

> is a deliberate repetition of the confessional use of the tetragrammaton . . . emphasizing the reality of Yahweh present in his very being, linking this proof to Moses to the earlier proof-of-Presence narratives that are begun in Exod. 3, and providing an anchor line for the last of five descriptive phrases to follow, phrases that define how Yahweh, 'The One Who Always Is,' really is.[264]

That YHWH 'called' (וַיִּקְרָא) his name before Moses is, as Wright notes, a remarkable and gracious expression, since it is normally humans who call on YHWH.[265] Widmer notes:

> Concerning the fact that YHWH proclaims His name in the third person singular, rather than in the first person, as one might expect at first sight, we followed an old Jewish tradition, which suggests that YHWH assumed the role of a *Vorbeter* [prayer leader]. In other words, YHWH teaches Moses how to use the divine name in subsequent prayer by revealing His name. If this line of interpretation is close to the logic of the final form of the text, that would endorse our contention that theology in its purest form (i.e. revealed by God Himself) is intrinsically linked to prayer.[266]

The adjective רַחוּם (merciful) speaks of YHWH's compassion for his people (cf. Ps. 103.13). חַנּוּן (gracious) is used only for God (cf. Exod. 22.26(27)). Both adjectives evoke YHWH's deep concern and care for his people, perhaps as familial or parental metaphors (cf. Exod. 2.6, using the different verb חָמַל). Widmer notes of חַנּוּן that '[i]t adds, however, the sense of a sovereign and generous king who is favourably inclined towards the weaker party (cf. 22:26, Ps. 86:15–16)'. חַנּוּן connects with Moses' previous prayer in which the phrase 'having found

---

261 Sarna 1991, 216.

262 See the chart on Widmer 2004, 184.

263 This is the only place where this occurs in the OT and different proposals are made for translating it. Cf. Widmer 2004, 172–3.

264 Durham 1987, 453.

265 C. Wright 2021, 582.

266 Widmer 2004, 202.

חֵן [grace] in YHWH's eyes' occurs six times (33.12–17; 34.9). Just as Moses found favour in the eyes of YHWH, so too will the people.[267]

YHWH is אֶרֶךְ אַפַּיִם (slow to anger), an attribute which ought to remind the Israelites just how seriously he takes idolatry. If he is slow to anger he abounds in other attributes: וְרַב־חֶסֶד וֶאֱמֶת (abounding in steadfast love and faithfulness); חֶסֶד (steadfast love) is repeated immediately in verse 7. Spieckermann thinks it is the main term in verses 6–7 and that the other adjectives are an expansion of it (cf. Exod. 20.6).[268] It seems to be closely related to the notion of covenant and to mean something like covenant fidelity or faithfulness but here goes beyond the idea of obligation to grace. אֱמֶת means both faithfulness and truth. YHWH does not gloss over idolatry; he calls it for what it is. But, simultaneously, he remains faithful; indeed he would not be faithful if he ignored the seriousness of idolatry. In verse 7 he keeps חֶסֶד and forgives. Verse 7 contains all the OT's major words for sin: עָוֺן וָפֶשַׁע וְחַטָּאָה (iniquity, transgression, sin).[269] As Knierim points out, as such they express the totality of sin against YHWH.[270] נֹשֵׂא (forgiving) may have connotations of a vicarious carrying of Israel's sins.[271] The rest of verse 7 turns attention to YHWH's justice.[272]

This proclamation of YHWH by YHWH is wonderfully rich and a good point on which to end our foray into the character of YHWH. It reminds us that YHWH not only acts in history but simultaneously explains his acts and his character. He reveals himself and thus offers himself to his people, as we will see below, in both deed and word.

---

267 Widmer 2004, 186.

268 Spieckermann 2000, 310.

269 See Widmer 2004, 189–91.

270 Knierim 1965.

271 Widmer 2004, 190–2.

272 Widmer (2004, 192–4) points out that וְנַקֵּה לֹא יְנַקֶּה (yet by no means clearing the guilty) is patent of two readings: YHWH does not entirely forgive or YHWH will not neglect just punishment. Widmer rightly notes that the interpretation must be constrained by the rest of the verse. This too is complex and he explores three options: collective punishment, trans-generational punishment and deferred punishment. Widmer (2004, 148) finds all three wanting and argues that 'in important ways Numbers 14 functions as a commentary on the divine name. In other words, I shall argue that YHWH's sentence, pronounced to Moses and Aaron in Numbers 14:20–35, comes as an intertextual hermeneutical key to the complex concept of YHWH's visitation of the iniquities of the fathers upon children to the fourth generation. We shall see that the children of the sinful generation only share in their parents' punishment insofar as they share in the "wilderness experience" until their parents die of natural death (Nu. 14:33).' Widmer (2004, 201) follows Scharbert's proposal that 'YHWH comes first to examine or to assess the moral standing of successive generations before appropriate measures are being taken. He is visiting with [a] view *to examine the iniquities of the fathers onto the third and fourth generations.*' Emphasis original.

However, divine action, and particularly special divine action (SDA), has not fared well in much theology and OT study in recent years. It is to this topic that we turn, after which we will revisit historical criticism.

# 8 Divine action in the Old Testament

## (a) Modernity revisited

Clearly, YHWH is portrayed in the OT as a God who acts, so that one would anticipate that divine action would be central to any discussion of the OT. Alas, a legacy of the modern critical approach to the OT is that in far too many cases the very possibility of YHWH's acting has been moved to the margins or become taboo. Ironically, and tellingly, as YHWH has been disallowed action the proposal for human actors/action in the production of the OT has multiplied exponentially so that it is no longer surprising to find the hands (actions) of multiple redactors identified in a short stretch of OT text. We saw this, for example, with Exodus 34.6–7 above. While the possibility of YHWH's having revealed himself to Moses and spoken these words receives scant or no attention in many major commentaries, the proposal for seeing the hands of different schools and multiple redactors at work abounds. At points like this it is hard not to recall C. S. Lewis's essay 'Fern-Seed and Elephants'.[273] Scholars claim to be able to discern the most minute fern-seed in the OT texts but are unable to attend to the elephant right in front of them, namely YHWH.

One of the attractive aspects of historical criticism pre-Wellhausen was that scholars would spend a considerable amount of time setting out their philosophy of religion so that one could then see how it influenced their reading of the OT. As we have seen, Wellhausen notoriously argued that philosophy follows but does not precede a critical reading of the OT, thereby obscuring the presuppositions brought to the text by many modern scholars and presenting a critical reading as objective and scientific, with religious readings automatically cast as ideological. In the twentieth century this move, perpetuated by OT luminaries such as James Barr and John Barton,[274] was unhelpful for mainstream OT scholarship that attempted to take divine action seriously, as we will see.

In his *Divine Revelation and the Limits of Historical Criticism*, William Abraham helps us to see why this is the case. Abraham notes that within the

---

273 Lewis 1975.
274 See above.

Christian tradition some sense of divine action and intervention is understood to be essential. 'On the other side there is the conviction that the contemporary theologian [OT scholar], if he is to be really honest and at home in recent developments, simply cannot appropriate the classical heritage at this point.'[275] Abraham then makes this crucial point:

> We should note immediately that this conviction is a *philosophical* conviction . . . It is a thesis about the compatibility of traditional Christian belief with contemporary canons of judgment in history and science, and even to state this with any degree of sophistication demands the exercise of philosophical judgment. The thesis is a *philosophical* one that calls for *philosophical* scrutiny . . . In this instance a body of agreed evidence to resolve the philosophical issue in one direction rather than another is just not available.[276]

Of course, if we follow Wellhausen and Barr in arguing that philosophy has little or no influence on OT criticism, then we will never see the need to scrutinize the philosophical presuppositions that much OT scholarship brings to its analysis of the text.

However, it is simply wrong to deny the influence of philosophy on modern OT studies and such a denial needs to be rejected once and for all. If one rejects Spinoza's pantheistic monism or Kant's idealism, as do I, then there is simply no reason to follow them in their rejection of divine action and historical narrative in the OT.

The reader may well still wonder: how is it that such a rejection of divine action as relevant to study of the OT has so often been uncritically assumed when the OT itself, as we have seen, asserts that YHWH can only be known through his action in history? How is it that so many OT scholars are able to devote so much attention to reconstructing stages in the development of the OT without having to scrutinize their philosophical presuppositions and account for their philosophy of religion? The answer is that the modern approach to the OT develops within modernity, and modernity has a vested interest in privatizing religion and in maintaining its standard narrative[277] whereby scholarship operating within its rules is simply neutral, objective,

---

275  Abraham 1982, 2.

276  Abraham 1982, 2–3. Emphasis added.

277  cf. Toulmin above.

autonomous scholarship. Deviation from its rules needs justification, but the standard narrative can simply be accepted as scientific and rational.

Modernity is the matrix within which historical criticism developed, and, as Scholder argues, what it does is read the Bible through the grid of the modern world view.[278] Modernity is a complex phenomenon so that there is real value in speaking of modernities just as there is value in speaking of historical criticisms. However, it is worth remembering that one thing philosophers do is to look for overarching patterns. We might well, therefore, ask: are there overarching patterns to modernity that can help orient OT scholars in terms of the impact of modernity on our discipline? There are, and I am glad to draw at this point on Richard Tarnas's fine volume, *The Passion of the Western Mind*, which is a wonderfully useful primer in the long story of philosophy. Tarnas's identification of the major characteristics of modernity helps us to see what is at stake in this discussion. At the end of his chapter, 'The Modern World View', Tarnas sets out seven characteristics of modernity, as follows.

i   Whereas, according to the medieval Christian world view, the personal and all-powerful God created and providentially ruled over the world, according to the modern world view the universe is impersonal, is regulated by natural laws and can be understood in purely mathematical and physical ways. 'God was now distantly removed from the physical universe, as creator and architect, and was now less a God of love, miracle, redemption, or historical intervention than a supreme intelligence and first cause, who established the material universe and its immutable laws and then withdrew from further direct activity.'[279]

ii   Whereas the Christian world view asserted the priority of the transcendent and spiritual over the earthly, this dualism was now inverted, with the material and concrete becoming the focus of attention.[280]

iii   Whereas the modern world view shares with the Greek world view a belief in an inherent order in the universe, by contrast it no longer locates the origin of this in a divine intelligence on which the mind could draw. The order is immanent within the universe and can be discerned through

---

278   Scholder 1990.
279   Tarnas 2010, 285.
280   Tarnas 2010, 286.

human investigation. However, 'the two realms, subjective mind and objective world, were now fundamentally distinct and operated on different principles'.[281]

iv In comparison with the Greeks' emphasis on a number of integrated cognitive modalities, the modern cosmos was able to be understood by humankind's empirical and rational faculties alone, while other parts of human nature – emotional, aesthetic, imaginative and so on – were generally seen as irrelevant or skewing for objective knowledge of the world.[282]

v In contrast to the medieval Christian world view, the modern world view conceived of the earth as a planet located within a neutral, infinite space, thereby eliminating the transcendent–terrestrial distinction.[283] Tarnas points out that in the process,

> [a]ll specifically human or personal qualities formerly attributed to the outer physical world were now recognized as naive anthropomorphic projections and deleted from the objective scientific perception. *All divine attributes were similarly recognized as the effect of primitive superstition and wishful thinking, and were removed from serious scientific discourse.* The universe was impersonal, not personal; nature's laws were natural, not supernatural.[284]

vi With the development of the theory of evolution and its implications for all fields of study, the question of what it means to be human and the intricacies of nature and its development were now related entirely to natural causes and processes that are observable empirically.[285]

vii Whereas in the medieval Christian world view, the human being was thought to be a creature and radically dependent on the living God, the modern world view asserted human independence and autonomy. 'While the purpose of knowledge for the medieval Christian was to better obey

---

281 Tarnas 2010, 286–7.
282 Tarnas 2010, 287.
283 Tarnas 2010, 287.
284 Tarnas 2010, 288. Emphasis added.
285 Tarnas 2010, 288.

God's will, its purpose for modern man was to better align nature to man's will.'[286] If the telos of the Christian perspective was to reconcile humankind and the world with God, the modern world view sought to achieve maximum freedom for humans.[287]

It needs to be stressed that what Tarnas is doing here is helpfully identifying the overarching patterns of the modern world view. Now, what I encourage the reader to do is twofold:

- Accept for argument's sake that Tarnas has accurately set out the major elements of the modern world view. Now, imagine yourself in the situation where these beliefs are simply accepted as normal and rational, namely, in the heart of modernity.
- Then, reflect on the emphasis in the Christian tradition on the living God as the one who acts and speaks, and try to interpret that through the grid of the modern world view. I suspect that the challenge and the resultant problem will speak for itself. Try as one might, there is something *irreconcilable* between the two. In practice, if not in theory, an informed choice has to be made, and time and again the mainstream OT guild has come down on the side of modernity.

One feels the need to issue several caveats at this point lest one is misunderstood. This is not an anti-modern rampage. There is a great deal about the modern world view that is good and to be celebrated. Under the influence of Platonism, for example, there was indeed an unhealthy overemphasis on the transcendent in the medieval era which needed to be subverted in order to allow the earthly to come properly into focus. The appropriation of the Aristotelian tradition in this respect was crucial and worked with the Christian tradition and the reappropriation of the Greek tradition in the Renaissance to light the flame of science and so much more. I, for one, have no desire to live pre-anaesthetic. Comparably, modern biblical studies has yielded enormous insights and we should not forgo these in an attempted return to 'pre-critical' interpretation alone. What we need is a nuanced discussion about the modern world view, its implications for the Christian tradition, what Christians should appropriate from it and where they need to hold their nerve against aspects of the modern world view.

---

286  Tarnas 2010, 289–90.
287  Tarnas 2010, 290.

In my opinion, it is particularly in one's view of God and in divine action and intervention that Christian scholars need to hold their nerve, lest we evacuate the Christian tradition of any distinctive content, as Gellner notes Christian scholars are prone to do.[288] I wish to defend the right of the many who desire to continue doing OT studies through the grid of the modern world view, and I recognize that I have a lot to learn from them. Postmodernism went a long way towards laying bare the assumptions of modernity, so that one would hope that they can no longer just be taken for granted but instead need to be argued for. One would like to hear such arguments! Whereas postmodernism ushered in a wild pluralism in OT studies, it was almost entirely 'deconstructive' rather than constructive in the sense of charting a new way forward, with the result that as it has declined historical criticism has moved to the fore again as the default mode of much rigorous OT study, now in an often-hardened secular mode. Again, I defend the right for such work but would love to hear the arguments for its presuppositions.

My plea is for a post-critical option in OT studies alongside other approaches. As I envisage it, this would be one in which the great Christian tradition of the living God and of divine action and intervention could be taken with full seriousness. My sense is that this would not solve the myriad of challenging problems within OT studies, but it would recast the discipline profoundly, and might contain the ring within which surprising solutions could be found.

## (b) The great acts of God revisited

The reader with a sense of history in OT studies may wonder if my project is simply an attempt to resurrect the discredited Biblical Theology Movement (BTM) of the mid twentieth century. This is a good question since the BTM has long been an interest of mine. As with so much of this discussion, the answer is not a simple one. Amid the challenges of modernity the BTM was a major attempt, with God's great acts at its heart, to retrieve the Bible for the Church.[289]

The era of the BTM can be set out with a degree of precision, namely from about 1945 to 1961. However, criticism of the BTM by Langdon Gilkey and James Barr, in particular, is thought to have sunk the movement once and for all. The BTM was primarily Protestant and American. Arising as it did around 1945, one is not surprised that it was influenced by Barthianism, although it was wary of Barth's perceived aversion to historical criticism. Emil Brunner, rather than Barth, was the stronger theological influence.

---

288 Gellner 1992.

289 For a robust analysis see Abraham 2017a, ch. 2.

The major emphases of the BTM were:[290]

1 The retrieval of the Bible as a *theological* book. Historical criticism has an important place in biblical studies but it represents the beginning and not the end; it should lead us to attend to God through his word, and biblical theology is a vital means in this respect.

2 *The unity of the Bible* as a whole. Scholars aligned with the BTM believed it to be crucial that we overcome the divide that had opened up between the OT and the NT.

3 A focus on God's great acts in history, thereby making *God's revelation of himself in history* central to biblical theology. Israel was regarded in this respect as unique among the ANE nations, and it was believed that God reveals his being and will through his great acts; in the OT, especially through the exodus.

4 The *distinctiveness* of the resulting biblical perspective.

By 1961, the BTM was close to collapse. Why? In Childs' view, there was a series of unresolved tensions in the BTM that eroded it from inside and left it vulnerable to the attacks from Barr, Gilkey and others from without. Childs argues that:

1 The thorny issue of the authority of the Bible was never resolved by the BTM. It rejected both fundamentalism and Barth's approach but without providing a viable alternative. The BTM failed to generate major commentaries and seemed to confine its attention to select books of the Bible.

2 The product of the BTM was rarely developed into the educational and curriculum strategies of the seminaries.

3 By the end of the 1950s and in the 1960s the Church was experiencing a great need to respond to the modern world and its challenges. The BTM appeared to be seriously lacking in this respect; it had not generated a new style of preaching, and theological ethics seemed to be moving forward well apart from it.

4 The BTM's emphasis on God's acts *in history* as inherently revelatory, as opposed to God's deed and word, appeared to solve many problems but hid major cracks in its edifice, cracks exploited by James Barr, Langdon Gilkey and others.

---

290 Here I am leaning on Childs 1970.

In my view, the BTM was a serious and courageous attempt to retrieve divine action in biblical studies, but – understandably for its time – it placed one foot in the Christian tradition and the other in the modern world view and the modern theology of its day, without recognizing that such a stance was unsustainable. Especially in relation to divine action, irreconcilable differences were at play in the two approaches so that inevitably this became an impossible place to stand for long.

Some 70 plus years later, a reassessment of the BTM is well overdue. Were the criticisms that facilitated its demise as strong as they appeared to be at the time? For Gilkey, the BTM got caught uncomfortably between being half liberal/modern and half biblical/orthodox: 'its world view or cosmology is modern, while its theological language is biblical and orthodox.'[291] In response to liberal theology, BTM scholars asserted that God revealed himself in his mighty acts, while simultaneously they affirmed the modern doctrine of the causal continuum. However, if the latter is true, then most of the biblical 'events' did not actually take place. They become, according to Gilkey, symbols instead:[292] 'we believe that the biblical people lived in the same causal continuum of space and time in which we live, and so one in which no divine wonders transpired and no divine voices were heard.'[293]

Gilkey finds the writings of the BTM riddled with contradictions in this respect. For him the implication is that, according to the BTM, the Bible is a book of great acts which the Hebrews believed God to have performed but which, in fact, we know he did not.[294] Thus, the great acts of God are reduced to God's 'inward incitement of a religious response to an ordinary event within the space-time continuum',[295] comparable to Schleiermacher's emphasis on religious experience, the precise sort of liberal theology from which the BTM was seeking to escape. Gilkey perceptively argued that the BTM needs a far more sophisticated view of how language works and a theological ontology. Gilkey might, at this point, have helped secure the BTM's anchorage to the Christian tradition and its insistence on divine action and intervention, but instead he moves in a liberal direction. For Gilkey, the biblical telling of God's great deeds must be distinguished from our recital of them; the biblical writers use language *univocally*, but as moderns – under

---

291  Gilkey 1961, 194.

292  Note Eco's (1984) distinction between a symbol and a metaphor.

293  Gilkey 1961, 196. Emphasis original.

294  For the implications for the exodus and Sinai events see Abraham's (2017a, 68–9) comments.

295  Gilkey 1961, 201.

the influence of the modern world view – we know that we can only speak of God *analogically*.

Seventy years on, I find it remarkable to think how effective was Gilkey's argument. He implicitly assumes the modern doctrine of progress as opposed to the Christian doctrine of providence.[296] The crucial question was whether or not the BTM could have been shored up with robust understandings of how language works and a sophisticated theology of reality (ontology). It is now clear that Gilkey overstepped the mark in appropriating the perspective of modernity, as well as misrepresenting the Christian tradition. Even in the Bible there is a consciousness that its language about God is not univocal; certainly, the Christian tradition is well aware of the complexity of religious language. In Aquinas, for example, we find a careful distinction between univocal, equivocal and analogical language. In recent decades, Christian philosophers such as William Alston, and Christian theologians such as Kevin Vanhoozer and Anthony Thiselton have leveraged Speech Act Theory in dazzlingly nuanced ways that leave wide-open space for divine activity. What Gilkey needed to interrogate was the modern belief in a closed causal continuum. Alas, he did not pursue this route.

James Barr's critique of the BTM focuses on two areas: the views of revelation and history at the heart of the BTM.[297] Barr's critique of the historical emphasis of the BTM is akin to Gilkey's. He attends to the antinomy or 'double talk' involved in confessing God's great acts while approaching history through critical examination of the biblical data. Barr also argues that the Bible does not emphasize history nearly as much as the BTM would like us to think.

Barr is well known for his critique of the BTM's abuse of word studies and the Greek–Hebrew contrast in views of the world, of its failure to take modern semantics into account and thus to become guilty repeatedly of 'illegitimate totality transfer', inappropriately reading meanings into words. Barr criticizes the BTM for discerning the distinctive theological content of the Bible in its vocabulary, as embodied in the Kittel-Friedrich dictionary.

Barr's and Gilkey's critiques were needed. The BTM needed to become theologically and linguistically sophisticated. However, Francis Watson[298] has rightly argued that Barr's linguistic critique of the BTM is not as devastating as is often thought, not least by Barr himself. According to Watson,

---

296  According to Graham 1997, these remain the two major options today.
297  Barr 1963.
298  Watson 1997.

Barr develops his wide-ranging criticism on a narrow foundation and wrongly argues that its linguistic errors are catastrophic for the entire project of the BTM. Watson revisits Oscar Cullmann's well-known work on time, a particular object of Barr's critique, and shows how Cullmann manifests awareness of the different ways in which the NT vocabulary for time is used, but elects consciously to attend to those occasions which are theologically rich and significant. Watson defends such an approach as legitimate.

Barr also critiques Cullmann in relation to his contrast between Hebrew and Greek thought. Cullmann contrasts the NT view of the resurrection of the body with the 'Greek' conception of immortality. As Watson shows, Cullmann is right in this regard. Watson concludes: 'there is little basis for his [Barr's] claim that "biblical theology" as once practised was fundamentally and irretrievably flawed. If biblical theology collapsed, it did not do so because of the overwhelming force of its critics' arguments.'[299] Indeed, '[t]here is, then, little or nothing in this piece of modern theological history to deter one from attempting to renew and to redefine biblical theology'.[300]

I am deeply interested in biblical theology, but that is not our concern here. Our concern is whether or not rigorous OT study can operate with a rich understanding of divine action and intervention as found in the Christian tradition. Gilkey thought not and Barr downplays the role of history in the OT. Gilkey was happy to retain God as creator and God as sustainer of the universe but could not find a place for divine intervention. Clearly, if one is going to emphasize the great acts of God in history then one needs to have a thick place for special divine action or intervention in one's toolbox. Gilkey could not find such a place.

Of course, we have spent much of Part 1 of this book setting up an alternative place from which to approach these issues in the OT. Having seen how utterly central divine action is to the OT and its presentation of YHWH, we will now return more closely to the issue of divine action, seeking an approach that is both informed by the OT and able to provide us with a theology of divine action with which we can read the OT.

## (c) The theology of divine action

In modernity the attack on divine action and especially divine intervention comes from philosophy through the twin prongs of science and history. The

---

299 Watson 1997, 24.

300 Watson 1997, 26. Intriguingly, Abraham, who helpfully revisits the BTM in his work on divine action, expresses no interest in biblical theology!

idea of a closed causal continuum that excludes the possibility of special divine action runs like a leitmotif through both of these. When Abraham published his *Divine Revelation and the Limits of Historical Criticism* in 1952, he attended to the historical challenge and said of the scientific one: 'There is little to suggest that theologians have sold their intellectual souls to scientists in return for the benefits of a scientific mode of reasoning.'[301] He also wrote at a time when serious reservations were starting to be expressed about historical criticism.

Scroll forward to today and the situation is significantly different. Again and again theological works on divine action and creation make *science* their primary dialogue partner. It often feels to this author as though science has appeared as a new magisterium in the theological arena. Lydia Jaeger perceptively notes that '[t]here is one unchallenged presupposition in most current models of divine action: it has to comply with the picture which science, and more specifically physics (perhaps suitably perfected in the future), offers us of the world'.[302] Major projects have been launched in this area and perhaps none as ambitious as the Divine Action Project (DAP), a whole series of conferences and books that began in 1988.[303] Abraham notes that 'the turn to science as a way to resolve fundamental queries about the nature and scope of divine action has been deliberate, well resourced, and pursued with enthusiasm and persistence'.[304] In relation to the DAP, Abraham[305] focuses in particular on the work of Robert John Russell and his evocative article, 'Does "The God Who Acts" Really Act?'[306] Readers are referred to Russell's work and Abraham's discussion of it for the details. The title of Russell's article evokes the BTM and Gilkey's criticism of it. Abraham identifies three major elements in Russell's approach:

1   Nature should be viewed as a hierarchy of emerging phenomena.
2   Russell adopts the Copenhagen understanding of quantum physics.
3   The theologian can therefore make two assertions about God and divine action: God acts at the level of quantum physics, and God acts in particular quantum events so as indirectly to produce a specific event at the macroscopic level. We can call such an event one of special providence.

---

301   Abraham 1982, 6.
302   Jaeger 2012, 304.
303   See Abraham 2017a, 164, n. 2, for details of the project.
304   Abraham 2017a, 147.
305   See Abraham 2017a, ch. 9.
306   Russell 1997, 44–65.

Quantum physics and Russell's theory are complex. Suffice it here to note Russell's conclusion that *'we can now understand special providence as the objective acts of God in nature and history, to which we respond, and we can understand these acts in a non-interventionist manner consistent with science'.*[307] Russell's hope is that if his approach is successful, it will fulfil Gilkey's hope of a theory that allows for belief in some of God's great acts in history.

Abraham acknowledges the brilliance and motivation behind Russell's work. However, he is, rightly in my view, less hopeful:

> On the newer version, while God objectively and directly acts, the effects are utterly undetectable. Thus it looks as if Russell will have to fall back on our subjective response as the criterion for picking out special acts of God in providence.[308]

For Abraham, the real problem lies at a deep level and not least in the assumption that the theologian is dependent on the scientist for any hope of retrieving divine action and intervention.

> The assumption seems to be that scientists are in a position to make significant, material contributions to theology, not least, to resolve crucial theological questions about divine action. This is patently false, given the constraints and limitations of scientific investigation.[309]

This is to ask for what science cannot deliver: 'we are asking physics and its modes of inquiry to resolve questions that belong in an entirely different domain.'[310]

The body of work that the BTM produced has largely disappeared. What is clear from Gilkey's and Barr's engagements with the BTM is that they emerge from particular theological and philosophical outlooks. There is nothing unusual about this, but it should make us examine their presuppositions as part of the whole picture, including their insightful critiques of the BTM. The demise of the BTM is connected with the radicalization of modern theology at the time, and Barr, for example, appeals to this 'progress' as part of his critique. What I find missing in Barr's and Gilkey's approaches is a sense of plurality in theology and philosophy and the ways in which

---

307  Russell 1997, 45. Emphasis original.

308  Abraham 2017a, 156.

309  Abraham 2017a, 160.

310  Abraham 2017a, 161.

different theological and philosophical perspectives might engage with the BTM. Theological and philosophical contexts make a major difference when it comes to (the very possibility of) divine action and intervention.

Of course, it is far easier to make this point situated where we are now – in the wake of the wild pluralism of postmodernism and with the benefit of the extraordinary renaissance of Christian philosophy over recent decades, spearheaded by luminaries such as Alvin Plantinga, William Alston, Nicholas Wolterstorff, C. S. Evans, Eleanora Stump and so many others. Abraham rightly notes of G. E. Wright's work that:

> Looking back it is easy to see that Wright was caught between a rock and a hard place. On the one hand, he wanted to highlight the central place of divine action in the scriptural traditions and in the Christian tradition; on the other hand, he did not have the conceptual or philosophical resources to bring his wares to the table.[311]

The same cannot be said of us. After postmodernism we are far more sensitive to the plurality of views in the academy, including in theology, and the astonishing corpus of outstanding work in Christian philosophy provides us with razor-sharp linguistic (cf. Alston), epistemological (cf. Plantinga and Wolterstorff) and – to a lesser extent – ontological resources. Take the issue of science and divine action, for example. Plantinga has attended to this repeatedly. In his *Where the Conflict Really Lies*, he lucidly examines the issues and concludes that 'what we've seen is that there is nothing in science, under either the old or the new picture, that conflicts with or even calls into question special divine action, including miracles'.[312]

In theology, recognition must be given to William Abraham, who has addressed divine action in a whole variety of ways but most recently and most comprehensively in his recent four-volume work, *Divine Agency and Divine Action*.[313] In volume 1 Abraham reviews the debate about divine action over the last seventy years or so, ranging from the BTM, to demythologization (Ogden and Bultmann), to analytic philosophy, to process theology, to science as we noted above, to neo-Thomism, and the grammatical approach of Kathryn Tanner. In volume 2 Abraham explores the resources in

---

311  Abraham 2017a, 32.

312  Plantinga 2011, 121–2.

313  Other major contributions have also been made, e.g. Schwöbel 1992, which we will discuss in detail in the following section.

the Christian tradition for a robust theology of divine agency. In volumes 3 and 4 he moves on to the constructive work of articulating a theology of divine agency and intervention. Abraham skilfully navigates his way in depth across the history of the recent debates about divine action (he got to know some of the major players while at Oxford), has no problem plunging into the philosophy of action and divine action – a route that he astutely notes is cut off to followers of Barth with his antipathy towards philosophy, hauls old and new out of the Christian tradition, rightly discerns 'God as Agent' as absolutely central to theology and thus produces a virtual short systematics in the third volume, and so on and so forth. His engaging style and great use of metaphors and examples make this high-level work eminently accessible. Clearly, we cannot review it in any detail. Suffice it here to alert the reader to central insights that relate to our project.

Overall, Abraham's goal is unashamedly *theological*: 'I seek in time to articulate as a theologian a rich vision of divine action that runs from conversion back to creation and forward to the eschaton.'[314] He notes that discussions of divine action simply cannot avoid making epistemological assumptions. Theologians have their own critical resources which bear on such assumptions, and they cannot do their work without them. For Abraham, *'the last thing the theologian should do is resist crossing over into the new world opened up in the church by divine revelation'*.[315] It is within that new world that the theologian finds rich resources for understanding divine action and thereby explicating the nature of God and his acts. Indeed, it is the responsibility of the theologian to enter fully into this new world, including its rich tradition of reflection and commentary, and to get on with leveraging these resources to reflect on God and his acts. For Abraham we have had enough throat-clearing and endless detours by theologians; a feast of rich and creative work awaits.

Early in volume 3 Abraham evocatively opens up the role of commitment in theology:

> I desire to speak directly and frankly about God in his amazing work of creation and redemption. And we cannot speak of God in a neutral tone of voice; we are not dealing here with a prosaic item like a cat on a mat, or a complex item, like a quark or the intricacy of constitutional law. We are dealing with our extraordinary Creator and Savior, with nothing less than the God who is named as Father, Son, and Holy Spirit and upon

---

314 Abraham 2017a, 14.

315 Abraham 2017a, 163. Emphasis added.

whom we depend for the very air we breathe. This is a daring and dangerous enterprise that we approach in fear and trembling, and with joy and adoration.[316]

Having noted this, for Abraham faith and the work of theology is no straitjacket; he extends forays far and wide. A major insight is that contrary to much analytic philosophy, 'action' is an *open concept* with a smorgasbord of context-related criteria.[317] Abraham explores and critiques closed concepts of *human* action which scholars then attempt to apply analogously to God. They quickly run into entirely predictable problems, such as because human action is always embodied whereas God is incorporeal and does not possess a body, we cannot speak sensibly and meaningfully of divine action. If this sounds strange, it is not an uncommon view. At a presentation I gave in Jerusalem a philosopher argued that God cannot speak because he does not have a voice box! Abraham, and philosophers like Alston,[318] respond rigorously to such reductionistic and anthropocentric views of human and divine action.[319] Abraham notes our tendency to suffer from mental cramp and diagnoses it astutely:

> The mental cramp, to repeat, is this: we have assumed that there is a single concept of action that can be gleaned by focusing on cases of human action; we have thought that by reflection on that concept we can understand divine action.[320]

Abraham argues that there is not one paradigm case of action around which all others can be situated but rather a multitude of paradigm cases. He follows Weitz in affirming that there is a whole host of contexts in which we can speak of human action.[321] In reaching for a definition Abraham writes:

> So we might say initially that action as an open concept has the following features: (a) it is open-ended in its meaning; (b) it calls for the specification of its context if it is to be clarified; (c) it requires specification in its content if it is to be understood.[322]

---

316  Abraham 2018, 7–8.
317  See esp. Abraham 2017a, ch. 6.
318  See Abraham 2017a, ch. 7, for his discussion of Alston.
319  See Abraham 2017a, 58–67.
320  Abraham 2017a, 87.
321  Abraham 2017a, 99.
322  Abraham 2017a, 101.

In the final chapter of his first volume he finds resources in the common-sense realism of Thomas Reid, who sees the concepts of action and agent as 'logically primitive'.

Thus, there is no problem philosophically in speaking about divine action. We are liberated from an Aristotelian framework of substance and accidents, of a philosophy of being, and so on. We are not constrained by the limits of projecting a philosophy of human action on to God. Instead, we can expand our view of agency to include God, who has diverse powers of action. Ontologically, we can affirm the crucial distinction between God and the world, while the world remains utterly dependent on God and his providence. At the same time, we can gladly affirm that this God acts in his world to redeem it.[323]

Indeed, '[i]f we think God exists, it is surely equally wise to let God set the agenda for what he does',[324] but affirming divine action and intervention is the beginning and not the end of such exploration because, as we attend to specific divine actions in Scripture, '[w]e need to work through the distinction between literal and non-literal as applied to divine action discourse. We will have to look at a whole range of tropes: analogy, metaphor, image, myth, allegory, typology, and the like.'[325] As part of this work we will need to excavate the Christian tradition to find rich nodes of a theology of divine action (Abraham's second volume).

> The fruitful way forward is to work with an open-textured concept of action, and deploy the doctrine of analogy in an apt way by exploring the relevant language strata in play and by working from specific instances of divine action discourse.[326]

Earlier, we noted how Abraham helps us to see that the veto in OT studies on divine action and intervention is a philosophical position. Now, however, he announces that:

> Negatively, the days of the philosophical veto are over. It is time to turn the tables firmly and unapologetically. We should veto any and every effort to approach discourse about divine agency and divine action with

---

323  Abraham 2017a, 220.

324  Abraham 2017a, 209.

325  Abraham 2017a, 105.

326  Abraham 2017a, 210.

a hermeneutic of suspicion. The veto business has run out of capital; it is time to shut it down and get on with the work of theology.[327]

Abraham asserts that claims about divine action are theological through and through. For far too long theologians have endlessly cleared their throats in this regard, being intimidated by unhelpful and incorrect philosophies of agency. It is as though they were secretly given a contraceptive to guard against divine action! They urgently need to wean themselves off such contraceptives, recover their courage, rediscover the rich Christian tradition in this area and get on with witnessing through their work to the *magnalia Dei*.[328]

Abraham moves to the constructive theological task in his volumes 3 and 4. At the outset of volume 3 Abraham engages with Provan's typology of five ways in which we can engage with the Bible:[329]

1　We can continue with historical study of the Bible.
2　We can follow the postmodern route.
3　We can adopt the 'Chicago' option of inerrancy.
4　We can pursue a counter-Reformational Protestantism.
5　We can retrieve the Reformers' view of the Bible as the norm for theology and its perspicuity.

Provan opts for the fifth one, and Abraham is sympathetic towards this but notes that his view of the canon differs from that of Provan. Abraham concedes that while in so many ways biblical studies is the crown jewel of theology, it 'now has many lives of its own that cannot carry the burden assigned by theology; these lives display rival ontological and epistemological commitments'.[330] Alas, biblical studies 'no longer is in the mood to deliver the resources theologians at one time ordered for timely delivery at the outset of their journey'.[331]

There is not a lot of engagement with the Bible in Abraham's four volumes, but when there is, it is often scintillating. For example, in relation to popular, contemporary views of God, he declares:

---

327　Abraham 2017a, 222.
328　Abraham 2017a, 15.
329　Provan 2017.
330　Abraham 2018, 25.
331　Abraham 2018, 36.

Compare all these with the God of the Exodus. Whatever we may say about the God of this little slice of the canonical heritage, we cannot say that this God is boring or operates at our behest. This God is an extraordinary agent who makes covenants with a people not just for their sake but for the sake of the whole world, who shows up in a burning bush, who argues with Moses until he is speechless, who ingeniously hardens Pharaoh's heart, who keeps promises to a group of despairing workers who have forgotten their ancestral birthright, who sends plagues in the dead of night, who thunders in lightning from Sinai, and who then turns around and gives in to Moses when he argues that Israel should be spared an act of divine genocide, and on and on. This is an awesome deity, a deity surrounded at once in light and darkness, a deity who is at once known and unknown, a deity who is both hidden and revealed, a deity under no human control and yet subject to human persuasion.[332]

In his discussion of the attributes of the Trinitarian God, Abraham intriguingly turns to Exodus 3.19 and 34.6–7, a passage we discussed above. In comparison with so much thin OT exegesis of these verses, Abraham notes that '[t]he initial predicates applied to God here are these: good, gracious, merciful, faithful, forgiving, and slow to anger. This suggests a cluster of attributes that we might more formally identify in and around the goodness of God.'[333] The attributes he identifies are:

• God is all-loving;
• God is the source of human flourishing;
• God is worthy of worship;
• God is just;
• God is holy;
• God is righteous, 'intervening in history to fulfill his covenant promises, to put things right when they go wrong, and to vindicate those who put their trust in him';[334]
• God is free: 'When God acts or engages in any activity, God freely and fully forms God's own intentions in such action or activity.'[335]

---

332 Abraham 2018, 41.
333 Abraham 2018, 57.
334 Abraham 2018, 57.
335 Abraham 2018, 58.

Similarly, from Exodus 6.6–8 Abraham develops the following attributes:

- God is all-powerful;
- God is eternal and everlasting;
- God is all-knowing;
- God is omnipresent;
- God is impassible;
- God is immutable;
- God's existence is necessary.

He notes that, '[t]aken together, lists like these begin to summarize the crucial ingredients that constitute a Christian doctrine of the attributes of God',[336] and God's attributes accurately reflect his nature.

Surprisingly, Abraham's third volume ranges across all the loci of doctrine, thus becoming a short but stimulating systematic theology. I say 'surprisingly' because one anticipates a major focus on divine action. However, for Abraham, 'the ultimate category for understanding God is that of a unique, mysterious, tripersonal Agent. Agents are made known through what they do.'[337] It seems to me that Abraham is right to make agency central to our understanding of God, and it is this that leads him to spread his discussion across the loci. If action is as central to God as Abraham thinks, then it also alerts us to *just* how deficient a reading of the OT is when it resists taking divine *action* into account.

All of this is to say that there is no good reason why the Christian OT scholar should not carry with him or her a robust account of divine action and intervention into the heart of a most rigorous study of the OT. To do so, we do not have to fall back on the aporias of the BTM. Rather, in our studies we are on solid ground philosophically, theologically, scientifically and historically – which we discussed above and will return to below.

Two caveats as we draw this discussion to a close. First, I am arguing for the right of the Christian OT scholar to operate in this way without being marginalized as somehow unscholarly and unacademic. Time and again I have noted that my plea is for a genuine pluralism in OT studies, and drawing on other typologies it is fairly easy to map out what some of the major streams might look like, according to their point of view; namely:

---

336 Abraham 2018, 60.
337 Abraham 2018, 55.

- the view that Christian faith and theology should be kept entirely apart from scientific OT studies;
- the view that Christian faith and theology should operate alongside OT studies in an uneasy tension;
- the view that OT studies should operate according to the rules of the guild with the results taken up and perfected by Christian theology;
- the view that Christian faith and theology should play an integral role in OT studies.

I am, of course, opting for the final stream, which brings me to my second caveat. The fear of some will be that such an approach provides a useful fire escape from all the challenges of OT study and the many, many difficult issues foregrounded by historical criticism. As we move on to discuss the divine action of revelation in the OT below, it will become clear that this is simply not the case.

## (d) Revelation in/and the Old Testament

The idea of revelation in and through the OT has not always fared well in recent times. Childs reviews the critiques of James Barr and F. G. Downing as well as Gottwald's sociological analysis in this respect.[338] Remarkably, Downing had concluded: 'The Old Testament writers do not pretend that the relation of God and man is close enough and clear enough for God to be said to have revealed himself'.[339] To be sure, God emerges from hiding to act on Israel's behalf but, according to Downing, no connection is forged between his alleged action and his character. For Barr, the term 'revelation' arises in modern theology and unhelpfully sets up a polarity between divine intervention (revelation) and reason and religion, that is, other ways of learning about God. Terminology for revelation is minimal in the Bible and to use the term is to import pre-critical baggage into discussions of the OT, the baggage of the Bible containing timeless propositions, whereas historical criticism has helped us to see that the OT is historically conditioned, emerged over a long period of time, and contains truth and error.[340]

Childs' response is robust and correct:

the knowledge of God in the Old Testament (and the New) involves a great variety of things far transcending the simple, common-sense definitions

---

338 For the latter see Childs 1985, 24–7.

339 Downing 1964, 47. Quoted in Childs 1985, 21.

340 Barr 1963.

offered. It includes events which are experiential and also cognitive, which are directed to the past and the future. The theological term 'revelation' is, in other words, an inadequate shorthand expression which seeks to encompass an enormous range of activities related to God's relation to his people . . . [N]o better term has emerged which even begins to convey the full range of meanings associated with the disclosure of God in the Bible.[341]

Using an extensive range of terminology, 'the Bible bears testimony to a *divine activity* which breaks into human society in countless unexpected ways'.[342] Childs then proceeds to discuss how God is revealed through creation, wisdom, history and the name YHWH.

Childs discerns the following features of God's revelation in the OT:

- God takes the initiative.
- God is never restricted to one mode of revelation but rather his appearance is a surprise.
- God reveals but also conceals his identity to Israel (cf. Exod. 33.23).
- God's revelation characteristically moves speedily from vison to speech. '*Because God speaks*, his primary medium is his word. He communicates to the patriarchs by calling them by name. If at times his voice is in the thunder, the *qôl* [voice of YHWH] soon becomes an interpreted word which Israel can understand.'[343]
- God is seen neither as monolithic nor unchanging. His transcendence is held in tension with his immanence, his hiddenness with his presence, and so on.

Revelation is interpersonal self-disclosure. In the case of the OT it is divine interpersonal self-disclosure. Just as humans can disclose themselves to one another in a huge variety of ways, it is the same with God. It is hard to see how one can avoid seeing 'revelation', in this sense, all over the OT. One would need to close this emphasis down by imposing a closed-continuum historical-critical approach or reduce revelation to rational propositions. It is not only certain fundamentalists who reduce revelation to rational propositions. In the Jewish tradition, for example, there is a strain of thought which reads God's call to Abraham as Abraham reasoning himself to monotheism! Childs provocatively and insightfully notes that:

---

341 Childs 1985, 22.
342 Childs 1985, 25. Emphasis added.
343 Childs 1985, 41. Emphasis added.

Actually the use of the term revelation in respect of the Bible entails a far greater threat than that envisioned by any of its recent critics. It is constitutive of human sinfulness to turn the witness to God through the scriptures into a manageable object and thus fail to reckon with revelation as a means of encountering the living God on his own terms.[344]

## The concept of revelation

Revelation is not simple, but complex, and what we urgently need is a model for the sort of disclosure events we find in the OT. A very rich one is that of Schwöbel in his *God: Action and revelation*.[345] It comes in his chapter on 'Revelation and "Experience"'. Schwöbel points out that theology is inevitably done through the thought world of one's time, but theologians should, nevertheless, function not only as fashion designers but also as fashion critics. In terms of our theological context, he notes that from 1945 until the 1960s *revelation* was dominant in theology. From the 1970s until the present, this shifted to an emphasis on *experience*, drawing *inter alia* on the social sciences. Schwöbel helpfully poses the question whether grounding theology solely in revelation *or* experience is a false dichotomy. Can we not articulate the relationship between revelation and experience in such a way that we avoid the problems with a sole focus on only one of these, seeing them instead as complementary?

Schwöbel proceeds to set forth a model in which both concepts play a central, albeit different, role. He defines revelation as 'the act of divine self-communication in which the triune God communicates himself through the medium of created reality as the ground and the author of creation, reconciliation and salvation of created being'.[346] Such self-revelation by God puts humans in a position to respond as persons to the personal God. Schwöbel elaborates on this by reaching for Ian Ramsey's notion of the 'disclosure event'[347] and exploring its formal structure.

Schwöbel proposes that we conceive of revelation[348] as a relational event consisting of the following five elements:

---

344  Childs 1985, 26.

345  I discuss this briefly in Bartholomew 2020.

346  Schwöbel 1992, 86.

347  Ramsey 1973. Schwöbel also draws on Herms 1984, 11–54. See also Schwöbel 1992, 168–298.

348  Schwöbel acknowledges his indebtedness to Dalferth's (1988, 39–46) exposition of revelation.

  i  the author of revelation;
  ii  the situation or context of revelation;
 iii  the content of revelation;
 iv  the recipient/s of revelation;
  v  the result of revelation.

### (i) The author of revelation

Theologically, the author is the Trinitarian God who, through the disclosure event, relates 'actively, directly and efficaciously to particular persons'.[349] Such an event is an intentional act of God and thus is grounded in God's freedom. It is asymmetrical and contingent in relation to the recipient/s, and cannot be constructed or arrived at logically from conditions in alternative contexts. This implies that one cannot project the limitations of human agency on to God – for example embodiment, as discussed above. Unlike human actions, there are no external constraints on God's actions and no gap between his intentions and bringing them about. According to the theological tradition, there is no conflict between his will and his being so that his action is unified. 'This necessitates an analysis of the concept of revelation which adequately expresses the unity of divine action in creation, reconciliation and salvation while taking the internal differentiation of different modes of action into account.'[350]

### (ii) The situation or context of revelation

In theology, the Christ event is typically seen as the paradigmatic event of God's disclosure. God reveals himself within his creation, including history and the capacity for linguistic expression.[351] 'The Christ event is therefore a complex occurrence comprising a variety of different connections which becomes a disclosure situation only in the connection of its constituent dimensions.'[352] Thus, the historical matrix in which revelation takes place is vital, as is the role of the historical recipients. Revelation involves, contrary to some proponents of the BTM, not just a series of brute facts concerning a sequence of events but also the claims embodied in the events and the witness of the recipients. Schwöbel therefore says of the Christ event:

---

349  Schwöbel 1992, 87.

350  Schwöbel 1992, 88.

351  See Davies 2004, who draws on Johann Georg Hamann (1730–88) to argue for the continuity between language and creation. See also Gunton 2002.

352  Schwöbel 1992, 88.

The combination of both dimensions means that the self-interpretation of Jesus, as it is mediated by his message of God the Father and the present coming of the Kingdom, becomes part of the interpretation of his history and fate by his followers.[353]

### (iii) The content of revelation

This third element moves into the foreground once the self-interpretation of God and the interpretation by the recipients are in place. In terms of Trinitarian theology, Schwöbel highlights at this point the work of the Spirit. The work of the Spirit does not only follow the disclosure event but is also constitutive of it. For those generations following God's self-disclosure it is mediated through the witness of the recipients to the self-disclosure. This does not collapse the witness into the revelatory self-disclosure.

Referring to the Christ event, Schwöbel notes that the witness needs validation and this occurs when those who hear the good news of Jesus become convinced that it discloses the truth about their own lives and about all of life. The certainty of faith is 'certainty that the Christ event is the self-disclosure of God as the ground of the being, reconciliation and salvation of creation'.[354]

Schwöbel is clear that God's self-disclosure in Christ relates to the whole of the creation:

> The personally disclosed truth about God's self-disclosure in the Christ event includes certainty about God as the ground, meaning and end of all created reality and makes thereby the whole of created reality the context of validation for the truth of revelation.[355]

In this way, 'created reality as a whole becomes a disclosure situation'.[356]

### (iv) The recipient/s of revelation

Schwöbel rightly and profoundly notes that 'God does not reveal propositions about God, God reveals himself'.[357] This is not to say that revelation excludes noetic content but that it is interpersonal and thus both affective and noetic. God's self-revelation involves God's giving of himself. This does not mean

---

353  Schwöbel 1992, 88.
354  Schwöbel 1992, 89.
355  Schwöbel 1992, 90.
356  Schwöbel 1992, 90.
357  Schwöbel 1992, 90.

that God's essence becomes the possession of the recipients; God remains the *Deus revelatus* and the *Deus absconditus*. Nevertheless, his self-revelation does provide true, albeit constrained, knowledge of God, appropriate to human creatures. 'As the personal self-communication of God it addresses the recipients in their personal being in the relational constitution of human existence as a relationship to God, to the world and as a self-relationship.'[358] As noted above, divine revelation involves an asymmetrical relationship between God and those to whom he reveals himself. 'Self-identification is therefore "identification of somebody as himself for us" which enables us to identify the author of this self-identification.'[359] As a result it always has a historical character. As does Abraham, Schwöbel here stresses the importance of the doctrine of creation and of human beings having been made in the *imago Dei*.

> Human personhood is realized in the mode of actively relating to God, to the world, to itself and other human persons and is therefore characterized by finite freedom. Human beings therefore are the creatures who can correspond to their creator or contradict their creator.[360]

Our world and existence is constituted by its relationship to God, and being in the *imago Dei* means that within our creaturely limits and freedom we can actively respond to God as the one who constitutes our world and being.

Above we noted Childs' comments about how revelation may be more radical and dangerous than is often noted because it fingers our sinfulness. Schwöbel discusses the freedom of humans to resist God, noting that such 'contradicting' of God always involves us in self-contradiction. By themselves, humans cannot overcome the distortion in their relationship with God. This inability is a sign of the asymmetry between God and humankind. Autonomous attempts to overcome the distortion simply accentuate it. Revelation thus functions both as the judgement of God for human abuse of human freedom and as the grace of God to overcome the resulting alienation through reconciliation. In his revelation God is revealed to be both creator and reconciler:

> The fact that the recipients of revelation are addressed in God's self-disclosure in commission and promise includes not only that humans

---

358 Schwöbel 1992, 93.

359 Schwöbel 1992, 91.

360 Schwöbel 1992, 93.

are destined to be persons, but also that they can be held accountable for their destiny and are able to actualize this call to personhood – in self-failure or self-fulfilment.[361]

The call to personhood is always personal, particular and concrete.

### (v) The result of revelation

When the self-disclosure of God is received by the recipients as 'commission and promise of authentic personhood', faith results, and it is neither entirely passive nor simply an act of decision.

> Faith is the act of acknowledging that the condition of its possibility cannot be constituted by human action; because it is constituted in God's self-disclosing action, it can only be received passively. Faith is therefore the active acknowledgement of its passive constitution in God's revelatory action.[362]

Faith is far more than the acceptance of a set of propositions; it is existential and manifests itself as profound trust in God. It frees the human from autonomy and for the telos of humanity along the grain of the creation and as revealed in the disclosure event.

The way in which faith relocates the human within the structures of creation alerts us to the profound implications of faith: 'faith is not a marginal theme of ontology, but rather the fundamental ontological datum which defines the perspective from which an ontology can be developed in the reflection of Christian faith.'[363] Schwöbel identifies three implications of this:

1 We must resist the tendency, common as it is in modern philosophy, to think of being or substance as independent and autonomous, with concepts such as space, time, change and events as primitive in the sense of foundationally basic. The creation is contingent and dependent for every moment of its existence on being sustained in existence by God. The concepts in our view of reality (ontology) must be explicated in relation to God's self-disclosure. 'This excludes, for instance, an

---

361 Schwöbel 1992, 94–5.
362 Schwöbel 1992, 96.
363 Schwöbel 1992, 97.

analysis of the relationship between God and humanity as a relationship between two self-sufficient causally interacting substances.'[364]

2 Being and consciousness should not be regarded as two separate and relatively unrelated aspects of reality (cf. Tarnas's characteristics of modernity above). God reveals himself to be the ground of both being and human consciousness, and thus the two are integrally related.

3 There is no gaping ditch between being and meaning so that the world only becomes meaningful when we impose meaning on it. Instead, 'the meaning of being is precisely the actualisation of the will of the creator in creation'.[365]

If faith has implications for our view of reality, it also has implications for our view of knowledge of the world, for our epistemology. Schwöbel points out that the knowledge issuing from faith which consists in our attempts to express the content of faith in terms understandable to our day cannot be equated with factual knowledge, conceptual knowledge, normative knowledge or self-knowledge. 'As ontological knowledge the knowledge of faith is the foundation of all these forms of knowledge and determines their function.'[366] The different types of knowledge mentioned above are expressions of the convictions contained in the knowledge of faith.

As regards factual and conceptual knowledge, creation means that the world 'is a contingent nexus of events' grounded in divine action.[367] In my words, creation implies a form of realism so that true insights about the creation can be expressed in language. However, faith always sees that which it sees in relation to God's telos for his creation, so that being is not value-neutral.

The knowledge of faith not only provides a normative framework within which the conditions and guide-lines of human agency are explicated; it also asserts an intrinsic connection between being and obligation, between 'is' and 'ought,' insofar as both are seen as grounded in the will of the creator.[368]

---

364  Schwöbel 1992, 97.
365  Schwöbel 1992, 97.
366  Schwöbel 1992, 98.
367  Schwöbel 1992, 99.
368  Schwöbel 1992, 99.

This normative framework extends to 'self-interpretation in human knowledge of reflection'.[369] The human capacity for reflection is not primordially basic but contingent, and constituted by and in relation to God.

## The concept of experience

As with revelation, Schwöbel attends to the Christ event in particular:

> The different strands of the proclamation, interpretation and explication of the Gospel of Christ in the New Testament show that the Christ event is presented as a particular *experience* in the light of which the universal truth about God's relationship to humanity and the world is disclosed. This particular experience includes all aspects which we have tried to develop in the analysis of the concept of experience.[370]

Schwöbel highlights the centrality of perception in the accounts of the Christ event and notes that this is always grounded in historical existence. Jesus' perceived historical existence is a necessary – although not sufficient – condition of the truth of the NT witness to Christ.

Experience, like revelation, is complex, and problems emerge when a simplified concept of experience is adopted. Since John Locke answered the question 'Whence has it [the mind] all the materials of reason and knowledge?' by answering 'from experience',[371] experience has become a central domain in which theology is called to defend itself. Schwöbel develops the following equation for experience:

*(A experiences) A experiences x as y, insofar as x is integrated into the interpretative framework I by interpreting it as y*

Experience proceeds by seeing something (x) as part of the class y. The individual Jesus (x) is predicated as y through the christological titles in the NT. These predicates refer to the message, praxis, life, death and resurrection of Jesus. General concepts, however, exist as part of a web of predicates, and thus experience integrates x as y into a framework of interpretation.

---

369  Schwöbel 1992, 99.
370  Schwöbel 1992, 113. Emphasis added.
371  Locke 1825, 51.

The integration of the Christ event into the already existing interpretive framework of the faith of Israel indicates the decisive role of contemporary beliefs and convictions of faith for the Christ event as a particular experience, and points to the essential connection between Christian faith and the faith of Israel.[372]

This framework is historically specific and embedded in a tradition of interpretation, which may include multiple regional frameworks of interpretation. Experience is not empirical alone but includes the role of the subject. Experience 'is also the process in which the possibility of experience as it is given to human subjects is actualized'.[373] There is a flexibility and openness to experience as the subject can employ the tools of the framework creatively. The framework exists only as 'personal appropriation'.

Those who experience and embrace the disclosure offered in the Christ event are given a new understanding of what it means to be human, and become part of a community in which the revelation in/of Christ is absolutely foundational. In this revelation Christ is shown to be the condition for all experience because he reveals God's agency as the condition of human experience. Schwöbel resituates general and special revelation within this framework. General revelation evokes the openness of human experience and the fact that it is not self-constituted. Special revelation designates the communication of the Trinitarian God, indicating the openness of human experience as the openness to the world as God's creation, and to faith in the Trinitarian God as truthful.[374]

For Schwöbel, therefore, revelation and experience connect in the relationship between divine agency and human action and, as such, should be of major theological concern. God's self-disclosure reveals his action in creation and redemption as the very condition for human experience. Both concepts need to be sufficiently radically understood if their integrality is to be maintained.

## Revelation, experience and the Old Testament

There is thus good reason to retain revelation as a central concept in the OT. God reveals himself in multiple different ways, including SDAs. Both revelation and experience are complex entities and we need a model like that of Schwöbel for grasping the different dimensions of OT revelation. Schwöbel,

---

372  Schwöbel 1992, 113.
373  Schwöbel 1992, 107.
374  Schwöbel 1992, 118.

not surprisingly as a Christian theologian, focuses on the Christ event, but, as I have argued, his model is remarkably fertile for the Sinai event as well,[375] and by extension to other events of divine self-disclosure in the OT.

The author (i) of the Sinai event is YHWH, revealing himself in a historically particular situation to the Israelites who were recently enslaved in Egypt. As with the Christ event, the disclosure of YHWH at Sinai is strongly asymmetrical, with YHWH taking the initiative, and the Israelites experiencing and recognizing him as God through his theophany on Sinai and his address directly to them and through Moses as mediator of God's speech. The asymmetrical nature of the interpersonal revelation means that aspects of human agency such as embodiment cannot be projected on to YHWH. The Sinai event is awash with metaphors for divine action, as befits such a time of heightened self-disclosure by YHWH, and thus, far from detracting from the revelation, draws attention to the divine agency at work. As Exodus 1—18 demonstrates unequivocally, YHWH is no national god; he is as capable of taking on Pharaoh, himself a god, as he is of meeting with the Israelites in the desert and disclosing himself to them. All of this activity by YHWH takes place way outside the land of Israel. YHWH is the redeemer God – he has brought Israel to himself (Exod. 19.4) – but he is also the Creator God; all the earth is his (Exod. 19.5).

The context of YHWH's self-disclosure (ii) to the liberated slaves is a desert mountain in the ANE not far from Egypt. Thus, his revelation is historically and geographically particular and is provided in terms that the Israelites can begin to grasp. YHWH comes to them, as it were, clothed in the garments of the ANE. The disclosure occurs through word and deed. YHWH's instructions or boundaries around the mountain, for example, inform the liberated slaves about YHWH's holiness, instructions that will be ritualized in the cultus. If Berman is right, the tabernacle is deliberately modelled on Ramesses II's war tent and would evoke for the Israelites YHWH's nature as the true King and the warrior on their behalf.

The content of the revelation at Sinai (iii) involves many aspects: fire, lightning, deep darkness and an overwhelming sense of YHWH's presence once he descends on to Mount Sinai. There is a strong sensory dimension to YHWH's revelation of himself. However, YHWH speaks, and his revelation in deed is accompanied by his revelation in word, explaining to the Israelites what he has done for them in the exodus and what he is doing for them in forming them into his covenant people, as well as, at points, providing profound insight into

---

375 Bartholomew 2020.

his character (cf. Exod. 34.6–7). Torah forms a major part of YHWH's revelation at Sinai, and in volume 2 of this series we will see how the law is a fundamental disclosure of the character of YHWH.

The recipients of the revelation (iv) are the recently liberated slaves. If they had been in Egypt for generations, then it is likely that the faith of their ancestors – trust in the God of Abraham, Isaac and Jacob – was but a distant memory and that in myriad ways they would have adopted the interpretative framework/s of Egypt. Unlike with the Christ event, they have no 'faith of Israel' which they can leverage to make sense of YHWH's self-disclosure and so considerable effort will need to go into the construction of such an interpretative framework. We can see this with the gradations of holiness at Sinai, with YHWH's sensory revelation of himself, with the giving of *torah*, and especially with the construction of the tabernacle, Israel's first great building project. As Jon Levenson has perceptively noted, the tabernacle is a microcosm of the macrocosm, providing continual and visible instruction in a definitive interpretation of the world.

Through it all, YHWH gives the gift of himself to the Israelites, in a deeply existential way which can never be fully captured by propositions or rationality. This is not to say they know God's essence: the deep darkness of Sinai reminds the Israelites that God is God, and that he cannot be mastered either in practice or rationally by humans. Nevertheless, within limits they are given to know YHWH truly. This interpersonal encounter and revelation alerts us unequivocally to the fact that defining revelation in the OT as the unveiling of truths that are not available to reason is woefully inadequate and reductionistic. Baillie comments: 'in the last resort it is not information about God that is revealed, but very God himself.'[376] As Abraham notes: 'Divine revelation must not be approached in independence from delineating the divine activity through which God reveals himself.'[377] And the Israelites give themselves to YHWH. It is important to recognize that, unlike in Egypt, the freedom of the Israelites is respected. The covenant is not imposed on them, but has to be agreed to by them.

The result of YHWH's self-disclosure (v) is faith or trust in him, manifested in agreeing to the covenant. This will soon undergo considerable testing in Exodus 32—34, in the process of which YHWH will reveal himself more fully and the trust of the Israelites will be enhanced. Unlike in the NT, there is, of course, a corporate aspect to the Israelites' response to

---

376 Baillie 1956, 28. Quoted in Abraham 1982, 21.
377 Abraham 1982, 13.

YHWH, a response which forms them not only into a community but also into a nation. Significantly, they become and are referred to as a nation before they possess a land.

The Israelites as recipients of YHWH's self-disclosure are an integral part of the event of revelation. For the self-disclosure to succeed, it needs to be received, understood and witnessed to. The relationship with YHWH is asymmetrical, but without Israel and Moses, in particular, to bear witness to the events of Sinai and to interpret them within the framework provided by Sinai, there would be no revelation. In Exodus 15, for example, Moses in his Song bears witness to the event of the exodus and provides an interpretation of it, all part of a developing interpretative framework.

There is thus an indispensably *human dimension* to revelation, received and passed on to future generations through memory, story, ritual, writing and song – all indispensable elements in enabling future generations to be brought to stand before YHWH at Sinai, as indeed they must be if Israel is to survive and flourish. None of this detracts from the importance of the basic historicity of the Sinai event. Indeed, it is the very historicity of the Sinai event that generates the interpretative framework handed down through generations and encapsulated in the writings of the OT.

What strikes me as well with the Sinai event is that the ontological and epistemological dimensions that Schwöbel identifies in the Christ event are present, at least *in nuce*, at Sinai. Abraham perceptively comments that 'God's word to the prophets and apostles is not just part of that wider activity of God that is the salvation of our souls. It is also the salvation of our theology and philosophy.'[378] We have noted, above, Ricoeur's statement about the relationship between creation and salvation and how this is the burning issue for OT studies. Schwöbel helps us to see even more than Ricoeur just how important this relationship is for our understanding of God and the world, including our ontology (view of reality) and epistemology, not least of experience. If YHWH is merely a local storm god or even a national god then the larger interpretative framework is subverted and lost. Of course, one can argue, as do many, that Israel's view of God developed over centuries from a local god to a national god to the one God YHWH. The final stages of such monotheistic development are seen as occurring very late in the history of Israel, as we have seen, in her periods of decline and as a result of reflection rather than disclosure by YHWH. One can argue that the final stage is the normative one, although many

---

378  Abraham 1982, 19.

profess to want to take all identifiable stages as potentially normative.[379] This developmental hypothesis has little place for YHWH's disclosure of himself in history to the Israelites. However, if YHWH did disclose himself at Sinai, and if the human account of that historical revelation in ANE garb is accurate, then early in the history of Israel we have this momentous eruption of revelation whose effect we still feel today.

Once the Sinai event comes into view as YHWH's self-disclosure, intriguingly, because recipients and experience are an integral part of that disclosure event, so too do Israel and Moses move into focus. A robust doctrine of divine action radically changes how we approach Sinai, and facilitates a reappearance of the historical Moses, a reappearance that much OT study resists.

## (e) The reappearance of Moses

As modern philosophy gathered momentum, God moved to the margins until he virtually disappeared. The focus became exclusively on this earthly realm. One might expect, therefore, that modern philosophy would invariably yield rich, visceral, textured understandings of the world. In some cases this has been the case. Husserl's phenomenology is quintessentially modern in its attempt to rescue the Enlightenment project, and some phenomenological analysis is indeed rich and textured. One thinks, for example, of Edward Casey's phenomenological analysis of place, as well as of memory, imagination and remembrance.[380] However, a marked characteristic of modern philosophy as it lost sight of God is that it became increasingly reductionistic, with such human qualities as beauty and emotion seen as less than real. Casey himself tracks the way in which place virtually disappeared from modern philosophy. Hamann captures this philosophical reductivism exquisitely: 'All the colors of this most beautiful world grow pale once you extinguish its light, the first-born of creation.'[381] Hamann is, of course, referring to Jesus as God's firstborn from the dead, but we should not forget that Israel is first described as YHWH's firstborn.

A similar move takes place in historical-critical readings of the OT that have lost sight of God and the possibility of divine action. One might expect that Moses and Israel would move front and centre, but in actuality the reverse has been the case. It is not at all unusual nowadays to dismiss Moses as

---

379 cf. here Moran's (1973) view of revelation as a continuing process at a preconceptual level, and Abraham's (1982, 13–14) critique of it. Intriguingly, Abraham (1982, 14) notes: 'I find Moran's assumptions about *experience* unintelligible.' Emphasis added.

380 Casey 2009.

381 Hamann 2007, 78.

a historical figure as well as the Sinai event, and Israel herself has come under threat.[382] John Van Seters, for example, asserts that '[t]he quest for the historical Moses is a futile exercise. He now belongs only to legend.'[383] We saw above how Assmann claims that Akhenaten was historical but his 'monotheism' forgotten, whereas the Mosaic distinction has endured while Moses was not a historical figure.

By contrast, Albright asserted that 'it is absurd to deny that Moses was actually the founder of the Israelite commonwealth and the framer of Israel's religious system'.[384] Albright's view is considerably strengthened once we take seriously the notion of divine action and YHWH's capacity for speaking. Abraham comments:

> As I read it, it is simply impossible to replace the direct disclosure of God's will with surplus amounts of profound human insight. Divine revelation is not a pious way of doing justice to the genius of human discovery. It stands on its own as a marvellous expression of divine grace, mercy, and love.[385]

Thus:

> we should take the traditional emphasis on divine speaking with the utmost seriousness. It is only because God has spoken His word that we can have any assurance about what He has done in creation and history and about His intentions and purposes in acting in creation and history.[386]

Once we take YHWH's self-disclosure at Sinai seriously, as per Schwöbel's model above, the historical context and the human recipients of that disclosure come into focus, and among them none is more central in the Pentateuch than Moses.

In an important work, Knierim notes the contradictions that plague OT scholarship in relation to Moses. He points out that it has become the *opinio communis* (prevailing doctrine) to see Exodus–Deuteronomy as about *Israel*. This view is largely the result of the critical reconstruction of the history of

---

382 For a recent review of the ancient and modern literature on Moses, see Hoffmeier 1986; 1996; Beegle 1992.
383 Van Seters 1983, 23.
384 Albright 1957, 258.
385 Abraham 1982, 19.
386 Abraham 1982, 21.

Israel rather than an exploration of the literary nature of the Pentateuch. 'In this critical reconstruction of Israel's historical beginnings, Moses has played an ever-decreasing role which is the exact opposite of the ever-increasing role asserted for Moses in the tradition-historical process resulting in the Pentateuch.'[387] The history of research of Moses has been dominated almost exclusively by what we can know about the historical Moses and the portrait of Moses *before* its final shape in the Pentateuch.[388]

> Due to the prevalent historical interest, the importance of Moses in the late form of Exodus-Deuteronomy has played no role in modern scholarship ... and the late form of the Pentateuch itself has not been worth studying, neither literarily nor historically.[389]

Far too much historical criticism thus failed to focus on the literary shape of OT texts before plunging into what lies behind them. In this context

> the serious study of the literary form and genre of the extant Pentateuch, and with it the story of the portrait of Moses, is just as necessary as the study of the historical Moses or of the Moses in the pre-Pentateuchal traditions.[390]

As Knierim points out, in Exodus–Deuteronomy Moses is mentioned more often than Israel, some 510 against 460 times.[391] Indeed, Knierim proposes that we see the Pentateuch as the biography of Moses:

> We must be prepared for the thesis that *the Pentateuch is not the story or history of Israel's beginnings but the story of the life of Moses which is fundamental for the beginnings of Israel's history; that it is the vita, or the biography, of Moses.*[392]

In terms of a triadic approach to OT texts, it is thus clear that divine action leads us to attend afresh to Moses, and the question of Moses pushes us to investigate the literary shape of the Pentateuch and Moses' centrality to the

---

387 Knierim 1995, 371.
388 Knierim (1995, 371) mentions one exception: Cazelles, ed., 1955.
389 Knierim 1995, 371.
390 Knierim 1995, 372.
391 Knierim 1995, 372.
392 Knierim 1995, 372. Emphasis original.

Pentateuch as literature.[393] The narrative of Moses holds together Exodus–Deuteronomy so that the Pentateuch is essentially bipartite: before Moses (Genesis) and the time of Moses (Exodus–Deuteronomy). Genesis is the introduction, the prelude, to the time of Moses. The link between the two parts is vital since it shows that

> the time of Moses must be understood in world-historical perspective as the culmination of the long process of world history in one short period. The Pentateuch is the story, or history, of the time of Moses in the light of universal creation and history, or the history of universal creation and history culminating in the time of Moses.[394]

Moses is the link between creation and Israel, a theologically crucial link:

> in Moses' mediation of the revelation of Sinai as well as in his testament, the program is laid down by which Israel is called to be the paradigm for humanity in God's/Yahweh's creation. The decisive person for mediating this revelatory paradigm is Moses. Thus, just as Moses is seen as the single most decisive person for Israel's history and existence, so is he the decisive person for all of humanity's history and existence.[395]

The literary dimension is thus inseparably connected with the theological, and with the historical. What is missing from Knierim's analysis, in my view, is the fundamental role of YHWH, and his role foregrounds the theological and historical dimensions of the Pentateuch. The literary foregrounds the human role in receiving God's revelation and rendering it understandable for present and future generations. Moses may be central but not nearly so much as YHWH, who leads the way at every point, forms Moses as a leader and mediator, and is undoubtedly *the* central character in the Pentateuch. Thus, I would not recommend seeing the Pentateuch as the biography of Moses. Exodus–Deuteronomy is better seen as the story of YHWH forming his people, with Moses as the leader through whom YHWH works in this process.

---

393  cf. Knierim 1995, 351–79.
394  Knierim 1995, 355.
395  Knierim 1995, 378.

# (f) YHWH and historical criticism: historical criticism revisited

We are now in a position where we have a robust theology of divine action and a theology of revelation which fit with YHWH as the God who acts in history. Where then does this leave us in terms of historical criticism, which remains the default mode in so much mainstream OT study?

## Historical criticism and the literary turn

During the 1970s and 1980s, there was a flurry of works raising serious questions about the limits[396] and validity of historical criticism in the interpretation of the OT. Source criticism was often referred to as 'literary' criticism, but the literary turn soon made it obvious that source criticism moved far too quickly towards determining the sources underlying OT texts without first pursuing a rigorous synchronic reading of the text.

Writing in 1956, Hahn said:

> No historian of the nineteenth century, trained in the methods of scientific research, undertook to expound a historical development without first examining the available written sources critically. The initial task of the higher critics, accordingly, was a purely technical one: the careful analysis of the composition of the books of the Old Testament . . . [B]efore criticism could proceed with its task of investigating the historical circumstances under which the writings had been produced, the problem of defining the textual limits and the special characteristics of the underlying sources must be solved.[397]

As anyone familiar with source criticism of the OT will know, the identification of sources depended on criteria by which to identify the sources, criteria such as doublets, changes in the divine name, linguistic features, distinctive theologies and so on. Alter and Kermode note that:

> This 'scientific' criticism was of great cultural and doctrinal importance; but, as we have said, it diverted attention from biblical narrative, poetry, and prophecy as literature, treating them instead as more or less distorted historical records. The characteristic move was to infer the existence of

---

396  Brevard Childs' canonical hermeneutic is especially significant for raising questions about the limits of historical criticism.

397  Hahn 1956, 3.

some book that preceded the one we have . . . The effect of this practice was curious: one spoke of the existing books primarily as evidence of what must once have been available in an original closer to what actually happened. That was their real value – as substitutes for what has unfortunately been lost.[398]

The tsunami of historical criticism seemed irresistible, but the literary turn has changed that; 'what has happened now is that the interpretation of the texts as they actually exist has been revalidated.'[399] Alter and Kermode note the landmark impact of Auerbach's *Mimesis* on this revalidation, a book we discussed earlier. Rather than the referential aspects, the literary turn attends to the internal aspects of the biblical texts with a view to responding to our 'urgent need to learn how to read the Bible again'.[400]

In his 'Introduction to the Old Testament' Alter does not downplay the heterogeneity of the material. However, in relation to what we nowadays call 'intertextuality', Alter observes that because the OT 'so frequently articulates its meanings by recasting texts within its own corpus', it is on the way to becoming an integrated work.[401] Alter asserts:

The evidence of the texts suggests that the literary impulse in ancient Israel was quite as powerful as the religious impulse, or, to put it more accurately, that the two were inextricable, so that in order to understand the latter, you have to take full account of the former. In all biblical narrative and in a good deal of biblical poetry as well, the domain in which literary invention and religious imagination are joined is history, for all these narratives, with the exception of Job and possibly Jonah, purport to be true accounts of things that have occurred in historical time.[402]

Alter points out the difficulty of separating fiction from history but insists that attention to the OT as literature is essential to its understanding. If we ignore the literary poetics we will 'grasp the meanings at best imperfectly'.[403] Alter professes no quarrel with the 'courage of conjecture' of historical critics

---

398  Alter and Kermode, eds, 1987, 3.
399  Alter and Kermode, eds, 1987, 4.
400  Alter and Kermode, eds, 1987, 5.
401  Alter and Kermode, eds, 1987, 13.
402  Alter 1987, 16–17.
403  Alter 1987, 21.

engaged in what Edmund Leach called 'unscrambling the omelette', but he maintains that 'the essential point for the validity of the literary perspective is that we have in the Bible, with far fewer exceptions than the historical critics would allow, a very well-made omelette indeed'.[404] The OT manifests a profound poetics, and so 'it will not be surprising that the new literary criticism of the Bible has tended to uncover unities where previous biblical scholars, following the hidden imperative "the more atomistic, the more scientific," found discontinuities, contradictions, duplications, fissures'.[405]

Above we have drawn attention to challenging developments in textual criticism. Intriguingly, Alter already addresses this issue in 1987, and perceptively notes that literary analysis should be a precondition for textual analysis. He quotes Polzin, who assigns 'an operational priority to literary analysis at the preliminary stage of research'.[406] Alter explains: 'before you can decide whether a text is defective, composite, or redundant, you have to determine to the best of your ability the formal principles on which the text is organized.'[407] Throughout his Introduction, Alter provides particular examples from the Hebrew Bible. He concludes:

> Sometime in the latter part of the second millennium B.C.E., the spiritual avant-garde of the Hebrew people began to imagine creation and creator, history and humankind, in a radically new way. This radicalism, though it would never produce anything like unanimity, generated certain underlying patterns of literary expression in the centuries that followed . . . In the prose narratives, one may infer that these patterns became the very matrix of an extraordinary new kind of representation of action, character, speech, and motive. In both cases, the imaginative recurrence, for all the diversity, to the bedrock assumptions of biblical monotheism about the nature of reality weaves tensile bonds among the disparate texts.[408]

Taking this into account, I invite the reader to reconsider part of the quote from Hahn above, namely:

---

404  Alter 1987, 25.
405  Alter 1987, 25.
406  Alter 1987, 26.
407  Alter 1987, 26.
408  Alter 1987, 34.

The initial task of the higher critics, accordingly, was a purely technical one: the careful analysis of the composition of the books of the Old Testament ... [B]efore criticism could proceed with its task of investigating the historical circumstances under which the writings had been produced, the problem of defining the textual limits and the special characteristics of the underlying sources must be solved.

Clearly, the literary turn has problematized aspect after aspect of the sure foundations of historical criticism, such that we would expect a reconsideration of the entire enterprise. Why has this not happened?

On the one hand, generations and lifetimes of back-breaking and rigorous work have been devoted to historical criticism of the OT, so it is understandable if proponents are reluctant to face the profound challenges of the literary turn. On the other hand, the challenge of the literary turn remains, and this brings us back to the importance of a triadic approach to OT texts which integrates their historical, literary, and theological or kerygmatic dimensions. Our discussion above, not least of the theology of divine action, alerts us to the fact that there are deeper theological and philosophical issues beneath this triad, issues which shape how we think about the three dimensions.

In his epochal work *Mimesis*, Auerbach remarkably relates the revolution in literature he discerns in the Bible to the Incarnation. Taking divine action in the OT seriously points us to a similar proposal, namely that it was YHWH's immersion in the life of Israel, exemplified in the Sinai event, that resulted in the emergence of such an extraordinary body of literature. As Kass points out, Israel's first great building project, namely that of the tabernacle, is full of *torah*/instruction about art and the role of creativity within the service of YHWH. Divine action leads us to see that we may well have underestimated the consequences for all of life, including literature and its poetics, in YHWH's presence amid his people, Israel.

## The criterion of similarity

Above we have seen how the literary turn presents a radical challenge to much historical criticism and has still to be fully appropriated in OT studies. However, surprisingly and wonderfully, the impetus for the literary turn came primarily from Jewish *literary* scholars, the luminaries being Robert Alter and Meir Sternberg. Their contribution has been huge, but, as Sternberg notes, their approach to the poetics of the Hebrew Bible is primarily an inductive one, assembling the poetics of the OT from the ground up, as it were, from the data of the OT through the lens of their literary intuition. This is surely valid and the fruits speak for themselves.

However, a question lingers, one which we foregrounded above. How do we account for the poetics of the OT and how does it relate to the poetics of ANE literature? Take the major repetition in Exodus 35—40 for example. Berman notes Gersonides' perceptive comment that this may relate to the literary conventions of the time which differ from those of his time. Berman observes that:

> There should be no delusion, however, that this critical reservoir of comparative data from the cognate literature will become fully available any time soon. The problem is particularly acute with regard to the genre of narrative. We have fine studies that survey the poetics of narrative in biblical literature. To date, however, no comparable work has been written for any of the cognate narrative corpuses of the ancient Near East. There has been no survey of Egyptian narrative techniques, nor of the poetics of Mesopotamian narrative that would allow us to test the bounds of literary unity in narrative for these ancient writers.[409]

How significant, we might well ask, could such comparative work be? Of course, we cannot have any degree of certainty until such work is done. The value of inductive studies on the OT will remain, but it is likely that such comparative studies will inform and constrain a poetics of the OT. Scholars inevitably work with an intuition of what literature is and how it operates, but such intuitions are always in danger of being informed by modern rather than ANE sensibilities about literature. Berman asserts: 'The ancient text is a minefield of literary phenomena that are culturally dependent.'[410] Let me provide one example. In Exodus, Pharaoh is never mentioned by name. Literary scholars alert us to gaps in literature and it is easy to assume that the failure to mention Pharaoh by name is an intentional gap calling for interpretation.[411] However, as Berman notes elsewhere,[412] in the Egyptian literature from the mid second millennium until the tenth century BC it was common Egyptian practice to refer to the pharaoh in this way. Only later did it become common practice to refer to Pharaoh Necho and so on.

---

409 Berman 2017, 276.

410 Berman 2017, 4.

411 cf. Kass 2021 on names and the lack of names in the early chapters of Exodus.

412 Berman 2020, 53.

Thus, what looks like a fairly obvious literary trope may turn out not to be one at all.

What is intriguing is Berman's claim that source criticism of the Pentateuch also emerged from inside the OT, as it were, dependent on the literary intuitions of the early historical critics and not through comparative study of ANE literature. It is important here to distinguish the literary sensibility of an Alter and a Sternberg from that of the early source critics; the former have a profound sense of the OT as literature whereas the latter operate with a naive, often untested view. Speaking of a new approach to the literature of the Pentateuch, of which Berman is a part, he notes that '[t]he root of the problem heretofore, according to this movement, is that scholars have rooted their compositional theories for the growth of the biblical text entirely in their own intuition of what constitutes literary unity'.[413]

As is apparent from this volume, the historical and cultural context of Israel in the ANE is of indispensable value in understanding the OT. Berman's plea is that the historical-critical approach to the OT as it has developed be appraised in relation to the comparative literature of the ANE. He calls this an 'empirical' approach, and identifies scholars such as van der Toorn and David Carr as part of this 'movement'. Around the time of the literary turn in the 1970s and 1980s, there was much talk about a crisis in historical criticism, less so now. However, the crisis remains.

In 2012–13, the Israel Institute for Advanced Study sponsored a residential group of eight of the top names in Pentateuchal historical criticism, tasked with identifying common ground in the divergent approaches to the Pentateuch.[414] They were asked to attend to such questions as:

- Should we identify extended narrative sources or attend to smaller blocks and themes?
- How are the units to be identified?
- Does redaction result in a cohesive text or is cohesion only a property of an underlying source?
- What exactly is meant by 'source', 'layer' and 'supplement'?
- And so on.

This year of intensive research and dialogue culminated in a conference in May 2013, entitled 'Convergence and Divergence in Pentateuchal Theory: Bridging

---

413 Berman 2017, 2–3.
414 Berman 2017, 1.

the Academic Cultures of Israel, North America, and Europe', attended by some 100 scholars from around the world.[415] Berman reports that:

> The conference opened with a report of the group's accomplishments over that time. Speaking on behalf of the conveners, Bernard M. Levinson explained that the discipline is in *a state of fragmentary discourse*, where scholars talk past each other, and mean different things even when they use the same terms. As he put it, 'scholars tend to operate from such different premises, employing such divergent methods, and reaching such inconsistent results, that meaningful progress has become impossible. The models continue to proliferate, but the communication seems only to diminish.'[416]

Source criticism is so deeply embedded in mainstream Pentateuchal scholarship that it is unlikely that this paradigm of reading the Pentateuch will soon be dislodged. In my view, it needs to be. Not only has this approach signally failed to produce 'assured results' in its attempt to approach the OT 'scientifically', but the challenges to it continue to grow. Berman's 2017 rich and fecund *Inconsistency in the Torah: Ancient literary convention and the limits of source criticism* is a case in point.

We noted above that Berman sees himself as a part of a group of scholars seeking a more empirical approach to the OT. However, he also comments:

> Whereas other scholars have examined the editorial practices of ancient scribes, I seek here to question our own notions of consistency and unity in a text, in light of what we discover from the writings of the ancient Near East.[417]

Again and again Berman foregrounds ANE data that challenges the assumptions of source criticism. For example, the criterion of divine names has been a staple for identifying different sources in the Pentateuch, as the term JEDP signifies. However, Berman points out that ANE authors were quite comfortable with referring to a god by different names in a short passage.[418] Particularly in the critical study of Deuteronomy, there is a long history of attending to the shift between second-person singular and second-person plural forms of address as

---

415  For the conference proceedings see Gertz, Levinson, Rom-Shiloni and Schmid, eds, 2016.
416  Berman 2017, 1–2. Emphasis added.
417  Berman 2017, 3.
418  Berman (2017, 3) references Tablet IV of the Baal Cycle.

a means of identifying different layers or strata. However, this phenomenon is found in the Sefire Treaty, a unified document. Berman is quick to note that such phenomena do not prove that this is how the OT must also be read, but they do give one pause. 'Perhaps the most prudent lesson from such examples is that we must attain competency as readers before we engage the text – and this we can do only by canvassing the available cognate materials.'[419]

What follows in Berman's *Inconsistency* is a wide-ranging and rich agenda crying out for further work in all sorts of areas. Much of this will be taken up in detail in subsequent volumes in this series. For now, however, it is important to provide an overview of Berman's work so that the reader can see the extent to which his empirical, comparative approach challenges the standard, critical approaches to the Pentateuch. Berman's *Inconsistency* consists of three parts: 'Inconsistency in Narrative', 'Inconsistency in Law' and a third section on renewing biblical criticism.

In Exodus 14 and 15 we have a prose account of the crossing of the Red Sea juxtaposed with a poetic account, with different emphases – contradictions? – in the two. Berman finds a parallel to such juxtaposition, by one author, in the Kadesh narratives: poems and reliefs commissioned by Ramesses II – the one official 'author' – after his defeat of the Hittites at Kadesh. Berman shows that

the Exodus sea account bears strong affinities with the Kadesh Poem of Ramesses II. The two compositions share a lengthy and distinct common plot structure that features many tropes which are distinct to these two works alone. I claim that the Exodus sea account is an appropriation of the Kadesh Poem as part of an ideological battle with Ramesses II, who ruled Canaan for the better part of the thirteenth century BCE. Importantly for our purposes, I show how the differences between the prose and poetic accounts of the crossing of the sea in Exodus chapters 14 and 15 are highly reminiscent of the types of differences that we see between the multiple versions of the battle of Kadesh that Ramesses commissioned upon his return home from battle with the Hittites at Kadesh. I also demonstrate that the longest of the three inscriptions, the Kadesh Poem, which is universally understood as composed by one agent, is nevertheless rife with the types of inner tensions and contradictions that often lead modern critics to the conclusion of revision and redaction within the texts of the Hebrew Bible.[420]

---

419  Berman 2017, 4.
420  Berman 2017, 5–6. See Berman 2017, chs 1–2.

In source criticism, divergent accounts of an event – for example the exodus, Sinai, the giving of the law – are regularly taken to be indicative of different sources. Berman attends to Hittite treaties in which Hittite kings would rehearse the history of their relationship to the vassal in question, and discovers that in subsequent communications the kings felt free to redraft the history without for a moment erasing the earlier version. Berman then relates this insight to the relationship between Deuteronomy and earlier accounts in Exodus–Numbers of events to which Deuteronomy refers. Berman argues that 'what we witness in the Torah – namely, rewritten history that does not displace earlier, conflicting versions of those same events – may be understood with recourse to the Late Bronze Age Hittite treaty prologue tradition'.[421]

OT law has long been a mine for source-critical excavations. In the six chapters of his Part 2, Berman tackles with aplomb the challenges of the OT law collections and their confusing differences. He argues that source critics have for too long worked with the anachronistic idea of OT law as statutory whereas ANE law is non-statutory. Statutory law implies strict construction and this distorts our understanding of how ANE law worked. Berman draws on Barry Eichler's illuminating analysis of the Laws of Eshnunna §§25–29 in relation to the logic of composition of ANE laws and inconsistencies. 'The inconsistencies, however, are deliberate, and reflect rhetorical and ideological needs.'[422] Berman uses this comparative material to show how it sheds light on the inconsistencies between the laws relating to freeing slaves in Exodus 21.1–6 and Leviticus 25.39–46.

Berman has done fascinating work on the relationship between Ruth and Deuteronomy 24.16—25.10. Structurally, Ruth's plot follows the orders of the laws in this section of Deuteronomy, but intriguingly the practice of law in Ruth is inconsistent with the very laws to which it pays homage! What is most intriguing is that Hurowitz observed a comparable phenomenon in the use of the Laws of Hammurabi 1–5 in the Neo-Babylonian work, Nebuchadnezzar King of Justice. As Berman notes: 'The phenomenon challenges us to understand how these ancient writers related to venerated legal texts and the provisions they contain.'[423]

Legal blending is a phenomenon of OT texts in which a text will use different versions of laws from different collections and blend them into one. Typically, critics see this as a late, post-exilic phenomenon aimed at supplanting

---

421  Berman 2017, 6. See Berman 2017, chs 3–4.
422  Berman 2017, 7.
423  Berman 2017, 7. See Berman 2017, chs 5–7.

the earlier versions. Berman argues for a complementary rather than a super-sessionary model, affirming 'more recent models of Pentateuch redaction that see here instead a creative melding of reapplications of God's word'.[424]

Not surprisingly after this tour de force, Berman's Part 3 is about renewing biblical criticism. Appropriately, he begins by reviewing the history of OT criticism, noting how the earliest critics such as Spinoza and Astruc held a much healthier view of what we cannot know, compared with later critics who thought that because they could ask the critical question, they could also answer it. Surprisingly, to me,[425] Berman calls for a return to a Spinozan hermeneutic. Berman's work is always helpfully grounded in actual exegesis and he discusses the tendency of critics to negate relevant evidence in Exodus 2.1–10, the rescue of Moses, and then revisits a seminal site for source critics, namely the flood narrative in Genesis. In a refreshing move, Berman foregrounds the highly creative work by Gordon Wenham on the unity of this narrative when read against the backdrop of Mesopotamian accounts of the Flood, noting that Wenham's work has largely been ignored. Berman retrieves Wenham's work and develops it further, while also exposing the inadequacies of source-critical analysis of the flood narrative. He argues that his examination of the source criticism of the flood narrative reveals no fewer than eight methodological errors:

- foundationalist epistemological assumptions;
- allowing theory to overpower and complicate the text;
- ignoring the rhetorical conventions of the ANE;
- reductive readings of inconvenient passages;
- a view of how redaction works that contradicts its own assumptions;
- a view of redaction that is not grounded empirically;
- an approach to redaction lacking a clear rationale;
- failure to engage with critical scholarship working with different assumptions.

In conclusion, Berman calls for:

- an epistemology of modesty which faces up to the limits of our evidence;
- an approach which is constrained by the practices of composition of the ANE.

---

424 Berman 2017, 8. See Berman 2017, chs 8–10.
425 See Bartholomew 2020.

Significantly, Berman observes that:

> A survey of six primers for source-critical methodology reveals a telling lacuna: all offer detailed examples of how to identify inconsistencies, tensions, and contradictions within the texts of the Torah as telltale signs of revision. But all assume that the modern exegete will be able to correctly flag these, on the basis of his or her own notion of consistency and literary unity. Not one of these primers suggests that competency in the writings of the ancient world is necessary in order to avoid anachronism.[426]

Finally, Berman refers to a project he and a colleague have developed, namely *Tiberias Project: A web application for the stylistic analysis and categorization of Hebrew scriptures*, and flags its potential for further work.[427]

Berman's work is an overwhelming and persuasive apology for what I here call the 'criterion of similarity'. The OT is ANE literature and we ought to leverage all the exponentially growing ANE resources for understanding the OT. Berman's work also demonstrates that the tools of historical criticism are not simply neutral. No one would deny that sources can be invaluable in rightly interpreting a book. However, the type of source criticism or literary criticism practised by historical critics is of a very particular type, speculatively developing sources from the form of the OT text in which we have received it. The examination of genre has been wonderfully fruitful in OT studies, but form criticism in which the smallest unit of a text is identified and then the history of its form traced back into the *Sitz im Leben* in the life of Israel is surely another thing altogether. So too with editing. It is obviously helpful to attend to ways in which the OT books have been edited into the shape in which we have received them. However, as Berman demonstrates, the notion of redaction is complex and needs to be constrained by ANE evidence. The OT contains many theological traditions and it is very illuminating if we can trace how such ideas developed in the life of Israel. But tradition history as practised builds on source, form and redaction criticism and too often lacks the modesty for which Berman appeals.

Harrisville, whose work I always find stimulating and congenial, asserts that:

---

426 Berman 2017, 275.

427 Available at <https://tiberias.dicta.org.il/#/> under the name Tiberias Stylistic Classifier for the Hebrew Bible.

An alternative to historical criticism does not exist; writing of its 'end' is a wish-fulfillment dream. The reasons are myriad. The historical question will not down because an author, real or 'implied,' is not merely after achieving dramatic results, but after linking them to some independent reality. It will not down because faith or other 'interested' interpretations cannot remain aloof from critical testing . . . [A]s long as there is the slightest interest in what the biblical texts say of their own time or of their addressees, historical criticism of one type or another will be in play.[428]

I agree with Harrisville, as this volume demonstrates, that any serious engagement with the OT will attend to its telling of history and explore the OT thoroughly in the context of the ANE. As Levenson asserts: 'The question is not whether we make historical judgments; the question can only be whether we do so poorly or well.'[429] The historical strand of an OT hermeneutic is non-negotiable. However, this is a vastly different thing from saying that an alternative to historical criticism does not exist.

Historical criticism has taken a particular form in modern OT studies, so that Alvin Plantinga is insightful when he alerts us to '[o]ne very important caution: HBC [historical biblical criticism] is a *project* rather than a *method*'.[430] This distinction enables Plantinga to go on to distinguish between Troeltschian HBC and Duhemian HBC, and to find both wanting philosophically.[431] Levenson comparably notes that

historical criticism is the form of biblical studies that corresponds to the classical liberal political ideal. It is the realization of the Enlightenment project in the realm of biblical studies. Like citizens in the classic liberal state, scholars practicing historical criticism of the Bible are expected to eliminate or minimize their communal loyalties, to see them as legitimately operative only within associations that are private, nonscholarly, and altogether voluntary.[432]

---

428 Harrisville 2014, 302. Readers should note that Harrisville's book is rich and full of vital insights. It is far more creative than its subtitle suggests, i.e. *An examination and defense of historical-critical method and its master practitioners.*

429 Levenson 1993, 110.

430 Plantinga 2015, 99. Emphasis original.

431 For Plantinga's detailed analysis see his *Warranted Christian Belief* (2000).

432 Levenson 1993, 118.

One can certainly call traditional historical criticism 'historical criticism', as well as Berman's new empirical approach. Indeed, both lay claim to being empirical, but clearly we need to have ways to distinguish the one from the other.

Berman identifies one of the errors of source criticism as failure to engage with critical scholarship working with different assumptions. It needs to be noted that this extends beyond OT studies, narrowly conceived. If OT study operates not just with neutral methods but as a project/s with a philosophical matrix out of which it proceeds, then critical attention to that matrix is vital for its results to be considered scientific. We live amid a remarkable renaissance of Christian philosophy, and some of its major proponents have specifically engaged with biblical studies. I think here of the work of Alvin Plantinga, C. S. Evans, Nicholas Wolterstorff, Eleonore Stump, William Alston and others. At one of our Scripture and Hermeneutic seminars, we facilitated a dialogue on biblical interpretation between Alvin Plantinga and Robert Gordon, the then Regius Professor of Hebrew at Cambridge University, and me, later published in *'Behind' the Text: History and biblical interpretation*. However, such interaction of OT scholars with philosophers is far too rare, and Plantinga's work cries out for serious engagement by OT scholars.

As we noted above, an implication of Psalm 93's statement about reality is that we cannot and should not ignore the question of the OT and history. Here, I side with historical criticism and against those proponents of the literary approach who are happy to develop rich, creative readings of OT texts while ignoring the question of historical reference. However, we need to rethink questions such as: What is history? How, to refer to the quote from Levenson above, do we determine what a good and what a poor historical judgement is in relation to the OT? What kind of history do we find in the OT? Much of this we attended to above in our critical realist discussion of history. To reiterate, we need above all to be aware of how we read OT texts in a non-reductionistic way so as to do justice to their literary, historical *and* kerygmatic dimensions. In this context we can then ask how source analysis, analysis of form, history of traditions, and redaction criticism can be rethought and recontextualized within such a paradigm.

## The criterion of dissimilarity

Berman advocates for a new empirical approach and for a revival of a Spinozan hermeneutic. I take Berman's point that Spinoza's emphasis on what we cannot know is helpful, but the philosophical and philosophy-of-religion baggage that Spinoza brings to the OT deters me from finding this a viable hermeneutic.[433]

---

433 Bartholomew 2020.

Berman would undoubtedly agree with me that in many, many ways the OT is unique among ANE literature. Of course, a fundamental way in which this surfaces is precisely through the comparative approach that Berman proposes. Again and again in this volume, we have found alerts to the unique nature of the OT from surprising sources, surprising at least for an OT scholar like myself.

However, when it comes to dissimilarity between the OT and ANE literature, the difference can be summed up in one word, namely YHWH. We began this book by noting that Israel is a God-trodden land. That it indeed is, and it is in the literature of the OT that we find the residue of his walk with Israel over centuries. We saw above how at Sinai YHWH gives himself to the Israelites, and at the heart of this collection of works that we call the Hebrew Bible, or the Old Testament, is this same offer of relationship and disclosure. The question is whether or not even so rich an empirical approach as that of Berman can do justice to this invitation. My sense is that, as obviously fertile as is Berman's approach, it runs aground as we head towards hearing the OT as God's address, his revelation of himself and his invitation to us to respond.

As I have argued in this volume, to do justice to such an acoustics for the OT, we will need more than a revised historical criticism. We will need a paradigm for hearing the OT that takes with full seriousness the divine agency of YHWH. As Benjamin Sommer's work makes clear,[434] a question like whether or not God speaks or can speak makes a huge difference to how one approaches and interprets an event like that of Sinai. And our attention to Schwöbel's model of divine agency alerted us to the magnitude of the sort of divine self-disclosure we find at Sinai, far more radical than we might imagine. YHWH reveals himself in such a way as to help us develop an interpretative framework – a world view – which sees the world as God's creation, and ourselves as his image-bearers whose real but limited agency depends on our being constituted by him and caught up in his purpose of blessing the world. Schwöbel helps us to see that YHWH's self-disclosure has major ontological, epistemological and ethical implications. As Herman Bavinck comparably says of the person of Christ:

> Revelation, while having its centre in the Person of Christ, in its periphery extends to the uttermost ends of creation. It does not stand isolated in nature and history, does not resemble an island in the ocean, nor a drop of oil upon water. With the whole of nature, with the whole of history, with

---

434  Sommer 2015.

the whole of humanity, with the family and society, with science and art it is intimately connected.

The world itself rests on revelation; revelation is the presupposition, the foundation, the secret of all that exists in all its forms. The deeper science pushes its investigations, the more clearly will it discover that revelation underlies all created being. In every moment of time beats the pulse of eternity; every point in space is filled with the omnipresence of God; the finite is supported by the infinite, all becoming is rooted in being.[435]

Harrisville betrays, I suspect, his Lutheran world view[436] when he asserts that '[t]he faith required for the reading and interpretation of the Bible is not a world view, or dogmatic principle, an extra-something brought to the task'.[437] World views are often held unconsciously but they are not so easily disposed of. As we have seen, at a deep level world views underlie philosophical assumptions and orient a person towards the world in a particular way. Although I value the recent philosophical approaches to the OT, I do not think that the OT is a philosophical book. In it we encounter YHWH, and through that encounter we are inducted into a way of orienting ourselves in relation to the world – a world view. The OT in this way performs two tasks: it introduces us to YHWH, and through that introduction provides us with an interpretative framework for describing and living in the world.

# 9 Conclusion

It is a privilege, sheer delight and yet a challenge to work away in the fields of the OT. Our discipline is in a state of turbulence and pluralism, with old paradigms challenged, postmodernism now in demise, hard secularism making itself felt, and so on. This is also a time of great opportunity, a time to craft healthy ways forward which respect the genuine pluralism of the academy.

Healthy and rigorous attention to the historicity of the OT, to OT origins, will inevitably be bound up with the literature and kerygma of the text, and thus with repeated encounter with YHWH. To contextualize Tom Wright in relation to OT studies, if I may:

---

435 Bavinck 1909, 1979, 27.
436 See Bartholomew 2017.
437 Harrisville 2014, 312.

In too much OT study YHWH comes to us as one unknown. Epistemologically, if I am right, this is the wrong way round. We come to him as ones unknown, crawling back from the far country, where we had wasted our substance on riotous but ruinous historicism. But the swinehusks – the 'assured results of modern criticism' – reminded us of that knowledge which arrogance had all but obliterated, and we began the journey home. But when we approach, as we propose to do in this [series of books], we will find him running to us as one clothed in the garments of the ANE and yet as one well known, whom we had spurned in the name of scholarship or even of faith, but who was still patiently waiting to be sought and found once more. And the ring on our finger and the shoes on our feet assure us that, in celebrating his kingdom and feasting at his table, we shall discover again and again not only who he is but [also] who we ourselves are: as unknown and yet well known, as dying and behold we live.[438]

---

438  Wright 1996, 662.

# Bibliography

Abbagnano, N. 1967. 'Positivism.' In P. Edwards, ed., *The Encyclopedia of Philosophy*, vols 5 and 6. New York, NY: Macmillan and Free Press, 414–19.

Abraham, William J. 1982. *Divine Revelation and the Limits of Historical Criticism*. Oxford: OUP.

——. 2017a. *Divine Agency and Divine Action, Volume 1: Exploring and Evaluating the Debate*. Oxford: OUP.

——. 2017b. *Divine Agency and Divine Action, Volume 2: Soundings in the Christian Tradition*. Oxford: OUP.

——. 2018. *Divine Agency and Divine Action, Volume 3: Systematic Theology*. Oxford: OUP.

——. 2021. *Divine Agency and Divine Action, Volume 4: A Theological and Philosophical Agenda*. Oxford: OUP.

Abusch, T. 1999. 'Marduk.' *DDD*, 543–9.

Ackerman, Robert. 1991. *The Myth and Ritual School: J. G. Frazer and the Cambridge ritualists*. New York, NY, and London: Routledge.

Agut–Labordère, Damien. 2016. 'Beyond the Persian Tolerance Policy: Great Kings and Egyptian Gods during the Achaemenid Period.' In Edelman et al., eds, *Religion in the Achaemenid Period*, 319–48.

Aharoni, Yohanan. 1962, 1967. *The Land of the Bible: A historical geography*. Tr. A. F. Rainey. London: Burns & Oates.

Albrektson, Bertil. 1967. *History and the Gods: An essay on the idea of historical events as divine manifestations in the Ancient Near East and in Israel*. ConBOT 1. Lund: CWK Gleerup.

Albright, William F. 1957. *From the Stone Age to Christianity: Monotheism and the historical process*. 2nd edn. New York, NY: Doubleday.

Algaze, Guillermo. 1993, 2005. *The Uruk World System: The dynamics of expansion of early Mesopotamian civilization*. 2nd edn. Chicago, IL: University of Chicago Press.

——. 2008. *Ancient Mesopotamia at the Dawn of Civilization: The evolution of an urban landscape*. Chicago, IL: University of Chicago Press.

Allen, Spencer L. 2015. *The Splintered Image: A study of Ištar, Baal and Yahweh: divine names and divine multiplicity in the Ancient Near East*. SANER 9. Berlin: De Gruyter.

Alparslan, Metin. 2012. 'Recording the Past: Hittite Historiography.' In
    Doğan-Alparslan and Alparslan, eds, *Hittites: An Anatolian empire*, 48–61.

Alster, Bendt. 1997. *Proverbs of Ancient Sumer: The world's earliest proverb collections*, vol. 1. Bethesda, MD: CDL.

Alston, William. 1989. *Divine Nature and Human Language*. Eugene, OR: Wipf & Stock.

——. 2002. 'What Metaphysical Realism Is Not.' In William Alston, ed., *Realism and Anti-Realism*. Ithaca, NY: Cornell University Press, 97–118.

Alter, Robert. 1987. 'Introduction to the Old Testament.' In Alter and Kermode, eds, *The Literary Guide to the Bible*, 11–35.

——. 2011. *The Art of Biblical Narrative*. 2nd edn. New York, NY: Basic Books, 2011.

Alter, Robert, and Frank Kermode. 1987. 'General Introduction.' In Alter and Kermode, eds, *The Literary Guide to the Bible*, 1–8.

Alter, Robert, and Frank Kermode, eds. 1987. *The Literary Guide to the Bible*. London: Fontana.

Amrhein, Anastasia, and Elizabeth Knott. 2019a. 'Conclusion: Beholding Babylon's Ishtar Gate.' In Amrhein, Fitzgerald and Knott, eds, *A Wonder to Behold*, 145–53.

——. 2019b. 'Introduction: Sacred Materials, Sacred Skills.' In Amrhein, Fitzgerald and Knott, eds, *A Wonder to Behold*, 25–39.

Amrhein, Anastasia, Clare Fitzgerald and Elizabeth Knott, eds. 2019. *A Wonder to Behold: Craftmanship and the creation of Babylon's Ishtar Gate*. Princeton, NJ: Princeton University Press.

Anderson, Bernhard W. 1978, 1987. 'Politics and the Transcendent: Voegelin's Philosophical and Theological Exposition of the Old Testament in the Context of the Ancient Near East.' In Stephen A. McKnight, ed., *Eric Voegelin's Search for Order in History*. 2nd edn. Lanham, MD: University Press of America.

Anderson, Bernhard W., ed. 1984. *Creation in the Old Testament*. Minneapolis, MN: Fortress.

Anderson, James S. 2015. *Monotheism and Yahweh's Appropriation of Baal*. Library of Biblical Studies. London: T&T Clark.

——. 2016. 'Creating Dialectical Tensions: Religious Developments in Persian-Period Yehud Reflected in Biblical Texts.' In Edelman et al., eds, *Religion in the Achaemenid Period*, 9–23.

Ankersmit, F. R. 1983. *Narrative Logic: A semantic analysis of the historian's language*. The Hague: Martinus Nijhoff.

——. 2001. *Historical Representation*. Stanford, CA: Stanford University Press.

——. 2009. 'Narrative and Interpretation.' In Tucker, ed., *A Companion to the Philosophy of History and Historiography*, 199–208.

Arnold, Bill T. 2004. *Who Were the Babylonians?* Atlanta, GA: SBL.

Ashford, Bruce R., and Craig G. Bartholomew. 2020. *The Doctrine of Creation: A constructive Kuyperian approach*. Downers Grove, IL: IVP Academic.

Assmann, Jan. 1990. 'Guilt and Remembrance: On the Theologization of History in the Ancient Near East.' *History and Memory* 2: 5–33.

——. 1997. *Moses the Egyptian: The memory of Egypt in Western monotheism*. Cambridge, MA: Harvard University Press.

——. 2001. *The Search for God in Ancient Egypt*. Tr. David Lorton. Ithaca, NY: Cornell University Press.

——. 2002. *The Mind of Egypt: History and meaning in the time of the pharaohs*. Tr. Andrew Jenkins. New York, NY: Metropolitan.

——. 2004. 'Monotheism and Polytheism'. In *RAW*, 17–31.

——. 2006. *Religion and Cultural Memory: Cultural memory in the present*. Tr. Rodney Livingstone. Stanford, CA: Stanford University Press.

——. 2008. *Of God and Gods: Egypt, Israel, and the rise of monotheism*. Madison, WI: Wisconsin University Press, 2008.

——. 2010. *The Price of Monotheism*. Tr. Robert Savage. Stanford, CA: Stanford University Press.

——. 2014a. *From Akhenaten to Moses: Ancient Egypt and religious change*. Cairo and New York, NY: The American University in Cairo Press.

——. 2014b. *Religio Duplex: How the Enlightenment reinvented Egyptian religion*. Tr. Robert Savage. Cambridge: Polity.

——. 2018. *The Invention of Religion: Faith and covenant in the book of Exodus*. Tr. Robert Savage. Princeton, NJ: Princeton University Press, 2018.

Aubet, Maria Eugenia. 2001. *The Phoenicians and the West: Politics, colonies, and trade*. Tr. Mary Turton. 2nd edn. Cambridge: CUP.

——. 2013. *Commerce and Colonization in the Ancient Near East*. Tr. Mary Turton. Cambridge: CUP.

Auerbach, Erich. 1953, 2003. *Mimesis: The representation of reality in Western literature*. 50th anniversary edn. Princeton Classics. Princeton, NJ: Princeton University Press.

Austin, J. L. 1975. *How to Do Things with Words*. 2nd edn. Oxford: OUP.

Averbeck, Richard E. 2002. 'Sumer, the Bible, and Comparative Method.' In Mark W. Chavalas and K. Lawson Younger Jr, eds, *Mesopotamia and the Bible: Comparative explorations*. JSOTSup 341. Sheffield: Sheffield Academic Press, 88–125.

——. 2003a. 'Daily Life and Culture in "Enki and the World Order" and Other Sumerian Literary Compositions.' In Averbeck, Chavalas and Weisberg, eds, *Life and Culture in the Ancient Near East*, 23–61.

——. 2003b. 'Myth, Ritual and Order in "Enki and the World Order".' *JAOS* 123/4: 757–71.

——. 2004. 'Ancient Near Eastern Mythography as It Relates to Historiography in the Hebrew Bible: Genesis 3 and the Cosmic Battle.' In Hoffmeier and Millard, eds, *The Future of Biblical Archaeology*, 328–56.

——. 2018a, tr. 'Enki and the World Order (4.91).' In *COS* IV, 340–51.

——. 2018b, tr. 'KAR 4: The Creation of Humanity (4.90).' In *COS* IV, 334–40.

Averbeck, Richard E., Mark W. Chavalas and David B. Weisberg, eds. 2003. *Life and Culture in the Ancient Near East*. Bethesda, MD: CDL.

Bailey, Clinton. 2018. *Bedouin Culture in the Bible*. New Haven, CT: Yale University Press.

Baillie, John. 1956. *The Idea of Revelation in Recent Thought*. New York, NY: Columbia University Press.

Baines, John. 2000. 'Egyptian Deities in Context: Multiplicity, Unity, and the Problem of Change.' In Porter, ed., *One God or Many?*, 9–78.

Ballentine, Debra Scoggins. 2015. *The Conflict Myth and the Biblical Tradition*. Oxford: OUP.

Barr, James. 1959. 'The Meaning of "Mythology" in Relation to the Old Testament.' *VT* 9/1: 1–10.

——. 1963. 'Revelation through History in the Old Testament and Modern Theology.' *Interpretation* 17: 193–205.

——. 1981. *Fundamentalism*. 2nd edn. London: SCM.

Barth, Karl. 1936–69. *Church Dogmatics*. Edinburgh: T&T Clark.

Barthes, Roland. 1986. *The Rustle of Language*. Tr. Richard Howard. New York, NY: Farrar, Straus & Giroux.

Bartholomew, Craig G. 1995. 'Review of J. Levenson, *The Hebrew Bible, the Old Testament, and Historical Criticism* (1993).' *CTJ* 30/2: 525–30.

——. 1998. *Reading Ecclesiastes: Old Testament exegesis and hermeneutical theory*. AnBib 139. Rome: Pontificio Istituto Biblico.

——. 2009. *Ecclesiastes*. BCOTWP. Grand Rapids, MI: Baker Academic.

——. 2011. *Where Mortals Dwell: A Christian view of place for today*. Grand Rapids, MI: Baker Academic.

——. 2015. *Introducing Biblical Hermeneutics: A comprehensive framework for hearing God in Scripture*. Grand Rapids, MI: Baker Academic.

——. 2017. *Contours of the Kuyperian Tradition: A systematic introduction*. Downers Grove, IL: IVP Academic.

——. 2020. *The God Who Acts in History: The significance of Sinai*. Grand Rapids, MI: Eerdmans.

——. Forthcoming in French 2022 and English 2024. 'The Bible and History.'

Bartholomew, Craig G., and Michael W. Goheen. 2013. *Christian Philosophy: A systematic and narrative introduction*. Grand Rapids, MI: Baker Academic.

——. 2014. *The Drama of Scripture: Finding our place in the biblical story*. 2nd edn. Grand Rapids, MI: Baker Academic.

Bartholomew, Craig G., et al., eds. 2003. *'Behind' the Text: History and biblical interpretation*. SAHS 4. Grand Rapids, MI: Zondervan.

Bartholomew, Craig G., and Istine Rodseth Swart, eds. 2021. *Søren Kierkegaard and Spirituality: A dialogue with C. Stephen Evans*. Cambridge: Kirby Laing Centre.

Barton, John. 2007. *The Nature of Biblical Criticism*. Louisville, KY: Westminster John Knox.

Batto, Bernard F. 1992. *Slaying the Dragon: Mythmaking in the biblical tradition*. Louisville, KY: Westminster John Knox.

Bauckham, Richard. *Bible and Mission: Christian witness in a postmodern world*. Grand Rapids, MI: Baker Academic, 2003.

Bauman, Zygmunt. 1989. *Modernity and the Holocaust*. Cambridge: Polity.

Baumgartner, H. M. 1972. *Kontinuität und Geschichte*. Frankfurt: Suhrkamp Verlag.

Bautch, Richard J., and Mark Lackowski, eds. 2019. *On Dating Biblical Texts to the Persian Period*. FzAT 101. Tübingen: Mohr Siebeck.

Bavinck, Herman. 1909, 1979. *The Philosophy of Revelation*. Grand Rapids, MI: Baker.

Bazak, Amnon. 2020. *To This Very Day: Fundamental questions in Bible study*. Maggid Tanakh Companions. Jerusalem: Maggid.

Beaulieu, Paul-Alain. 2018. *A History of Babylon 2200 BC – AD 75*. Blackwell History of the Ancient World. Chichester: Wiley-Blackwell.

Becking, Bob, Meindert Dijkstra, Marjo C. A. Korpel and Karel J. H. Vriezen. 2001. *Only One God? Monotheism in Ancient Israel and the veneration of the goddess Asherah*. Sheffield: Sheffield Academic Press.

Beckman, Gary. 1995. 'The Siege of Uršu Text (CTH 7) and Old Hittite Historiography.' *JCS* 47: 32.

Beegle, Dewey M. 1992. 'Moses.' *ABD*, vol. 4, 909–21.

Beldman, David J. H. 2020. *Judges*. THOTC. Grand Rapids, MI: Eerdmans.

Bellah, Robert N. 2011. *Religion in Human Evolution: From the Paleolithic to the Axial Age*. Cambridge, MA: Belknap.

Benedict XVI. 2014. *The Ten Commandments*. Catholic Foundation Stones. London: St Pauls Publishing UK. Kindle edn.

Berkhof, Hendrikus. 1966. *Christ the Meaning of History*. Tr. Lambertus Buurman. Grand Rapids, MI: Baker.

Berlinerblau, Jacques. 2002. '"Poor Bird, Not Knowing Which Way to Fly": Biblical Scholarship's Marginality, Secular Humanism, and the Laudable Occident.' *BibInt* 10: 267–304.

Berman, Joshua A. 2011. 'CTH 133 and the Hittite Provenance of Deuteronomy 13.' *JBL* 130: 25–44.

——. 2013a. 'Historicism and Its Limits: A Response to Bernard M. Levinson and Jeffrey Stackert.' *JAJ* 4: 297–309.

——. 2013b. 'Histories Twice Told: Deuteronomy 1–3 and the Hittite Treaty Prologue Tradition.' *JBL* 132: 229–50.

——. 2017. *Inconsistency in the Torah: Ancient literary conventions and the limits of source criticism*. Oxford: OUP.

——. 2020. *Ani Maamin: Biblical criticism, historical truth, and the Thirteen Principles of Faith*. Jerusalem: Maggid.

Bettelheim, Bruno. 1976. *The Uses of Enchantment: The meaning and importance of fairy tales*. New York, NY: Alfred A. Knopf.

Bhaskar, Roy. 1998. 'General Introduction.' In Margaret Archer, Roy Bhaskar, Andrew Collier, Tony Lawson and Alan Norrie, eds, *Critical Realism: Essential readings*. Critical Realism: Interventions. New York, NY: Routledge, ix–xxiv.

Block, Daniel I. *Judges, Ruth*. 1999. NAC 6. Nashville, TN: Broadman & Holman.

Bodde, Derk, and Clarence Morris. 1967. *Law in Imperial China: Exemplified by 190 Ch'ing Dynasty cases (translated from the Hsing-an hui-lan), with historical, social, and juridical commentaries*. Harvard Studies in East Asian Law. Cambridge, MA: Harvard University Press.

Bottéro, Jean. 1977. 'Les Noms de Marduk, l'écriture, et la "logique" en Mésopotamie ancienne.' In Maria de Jong Ellis, ed., *Essays on the Ancient Near East in Memory of Jacob Joel Finkelstein*. Hamden, CT: Archon, 5–28.

——. 2001. *Religion in Ancient Mesopotamia*. Tr. Teresa Lavender Fagan. Chicago, IL, and London: University of Chicago Press.

Brague, Rémi. 2007. *The Law of God: The philosophical history of an idea*. Tr. Lydia G. Cochrane. Chicago, IL: University of Chicago Press.

Breasted, James H. 1912, 1972. *Development of Religion and Thought in Ancient Egypt*. Philadelphia, PA: University of Pensylvannia Press.

Brettler, Marc Zvi. 1989. *God Is King: Understanding an Israelite metaphor.* JSOTSup 76. Sheffield: Sheffield Academic Press.

Briant, Pierre. 2002. *From Cyrus to Alexander: A history of the Persian Empire.* Winona Lake, IN: Eisenbrauns.

Brichto, Herbert C. 1992. *Toward a Grammar of Biblical Poetics: Tales of the prophets.* Oxford: OUP.

Brisch, Nicole. 2013. 'History and Chronology.' In Crawford, ed., *The Sumerian World,* 111–127.

Bronner, Leah. 1968. *The Stories of Elijah and Elisha: As polemics against Baal worship.* Pretoria Oriental Series 6. Leiden: Brill.

Brooks, C. 1975. *The Well Wrought Urn: Studies in the structure of poetry.* London: Harcourt Brace Jovanich.

Brotzman, Ellis R., and Eric J. Tully. 1994, 2016. *Old Testament Textual Criticism: A practical introduction.* Grand Rapids, MI: Baker Academic.

Brueggemann, Walter. 2021. *Delivered out of Empire: Pivotal moments in the book of Exodus, Part One.* Louisville: KY: Westminster John Knox.

Brunner, Emil. 1949. *The Christian Doctrine of God.* Tr. Olive Wyon. Dogmatics 1. Philadelphia, PA: Westminster.

Bryce, Trevor. 2002. *Life and Society in the Hittite World.* Oxford: OUP.

——. 2014. *Ancient Syria: A three thousand year history.* Oxford: OUP.

——. 2016. *Babylonia: A very short introduction.* Oxford: OUP.

Bryce, Trevor, and Jessie Birkett-Rees. 2016. *Atlas of the Ancient Near East: From prehistoric times to the Roman imperial period.* New York, NY: Routledge.

Buckley, Michael. 1990. *At the Origins of Modern Atheism.* Rev. edn. New Haven, CT: Yale University Press.

Budge, E. A. Wallis. 1904. *The Gods of the Egyptians, or Studies in Egyptian Mythology,* vol. 1. New York, NY: Dover.

Burke, Sean. 1992. *The Death and Return of the Author: Criticism and subjectivity.* Edinburgh: Edinburgh University Press.

Butterfield, Herbert. 1981. *The Origins of History.* New York, NY: Basic Books.

Caquot, André, and Maurice Sznycer. 1980. *Ugaritic Religion.* Iconography of Religions 15/8. Leiden: Brill.

Carr, David M. 1986a. 'Narrative and the Real World.' *History and Theory* 25: 117–32.

——. 1986b. *Time, Narrative and History.* Bloomington, IN: Indiana University Press.

——. 2005. *Writing on the Tablet of the Heart: Origins of Scripture and literature.* New York, NY: OUP.

Casey, Edward S. 2009. *Getting Back into Place: Toward a renewed understanding of the place-world*. 2nd edn. Indianapolis, IN: Indiana University Press.

Cashdollar, C. D. 1989. *The Transformation of Theology: Positivism and Protestant thought in Britain and America*. Princeton, NJ: Princeton University Press.

Cassirer, Ernst. 1955. *The Philosophy of Symbolic Forms, Volume 2: Mythical Thought*. New Haven, CT: Yale University Press.

Casson, Lionel. 1971. *Ships and Seamanship in the Ancient World*. Princeton, NJ: Princeton University Press.

Cassuto, U. 1975. *Biblical and Oriental Studies, Volume 2: Bible and Ancient Oriental Texts*. Tr. Israel Abrahams. Jerusalem: Magnes.

Cataldo, Jeremiah W. 2012. *Breaking Monotheism: Yehud and the material formation of monotheistic identity*. LHBOTS 565. London: T&T Clark.

Cazelles, H., ed. 1955. *Moïse: L'Homme de l'alliance*. Paris: Desclée.

Chalmers, A. F. 1990. *Science and Its Fabrication*. Milton Keynes: Open University Press.

——. 1999. *What Is This Thing Called Science?* 3rd edn. Indianapolis, IN, and Cambridge: Hackett.

Charpin, Dominique. 2010. *Reading and Writing in Babylon*. Tr. Jane Marie Todd. Cambridge, MA: Harvard University Press.

Childs, Brevard S. 1962. *Myth and Reality in the Old Testament*. 2nd edn. SBT. London: SCM.

——. 1970. *Biblical Theology in Crisis*. Philadelphia, PA: Westminster.

——. 1974. *The Book of Exodus*. OTL. Louisville, KY: Westminster John Knox.

——. 1979. *Introduction to the Old Testament as Scripture*. Philadelphia, PA: Fortress.

——. 1985. *Old Testament Theology in a Canonical Context*. London: SCM.

Chrétien, Jean-Paul. 2004. *The Ark of Speech*. Tr. Andrew Brown. New York, NY: Routledge.

——. 2015. *Under the Gaze of the Bible*. Tr. John M. Dunaway. Perspectives in Continental Philosophy. New York, NY: Fordham University Press.

——. 2019. *Spacious Joy: An essay in phenomenology and literature*. Tr. Anna A. Davenport. New York, NY: Rowman & Littlefield.

Christensen, Duane L. 2002. *Deuteronomy 21:10 – 34:12*. WBC 6B. Nashville, TN: Thomas Nelson.

Clifford, Richard J. 1990. 'Phoenician Religion.' *BASOR* 279: 55–64.

——. 1994. *Creation Accounts in the Ancient Near East and in the Bible*. CBQMS 26. Washington, DC: Catholic Biblical Association of America.

Clouser, Roy. 1991. *The Myth of Religious Neutrality: An essay on the hidden role of religious beliefs in theories*. Notre Dame, IN: University of Notre Dame Press.

Collingwood, R. G. 1946. *The Idea of History*. Oxford: OUP.

Collins, Billie J. 2007. *The Hittites and Their World*. Atlanta, GA: SBL.

Coogan, Michael. 2014. *The Ten Commandments: A short history of an ancient text*. New Haven, CT: Yale University Press.

Cotterell, Arthur. 2019. *The First Great Powers: Babylon and Assyria*. London: Hurst.

Craigie, P. C. 1976. *The Book of Deuteronomy*. NICOT. Grand Rapids, MI: Eerdmans.

Crawford, Harriet. 1991. *Sumer and the Sumerians*. Cambridge: CUP.

——. 1998. *Dilmun and Its Gulf Neighbours*. Cambridge: CUP.

Crawford, Harriet, ed. 2013, 2017. *The Sumerian World*. London: Routledge.

Cross, Frank M. 1947. 'The Tabernacle: A Study from an Archeological and Historical Approach.' *BA* 10/3: 45–68.

——. 1973. *Canaanite Myth and Hebrew Epic: Essays in the history of the religion of Israel*. Cambridge, MA: Harvard University Press.

——. 1998. *From Epic to Canon: History and literature in Ancient Israel*. Baltimore, MD, and London: Johns Hopkins University Press.

Crossan, John D. 1998. *The Birth of Christianity: Discovering what happened in the years immediately after the execution of Jesus*. San Francisco, CA: HarperSanFrancisco.

Culp, A. J. 2020. *Memoir of Moses: The literary creation of covenantal memory in Deuteronomy*. Lanham, MD: Lexington Books / Fortress Academic.

Curtis, John. 1998, 2000. *Ancient Persia*. London: British Museum.

Dalferth, Ingolf U. 1988. *Theology and Philosophy*. Eugene, OR: Wipf & Stock.

Damrosch, David. 1987. *The Narrative Covenant: Transformations of genre in the growth of biblical literature*. Ithaca, NY: Cornell University Press.

Danto, A. C. 1985. Reissued 2007. *Narration and Knowledge*. New York, NY: Columbia University Press.

Davia, Michèle, John W. Wevers and Michael Weigl, eds. 2001a. *The World of the Aramaeans, Volume 1: Biblical Studies in Honour of Paul-Eugène Dion*. JSOTSup 324. Sheffield: Sheffield Academic Press.

——, eds. 2001b. *The World of the Aramaeans, Volume 3: Studies in Language and Literature in Honour of Paul-Eugène Dion*. JSOTSup 326. Sheffield: Sheffield Academic Press, 2001.

Davies, Oliver. 2004. *The Creativity of God: World, Eucharist, reason*. Cambridge: CUP.

Davies, Philip R. 2016. 'Monotheism, Empire, and the Cult(s) of Yehud in the Persian Period.' In Edelman et al., *Religion in the Achaemenid Period*, 24–35.

De Martino, Stefano. 2012. 'Religion and Mythology.' In Doğan-Alparslan and Alparslan, eds, *Hittites: An Anatolian empire*, 410–29.

Dentan, R.C. 'The Literary Affinities of Exodus xxxiv 6f.' *VT* 13:34–51.

Derrida, Jacques, and Gianni Vattimo, eds. 1998. *Religion*. Tr. J. Geiger, S. Weber and D. Webb. Cambridge: Polity.

Dickson, D. Bruce. 2013. 'Kingship as Racketeering: The Royal Tombs and Death Pits at Ur, Mesopotamia Reinterpreted from the Standpoint of Conflict Theory.' In Hill et al., eds, *Experiencing Power, Generating Authority*, 311–28.

Dilthey, W. 1976. *Selected Writings*. Ed. H. P. Rickman. Cambridge: CUP.

Dinçol, Belkis. 2012. 'Hittite Laws.' In Doğan-Alparslan and Alparslan, eds, *Hittites: An Anatolian empire*, 520–9.

Doak, Brian R. 2015. *Phoenician Aniconism in Its Mediterranean and Ancient Near Eastern Contexts*. Atlanta, GA: SBL.

Doğan-Alparslan, Meltem, and Metin Alparslan, eds. 2012. *Hittites: An Anatolian empire*. Istanbul: Ege Yayinlari.

Dorsey, David A. 1991. *The Roads and Highways of Ancient Israel*. Eugene, OR: Wipf & Stock.

Douglas, Mary. 1999. *Leviticus as Literature*. Oxford: OUP.

Downing, Francis G. 1964. *Has Christianity a Revelation?* London: SCM.

Durham, John I. 1987. *Exodus*. WBC 3. Nashville, TN: Thomas Nelson.

Dusinberre, Elspeth R. M. 2013. *Empire, Authority, and Autonomy in Achaemenid Anatolia*. Cambridge: CUP.

Eco, Umberto. 1984. *Semiotics and the Philosophy of Language*. Bloomington, IN: Indiana University Press.

Edelman, Diana, Anne Fitzpatrick-McKinley and Philippe Guillaume, eds. 2016. *Religion in the Achaemenid Persian Empire: Emerging Judaisms and trends*. ORA 17. Tübingen: Mohr Siebeck.

Edzard, Dietz Otto. 1997. *Gudea and His Dynasty*. The Royal Inscriptions of Mesopotamia: Early Periods 3/1. Toronto: University of Toronto Press.

Eichrodt, Walther. 1951. *Man in the Old Testament*. SBT 4. London: SCM.

Elnes, E. E., and Patrick D. Miller. 1999. 'Elyon.' *DDD*, 293–9.

Elrefaei, Aly. 2016. *Wellhausen and Kaufmann: Ancient Israel and its religious history in the works of Julius Wellhausen and Yehezkel Kaufmann*. BZAW 490. Berlin: De Gruyter.

Finkel, Irving. 2018. 'Ashurbanipal's Library: Contents and Significance.' In Gareth Brereton, ed., *I Am Ashurbanipal: King of the world, king of Assyria*. London: British Museum, 80–7.

Finkel, Irving, and Michael Seymour. 2008. *Babylon: City of wonders*. London: British Museum.

Fish, Stanley. 1980. *Is There a Text in This Class? The authority of interpretive communities*. Cambridge, MA: Harvard University Press.

Fishbane, Michael. 1985. *Biblical Interpretation in Ancient Israel*. Oxford: Clarendon.

Fisher, Loren R. 2015. *The Eloquent Peasant*. 2nd edn. Eugene, OR: Cascade.

Fitzpatrick-McKinley, Anne. 2016. 'Continuity between Assyrian and Persian Policies toward the Cults of Their Subjects.' In Edelman et al., eds, *Religion in the Achaemenid Persian Empire*, 137–71.

Fokkelman, J. P. 1991. *Narrative Art in Genesis: Specimens of stylistic and structural analysis*. The Biblical Seminar 12. Eugene, OR: Wipf & Stock.

Foster, Benjamin R. 2005. *Before the Muses: An anthology of Akkadian literature*. 3rd edn. Bethesda, MD: CDL.

Foucault, Michel. 2003. *'Society Must Be Defended': Lectures at the Collège de France, 1975–76*. Tr. David Macey. London: Penguin.

Frankfort, Henri. 1948, 1975. *Ancient Egyptian Religion: An interpretation*. New York, NY: Dover.

——. 1956. *The Birth of Civilization in the Near East*. New York, NY: Doubleday/ Anchor.

Frankfort, Henri, H. A. Frankfort, John A. Wilson, Thorkild Jacobsen and William A. Irwin. 1946. *The Intellectual Adventure of Ancient Man: An essay on speculative thought in the Ancient Near East*. Chicago, IL: University of Chicago Press.

Friedman, Richard E. 2017. *The Exodus: How it happened and why it matters*. New York, NY: HarperOne.

Friedman, Richard E., ed. 1983. *The Poet and the Historian: Essays in literary and historical biblical criticism*. Harvard Semitic Studies 26. Chico, CA: Scholars.

Gadamer, Hans-Georg. 1989. *Truth and Method*. Tr. Joel Weinsheimer and Donald G. Marshall. 2nd rev. edn. London: Sheed & Ward.

Gadotti, Alhena. 2014. *'Gilgamesh, Enkidu and the Netherworld' and the Sumerian World*. Untersuchungen zur Assyriologie und vorderasiatischen Archäologie 10. Berlin: De Gruyter.

Gammie, John G. 1989. *Holiness in Israel*. Overtures to Biblical Theology. Minneapolis, MN: Fortress.

Garnett, Anna. 2015. *The Colossal Statue of Ramesses II*. London: British Museum.

Geller, Stephen A. 2000. 'The God of the Covenant.' In Porter, ed., *One God or Many?*, 273–319.

Gellner, Ernest. 1992. *Postmodernism, Reason and Religion*. New York, NY: Routledge.

Gertz, Jan C., B. M. Levinson, D. Rom-Shiloni and K. Schmid, eds. 2016. *The Formation of the Pentateuch: Bridging the academic cultures of Europe, Israel, and North America*. FzAT 111. Tübingen: Mohr Siebeck.

Gibbs, R. W. 1994. *The Poetics of Mind: Figurative thought, language, and understanding*. Cambridge: CUP.

Gibbs, R. W., ed. 2008. *The Cambridge Handbook of Metaphor and Thought*. Cambridge: CUP.

Gilkey, Langdon. 1961. 'Cosmology, Ontology and the Travail of Biblical Language.' *JR* 41: 194–205.

Giovino, Mariana. 2007. *The Assyrian Sacred Tree: A history of interpretations*. Orbis Biblicus et Orientalis 230. Fribourg: Academic Press; Göttingen: Vandenhoeck & Ruprecht.

Girard, René. 1965. *Deceit, Desire, and the Novel: Self and other in literary structure*. Tr. Y. Freccero. Baltimore, MD: Johns Hopkins University Press.

——. 2001. *I See Satan Fall Like Lightning*. Tr. James G. Williams. New York, NY: Orbis.

Glassner, Jean-Jacques. 2003. *The Invention of Cuneiform: Writing in Sumer*. Tr. Zainab Bahrani and Marc Van De Mieroop. Baltimore, MD: Johns Hopkins University Press.

Gnuse, Robert K. 1997. *No Other Gods: Emergent monotheism in Israel*. JSOTSup 241. Sheffield: Sheffield Academic Press.

Goheen, Michael W., and Craig G. Bartholomew. 2008. *Living at the Crossroads: An introduction to Christian worldview*. Grand Rapids, MI: Baker Academic.

Goldman, Solomon. 1963. *The Ten Commandments*. Chicago, IL: Phoenix.

Goodman, Nelson. 1976. *Languages of Art: An approach to a theory of symbols*. Indianapolis, IN: Hackett.

Gordon, Cyrus H. 1949. *Ugaritic Literature: A Comprehensive Translation of the Poetic and Prose Texts*. Rome: Pontificium Institutum Biblicum, 1949.

——. 1962, 1965. *The Common Background of Greek and Hebrew Civilizations*. New York, NY: Norton.

Gottwald, Norman K. 1979. *The Tribes of Yahweh: A sociology of the religion of liberated Israel, 1250–1050 B.C.E.* London: SCM.

Goudzwaard, Bob, and Craig G. Bartholomew. 2017. *Beyond the Modern Age: An archaeology of contemporary culture*. Downers Grove, IL: IVP Academic.

Graham, Gordon. 1997. *The Shape of the Past: A philosophical approach to history*. Oxford: OUP.

Greenberg, Moshe. 1969. *Understanding Exodus: The heritage of biblical Israel*. New York, NY: Jewish Theological Seminary of America.

——. 2013. *Understanding Exodus: A holistic commentary on Exodus 1–11*. 2nd edn. Eugene, OR: Cascade.

Greenfield, J. C. 1999. 'Hadad.' *DDD*, 377–82.

Grottanelli, Cristiano. 1999. *Kings and Prophets: Monarchic power, inspired leadership, and sacred texts in biblical narrative*. Oxford: OUP.

Gunkel, Hermann. 1998. *Introduction to Psalms: The genres of the religious lyric of Israel*. Tr. James D. Nogalski. Eugene, OR: Wipf & Stock.

Gunton, Colin E. 2002. *Act and Being: Towards a theology of the Divine Attributes*. Grand Rapids, MI: Eerdmans.

Gurney, O. R. 1977. *Some Aspects of Hittite Religion*. The Schweich Lectures 1976. Oxford: OUP.

Hacking, Ian. 2012. 'Introductory Essay'. In Kuhn, *The Structure of Scientific Revolutions*, vii–xxxvii.

Hahn, Herbert F. 1956. *The Old Testament in Modern Research*. London: SCM.

Hahn, Scott W., and Jeffrey L. Morrow. 2020. *Modern Biblical Criticism as a Tool of Statecraft (1700–1900)*. Steubenville, OH: Emmaus.

Hahn, Scott W., and Benjamin Wiker. 2013. *Politicizing the Bible: The roots of historical criticism and the secularization of Scripture, 1300–1700*. New York, NY: Herder & Herder.

Halbwachs, Maurice. 1980. *The Collective Memory*. New York, NY: Harper Colophon.

Halevi, Z'ev ben Shimon. 1988. *Kabbalah and Exodus*. New York, NY: Samuel Weiser.

Hall, Edward T. 1959, 1981. *The Silent Language*. New York, NY: Anchor.

Hallo, W. W. 1988. 'Sumerian Literature: Background to the Bible.' *BR* 4:28–38.

——. 1996. *Origins: The Ancient Near Eastern background of some modern Western institutions*. Leiden: Brill.

Halpern, Bruce. 1988. *The First Historians: The Hebrew Bible and history*. San Francisco, CA: Harper & Row.

Hamann, Johann Georg. 2007. *Writings on Philosophy and Language*. Cambridge Texts in the History of Philosophy. Cambridge: CUP.

Harrisville, Roy A. 2014. *Pandora's Box Opened: An examination and defense of historical-critical method and its master practitioners*. Grand Rapids, MI: Eerdmans.

Hayes, Christine. 2015. *What's Divine about Divine Law? Early perspectives*. Princeton, NJ: Princeton University Press.

Heidegger, Martin. 1982. *The Basic Problems of Phenomenology*. Tr. Albert Hofstadter. Bloomington, IN: Indiana University Press.

Hendel, Ronald. 1988. *The Epic of the Patriarch: The Jacob cycle and the narrative traditions of Canaan and Israel*. Harvard Semitic Monographs 42. Leiden: Brill.

——. 1995. 'Dating the Patriarchal Age.' *BAR* 21/4: 56–7.

——. 1997. 'Aniconism and Anthropomorphism in Ancient Israel.' In Karel van der Toorn, ed., *The Image and the Book: Iconic cults, aniconism, and the rise of book religion in Israel and the Ancient Near East*. Leuven: Peeters, 205–28.

——. 2005. *Remembering Abraham: Culture, memory, and history in the Hebrew Bible*. Oxford: OUP.

Herberg, Will. 1976. *Faith Enacted as History: Essays in biblical theology*. Ed. Bernhard W. Anderson. Philadelphia, PA: Westminster.

Herms, Eilert. 1984. 'Offenbarung.' In *Funkkolleg Religion*. Studienbegleitbrief 7. Weinheim/Basel: Beltz Verlag, 11–54.

——. 1992. *Offenbarung und Glaube: zur Bildung des christlichen Lebens*. Tübingen: Mohr Siebeck.

Herrera, R. A. 2001. *Reasons for Our Rhymes: An inquiry into the philosophy of history*. Grand Rapids, MI: Eerdmans.

Herrmann, W. 1999. 'El.' In *DDD*, 274–80.

Hertog, Cornelis den. 2012. *The Other Face of God: 'I Am that I Am' reconsidered*. Hebrew Bible Monographs 32. Sheffield: Sheffield Phoenix.

Heslam, Peter. 1998. *Creating a Christian Worldview: Abraham Kuyper's lectures on Calvinism*. Grand Rapids, MI: Eerdmans.

Hess, Richard S. 2007. *Israelite Religion: An archaeological and biblical survey*. Grand Rapids, MI: Baker Academic.

——. 2009. *Studies in the Personal Names of Genesis 1–11*. Winona Lake, IN: Eisenbrauns.

Hesse, Mary. 1994. 'How to Be Postmodern without Being a Feminist.' *The Monist* 77/4: 445–61.

Hill, Jane A., Philip Jones and Antonio J. Morales, eds. 2013. *Experiencing Power, Generating Authority: Cosmos, politics, and the ideology of kingship in Ancient Egypt and Mesopotamia*. Penn Museum International Research

Conferences. Philadelphia, PA: University of Pennsylvania Museum of Archaeology and Anthropology.

Himmelfarb, Gertrude. 1994. *On Looking into the Abyss: Untimely thoughts on culture and society*. New York, NY: Vintage.

Hoffmeier, James K. 1986. 'Moses.' In *ISBE*, vol. 3, 415–25.

——. 1996. *Israel in Egypt: The evidence for the authenticity of the exodus tradition*. Oxford: OUP.

——. 2003. 'Everyday Life in Ancient Egypt'. In Averbeck et al., eds, *Life and Culture in the Ancient Near East*, 327–51.

——. 2005. *Ancient Israel in Sinai: Evidence for the authenticity of the wilderness tradition*. Oxford: OUP.

——. 2015. *Akhenaten and the Origins of Monotheism*. Oxford: OUP.

Hoffmeier, James K., and Alan Millard, eds. 2004. *The Future of Biblical Archaeology: Reassessing methods and assumptions*. Grand Rapids, MI: Eerdmans.

Hoffner Jr, Harry A. 1990. *Hittite Myths*. Atlanta, GA: Scholars.

——. 1997. *The Laws of the Hittites: A critical edition*. Leiden: Brill.

Hoffner Jr, Harry A., and Gary M. Beckman, eds. 1986. *Kaniššuwar: A tribute to Hans G. Güterbock on his seventy-fifth birthday, May 27, 1983*. Assyriological Studies 23. Chicago, IL: Oriental Institute of the University of Chicago.

Holloway, Steven W. 2002. *Aššur Is King! Aššur Is King! Religion in the exercise of power in the Neo-Assyrian Empire*. Culture and History of the Ancient Near East 10. Leiden: Brill.

Homan, Michael M. 2000. 'The Divine Warrior in His Tent: A Military Model for Yahweh's tabernacle.' *BRev* 16/6: 22–33.

——. 2002. *To Your Tents, O Israel! The terminology, function, form, and symbolism of tents in the Hebrew Bible and the Ancient Near East*. Leiden: Brill.

Hornung, Erik. 1982. *Conceptions of God in Ancient Egypt: The one and the many*. Tr. John Baines. Ithaca, NY: Cornell University Press.

——. 1999. *Akhenaten and the Religion of Light*. Tr. David Lorton. Ithaca, NY: Cornell University Press.

Horowitz, Wayne. 1998, 2011. *Mesopotamian Cosmic Geography*. Winona Lake, IN: Eisenbrauns.

Human, Dirk J., ed. 2007. *Psalms and Mythology*. LHBOTS 462. London: T&T Clark.

Hurowitz, Victor. 1992. *I Have Built You an Exalted House: Temple building in light of Mesopotamian and North-West Semitic writings*. JSOTSup 115. Sheffield: Sheffield Academic Press.

Hurtado, Larry W. 2015. *One God, One Lord: Early Christian devotion and ancient Jewish monotheism*. 3rd edn. London: Bloomsbury.

Imes, Carmen J. 2018. *Bearing YHWH's Name at Sinai: A reexamination of the name command of the Decalogue*. BBRSup 19. University Park, PA: Eisenbrauns.

Irwin, William A. 1946. 'The Hebrews.' In Frankfort et al., *The Intellectual Adventure of Ancient Man*, 223–360.

Israel, Jonathan I. 2001. *Radical Enlightenment: Philosophy and the making of modernity, 1650–1750*. Oxford: OUP.

Jacobsen, Thorkild. 1946. 'Mesopotamia.' In Frankfort et al., *The Intellectual Adventure of Ancient Man*, 125–219.

——. 1987. *The Harps That Once . . . Sumerian poetry in translation*. New Haven, CT: Yale University Press.

Jaeger, Lydia. 2012. 'Against Physicalism-Plus-God: How Creation Accounts for Divine Action in Nature's World.' *Faith and Philosophy* 29: 295–312.

Janzen, Waldemar. 1992. 'Land.' In *ABD*, vol. 3, 237–49.

Jefferson, A., and Robey, D. 1986. *Modern Literary Theory: A comparative introduction*. 2nd edn. London: Batsford.

Jigoulov, Vadim S. 2010. *The Social History of Achaemenid Phoenicia: Being a Phoenician, negotiating empires*. New York, NY: Routledge.

Johnson, A. R. 1961. *The One and the Many in the Israelite Conception of God*. Cardiff: University of Wales Press Board.

Johnston, Sarah I., ed. 2004. *Religions of the Ancient World: A guide*. Cambridge, MA: Belknap.

Kass, Leon R. 1994, 1999. *The Hungry Soul: Eating and the perfecting of our nature*. Chicago, IL: University of Chicago Press.

——. 2003. *The Beginning of Wisdom: Reading Genesis*. Chicago, IL: University of Chicago Press.

——. 2021. *Founding God's Nation: Reading Exodus*. New Haven, CT: Yale University Press.

Kass, Leon, Michael Fishbane, Peter Berkowitz, Gilbert Meilaender and Meir Soloveichik. 2013. 'The Ten Commandments: Why the Decalogue Matters.' *Mosaic*, June. Kindle edn.

Kaufmann, Yehezkel. 1960. *The Religion of Israel: From its beginnings to the Babylonian exile*. Tr. and ed. Moshe Greenberg. Chicago, IL: University of Chicago Press.

Kawashima, Robert S. 2004. *Biblical Narrative and the Death of the Rhapsode*. Bloomington and Indianapolis, IN: Indiana University Press.

Kemp, Barry. 2012. *The City of Akhenaten and Nefertiti: Amarna and its people*. London: Thames & Hudson.

Kitchen, Kenneth. 2003. *On the Reliability of the Old Testament*. Grand Rapids, MI: Eerdmans.

Kitchen, Kenneth A., and Paul J. N. Lawrence. 2012a. *Treaty, Law and Covenant in the Ancient Near East, Part 1: The Texts*. Wiesbaden: Harrassowitz Verlag.

——. 2012b. *Treaty, Law and Covenant in the Ancient Near East, Part 2: Text, Notes and Chromograms*. Wiesbaden: Harrassowitz Verlag.

——. 2012c. *Treaty, Law and Covenant in the Ancient Near East, Part 3: Overall Historical Survey*. Wiesbaden: Harrassowitz Verlag.

Knauf, E. A. 1999. 'Shadday.' *DDD*, 749–53.

Knierim, Rolf P. 1965. *Die Hauptbegriffe fur Sünde im Alten Testament*. Gütersloh: Gerd Mohn.

——. 1995. *The Task of Old Testament Theology: Substance, method, and cases*. Grand Rapids, MI: Eerdmans.

Köckert, M. 1999. 'Fear of Isaac.' In *DDD*, 329–31.

Kolakowski, L. 1968, 1972. *Positivist Philosophy: From Hume to the Vienna Circle*. London: Penguin.

König, Adrio. 1982. *Here Am I! A Christian reflection on God*. Grand Rapids, MI: Eerdmans.

Kövecses, Z. 2010. *Metaphor: A practical introduction*. 2nd edn. Oxford: OUP.

Kramer, Samuel N. 1959. 'Sumerian Literature and the Bible.' In *Studia Biblica et Orientalia*. AnBib 12. Rome: Pontificio Istituto Biblico, 185–204.

——. 1961, 1972. *Sumerian Mythology: A study of spiritual and literary achievements in the third millennium B.C.* Philadelphia, PA: University of Philadelphia Press.

——. 1963. *The Sumerians: Their history, culture, and character*. Chicago: University of Chicago Press.

——. 1981. *History Begins at Sumer: Thirty-nine firsts in man's recorded history*. 3rd edn. Philadelphia, PA: University of Pennsylvania Press.

Krupnick, M. 1994. 'Steiner's Literary Journalism: "The Heart of the Maze".' In Scott and Sharp, eds, *Reading George Steiner*, 43–57.

Kuhn, Thomas S. 2012. *The Structure of Scientific Revolutions*. 50th anniversary edn. Chicago, IL: University of Chicago Press.

Kuhrt, Amélie. 2007, 2010. *The Persian Empire: A corpus of sources from the Achaemenid period*. London: Routledge.

LaCocque, André, and Paul Ricoeur. 1998. *Thinking Biblically: Exegetical and hermeneutical studies*. Tr. David Pellauer. Chicago, IL: University of Chicago Press.

Lafont, Sophie. 2003. 'Middle Assyrian Period.' In Westbrook, ed., *A History of Ancient Near Eastern Law*, vol. 1, 521–63.

Lakoff, G., and M. Turner. 1989. *Cool Reason: A field guide to poetic metaphor*. Chicago, IL: University of Chicago Press.

Lambert, W. G. 1980–3. 'Kosmogonie.' In E. Ebeling and B. Meissner, eds, *Reallexikon der Assyriologie*, vol. 6. Berlin: De Gruyter, 218–22.

Leick, Gwendolyn. 2001. *Mesopotamia: The invention of the city*. London: Penguin.

Leitz, Christian. 'Deities and Demons.' In *RAW*, 392–6.

Levenson, Jon D. 1993. *The Hebrew Bible, the Old Testament, and Historical Criticism: Jews and Christians in biblical studies*. Louisville, KY: Westminster John Knox.

——. 2012. *Inheriting Abraham: The legacy of the patriarch in Judaism, Christianity and Islam*. Princeton, NJ: Princeton University Press.

Levinson, Bernard M., and Jeffrey Stackert. 2012. 'Between the Covenant Code and Esarhaddon's Succession Treaty: Deuteronomy 13 and the Composition of Deuteronomy.' *JAJ* 3: 123–40.

Levy, Thomas E., Thomas Schneider and William H. C. Propp, eds. 2015. *Israel's Exodus in Transdisciplinary Perspective: Text, archaeology, culture, and geoscience*. Cham: Springer.

Lewis, C. S. 1971. *Undeceptions: Essays on theology and ethics*. London: Bles.

——. 1975. *Fern-Seed and Elephants and Other Essays on Christianity*. London: Fount.

Lewis, Theodore J. 2020. *The Origin and Character of God: Ancient Israelite religion through the lens of divinity*. Oxford: OUP.

Lilla, Mark. 2007, 2008. *The Stillborn God: Religion, politics, and the modern West*. New York, NY: Vintage.

Lipiński, Edward. 2000. *The Aramaeans: Their ancient history, culture, religion*. OLA. Leuven: Peeters.

Lisman, Jan J. W. 2013. *Cosmogony, Theogony, and Anthropogeny in Sumerian Texts*. AOAT 409. Münster: Ugarit-Verlag.

Liverani, Mario. 2005. *Israel's History and the History of the Bible*. Tr. Chiara Peri and Philip R. Davies. London: Routledge.

——. 2014. *The Ancient Near East: History, society and economy*. New York, NY: Routledge.

——. 2017. *Assyria: The imperial mission*. Winona Lake, IN: Eisenbrauns.

Livingstone, A. 1999. 'Assur.' In *DDD*, 108–9.

Locke, John. 1825. *An Essay Concerning Human Understanding*. London: Griffin & Co.

Lodge, David, ed. 1972. *Twentieth Century Literary Criticism: A reader.* London: Longman.

Lorton, David. 2004. 'Ethics and Law Codes.' In *RAW*, 514–16.

Losch, Richard R. 2005. *The Uttermost Part of the Earth: A guide to places in the Bible.* Grand Rapids, MI: Eerdmans.

Lyotard, J.-F. 1984. *The Postmodern Condition: A report on knowledge.* Minneapolis, MN: University of Minneapolis Press.

McCann Jr, J. Clinton. 1993. *A Theological Introduction to the Book of Psalms: The psalms as torah.* Nashville, TN: Abingdon.

McCarthy, D. J. 1978. 'Exod 3:14: History, Philology and Theology.' *CBQ* 40/3: 311–22.

MacDonald, Nathan. 2012. *Deuteronomy and the Meaning of 'Monotheism'.* 2nd edn. FzAT 2/1. Tübingen: Mohr Siebeck.

McGrath, Alister. 2002. *A Scientific Theology, Volume 2: Reality.* Grand Rapids, MI: Eerdmans.

Machinist, Peter. 1991. 'The Question of Distinctiveness in Ancient Israel: An Essay.' In Mordechai Cogan and Israel Eph'al, eds, *Ah, Assyria . . . Studies in Assyrian history and Ancient Near Eastern historiography presented to Hayim Tadmor.* Scripta Hierosolymitana 33. Jerusalem: Magnes, 196–212.

——. 2006. 'Final Response: On the Study of the Ancients, Language, Writing, and the State.' In Seth L. Sanders, ed., *Margins of Writing, Origins of Cultures: New approaches to writing and reading in the Ancient Near East.* Chicago, IL: Oriental Institute Press, 291–300.

MacIntyre, Alasdair. 1988. *Whose Justice? Which Rationality?* London: Duckworth.

——. 1997. 'Epistemological Crises, Dramatic Narrative, and the Philosophy of Science.' In Stanley Hauerwas and L. Gregory Jones, eds, *Why Narrative? Readings in narrative theology.* Eugene, OR: Wipf & Stock, 138–57.

——. 2007. *After Virtue: A study in moral theory.* 3rd edn. Notre Dame, IN: University of Notre Dame Press.

Macquarrie, John. 1969. *Prayer Is Thinking.* New York, NY: Sentinel.

Malamat, A. 1973. 'The Aramaeans.' In Wiseman, ed., *Peoples of Old Testament Times*, 134–55.

Mandelbaum, M. 1967. 'Historicism.' In P. Edwards, ed., *The Encyclopedia of Philosophy*, vols 3 and 4. New York, NY: Macmillan and Free Press, 22–5.

Manetti, Giovanni. 1993. *Theories of the Sign in Classical Antiquity.* Tr. C. Richardson. Bloomington, IN: Indiana University Press, 1993.

Martino, Stefano de. 2012. 'Religion and Mythology.' In Doğan-Alparslan and Alparslan, eds, *Hittites: An Anatolian empire*, 410–29.

Masterman, Margaret. 1970. 'The Nature of a Paradigm.' In Imre Lakatos and Alan Musgrave, eds, *Criticism and the Growth of Knowledge*. Cambridge: CUP, 59–89.

Matthiae, Paolo. 2021. *Ebla: Archaeology and history*. Tr. Richard Bates, Mattia Bilardello and Anita Weston. New York, NY: Routledge.

Mays, James L. 1994. *The Lord Reigns: A theological handbook to the Psalms*. Louisville, KY: Westminster John Knox.

——. 2011. *Psalms*. Interpretation. Louisville, KY: Westminster John Knox.

Mazar, Amihai. 1990. *Archaeology of the Land of the Bible, 10,000–586 B.C.E.* New York, NY: Doubleday.

Mendenhall, G. E. 1955. *Law and Covenant in Israel and the Ancient Near East*. Pittsburgh, PA: The Biblical Colloquium.

Meskell, Lynn. 2002. *Private Life in New Kingdom Egypt*. Princeton, NJ: Princeton University Press.

Mettinger, Tryggve N. D. 1988. *In Search of God: The meaning and message of the everlasting names*. Tr. Frederick H. Cryer. Philadelphia, PA: Fortress.

——. 1995. *No Graven Image? Israelite Aniconism in Its Ancient Near Eastern Context*. Stockholm: Almqvist & Wiksell.

Meyer, Ben F. 1989. *Critical Realism and the New Testament*. Princeton Theological Monograph Series 17. Allison Park, PA: Pickwick.

Midgley, Mary. 2003. *The Myths We Live By*. New York, NY: Routledge.

Milbank, John. 1997. *The Word Made Strange: Theology, language, and culture*. Oxford: Blackwell.

Millard, Alan R., and Donald J. Wiseman, eds. 1980. *Essays on the Patriarchal Narratives*. Leicester: IVP.

Miller, Patrick D. 2000. *The Religion of Ancient Israel*. London: SPCK; Louisville, KY: Westminster John Knox.

——. 2004, 2007a. 'The Psalter as a Book of Theology.' In Miller, *The Way of the Lord*, 214–25.

——. 2004, 2007b. *The Way of the Lord: Essays in Old Testament theology*. Grand Rapids, MI: Eerdmans.

Mink, L. O. 1987. *Historical Understanding*. Ithaca, NY, and London: Cornell University Press.

Moberly, R. W. L. 1992. *The Old Testament of the Old Testament: Patriarchal narratives and Mosaic Yahwism*. Minneapolis, MN: Fortress.

——. 2020. *The God of the Old Testament: Encountering the divine in Christian Scripture*. Grand Rapids, MI: Baker Academic.

Moi, Toril. 2017. *Revolution of the Ordinary: Literary studies after Wittgenstein, Austin, and Cavell*. Chicago, IL: University of Chicago Press.

Monson, John. 2018. 'Original Context and Canon.' In Andrew T. Abernethy, ed., *Interpreting the Old Testament Theologically: Essays in honor of Willem A. VanGemeren*. Grand Rapids, MI: Zondervan, 25–42.

Moor, J. C. de. 1997. *The Rise of Yahwism: The roots of Israelite monotheism*. 2nd edn. BETL 91A. Leuven: Peeters.

Moore, Megan Bishop, and Brad E. Kelle. 2011. *Biblical History and Israel's Past: The changing study of the Bible and history*. Grand Rapids, MI: Eerdmans.

Morales, L. Michael, ed. 2014. *Cult and Cosmos: Tilting toward a temple-centered theology*. Leuven: Peeters.

Moran, Gabriel. 1973. *Theology of Revelation*. London: Search Press.

Morris, Ellen. 2013. 'Propaganda and Performance at the Dawn of the State.' In Hill et al., eds, *Experiencing Power, Generating Authority*, 33–64.

Mouton, Alice. 2015. 'The Sacred in Hittite Anatolia: A Tentative Definition.' *History of Religions* 55/1: 41–64.

Mowinckel, S. 1922. *Psalmenstudien, Volume 2: Das Thronbesteigungsfest Jahwäs und der Ursprung der Eschatologie*. Amsterdam: P. Schippers and B. R. Grüner.

——. 1961. 'The Name of the God of Moses.' *HUCA* 32: 121–33.

Mullen Jr, E. T. 1980. *The Divine Council in Canaanite and Early Hebrew Literature*. Harvard Semitic Monographs 24. Chico, CA: Scholars.

Müller, H.-P. 1999. 'Chemosh.' In *DDD*, 186–9.

Munslow, Alun. 1997. *Deconstructing History*. London and New York, NY: Routledge.

Naugle, David. 2002. *Worldview: The history of a concept*. Grand Rapids, MI: Eerdmans.

Neill, Stephen, and Tom Wright. 1988. *The Interpretation of the New Testament, 1861–1986*. 2nd edn. Oxford: OUP.

Newbigin, Lesslie. 1989. *The Gospel in a Pluralist Society*. Grand Rapids, MI: Eerdmans.

——. 1995. *Proper Confidence: Faith, doubt, and certainty in Christian discipleship*. Grand Rapids, MI: Eerdmans.

Niesiolowski-Spano, Lucasz. 2016. *Origin Myths and Holy Places in the Old Testament: A study of aetiological narratives*. Tr. Jacek Laskowski. New York, NY: Routledge.

Nietzsche, Friedrich. 1974. *The Gay Science*. Tr. Walter Kaufmann. New York, NY: Random House Vintage.

Norris, Christopher. 1994. *Truth and the Ethics of Criticism*. Manchester: Manchester University Press.

Östborn, Gunnar. 1950. *Cult and Canon: A study in the canonization of the Old Testament.* Uppsala: A. B. Lundequistska.

Oswalt, John N. 2009. *The Bible among the Myths: Unique revelation or just ancient literature?* Grand Rapids, MI: Zondervan.

Otto, Eckart. 2006. *Mose: Geschichte und Legende.* Munich: C. H. Beck.

Otto, Rudolf. 1950. *The Idea of the Holy: An inquiry into the non-rational factor in the idea of the divine and its relation to the rational.* Tr. John W. Harvey. 2nd edn. Oxford: OUP.

Pardee, Dennis. 2002. *Ritual and Cult at Ugarit.* Ed. Theodore J. Lewis. Writings from the Ancient World 10. Atlanta, GA: SBL.

——. 2012. *The Ugaritic Texts and the Origins of West-Semitic Literary Composition.* Oxford: OUP.

Pardes, Ilana. 2000. *The Biography of Ancient Israel: National narratives in the Bible.* Berkeley, CA: University of California Press.

Parkinson, R. B., tr. 1997. *The Tale of Sinuhe and Other Ancient Egyptian Poems, 1940–1640 BC.* Oxford: OUP.

Parpola, Simo. 2000. 'Monotheism in Ancient Assyria.' In Porter, ed., *One God or Many?*, 165–209.

Peckham, J. Brian. 2014. *Phoenicia: Episodes and anecdotes from the Ancient Mediterranean.* Winona Lake, IN: Eisenbrauns.

Peker, Hasan. 2012. 'International Relationships and Political Instruments of the Hittite State.' In Doğan-Alparslan and Alparslan, eds, *Hittites: An Anatolian empire*, 64–79.

Penchansky, David. 1995. *The Politics of Biblical Theology: A postmodern reading.* Studies in American Biblical Hermeneutics 10. Macon, GA: Mercer.

Pepper, S. C. 1942. *World Hypotheses: Prolegomena to systematic philosophy and a complete survey of metaphysics.* Berkeley, CA: University of California Press.

Perlitt, L. 1965. *Vatke und Wellhausen: Geschichtsphilosophische Voraussetzungen und historiographische Motive für die Darstellung der Religion und Geschichte Israels durch Wilhelm Vatke und Julius Wellhausen.* BZAW 94. Berlin: Alfred Töpelmann.

Petersen, Allan R. 1998. *The Royal God: Enthronement festivals in Ancient Israel and Ugarit?* Copenhagen International Seminar. JSOTSup 259. Sheffield: Sheffield Academic Press.

Pettinato, G. 1971. *Das altorientalische Menschbild und die sumerischen und akkadischen Schöpfungsmythen.* Heidelberg: Abhandlungen der Heidelberger Akadamie der Wissenschaften, Phil-Hist. Klasse.

Pike, D. M. 1990. 'Israelite Theophoric Personal Names in the Bible and Their Implications for Religious History.' PhD thesis. University of Pennsylvania.

Plantinga, Alvin. 1984. 'Advice to Christian Philosophers.' *Faith and Philosophy* 1/3: 253–71.

——. 1995. 'Christian Philosophy at the End of the 20th Century.' In S. Griffioen and B. M. Balk, eds, *Christian Philosophy at the Close of the Twentieth Century: Assessment and perspective*. Kampen: Kok, 29–53.

——. 2000. *Warranted Christian Belief*. New York, NY: OUP.

——. 2011. *Where the Conflict Really Lies: Science, religion, and naturalism*. Oxford: OUP.

——. 2015. *Knowledge and Christian Belief*. Grand Rapids, MI: Eerdmans.

Pongratz-Leisten, Beate. 2011. 'A New Agenda for the Study of the Rise of Monotheism.' In Pongratz-Leisten, ed., *Reconsidering the Concept of Revolutionary Monotheism*, 1–40.

——. 2017. *Religion and Ideology in Assyria*. SANER 6. Berlin: De Gruyter.

Pongratz-Leisten, Beate, ed. 2011. *Reconsidering the Concept of Revolutionary Monotheism*. Winona Lake, IN: Eisenbrauns.

Porter, Barbara N. 1993. 'Sacred Trees, Date Palms, and the Royal Persona of Ashurnasirpal II.' *JNES* 52/2: 129–39.

——. 2000. 'The Anxiety of Multiplicity: Concepts of Divinity as One and Many in Ancient Assyria.' In Porter, ed., *One God or Many?*, 211–71.

Porter, Barbara N., ed. 2000. *One God or Many? Concepts of divinity in the ancient world*. Transactions of the Casco Bay Assyriological Institute 1. Chebeague, ME: Casco Bay Assyriological Institute.

Postgate, Nicholas. 2010. 'Dismembering Enki and Ninhursaga.' In Heather D. Baker, Eleanor Robson and Gábor Zólyomy, eds, *Your Praise Is Sweet: A memorial volume for Jeremy Black from students, colleagues and friends*. London: British Institute for the Study of Iraq, 237–44.

Pritchard, James B., ed. 2011. *The Ancient Near East: An anthology of texts and pictures*. Princeton, NJ: Princeton University Press.

Propp, William H. C. 1999. *Exodus 1–18*. AB. New York, NY: Doubleday.

——. 2006. *Exodus 19–40*. AB. New York, NY: Doubleday.

Provan, Iain. 2017. *The Reformation and the Right Reading of Scripture*. Waco, TX: Baylor University Press.

Provan, Iain, V. Philips Long and Tremper Longman III. 2003. *A Biblical History of Israel*. Louisville, KY: Westminster John Knox.

Raaflaub, Kurt A., ed. 2016. *The Adventure of the Human Intellect: Self, society, and the divine in ancient world cultures*. Chichester: Wiley-Blackwell.

Radner, Karen. 2003. 'Neo-Assyrian Period.' In Westbrook, ed., *A History of Ancient Near Eastern Law*, vol. 2, 883–910.

——. 2015. *Ancient Assyria: A very short introduction*. Oxford: OUP.

Radner, Karen, and Eleanor Robson, eds. 2011. *The Oxford Handbook of Cuneiform Culture*. Oxford: OUP.

Ramsey, Ian T. 1973. *Models for Divine Activity*. Eugene, OR: Wipf & Stock.

Redford, Donald B., ed. 2002. *The Ancient Gods Speak: A guide to Egyptian religion*. Oxford: OUP.

Redford, Donald B., William G. Dever, P. Kyle McCarter Jr and John J. Collins. 2012. *Aspects of Monotheism: How God is one*. Ed. Hershel Shanks and Jack Meinhardt. Washington, DC: Biblical Archaeology Society.

Reinhold, Gotthard G. G. 2016. *The Rise and Fall of the Aramaeans in the Ancient Near East, from Their First Appearance until 732 B.C.E.* New Studies on Aram and Israel. Frankfurt: Peter Lang.

Reymond, E. A. E. 1969. *The Mythical Origin of the Egyptian Temple*. Manchester: Manchester University Press.

Ribichini, S. 1999. 'Melqart.' In *DDD*, 563–5.

Ricoeur, Paul. 1967. *The Symbolism of Evil*. Tr. Emerson Buchanan. Boston, MA: Beacon.

——. 1984, 1985, 1988. *Time and Narrative*. 3 vols. Tr. Kathleen McLaughlin and David Pellauer. Chicago, IL: Chicago University Press.

——. 1991, 2007. *From Text to Action: Essays in hermeneutics, II*. Tr. Kathleen Blamey and John B. Thompson. Evanston, IL: Northwestern University Press.

——. 2004. *Memory, History, Forgetting*. Tr. Kathleen Blamey and David Pellauer. Chicago, IL: University of Chicago Press.

Rieff, Philip. 1973. *Fellow Teachers*. New York, NY: Dell.

Roaf, Michael. 1990. *Cultural Atlas of Mesopotamia and the Ancient Near East*. Oxford: Equinox.

Robson, Eleanor. 2019. *Ancient Knowledge Networks: A social geography of cuneiform scholarship in first-millennium Assyria and Babylon*. London: UCL.

Rochberg, Francesca. 2011. 'Observing and Describing the World through Divination and Astronomy.' In Radner and Robson, eds, *The Oxford Handbook of Cuneiform Culture*, 618–36.

——. 2016. *Before Nature: Cuneiform knowledge and the history of science*. Chicago, IL: University of Chicago Press.

Rogers, Katherin A. 2000. *Perfect Being Theology*. Reason and Religion. Edinburgh: Edinburgh University Press.

Röllig, W. 1999. 'El-Creator-of-the-Earth.' In *DDD*, 280–1.

Römer, Thomas. 2015. *The Invention of God*. Tr. Raymond Geuss. Cambridge, MA: Harvard University Press.

Rupprecht, W. 1964. In H. Breit and C. Westermann, eds, *Die alttestamentliche Texte*. Calwer Predighthilfen 3. Stuttgart: Calwer Verlag, 143–53.

Russell, Robert John. 1997. 'Does "The God Who Acts" Really Act?' *Theology Today* 54: 44–65.

Saggs, H. W. F. 1973. 'The Assyrians.' In D. J. Wiseman, ed., *Peoples of Old Testament Times*, 156–78.

——. 1984. *The Might That Was Assyria*. London: Sidgwick & Jackson.

——. 1989. *Civilization before Greece and Rome*. New Haven, CT: Yale University Press.

Said, Edward W. 1953, 2003. 'Introduction to the Fiftieth-Anniversary Edition.' In Auerbach, *Mimesis: The representation of reality in Western literature*, ix–xxxii.

Sanders, Seth L. 2009. *The Invention of Hebrew*. Traditions. Urbana, IL: University of Illinois Press.

Sarna, Nahum M. 1986, 1996. *Exploring Exodus: The origins of biblical Israel*. New York, NY: Schocken.

——. 1989. *Genesis*. JPS Torah Commentary. Jerusalem: JPS.

——. 1991. *Exodus*. JPS Torah Commentary. Jerusalem: JPS.

Schachner, Andreas. 2012. 'Hattuša, the Capital City of the Hittite Empire.' In Doğan-Alparslan and Alparslan, eds, *Hittites: An Anatolian empire*, 150–75.

Schart, Aaron. 1998. *Die Enstehung des Zwölfprophetenbuchs: Neubearbeitungen von Amos im Rahmen schriftenübergreifender Redaktionsprozesse*. BZAW 260. Berlin: De Gruyter.

Schmid, H. H. 1984. 'Creation, Righteousness, and Salvation: "Creation Theology as the Broad Horizon of Biblical Theology".' In Anderson, ed., *Creation in the Old Testament*, 102–17.

Schmid, Konrad. 2019. *A Historical Theology of the Hebrew Bible*. Tr. Peter Altmann. Grand Rapids, MI: Eerdmans.

Schneider, Tammi J. 2011. *An Introduction to Ancient Mesopotamian Religion*. Grand Rapids, MI: Eerdmans.

Schniedewind, William M. 2004. *How the Bible Became a Book*. Cambridge: CUP.

——. 2013. *A Social History of Hebrew: Its origins through the rabbinic period*. New Haven, CT: Yale University Press.

——. 2019. *The Finger of the Scribe: How scribes learned to write the Bible*. Oxford: OUP.

Scholder, Klaus. 1990. *The Birth of Modern Critical Theology: Origins and problems of biblical criticism in the seventeenth century.* Tr. John Bowden. London: SCM.

Schutte, Flip. 2007. 'Myth as Paradigm to Read a Text.' In Human, ed., *Psalms and Mythology*, 1–8.

Schwemer, Daniel. 2012. 'The Cult of the Dead, Magic Rituals, and the Care of the Dead.' In Doğan-Alparslan and Alparslan, eds, *Hittites: An Anatolian empire*, 432–49.

Schwöbel, Christoph. 1992. *God: Action and revelation.* Kampen: Kok Pharos.

Scott, N. A. 1994. 'Steiner on Interpretation.' In Scott and Sharp, eds, *Reading George Steiner*, 1–13.

Scott, N. A., and R. A. Sharp, eds. 1994. *Reading George Steiner.* Baltimore, MD, and London: Johns Hopkins University Press.

Scurlock, Joann, and Richard H. Beal, eds. 2013. *Creation and Chaos: A reconsideration of Hermann Gunkel's Chaoskampf hypothesis.* Winona Lake, IN: Eisenbrauns.

Seerveld, Calvin G. 2012. 'Footprints in the Snow.' *Comment*, March. <www.cardus. ca/comment/article/footprints-in-the-snow>. Accessed 11 August 2021.

Segal, Robert A. 1999. *Theorizing About Myth.* Amherst, MA: University of Massachusetts Press.

——. 2015. *Myth: A very short introduction.* Oxford: OUP.

Sekine, Seizo. 2014. *Philosophical Interpretations of the Old Testament.* Tr. J. Randall Short. BZAW 458. Berlin: De Gruyter.

Sellin, Ernst. 1936. *Theologie des Alten Testaments.* 2nd edn. Leipzig: Quelle & Meyer.

Selz, Gebhard J., ed. 2011. *The Empirical Dimension of Ancient Near Eastern Studies.* Wiener Offene Orientalistik 6. Vienna: LIT Verlag.

Semino, E., and G. Steen. 2008. 'Metaphor and Thought.' In R. W. Gibbs, ed., *The Cambridge Handbook of Metaphor and Thought.* Cambridge: CUP, 232–46.

Sertillanges, A. G. 1960. *The Intellectual Life: Its spirit, conditions, method.* Westminster, MA: Newman.

Seyfried, Friederike, ed. 2012. *In the Light of Amarna: 100 years of the Nefertiti discovery.* Berlin: Staatliche Museen zu Berlin.

Shannon, Avram R. 2007. 'The Achaemenid Kings and the Worship of Ahura Mazda: Proto-Zoroastrianism in the Persian Empire.' *Studia Antiqua* 5/2: 79–85.

Sheehan, Jonathan. 2005. *The Enlightenment Bible: Translation, scholarship, culture.* Princeton, NJ, and Oxford: Princeton University Press.

Silverman, James. 2016. 'Was There an Achaemenid "Theology" of Kingship? The Intersection of Mythology, Religion, and Imperial Policy.' In Edelman et al., eds, *Religion in the Achaemenid Persian Empire*, 172–96.

Singer, Itamar. 2012. 'Pleading to the Gods.' In Doğan-Alparslan and Alparslan, eds, *Hittites: An Anatolian empire*, 494–501.

Sire, James. 2015. *Naming the Elephant: Worldview as a concept*. Downers Grove, IL: IVP.

——. 2020. *The Universe Next Door: A basic worldview catalog*. 6th edn. Downers Grove, IL: IVP Academic.

Smit, M. C. 2002. *Toward a Christian Conception of History*. Ed. and tr. Herbert Donald Morton and Harry Van Dyke. Lanham, MD: University Press of America.

Smith, Jonathan Z. 2004. *Relating Religion: Essays in the study of religion*. Chicago, IL: University of Chicago Press.

Smith, Mark S. 1994. *The Ugaritic Baal Cycle, Volume 1: Introduction with Text, Translation and Commentary of KTU 1.1–1.2*. VTSup 55. Leiden: Brill.

——. 1997. *The Pilgrimage Pattern in Exodus*. Sheffield: Sheffield Academic Press.

——. 2001. *The Origins of Biblical Monotheism: Israel's polytheistic background and the Ugaritic texts*. Oxford: OUP.

——. 2004. *The Memoirs of God: History, memory, and the experience of the divine in Ancient Israel*. Minneapolis, MN: Fortress, 2004.

——. 2008. *God in Translation: Deities in cross-cultural discourse in the biblical world*. Grand Rapids, MI: Eerdmans.

——. 2011. *Exodus*. New Collegeville Bible Commentary. Collegeville, MN: Liturgical Press.

——. 2016. *Where the Gods Are: Spatial dimensions of anthropomorphism in the biblical world*. New Haven, CT, and London: Yale University Press.

Snell, Daniel C., ed. 2005. *A Companion to the Ancient Near East*. Blackwell Companions to Philosophy. Oxford: Blackwell.

Sommer, Benjamin D. 2015. *Revelation and Authority: Sinai in Jewish scripture and tradition*. New Haven, CT: Yale University Press.

Sonderegger, Katherine. 2015. *Systematic Theology, Volume 1: The Doctrine of God*. Minneapolis, MN: Fortress.

Sparks, Adam. 2010. *One of a Kind: The relationship between old and new covenants as the hermeneutical key for Christian theology of religions*. Eugene, OR: Pickwick.

Spieckermann, Hermann. 2000. 'God's Steadfast Love: Towards a New Conception of Old Testament Theology.' *Biblica* 81: 305–27.

Spina, Frank A. 2005. *The Faith of the Outsider: Exclusion and inclusion in the biblical story*. Grand Rapids, MI: Eerdmans.

Spykman, Gordon, Guillermo Cook, Michael Dodson, Lance Grahn, Sidney Rooy and John Stam. 1998. *Let My People Live: Faith and struggle in Central America*. Grand Rapids, MI: Eerdmans.

Stager, L. E. 1998. 'Forging an Identity: The Emergence of Ancient Israel.' In M. D. Coogan, ed., *The Oxford History of the Biblical World*. New York, NY: OUP, 90–131.

Steele, Francis R. 1948. *The Code of Lipit-Ishtar*. Philadelphia, PA: University Museum, University of Pennsylvania Press.

Steiner, George. 1988. 'Books: The Good Books.' *The New Yorker*, 11 January: 94–8.

——. 1989. *Real Presences: Is there anything in what we say?* London and Boston, MA: Faber & Faber.

——. 1994. 'A Responsion.' In Scott and Sharp, eds, *Reading George Steiner*, 275–85.

——. 1998. *After Babel: Aspects of language and translation*. 2nd edn. Oxford: OUP.

Steinkeller, Piotr. 1992. 'Early Semitic Literature and Third Millennium Seals with Mythological Motifs.' In P. Fronzaroli, ed., *Literature and Literary language at Ebla*. Quaderni di Semitistica 18. Florence: Dipartimento di Linguistica, Università di Firenze, 243–75.

——. 2002. 'Archaic City Seals and the Question of Early Babylonian Unity.' In T. Abusch, ed., *Riches Hidden in Secret Places: Ancient Near Eastern studies in memory of Thorkild Jacobsen*. Winona Lake, IN: Eisenbrauns, 249–57.

——. 2019. *History, Texts, and Art in Early Babylonia: Three essays*. SANER 15. Berlin: De Gruyter.

Sternberg, Meir. 1985. *The Poetics of Biblical Narrative: Ideological literature and the drama of reading*. Bloomington, IN: Indiana University Press.

Stiver, Dan. 1996. *The Philosophy of Religious Language: Sign, symbol and story*. Oxford: Blackwell.

Stol, M. 1999. 'Sîn.' In *DDD*, 782–3.

Süel, Aygül, and Mustafa Süel. 2012. 'Šapinuwa: Another Capital City of Hittite State.' In Doğan-Alparslan and Alparslan, eds, *Hittites: An Anatolian empire*, 178–93.

Surls, Austin. 2017. *Making Sense of the Divine Names in Exodus: From etymology to literary onomastics*. BBRSup 17. Winona Lake, IN: Eisenbrauns.

Sweeney, Marvin A. 2007. *I and II Kings*. OTL. Louisville, KY: Westminster John Knox.

Taggar-Cohen, Ada. 2014. 'Concept of the Divine in Hittite Culture and Hebrew Bible: Expression of the Divine.' *JISMOR* 9: 29–50.

Tarnas, Richard. 2010. *The Passion of the Western Mind: Understanding the ideas that have shaped our world view.* London: Pimlico.

Tate, A. 1955. *The Man of Letters in the Modern World: Selected essays, 1928–1955.* New York, NY: Meridian.

Teeter, Emily. 1997. *The Presentation of Maat: Ritual and legitimacy in Ancient Egypt.* SAOC 57. Chicago, IL: Oriental Institute of the University of Chicago.

——. 2002. 'Maat.' In Redford, ed., *The Ancient Gods Speak,* 189–91.

——. 2011. *Religion and Ritual in Ancient Egypt.* Cambridge: CUP.

Thiselton, Anthony C. 1999. 'Communicative Action and Promise in Interdisciplinary, Biblical, and Theological Hermeneutics.' In R. Lundin, C. Walhout and A. C. Thiselton, eds, *The Promise of Hermeneutics.* Grand Rapids, MI: Eerdmans, 133–239.

Thompson, James Westfall, and Bernard J. Holm. 1942. *A History of Historical Writing,* vol. 1. New York, NY: Macmillan.

Toulmin, Stephen. 1990. *Cosmopolis: The hidden agenda of modernity.* Chicago, IL: University of Chicago Press.

Tov, Emmanuel. 2012. 'Post-Modern Textual Criticism?' In Timothy M. Law and Alison Salvesén, eds, *Greek Scripture and the Rabbis.* Contributions to Biblical Exegesis and Theology 66. Leuven: Peeters, 1–18.

Tucker, Aviezer, ed. 2009. *A Companion to the Philosophy of History and Historiography.* Blackwell Companions to Philosophy. Oxford: Blackwell.

Tugendhaft, Aaron. 2018. *Baal and the Politics of Poetry.* The Ancient Word 1. London and New York, NY: Routledge.

Tyldesley, Joyce. 2000. *Ramesses: Egypt's greatest pharaoh.* London: Penguin.

Ulrich, Eugene. 1999. *The Dead Sea Scrolls and the Origin of the Bible: Studies in the Dead Sea Scrolls and related literature.* Grand Rapids, MI: Eerdmans.

Ünal, Ahmet. 2012a. 'Divination and Prophecy.' In Doğan-Alparslan and Alparslan, eds, *Hittites: An Anatolian empire,* 452–73.

——. 2012b. 'Dream in the Hittite World.' In Doğan-Alparslan and Alparslan, eds, *Hittites: An Anatolian empire,* 476–91.

Van De Mieroop, Marc. 1999. *Cuneiform Texts and the Writing of History.* London: Routledge.

——. 2005. *King Hammurabi of Babylon: A biography.* Oxford: Blackwell.

——. 2016. *Philosophy before the Greeks: The pursuit of truth in Ancient Babylonia.* Princeton, NJ: Princeton University Press.

Van den Hout, Theo P. J. 2012. 'A Short History of the Hittite Kingdom and Empire.' In Doğan-Alparslan and Alparslan, eds, *Hittites: An Anatolian empire*, 22–44.

Van der Merwe, Christo H. J., Jacobus A. Naudé and Jan H. Kroeze. 2017. *A Biblical Hebrew Reference Grammar*. London: Bloomsbury T&T Clark.

Van der Toorn, Karel. 2007. *Scribal Culture and the Making of the Hebrew Bible*. Cambridge, MA: Harvard University Press.

Van der Toorn, Karel, Bob Becking and Pieter van der Horst, eds. 1999. *Dictionary of Deities and Demons in the Bible*. 2nd edn. Leiden: Brill; Grand Rapids, MI: Eerdmans.

Van Driel, G. 1969. *The Cult of Aššur*. Assen: Van Gorcum.

Van Gessel, Ben H. L. 1998–2001. *Onomasticon of the Hittite Pantheon*. 3 vols. Leiden and New York, NY: Brill.

Van Huyssteen, Wentzel. 1989. *Theology and the Justification of Faith: Constructing theories in systematic theology*. Grand Rapids, MI: Eerdmans.

Van Seters, John. 1983. *In Search of History: Historiography in the ancient world and the origins of biblical history*. New Haven, CT: Yale University Press.

Vernoff, Charles E. 1986. 'The Contemporary Study of Religion and the Academic Teaching of Judaism.' In Zev Garber, ed., *Methodology in the Academic Teaching of Judaism*. Studies in Judaism. Lanham, MD: University Press of America, 15–40.

Voegelin, Eric. 1997. *Science, Politics, and Gnosticism*. Tr. William J. Fitzpatrick. Washington, DC: Regnery.

Von Rad, Gerhard. 1966a. *From Genesis to Chronicles: Explorations in Old Testament theology*. Edinburgh: Oliver & Boyd.

——. 1966b. *The Problem of the Hexateuch and Other Essays*. Tr. E. W. Trueman Dicken. Edinburgh: Oliver & Boyd.

——. 1972. *Genesis*. OTL. Original tr. John H. Marks. Rev. edn. London: SCM.

——. 1984. 'The Theological Problem of the Old Testament Doctrine of Creation.' In Anderson, ed., *Creation in the Old Testament*, 53–64.

——. 1991. *Holy War in Ancient Israel*. Tr. Marva J. Dawn. Grand Rapids, MI: Eerdmans.

Vriezen, Th. C. 1970. *An Outline of Old Testament Theology*. 2nd edn. Oxford: Basil Blackwell.

Wallace, Mark I. 1995. 'Introduction.' In Paul Ricoeur, *Figuring the Sacred: Religion, imagination, and narrative*. Tr. David Pellauer. Minneapolis, MN: Augsburg Fortress, 1–32.

Walton, John H., and D. Brent Sandy. 2013. *The Lost World of Scripture: Ancient literary culture and biblical authority.* Downers Grove, IL: IVP.

Waters, Matt. 2014. *Ancient Persia: A concise history of the Achaemenid Empire, 550–330 BCE.* Cambridge: CUP.

Watson, Francis. 1994. *Text, Church and World: Biblical interpretation in theological perspective.* Edinburgh: T&T Clark.

——. 1997. *Text and Truth: Redefining biblical theology.* Edinburgh: T&T Clark.

Wazana, Nili. 2003. 'From Dan to Beer-Sheba and from the Wilderness to the Sea: Literal and Literary Images of the Promised Land in the Bible.' In Mary N. MacDonald, ed., *Experiences of Place.* Cambridge, MA: Center for the Study of World Religions, 45–85.

——. 2013. *All the Boundaries of the Land: The promised land in biblical thought in light of the Ancient Near East.* Tr. Liat Qeren. Winona Lake, IN: Eisenbrauns.

Weinfeld, Moshe. 1993. *The Promise of the Land: The inheritance of Canaan by the Israelites.* Berkeley, CA: University of California Press.

Weiss, M. 1984. *The Bible from Within: The method of total interpretation.* Jerusalem: Magnes.

Wellek, R., and A. Warren. 1963. *Theory of Literature.* 3rd edn. London: Penguin.

Welten, P. 1982. 'Königsherrschaft Jahwes und Thronbesteigung.' *VT* 32: 297–310.

Wenham, Gordon J. 1980. 'The Religion of the Patriarchs.' In Millard and Wiseman, eds, *Essays on the Patriarchal Narratives*, 161–95.

——. 1981. *Numbers.* TOTC. Leicester: IVP.

——. 1987. *Genesis 1–15.* WBC 1. Waco, TX: Word.

——. 1994. *Genesis 16–50.* WBC 2. Dallas, TX: Word.

Westbrook, Raymond, ed. 2003. *A History of Ancient Near Eastern Law.* 2 vols. Leiden: Brill.

Westermann, Claus. 1984. *Genesis 1–11: A commentary.* Tr. John J. Scullion. Minneapolis, MN: Fortress.

White, Ellen. 2014. *Yahweh's Council: Its structure and membership.* FzAT 2/65. Tübingen: Mohr Siebeck.

White, H. V. 1973. *Metahistory: The historical imagination in nineteenth-century Europe.* Baltimore, MD: Johns Hopkins University Press.

——. 1978. *Tropics of Discourse: Essays in cultural criticism.* Baltimore, MD: Johns Hopkins University Press.

——. 1987. *The Content of the Form: Narrative discourse and historical representation.* Baltimore, MD: Johns Hopkins University Press.

Whybray, Norman. 1987. *The Making of the Pentateuch: A methodological study.* JSOTSup 53. Sheffield: Sheffield Academic Press.

Widengren, Geo. 1955. *Sakrales Königtum im Alten Testament und im Judentum*. Stuttgart: W. Kohlhammer.

——. 1973. 'The Persians.' In Wiseman, ed., *Peoples of Old Testament Times*, 312–57.

Widmer, Michael. 2004. *Moses, God, and the Dynamics of Intercessory Prayer*. FzAT 8. Tübingen: Mohr Siebeck.

Wiener, Nancy H., and Jo Hirschmann. 2014. *Maps and Meaning: Levitical models and contemporary care*. Minneapolis, MD: Fortress.

Wiesehöfer, Josef. 1996, 2001. *Ancient Persia from 550 BC to 650 AD*. Tr. Azizeh Azodi. London: I. B. Taurus.

Wildman, Wesley J. 2017. *In Our Own Image: Anthropomorphism, apophaticism, and ultimacy*. Oxford: OUP.

Williamson, H. G. M. 2014. *Isaiah 1–5*. ICC. London: Bloomsbury.

Wilken, Robert L. 1992. *The Land Called Holy: Palestine in Christian thought and history*. New Haven, CT, and London: Yale University Press.

Wilkinson, Richard H. 2000. *The Complete Temples of Ancient Egypt*. New York, NY: Thames & Hudson.

——. 2003. *The Complete Gods and Goddesses of Ancient Egypt*. New York, NY: Thames & Hudson.

Wilkinson, Richard H., ed. 2008. *Egyptology Today*. Cambridge: CUP.

Wilkinson, Toby. 2010. *The Rise and Fall of Ancient Egypt*. New York, NY: Random.

——. 2014. *The Nile: Travelling downriver through Egypt's past and present*. New York, NY: Vintage.

Wilson, John A. 1946. 'Egypt.' In Frankfort et al., *The Intellectual Adventure of Ancient Man*, 31–122.

Windelband, W. 1901. *A History of Philosophy*. 2nd edn. New York, NY: Macmillan.

Winter, Irene J. 1992. '"Idols of the King": Royal Images as Recipients of Ritual Action in Ancient Mesopotamia.' In *Journal of Ritual Studies* 6/1 (special issue: *Art in Ritual Context*, ed. Kathleen Ashley and Irene J. Winter): 12–42.

Wiseman, Donald J. 1973. 'Introduction.' In Wiseman, ed., *Peoples of Old Testament Times*, xv–xxi.

Wiseman, Donald J. ed. 1973. *Peoples of Old Testament Times*. Oxford: Clarendon.

Wittgenstein, Ludwig. 1922. *Tractatus Logico-Philosophicus*. Sweden: Chiron.

Wolters, Al. 1981. 'Facing the Perplexing History of Philosophy.' *Tydskrif vir Christelike Wetenskap*17: 1–17.

Woolmer, M. 2017. *A Short History of the Phoenicians*. London: Tauris.

Wright, Andrew. 2013. *Christianity and Critical Realism: Ambiguity, truth and theological literacy*. New York, NY: Routledge.

Wright, Christopher J. H. 1990. *God's People in God's Land: Family, land, and property in the Old Testament*. Grand Rapids, MI: Eerdmans.

——. 2004. *Old Testament Ethics for the People of God*. Leicester: IVP.

——. 2021. *Exodus*. The Story of God Bible Commentary. Grand Rapids, MI: Zondervan.

Wright, G. Ernest. 1950. *The Old Testament against Its Environment*. SBT 2. London: SCM.

——. 1955. *God Who Acts: Biblical theology as recital*. London: SCM.

Wright, N. T. 1992. *The New Testament and the People of God*. Christian Origins and the Question of God 1. London: SPCK.

——. 1996. *Jesus and the Victory of God*. Christian Origins and the Question of God 2. London: SPCK.

Wright, Tom. 2018. *Paul: A biography*. London: SPCK.

Xeller, P. 1999. 'Resheph.' In *DDD*, 700–3.

Yamauchi, Edwin M. 1990, 1996. *Persia and the Bible*. Grand Rapids, MI: Baker.

Yaron, Reuven. 1988. *The Laws of Eshnunna*. 2nd edn. Jerusalem: Magnes.

Yerushalmi, Yosef H. 1989. *Zakhor: Jewish history and Jewish memory*. New York, NY: Schocken.

Younger Jr, K. Lawson. 2016. *A Political History of the Arameans: From their origins to the end of their polities*. Archaeology and Biblical Studies 13. Atlanta: SBL.

Zamazalová, Sylvie. 2011. 'The Education of Neo-Assyrian Princes.' In Radner and Robson, eds, *The Oxford Handbook of Cuneiform Culture*, 313–30.

Zevit, Ziony. 1976. 'The Priestly Redaction and Interpretation of the Plague Narrative in Exodus.' *JQR* 66: 194–205.

——. 2021. *The Religions of Ancient Israel: A synthesis of parallactic approaches*. London: Continuum.

Zimmerli, Walther. 1982. *I Am Yahweh*. Ed. Walter Brueggemann. Tr. Douglas W. Stott. Atlanta, GA: John Knox.

# Index of Scripture references

# Index of subjects

paradigm, 63, 73–9, 85–7, 93, 96–7, 102, 116–19, 152, 180, 189, 192, 194, 298, 389, 407, 428, 451, 470, 490, 511, 518, 524–5; *see also* tradition

Parpola, Simo, 302–3, 306, 378

particularity, 8–9, 111, 127, 312, 466, 470

pattern, 7, 43, 60, 184, 205, 209, 267, 409, 478, 480, 514

Paul (apostle), 80–2, 145–6

Pentateuch, 29, 42, 44–5, 57, 102–3, 114, 119, 188, 212, 273, 289, 379, 430, 433, 435, 445, 452–3, 457, 464, 509–11, 517–19, 521

Persia *see* world view, Persian

pharaoh, 4, 199–202, 212–13, 218–20, 223–4, 226, 229, 233–7, 239, 242–4, 291, 311, 387, 400, 422, 445, 447–9, 451, 454–5, 457, 493, 505, 516

philology, 29–30, 327, 420

philosophy, 29, 38, 47, 60, 65, 68, 70, 86–93, 97, 113–14, 117, 129, 147–50, 153–6, 163–4, 186–9, 204, 206–7, 223, 246, 302, 327, 330, 403, 405–7, 421, 425, 427, 476–8, 485, 487–91, 501, 507–8, 524; of history, 62, 86, 89, 155, 161, 166, 173, 414, 416; of religion, 114, 211, 402, 407, 476–7, 524; of science, 50, 70, 116, 185, 190–1

Phoenicia, Phoenician(s), 12–13, 15, 245, 335, 338–50, 358–9, 376, 385, 398, 432–3, 446; *see also* world view, Phoenician

plague(s), 169, 212, 219, 247, 285, 429, 493, 509

Plantinga, Alvin, 46, 86, 90, 92, 104, 126, 155, 158, 186, 190, 407, 488, 523–4

Plato, 46, 53, 56, 207, 332, 480

plot, 141–4, 163, 227, 325, 383, 519–20; *see also* emplotment

pluralism, 1, 51, 75–7, 91, 118, 134, 140, 365, 481, 488, 494, 526

poem, 127, 131–2, 136, 305, 355–6, 377, 379, 388, 448–50, 519

poetics, 36, 47, 99, 137, 139–40, 144, 162, 167, 170–2, 182, 360, 392, 513–16

poetry, 30, 54, 132, 134, 150, 177, 360, 373, 387, 439, 450, 512–13

polemic, 24, 51, 126, 375–6, 379, 399, 403, 405, 447–8

politics, 29, 37, 68, 199, 201–2, 212, 244, 246, 271, 280, 282, 284, 311, 339, 345, 352, 364, 366, 470

polytheism, 57, 204–5, 214–15, 226–7, 232, 243, 280, 291, 302–5, 311, 325, 337, 350, 357, 359–60, 364, 366, 368–9, 371, 377–80, 382, 390, 393, 420, 423

post-Enlightenment, 76, 100, 115, 117, 148, 165, 171–2, 180–1, 183–4, 192–4, 211, 313

postmodernism, 1, 38, 46–7, 67, 75–7, 85, 88, 90–2, 98, 100, 118, 126, 131, 134, 137, 155, 162, 164–6, 180, 389, 481, 488, 526

power, 6, 28–30, 32–5, 37, 52, 57, 61, 66, 90, 103, 107, 141, 154, 161, 174, 193, 200–2, 215, 217–18, 221, 223, 225–6, 243, 249, 260, 276, 278, 285, 287–8, 291–3, 297, 304, 306, 310–13, 316, 320–1, 324, 326, 331, 338, 344, 346, 352, 356, 361, 364, 366, 371–2, 375, 378–80, 385–6, 405, 411, 417, 427, 437–8, 443–4, 446, 448, 451, 454–5, 460, 462, 469–70

practices, 11, 72, 112, 233, 292, 310, 332, 346, 359, 418, 435, 468, 518, 521; *see also* praxis

praxis, 158, 199, 503; *see also* practices

prayer, 108, 233, 263, 279, 284, 287, 299, 301, 305, 307, 325, 414, 416, 463, 465–6, 474

priest(s), 107, 177, 229, 232, 234, 253, 280, 286, 302, 306–7, 345, 348, 357, 441–2

writing, 1, 3–5, 33, 35–6, 39, 41, 53, 56–7,
60, 87, 89, 120–2, 130, 141–2, 144, 147,
161–2, 164, 166, 170, 177–8, 246–7,
265, 271, 286, 292, 299, 309, 314, 319,
327–8, 330–1, 333–5, 341, 365–7, 370,
391, 421, 427, 438, 507, 512, 523

Zion, 11, 292, 341, 410–12, 415